# Lecture Notes in Artificial Intelligence 13307

Subseries of Lecture Notes in Computer Science

## Series Editors

Randy Goebel
*University of Alberta, Edmonton, Canada*

Wolfgang Wahlster
*DFKI, Berlin, Germany*

Zhi-Hua Zhou
*Nanjing University, Nanjing, China*

## Founding Editor

Jörg Siekmann
*DFKI and Saarland University, Saarbrücken, Germany*

More information about this subseries at https://link.springer.com/bookseries/1244

Don Harris · Wen-Chin Li (Eds.)

# Engineering Psychology and Cognitive Ergonomics

19th International Conference, EPCE 2022
Held as Part of the 24th HCI International Conference, HCII 2022
Virtual Event, June 26 – July 1, 2022
Proceedings

 Springer

*Editors*
Don Harris
Coventry University
Coventry, UK

Wen-Chin Li
Cranfield University
Cranfield, UK

ISSN 0302-9743      ISSN 1611-3349 (electronic)
Lecture Notes in Artificial Intelligence
ISBN 978-3-031-06085-4      ISBN 978-3-031-06086-1 (eBook)
https://doi.org/10.1007/978-3-031-06086-1

LNCS Sublibrary: SL7 – Artificial Intelligence

This Springer imprint is published by the registered company Springer Nature Switzerland AG
The registered company address is: Gewerbestrasse 11, 6330 Cham, Switzerland

# Foreword

Human-computer interaction (HCI) is acquiring an ever-increasing scientific and industrial importance, as well as having more impact on people's everyday life, as an ever-growing number of human activities are progressively moving from the physical to the digital world. This process, which has been ongoing for some time now, has been dramatically accelerated by the COVID-19 pandemic. The HCI International (HCII) conference series, held yearly, aims to respond to the compelling need to advance the exchange of knowledge and research and development efforts on the human aspects of design and use of computing systems.

The 24th International Conference on Human-Computer Interaction, HCI International 2022 (HCII 2022), was planned to be held at the Gothia Towers Hotel and Swedish Exhibition & Congress Centre, Göteborg, Sweden, during June 26 to July 1, 2022. Due to the COVID-19 pandemic and with everyone's health and safety in mind, HCII 2022 was organized and run as a virtual conference. It incorporated the 21 thematic areas and affiliated conferences listed on the following page.

A total of 5583 individuals from academia, research institutes, industry, and governmental agencies from 88 countries submitted contributions, and 1276 papers and 275 posters were included in the proceedings to appear just before the start of the conference. The contributions thoroughly cover the entire field of human-computer interaction, addressing major advances in knowledge and effective use of computers in a variety of application areas. These papers provide academics, researchers, engineers, scientists, practitioners, and students with state-of-the-art information on the most recent advances in HCI. The volumes constituting the set of proceedings to appear before the start of the conference are listed in the following pages.

The HCI International (HCII) conference also offers the option of 'Late Breaking Work' which applies both for papers and posters, and the corresponding volume(s) of the proceedings will appear after the conference. Full papers will be included in the 'HCII 2022 - Late Breaking Papers' volumes of the proceedings to be published in the Springer LNCS series, while 'Poster Extended Abstracts' will be included as short research papers in the 'HCII 2022 - Late Breaking Posters' volumes to be published in the Springer CCIS series.

I would like to thank the Program Board Chairs and the members of the Program Boards of all thematic areas and affiliated conferences for their contribution and support towards the highest scientific quality and overall success of the HCI International 2022 conference; they have helped in so many ways, including session organization, paper reviewing (single-blind review process, with a minimum of two reviews per submission) and, more generally, acting as goodwill ambassadors for the HCII conference.

This conference would not have been possible without the continuous and unwavering support and advice of Gavriel Salvendy, founder, General Chair Emeritus, and Scientific Advisor. For his outstanding efforts, I would like to express my appreciation to Abbas Moallem, Communications Chair and Editor of HCI International News.

June 2022                                                          Constantine Stephanidis

# HCI International 2022 Thematic Areas and Affiliated Conferences

**Thematic Areas**

- HCI: Human-Computer Interaction
- HIMI: Human Interface and the Management of Information

**Affiliated Conferences**

- EPCE: 19th International Conference on Engineering Psychology and Cognitive Ergonomics
- AC: 16th International Conference on Augmented Cognition
- UAHCI: 16th International Conference on Universal Access in Human-Computer Interaction
- CCD: 14th International Conference on Cross-Cultural Design
- SCSM: 14th International Conference on Social Computing and Social Media
- VAMR: 14th International Conference on Virtual, Augmented and Mixed Reality
- DHM: 13th International Conference on Digital Human Modeling and Applications in Health, Safety, Ergonomics and Risk Management
- DUXU: 11th International Conference on Design, User Experience and Usability
- C&C: 10th International Conference on Culture and Computing
- DAPI: 10th International Conference on Distributed, Ambient and Pervasive Interactions
- HCIBGO: 9th International Conference on HCI in Business, Government and Organizations
- LCT: 9th International Conference on Learning and Collaboration Technologies
- ITAP: 8th International Conference on Human Aspects of IT for the Aged Population
- AIS: 4th International Conference on Adaptive Instructional Systems
- HCI-CPT: 4th International Conference on HCI for Cybersecurity, Privacy and Trust
- HCI-Games: 4th International Conference on HCI in Games
- MobiTAS: 4th International Conference on HCI in Mobility, Transport and Automotive Systems
- AI-HCI: 3rd International Conference on Artificial Intelligence in HCI
- MOBILE: 3rd International Conference on Design, Operation and Evaluation of Mobile Communications

# List of Conference Proceedings Volumes Appearing Before the Conference

1. LNCS 13302, Human-Computer Interaction: Theoretical Approaches and Design Methods (Part I), edited by Masaaki Kurosu
2. LNCS 13303, Human-Computer Interaction: Technological Innovation (Part II), edited by Masaaki Kurosu
3. LNCS 13304, Human-Computer Interaction: User Experience and Behavior (Part III), edited by Masaaki Kurosu
4. LNCS 13305, Human Interface and the Management of Information: Visual and Information Design (Part I), edited by Sakae Yamamoto and Hirohiko Mori
5. LNCS 13306, Human Interface and the Management of Information: Applications in Complex Technological Environments (Part II), edited by Sakae Yamamoto and Hirohiko Mori
6. LNAI 13307, Engineering Psychology and Cognitive Ergonomics, edited by Don Harris and Wen-Chin Li
7. LNCS 13308, Universal Access in Human-Computer Interaction: Novel Design Approaches and Technologies (Part I), edited by Margherita Antona and Constantine Stephanidis
8. LNCS 13309, Universal Access in Human-Computer Interaction: User and Context Diversity (Part II), edited by Margherita Antona and Constantine Stephanidis
9. LNAI 13310, Augmented Cognition, edited by Dylan D. Schmorrow and Cali M. Fidopiastis
10. LNCS 13311, Cross-Cultural Design: Interaction Design Across Cultures (Part I), edited by Pei-Luen Patrick Rau
11. LNCS 13312, Cross-Cultural Design: Applications in Learning, Arts, Cultural Heritage, Creative Industries, and Virtual Reality (Part II), edited by Pei-Luen Patrick Rau
12. LNCS 13313, Cross-Cultural Design: Applications in Business, Communication, Health, Well-being, and Inclusiveness (Part III), edited by Pei-Luen Patrick Rau
13. LNCS 13314, Cross-Cultural Design: Product and Service Design, Mobility and Automotive Design, Cities, Urban Areas, and Intelligent Environments Design (Part IV), edited by Pei-Luen Patrick Rau
14. LNCS 13315, Social Computing and Social Media: Design, User Experience and Impact (Part I), edited by Gabriele Meiselwitz
15. LNCS 13316, Social Computing and Social Media: Applications in Education and Commerce (Part II), edited by Gabriele Meiselwitz
16. LNCS 13317, Virtual, Augmented and Mixed Reality: Design and Development (Part I), edited by Jessie Y. C. Chen and Gino Fragomeni
17. LNCS 13318, Virtual, Augmented and Mixed Reality: Applications in Education, Aviation and Industry (Part II), edited by Jessie Y. C. Chen and Gino Fragomeni

18. LNCS 13319, Digital Human Modeling and Applications in Health, Safety, Ergonomics and Risk Management: Anthropometry, Human Behavior, and Communication (Part I), edited by Vincent G. Duffy
19. LNCS 13320, Digital Human Modeling and Applications in Health, Safety, Ergonomics and Risk Management: Health, Operations Management, and Design (Part II), edited by Vincent G. Duffy
20. LNCS 13321, Design, User Experience, and Usability: UX Research, Design, and Assessment (Part I), edited by Marcelo M. Soares, Elizabeth Rosenzweig and Aaron Marcus
21. LNCS 13322, Design, User Experience, and Usability: Design for Emotion, Well-being and Health, Learning, and Culture (Part II), edited by Marcelo M. Soares, Elizabeth Rosenzweig and Aaron Marcus
22. LNCS 13323, Design, User Experience, and Usability: Design Thinking and Practice in Contemporary and Emerging Technologies (Part III), edited by Marcelo M. Soares, Elizabeth Rosenzweig and Aaron Marcus
23. LNCS 13324, Culture and Computing, edited by Matthias Rauterberg
24. LNCS 13325, Distributed, Ambient and Pervasive Interactions: Smart Environments, Ecosystems, and Cities (Part I), edited by Norbert A. Streitz and Shin'ichi Konomi
25. LNCS 13326, Distributed, Ambient and Pervasive Interactions: Smart Living, Learning, Well-being and Health, Art and Creativity (Part II), edited by Norbert A. Streitz and Shin'ichi Konomi
26. LNCS 13327, HCI in Business, Government and Organizations, edited by Fiona Fui-Hoon Nah and Keng Siau
27. LNCS 13328, Learning and Collaboration Technologies: Designing the Learner and Teacher Experience (Part I), edited by Panayiotis Zaphiris and Andri Ioannou
28. LNCS 13329, Learning and Collaboration Technologies: Novel Technological Environments (Part II), edited by Panayiotis Zaphiris and Andri Ioannou
29. LNCS 13330, Human Aspects of IT for the Aged Population: Design, Interaction and Technology Acceptance (Part I), edited by Qin Gao and Jia Zhou
30. LNCS 13331, Human Aspects of IT for the Aged Population: Technology in Everyday Living (Part II), edited by Qin Gao and Jia Zhou
31. LNCS 13332, Adaptive Instructional Systems, edited by Robert A. Sottilare and Jessica Schwarz
32. LNCS 13333, HCI for Cybersecurity, Privacy and Trust, edited by Abbas Moallem
33. LNCS 13334, HCI in Games, edited by Xiaowen Fang
34. LNCS 13335, HCI in Mobility, Transport and Automotive Systems, edited by Heidi Krömker
35. LNAI 13336, Artificial Intelligence in HCI, edited by Helmut Degen and Stavroula Ntoa
36. LNCS 13337, Design, Operation and Evaluation of Mobile Communications, edited by Gavriel Salvendy and June Wei
37. CCIS 1580, HCI International 2022 Posters - Part I, edited by Constantine Stephanidis, Margherita Antona and Stavroula Ntoa
38. CCIS 1581, HCI International 2022 Posters - Part II, edited by Constantine Stephanidis, Margherita Antona and Stavroula Ntoa

39. CCIS 1582, HCI International 2022 Posters - Part III, edited by Constantine Stephanidis, Margherita Antona and Stavroula Ntoa
40. CCIS 1583, HCI International 2022 Posters - Part IV, edited by Constantine Stephanidis, Margherita Antona and Stavroula Ntoa

**http://2022.hci.international/proceedings**

# Preface

The 19th International Conference on Engineering Psychology and Cognitive Ergonomics (EPCE 2022) is an affiliated conference of the HCI International Conference. The first EPCE conference was held in Stratford-upon-Avon, UK in 1996, and since 2001, EPCE has been an integral part of the HCI International conference series. Over the last 25 years, over 1,000 papers have been presented in this conference, which attracts a world-wide audience of scientists and human factors practitioners. The engineering psychology submissions describe advances in applied cognitive psychology that underpin the theory, measurement and methodologies behind the development of human-machine systems. Cognitive ergonomics describes advances in the design and development of user interfaces. Originally, these disciplines were driven by the requirements of high-risk, high-performance industries where safety was paramount, however the importance of good human factors is now understood by everyone for not only increasing safety, but also enhancing performance, productivity and revenues.

One volume of the HCII 2022 proceedings is dedicated to this year's edition of the EPCE Conference and focuses on topics related to the human-centered design of equipment and human performance in the working environment. Application areas encompass human-robot interaction, wearable devices and web-interfaces. The working environment can be particularly demanding. Modern technology has resulted in new manifestations of stress at work. This is addressed in a number of papers covering its identification, measurement and mitigation. The aerospace environment is particularly demanding of the performance required of both equipment and its users. The last two years during the global pandemic have placed additional stresses on staff. These issues are covered in several papers in the final section of the proceedings, along with descriptions of various non-intrusive physiological measures for assessing cognitive load and performance and the evaluation of new flight deck interfaces.

Papers of this volume are included for publication after a minimum of two single–blind reviews from the members of the EPCE Program Board or, in some cases, from members of the Program Boards of other affiliated conferences. We would like to thank all of them for their invaluable contribution, support and efforts.

June 2022

Don Harris
Wen-Chin Li

# 19th International Conference on Engineering Psychology and Cognitive Ergonomics (EPCE 2022)

Program Board Chairs: **Don Harris,** Coventry University, UK and **Wen-Chin Li,** Cranfield University, UK

- Wesley Chan, Cathay Pacific Airways, Hong Kong
- Iveta Eimontaite, Cranfield University, UK
- Sarah Fletcher, Cranfield University, UK
- Maik Friedrich, German Aerospace Center (DLR), Braunschweig, Germany
- Hannes Griebel, CGI UK, UK
- Iris Hsu, Taiwan Transportation Safety Board, Taiwan
- Hannu Karvonen, VTT Technical Research Centre of Finland Ltd., Finland
- John J. H. Lin, National Taiwan Normal University, Taiwan
- Maggie Ma, The Boeing Company, USA
- Pete McCarthy, Cathay Pacific Airways, UK
- Jose Luis Munoz Gamarra, Aslogic, Spain
- Tatiana Polishchuk, Linköping University, Sweden
- Dujuan Sevillian, Human Factors Expert, USA
- Lei Wang, Civil Aviation University of China, China
- Chung-San Yu, Air Force Academy, Taiwan
- Jingyu Zhang, Institute of Psychology, Chinese Academy of Sciences, China

The full list with the Program Board Chairs and the members of the Program Boards of all thematic areas and affiliated conferences is available online at

**http://www.hci.international/board-members-2022.php**

# HCI International 2023

The 25th International Conference on Human-Computer Interaction, HCI International 2023, will be held jointly with the affiliated conferences at the AC Bella Sky Hotel and Bella Center, Copenhagen, Denmark, 23–28 July 2023. It will cover a broad spectrum of themes related to human-computer interaction, including theoretical issues, methods, tools, processes, and case studies in HCI design, as well as novel interaction techniques, interfaces, and applications. The proceedings will be published by Springer. More information will be available on the conference website: http://2023.hci.international/.

General Chair
Constantine Stephanidis
University of Crete and ICS-FORTH
Heraklion, Crete, Greece
Email: general_chair@hcii2023.org

**http://2023.hci.international/**

# Contents

**Cognition in Human-Centred Design**

Effects of Filled Pauses on Memory Recall in Human-Robot Interaction
in Mandarin Chinese ............................................... 3
   *Xinyi Chen, Andreas Liesenfeld, Shiyue Li, and Yao Yao*

Investigation of Temporal Changes of Gaze Locations During
Characteristic Evaluation When Viewing Whole-Body Photos ............... 18
   *Fuyuko Iwasaki, Masashi Nishiyama, and Yoshio Iwai*

Swiping Angles Differentially Influence Young and Old Users'
Performance and Experience on Swiping Gestures ........................ 33
   *Jiali Jiang, Zheng Wei, Tong Yang, Yanfang Liu, Bingxin Li, and Feng Du*

Development of a Concept of Operations for a Counter-Swarm Scenario ...... 49
   *Jari Laarni, Antti Väätänen, Hannu Karvonen, Toni Lastusilta,*
   *and Fabrice Saffre*

Integrated Sensors Platform: Streamlining Quantitative Physiological Data
Collection and Analysis ............................................ 64
   *Harry X. Li, Vincent Mancuso, and Sarah McGuire*

Usability Evaluation of a Web Interface for Passengers' Health Monitoring
System on Detecting Critical Medical Conditions ........................ 74
   *Elizabeth Manikath and Wen-Chin Li*

Effects of Background Music on Visual Short-Term Memory:
A Preliminary Study ............................................... 85
   *Fatih Baha Omeroglu and Yueqing Li*

Do Mathematical Typesetting Applications Affect User Manipulation
of Fractions? Evidence from an Eye-Tracking Experiment .................. 97
   *Francis Quinby, Marco Pollanen, Wesley S. Burr,*
   *and Michael G. Reynolds*

Effects of a Robot Human-Machine Interface on Emergency Steering
Control and Prefrontal Cortex Activation in Automatic Driving ............. 108
   *Hiroko Tanabe, Yuki Yoshihara, Nihan Karatas, Kazuhiro Fujikake,*
   *Takahiro Tanaka, Shuhei Takeuchi, Tsuneyuki Yamamoto,*
   *Makoto Harazawa, and Naoki Kamiya*

The Influence of Font Size, Contrast, and Weight on Text Legibility
for Wearable Devices ................................................... 124
    *Xiaoyu Wang, Huihui Zhang, Miao He, Yanfang Liu, and Liang Zhang*

Aesthetic Preference in the Composition Ratios of Graphic Designs .......... 137
    *Yao-Sheng Wu*

**Cognition at Work**

Influence of Technostress on Work Engagement and Job Performance
During Remote Working ................................................. 149
    *Michele Di Dalmazi, Marco Mandolfo, Chiara Stringhini,
    and Debora Bettiga*

Applying Hierarchical Task Analysis to Identify the Needs of Intelligent
Equipment for Traffic Police in China .................................... 164
    *Wenxuan Duan, Yan Shang, Jingyu Zhang, Huiyun Wang,
    and Xiangying Zou*

Social Exposure and Burnout During the Pandemic: An Investigation
on Three Different Positions of Frontline Metro Staffs ..................... 179
    *Yao Fu, Ranran Li, Jingyu Zhang, Zizheng Guo, and Guo Feng*

User-Centered Interface Design and Evaluation for Teleoperated Cranes
with Boom Tip Control .................................................. 189
    *Lorenz Prasch, Felix Top, Jonas Schmidtler, Klaus Bengler,
    and Johannes Fottner*

A Study on the Influence of Personality on the Performance
of Teleoperation Tasks in Different Situations ............................ 212
    *Kuo Qin, Yijing Zhang, and Jingyu Zhang*

An Emergency Centre Call Taker Task Analysis ........................... 225
    *Norman G. Vinson, Jean-François Lapointe, and Noémie Lemaire*

**Cognition in Aviation and Space**

Cultural Effects on the Selection of Aviation Safety Management Strategies .... 245
    *Wesley Tsz-Kin Chan and Wen-Chin Li*

Improved Spectral Subtraction Method for Civil Aircraft Approach
and Landing Crew Interactive Voice Enhancement ....................... 253
    *Nongtian Chen, Weifeng Ning, Yongzheng Man, and Junhui Li*

Active Supervision in a Remote Tower Center: Rethinking of a New
Position in the ATC Domain .......................................... 265
   *Maik Friedrich, Felix Timmermann, and Jörn Jakobi*

Effects of Intensity of Short-Wavelength Light on the EEG
and Performance of Astronauts During Target Tracking .................... 279
   *Yang Gong, Ao Jiang, ZiJian Wu, Xinyun Fu, Xiang Yao,*
   *Caroline Hemingray, Stephen Westland, and WenKai Li*

The Effect of Pilots' Expertise on Eye Movement and Scan Patterns
During Simulated Flight Tasks ........................................ 290
   *Yue Hua, Shan Fu, and Yanyu Lu*

The Effect of the COVID-19 Pandemic on Air Traffic Controllers'
Performance: Addressing Skill Fade Concerns in Preparation for the Return
to Normal Operations ................................................ 300
   *Shane Kenny and Wen-Chin Li*

Investigating Pilots' Operational Behaviours While Interacting
with Different Types of Inceptors ...................................... 314
   *Wojciech Tomasz Korek, Wen-Chin Li, Linghai Lu, and Mudassir Lone*

Assessments on Human-Computer Interaction Using Touchscreen
as Control Inputs in Flight Operations ................................. 326
   *Wen-Chin Li, Yung-Hsiang Liang, Wojciech Tomasz Korek,*
   *and John J. H. Lin*

Establishment of a Situation Awareness Analysis Model for Flight Crew
Alerting ........................................................... 339
   *Xianxue Li*

Ergonomic Evaluation of the Touch Screen in the Cockpit Under
Stationary and Vibration Conditions ................................... 349
   *Ang Liu, Zhen Wang, and Shan Fu*

Content and Context Analysis of Fatigue Management Regulations
for Flight Crew in the South Asian Region .............................. 358
   *Chanika Mannawaduge Dona and Silvia Pignata*

Stabilise, Solve, Execute Creating a Management Model for Resilient
Flight Deck Operations ............................................... 373
   *Pete McCarthy, Gregory Benichou, and Peter Hudson*

Clipped Wings: The Impact of the COVID-19 Pandemic on Airline Pilots
and Influence on Safety Climate ......................................... 384
*Andrew Mizzi, Gui Lohmann, and Guido Carim Junior*

Degrading Human Factors Through the Invisible 'Freaky 13th' Element ....... 397
*Angeline Ram*

Experimental Assessment of Fixation-Based Attention Measurement
in an Aircraft Cockpit ................................................... 408
*Simon Schwerd and Axel Schulte*

Is There a Relationship Between Pilot Stress and Short- and Long- Haul
Flights? ................................................................. 420
*Khai Sheng Sew, Jongwoo Jung, Kin Wing Lo, Lucus Yap,
and Silvia Pignata*

Evaluation of User Experience of Self-scheduling Software for Astronauts:
Defining a Satisfaction Baseline ......................................... 433
*Shivang Shelat, John A. Karasinski, Erin E. Flynn-Evans,
and Jessica J. Marquez*

Pilot Fatigue Evaluation Based on Eye-Movement Index and Performance
Index ................................................................... 446
*Hongjun Xue, Xiaotian Chen, Xiaoyan Zhang, Ziqi Ma, and Kai Qiu*

Study on the Mechanism of Pilot Fatigue on Performance ................... 461
*Hongjun Xue, Ziqi Ma, Xiaoyan Zhang, Xiaotian Chen, Kai Qiu,
and Jie Li*

Preliminary Research on Evaluation Index of Professional Adaptability
for Airline Transport Pilot .............................................. 473
*Mengxi Zhang, Lei Wang, Ying Zou, Jiahua Peng, Yiwei Cai, and Shu Li*

The Assessment of Aviation Situation Awareness Based on Objective
Behavior Methods ....................................................... 488
*Hao Zhou, Yanyu Lu, and Shan Fu*

**Author Index** ....................................................... 505

# Cognition in Human-Centred Design

# Effects of Filled Pauses on Memory Recall in Human-Robot Interaction in Mandarin Chinese

Xinyi Chen[1], Andreas Liesenfeld[2], Shiyue Li[1], and Yao Yao[1]([✉])

[1] The Hong Kong Polytechnic University, Hung Hom, Hong Kong
xysimba.chen@connect.polyu.hk, {shiyue1.li,y.yao}@polyu.edu.hk
[2] Radboud University, Nijmegen, Netherlands
andreas.liesenfeld@ru.nl

**Abstract.** In recent years, voice-AI systems have seen significant improvements in intelligibility and naturalness, but the human experience when talking to a machine is still remarkably different from the experience of talking to a fellow human. In this paper, we explore one dimension of such differences, i.e., the occurrence of disfluency in machine speech and how it may impact human listeners' processing and memory of linguistic information. We conducted a human-machine conversation task in Mandarin Chinese using a humanoid social robot (Furhat), with different types of machine speech (pre-recorded natural speech vs. synthesized speech, fluent vs. disfluent). During the task, the human interlocutor was tested in terms of how well they remembered the information presented by the robot. The results showed that disfluent speech (surrounded by "um"/"uh") did not benefit memory retention both in pre-recorded speech and in synthesized speech. We discuss the implications of current findings and possible directions of future work.

**Keywords:** Human-robot interaction · Humanoid robot · Spoken disfluency

## 1  Introduction

With the development of smart phones and smart home devices, voice user interface (VUI), such as Alexa, Google Assistant and Siri, has been increasingly widely used in people's daily life. People speak with these devices mostly for tasks such as playing music, searching without typing, and controlling smart home devices [1]. However, human users may encounter problems communicating with such devices even in such relatively simple interactions [2]. One side of the problem is that natural human speech comes with many subtle features that aid action formation and scaffold successful communication, such as response tokens, interjections, and other short, time-sensitive cues [3]. Many automatic speech recognition (ASR) systems are still blind to such liminal signs, which may cause problems computing speaker intention and rendering the voice assistant

© The Author(s), under exclusive license to Springer Nature Switzerland AG 2022
D. Harris and W.-C. Li (Eds.): HCII 2022, LNAI 13307, pp. 3–17, 2022.
https://doi.org/10.1007/978-3-031-06086-1_1

unable to provide appropriate responses. Thus, efforts have been devoted to draw attention to more features of human speech, tackling questions such as detecting disfluency in speech [4] and tuning the voice assistant system accordingly [5,6]. Another side lies in how these devices sound. One common complaint is the way they speak is "robotic", and that this unnaturalness affects communicative success. An increasing amount of research [7,8] looks into design strategies to make VUI voices more feature-rich and adaptive to interactional cues. For example, there have been multiple attempts to enable voice-AI systems to better mimic disfluency, hesitation, and timing of natural talk [9–14].

Device related considerations aside, whether humans will exhibit the same behavior in human-robot interaction as they interact with a human companion is still in question. One approach is to aim for a humanoid social robot design that strives to mimic HHI (human-human interaction) based on models of ostensible communicative behavior, assuming that robots with human-like appearance and behavior might eventually be perceived as human-like conversational partners [15]. Furthermore, in terms of speech, there are studies showing that humans tend to adjust their speech rate [16] and exhibit phonetic alignment [17] towards voice AI. Nevertheless, [18] found that when working on a picture naming task with a robot partner, human talkers did not show the partner-elicited inhibitory effects reported for the same task when speakers were paired with a human partner.

Speech and voice effects in human-robot interaction have been widely investigated. For example, [19] has manipulated a female-like humanoid robot's speech in three aspects, voice pitch, humor, and empathy. They found that the voice pitch significantly affected the perceived attractiveness of the robot. Humour and empathy also positively affected how the users perceived the interaction. [20] compared three voices, human voice, humanoid voice, and synthesized voice. Human participants gave human voices higher scores on appeal, credibility, and human likeness except for eeriness. Moreover, more similarity to human voice in synthesized voice was rated as more likable.

We mainly look at the voice aspects in this study, specifically, we ask the question of how people would behave when they hear robot speech with filled pauses. Disfluency is an important feature of human conversation. Inter alia, human conversationalists can use disfluency to mark upcoming utterances for various communicative purposes. For instance, there are studies showing that disfluency can benefit listener comprehension [21–24], and improve memory recall [23,25]. Among the different disfluency types, filled pause, also called "filler", is a frequently investigated type and also has been found [26,27] to facilitate memory recall, but [28] has failed to replicate this effect in their online experiments. In the current study, we attempt to replicate the memory recall experiment with human-computer conversations. We hypothesize that the same memory advantage associated with disfluency would be observed when a robot conversational partner produces disfluent speech. Since the existing text-to-speech (TTS) systems may not be able to produce natural-sounding disfluent speech, we included both pre-recorded speech produced by a human reader and the synthesized speech generated by a TTS system.

## 2  Methodology

We used a humanoid robot Furhat [29], a talking head that can display realistic facial features both static and in motion (i.e., lip movements, blinking, and facial expressions such as smiling or frowning) through an internal projector. Using a built-in camera, Furhat can track human speakers in its surroundings and turn itself toward the interlocutor during speech. [30] has discussed the advantage of physical robots in interaction with people compared with virtual agents in multiparty and dyadic settings, with more timely turn-taking. Another study [31] investigated how different kinds of counterparts influence people's decisions based on trust. It was found that, with the same speaking material, compared with a light-emitting audio computer box, a realistic humanoid robot inspired more trust in human participants when the artificial agent was perceived very similar to a human being.

We mainly looked at the memory retention performance of human participants in a human-robot dialogue in Mandarin Chinese. During the interaction, Furhat told three short stories and asked the human listener questions about the details. For the experiment, a 2 (Furhat voice: pre-recorded natural voice vs. synthetic voice) × 2 (Presence of disfluency: fluent vs. disfluent) between-subject design was used.

Natural speech was recorded by a female Mandarin speaker in her 20s (i.e., the reader), while synthesized speech was generated using the Amazon Polly TTS system with the Zhiyu Chinese female voice. Disfluent speech was featured by the insertion of fillers "um" and "uh" at utterance-initial positions every two or three sentences. There is no added surrounding silence, consistent with the findings in [32] of fillers' environment in Mandarin Chinese. Each participant was randomly assigned to one of the four conditions. Mean memory accuracies were compared across conditions. In the space below, we report more details of the experimental methods.

**Table 1.** Story duration (seconds) by experiment condition

| Experiment condition | | Story 1 | Story 2 | Story 3 |
|---|---|---|---|---|
| Pre-recorded speech | Fluent | 79 | 79 | 121 |
| | Disfluent | 82 | 81 | 124 |
| Synthesized speech | Fluent | 91 | 84 | 123 |
| | Disfluent | 93 | 89 | 126 |

## 2.1 Participants

All the participants are native Mandarin speakers from Mainland China recruited from a local university in Hong Kong. The study was approved by the ethics committee of the Hong Kong Polytechnic University, and all participants gave written consent prior to the experiment. None of the participants studied linguistics, psychology, or computer science; in general, the participants had little or no experience interacting with a humanoid robot, although some had used their smart phone voice assistants or interacted with a robot "waiter" bringing takeout, but not experienced users of social robots. In this paper, we report the results with 71 participants (28M, 43F; 18–36 y.o., mean = 23.93, sd = 4.40), 18 each for the two fluent conditions and 19 each for the two disfluent conditions.

## 2.2 Materials

The critical materials of this experiment are three stories for the memory test: a short story about the *Little Prince* (Story 1), a fantasy story constructed by the authors (Story 2), and a short story from *Alice in the Wonderland* (Story 3) that was translated from one of the stories used in [26]. Each story had a few hundred Chinese characters (Story 1: 293; Story 2: 324; Story 3: 499). The story duration by experiment condition is in Table 1. In the disfluent version, "um"/"uh" was inserted at utterance-initial positions every two or three sentences with equal chance between the two markers. Both Story 1 and Story 2 were followed by two multiple-choice questions (each with four choices) regarding some factual detail presented in the story (e.g., "What is the nationality of the author of *Little Prince*? American, British, German, or French?"). Sentences that contained answers to the questions all appeared with an utterance initial "um"/"uh" in the disfluent version of the story. After hearing Story 3, the participant would be asked to retell the story with as much detail as they could remember. Six (out of 14) plot points in Story 3 occurred with an utterance initial "um"/"uh" in the disfluent version (crucial), while the remaining 8 plot points did not vary between the fluent and disfluent versions (control).

The natural speech stimuli were recorded in a soundproof booth, using an AKG C520 head-mounted microphone connected to a UR22MKII interface. Before the recording, the reader listened to a sample of the synthesized speech so that she could match in speech rate and style in her own production. To create natural disfluent stimuli, we elicited naturally produced tokens of "um" and "uh" by asking the reader to retell the stories from memory, and then inserted the clearest disfluency tokens to the designated locations in the fluent productions.

The TTS system was overall successful in generating fluent synthesized speech, but the synthesis of disfluent speech proved to be challenging. This is not surprising, given the well-known difficulty in modeling of naturally produced disfluencies in TTS systems. When conventional spellings of disfluency markers ("um"/"uh"/"恩"/"啊"/"額"/"哦") were inserted into the Chinese text, the resulting synthesized speech was so unnatural that intelligibility was greatly compromised. We ended up using two third tone characters "崀" (for "um") and

"馬我" (for "uh") for most fillers which gave the best synthesis results among all the characters with similar pronunciations. And two first tone characters "恩" and "婀" each once in the second story, because in these two places, the two third tone characters sounded too loud and abrupt. Disfluency tokens are usually lengthened in speech, so we adjusted the speech rate at word level for these disfluency tokens separately, we were able to keep consistency in the story level. The duration of the pre-recorded filler and synthesized fillers are presented in order in Table 2.

**Table 2.** Filler duration (milliseconds) in order in each story

|  | Pre-recorded | Synthesized |
|---|---|---|
| Story1_um_1 | 800 | 460 |
| Story1_um_2 | 460 | 430 |
| Story1_uh_1 | 730 | 500 |
| Story1_uh_2 | 570 | 500 |
| Story1_uh_3 | 640 | 450 |
| Story1_um_3 | 640 | 550 |
| Story2_uh_1 | 740 | 400 |
| Story2_um_1 | 730 | 430 |
| Story2_uh_2 | 480 | 450 |
| Story2_um_2 | 490 | 300 |
| Story2_um_3 | 460 | 430 |
| Story2_uh_3 | 640 | 510 |
| Story3_um_1 | 730 | 340 |
| Story3_uh_1 | 750 | 350 |
| Story3_uh_2 | 640 | 440 |
| Story3_um_2 | 510 | 360 |
| Story3_uh_3 | 640 | 370 |
| Story3_um_3 | 620 | 340 |

## 2.3 Procedure

The human-computer dialogue task occurred in a soundproof booth, with Furhat (410 mm (H) × 270 mm (W) × 240 mm (D)) placed on a table against the wall and the participant seated in a chair about 85 cm away, facing Furhat and roughly at the same eye level. The session was recorded by two video cameras, placed on nearby tables and directed at Furhat and the participant, respectively. The participant's verbal responses were also recorded by Furhat's built-in microphone. After the participant sat down, upon detecting the presence of the participant,

Furhat would "wake up" from the sleep state and initiate the dialogue routine. The routine consisted of five sections, all led by Furhat: (1) greeting and self-introduction (e.g., "My name is Furhat. We will play a game today."), (2) small talk (e.g., "Have you spoken to a robot before?"), (3) practice multiple-choice questions (e.g., "Which one of the following is a Chinese musical instrument?"), (4) story telling and memory test (e.g., "Next, I will tell you a story and then ask you some questions."), (5) ending (e.g., "Thank you. The task has completed. You can leave the room now.").

A complete session lasted about 15 min. The critical section for analysis is (4), which contains all three stories. The preceding sections (i.e., (1)–(3)) serve to familiarize the participant with the interaction with Furhat. Throughout the conversation, Furhat's speech was accompanied by constant lip movements and occasional facial expressions (e.g., smiling, eyebrow movements). For comprehension, Furhat used the Google Cloud speech-to-text system; when recognition failed, we designed subroutines for Furhat to ask for maximally two repetitions from the participant for each response. Based on the participant's responses to multiple-choice questions in sections (3) and (4), Furhat would keep track of and report the participant's cumulative points after each answer.

After the dialogue task completed, the participant would leave the booth and complete a poststudy interview with a human researcher, where the participant would evaluate their experience of interacting with Furhat and provide ratings of naturalness and friendliness for Furhat's speech.

## 3   Results

### 3.1   Memory and Recall Accuracy

We had 74 participants in total, 1 was excluded because of lower than chance level performance, 2 was excluded because they have a linguistic background. We analyzed the accuracy of the remaining 71 participants' verbal responses in the memory recall test. For the multiple-choice questions after Stories 1 and 2, a correct answer gets 1 point and a wrong answer gets 0. If the participant answered wrong first and then changed to the correct answer, they would get a half point. For Story 3, we followed the grading rubrics in [26], the participant gets 1 point for the correctly remembered plot and 0 otherwise. The total points were divided by the number of questions (or plot points) to derive accuracy scores in the range of 0–100%. We built generalized mixed effects models (using the lme4 package [33]) to examine the effects of disfluency (fluent vs. disfluent) and type of speech(pre-recorded vs. synthesised) and their interaction on response accuracy, with by-participant and by-question/plot random effects. Naturalness and friendliness ratings are modeled separately in ordinal logistic regression models (using the MASS package [34]) with similar structure as the accuracy models. Figure 1 and Fig. 2 plots the mean accuracy scores by experimental conditions.

As shown in Fig. 1, overall, participants' response accuracy for the multiple-choice questions in stories 1 and 2 (mean accuracy = 73.37%, baseline = 25%)

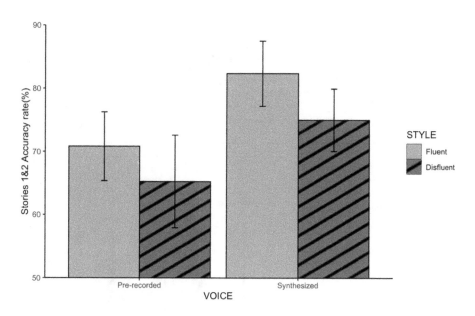

**Fig. 1.** Mean accuracy scores (%) of multi-choice questions by experimental condition in stories 1&2.

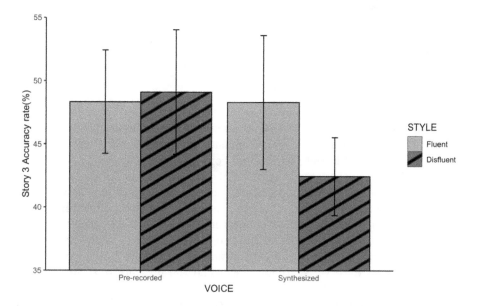

**Fig. 2.** Mean accuracy scores (%) of retelling story task by experimental condition in story 3

is much higher than the retelling in story 3 (mean accuracy = 48.31%) in Fig. 2. In addition, when we look at the accuracy result in crucial and control groups in Fig. 3 we observe similar patterns across stories: (1) when Furhat produces synthesized speech, disfluent speech seems to elicit lower accuracy rates; (2) in the retelling task of story 3, the general accuracy rate is higher in crucial conditions than in control conditions. Neither of these patterns reached statistical significance (ps > 0.05).

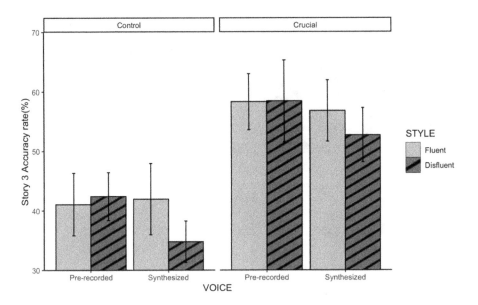

**Fig. 3.** Mean accuracy scores (%) of retelling story task by group in story 3

**Comparing Memory and Recall Accuracy Across Tasks.** Comparing the accuracy result between fluent and disfluent conditions in Fig. 1 and in Fig. 2, we see that the trend in the pre-recorded voice condition of story three is opposite than the three other scenarios where the accuracy rates are generally lower in disfluent conditions. Not only we did not see an evident gap between fluent and disfluent conditions, in this case, we see a very slight advantage in the disfluent condition (about 0.8%). This reverse trend made us wonder how different it is between story three and the two previous stories. We carried out an additional analysis adding a third explanatory variable *story* besides voice (pre-recorded natural voice vs. synthetic voice) and the presence of disfluency. We again employed a generalized mixed effects model [33] to examine the three independent variables and their interaction on response accuracy, with by-participant and by-question/plot random effects. random effect. No statistically significant (p < 0.05) main effect or interaction effect was observed, but at the 0.1 significance level, there is a main effect of story three ($\beta = -1.19, p = 0.0977$), the accuracy was lower in story three and higher in stories one and two, and an interaction of synthesized voice and story three: in fluent speech, the difference between synthesized voice and pre-recorded voice is lower for story three than for stories one and two ($\beta = -0.84, p = 0.0902$). We also employed a linear mixed effects model [33] to examine the three independent variables and their interaction on response accuracy, with by-participant as the random effect. We obtained a significant main effect of story three (ps < 0.001), but no statistically significant interaction effects were observed.

## 3.2   Post-study Interview Results

Figures 4 and 5 shows the naturalness and friendliness scores obtained from the post-study interviews. The naturalness rating did not differ much across conditions except for the lowest rating for disfluent synthesized speech, suggesting that the participants were indeed sensitive to the unnaturalness of synthesized disfluent speech. Meanwhile, for friendliness rating, fluent pre-recorded speech tends to be more preferred over disfluent pre-recorded speech. In contrast, the opposite trend seems present for synthesized speech, suggesting a possible compensation for the phonetic awkwardness of disfluent synthesized speech, although neither trend reaches statistical significance.

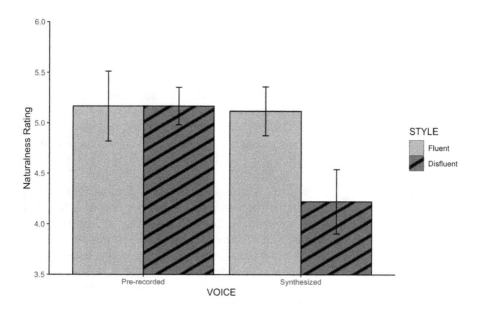

**Fig. 4.** Mean naturalness scores by experimental condition.

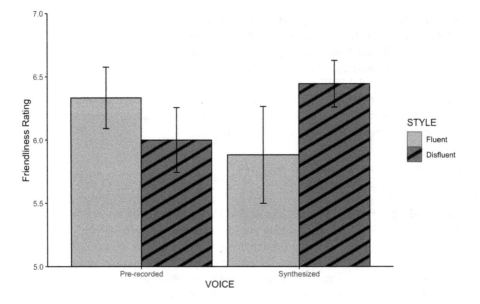

**Fig. 5.** Mean friendliness scores by experimental condition.

## 4  Discussion

This study aims to investigate whether disfluency in machine speech may influence human listeners' memory retention of linguistic information. Looking at Fig. 1 and Fig. 2, what stands out in these two figures is the general pattern of better accuracy in the fluent speech condition than in the disfluent speech condition. However, this advantage of fluent speech over disfluent speech seems to be subdued in the retelling task (story 3) with pre-recorded natural speech. Recall that the existing literature shows mixed findings regarding the disfluency advantage in memory and recall. While some studies (e.g., [26]) found better memory performance when exposed to disfluent speech, others found null effects. Our results contribute further data to the complexity of the (dis)fluency effects on memory retention. To account for the observed results, we propose that there are two competing forces: on one hand, disfluency in speech may lead to heightened attention from the listener and therefore boost recall performance (i.e., the disfluency advantage); on the other hand, disfluencies may also cause disruptions in speech comprehension and thus hinder the processing and memorizing of the information (i.e., the disfluency disadvantage). Both forces co-exist in any speech comprehension task, but their relative strengths may differ as a function of speech naturalness (especially regarding the disfluency tokens), nature of the memory task (and task difficulty), and other factors. In a given task, if the disfluency advantage overwhelms the disfluency disadvantage, we should observe overall better memory performance with disfluent speech; on the contrary, if the disfluency disadvantage overwhelms the disfluency advantage, we should observe overall worse performance with disfluent speech; if the disfluency advantage and disadvantage are similar in strength, we would observe a null effect of disfluency on memory performance.

If we compare the current study with that of [26], the experimental design of [26] is most similar to the condition of story retelling task (story 3) with pre-recorded fluent/disfluent speech in the current study. Importantly, it is also in this condition where we observed the least amount of overall disfluency disadvantage (or the highest level of disfluency advantage). In the rest of this section, we discuss possible reasons why other experimental conditions show a lesser degree of disfluency advantage in comparison.

## 4.1    Task Differences

Two memory tasks were used in the current study. In the first two stories (stories 1 and 2), the participants answered the multiple-choice questions, whereas for story 3, the participants were asked to retell the whole story. The two tasks differ significantly in terms of the nature of the task and the level of difficulty. Answering multiple-choice questions mainly requires recognition memory [35], as the listener chooses the choice that best matches the information extracted from memory as the most plausible answer to the question. In a retelling task, however, the listener needs to not only extract information from memory but also bind the information together, which often requires information reorganization and is thus a more challenging memory task.

In the current study, the participants achieved significantly higher accuracy in the multiple-choice task (stories 1 and 2) than in the retelling task (story 3). This is in line with the task differences discussed above. Furthermore, we also observed a more evident trend of disfluency disadvantage (i.e., higher accuracy with fluent speech than with disfluent speech) in the easier, multiple-choice task than in the retelling task. This indicates that when the task is easier, the disfluency disadvantage overpowers any potential disfluency advantage related to heightened attention, probably because an easier task does not require a high level of attention after all.

## 4.2    Synthesized Filled Pauses

In the more difficult story retelling task of this study, where memory performance may be more sensitive to attention levels and thus more likely to show a disfluency advantage, we still observed a trend of overall disfluency disadvantage with synthesized speech, but with pre-recorded natural speech, this trend seems to have disappeared, suggesting that the disfluency advantage is strong enough to cancel out the disfluency disadvantage. We argue that the discrepancy between the results from synthesized speech and those from pre-recorded natural speech is mainly due to the perceptual unnaturalness of the synthesized disfluency tokens (filled pauses) in the former condition.

Compared with the naturally produced filled pauses, the synthesized ones used in the current study are different in several acoustic dimensions. Most importantly, the synthesizer we used did not have a separate module for synthesizing disfluency tokens, so we had to generate filled pauses by synthesizing real words that are phonetically similar. Previous studies have shown that naturally produced filled pauses should be longer than phonetically similar real words. In the current study, the pre-recorded natural filled pauses are clearly longer than the synthesized ones (see Table 2), and the filled pauses used in previous studies like [26] and [36] were even longer (e.g., the "um" tokens used in these studies were longer than 1000 ms). In addition to duration, the vowels in the synthesized filled pauses of the current study may also pose naturalness concerns. In naturally produced speech, the vowels in "um" and "uh" are not exactly the same as [a] or schwa in real words; [11] demonstrates that it is preferable to use a distinct phone (i.e., one that is different from the sounds of real words) when synthesizing filled pauses. Given both the shorter duration and the less-than-natural sounding vowels, it is not surprising that synthesized disfluent speech received the lowest naturalness ratings from the participants of the current study, compared with pre-recorded fluent and disfluent speech and synthesized fluent speech (see Fig. 4).

Given the low naturalness of the synthesized filled pauses, the disadvantage associated with disfluency may be exacerbated, as listeners experience greater disruptions and confusion in speech comprehension and information processing, which in turn leads to memory difficulties. In some sense, the comprehension of unnatural disfluent speech may be comparable to the comprehension of heavily accented speech. As found in [37], when the acoustic signals substantially deviate from listeners' expectations for the upcoming message, cognitive resources will be strained, and verbal working memory and cognitive control will be impaired.

Finally, the literature has also shown that in naturally produced spontaneous speech, the distribution of disfluencies is often related to planning difficulties and the accessibility of the upcoming linguistic units. Correspondingly, listeners may use the presence of disfluencies to predict the content of the upcoming message (e.g., [22]). In the current study, disfluency tokens are inserted roughly equidistantly in the stories, without considering the accessibility of the following noun or verb. We suggest that this design may also cause some disruption in speech comprehension for both pre-recorded and synthesized speech, and hence undermine the potential benefit of disfluency on memory retention.

### 4.3 Naturalness vs. Friendliness

In the post-study interview results, we observe a discrepancy between the naturalness ratings and the friendliness ratings. Specifically, the synthesized disfluent condition sees the lowest ratings in naturalness but the highest ratings in friendliness, compared with all the other three conditions. It is not yet clear to us why a less natural sounding robot would sound more friendly to the user. Is it because human interlocutors feel less intimidated by a disfluent and less natural sounding robot partner? We hope to explore a wider spectrum of user evaluations of robot speech (e.g., [12]) and human-computer interactions in the future.

# 5   Conclusion

In this study, we investigated the influence of disfluency in robot speech on Mandarin listeners' memory retention. We used a human-computer dialogue task, with a humanoid robot Furhat implemented with two types of robot voice (pre-recorded natural speech and synthesized speech). For the memory test, human listeners were asked to either answer multiple-choice questions or retell the story they have just heard. Our results showed that in three out of the four experimental conditions (multiple-choice with pre-recorded voice, multiple-choice with synthesized voice, story retelling with synthesized voice), there is a trend for lower memory accuracy with disfluent speech, evidencing a disfluency disadvantage. Only in one condition, i.e., story telling with pre-recorded voice, did we see an overall null effect of disfluency, suggesting that the disfluency advantage was cancelled out by the potential benefit of disfluency.

Although we did not find a clear effect of disfluency advantage, as showed in [26], our results do suggest that the effect would be more likely observed using natural-sounding disfluent speech and a challenging memory task like story retelling (which is also what [26] used).

Our results with disfluent synthesized speech join the existing literature on the processing of robot speech disfluency (e.g., [38,39]) in showing that disfluent synthesized speech is harder for human listeners to process than fluent synthesized speech is, probably due to low naturalness.

In future research, we hope to continue to explore the effects of disfluency in robot speech on human listeners' speech comprehension.

**Acknowledgement.** We thank Albert Chau, Sarah Chen, Yitian Hong, and Xiaofu Zhang for their assistance with the experiment.

# References

1. Ammari, T., Kaye, J., Tsai, J., Bentley, F.: Music, search, and IoT: how people (really) use voice assistants. ACM Trans. Comput.-Hum. Interact. **26** (2019). https://doi.org/10.1145/3311956
2. Kopp, S., Krämer, N.: Revisiting human-agent communication: the importance of joint co-construction and understanding mental states. Front. Psychol. **12** (2021). https://www.frontiersin.org/articles/10.3389/fpsyg.2021.580955/full
3. Dingemanse, M.: Between sound and speech: liminal signs in interaction. Res. Lang. Soc. Interact. **53**, 188–196 (2020)
4. Shriberg, E.: Spontaneous speech: how people really talk and why engineers should care. In: Interspeech 2005, pp. 1781–1784 (2005). https://www.isca-speech.org/archive/interspeech_2005/shriberg05_interspeech.html
5. Mitra, V., et al.: Analysis and tuning of a voice assistant system for dysfluent speech. In: Interspeech 2021, pp. 4848–4852 (2021). https://www.isca-speech.org/archive/interspeech_2021/mitra21_interspeech.html
6. Wu, J., Ahuja, K., Li, R., Chen, V., Bigham, J.: ScratchThat: supporting command-agnostic speech repair in voice-driven assistants. Proc. ACM Interact. Mob. Wearable Ubiquitous Technol. **3** (2019). https://doi.org/10.1145/3328934

7. Sutton, S., Foulkes, P., Kirk, D., Lawson, S.: Voice as a design material: sociophonetic inspired design strategies in human-computer interaction. In: Conference on Human Factors in Computing Systems - Proceedings, pp. 1–14 (2019)

8. Schmitt, A., Zierau, N., Janson, A., Leimeister, J.: Voice as a contemporary frontier of interaction design. In: European Conference On Information Systems (ECIS) (2021)

9. Adell, J., Escudero, D., Bonafonte, A.: Production of filled pauses in concatenative speech synthesis based on the underlying fluent sentence. Speech Commun. **54**, 459–476 (2012). https://www.sciencedirect.com/science/article/pii/S0167639311001580

10. Betz, S., Wagner, P., Schlangen, D.: Micro-structure of disfluencies: basics for conversational speech synthesis. In: Interspeech 2015, pp. 2222–2226 (2015). https://www.isca-speech.org/archive/interspeech_2015/betz15_interspeech.html

11. Dall, R., Tomalin, M., Wester, M.: Synthesising filled pauses: representation and datamixing. In: Proceedings of the 9th ISCA Workshop On Speech Synthesis Workshop (SSW 9), pp. 7–13 (2016)

12. Betz, S., Carlmeyer, B., Wagner, P., Wrede, B.: Interactive hesitation synthesis: modelling and evaluation. Multimodal Technol. Interact. **2**, 9 (2018). http://www.mdpi.com/2414-4088/2/1/9

13. Carlmeyer, B., Betz, S., Wagner, P., Wrede, B., Schlangen, D.: The hesitating robot - implementation and first impressions. In: Companion of the 2018 ACM/IEEE International Conference on Human-Robot Interaction, pp. 77–78 (2018). https://doi.org/10.1145/3173386.3176992

14. Székely, É., Henter, G., Beskow, J., Gustafson, J.: How to train your fillers: uh and um in spontaneous speech synthesis. In: 10th ISCA Workshop On Speech Synthesis (SSW 10) (2019)

15. Zonca, J., Folsø, A., Sciutti, A.: The role of reciprocity in human-robot social influence. IScience **24**, 103424 (2021). https://www.sciencedirect.com/science/article/pii/S258900422101395X

16. Cohn, M., Liang, K., Sarian, M., Zellou, G., Yu, Z.: Speech rate adjustments in conversations with an Amazon Alexa socialbot. Front. Commun. **6**, 1–8 (2021)

17. Zellou, G., Cohn, M., Kline, T.: The influence of conversational role on phonetic alignment toward voice-AI and human interlocutors. Lang. Cogn. Neurosci. 1–15 (2021). https://doi.org/10.1080/23273798.2021.1931372

18. Wudarczyk, O., et al.: Robots facilitate human language production. Sci. Rep. **11**, 16737 (2021)

19. Niculescu, A., van Dijk, B., Nijholt, A., Li, H., See, S.L.: Making social robots more attractive: the effects of voice pitch, humor and empathy. Int. J. Soc. Robot. **5**(2), 171–191 (2012). https://doi.org/10.1007/s12369-012-0171-x

20. Kühne, K., Fischer, M., Zhou, Y.: The human takes it all: humanlike synthesized voices are perceived as less eerie and more likable. Evidence from a subjective ratings study. Front. Neurorobot. **14** (2020). https://www.frontiersin.org/article/10.3389/fnbot.2020.593732

21. Arnold, J., Tanenhaus, M., Altmann, R., Fagnano, M.: The old and thee, uh, new: disfluency and reference resolution. Psychol. Sci. **15**, 578–582 (2004)

22. Arnold, J., Tanenhaus, M.: Disfluency Effects in Comprehension: How New Information Can Become Accessible. The Processing and Acquisition of Reference (2011)

23. MacGregor, L., Corley, M., Donaldson, D.: Listening to the sound of silence: disfluent silent pauses in speech have consequences for listeners. Neu-

ropsychologia **48**, 3982–3992 (2010). https://linkinghub.elsevier.com/retrieve/pii/S0028393210004148

24. Corley, M., MacGregor, L., Donaldson, D.: It's the way that you, ER, say it: hesitations in speech affect language comprehension. Cognition **105**, 658–668 (2007). https://www.sciencedirect.com/science/article/pii/S0010027706002186

25. Collard, P., Corley, M., MacGregor, L., Donaldson, D.: Attention orienting effects of hesitations in speech: evidence from ERPs. J. Exp. Psychol. Learn. Mem. Cogn. **34**, 696–702 (2008). http://doi.apa.org/getdoi.cfm?doi=10.1037/0278-7393.34.3.696

26. Fraundorf, S., Watson, D.: The disfluent discourse: effects of filled pauses on recall. J. Mem. Lang. **65**, 161–175 (2011)

27. Bosker, H., Tjiong, J., Quené, H., Sanders, T., De Jong, N.: Both native and non-native disfluencies trigger listeners' attention. In: The 7th Workshop on Disfluency in Spontaneous Speech (DiSS 2015) (2015)

28. Muhlack, B., et al.: Revisiting recall effects of filler particles in German and English. In: Proceedings of Interspeech 2021 (2021)

29. Al Moubayed, S., Beskow, J., Skantze, G., Granström, B.: Furhat: a back-projected human-like robot head for multiparty human-machine interaction. In: Esposito, A., Esposito, A.M., Vinciarelli, A., Hoffmann, R., Müller, V.C. (eds.) Cognitive Behavioural Systems. LNCS, vol. 7403, pp. 114–130. Springer, Heidelberg (2012). https://doi.org/10.1007/978-3-642-34584-5_9

30. Skantze, G.: Turn-taking in conversational systems and human-robot interaction: a review. Comput. Speech Lang. **67**, 101178 (2021)

31. Cominelli, L., et al.: Promises and trust in human-robot interaction. Sci. Rep. **11**, 9687 (2021)

32. Zhao, Y., Jurafsky, D.: A preliminary study of Mandarin filled pauses (2005)

33. Bates, D., Mächler, M., Bolker, B., Walker, S.: Fitting linear mixed-effects models using LME4. J. Stat. Softw. **67**, 1–48 (2015)

34. Venables, W., Ripley, B., Venables, W.: Modern Applied Statistics with S. Springer, Cham (2002).OCLC: ocm49312402

35. Voskuilen, C., Ratcliff, R., Fennell, A., McKoon, G.: Diffusion models of memory and decision making. Learn. Mem. Comprehensive Reference 227–241 (2017). https://linkinghub.elsevier.com/retrieve/pii/B9780128093245210456

36. Corley, M., Hartsuiker, R.: Why um helps auditory word recognition: the temporal delay hypothesis. Plos One **6**, e19792 (2011). https://journals.plos.org/plosone/article?id=10.1371/journal.pone.0019792

37. Van Engen, K., Peelle, J.: Listening effort and accented speech. Front. Hum. Neurosci. **8** (2014). https://www.frontiersin.org/article/10.3389/fnhum.2014.00577

38. Carlmeyer, B., Schlangen, D., Wrede, B.: Look at me: self-interruptions as attention booster? In: Proceedings of the Fourth International Conference on Human Agent Interaction, pp. 221–224 (2016). https://dl.acm.org/doi/10.1145/2974804.298048

39. Carlmeyer, B., Schlangen, D., Wrede, B.: Exploring self-interruptions as a strategy for regaining the attention of distracted users. In: Proceedings of the 1st Workshop on Embodied Interaction with Smart Environments - EISE 2016, pp. 1–6 (2016). http://dl.acm.org/citation.cfm?doid=3008028.3008029

# Investigation of Temporal Changes of Gaze Locations During Characteristic Evaluation When Viewing Whole-Body Photos

Fuyuko Iwasaki, Masashi Nishiyama[✉] [iD], and Yoshio Iwai[✉]

Graduate School of Engineering, Tottori University,
101 Minami 4-chome, Koyama-cho, Tottori 680-8550, Japan
nishiyama@tottori-u.ac.jp

**Abstract.** We investigated how the observer's gaze locations temporally shift over the body parts of a subject in an image when the observer is tasked to evaluate the subject's characteristics. We also investigated how the temporal changes of the gaze locations vary when different characteristic words are contained in the tasks. Previous analytical studies did not consider time-series gaze locations, although they did determine that the initial location that the observer's gaze fixates on is the subject's face. In our analysis, we assigned characteristic evaluation tasks to observers and measured their gaze locations temporally while they viewed human images. We computed the distance from the observer's gaze location to the subject's body part at each time point and evaluated the temporal difference of the distances between the tasks. We found that the observer's gaze fixated on the face initially and shifted to the upper and lower body parts. We determined a common pattern of time-series signals of gaze locations among many participants and individual patterns among a few participants. Furthermore, we found that the temporal changes of the gaze locations became similar or dissimilar according to the characteristic words contained in the tasks.

**Keywords:** Gaze · Temporal change · Subject's characteristic

## 1 Introduction

Interactions through displays, such as online presentations and parties, are becoming increasingly popular. In the future, it may be common to interact with others using large displays that show whole bodies (Fig. 1). These potential future online interactions will offer opportunities to gauge other people's characteristics through display images. In formal, real-world scenarios, it is essential to make a favorable impression on others, and this is likely to remain important in the online space. In this paper, we consider how observers alter their behavior when perceiving unfamiliar subjects' characteristics through display images in formal scenarios.

D. Harris and W.-C. Li (Eds.): HCII 2022, LNAI 13307, pp. 18–32, 2022.
https://doi.org/10.1007/978-3-031-06086-1_2

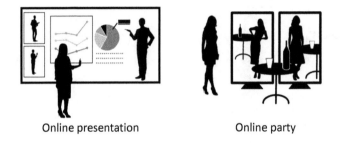

Online presentation                Online party

**Fig. 1.** Future interactions on large displays, in which people use their whole bodies. We consider that people hold online presentations and parties when far away from each other. Observers have more opportunities to perceive subjects' characteristics through images on large displays. In these opportunities, conveying the characteristic that the observers feel favorable is essential, as well as the interaction in real space.

In real-space interactions, observers obtain a large amount of information through vision when they evaluate the characteristics of other people [2, 10, 11, 13]. These visual functions play an important role when evaluating subjects' characteristics on display images. In this study, we consider gaze behavior as a visual function. Specifically, we consider the case in which observers direct their gaze to a subject's face, upper body, lower body, and other body parts.

In analytical studies [7, 14] in cognitive science, researchers investigated the initial gaze locations of observers performing characteristic evaluation tasks. These researchers reported that the gaze first fixates on subjects' faces in images. Based on this observation, we can assume that the face is an important cue in evaluating subjects' characteristics. However, in these analytical studies, the researchers did not investigate how gaze locations temporally shift over other body parts after the observer first looks at a face.

In this study, we investigated how the gaze locations of observers, who are tasked to evaluate characteristics, temporally shift over body parts after the observer first looks at a face. We also investigated whether the temporal changes of the gaze locations varied when the characteristic word included in the task changed. To achieve this, we displayed a stimulus image containing a subject on the display screen. We measured the time series of gaze locations of an observer looking at the stimulus image. We assigned observers the task of evaluating a characteristic word and asked them whether they considered the word to match the stimulus image. We calculated the distance from the body part of the subject in the image to the gaze location measured from the observer and evaluated the time-series signals of the distances. The experimental results demonstrated that the observer's gaze fixated on the face initially, and moved away from the face and variously to the upper and lower body parts as time passed. We found a common pattern of time-series signals of gaze locations among many participants and individual patterns among a small number of participants. We also found that some of the characteristic words included in the tasks had similar time-series signals to the gaze locations, whereas others did not have those of the gaze locations.

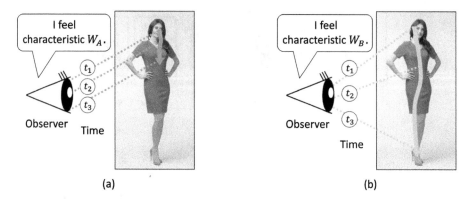

(a)                              (b)

**Fig. 2.** We assumed that the gaze location of the observer shifted over the body parts of the subject in the image as time passed when the observer was tasked to evaluate characteristic words $W_A$ and $W_B$.

## 2    Analysis of Temporal Changes of the Gaze Locations

### 2.1    Hypotheses

We formulated hypotheses to analyze the time-series signals of the gaze locations measured in the task of evaluating characteristics of human images as follows:

H1: When the participants are tasked to evaluate the characteristics of subjects, the participants' gaze locations temporally shift from the faces of the subjects to other body parts.

H2: When the characteristic words included in the task change, the time-series signals of the gaze locations described in Hypothesis H1 change.

In this study, we define the gaze location as the point where the gaze direction vector intersects the stimulus image on the display screen at a certain time.

First, we present a specific example (Fig. 2(a)) of what is expected for H1. We consider the case in which a task containing characteristic word $W_A$, such as gentle or intellectual, is assigned to a participant. We consider that the gaze first fixates on the subject's face, as described in [1,7–9,12,14,15]. Then the gaze location shifts from the face to other body parts, such as the chest, as time passes. When we assign a task with another characteristic word $W_B$, we consider the gaze locations to shift differently over time, as shown in Fig. 2(b). Second, we present a specific example of what is expected for H2. When we compare the time-series signals of the gaze locations between Figs. 2(a) and (b), we consider that the gaze location at each time point differs because of the difference in the characteristic words included in the tasks. To confirm these two hypotheses, we design an experimental method for measuring and analyzing gaze locations. We describe the details below.

## 2.2   Task

We explain the characteristic words contained in the task. We use characteristic words that often apply to formal scenarios in which many people share social conventions. Specifically, we target characteristic words used in formal scenarios, such as presentations and parties. Note that formal scenarios make people likely to hope to make a positive impression on another person; hence, we exclude words that express negative characteristics.

We had a free discussion to select the characteristic words that fit formal scenarios. As a result, we chose the following six characteristic words used in our analysis:

- Gentle
- Ambitious
- Unique
- Rich
- Intellectual
- Stylish

In our analysis, we assign observers the task of evaluating the characteristic words used in the formal scenario to measure the observers' gaze locations. The tasks are as follows:

$T_1$: Do you feel the subject is gentle?
$T_2$: Do you feel the subject is ambitious?
$T_3$: Do you feel the subject is unique?
$T_4$: Do you feel the subject is rich?
$T_5$: Do you feel the subject is intellectual?
$T_6$: Do you feel the subject is stylish?

We asked the participants to complete each task by answering yes or no in our analysis.

## 2.3   Stimulus Images

We describe the details of the stimulus images observed by the participants. For each participant, we used 100 stimulus images containing subjects. Figure 3 shows a sample of the stimulus images used in our analysis. We only used images containing standing subjects, which are often encountered in formal scenarios, such as poster presentation areas and standing party receptions. The hands and feet were not aligned between the subjects. We assumed that the subject's body area was visible from head to toe and that the subject's face was close to the front. We excluded sitting and supine postures. We used only one  subject per

**Fig. 3.** Sample of stimulus images used in our analysis.

stimulus image. We set the ratio of female to male subjects to 1:1, with 50 males and 50 females. We chose the subject's clothing to be appropriate for formal scenarios such as presentations and parties. We set the subject's facial expression to either smiling or neutral. We assumed that there was no background object in the stimulus image that was more prominent than the subject. We also assumed that there were no other objects in front of the subject. We resized the image to 972 pixels in height. We maintained the aspect ratio of the original image. The average size of the image width was $447.2 \pm 82.5$ pixels. We collected images from the photo website[1].

---

[1] https://www.photo-ac.com/.

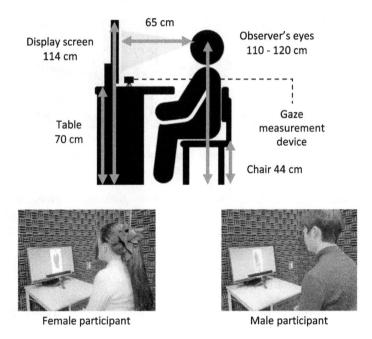

**Fig. 4.** Experimental settings for gaze measurement.

## 2.4   Settings

Twenty-four participants (12 males and 12 females, with an average age of $22.0\pm$ 1.2 years old, Japanese students) participated in the study. We fully explained the disadvantages of gaze measurement to the participants and obtained their consent on a form. The participants and the subjects in the stimulus images were not directly acquainted with each other. During gaze measurement, we required the participants to complete all tasks $(T_1, \ldots, T_6)$. The procedure followed by the participants performing tasks is described in Sect. 2.5.

In this section, we describe the settings for our analysis. The participant was seated on a chair at a distance of 65 cm horizontally from the display screen. The height of the chair was 44 cm from the floor. The eye height of the participant was between 110 and 120 cm from the floor. We used the settings shown in Fig. 4 to measure the gaze locations of the participants. We displayed the stimulus image on the 24-in. display screen (AOC G2460PF, resolution $1920 \times 1080$ pixels, refresh rate 59.94 Hz) to measure the gaze locations. Figure 5 shows examples of the stimulus images on the display screen. We displayed the stimulus images at random locations on the screen to avoid center bias [3,4]. We used Gazepoint GP3 HD as the gaze measurement device. The sampling rate of this device was 150 Hz. In practice, the interval of the measurement time of the gaze location varied. Thus, we resampled at 60 Hz to make the interval equal using bilinear interpolation.

**Fig. 5.** Examples of stimulus images displayed on the screen.

As a preliminary experiment, we evaluated the gaze measurement error using these settings. We showed reference images containing six reference points with known locations to seven people on the screen. The average error from the reference points to the gaze locations was $71.4 \pm 32.0$ pixels.

### 2.5    Gaze Measurement Procedure

We used the following procedure to measure the gaze locations of the participants in our analysis.

$P_1$: We randomly selected one participant for gaze measurement.

$P_2$: We randomly set the order of tasks $(T_1, \ldots, T_6)$ to be assigned to the participant.

$P_3$: We explained the task given to the participant, and the measurement procedure.

$P_4$: We displayed a gray image on the screen for one second.

$P_5$: We randomly selected one stimulus image from all the stimulus images, without overlap.

$P_6$: We displayed the selected stimulus image on the screen for six seconds and recorded the time-series gaze locations of the participant.

$P_7$: We displayed a black image on the screen for three seconds.

$P_8$: We asked the participant to provide an answer for completing the task explained in $P_3$.

$P_9$: We repeated the procedure from $P_4$ to $P_8$ until we used all the stimulus images.

$P_{10}$: We repeated the procedure from $P_3$ to $P_9$ until all tasks were completed according to the task order set in $P_2$.

$P_{11}$: We repeated the procedure from $P_1$ to $P_{10}$ until all participants had completed the tasks.

### 2.6    Body Parts Used in Our Analysis

The subjects in the stimulus images used in our analysis were in standing postures, as described in Sect. 2.3. The subjects' hands and feet were freely positioned. When the subjects in the images were in various standing postures, the

$b_1$ : Nose

$b_2$ : Right shoulder                           $b_3$ : Left shoulder

$b_4$ : Right elbow                              $b_5$ : Left elbow

$b_6$ : Right wrist                              $b_7$ : Left wrist

$b_8$ : Waist

$b_9$ : Right knee                               $b_{10}$ : Left knee

$b_{11}$ : Right toes                            $b_{12}$ : Left toes

(a)

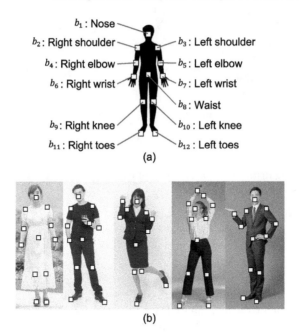

(b)

**Fig. 6.** (a) Body parts used for our analysis. (b) Examples of the body parts detected from the stimulus images.

positions of the body parts differed between the stimulus images. Thus, we cannot directly compare the measured gaze locations between the stimulus images. We considered detecting body parts from the stimulus images and calculated the relative distances between the body parts and the gaze locations. We explain how we calculated the distance in Sect. 2.7.

In this section, we explain body parts $b \in \{b_1, \cdots, b_{12}\}$ in Fig. 6(a) used in our analysis. We used 12 body parts: the nose in the center of the head region, the right and left shoulders in the torso region, the waist, two right and two left joints in the arms, and two right and two left joints in the feet. To detect the body parts of the subjects in the stimulus images, we used OpenPose [5]. Note that we excluded body parts with close distances between joints, such as palm joints and toe joints, and used only body parts with far distances between joints. Figure 6(b) shows examples of body parts detected in the stimulus images.

## 2.7   Calculation of the Temporal Changes of the Gaze Locations

In our analysis, we used the distance from the measured gaze location to the body part. We describe the method used to calculate the distance below. Suppose gaze location $x(t, i, T, \mathcal{X})$ measured at time $t$ when participant $i$ observes stimulus image $\mathcal{X}$ when task $T \in \{T_1, \cdots, T_6\}$ is given. Distance $d(t, b, i, T, \mathcal{X})$ from gaze location $x(t, i, T, \mathcal{X})$ to location $p(b, \mathcal{X})$ of body part $b$ of the subject in the stimulus image is expressed as

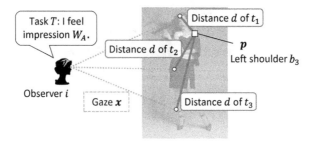

**Fig. 7.** Calculating distance $d(t, b_3, i, T, \mathcal{X})$ of time $t$ between gaze location $\boldsymbol{x}(t, i, T, \mathcal{X})$ and left shoulder location $\boldsymbol{p}(b_3, \mathcal{X})$.

$$d(t, b, i, T, \mathcal{X}) = \frac{\check{D}_\mathcal{X}}{D_\mathcal{X}} \|\boldsymbol{x}(t, i, T, \mathcal{X}) - \boldsymbol{p}(b, \mathcal{X})\|_2. \tag{1}$$

We use the L2 norm as the distance metric. Let $D_\mathcal{X}$ be the distance from the midpoint of the left and right shoulders to the waist point on each stimulus image, and let $\check{D}_\mathcal{X}$ be the average value of $D_\mathcal{X}$ computed from all the stimulus images. In our analysis, $\check{D}_\mathcal{X}$ was 250.0 pixels. As an example, the case of measuring distance $d(t, b_3, i, T, \mathcal{X})$ for left shoulder $b_3$ is shown in Fig. 7.

Next, using the set $\mathcal{S}$ containing all the stimulus images, we calculate the average distance for body part $b$ at time $t$ as

$$d(t, b, i, T) = \frac{1}{X} \sum_{\mathcal{X} \in \mathcal{S}} d(t, b, i, T, \mathcal{X}), \tag{2}$$

where $X$ is the number of stimulus images. In our analysis, we measured the gaze location at 60 Hz for 6 s; hence, the total number of gaze locations sampled in the procedure $P_6$ of Sect. 2.5 was 360. We had to pay attention to eye blinking, which often resulted in times when the gaze location was not measured. In this case, we did not include times that corresponded to blinking when we calculated the distance.

Finally, we refer to the time-series signal for which the values of distance $d(t, b, i, T)$ at each time point $t$ were aligned in the time direction as the temporal change of the gaze locations.

## 3    Experimental Results

### 3.1    Analysis of the Average Temporal Changes of the Gaze Locations

We investigated hypothesis H1 described in Sect. 2.1 by computing the average temporal changes of the gaze location using distance $d(t, b)$ of time $t$ between the measured gaze and each body part $b$ as follows:

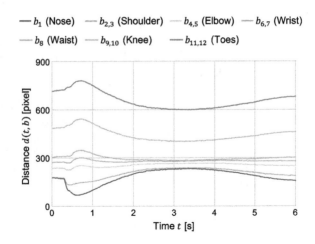

**Fig. 8.** Average temporal changes of the gaze location for each body part $b$. Average distance $d(t,b)$ at each time point $t$ was computed from the results for all tasks and participants.

$$d(t,b) = \frac{1}{6I} \sum_{T \in \mathcal{T}} \sum_{i \in \mathcal{I}} d(t,b,i,T), \qquad (3)$$

where $d(t,b,i,T)$ is the distance in Eq. (2), $\mathcal{T}$ is the set of tasks $\{T_1, \cdots, T_6\}$, $I$ is the number of participants, and $\mathcal{I}$ is the set containing all participants.

Before evaluating distance $d(t,b)$, we checked distance $d(t,b,i,T)$ calculated from the symmetrical body parts. Differences in the distance were minimal between the right and left shoulders, between the right and left elbows, between the right and left wrists, between the right and left knees, and between the right and left toes. Thus, we averaged the distances between the left and right body parts for symmetrical cases. In our analysis, to calculate the distance, we used the following body parts: shoulder $B_{2,3}$, elbow $B_{4,5}$, wrist $B_{6,7}$, knee $B_{9,10}$, and toes $B_{11,12}$.

Figure 8 shows the average temporal changes of the gaze location using distance $d(t,b)$ for each body part $b$. The vertical axis represents the magnitude of the value of $d(t,b)$. If this magnitude is small, the gaze location is close to the body part location on average. The horizontal axis represents time $t$ when the gaze location was measured.

Between $t = 0$ s and 0.3 s, there was a period when the average distance was almost unchanged. We consider that the participants' brains worked to respond in some way to the stimulus image in this period. After $t = 0.3$ s, the average distance for the nose $b_1$ continually became smaller, reaching a minimum distance at 0.6 s. We consider that the participants shifted their gaze to the subject shown at a random position on the display screen and started to observe the subject's face. This result shows the same tendency as the results in previous analytical studies [7,14]. After $t = 0.6$ s, the average distance for the nose $b_1$ tended to increase toward 3.1 s, and this increase gradually became smaller. By contrast, the average distance for the toes $b_{11,12}$ tended to decrease, and this decrease gradually became smaller. We did not determine any particular body part for which the average distance was extremely small in this period. Between $t = 3.1$ s and 6 s, the average distance for the nose $b_1$ gradually decreased, and conversely, the average distance for the toes $b_{11,12}$ gradually increased.

We summarize the results of our analysis of hypothesis H1. The participants not only looked at the face at all times but also observed other body parts in addition to the face after first looking at it. However, we cannot say that the body part where the gaze fixated was common among the participants or stimulus images. We confirmed that the gaze locations variously shifted to upper and lower body parts over time.

## 3.2    Temporal Changes of the Gaze Locations of Each Participant

We evaluated the temporal changes of the gaze locations of each participant. We computed distance $d(t, b, i)$ of participant $i$ as

$$d(t, b, i) = \frac{1}{6} \sum_{T \in \mathcal{T}} d(t, b, i, T), \tag{4}$$

where $d(t, b, i, T)$ is the distance in Eq. (2) for each task $T$ and $\mathcal{T}$ is the set of tasks $\{T_1, \cdots, T_6\}$. We used seven body parts $b$ as follows: nose, shoulders, elbows, wrists, waist, knees, and toes.

We applied hierarchical clustering to visualize the temporal change patterns of the gaze location. First, we computed distance $d(t, b, i)$ using Eq. (4) at body part $b$ for time $t$ for each participant $i$ by averaging the distances for all stimulus images and all tasks. Next, we generated a matrix with $d(t, b, i)$ elements for each participant. The size of the matrix was $360 \times 7$. Each matrix corresponded to a specific participant. We used the Frobenius norm as the distance metric between matrices. We set the number of clusters to four.

We applied hierarchical clustering to the temporal changes of the gaze locations of 24 participants and found that 17 belonged to cluster 1, 3 to cluster 2, 2 to cluster 3, and 2 to cluster 4. Figure 9 shows the representative temporal change of the gaze location for one participant in each cluster. The vertical axis represents the magnitude of $d(t, b, i)$. A small value indicates that the gaze location was close to the location of body part $b$. In the figure, we show the temporal changes of gaze location for one of the participants of the pair with the smallest norm in each cluster. Figure 9(a) shows the temporal change of the gaze location in cluster 1, which included most participants. In this cluster, participants not only looked at the face at all times but also observed other body parts after first looking at the face. The remaining clusters are shown in Figs. 9(b)–(d). Although the number of participants that belonged to the cluster was small, each cluster demonstrated an individual pattern of temporal change of gaze location. In cluster 2, the participants' gaze first gathered at the nose and continued to stay near the face. In clusters 3 and 4, the participants shifted their gaze more to the lower part of the body, such as the feet, compared with the results in cluster 1. From

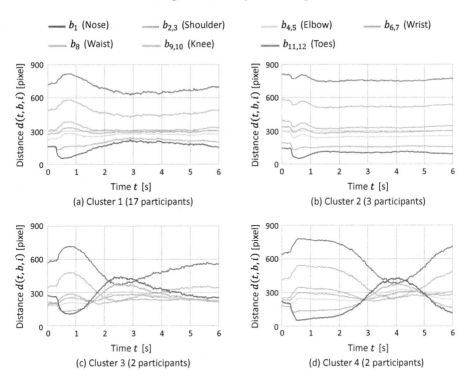

**Fig. 9.** Temporal changes of gaze locations $d(t, b, i)$ for representative participant $i$. We performed hierarchical clustering using all participants.

these results, we believe that there was a common pattern of temporal change of gaze location among many participants and individual patterns among a small number of participants.

## 3.3 Comparison of the Temporal Changes of the Gaze Locations Between Characteristic Words

We investigated hypothesis H2 described in Sect. 2.1 by visualizing the differences in the temporal change of the gaze locations between tasks containing different characteristic words. In this analysis, we focused on the body part of the nose $b_1$. We computed distance $d(t, b_1, T)$ for each task $T \in \{T_1, \ldots, T_6\}$ as

$$d(t, b_1, T) = \frac{1}{I} \sum_{i \in \mathcal{I}} d(t, b_1, i, T), \tag{5}$$

where $d(t, b_1, i, T)$ is the distance in Eq. (2), $I$ is the number of participants, and $\mathcal{I}$ is the set containing all participants. Figure 10 shows the time-series signals of distance $d(t, b_1, T)$. Between $t = 0$ s and 0.6 s, the distances were almost common among all tasks. Between 0.6 s and 6 s, the distances increased and decreased

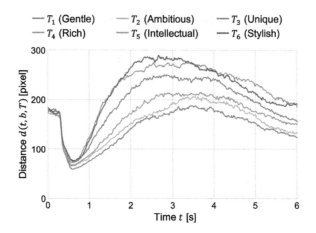

**Fig. 10.** Visualization of the temporal changes of the gaze locations $d(t, b_1, T)$ for each task $T \in \{T_1, \ldots, T_6\}$ of each characteristic word. We computed these temporal changes for the body part of the nose $b_1$.

**Table 1.** We computed the distance matrix between the task vectors using the temporal changes of the gaze locations $d(t, b_1, T)$. $T_1$: Gentle, $T_2$: Ambitious, $T_3$: Unique, $T_4$: Rich, $T_5$: Intellectual, $T_6$: Stylish.

|       | $T_1$  | $T_2$  | $T_3$  | $T_4$  | $T_5$  | $T_6$  |
|-------|--------|--------|--------|--------|--------|--------|
| $T_1$ | 0      | 254.5  | 1040.2 | 1548.1 | 512.9  | 1562.6 |
| $T_2$ | 254.5  | 0      | 823.2  | 1325.5 | 302.6  | 1348.8 |
| $T_3$ | 1040.2 | 823.2  | 0      | 536.5  | 547.7  | 537.3  |
| $T_4$ | 1548.1 | 1325.5 | 536.5  | 0      | 1049.8 | 218.8  |
| $T_5$ | 512.9  | 302.6  | 547.7  | 1049.8 | 0      | 1070.4 |
| $T_6$ | 1562.6 | 1348.8 | 537.3  | 218.8  | 1070.4 | 0      |

over time for all tasks. Additionally, there were differences in the timing of the increase and decrease among the tasks. The experimental results demonstrated that the tendency was similar in all tasks; that is, the gaze locations approached the nose first and then left. We found that the timing of the gaze shift after the participant looked at the nose differed between tasks.

We further investigated the differences in the temporal changes of the gaze locations. We generated a task vector for each task's $d(t, b_1, T)$ values, arranged in ascending order at time $t$. We calculated the distance matrix between the task vectors using the L2 norm. Table 1 shows the distance matrix between the task vectors. We applied the metric multidimensional scaling (MDS) [6] to the distance matrix and placed the task vectors on a two-dimensional plane, as shown in Fig. 11. The distance between gentle $T_1$ and ambitious $T_2$ was small, which indicates that the temporal changes of the gaze locations were similar to each other. Similarly, the distance between rich $T_4$ and stylish $T_6$ was small,

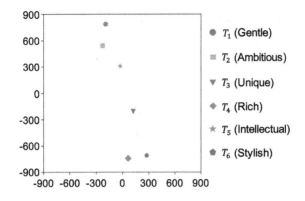

**Fig. 11.** Results of placing each temporal change of the gaze location for each characteristic word on a two-dimensional plane. We calculated metric MDS using the distance matrix of the task vector.

which indicates that the temporal changes of the gaze locations were similar to each other. $T_1$ and $T_2$ were placed further away from $T_4$ and $T_6$, which indicates that the temporal changes of the gaze locations were not similar. In particular, the distance between $T_1$ and $T_6$ was the largest. For the unique $T_3$, there was nothing placed particularly close to it. The intellectual $T_5$ was placed close to $T_2$. From the results of our analysis into hypothesis H2, we found that there were words with similar and dissimilar temporal changes of the gaze locations among the characteristic words included in the tasks. This suggests that changes in characteristic words probably cause differences in the temporal changes of the gaze locations.

## 4   Conclusions

We investigated how observers temporally view the body parts of subjects in images when they are assigned a task to evaluate characteristics. We also investigated whether the temporal changes of the gaze locations differed when the characteristic words in the task changed. We calculated the distance from the body part of the subject in the image to the measured gaze location. We compared the time-series signals of the calculated distance. From the experimental results, we confirmed that the observer's gaze initially fixated on the face, then moved away from the face and variously shifted to the upper and lower body parts as time passed. We also confirmed a common pattern of temporal change of gaze locations among many participants and individual patterns among a small number of participants. Furthermore, we determined characteristic words with similar and dissimilar temporal changes of the gaze locations.

In future work, we will analyze the temporal changes of the gaze locations measured using various characteristic words. We will also expand our analysis to various subjects' appearances, such as age, body shape, and race, in the stimulus images.

**Acknowledgment.** This work was partially supported by JSPS KAKENHI Grant No. JP20K11864. We would like to thank Ms. Nonoka Kawaguchi for her cooperation in our evaluation and data collection.

# References

1. Bareket, O., Shnabel, N., Abeles, D., Gervais, S., Yuval-Greenberg, S.: Evidence for an association between men's spontaneous objectifying gazing behavior and their endorsement of objectifying attitudes toward women. Sex Roles **81**, 245–256 (2018)
2. Bente, G., Donaghy, W.C., Suwelack, D.: Sex differences in body movement and visual attention: an integrated analysis of movement and gaze in mixed-sex dyads. J. Nonverbal Behav. **22**, 31–58 (1998)
3. Bindemann, M.: Scene and screen center bias early eye movements in scene viewing. Vis. Res. **50**(23), 2577–2587 (2010)
4. Buswell, G.T.: How People Look at Pictures: A Study of the Psychology of Perception of Art. University of Chicago Press (1935)
5. Cao, Z., Hidalgo, G., Simon, T., Wei, S.E., Sheikh, Y.: OpenPose: realtime multi-person 2D pose estimation using part affinity fields. IEEE Trans. Pattern Anal. Mach. Intell. **43**(1), 172–186 (2021)
6. Cox, M., Cox, T.: Multidimensional scaling. In: Cox, M., Cox, T. (eds.) Handbook of Data Visualization, pp. 315–347. Springer, Cham (2008). https://doi.org/10.1007/978-3-540-33037-0_14
7. Gervais, S.J., Holland, A.M., Dodd, M.D.: My eyes are up here: the nature of the objectifying gaze toward women. Sex Roles **69**, 557–570 (2013)
8. Hollett, R.C., Morgan, H., Chen, N.T.M., Gignac, G.E.: Female characters from adult-only video games elicit a sexually objectifying gaze in both men and women. Sex Roles **83**, 29–42 (2020)
9. Kinoshita, K., Inoue, M., Nishiyama, M., Iwai, Y.: Body-part attention probability for measuring gaze during impression word evaluation. In: Stephanidis, C., Antona, M., Ntoa, S. (eds.) HCII 2021. CCIS, vol. 1420, pp. 105–112. Springer, Cham (2021). https://doi.org/10.1007/978-3-030-78642-7_15
10. Mason, M.F., Tatkow, E.P., Macrae, C.N.: The look of love: gaze shifts and person perception. Psychol. Sci. **3**, 236–239 (2005)
11. Mehrabian, A.: Silent Messages: Implicit Communication of Emotions and Attitudes. Wadsworth Publishing Company (1971)
12. Nishiyama, M., Matsumoto, R., Yoshimura, H., Iwai, Y.: Extracting discriminative features using task-oriented gaze maps measured from observers for personal attribute classification. Pattern Recogn. Lett. **112**, 241–248 (2018)
13. Pfeiffer, U.J., Vogeley, K., Schilbach, L.: From gaze cueing to dual eye-tracking: novel approaches to investigate the neural correlates of gaze in social interaction. Neurosci. Biobehav. Rev. **37**(10), 2516–2528 (2013)
14. Philippe, B., Gervais, S.J., Holland, A.M., Dodd, M.D.: When do people "check out" male bodies? Appearance-focus increases the objectifying gaze toward men. Psychol. Men Masculinity **19**(3), 484–489 (2018)
15. Riemer, A.R., Haikalis, M., Franz, M.R., Dodd, M.D., Dilillo, D., Gervais, S.J.: Beauty is in the eye of the beer holder: an initial investigation of the effects of alcohol, attractiveness, warmth, and competence on the objectifying gaze in men. Sex Roles **79**, 449–463 (2018)

# Swiping Angles Differentially Influence Young and Old Users' Performance and Experience on Swiping Gestures

Jiali Jiang[1,2], Zheng Wei[1,2], Tong Yang[3], Yanfang Liu[3], Bingxin Li[1(✉)], and Feng Du[1,2(✉)]

[1] CAS Key Laboratory of Behavioral Science, Institute of Psychology, Chinese Academy of Sciences, Beijing, China
{libx,duf}@psych.ac.cn
[2] Department of Psychology, University of Chinese Academy of Sciences, Beijing, China
[3] Huawei & Chinese Academy of Sciences UX Design Human Factors Joint Lab, Beijing, China

**Abstract.** The efficiency and convenience of gesture shortcuts have an important influence on user experience. However, it is unknown how the number of permitted swiping angles and their allowable range affect users' performance and experience. In the present study, young and old users executed swiping in multiple directions on smartphones. Results showed that multiple allowable angles resulted in slower swiping speed and poorer user experience than the single allowable angle condition. However, as the number of allowable angles increased, only old users showed a significant decrease in swiping accuracy. Vertical-up and upper-right swiping were faster than swiping in the horizontal directions. Furthermore, narrower operable range of swiping only reduced swiping accuracy in the tilted direction. Though old users performed worse on swiping than younger users, their subjective ratings were more positive than younger users'. Suggestions on how to design swiping gestures on the human-mobile interface were discussed.

**Keywords:** Gesture shortcuts · Swipe gestures · Swipe angle · Age difference · User experience

## 1 Introduction

Touchscreen mobile phones have become an essential tool for people's daily life because of their powerful functions associated with communication, consumption and entertainment. It has been shown that in 2020 the average smartphone user had 40 applications installed on their phone [1]. Using touchscreen gestures is the most common way for users to interact with their phones. Among the commonly used touchscreen gestures (e.g., tapping, swiping, rotating, zooming), the swiping gestures is the most frequently used. For example, by swiping up from the bottom edge of the screen, users can return to the phone's home screen while using an app. Moreover, swiping inward from either the left or right edge of the screen has been used as a shortcut for going back to the previous screen at any point.

D. Harris and W.-C. Li (Eds.): HCII 2022, LNAI 13307, pp. 33–48, 2022.
https://doi.org/10.1007/978-3-031-06086-1_3

Phone designers may hope to provide as many shortcut gestures or swipe gestures as possible to execute important commands quickly. One possible approach to achieve this goal is to divide the operating area into sections by angles and associate different swiping directions with different commands. However, two crucial issues arise for this approach.

Firstly, it is problematic for users to differentiate between those gestures on a typical mobile phone with a limited screen size. Studies in which users operated on tablets and pads with relatively larger touching space revealed that swipes in the vertical direction were associated with slower swiping speed and worse subjective ratings of gestures compared to horizontal swipes [2, 3]. Nevertheless, a study on smartphones showed a different result. Warr and colleagues compared users' performance and subjective evaluation of vertical and horizontal swipes and found that the vertical swipes were on average faster and less frustrating [4]. These studies imply that the allowable operating space and direction of swipes do play a role that affects swiping performance.

Secondly, differentiating between multiple operations in one interface will lead to increased cognitive load and a higher probability of misoperation. It is well known that users always prefer simple gestures with reduced cognitive loads and quick shortcuts which can easily access the target interface [7–10]. Evidence that high cognitive load decreases performance also comes from studies on age differences [5, 6]. For example, Nathalie and colleagues found that the elderly showed significantly longer time and they needed additional assistance when performing tasks (e.g., change font size, set timer) on a smartwatch by gestures [5]. By examining the operating performance of two types of touchscreen gestures (e.g., double-tapping, dragging) to switch off an alarm, researchers also found that the task completion time increased with age [6].

Therefore, the primary purpose of the present study is to explore how the number of permitted swiping/sliding angles and the allowable scope for swiping would influence task performance and user experience. We also studied the effect of different swiping angles and age-related differences on the swiping task performance.

## 2   Materials and Method

### 2.1   Users

Twenty young phone users (9 males; mean age = 24.25 years, $SD$ = 2.34, age ranged between 21–29 years) and 20 old users (10 males; mean age = 65.15 years, $SD$ = 3.45, age ranged between 60–75 years) who had normal or corrected-to-normal vision took part in the experiment for a cash reward. They were all right-handed and both groups had similar experiences in using touchscreen mobile phones. All users signed informed consent form before the experiment and received cash rewards after the experiment.

The study was approved by the institutional review board of the Institute of Psychology, Chinese Academy of Sciences. All procedures were performed by relevant guidelines and regulations.

There were three experimental levels: a gesture allowing only one swiping angle with the range of 45° (level of 1–45 thereafter), a gesture allowing only one swiping angle with the range of 90° (level of 1–90 thereafter), and a gesture allowing five different swiping angles and each had a range of 45° (level of 5–45 thereafter). The number of angles (1–45 vs. 5–45) and the allowable swiping range (1–45 vs. 1–90) were both within-subjects variables.

There were a total of 5 specific swiping directions (as shown in the Fig. 1a): swiping vertically up, swiping to the upper left corner (*upper left*), swiping to the upper right corner from the bottom edge of the screen (*upper right*), and horizontal swiping left (*horizontal left*) and right (*horizontal right*).

The primary dependent variables were reaction time, response accuracy, and swiping speed. Fatigue, emotional experience, and general evaluation (e.g., perceived usability) of gestures were recorded serving as key dependent variables.

## 2.2 Apparatus and Materials

Users were instructed to perform the swiping task and rate their fatigue and emotional experience on a HUAWEI nova 8 SE mobile phone with a 6.53-in. screen and Android 10.0. A gesture evaluation survey was completed on the laptops with a 14-in. screen for evaluating the usability of gestures. Each statement was measured on a 7-point Likert scale ranging from 1 (strongly disagree) to 7 (strongly agree). In addition, users were asked to answer three general questions indicating the likelihood to use each gesture in the real-word interaction, the possibility to recommend every gesture to other users and whether they were satisfied with the gesture, "0" means "absolutely impossible to reuse/recommend and very dissatisfied", and "10" means "very likely to reuse/recommend and very satisfied".

A standard Visual Analogue Scale (VAS) was used to assess current fatigue, ranging from 0 (relaxed, not tired) to 10 (very tired). Users were also instructed to rate the statement along the dimensions of valence and arousal; ratings for positive emotion were scored from 0 (very unpleased/uncomfortable) to 10 (very happy/comfortable) and negative emotion was scored from 0 (very not discouraged/fidget) to 10 (very discouraged/fidget). Ratings for arousal were scored from one (very calm) to 10 (very aroused).

## 2.3 Procedure

Users learned the gestures of different angles and ranges via videos to familiarize themselves with how to perform each gesture in the experiment. Users were allowed to practice the gestures until they understood the task instructions and all gestures. After the practice, baseline fatigue, emotional valence, and arousal were measured before the task began.

There were two critical experiment blocks, which were further divided into 10 subblocks. Each subblock consisted of conditions that allowed either 1 or 5 different swiping angles, showing in random order. Swiping ranges were manipulated between two blocks. Users were instructed about the number of angles and angle range allowed in the upcoming task. As soon as the message "Start to swipe" appeared in the center of the screen, the user had to perform the gesture as quickly and accurately as possible. All users held the mobile phone with their left hand while using the right thumb finger to finish the swiping task. Users received right or wrong feedback for their responses. The same trial would be repeated if the response was wrong. After a second interval, the next trial began. Breaks were allowed between subblocks (Fig. 2).

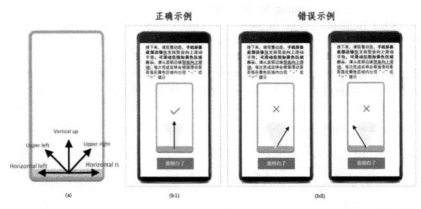

**Fig. 1.** (a) Five swipe angles in the experiment. (b) An example of the condition of 1–45 in the experiment. In this examplar, users were instructed to execute a vertical-up swipe from the bottom edge of the screen. Vertical swipes were only allowed within the yellow sector. It is defined as a correct swipe if the swiping track of the subject is always within the yellow area (b1); otherwise, it is a wrong swipe. (b2) The yellow area was not presented in the formal stage of the experiment. (Color figure online)

**Fig. 2.** Timeline of a trial in the formal stage of the experiment. In this examplar, users were instructed to execute a vertical-up swipe from the bottom edge of the screen. There were five allowable swiping angles in this examplar.

Scales of fatigue and emotions were filled out once after the two critical blocks respectively. Once the task was completed, users completed the gesture evaluation survey. It took about 45 min to complete all the tasks.

## 3   Results

All data were analyzed using R version 3.6.2 (R Core Team, 2019).

### 3.1   The Analysis of the Allowable Number of Angles

It should be noted that only the data of the level of 1–45 and 5–45 were included in the analysis of the allowable angle number, while the data of level 1–90 were excluded. A 2 (number of angles: 1 angle, 5 angles) × 5 (*vertical up, upper left, upper right, horizontal left,* and *horizontal right*) × 2 (age: younger, older) three-way ANOVA with mixed measurements was employed to compare the effect of the number of angles, specific angle, and age on reaction time, accuracy and speed.

**Reaction Time.** Descriptive statistical result for reaction time is illustrated in Appendix A. In the analysis of reaction time, trials with a precision error or out of three standard deviations were excluded (0.55% of the data). There was no significant main effect on the number of angles ($F = 0.74$). However, the main effect of specific angle was significant, $F(4, 152) = 2.73$, $p = .031$, $\eta_p^2 = 0.07$. Post-hoc analysis revealed that reaction time was longer for *horizontal left* than for *vertical up* swipes ($p = .040$). The main effect of age was also significant, $F(1, 38) = 26.52$, $p < .001$, $\eta_p^2 = 0.41$, with on average longer reaction time in the older group (mean reaction time of 667 ms) compared to the younger group (382 ms). No significant interaction was found between the factors on reaction time.

**Accuracy.** Descriptive statistical result for the accuracy is illustrated in Appendix B. There was a significant main effect of number of angles, $F(1, 38) = 33.6$, $p < .001$, $\eta_p^2 = 0.47$, with higher accuracy for level 1–45 (99.41%) than level 5–45 (96.50%). The main effect of specific angle was significant, $F(4, 152) = 4.91$, $p < .001$, $\eta_p^2 = 0.11$. Post-hoc analysis revealed that the accuracy of *vertical up* was higher than that of *upper left* ($p < .001$) and *upper right* ($p = .040$). The effect of age was also significant, $F(1, 38) = 8.32$, $p = .006$, $\eta_p^2 = 0.18$, with higher accuracy for the younger group (mean accuracy of 98.96%) compared to the older group (96.95%).

As Fig. 3 showed, we found a significant interaction between the number of angles and age, $F(1, 38) = 10.62$, $p = .002$, $\eta_p^2 = 0.22$. Post-hoc analysis revealed that accuracy was not different between level 1–45 and level of 5–45 (accuracy was 99.60% for 1–45 and 98.33% for 5–45; $p = .081$) in the younger group. However, the accuracy in level 1–45 (99.23%) was significantly higher than level 5–45 (94.68%) in the older group ($p < .001$).

**Speed.** Descriptive statistical result for the speed is illustrated in Appendix C. In the analysis of speed, trials with a precision error were excluded. There was a significant main effect of the number of angles, $F(1, 38) = 23.58$, $p < .001$, $\eta_p^2 = 0.38$, with higher speed for level 1–45 (1.76 px/ms) than level 5–45 (1.59 px/ms). The main effect of specific angle was significant, $F(4, 152) = 68.12$, $p < .001$, $\eta_p^2 = 0.64$. Post-hoc analysis revealed that there was no difference in the speed between *vertical up* and *upper right* ($p > .999$), and they both associated with higher speed than other specific angles (all $p < .05$); the speed of *horizontal left* was not different with *horizontal right* ($p = .104$) and they both were lower than other angles (all $p < .05$). The main effect of age was also significant, $F(1, 38) = 6.07$, $p = .018$, $\eta_p^2 = 0.14$; younger users (mean speed of 1.94 px/ms) performed the swiping gestures more quickly compared to the older users (1.41 px/ms).

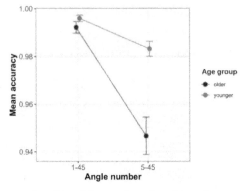

**Fig. 3.** Mean accuracy as a function of the number of angles and age group. Red and blue dots represent mean accuracy in the older and younger users, receptively. Error bars indicate standard error of the mean.

As Fig. 4 showed, number of angles interacted significantly with specific angle, $F(4, 152) = 2.68, p = .034, \eta_p^2 = 0.07$. Post-hoc analysis showed that the speed of level 1–45 was higher than level 5–45 in the angle *upper left*, *upper right*, *horizontal right*, and *vertical up* (all $p < .05$), while there was no difference between the speed of two angle numbers in the angle *horizontal left* ($p = .135$).

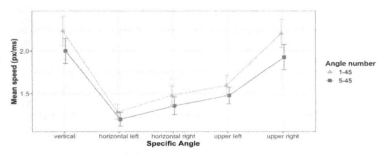

**Fig. 4.** Mean speed as a function of specific angle and angle number. Triangles and squares represent mean speed of levels of 1–45 and 5–45, respectively, in different specific angles. Error bars indicate standard error of the mean.

Importantly, as Fig. 5 showed, age interacted significantly with specific angle, $F(4, 152) = 6.23, p < .001, \eta_p^2 = 0.14$. Post-hoc analysis revealed that the younger users' speed was faster than the older users in the angle of *vertical up*, *horizontal right*, *upper left*, and *upper right* (for *vertical up*, *upper left*, *upper right*, $p < .05$; for *horizontal right*, $p = 0.063$). Similar speed was found between the two age groups in the angle of *horizontal left* ($p = .322$).

**Subjective Ratings.** A 2 (number of angles: 1 angle, 5 angles) × 2 (age: younger, older) two-way ANOVA with mixed measurements was employed to compare the effect of the number of angles and age on gesture evaluation scores and fatigue and emotional indicators.

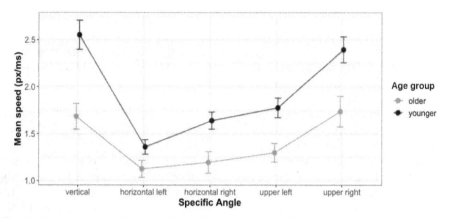

**Fig. 5.** Mean speed as a function of specific angle and age. Red and blue dots represent mean accuracy in the older and younger users, receptively. Error bars indicate standard error of the mean. (Color figure online)

*Gesture Evaluation Scores.* Descriptive statistical result for the gesture evaluation scores is illustrated in Appendix D. As shown in Fig. 6, all gesture evaluation scores of level 1–45 were higher than level 5–45 (all $p \leq .05$). In addition, scores of older users were higher than that of younger users (all $p < .05$), except ease of learning ($p = .941$) and generalization ($p = .333$). The two-way interaction between the number of angles and age did not reach significance on any gesture evaluation score (all $p > .05$).

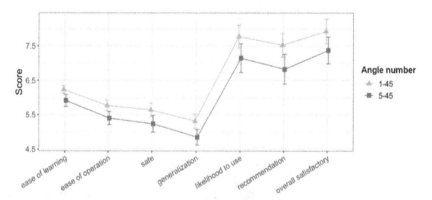

**Fig. 6.** Gesture evaluation scores as a function of the angle number. Triangles and squares represent gesture evaluation scores of levels of 1–45 and 5–45, respectively, in different specific angles. Error bars indicate standard error of the mean.

*Fatigue and Emotional Experience.* Descriptive statistical result for the rating scores of perceived fatigue and emotional experience before and after the task is illustrated in Appendix D. Rating score of fatigue and emotional experience was adjusted (by subtracting) for their baseline, indexing a difference or changes of the score pre- and post-task for each variable. There was a significant main effect of number of angles on negative emotion, $F(1, 38) = 5.52$, $p = .024$, $\eta_p^2 = 0.13$. Scores of negative emotion were increased more dramatically, with a larger change for the level of 5–45 compared to 1–45.

Particularly, as shown in Fig. 7, number of angles interacted significantly with age on the changes of negative emotion, $F(1, 38) = 5.96$, $p = .019$, $\eta_p^2 = 0.14$. Post-hoc analysis showed a significantly higher increment of negative emotion in level 1–45 than level 5–45 for the younger group ($p = .002$), whereas the effect for older users did not reach significance ($p = .948$). Moreover, the number of angles interacted significantly with age on the increment of emotional arousal, $F(1, 38) = 5.01$, $p = .031$, $\eta_p^2 = 0.12$. Post-hoc analysis revealed a marginally larger change of emotional arousal in level 5–45 than level 1–45 for the younger group ($p = .056$), whereas the effect for older users did not reach significance ($p = .240$).

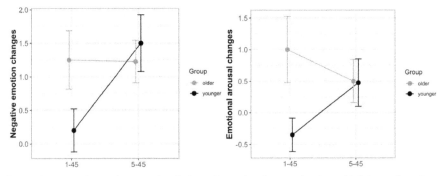

**Fig. 7.** Changes of negative emotion (left) and emotional arousal ratings (right) as a function of angle number and age. Red and blue dots represent mean accuracy in the older and younger users, receptively. Error bars indicate standard error of the mean. (Color figure online)

### 3.2   The Analysis of Allowable Angle Range

It should be noted that only the data of the level of 1–45 and 1–90 were included in the analysis of the allowable angle range, while the data of level 5–45 were excluded. A 2 (angle range: 1–45, 1–90) × 5 (specific angle: *vertical up, upper left, upper right, horizontal left*, and *horizontal right*) × 2 (age: younger, older) three-way ANOVA with mixed measurements was employed to compare the effect of the allowable angle range, specific angle, and age on reaction time, accuracy and speed.

**Reaction Time.** In the analysis of reaction time, trials with a precision error or out of three standard deviations were excluded (0.50% of the data). There was no significant effect of angle range ($F = 0.009$), neither was the specific angle ($F = 2.15$, $p = 0.077$). However, the main effect of age was significant, $F(1, 38) = 29.73$, $p < .001$, $\eta_p^2 = 0.44$, with longer reaction time for the older group (mean reaction time of 693 ms) compared to the younger group (377 ms). No significant interaction was found between the factors on reaction time.

**Accuracy.** There was a significant main effect of angle range, $F(1, 38) = 5.29, p = .027$, $\eta_p^2 = 0.12$, with higher accuracy for the level of 1–90 (99.83%) than 1–45 (99.41%). The main effect of age was also significant, $F(1, 38) = 4.62, p = .038, \eta_p^2 = 0.11$, with higher accuracy for the younger group (mean accuracy of 99.80%) compared to the older group (99.44%). The main effect of the specific angle did not reach significance ($F = 1.31, p = .270$) (Fig. 8).

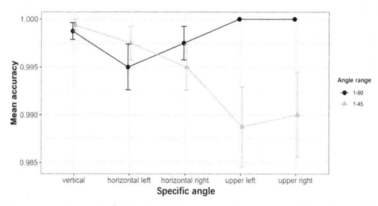

**Fig. 8.** Mean accuracy as a function of specific angle and angle range. Black dots and light grey triangles represent gesture evaluation scores of levels of 1–90 and 1–45, respectively, in different specific angles. Error bars indicate standard error of the mean.

Importantly, significant interaction was found between angle range and specific angle, $F(4, 152) = 3.8, p = .006, \eta_p^2 = 0.09$. Post-hoc analysis revealed that accuracy was not significantly different between the two levels of angle range when users performed horizontal or vertical swipes (*vertical up, horizontal left, horizontal right*, all $p > .05$); whereas the accuracy of level of 1–90 was significantly higher than 1–45 when users swiped along the inclined angles (*upper left, p = .001; upper right, p = .003*).

**Speed.** In the analysis of speed, trials with a precision error were excluded. The main effect of angle range was not significant ($F = 0.008$). However, we found a significant main effect of specific angle, $F(4, 152) = 6.58, p < .001, \eta_p^2 = 0.63$. Post-hoc analysis revealed that the speed of *vertical up* and *upper right* was not different ($p > .999$) and were significantly higher than other angles (all $p < .05$); the *horizontal left* was lower than all other angles (all p $< .05$). The speed of *horizontal left* and *horizontal right* was not significantly different ($p = .104$). There was a significant main effect of age, $F(1, 38) = 7.53, p = .009, \eta_p^2 = 0.17$, with higher speed for the younger users (mean speed of 2.07 px/ms) compared to the older users (1.45 px/ms).

Importantly, same as the result on angle number, age interacted significantly with specific angle, $F(4, 152) = 5.77, p < .001, \eta_p^2 = 0.13$. Post-hoc analysis revealed that the younger users swiped faster than the older users in the angle of *vertical up, horizontal right, upper left,* and *upper right* (all $p < .05$), but no significant difference was detected between the two age groups in the angle of *horizontal left* ($p = .259$).

**Subjective Ratings.** A 2 (angle range: 1–45, 1–90) × 2 (age: younger, older) two-way ANOVA with mixed measurements was also employed to compare the effect of the allowable angle range and age on the gesture evaluation scores and fatigue and emotional indicators.

*Gesture Evaluation Scores.* As Fig. 9 showed, scores of 1–45 were lower compared to 1–90 in all gesture evaluation ratings (all $p < .05$), except for the ease of learning ($p = .594$). In addition, we found that the main effects of age on all gesture evaluation scores were significant (all $p < .05$), with generally higher scores from older users than younger users, except for ease of learning ($p = .671$) and generalization ($p = .890$).

Importantly, we found significant interactions between angle range and age on several gesture evaluation scores, including ease of operation ($p = .002$), generalization ($p = .037$), recommendation ($p = .002$) and overall satisfactory ($p = .009$). Specifically, the younger users rated higher scores in the level of 1–90 than 1–45, while the older users indicated similar rating scores in the two levels.

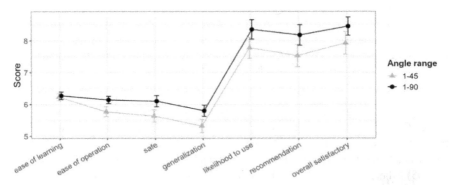

**Fig. 9.** Gesture evaluation scores as a function of the angle range. Black dots and light grey triangles represent gesture evaluation scores of levels of 1–90 and 1–45, respectively, in different specific angles. Error bars indicate standard error of the mean.

*Fatigue and Emotional Experience.* There was a significant main effect of age on the increment of emotional arousal, $F(1, 38) = 4.77, p = .035, \eta_p^2 = 0.11$, with higher increment of emotional arousal for older users. No other significant main effect or interaction was found in the analysis of the fatigue and emotional experience.

## 4   Discussion

The purpose of this study was to identify how the number of permitted swiping angles and the allowable scope for swiping would influence task performance and user experience. The present study revealed that on average users had slower swiping speed and poorer experience when multiple angles were allowable to swipe. There are two possible reasons. Firstly, users were slower and more cautious when operating in relatively complex scenarios with more response choices. As shown in the study of McDowd & Craik [11], participants were instructed to press the corresponding response key once the target presented at one of 2/4/6/8 positions. Results showed that as the alternative positions increased, participants responded with longer reaction time. Secondly, multiple permitted angles may make a feeling of narrowness and crowdedness for users and thereby affected their performance and satisfaction. Previous studies have shown that the completion time for users to click a specific item in an array of squares was significantly shorter when squares appeared with more space/distance between each other [12, 13].

Providing multiple swiping angles impaired swiping accuracy of older users but did not affect that of younger users. Consistent result was reported in a previous study. Anthony and colleagues indicated that older adults exhibited greater performance decline than younger adults when cognitive load increased [14]. Researchers interpreted that this may be due to the age-related attentional deficits which impaired the perceptual processing and encoding of stimuli in the high load condition. In an additional analysis on age, we again identified better performance in the younger users who responded faster compared to older users in most of the angles except swiping horizontally left. Swiping to the left has been found to be associated with a relatively lower speed in static and driving conditions [2]. Indeed, it is noted that even the younger users in the present study had certain difficulties showing rather slow speeds in the swiping left condition, which implies being cautious in offering options of leftward swipes, at least in the group of right-handed users.

Consistent with the previous study [4, 15], we also found that users swiped more quickly in the vertical-up and upward-right directions than in other directions. This may be determined by the kinematic characteristics of the human fingers. In the present study, users were instructed to swipe with their right thumb. Previous study has revealed that swiping with the right thumb in the vertical directions was associated with fewer metacarpal abduction, flexion, and carpometacarpal abduction compared to horizontal directions [15]. Therefore, the vertical-up and upward-right swiping might benefit from shorter wrist and hand movement compared with swiping in other directions.

To the best of our knowledge, we show for the first time that gesture performance can be modulated by different angle ranges of swiping. Specifically, we found that users' swipe precision in the diagonal directions significantly decreased by reducing the allowable swiping range from 90 to 45°. However, this was not the case when users swiped in either vertical or horizontal directions. These results indicated that users may be more susceptible to the swiping range in oblique angles than other angle conditions. Thus designers should provide users with a swiping range as wider as possible to reduce error rates for diagonal swiping gestures.

Comparing gesture evaluation scores between different numbers of angles and varying angle range in the younger and older user groups, both of them preferred fewer allowable swiping angles. Only the younger users decreased their scores when allowable swiping range became narrower while the older users rated equally high scores to the two levels of swiping range. In fact, despite performing poorly in accuracy and speed, older users showed higher gesture evaluation scores and reported similar emotional experiences between 1 and 5 numbers of angles. Similar results have been shown in previous research [12, 16, 17]. For instance, Gao and Sun found that although older users committed more errors and performed slower in four touchscreen gestures (e.g., clicking, dragging, zooming, and rotating) than younger users, they showed a more positive attitude about the gestures than younger participants did [12]. Gao offered an explanation that older people were inclined to express their preference of the novel matters, which made them a feeling of keeping up-to-date.

## 5  Conclusion

The present study provided straightforward evidence that providing multiple allowable angles resulted in worse accuracy, slower swiping speed, and poorer user experience than a single allowable angle, although younger users' swiping accuracy was independent of the number of angles. Subjects were fastest in the vertical-up and upper-right direction while slowest in the horizontal-left direction. Further, narrower operable range of swiping only reduced swiping accuracy in the tilted direction, which is a novel finding in the field of touchscreen gesture interaction. These discoveries may remind us that in the design of swiping interactive gestures, especially for touchscreen mobile phones, vertical swiping is optimal, and excessive swiping angles for diverse instructions should be avoided. If tilted swiping is necessary, designers should provide a large enough operable range to enable effective gesture performance.

**Acknowledgment.** This study was supported by a research grant from Huawei Corporation. J. J. and Z. W. contribute equally to this study.

## Appendix A. Mean Values (Standard Error) of the Reaction Time (ms)

| Exp level | Specific angle | Younger | Older | Average |
|---|---|---|---|---|
| 1–45 | a1 | 399(60) | 606(47) | 502(41) |
| | a2 | 387(54) | 645(37) | 516(38) |
| | h1 | 400(36) | 753(84) | 576(53) |
| | h2 | 358(40) | 745(69) | 552(50) |
| | v | 389(57) | 656(72) | 523(50) |
| | Average | 386(49) | 681(64) | 534(47) |
| 5–45 | a1 | 381(30) | 585(32) | 483(27) |

*(continued)*

(*continued*)

| Exp level | Specific angle | Younger | Older | Average |
|---|---|---|---|---|
| | a2 | 398(32) | 663(39) | 531(33) |
| | h1 | 410(30) | 804(130) | 607(73) |
| | h2 | 361(19) | 631(47) | 496(33) |
| | v | 339(24) | 584(34) | 461(28) |
| | Average | 378(28) | 653(69) | 515(43) |
| 1–90 | a1 | 334(27) | 663(78) | 498(48) |
| | a2 | 375(41) | 654(53) | 515(40) |
| | h1 | 420(37) | 768(89) | 594(55) |
| | h2 | 360(55) | 709(55) | 534(43) |
| | v | 347(35) | 731(77) | 539(52) |
| | Average | 367(35) | 705(71) | 536(48) |

## Appendix B. Mean Values (Standard Error) of the Accuracy (%)

| Exp level | Specific angle | Younger | Older | Average |
|---|---|---|---|---|
| 1–45 | a1 | 99(0.46) | 98.75(0.71) | 98.88(0.42) |
| | a2 | 99.75(0.25) | 98.25(0.83) | 99(0.45) |
| | h1 | 99.75(0.25) | 99.75(0.25) | 99.75(0.17) |
| | h2 | 99.5(0.34) | 99.5(0.34) | 99.5(0.24) |
| | v | 100(0) | 99.88(0.13) | 99.94(0.06) |
| | Average | 99.6(0.3) | 99.23(0.54) | 99.41(0.31) |
| 5–45 | a1 | 97.75(0.77) | 91.5(2.84) | 94.63(1.53) |
| | a2 | 98(1.05) | 94.5(1.02) | 96.25(0.77) |
| | h1 | 99(0.46) | 94(1.65) | 96.5(0.93) |
| | h2 | 97.5(0.57) | 94.75(1.6) | 96.13(0.87) |
| | v | 99.38(0.44) | 98.63(0.64) | 99(0.39) |
| | Average | 98.33(0.7) | 94.68(1.76) | 96.5(0.99) |
| 1–90 | a1 | 100(0) | 100(0) | 100(0) |
| | a2 | 100(0) | 100(0) | 100(0) |
| | h1 | 100(0) | 99(0.46) | 99.5(0.24) |
| | h2 | 100(0) | 99.5(0.34) | 99.75(0.17) |
| | v | 100(0) | 99.75(0.17) | 99.88(0.09) |
| | Average | 100(0) | 99.65(0.28) | 99.83(0.14) |

## Appendix C. Mean Values (Standard Error) of the Speed (px/ms)

| Exp level | Specific angle | Young | Old | Average |
|---|---|---|---|---|
| 1–45 | a1 | 1.84(0.17) | 1.35(0.14) | 1.6(0.12) |
| | a2 | 2.56(0.22) | 1.85(0.23) | 2.21(0.17) |
| | h1 | 1.37(0.12) | 1.2(0.13) | 1.28(0.09) |
| | h2 | 1.72(0.14) | 1.23(0.16) | 1.48(0.11) |
| | v | 2.7(0.25) | 1.77(0.19) | 2.24(0.17) |
| | Average | 2.04(0.22) | 1.48(0.18) | 1.76(0.15) |
| 5–45 | a1 | 1.71(0.12) | 1.25(0.14) | 1.48(0.1) |
| | a2 | 2.23(0.16) | 1.62(0.23) | 1.93(0.15) |
| | h1 | 1.35(0.1) | 1.05(0.12) | 1.2(0.08) |
| | h2 | 1.56(0.11) | 1.15(0.16) | 1.36(0.1) |
| | v | 2.41(0.18) | 1.6(0.2) | 2(0.15) |
| | Average | 1.85(0.16) | 1.33(0.18) | 1.59(0.13) |
| 1–90 | a1 | 1.91(0.18) | 1.33(0.12) | 1.62(0.12) |
| | a2 | 2.48(0.23) | 1.78(0.22) | 2.13(0.17) |
| | h1 | 1.44(0.11) | 1.05(0.09) | 1.24(0.08) |
| | h2 | 1.81(0.14) | 1.19(0.16) | 1.5(0.11) |
| | v | 2.86(0.26) | 1.8(0.21) | 2.33(0.19) |
| | Average | 2.1(0.22) | 1.43(0.18) | 1.76(0.15) |

## Appendix D. Mean Values (Standard Error) of the Subjective Ratings

| Scores | Exp level | Young | Old | Average |
|---|---|---|---|---|
| learn | 1–45 | 24.85(0.74) | 25(0.54) | 24.925(0.45) |
| | 5–45 | 23.65(0.85) | 23.65(1.12) | 23.65(0.69) |
| | 1–90 | 25.55(0.64) | 24.65(0.7) | 25.1(0.47) |
| operation | 1–45 | 26.55(1.2) | 31.15(0.64) | 28.85(0.77) |
| | 5–45 | 24.85(1.43) | 29.15(1.04) | 27(0.94) |
| | 1–90 | 30.3(0.92) | 31.1(0.71) | 30.7(0.58) |
| safe | 1–45 | 10.55(0.63) | 12(0.43) | 11.275(0.39) |
| | 5–45 | 9.35(0.7) | 11.6(0.59) | 10.475(0.49) |

(*continued*)

(*continued*)

| Scores | Exp level | Young | Old | Average |
|---|---|---|---|---|
| general | 1–90 | 11.6(0.62) | 12.8(0.3) | 12.2(0.35) |
| | 1–45 | 15.45(0.92) | 16.45(0.82) | 15.95(0.62) |
| | 5–45 | 13.9(0.96) | 15.2(0.95) | 14.55(0.67) |
| likelihood | 1–90 | 17.75(0.74) | 17.05(0.75) | 17.4(0.52) |
| | 1–45 | 6.75(0.54) | 8.8(0.23) | 7.775(0.33) |
| | 5–45 | 6.35(0.6) | 7.95(0.53) | 7.15(0.42) |
| recommend | 1–90 | 7.65(0.52) | 9.05(0.23) | 8.35(0.3) |
| | 1–45 | 6.4(0.53) | 8.65(0.28) | 7.525(0.35) |
| | 5–45 | 5.85(0.6) | 7.8(0.56) | 6.825(0.43) |
| satisfactory | 1–90 | 7.65(0.52) | 8.7(0.36) | 8.175(0.32) |
| | 1–45 | 6.6(0.54) | 9.25(0.22) | 7.925(0.36) |
| | 5–45 | 6.25(0.51) | 8.5(0.48) | 7.375(0.39) |
| diff_positive | 1–90 | 7.55(0.46) | 9.35(0.2) | 8.45(0.28) |
| | 1–45 | −0.25(0.37) | −0.95(0.64) | −0.6(0.37) |
| | 5–45 | −1.05(0.44) | −1.4(0.43) | −1.225(0.3) |
| diff_negative | 1–90 | −0.25(0.29) | −1.55(0.64) | −0.9(0.36) |
| | 1–45 | 0.2(0.32) | 1.25(0.43) | 0.725(0.28) |
| | 5–45 | 1.5(0.42) | 1.23(0.32) | 1.36(0.26) |
| diff_arousal | 1–90 | 0.55(0.32) | 1.05(0.44) | 0.8(0.27) |
| | 1–45 | −0.35(0.26) | 1(0.52) | 0.33(0.31) |
| | 5–45 | 0.475(0.38) | 0.5(0.34) | 0.49(0.25) |
| diff_fatigue | 1–90 | −0.15(0.34) | 0.2(0.2) | 0.03(0.2) |
| | 1–45 | 0.75(0.47) | 1.4(0.53) | 1.08(0.35) |
| | 5–45 | 1.45(0.46) | 1.5(0.42) | 1.48(0.31) |
| | 1–90 | 0.85(0.47) | 1.2(0.53) | 1.02(0.35) |

# References

1. 55+ App Usage Statistics and Trends for 2021 [Infographic]. https://techjury.net/blog/app-usage-statistics/. Accessed 11 Feb 2022
2. Burnett, G., Crundall, E., Large, D., Lawson, G., Skrypchuk, L.: A study of unidirectional swipe gestures on in-vehicle touch screens. In: Proceedings of the 5th International Conference on Automotive User Interfaces and Interactive Vehicular Applications - AutomotiveUI 2013, pp. 22–29 (2013)
3. Huang, J.H., et al.: Differences in muscle activity, kinematics, user performance, and subjective assessment between touchscreen and mid-air interactions on a tablet. Behav. Inf. Technol. (2021)

4. Warr, A., Chi, E.H.: Swipe vs. scroll: web page switching on mobile browsers. In: Proceedings of the SIGCHI Conference on Human Factors in Computing Systems, Paris, pp. 2171–2174. Association for Computing Machinery (2013)
5. Zotz, N., Saft, S., Rosenlöhner, J., Böhm, P., Isemann, D.: Identification of age-specific usability problems of smartwatches. In: Miesenberger, K., Kouroupetroglou, G. (eds.) ICCHP 2018. LNCS, vol. 10897, pp. 399–406. Springer, Cham (2018). https://doi.org/10.1007/978-3-319-94274-2_57
6. López, B.R., Benito, L.J., Llamas, V.S., Del Castillo, M.D., Serrano, J.I., Rocon, E.: Interaction with touchscreen smartphones in patients with essential tremor and healthy individuals. Neurologia **36**(9), 657–665 (2018)
7. Poppinga, B., Sahami Shirazi, A., Henze, N., Heuten, W., Boll, S.: Understanding shortcut gestures on mobile touch devices. In: Proceedings of the 16th International Conference on Human-Computer Interaction with Mobile Devices & Services (2021)
8. Zhang, C., Jiang, N., Feng, T.: Accessing mobile apps with user defined gesture shortcuts: an exploratory study. In: Proceedings of the 2016 ACM International Conference on Interactive Surfaces and Spaces, Niagara, pp. 385–390 (2016)
9. Aziz, N., Batmaz, F., Stone, R., Chung, P.: Selection of touch gestures for children's applications. In: 2013 Science and Information Conference, London, pp. 721–726 (2013)
10. Leitão, R., Silva, P.: A study of novice older adults and gestural interaction on smartphones. In: CHI 2013 Mobile Accessibility Workshop, Paris (2013)
11. McDowd, J.M., Craik, F.I.: Effects of aging and task difficulty on divided attention performance. J. Exp. Psychol. Hum. Percept. Perform. **14**(2), 267–280 (1988)
12. Gao, Q., Sun, Q.: Examining the usability of touch screen gestures for older and younger adults. Hum. Factors **57**(5), 835–863 (2015)
13. Hsieh, M.H., Ho, C.H., Lee, I.C.: Effects of smartphone numeric keypad designs on performance and satisfaction of elderly users. Int. J. Ind. Ergon. **87** (2022)
14. Zanesco, A.P., Witkin, J.E., Morrison, A.B., Denkova, E., Jha, A.P.: Memory load, distracter interference, and dynamic adjustments in cognitive control influence working memory performance across the lifespan. Psychol Aging **5**(5), 614–626 (2020)
15. Coppola, S.M., Lin, M., Schilkowsky, J., Arezes, P.M., Dennerlein, J.T.: Tablet form factors and swipe gesture designs affect thumb biomechanics and performance during two-handed use. Appl. Ergon. **69**, 40–46 (2018)
16. Giassi, B.H., Seabra, R.D.: Influence of age on the usability assessment of the Instagram application. In: Latifi, S. (ed.) Information Technology–New Generations (ITNG 2020). AISC, vol. 1134, pp. 423–428. Springer, Cham (2020). https://doi.org/10.1007/978-3-030-43020-7_56
17. Sonderegger, A., Schmutz, S., Sauer, J.: The influence of age in usability testing. Appl. Ergon. **52**, 291–300 (2016)

# Development of a Concept of Operations
# for a Counter-Swarm Scenario

Jari Laarni[✉], Antti Väätänen, Hannu Karvonen, Toni Lastusilta, and Fabrice Saffre

VTT Technical Research Centre of Finland Ltd., Espoo, Finland
jari.laarni@vtt.fi

**Abstract.** This paper describes a Concept of Operations (ConOps) for a counter-swarm scenario in which the defender side uses a swarm of drones to defend a target against an attacking drone swarm. A ConOps is a high-level conceptual description of how the elements of a system and entities in its environment interact in order to achieve their stated goals. It has shown to be a useful and integrative element in designing complex technical systems. The ConOps for a counter-swarm scenario presented in this paper will provide answers, among others, to the following questions: how the two drone swarms are deployed, how a scenario is introduced to the simulation system, and how its progress is monitored and supervised. A preliminary version of the ConOps for a counter-swarm scenario was drafted through by using a counter-swarm simulator and conducting discussions and interviews with military experts of the Finnish Defence Forces.

**Keywords:** Robotic swarm · Counter-swarming · Concept of Operations

## 1 Introduction

Highly autonomous and intelligent swarms of robotic vehicles are becoming more popular in the military domain, since swarm systems can perform many kinds of tasks more effectively and efficiently than a single device. Swarm robotics is a technical approach aiming to develop multi-robot systems, which are based on many cost-effective robots. Here, we present the development of a Concept of Operations (ConOps) for a counter-swarm scenario in which the defender side uses a swarm of drones to defend a target against an attacking drone swarm. A ConOps is a high-level conceptual description of how the elements of a system and entities in its environment interact in order to achieve their stated goals. It has shown to be a useful and integrative element in designing complex technical systems. The ConOps for a counter-swarm scenario will provide answers, among others, to the following questions: how the two swarms are deployed, how a scenario is introduced to the simulation system, and how its progress is monitored and supervised.

One key task in ConOps development is to define the main performance requirements for the system that is under development. We have conducted expert interviews, based on which we have drafted the key requirements for a swarm of robotic vehicles and counter-swarm actions, and compared them with the requirements identified in an earlier project.

In this paper, we will also outline control concepts for a high-level control of a swarm of robots, including tasks such as situation assessment, coordination of task progress, alarm handling, and alerting other law enforcement units and manned vehicles to the situation.

The remainder of the paper is structured as follows: First, we review some relevant literature on counter-swarming. Second, we define the meaning of a ConOps on a conceptual level, give some examples of ConOps for robotic swarms, and present an earlier ConOps for a swarm of autonomous robotic vehicles in the military domain. Third, we present the summary of our interview results and the objective and progress of the development of a ConOps for counter-swarming scenario.

## 2  Relevant Literature

First, we review some relevant literature on modelling and design of counter-swarming systems.

Several authors have reviewed possible ways of countering an attacking swarm of drones. According to [15], there are several methods of defending against an attacking swarm, which were classified into four groups, methods of destroying the attacker, collapsing, trapping and hijacking it. The first group is further divided into methods of shooting individual drones or their clusters with lasers, electromagnetic guns, or high-powered microwaves, or destroying an attacking swarm with another swarm. Kang et al. [9] published a detailed survey on counter unmanned vehicle systems in which they described some key counter UAV systems. First, they introduced several unmanned aerial vehicle (UAV) applications and regulations; second, they described various possible platforms, architectures, devices and functions of the counter UAV systems; and third, they reviewed the current features of the counter UAV markets.

Recently, Brust et al. [2] developed a swarm-based counter UAV defense system. The motivation for this study was that existing counter-unmanned aerial systems (C-UAS), which for the majority come from the military domain, lack scalability or induce collateral damages. Their system is based on an autonomous defense UAV swarm, capable of self-organizing its defense formation and to intercept a malicious UAV. The fully localized and GPS-free approach is based on modular design regarding the defense phases, and it uses a newly developed balanced clustering approach to realize intercept and capture formations. The authors also implemented a prototype UAV simulator. The resulting networked defense UAV swarm is claimed to be resilient to communication losses. Through extensive simulations, they demonstrated the feasibility and performance of their approach.

Strickland et al. [16] developed a responding system for unmanned aerial swarm saturation attacks with autonomous counter-swarms. The motivation to this study was that existing response systems are vulnerable to saturation attacks of large swarms of low-cost autonomous vehicles. One method of reducing this threat is the use of an intelligent counter swarm with tactics, navigation and planning capabilities for engaging the adversarial swarm. Both a Monte Carlo analysis in a simulation environment to measure the effectiveness of several autonomous tactics as well as an analysis of live flight experiments in swarm competitions were conducted in this study.

Several theses on counter-swarming have been written at Naval Postgraduate School in Monterey, California. Some of them have investigated the possibility to defend against attacking drone swarms by missile-based defense systems. Parsons' [13] thesis explored the design of a counter-swarm indirect fire capability within the existing Marine Corps ground-based air defense and fire support framework. He developed a novel solution by defining the parameters of an artillery shell with effects designed to disrupt UAV operations. Such a shell would target the electromagnetic spectrum vulnerabilities of UAVs by utilizing expendable jammers delivered as a payload in a cargo-carrying projectile. This capability is likely to be effective against the swarm threat and can be used from the rear in support of units under UAV attack anywhere within range of the artillery piece. Thyberg [17] designed a low-cost delivery vehicle capable of deploying multiple guided munitions laterally out of the missile body at an altitude greater than that of the drone swarm. The guided munitions would be tasked by a targeting hub that would remain aloft above the specific drones, providing unique guidance commands to each deployed unit. This thesis focused specifically on the deployment of the munitions from a flight system, utilizing both Computational Fluid Dynamics and real flight testing to design an effective ejection mechanism and tracking approach. Additionally, high-level design and analysis of a targeting system within the missile was performed. The aim was to give the more cost-symmetric options and capabilities when it comes to air defense against drone swarms in the future. Lobo [11] designed sub-munition for a low-cost small UAV counter-swarm missile. The starting point was the possibility of defenses getting overwhelmed and the large cost asymmetry between currently available defenses and the cost of these threats. A survivability methodology was used to study the susceptibility and vulnerability of threat vehicles. The designed sub-munition possesses a low-cost affecting mechanism, such that multiple units could be delivered by a low-cost delivery vehicle. Experimental testing demonstrated the viability of the designs and the ability to provide a defense against small UAV swarms with low-cost technologies. Grohe [7] designed and developed a counter swarm air vehicle prototype. The motivation for this research was the fact that current air defense systems are designed to counter low quantities of very capable but extremely expensive weapons, and in many cases cannot properly defend against attacks involving a large number of offensive weapons. To avoid the scenario of an opponent overmatching current defenses with emerging low-cost weapons, a missile-based interceptor system was proposed. The chosen scenario was investigated using 'Repast Simphony' agent-based simulation. The aim was to deliver a payload capable of defeating multiple units, while still remaining cost-effective against the threat of low-cost small UAVs.

Several theses at Naval Postgraduate School in Monterey have studied swarm tactics with modelling and simulation tools. Gaerther [6] investigated UAV swarm tactics with agent-based simulation and Markov process analysis. Both defensive and enemy forces had the ability to launch a swarm of 50 UAVs, which are able to cooperate among their respective agents. The mission was to protect their own home base (i.e., the high value target) and to destroy the opposing one. Each side had the same type of UAVs with the same specifications. The scenario started with UAVs already launched. During the experiments, relevant factors, such as the initial positioning, spatial and temporal coordination, number of flights, and tactical behavior, were varied. Agent-based simulation and an associated analytical model were formulated. In agent-based simulation a UAV was modelled as an agent that follows a simple rule set, which is responsible for the emergent swarm behavior relevant to defining swarm tactics. In addition, a two-level Markov process was developed to model the air-to-air engagements; the 1st level focused on one-on-one combat, and the 2nd level incorporated the results from the first and explores multi-UAV engagements. Diukman et al. [4] developed an integrative model to understand an opponent swarm. The integrative meta-model was based on an abstract description of the swarm objects (agents, C2 unit, and environment) and processes (transfer of EMMI (energy, material, material wealth, and information)). The Map Aware Non-Uniform Automata (MANA) agent-based simulation environment was used to explore different scenarios, such as Rally (attraction of swarm agents to one another in space), Avoid (swarm avoidance of a perceived threat object/entity), Integration (swarm agents capable of changing their local rule set in accordance to input stimuli), and Triangulation (locating the physical location of a LOS C2 unit based on observed swarm movement patterns). Day [3] studied multi-agent task negotiation among UAVs to defend against swarm attacks. Enemy agents sought to engage a high value defensive target. Defensive agents attempted to engage and eliminate enemy agents before they were able to reach the high value target. Baseline defensive strategy was a centralized solution to the optimal assignment problem. Centralized methods needed a centralized oracle that had near perfect situational awareness of the entire scenario at all times and near unlimited bandwidth to communicate with all of its assets. Distributed task assignment strategies were compared against the centralized baseline solution. They tried to remove above-mentioned constraints while striving to maintain solutions that approach optimal solutions otherwise found by centralized algorithms. In this study it was found that factors other than assignment method are more significant in terms of the effect on the percentage of enemies destroyed. These more significant factors were the number of defensive UAVs per enemies, the defensive probability of elimination and the speeds of defensive and enemy UAVs. Munoz [12] implemented an agent-based simulation and analysis of a defensive UAV swarm against an enemy UAV swarm. Enemy UAVs were programmed to engage a high value unit deployed in open waters, and a defensive UAV swarm aimed to counter the attack. The scenario was investigated using the above-mentioned open source simulation environment 'Repast Simphony'. Each defensive UAV launched has one enemy UAV assigned to it to engage. After its launch, the defensive UAV needs to predict the future position of the assigned enemy UAV. Then it needs to check the distance to the assigned enemy UAV. If the distance to the assigned enemy UAV is within the Blast Range, the defensive UAV blasts, and it has a probability of elimination associated with that explosion to determine if the assigned enemy UAV is eliminated or not. There were several controllable factors, such as enemy UAV speed, blast range, enemy UAV endurance, a critical number of enemy UAVs, detection range, and number of defensive UAVs launched per enemy. It was found that for defensive UAV to obtain a higher probability of elimination, the defensive UAV speed was recommended to be comparable, if not greater than, the enemy UAV attack speed. The number of direct hits the high value unit can withstand was significant.

According to the literature review, quite much theoretical research has been done about counter-swarming, but there are quite few real-life demonstrations – or at least public knowledge of them is limited.

## 3   Concept of Operations

The notion of Concept of Operations (ConOps) was introduced by Fairley and Thayer in the late nineties [5]. The first standard providing guidance on the desired format and contents of a ConOps document was IEEE standard 1362 [8]. Another relevance guide is the 2012 AIAA revision proposal Guide: Guide to the Preparation of Operational Concept Documents (ANSI/AIAA G-043A-2012) [1]. These documents define a ConOps as a description of a system's operational characteristics from the end user's viewpoint. The description can be considered as a boundary object aiming to communicate high-level quantitative and qualitative system information among the main stakeholders. ConOps documents can be presented in variety of ways due to the fact that they play different functions in different domains. Typically, ConOps documents are textual descriptions illustrated by images and informal graphics that portray the key features of the proposed system [18].

ConOps is considered as a knowledge artefact created during the early stages of the design process, but ConOps has potential to be used at all stages of the development process, and a high-level ConOps is a kind of template that can be modified and updated regarding specific needs and use cases [19].

A typical ConOps contains at a suitable level of detail the following kind of information [1]: possible existing systems and operations; proposed system operational overview, including items such as missions, operational policies and constraints, operational environment, personnel, and support concept and environment; system overview, including items such as system scope, goals and objectives, users and operators, system interfaces and boundaries, system states and modes, system capabilities and system architecture; operational processes; and analysis of the proposed system, including possible advantages and disadvantages, alternatives and trade-offs and regulatory impacts.

Typically, the ConOps development process includes at least three following main stages: First, background and motivation for the ConOps will be introduced, for example, by considering the operational task from an evolutionary perspective and by investigating how it has been developed throughout times. Second, the first version of the ConOps will be developed by identifying the preliminary needs, requirements and critical usage scenarios and outlining the first sketches of the system architecture, descriptions of user interaction with the system as well as conceptual illustrations and drawings. Third, all information is aggregated and synthesized as a final ConOps description specifying the main operational tasks and usage scenarios, and by this way laying the foundations for a well-grounded and shared understanding of the aimed future operation.

ConOps documents come in various forms, but at the system level, they typically describe the main system elements and their workings, stakeholders, tasks and functions, and goals and requirements.

## 3.1   Robotic Swarm ConOps for the Military Domain

Previously, we developed a ConOps for a swarm of autonomous robotic vehicles in the military domain in MATINE funded project entitled "Development of a Concept of Operations for the operation of a swarm of robots" (RoboConOps) [10]. Our aim was to demonstrate how autonomic robotic swarms can be deployed in different military branches, that is, coast guarding at the littoral zone by the navy, air surveillance by the Air Forces and support for the urban troops operations. Each branch-specific ConOps contained the description of the mission goal, critical scenario description, main system requirements, system structure in the general level, and human-system interaction. The representative scenarios were brief fictional stories, which describe possible operative situations in the near future, when robotic swarms play an important role in military operations. Both normal and demanding operating situations were described in the scenarios. Performance requirements for the proposed system were based on expert interviews and workshops. A major part of the identified requirements focused on issues such as level of autonomy, data collection and tracing procedures, swarm navigation, human-robot interaction, operational robustness, weather-proofness and serviceability. Three system architectures were generated for each military branch, all of them consisting of elements such as robot nodes of the swarm, internal and external communication system, sensors and actuators, target, environment and control center. In the coast guarding scenario, underwater sensors and surveillance unmanned air vehicles (UAVs) monitor surroundings and if something abnormal is detected, send possible alarms and notifications to the swarm operation center. Cargo UAVs carrying unmanned under-water vehicles (UUVs) or surface vehicles (USVs) play an important role, for example, in reconnaissance missions. The operators are sitting in the command and control center and formulate and design the missions, supervise their execution and communicate with other stakeholders. The air surveillance system architecture is composed of various types of UAVs, such as cost-effective mini-UAVs, long-range surveillance UAVs and multifunctional UAVs. It is also possible to include manned aircrafts into the system architecture. In the Ground Force scenario urban troops are equipped with a fixed sensor and camera network, surveillance and cargo UAVs and multifunctional unmanned ground vehicles (UGVs).

Three control concepts for supervising the autonomous robotic swarms were developed for each military branch. The concepts describe operator roles in a detailed level and how these roles are connected to the technical systems and to other actors related to each military branch's operations. Air Force and Navy scenarios have two operators monitoring and supervising autonomous swarms with a workstation-based user-interface setup. In the Air Force scenario, one operator conducts mission planning, supervises its progress and reacts to possible exceptions in the control center. Another operator is in an intelligence officer role, making plans for missions together with the other operator, building a common operational picture and analyzing and sharing gathered reconnaissance information. In the Navy scenario the command and control center is also manned with two operators. One of them monitors both the sensor network and the progress of the mission and manages alarms and unknown object information. Another one is responsible of special missions: he supervises robotic swarms during task execution and communicates awareness information for the land forces and manned vehicle units. In the Ground Force scenario one operator supervises the swarm in a workstation-based operation center, makes mission plans and monitors their progress. Another operator is working in the battleground and assigns detailed tasks such as building investigation and clearing missions to the swarm through a mobile user interface.

# 4  Objectives

## 4.1  Main Aim and Progress of Work

In the present study our main aim was to develop simulations of swarm-based counter-measures to an attack conducted using a swarm of autonomous drones. For instance, we tested a defensive strategy by simulating autonomous UAVs ("scouts") with the ability to call upon a larger force when detecting a potential threat [14]. We anticipated that between ten and a hundred autonomous units (depending on the scenario) will be suitable to demonstrate the advantages of swarm-based defense. The project consisted of the following tasks: 1) implementation of a realistic 3D flight model with adjustable parameters; 2) testing robustness of the swarming behavior to errors and environmental conditions; 3) performance evaluation of the counter-swarm; 4) identification and simulation of typical scenarios; and 5) deployment cost evaluation.

Representative scenarios were selected based on discussions with military experts of the Finnish Defence Forces. The potential example scenarios include both military/law enforcement (e.g., radar station) and civilian targets (e.g., power plants). Emergent properties that result from the interplay between exogenous (e.g., the geometry and topology of the environment) and endogenous factors (e.g., the collective decision-making functions governing the behavior of the swarm) were thoroughly investigated and leveraged.

## 4.2  Methods

Six military experts were interviewed in 2021. The experts represented the Headquarters of the Defence Forces, the Headquarters of the Land Forces, the Naval Academy and The Finnish Defence Research Agency [14]. The interviews were held remotely through Microsoft Teams by two or three researchers. Interviews were audio-recorded provided that the interviewees consented to the audio recording. If the consent was not given, detailed notes were taken during the interview. Each of the interviews and group discussions lasted for two to three hours, and they were divided into two main parts. First, there was a general discussion about the use of robotic swarms in military missions; and after that, there was a detailed discussion about the CounterSwarm simulator and the ways it could be further developed.

# 5  Results

## 5.1  Summary of Interview Results

Next, we present the main results of the expert interviews. This section is based on the MATINE summary report by Saffre et al. [14]. The summary of the interviews presents opinions of individual experts, and thus does not reflect a consensus among all interviewees. In general, the interviewees thought that autonomous robotic swarms can be seen as a potential game changer of how the warfare is conducted. For example, the boundaries of military branches may become blurry, if all types of robotic swarms can be used in all military branches. Robotic swarms can be used on land, at sea and in the air, and swarming can also be applied in cyberspace. A war between drone swarms is technically possible in the near future, but poor weather and environmental conditions may compromise their effective use.

In general, ethical and judicial restrictions will prevent the use of swarms of autonomous vehicles in straight military offences [14]. The role of humans is to set limits to the warfare between autonomous systems and prevent further escalation of the situation. However, this becomes more difficult, as the tempo of warfare increases.

Encirclement and simultaneity are key features of military swarming: swarming makes possible to encircle the enemy drones and attack them simultaneously from multiple directions. A surrounding swarm can also conduct pulsing hit-and-run attacks by appearing and disappearing repeatedly. In order to achieve these positive impacts, a high level of autonomy is required so that the members of the swarm decide on how to act. Decision making is to a large extent decentralized and conducted where the operation is carried out.

Swarming promotes flexibility: the mission can be continued, even though a large part of the drones has been destroyed. Disposability and cost-effectiveness are key indicators: if the swarm is composed of inexpensive drones, the whole swarm can be sacrificed if needed. It is not necessarily feasible to incorporate both manned and unmanned units into swarms, because they may restrict each other's abilities. In principle, the collaboration between manned and unmanned systems is challenging, because a manned system quite easily slows down the progress of a mission.

In the first phase, autonomous swarms can be used in surveillance/reconnaissance operations and in area monitoring. For example, a drone swarm could conduct long-term patrolling in a military area, detect and recognize possible unknown objects and react quickly to them. Swarming provides new opportunities to decoy the enemy by saturating the airspace or leading new swarms periodically to the airspace. From the defender's perspective, it is very difficult to recognize armed drones carrying explosives or weapons from harmless units, if the airspace is saturated with these drones.

Since it is difficult to detect an attacking swarm of drones if it does not emit anything, a layered system is required for the detection and identification of the swarm. The layered system should be composed of various nonphysical systems (e.g., sensors, radars and lasers).

The defensive maneuvers against robotic swarms should include interfering and/or preventing communication. In principle, the best method to neutralize an attacking swarm of drones is to break the electronics of a drone with an electro-magnetic pulse. The drawback of this method is that it easily causes collateral damage, for example, destroys one's own devices at the same time. Physical mitigators such as projectiles and drones are especially suitable for counter-swarming. As discussed above, in our simulation another swarm counters an attacking drone swarm, and the drones of both swarms are equipped with weapons.

During the latter part of the interview, we carried out some simulator runs and discussed with the experts the key features of the simulation and the ways it could be improved (Fig. 1).

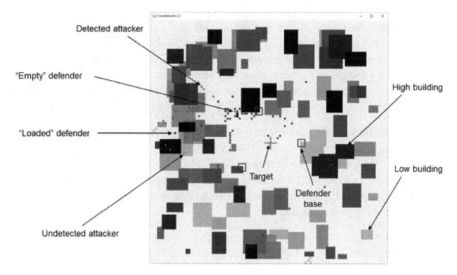

**Fig. 1.** CounterSwarm simulator's situational picture with legends of the used symbols [14].

One of the interviewers presented the simulator to the interviewee. The interviewer noted that the simulator enables the investigation of complex behavior of autonomous drone swarms. For example, it is possible to test the influence of critical variables such as the relative size of attacking and defending swarms; and assault and guarding distance, as well as properties of individual units, like speed and resilience. Furthermore, the systematic analysis of the impact of control parameters enables the implementation of various tactics in the form of combinations of parameter values for the functions governing autonomous decision making by individual units, for example, pursuit, encirclement and perimeter defense. The effects of some of these parameters were demonstrated to the interviewee.

The interviewees thought that the simulator is useful in promoting tactical thinking about counter-swarming [19]. Several parameters were recognized as relevant for controlling the behavior of attacking and defending swarms such as assault and counter-attack distance and probability of change of direction. The interviewees also thought that it is important to continue to study the impacts of various control parameters on swarm behavior in counter-swarming context. Several improvements were suggested to the tactical control of robotic swarms such as division of a swarm into smaller groups, introduction of sub-tasks, optimization of a counter-attack and programming of new scenarios (e.g., reconnaissance).

## 5.2  Main Elements of a ConOps for Counter-Swarming

Next we present the main characteristics of a ConOps for counter-swarming. The ConOps is based on information gathered through expert interviews and the results of simulations designed to study the performance of various attack and defence tactics.

**Mission Description.** The main objective is to prevent a drone swarm to reach a predefined high-valued target by attacking against it. Special defender tactics for preventing the enemy drone to achieve its objective were developed. According to gathered intelligence, there is a danger of terrorists attacking strategic targets in big cities using drone swarms. The defender side has also intelligence knowledge of possible enemy tactics. The level of preparedness was raised based on the updated situational awareness.

**Scenario Definition.** There is a big public event at a sports stadium. Terrorists make an attack by sending a drone swarm equipped with explosives towards the stadium. They have launched the swarm from a nearby air base, which has not been guarded. Provisions have been made for these kinds of attacks by identifying possible high-risk places (e.g., stadiums) and arming them with drone swarm stations or ordering moveable stations to the stadium for big public events.

Area surveillance is made by radars, and observations made about an approaching swarm triggers the operation of the defending swarm. Figure 2 illustrates the stadium defense scenario based ConOps diagram. The diagram visualizes and indicates the relationships between stakeholders, security control center with operators, and environment and air surveillance system with counter drone swarm units.

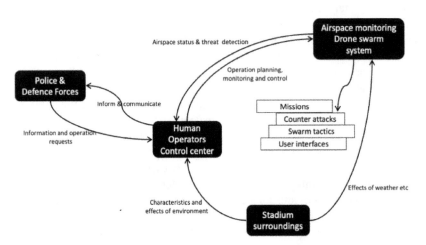

**Fig. 2.** ConOps diagram of the sport stadium surveillance and defense scenario.

**Main Stakeholders.** Public law authorities such as police take the main responsibility of organizing the swarm-based counter-swarm operation. Cooperation among authorities (e.g., with the defence forces) plays an important role. It is possible to purchase the counter-swarm service from private companies either partly or totally.

The station for a drone swarm with launch pads can be either moveable or immoveable. In the first case, it can be ordered by request to the place where the public event is held.

At the security control centre specialized operators plan, perform and manage the mission (intelligence operator, swarm operator etc.). Figure 3 shows the main tasks each of the operators are in charge of. An intelligence officer is responsible of mission planning and operation, a swarm operator is responsible of monitoring and control of the swarm, and a group of service personnel is responsible of the launch of the swarm and its return. In addition, operators at the control center have direct connection to the police headquarters, the defense forces and other authorities.

**Operational Environment.** The dogfight occurs in the airspace above the target city. It is summer weekend, the weather is fair, and wind conditions favorable for drone operations.

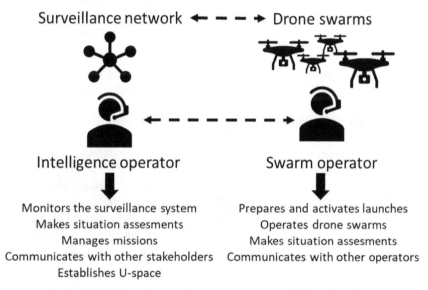

**Fig. 3.** Security control center operators and their tasks.

**Main Phases of the Scenario.** One of the main elements of the ConOps is the description of the main phases of the mission. The mission can be divided into the following phases:

1. The system is switched to the state of full readiness, and preparations are made to the swarm mission.
2. Airspace is monitored by a radar system.
3. An approaching enemy swarm is detected, identified and classified.
4. A temporary restricted space around the stadium is set up to automatically secure the area of an air battle (so called U-space).

5.  A method for countering the attacking swarm is selected (taken into account, e.g., the minimization of the risk of collateral damage).
6.  An air-raid alarm is triggered.
7.  The defender swarm is launched, and it is approaching the enemy swarm.
8.  Primary tactics for swarm confrontation is selected.
9.  The engagement between drone swarms starts.
10. Defender tactics is adjusted according to the enemy behavior.
11. The enemy mutually adjusts its tactics.
12. There is a culmination point of the air battle, after which the enemy swarm disengages the battle.
13. The defender swarm returns to the air base.
14. Maintenance and service operations are carried out.
15. Debriefing and reporting are completed.

**Performance Requirements.** Some key success criteria are skilled application of swarm tactics (e.g., encirclement, simultaneity and pulsing attack) and ability to flexibly change defender tactics. Air dominance can be most easily achieved by the number of drones, i.e., by saturation of the airspace.

A repertoire of tactics are available providing the defender drone swarm the best possible chance of repelling the attack. Three tactical rules turned out to be successful in simulations: 1) quick response, in which the drone flies toward the attacker to intercept it some distance from the target; 2) limited recruitment capability in which defenders are allowed to respond to a threat detected by others, but only when they are already close to the event; and 3) restricted perimeter in which a retreating attacker is chased only a short distance away from the target, to avoid falling for decoy manoeuvres [14].

Persistence is important, since operations may last a quite long period of time in variable weather and lighting conditions. Resilience is also needed so that the swarm is able successfully complete its mission, even when several defender drones are destroyed. Level of autonomy can be changed during the mission, positioning cannot be only based on GPS, and communication between drones should be resistant to disturbances and failures.

**Challenges and Risks.** Several challenges and risks have to be considered. For example, the risk of collateral damages is high in built environments; ethical and juridical challenges also have to be taken into account; and poor weather may compromise the defender tactics.

**System Interface (What is Included in the System and What is Not).** The system consists of an autonomous swarm of flying robotic systems. Individual drones are compact, adaptable, reliable, durable, effective, capable of learning, and equipped with various kinds of payloads. A compromise between weight and feature set must be carefully made, however, a mix of different drones can facilitate the choice.

The system also includes a computer system with programming software for learning robots, communication system, user interface for communication between operators and robots, and carriers and launch pads.

# 6 Discussion

In this research, a novel solution was developed against a hostile swarm of autonomous drones. Evaluation of the usefulness of the proposed counter-swarm approach helps to decide the applicability of the approach. For example, it can be determined in which scenarios (e.g., the protected area is of a specific size) it is viable to use the approach.

The ConOps approach makes it possible to understand and disclose motivations and possible barriers of usage activity among different user groups. The ConOps also helps to determine different modes for swarm management according to their complexity. In the lowest level of complexity, one operator executes one mission by monitoring and controlling one specific robot swarm, and in the highest levels of complexity, multiple robotic swarms, operators and troops from different military branches operate in the same area and accomplish joint missions. Even though technological and human factors issues are seldom a critical bottleneck for the deployment of autonomous swarm robot systems, they are highly important from the end users' perspective, and they must also be adequately addressed in the ConOps. A fluent interaction between human operators and a swarm of robots means specific requirements for the operator and the system. The operator must be aware of the system and mission status, and user interfaces must be designed to present situation-aware information in a right manner. On the other hand, the system must adapt to different situations and react to operator actions.

Some of the main prospects of swarming were raised in discussions with military experts. Swarming can in general support traditional victorious warfare tactics and actions. Simultaneity and encirclement indicate that it is possible to center power around the enemy troops and attack them simultaneously from multiple directions; increased flexibility and resilience, in turn, indicate that there are more opportunities to change tactics on the fly, and it is possible to continue a mission, even though part of the swarm has been destroyed. It is also possible to saturate the area by covering the space with a swarm of cost-effective drones and to sacrifice the whole swarm in order to achieve some goal (i.e., disposability). These prospects have implications for how military missions will be executed in the future, and how the roles of human operators and military troops operating in the battlefield will change. For example, it is possible that the boundaries of military branches become more blurred with the increasing role of autonomous systems; there are new possibilities to decoy the adversary, and the rhythm and tempo of warfare may drastically increase. In order to achieve these prospects, global behavior of a swarm is more than a sum of the behavior of its parts. A swarm of drones should, among others, exhibit a high level of autonomy, distributed decision-making, and short-range communications. All these changes, in turn, have implications to human-swarm interaction. Human operator can be or should be out-of-the-loop, when the situation in the battlefield evolves very fast. On the other hand, ethical and legislative concerns should not be insurmountable, if one swarm of autonomous robots attacks another one.

The Concept of Operations for our counter-swarm scenario is divided into two main parts, detection, identification and monitoring of the adversary and attacking and defending. Regarding detection and identification, there are several challenges from the defender's point of view. It is difficult to track the approaching swarm, and identify it, if the attacking swarm approaches quietly. In a war of swarms, the most obvious way to destroy the adversaries is to shoot them down or crash against them, but it may have unwanted side effects that have to be considered.

Promising application areas for autonomous/semi-autonomous swarm of drones are, for example, intelligence, surveillance and decoy operations and guarding a military airbase or a service harbor. A swarm of UUVs patrolling under water can be used in anti-submarine warfare, and mine search and minesweeping. A war of swarms was considered to be realistic in the near future (i.e., within five to ten years).

## 7  Conclusions

The paper describes a ConOps for a counter-swarm scenario in which the defender side uses a swarm of drones to defend a target against an attacking drone swarm. A ConOps is a high-level conceptual description of how the elements of a system and entities in its environment interact in order to achieve their stated goals. It has shown to be a useful and integrative element in designing complex technical systems. The ConOps for a counter-swarm scenario will provide answer, among others, to the following questions: how the two swarms are deployed, how the scenario is introduced to the simulation system, and how its progress is monitored and supervised. A preliminary version of the ConOps for a counter-swarm scenario was drafted through a counter-swarm simulator and discussions with military experts of the Finnish Defence Forces.

**Acknowledgements.** This research was funded by the Scientific Advisory Board for Defence (MATINE) in the CounterSwarm project. In addition, the Academy of Finland is acknowledged for part of the financial support from the project 'Finnish UAV Ecosystem' (FUAVE, project grant number 337878).

## References

1. American Institute of Aeronautics and Astronautics (AIAA): ANSI/AIAA guide for the preparation of operational concept document, G-043-1992. ANSI/AIAA G-043-1992, Reston, VA (1993)
2. Brust, M.R., Danoy, G., Stolfi, D.H., Bouvry, P.: Swarm-based counter UAV defense system. Discov. Internet Things **1**(1), 1–19 (2016)
3. Day, M.: Multi-agent task negotiation among UAVs to defend against swarm attacks. Naval Postgraduate School, Monterey, California (2012)
4. Diukman, A.G.: Swarm observations implementing integration theory to understand an opponent swarm. Naval Postgraduate School, Monterey, California (2012)
5. Fairley, R.E., Thayer, R.H.: The concept of operations: the bridge from operational requirements to technical specifications. Ann. Softw. Eng. **3**, 417–432 (1997)
6. Gaerther, U.: UAV swarm tactics: an agent-based simulation and Markov process analysis. Naval Postgraduate School, Monterey, California (2013)
7. Grohe, K.: Design and development of a counter swarm prototype air vehicle. Naval Postgraduate School Monterey United States (2017)
8. IEEE: IEEE Guide for Information Technology - System Definition - Concept of Operations (CONOPS) Document, IEEE Std 1362™, IEEE CONOPS Standard. IEEE, New York (1998)

9. Kang, H., Joung, J., Kim, J., Kang, J., Cho, Y.S.: Protect your sky: a survey of counter unmanned aerial vehicle systems. IEEE Access **8**, 168671–168710 (2020)
10. Laarni, J., Koskinen, H., Väätänen, A.: Concept of operations development for autonomous and semi-autonomous swarm of robotic vehicles. In: HRI 2017 Companion, 06–09 March 2017, Vienna, Austria. ACM (2017)
11. Lobo, K.B.: Submunition design for a low-cost small UAS counter-swarm missile. Naval Postgraduate School Monterey United States (2018)
12. Munoz, M.F.: Agent-based simulation and analysis of a defensive UAV swarm against an enemy UAV swarm. Naval Postgraduate School, Monterey, California (2012)
13. Parsons, M.D.: Feasibility of indirect fire for countering swarms of small unmanned aerial systems. Doctoral dissertation. Naval Postgraduate School, Monterey, CA (2020)
14. Saffre, F., Karvonen, H., Laarni, J., Lastusilta, T., Väätänen, A.: CounterSwarm – turning collective intelligence against hostile drone swarms. MATINE summary report (2021)
15. Scharre, P.: Counter-swarm: a guide to defeating robotic swarms—War on the rocks (2017)
16. Strickland, L., Day, M.A., DeMarco, K., Squires, E., Pippin, C.: Responding to unmanned aerial swarm saturation attacks with autonomous counter-swarms. In: Ground/Air Multisensor Interoperability, Integration, and Networking for Persistent ISR IX, vol. 10635, p. 106350Y. International Society for Optics and Photonics (2016)
17. Thyberg, R.I.: Design and testing of a multi-unit payload delivery and tracking system for guided munitions to combat UAV swarm threats. Naval Postgraduate School, Monterey, California, United States (2016)
18. Tommila, T., Laarni, J., Savioja, P.: Concept of operations (ConOps) in the design of nuclear power plant instrumentation & control systems. A working report of the SAREMAN project. VTT Working Report. VTT, Espoo (2013)
19. Väätänen, A., Laarni, J., Höyhtyä, M.: Development of a concept of operations for autonomous systems. In: Chen, J. (ed.) AHFE 2019. AISC, vol. 962, pp. 208–216. Springer, Cham (2020). https://doi.org/10.1007/978-3-030-20467-9_19

# Integrated Sensors Platform

## Streamlining Quantitative Physiological Data Collection and Analysis

Harry X. Li$^{(\boxtimes)}$ , Vincent Mancuso, and Sarah McGuire

Massachusetts Institute of Technology Lincoln Laboratory, Lexington, USA
`harry.li@ll.mit.edu`

**Abstract.** Human performance measurement for computer-based tasks is a critical need for assessing new capabilities and making inferences about their usability, utility and efficacy. Currently, many performance-based assessments rely on outcome-based measures and subjective evaluations. However, a quantitative method is needed to provide more fine-grained insight into performance. While there are some commercial solutions that integrate human sensors, in our exploration, these solutions have numerous limitations. We decided to build our own web application platform, the Integrated Sensors Platform (ISP), to collect, integrate, and fuse disparate human-based sensors, allowing users to link physio-behavioral outcomes to overall performance. Currently, we have integrated three sensors, two commercial and one custom, which together can help calculate various user metrics. While our focus has been using ISP to assess visualizations for cybersecurity, we hypothesize that it can have impact for both researchers and practitioners in the HCII community.

**Keywords:** Tool evaluation · User-centered design · Physio-behavioral monitoring

## 1 Introduction

When developing a new tool or application, it has become a common standard to incorporate the perspective of the user into the development. This process, also

DISTRIBUTION STATEMENT A. Approved for public release. Distribution is unlimited. This material is based upon work supported under Air Force Contract No. FA8702-15-D-0001. Any opinions, findings, conclusions or recommendations expressed in this material are those of the author(s) and do not necessarily reflect the views of the U.S. Air Force. ©2021 Massachusetts Institute of Technology. Delivered to the U.S. Government with Unlimited Rights, as defined in DFARS Part 252.227-7013 or 7014 (Feb 2014). Notwithstanding any copyright notice, U.S. Government rights in this work are defined by DFARS 252.227-7013 or DFARS 252.227-7014 as detailed above. Use of this work other than as specifically authorized by the U.S. Government may violate any copyrights that exist in this work.

© The Author(s), under exclusive license to Springer Nature Switzerland AG 2022
D. Harris and W.-C. Li (Eds.): HCII 2022, LNAI 13307, pp. 64–73, 2022.
https://doi.org/10.1007/978-3-031-06086-1_5

known as User-Centered design [4], is based on an explicit understanding of the users, task environments, and is driven and refined through multiple iterations. Throughout the process, designers ask questions about the usability (can the user interact with the tool), utility (does the system do something of value), and efficacy (how well does the tool support the user's goal). To be successful in this process, designers must incorporate the users throughout each phase of the design process: interviews and observations during requirements development, participatory design and feedback during the development, and iterative user testing during development and evaluation phases [1]. In this paper, we focus on the last phase and present a new tool we developed to enable researchers and practitioners to execute rigorous and quantitative evaluations based on physio-behavioral data.

## 2 Human-Centered Evaluations

Human-centered tool evaluations often rely on subjective evaluations, by the user or observers, and outcome-based measures. Surveys such as the System Usability Scale [5] allow assessors to quickly and easily understand a user's opinion on how well the tool functions and how well they were able to use it. Methods such as heuristic evaluation and cognitive walkthrough [3] allow a subject matter expert to walk through a system to identify issues with the usability of a system based on usability principles and expertise in the domain. Alternatively, evaluations can rely on behavioral and performance measurements. These measures rely on procedural-based metrics (e.g. response time, time spent in search, order of operations) as well as outcome-based metrics (e.g. task completion, accuracy). While these metrics provide insight into higher level processes and overall performance, they still exist one level above the higher-level cognitive functions that drive human behavior, understanding and decision making.

Within the research community, the emergent field of neuro-ergonomics [8] has focused on identifying physio-behavioral sensors and developing analyses to elicit cognitive states such as attention, cognitive workload, stress and fatigue. Research has shown that measures such as eye movement, heart rate, and even user activity can be used to make inferences on these constructs [9]. Traditionally this research has focused on the antecedents and dynamics of the various states, but as our understanding matures, there are new opportunities in applying this knowledge to inform the human-centered evaluation of tools. For example, Lukanov et al. [6] leveraged functional Near Infrared Spectroscopy (fNIRS) to assess mental workload during usability testing of a simple web form. Their findings showed that the fNIRS system provided insight into changes in mental workload, some of which were unexpected, and demonstrated a method for complimenting subjective responses with quantitative physiological data. While this approach is useful for webpages and other general use tools for a wide user base, these effects are even more magnified when discussing tools for operational users, such as air traffic controllers, cyber security analysts, pilots and military personnel.

The approach, methods and findings of Lukanov et al. demonstrate the enormous potential for these approaches for human-centered evaluations; however, the monetary costs and need for technical expertise limit the use of these methods within User-Centered Design. As of today, the cost and complexity of acquiring, integrating and analyzing the sensors and associated data makes applying these methods less practical for use in usability and tool evaluations. While there are some commercial solutions that work towards this goal, in our exploration, these solutions are costly and can be limiting. Most commercial solutions are locked into the company's ecosystem, requiring users to purchase separate compatible sensors, and not allowing them to use sensors they may already own, or that may be more appropriate to their research needs. The lack of physio-behavioral measurement and analysis remains a critical gap in human-centered tool evaluations, one which, if addressed, can further our ability to understand the impact of our design choices on more complex and nuanced human outcomes.

In this pursuit, we developed the Integrated Sensors Platform (ISP), a web application platform to help collect, integrate, and fuse disparate physio-behavioral sensors, to understand cognitive outcomes such as attention and workflow, and link to the overall performance of the users, while making it accessible and affordable to human-centered design researchers and practitioners. In the following sections we will document the overall architecture of the system, the design choices that were made, provide an overview of how it can be used to conduct a tool assessment, document how it can be leveraged by the wider community and discuss our future work.

## 3   Integrated Sensors Platform

The ISP is a tool aimed at integrating a multitude of commercial and experimental sensors. Built using open-source platforms, we have focused initially on low-cost sensors as a way to help lower the cost of entry for users. Additionally, we provided built-in integration and analysis capabilities to allow users who may not have a background in such analyses to benefit from the tool. In the following sections we present an overview of the system, including an initial set of sensors we selected, description of the architecture and walkthrough of the user interface.

### 3.1   Sensor Selection

To demonstrate our concept, we selected 3 minimally invasive sensors that cover a range of behavioral and physiological measures to integrate into the system. We did not want sensors that would impede an individual's normal movement by requiring them to be connected to extensive wires. We also did not want sensors that required long setup or calibration time, since the purpose of the ISP is to enable a wide range of users to quickly capture relevant measures. Also, the sensors had to either be internally developed or open-source so that they could be integrated within the platform.

**Heart Rate Monitor and Eye Tracker.** Based on these criteria, we first chose to integrate a Mionix NAOS GQ [7] computer mouse with an integrated optical sensor for measuring heart rate which can provide a measure of workload. We also integrated a GazePoint GP3 [2] eye tracker for capturing gaze position and blinks. These two commercial sensors come with software that makes the sensor data available through web server interfaces. It is important to note that we chose these sensors for the purpose of demonstration, and not necessarily based on comparisons to other commercially available models.

**Sensei Software Workflow Monitor.** Finally, we built and integrated a software workflow monitor called Sensei which records user actions in the browser and also captures periodic screenshots for associating mouse movements and eye tracking to portions of the computer screen.

Sensei is written in JavaScript and can be easily integrated into any browser-based website. It listens for user-initiated browser events (mouse movement, clicks, key presses, etc.) and can stream the data in real time or batches to a server via HTTP or WebSocket protocols. Moreover, Sensei can take periodic screenshots of a user's tab or entire screen, which can be used to record user workflow and tool usage, and link physiological data back to what was on the screen at the time of collection. We have integrated Sensei into the ISP for troubleshooting as well as into external web tools that we wanted to evaluate.

This demonstrates the advantage of our platform, which combines data collection from commercial and in-house sensors.

## 3.2 Architecture

The ISP system architecture is broken up into four components: the Sensors which collect the data (discussed in detail in the previous section), the Sensor Proxy which transmits data, the Client which displays the user interface, and the Server which stores the data (Fig. 1). The ISP Client is a website written in ReactJS, JavaScript and HTML 5 that can be opened from any modern browser and run independently from other software installed on the computer. It receives data from the Sensors and/or Sensor Proxy, then visualizes and performs analysis on the collected data.

The Sensor Proxy is written in NodeJS and acts as a middle man between the Sensor and the Client for Sensors that cannot be directly accessed within the browser. For example, the eye tracker makes its data available on a TCP socket, which is currently tricky for a browser to directly connect to. Instead, the Sensor Proxy connects to the eye tracker TCP socket, then proxies the data to the Client via a WebSocket. Similarly, an external Sensei instance running in another web client can send its data to the Sensor Proxy which passes it to the ISP Client.

Finally, the Server is written in NodeJS and saves the data from multiple concurrent Clients to a local SQLite3 database file. Every time an ISP Client starts a data collection session, the Server assigns that session an ID and labels all incoming sensor data with that session ID. Later, the Server can separate data from different sessions using the session ID. In the future, the local SQLite3 file could be changed to a database server if better performance were necessary.

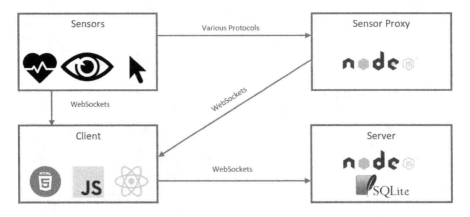

**Fig. 1.** Architecture diagram of ISP. Users access the Client in a browser like a normal website. The Client connects to the Sensors directly or indirectly through the Sensor Proxy. The Client then sends data to the Server to be saved.

### 3.3   User Interface (Client)

The user interface has three primary pages, aimed at supporting data collection and analysis. First, the Configuration Page allows users to input their task information and configure their sensors. Then, the Data Collection Page lets user select sensors for data collection and displays the statuses of the sensors. Finally, the Data Analysis Page consolidates data to be downloaded and can automatically generate some analysis based on sensor data.

**Configuration Page.** When first loaded, the ISP starts on the Configuration Page shown in Fig. 2, which allows the user to configure the data collection and record any necessary metadata. In the left column (Fig. 2A), the user has the ability to save information about the current data collection session, including information about the task, participant, station, and equipment being used for data collection. In the right columns (Fig. 2B), the user can configure the sensor data sources and where to save the data. The user can set the sample rate of the eye tracker (30 Hz) and workflow monitor sensor, including the rate of the "mouse move" web event (1 Hz), and configure how often to capture images of the user's screen (ex every 10 s). Finally, the user can configure the Client to collect data from a Sensor on a remote server by typing in the requisite URL or IP address.

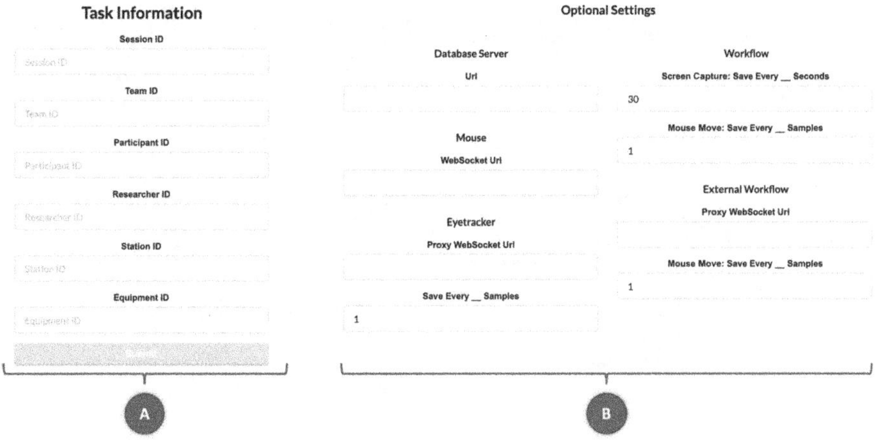

**Fig. 2.** Configuration page. A) The user can input information about the task and B) configure how and where to save data from the sensors

**Data Collection Page.** Once the user has entered the information in the Configuration Page, they can click the submit button to move to the Data Collection Page, shown in Fig. 3. At the top of the dashboard is a control bar (Fig. 3A), that shows the task information and has buttons to start or stop data collection. Each of the columns shows information for the sensors currently integrated. Users can choose whether to save data from a sensor and are able to view the total number of data samples for that sensor. The left column is the heart rate mouse (Fig. 3B), which displays the current heart rate. The next column is the eye tracker (Fig. 3C), which displays the current and recent eye position data. The last two columns show data from a software sensor developed by our team called Sensei, which records web events (mouse movement, clicks, key presses, etc.) and takes periodic screenshots. The third column is the internal Sensei (Fig. 3D), which displays the actions the user takes within the ISP Client and can be used for troubleshooting. The final column shows data from an external Sensei (Fig. 3E) integrated into a separate web application, which displays user actions taken within that external tool. Once a sensor is enabled, data is streamed to the server in real-time. When data samples are saved from a sensor, it updates the number of total saved samples so that the user can monitor the data collection. The interface allows the user to control data collection and monitor the data being collected in real time so as to ensure accurate data is captured throughout session.

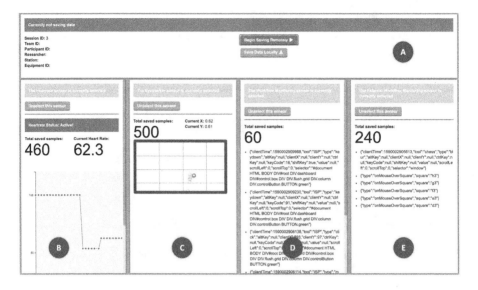

**Fig. 3.** Data collection page. A) The top control bar displays task information and has buttons to start and stop data collection. The bottom columns display sensor data and controls for the B) Heart Rate Monitor, C) Eye Tracker, D) Internal Sensei, E) External Sensei.

**Data Analysis Page.** After data has been collected, the user can access the Data Analysis Page (Fig. 4) where they can access an archive of the data on the server and can perform some analysis. In the left column (Fig. 4A), the user can configure where the Server is located. When the Client retrieves the data, the web page displays a list of all the data collection sessions stored in the database. The collections are sorted in order according to the datetime created and displays the task information that the user had entered in the Configuration Page at the beginning of data collection. When the user clicks on one of the tasks, the right column shows more information about the collected data (Fig. 4B). The user also has the option of downloading all the collected data from an individual session or all the sessions in JSON format.

To correlate the mouse and/or eye position data to user workflows, Sensei takes periodic screenshots that the Data Analysis Page uses to generate heatmaps (Fig. 4C). The user can select the source data (mouse or eye positions), and the Data Analysis page will generate heatmaps by downsampling and summing the position data into a lower resolution grid. As the screenshots are taken periodically, the heatmaps may not always accurately represent what the user was looking at in between the screenshot samples, so it is important that the user keep accurate records to ensure heatmap validity.

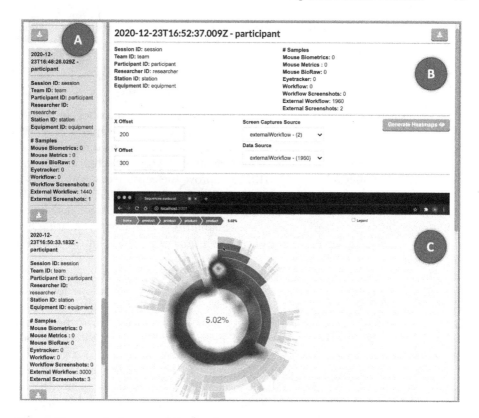

**Fig. 4.** Data analysis page. (A) list of data collection sessions, (B) more information about a particular session and (C) example heatmap generated by ISP based on usage of a sunburst visualization.

## 4   Applications of ISP

In developing the ISP, our main intent was to use it for evaluating analytic and visualization tools for cybersecurity. However, we hypothesize that there are more broad applications. By making a low cost, easy to use, and composable suite of tools, we aim to enable users, who may not have as rich of expertise, to leverage research on physio-behavioral monitoring in their human-centered evaluations.

ISP could be used, for example, to quantitatively evaluate the effectiveness of a computer operator or the usage of a prototype web tool. A researcher could conduct a study with ISP to collect data on participants as they perform computer tasks. Afterwards they could analyze the data to evaluate workload, fatigue, user workflow, or tool usage, then make quantitatively-backed recommendations to improve operator training or tool design.

Moving forward, our goal is to build on the ISP based on our own experience, and work with potential stakeholders to create a more holistic tool that enables users across multiple domains to understand physio-behavioral outcomes of their tools on users.

## 5    Future Work

As we continue to develop the ISP, we plan to expand the number and types of sensors into the system and expand the automatic analysis capability. There are several sensors that could be added to expand our current data collection ability, including a proximity sensor to measure collaboration, chat monitoring to measure communication, and fNIRS to improve the capture of cognitive load. We also hope to expand the capability to allow for different types of heart rate monitors (i.e. chest straps or wrist worn), and eye trackers. In addition, as remote human participant testing is increasing, capabilities for remotely capturing eye tracking and physiological measures using web cameras could be integrated into the system.

The automated analysis tool can also be greatly expanded to provide workload information from the heart rate and eye tracking data, and task performance measures could also be derived from Sensei-captured data, such as task completion time and tasks completed. Since our goal is for this system to be usable by both novices and experts in physio-behavioral data collection, better analysis capabilities could provide useful results for all experience levels.

Moreover, while we have currently only used ISP in small-scale testing and data collection performed by single team members, we would like to use ISP to capture data on multiple people collaborating, in order to test and demonstrate this capability. We also want to validate ease of set up: that the Sensors and Client can be set up on users' computers, and that the Sensor Proxy and Server can be set up on a server or virtual machine in the network. Finally, we want to validate that the Server is robust enough to concurrently collect data in a distributed environment, and that data collection is comprehensive and encompassing.

## 6    Conclusions

We developed the Integrated Sensor Platform to help users who are interested in evaluating tools, and conducting human-centered research to collect, integrate, and fuse data from multiple human-based sensors, and link them to factors such as stress, workflow, etc., and to the overall performance of the individuals and teams. We developed the platform with flexibility in mind, allowing for the addition of multiple types and brands of sensors to the system. By leveraging common, open-source web technologies, we designed a modular system that can be easy for developers to expand the capabilities based on their specific needs, available sensors and research questions. Our initial prototype system integrates three different sensors: a heart rate monitor that is built into a mouse, a low-cost eye tracking system, and an internally developed software workflow sensor called Sensei. In addition to flexibility in the code base, the ISP was developed to allow flexibility on the front end. The user interface allows individuals to select the sensors used and to monitor the data collection. Once collected they are able to easily access, download, and view initial analysis of the captured data. We have prototyped initial visualizations into our analysis system that will allow users without expertise in physio-behavioral data analysis to understand the data. By creating this system, we hope to reduce the barriers to collecting physio-behavioral measures making it more accessible to collect this data when performing usability assessments of technologies as they are developed or to capture quantitative measures of performance in research activities.

# References

1. Abras, C., Maloney-Krichmar, D., Preece, J.: User-centered design. In: Bainbridge, W. (ed.) Berkshire Encyclopedia of Human-Computer Interaction, pp. 445–456. Berkshire Publishing Group (2004)
2. GP3 Eye Tracking device. Gazepoint, 16 December 2021. https://www.gazept.com/product/gazepoint-gp3-eye-tracker/. Accessed 5 Jan 2022
3. Hollingsed, T., Novick, D.G.: Usability inspection methods after 15 years of re-search and practice. In: Proceedings of the 25th Annual ACM International Conference on Design of Communication, pp. 249–255. Association for Computing Machinery, New York (2007). https://doi.org/10.1145/1297144.1297200
4. International Organization for Standardization: ISO: 13407: Human-Centered Design Processes for Interactive Systems. International Organization for Standardization, Geneva (1999)
5. Lewis, J.R.: The system usability scale: past, present, and future. Null **34**(7), 577–590 (2018). https://doi.org/10.1080/10447318.2018.1455307
6. Lukanov, K., et al.: Using fNIRS in usability testing: understanding the effect of web form layout on mental workload. In: Proceedings of the 2016 CHI Conference on Human Factors in Computing Systems, pp. 4011–4016 (2016)
7. Mionix Naos QG. Mionix NOAS GQ. (n.d.). https://mionix.net/products/naos-qg. Accessed 5 Jan 2022
8. Parasuraman, R.: Neuroergonomics: research and practice. Theor. Issues Ergon. Sci. **4**(1–2), 5–20 (2003)
9. Parasuraman, R., Wilson, G.F.: Putting the brain to work: neuroergonomics past, present, and future. Hum. Factors **50**(3), 468–474 (2008)

# Usability Evaluation of a Web Interface for Passengers' Health Monitoring System on Detecting Critical Medical Conditions

Elizabeth Manikath[(✉)] [ID] and Wen-Chin Li[ID]

Safety and Accident Investigation Centre, Cranfield University, Cranfield, U.K.
elizabeth.manikath@cranfield.ac.uk

**Abstract.** Medical emergencies occurring on board an aircraft put flight and cabin crew into an extremely stressful situation. It is essential that the emergency is detected at an early point. Cabin crew play a vital role in aviation safety besides providing passenger services. Although cabin crew are trained in first aid, they might not be sufficiently qualified to detect critical conditions early. This study evaluated the usability and utility of a web interface for an onboard health monitoring system, which displays certain vital signs of the traveler and provides alerts to the cabin crew. Within the research project HOPEKI, Lufthansa Technik AG is currently developing a heath monitoring system. The optimal content and arrangement of information was assessed through a distributed questionnaire. The survey software "Qualtrics" was used for designing and distribution of the questionnaire. Cabin crew with experience handling medical emergencies were invited via social media (e.g. Yammer, LinkedIn) to participate in the study. SPSS was used for the descriptive statistical analysis. The usability of the interface was assessed using modified versions of SUS, PSSUQ and TUQ questionnaire and showed average usability and satisfaction scores. Improvements in the existing interface and an additional "emergency button" could support the cabin crew in early detecting medical emergencies on board.

**Keywords:** Health monitoring · Wearable technology · Measurement of vital signs · In-flight medical emergencies · Passenger safety · Cabin crew first aid training

## 1 Introduction

Medical emergencies occurring on board an aircraft put flight and cabin crew into an extremely stressful situation. The likelihood of a medical emergency on board an intercontinental flight is reported to be one event in every 10.000 to 40.000 passengers according to Graf et al. (2012, p. 591). Unfortunately, systematic approaches to report medical emergencies occurred on board of a commercial passenger aircraft do not exist and the procedures vary from airline to airline. According to Graf et al. (2012, p. 592) official figures of medical emergencies are not published by airlines. Neither a common database nor a general standard on how to classify medical emergencies is existing.

© The Author(s), under exclusive license to Springer Nature Switzerland AG 2022
D. Harris and W.-C. Li (Eds.): HCII 2022, LNAI 13307, pp. 74–84, 2022.
https://doi.org/10.1007/978-3-031-06086-1_6

Additionally, the EU GDPR further restricts the collection of sensitive data making it difficult to collect and store data of incidences and obtain validated statistics on the occurrence of medical emergencies on board. Graf et al. (2012, p. 592) reported 43% of the cases cardiovascular diseases and neurological conditions as a cause for medical emergencies on board a European carrier. It is essential that the emergency is detected at an early point. This is especially important in case of sudden cardiac arrests where early defibrillation improves the survival rates of the passenger [2]. Cabin crew play a vital role in aviation safety besides providing passenger services. In case of medical emergencies they are expected to manage the situation and provide first aid. Although cabin crew are trained in first aid they might not be qualified enough to firstly early detect critical conditions but also to handle them [3, 4]. Usually passengers are sleeping or resting in the aircraft, which makes it difficult to notice an acute collapse [2]. Additionally increasing workload, fatigue and stress levels on long-range flights might be factors, which distract the flight attendants of closely observing passengers' general condition.

An onboard health monitoring system, which displays certain vital signs of the traveler, could support the crew in their task of observing critical health conditions. Marinos et al. (2011, pp. 223–233) implemented and tested such a health monitoring system onboard an Airbus A340 cabin mock-up. The focus of this research was on sensor integration and connection to the airplanes existing network architecture [5]. However, the effect on cabin crew task performance, workload and stress levels have not been studied yet, as well as the optimal design of the GUI. The focus of this research is to evaluate the usability, learnability and interface quality of a web-based interface as developed by Lufthansa Technik AG.

To evaluate the usability of a product or system, there are a number of standardized questionnaires available such as e.g. System Usability Scale (SUS), Questionnaire for User Interaction Satisfaction (QUIS) and Post Study System Usability Questionnaire (PSSUQ) [6]. However, these questionnaires are evaluating usability in a simplified way and application for telehealth services is limited. Telehealth is defined as medical services provided using "electronic information and telecommunication technologies" to connect over a long-distance between a healthcare provider and a patient [7]. There are multiple surveys to assess telehealth services, which were mostly developed in the early 2000s [8]. Some of the questionnaires as mentioned by Parmanto et al. (2016, p. 4) such as Telemedicine Patient Questionnaire (TMPQ), Telemedicine Satisfaction Questionnaire (TSQ) and Telemedicine Satisfaction and Usefulness Questionnaire (TSUQ) were developed to evaluate specific videoconferencing systems. Typically, these questionnaires, including the Telehealth Usability Questionnaire (TUQ), contain a section, which evaluates the interaction quality between patient and clinician, which is unique to telehealth questionnaires [8]. However in case of a health monitoring system, measuring the interaction quality is not applicable since the system was not developed to interact with clinicians. Therefore, only the applicable questions from SUS, PSSUQ and TUQ were selected to evaluate usability of the user interface.

The German Federal Ministry for Economic Affairs and Energy (BMWi) funds the research project HOPE KI at Lufthansa Technik AG, which started in March 2021. The aim of the project is to analyze health risks for passenger and minimize these using new sensor technology and data analytics. The goal is to increase passenger safety but also well-being (e.g. reduction of flight anxiety, encouragement for mobility, sleep quality enhancement). The first proof of concept is using wearable technology (Apple Watch Series 6) as a sensor to transmit passenger's vital data (e.g. heart rate, oxygen saturation). Here the passenger actively needs to give consent in order to transmit the data to the server. The advantage of using wearable technology is that the passenger is deciding which information will be shared with the system; however, the limitation is that not every traveler possesses a wearable. The obtained data will be displayed on a web-based GUI for the cabin crew.

The overview page depicts the overall aircraft with the general status on each seat. "Inactive" means that the data sent via the sensors is older than 45 s. "Active" means real-time health data is sent from the passenger seat. Status "Warning" is the first of two warning messages indicating that the passenger's individual health parameters are out of the neutral range and there might be a health problem, whereas "Alert" means that there is a serious health problem (Fig. 1).

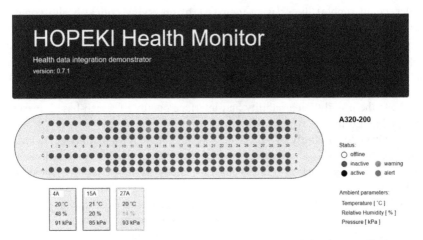

**Fig. 1.** Overview page of the web-based user interface (Color figure online)

To assess comfort levels in the cabin ambient parameters such as temperature, humidity and atmospheric pressure are displayed.

On the second screen, the operator can see detailed information about the passenger such as:

- Gender
- Age
- Seat number
- Heart rate
- Oxygen saturation
- Step count (how many steps did the passenger walk?) (Fig. 2).

**Fig. 2.**  Detailed view per passenger seat (Color figure online)

If a parameter is out of range, the color displayed will change accordingly to a visual warning either orange for "warning" or red for "alert". Additionally, the "tachometer" symbols indicate the "neutral" and "out-of-range" for the measured parameters.

## 2  Methodology

### 2.1  Participants

Participants were eligible if they were 18 years or older at the time of the study, were employed as flight attendants, had full proficiency in English language and had access to a computer with access to the internet. Cabin crew who did not experience medical emergencies during their career were not eligible for the study. Participation was voluntary and anonymously. Participants were able to exit the study at any time by closing the survey.

Participants were recruited in three ways: First: via social media platforms such as Yammer. LinkedIn or Facebook. The link to the survey was shared on the respective sites. Second: personal contacts were contacted directly via Email. Third: snowball sampling.

The institutional research ethics committee had granted ethics approval (CURES/14868/2021).

### 2.2  Material

Since not every question from the standardized questionnaires were applicable to evaluate a health monitoring system, only the relevant ones were chosen and a score for each modified questionnaire was calculated. Data were collected between December 2021 and January 2022.

The survey is divided into four sections: usability, interface quality, learnability and general closing questions. Each section will be described briefly.

**Ease of Use and Usability:**  The aim of this section is to evaluate how easy and simple the user interface can be used. The operator should feel confident and like using the tool.

The system shall not add additional complexity to the workload of cabin crew. Instead, it should support the user in their task completion. The questions in this section are mainly taken from the SUS and PSSUQ.

**Interface Quality:** The interaction between the operator and the user interface is assessed in this section. The scaling system rates how pleasant it was to use the system. Additionally it evaluates whether the display contained sufficient information to support task completion. The questions are mainly taken from the PSSUQ.

**Learnability:** This section evaluates whether the system could be used intuitively or additional/special training was necessary for operation. The user rates whether they would need to learn how to use the interface before working with it.

**General Ending Questions:** The general ending questions serve to rate the overall experience using the web-based interface. The user is evaluating whether the expectations on the system were fulfilled. Moreover, the operator is rating the overall satisfaction using the display.

A seven point Likert scale was used for the rating of all questions to get more responses that are accurate.

## 2.3  Research Design

The online survey software Qualtrics (www.qualtrics.com) was used to design and distribute the survey. The link to the questionnaire was published on social media platforms or distributed via Email. The link to the survey granted anonymous participation. The questionnaire consisted of three parts. The first block contained basic information about the study and the participant informed consent form. Active agreement of the participant was needed otherwise the questionnaire would be discontinued. After the introductory section, relevant basic demographic questions followed. The users were asked about their experience handling medical emergencies on board the aircraft. In the final section, the participants were asked to familiarize themselves with the user interface by firstly reading the user instructions and secondly logging into the web-based user interface. Afterwards the participant needed to evaluate the usability, interface quality and the learnability of the system.

Individual scores for SUS, PSSUQ and TUQ were calculated and compared.

SUS is a questionnaire consisting of ten items which uses a five point Likert scale [9]. For this study, nine questions were selected to evaluate the user interface. The following question has been intentionally left out "I thought the system was easy to use" because instead the following statement from PSSUQ "it was simple to use this system" was chosen to evaluate the usability. The statement from PSSUQ was selected because the phrasing is in an "active-voice". To calculate the scores for the SUS the scores for the seven-point Likert scale needed to be transformed into a five-point scale [10]. Therefore, the following formula was used [10]:

$$x_5 = (x_7 - 1) * (4/6) + 1 \tag{1}$$

To calculate the SUS score for the modified nine-item questionnaire the calculation formula needed to be adjusted. Instead of multiplying with 2.5 (=100/40) for the ten-item questionnaire the multiplier is 100/36 to compensate the left-out question [11]. According to Lewis, Sauro (2017, pp. 38–46) the effect of dropping one question in the SUS is marginal as long as afterwards the correct multiplier is used to calculate the overall score.

The PSSUQ version 3 is a 16-item questionnaire following a seven- point Likert scale and a "not applicable" option [12]. From the PSSUQ ten questions were selected. For the scoring of PSSUQ the left out questions were counted as "not applicable" with a score of zero.

The TUQ comprises 21 questions to evaluate five usability elements of telehealth systems such as ease of use, effectiveness, usefulness, satisfaction and reliability [13]. Items in the questionnaire are rated using a seven-point Likert scale. Four questions evaluating interface quality and "ease of use & learnability" were selected for the survey because these elements were not covered by SUS or PSSUQ. The total score for the TUQ questions were calculated as the overall score average of all questions.

## 3    Results

Statistical analysis were subject to descriptive statistical analysis using IBM SPSS (Version 28.0).

### 3.1    Demographics

In total 35 participants (13 male and 22 female) contributed to the study. Two of them were not cabin crew professionals (one Aeromedical Examiner and Cardiologist, one maintenance professional). Participants were recruited via social media and snowball sampling. The majority 76% (n = 25) had more than 10 years of experience and (39%) of the professionals were of European or Asian (24%) decent. 46% (n = 13) of the flight attendants had managing functions such as Purser, Lead cabin crew or Cabin service director. Of the 33 cabin crew professionals, only 21% stated that they are medically trained (beyond the mandatory first aid training) and 85% of the participants indicated that they had experienced a medical emergency during their career.

Twenty-nine percent of the cabin crew who had experience handling medical emergencies encountered at least 5 times a medical emergency on board during their career. Flight attendants with a tenure of more than 10 years encountered higher numbers (>10) of critical situations during their career. The majority of cabin crew 43% (n = 12) reported that emergencies occurred during long-haul flights (>7 h), which is consistent with what has been found in the literature (Graf et al. 2012, p. 592).

In case of a medical emergency 64% of the flight attendants described that they either were informed by the passenger's family, other passengers, and crewmembers or detected the critical health status by themselves. In 29%, the cabin crew stated that the emergency was recognized by coincidence. In such a case, some of the participants indicated that an additional "Medical Call Button" or an alert mode on the existing Call Button (e.g. pressing the button several times) could support the flight attendants to early detect critical situations.

## 3.2  Evaluation of the User Interface

A total of 35 participants consented to contribute to the survey, 33-cabin crew plus two non-cabin crew. Six participants were excluded because they did not have experience with medical emergencies on board an aircraft. Another 17 (76% female, 24% male) participants did not complete the survey. Finally, for data analysis 12 (50% female, 50% male) responses were used. Eighty-three percent of the flight attendants were in the age group of 30–50 and 82% had a work experience of greater than 10 years. The majority (55%, n = 9) were European flight attendants, 36% Asian and 9% African.

Elements from three different usability questionnaires (SUS, PSSUQ and TUQ) were chosen to evaluate the usability of the interface.

Eight of the eleven flight attendant participants (n = 8) filled out the nine questions from the SUS. A score of 68 is considered as average.

The mean value (58, 8) indicate that the usability evaluation according to SUS is below average. As a comparison the SUS score from the Aeromedical Examiner was 62 (Std. deviation: 2, 31), also below average indicating a subpar performance. The lower mean value for the cabin crew SUS scores shows that the usability of the interface should be improved. However, the score itself does not provide information about in which point the interface needs improvement. Interestingly, the scores from the medical expert are higher although the interface was primarily designed to support layperson. The major part (63%) of the professionals indicated that they felt confident to use the system.

The PSSUQ can be divided up into three subscales evaluating the system usefulness (SYSUSE), information quality (INFOQUAL) and interface quality (INTERQUAL) [12]. The overall score can be calculated by adding up the average scores of the total 16 questions. One (1) stands for "strongly agree" whereas seven (7) is "strongly disagree", meaning the lower the overall score the higher the user's perception of satisfaction.

Seven of the eleven participants (n = 7) filled out the eleven questions derived from the PSSUQ. The mean score as well as the overall score are low and indicate a very good perceived satisfaction of the user interface (see Table 1). Looking at the individual scores for SYSUSE, INFQUAL and INTERQUAL the scores for information quality were rated best with a mean of 1, 1. The scores for the interface quality were rated worst with a mean of 2, 3 (see Table 1).

**Table 1.**  Detailed PSSUQ scores

|            | Minimum | Maximum | Mean  | Std. deviation | 95% CI         |
|------------|---------|---------|-------|----------------|----------------|
| SYSUSE     | 1, 5    | 3, 3    | 2, 3  | 0, 6           | [1, 8; 2, 9]   |
| INFQUAL    | 1, 0    | 4, 3    | 2, 5  | 1, 0           | [0, 7; 1, 5]   |
| INTERQUAL  | 1, 0    | 3, 0    | 2, 3  | 0, 7           | [1, 7; 2, 9]   |
| Overall    | 0, 8    | 2, 1    | 1, 6  | 0, 4           | [1, 2; 2, 0)   |

The statement with the lowest rating with a mean of 3, 2 (Std. deviation: 2) was "I was able to complete the tasks and scenarios quickly using this system". It seems that not all of the participants found the system and its functionality useful. However, the best scores were for one of the concluding statements "this system has all the functions and capabilities I expect it to have" (mean: 2, 0; std. deviation: 0, 5) indicating that the overall functionality was rated good.

Comparing the scores from the layperson to the Aeromedical doctor the latter are higher indicating less perceived satisfaction (Overall PSSUQ Score: 2, 6; Std. deviation; 0, 5). The worst scores were achieved for the interface quality (INFQUAL: 6) and the best scores for system usefulness (SYSUSE: 2). Obviously, the amount of information is not sufficient for the Aeromedical expert to track the health status of passengers.

Four questions were chosen from the Telehealth Usability Questionnaire (TUQ). The total score is calculated by adding up the averages to each question, similar to the PSSUQ calculation. However, in contrast to the PSSUQ the higher the overall average scores, the higher the usability of the telehealth system [13]. Seven participants (n = 7) answered the questions from the TUQ. Looking at the mean value (5, 6; std. deviation: 0, 7), the usability results are good. The question "I like using the system" which the majority of the participants (n = 12) answered also had the highest rating with 5, 6 (std. deviation: 1, 5) reflecting the good overall usability assessment. Comparing the lowest scores (mean: 5, 1; std. deviation: 1, 4) were achieved for the question "This system is able to do everything I would want it to be able to do". This indicates that the overall functionality could be improved.

## 4  Discussion

In a medical emergency, every second counts and is vital for the survival rate of the passenger. In this study, 64% of the cabin crew stated that other passengers called out the attention on the medical emergency, which indicates that in most of these cases the detection time would have been longer without the support of the fellow travelers. Unfortunately, the outcome of the situation (e.g. survival rates), as well as the perceived workload of the flight attendants during the situation were not examined, which would have been useful to prove the hypothesis.

Although the sample size for this study was low the feedback of the participants regarding the usability of the onboard health monitoring system was positive. The assessments according to SUS, PSSUQ and TUQ revealed mostly an average usability for the user interface. The overall functionality was rated positively however the arrangement of information on the health status of the passengers was perceived too complex. Therefore a more simple depiction should be developed. Two of the participants mentioned that the system is "quite simple to use" and "kind of user-friendly". Additionally one flight attendant mentioned that it is a "great idea" to have a health monitoring system on board. Therefore, it needs to be evaluated whether a more simple system such as a "medical/emergency button" could create more awareness for the crew than a constant health monitoring.

### 4.1  Proposed Improvements to the User Interface

Some of the detailed feedback mentioned e.g. that the different warning colors is creating too much complexity in the aircraft environment ("please find an anxious-free way to displays the medical info, as on a plane of 100+ pax, I couldn't imagine the lights and colors vibing altogether!"). Moreover, another statement was that the cabin crew should be careful not to "over care" the passenger and that a red warning light should be enough to create awareness and achieve close monitoring. A resulting improvement to the overview page of the system could be only to display the passenger seats when there is an alert (see Fig. 3). The advantage would be that less color are used and that the attention of the cabin crew will only be drawn to the alerts and not distracted by too much information displayed.

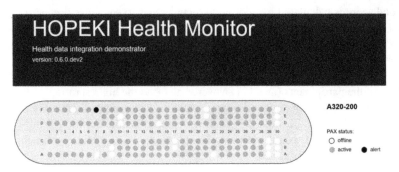

**Fig. 3.** Simplified overview page with only alert display (Color figure online)

Additionally on the detailed view page, the tachometer symbols could be replaced by arrow symbols indicating whether the health parameter is too low or too high. The disadvantage of using a colored tachometer symbol is that the operator would need to do two checks to see whether a parameter is out of range. The advantage of the arrow symbol is it clearly indicates a change of the measured parameter. Therefore, the user does not need to interpret another scale (e.g. the tachometer) to see the deviation to the neutral value (Fig. 4).

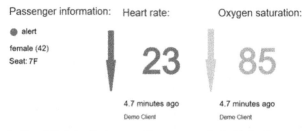

**Fig. 4.** Simplified detailed page with arrow symbols (Color figure online)

Additional user testing would be necessary to evaluate whether the proposed changes to the interface result in higher usability scores. A simulated test scenario in an aircraft environment with both interface designs measuring the operator's time for task completion would be necessary to see any changes in the reaction times.

## 4.2  Limitations

Availability of cabin crew to participate in the study are one main limitation of this study, as well as the snowball sampling method. It is likely that the study was more accessible to cabin crew using social media and who are comfortable with digital surveys. Additionally only participants with experience handling medical emergencies were admitted to evaluate the user interface in order to receive expert feedback. In a future study, feedback from non-expert should be included as a comparison to the expert-group responses. To get more reliable expert feedback a bigger sample size would be necessary. Moreover, multiple subject matter expert interviews combined with a system simulating different health conditions in an aircraft environment can lead to detailed feedback regarding arrangement of visual information.

## 4.3  Prospect Studies

Mass transport vehicles such as trains, busses, ship commonly have emergency/security alert buttons. However, in commercial aircraft only a general call button is available either for the passengers to alert the crew in case of an emergency or for service purposes. Three out of 35 participating cabin crew stated that a "medical emergency call/assistance button" or an additional emergency function (e.g. pressing the call button multiple times to trigger an alarm) to the existing call button could support the crew to react quickly in case of an emergency. Future research could focus on analyzing the workload of cabin crew during emergency, how medical training can be improved and standardizing onboard procedures for medical emergencies. Cabin crew are expected to manage medical emergencies on board, however the role distribution between cabin crew, medical volunteers (e.g. supporting doctors, nurses, paramedical) and the flight crew often is not clear [14]. The ultimate responsibility for all passengers on board is with the captain deciding whether to divert the aircraft, which can lead to a conflict with medical volunteers and cabin crew in between captain's and doctor's decision [15].

## 5  Conclusions

As expected the participating cabin crew reacted positively on the concept of a health monitoring system for aircraft. The overall usability scores were sufficient and indicated an average performance. However, the flight attendants stated that the displayed information could be simplified in terms of color and amount of information. Although medical experts are not the primary target group for the user interface, obviously the displayed information was not sufficient for task completion, which were also reflected in the lower usability scores. To evaluate the proposed changes to the interface additional user testing with a bigger sample size, as well as a simulation in an aircraft environment would be necessary.

For future studies, an alerting system triggered directly by the passengers ("medical emergency button") should be evaluated, since the participants mentioned this multiple times as an aid to create more situation awareness for emergencies. Moreover, it needs to be evaluated whether such an alerting system could replace a constant health monitoring of passengers in terms of cabin crew workload and reaction time.

# References

1. Graf, J., Stüben, U., Pump, S.: In-flight medical emergencies. Dtsch. Arztebl. Int. **109**(37), 591–602 (2012). https://doi.org/10.3238/arztebl.2012.0591
2. Brown, A.M., Rittenberger, J.C., Ammon, C.M., Harrington, S., Guyette, F.X.: In-flight automated external defibrillator use and consultation patterns. Prehospital Emerg. Care **14**, 235–239 (2010)
3. Kim, J.H., Choi-Kwon, S., Park, Y.H.: Comparison of inflight first aid performed by cabin crew members and medical volunteers. J. Travel Med. **24**, 1–6 (2016)
4. Mahony, P.H., Griffiths, R.F., Larsen, P., et al.: Retention of knowledge and skills in first aid and resuscitation by airline cabin crew. Resuscitation **76**, 413–418 (2008)
5. Marinos, D., Leonidas, F., Vlissidis, N., et al.: Medical and safety monitoring system over an in-cabin optical wireless network. Int. J. Electron. **98**(2), 223–233 (2010). https://doi.org/10.1080/00207217.2010.506846
6. Rotaru, O.A., Vert, S., Vasiu, R., Andone, D.: Standardised questionnaires in usability evaluation. Applying standardised usability questionnaires in digital products evaluation. In: Lopata, A., Butkienė, R., Gudonienė, D., Sukackė, V. (eds.) ICIST 2020. CCIS, vol. 1283, pp. 39–48. Springer, Cham (2020). https://doi.org/10.1007/978-3-030-59506-7_4
7. Official website of US Health Resources & Services Administration. https://www.hrsa.gov/rural-health/telehealth/what-is-telehealth. Accessed 15 Jan 2022
8. Parmanto, B., Lewis, A.N., Graham, K.M., Bertolet, M.H.: Development of the telehealth usability questionnaire (TUQ). Int. J. Telerehabil. **8**(1), 3–10 (2016)
9. SUS homepage. https://www.usability.gov/how-to-and-tools/methods/system-usability-scale.html. Accessed 31 Jan 2022
10. Scale convertion. https://measuringu.com/convert-point-scales/. Accessed 02 Feb 2022
11. Lewis, J.R., Sauro, J.: Can I leave this one out? The effect of dropping an item from the SUS. J. Usab. Stud. **13**(1), 38–46 (2017)
12. PSSUQ homepage. https://uiuxtrend.com/pssuq-post-study-system-usability-questionn aire/#interpretation. Accessed 01 Feb 2022
13. TUQ homepage. https://ux.hari.pitt.edu/v2/api/download/TUQ_English.pdf. Accessed 04 Feb 2022
14. Ho, S.F., Thirumoorthy, T., Boon, B., et al.: What to do during inflight medical emergencies? Practice pointes from a medical ethicist and an aviation medicine specialist. Singapore Med. J. **58**(1), 14–17 (2017). https://doi.org/10.11622/smedj.2016145
15. Bravermann, A., Clutter, P., Mannion, N.: Moral dilemmas of nurses and paramedics during in-flight medical emergencies on commercial airlines. J. Emerg. Nurs. **47**(3), 476–482 (2021). https://doi.org/10.1016/j.jen.2020.12.003

# Effects of Background Music on Visual Short-Term Memory: A Preliminary Study

Fatih Baha Omeroglu and Yueqing Li[✉]

Lamar University, Beaumont, TX 77705, USA
{fomeroglu,yueqing.li}@lamar.edu

**Abstract.** Effect of music has been studied over the years and it has been demonstrated that music significantly affects human brain in various ways. Music can change one's mood, energy, and motivation. Based on the music selection and type, music can induce various feelings and emotions in human mind. In this research, the effect of self-selected relaxing and disliked background music on visual short-term memory was studied. Electroencephalogram (EEG) data was collected while participants were performing the CBT task under three background music conditions: preferred relaxing music, disliked music, and no background music. Results showed that participants achieved significantly better CBT scores while listening to relaxing music. Additionally, relaxing music had a significant effect on beta power spectral density. This preliminary study shed some light on the relationship between self-selected background music, and short-term memory performance using EEG. Results of this study can be valuable guideline to understand how music affects our visual short-term memory and what kind of background music conditions can enhance our short-term memory performance.

**Keywords:** Background music · Cognitive task performance · EEG

## 1 Introduction

Background music has been commonly used in advertisements, workplaces, shopping areas, restaurants, and many entertainment venues (Herrington and Capella 1994). There are studies that indicates the effect of music on individuals' neurons and brain's functioning (Jausovec et al. 2006). Due to the significant music has on individuals over the years the effect of background music on mood, cognition and task performance have been researched deeply in the field of psychology (Savan 1999). Still up to today, studies are trying to find concrete evidence between music listening and human cognition.

### 1.1 Literature Review

One of the very well-researched topics has been the The Mozart Effect. The Mozart effect has become a known phenomenon and it has been previously demonstrated significant relationship between people who listened Mozart's music and their task performance (Mori et al. 2014). It was shown that Mozart's music was able to activate the parts of

© The Author(s), under exclusive license to Springer Nature Switzerland AG 2022
D. Harris and W.-C. Li (Eds.): HCII 2022, LNAI 13307, pp. 85–96, 2022.
https://doi.org/10.1007/978-3-031-06086-1_7

our brain that is responsible for attention and focus (Verrusio et al. 2015). Jausovec et al. (2006) observed that individuals who was exposed to Mozart's music has significantly performed better on digit span test. Classical music has also improved digit span task performance results in another study where it was concluded that the classical music significantly increased working memory functions of the brain (Mammarella et al. 2007). Another study found that undergraduate students performed better on an IQ subtest after listening to up tempo piece from Mozart and they performed worse when they listened down tempo classical piece from Albinoni (Schellenberg et al. 2007). Listening to Mozart's Sonata also found to be increasing the participants paper folding and cutting task performance (Rideout et al. 1998). Additional study demonstrated that instrumental music helped participants perform better on visual search task compared to silence or background talking noise conditions (Crust et al. 2004). Students who listened to instrumental music performed significantly better than students who listened to music with lyrics and vocals on performed sentence recall memory test (O'Hare 2011). It was found that speech in the background music and the vocals in songs found to be reducing task performance of the participants in another study (Alley and Greene 2008). It was concluded that instrumental music compared to music with vocals increased digit span task performance significantly (Alley and Greene 2008). Instrumental music also found to be increasing visual search task performance (Crust et al. 2004).

Some other studies presented conflicting findings regarding the effect of background music on task performance. It was found that background music can affect people's reading task performance in a negative way, Thompson et al. (2012) demonstrated that the even the instrumental music distracted participants from reading comprehension. Another study found no difference between instrumental music condition and lyrical music condition; however, it was found that background music had distracting effects on participants since participants achieved their best results in silence condition (Avila et al. 2012). Alley and Greene (2008) found no performance difference in working memory task when participants listened to vocal music or instrumental music. It was noted in another study that the experiment results provided best place for students to study was quiet room and students experienced a lot more distraction while listening to music especially the ones with lyrics (Chou 2010). It was observed that, some studies showed no significant difference in performance on even in digit span test under different background music conditions (Perham and Vizard 2011). Conflicting with the previous stated research regarding Mozart effect, Steele et al. (1997) found no difference on performance of digit span tasks when participants listened Mozart compared to not listening to any music.

Some of the recent research incorporated advance research methodologies to improve the analysis on effect of background music on performance and cognition. An fMRI study detected that, fast tempo music showed an increasing activity in brain areas where it can indicate better attentiveness and responsiveness (Bishop et al. 2014). Studies showed that music activates different parts of the brain (Kristeva et al. 2003). EEG has been a popular device to analyze these changes in the brain in various experimental conditions (Almudena et al. 2021). A study showed that left frontal activation of EEG alpha signals during up tempo, happy mood inducing songs, on the other hand slower tempo and sad songs led more prominent alpha activity on the right frontal part of the brain (Tsang et al. 2001). It was even observed that the perception of music task and imagination of sound elicited more alpha activity in the brain (Schaefer et al. 2011). Listening to pleasing music is also found to be increasing theta on the frontal midline of the brain (Sakharov et al. 2005). EEG studies also demonstrated that music increase in alpha and theta activity is also linked to attention and focus (Asada et al. 1999). Some EEG related studies indicated background music promoted more alpha, theta and beta waves, and these brains were previously linked to task performance in literature (Küssner et al. 2016). However, this study found no evident relationship between music and EEG, concluding that there is no relationship between background music condition and EEG signal (Küssner et al. 2016). Additionally, another recent research showed background music increasing alpha and theta activity. The study concluded self-selected preferred music increased task focus states and reduced mind wandering (Kiss and Linnell 2020). It was found that participants listening to the music they choose and prefer improved their visual search task performance (Mori et al. 2014). Nakamura et al. (1999) previously showed that there was a significant beta increase during music listening indicating the significant correlation between beta waves and music. Increase in beta power values were observed during tasks requires attention such as reading, searching and subtraction (Molteni et al. 2007). Participants who showed more prominent beta waves with increase in beta power values achieved better scores on cognitive tests (Fitzgibbon et al. 2004). It has previously been shown that there is a correlation between preferred music and beta activity; participants showed more beta activity when they listened to the activating happy music they preferred (Höller et al. 2012). Recent literature indicated that beta power changes might be an indication of task performance (Küssner et al. 2016). Based on these past studies, music might be considered as one of the main beta wave stimulants which is also previously been linked to better task performance.

Even though there is a significant amount of research out there, the effect of background music on task performance and cognition is still quite unknown and controversial. Most research is survey or questionnaire based and those which used EEG or other biometric measuring tools only focused on certain types of music genres or styles where subjects did not get to choose the music they prefer. Music is very subjective for each person and different types of music can significantly affect people in various ways. Preferred and non-preferred music is used in this study to eliminate the subjective differences and emotions towards different music types, so the relation between brain waves, preferred music choices, and task performance can be analyzed more objectively to create a more concrete relationship between these variables. To the best of our knowledge, no previous study has researched the relationship between task performance, and self-selected music using EEG. The goal of this study was to create a more concrete relationship between self-selected preferred background music, task performance, and human cognition with a deeper analysis on theta, alpha and beta brain waves.

## 2  Methodology

### 2.1  Participants

Ten (eight males, two females) volunteers are recruited for this study. The mean age was 29.3 and standard deviation was 4.7. Participants were not under the influence of any medication or stimulant at the time of the experiment. Three of the participants have some level of music training and they play a musical instrument. Other seven participants have never received any kind of music training. Institutional Review Board (IRB) fully approved the study to be conducted.

### 2.2  Data Acquisition

To acquire EEG signals from participants, G.Tec g.USBamp amplifier equipment was used alongside of g.Gammacap, g.GAMMAbox with g.Ladybird active wet Ag-AgCl electrodes. To save data and filter preprocess the data with filtering, BCI2000 software was used. Impedance was below 10 k$\Omega$ to ensure good signal quality. Total of 11 electrodes; F6, F5, Fz, Cz, Pz, C3, C4, P5, P6, O1, O2 sites were used based on International 10–20 electrode positioning method. Reference electrode was placed on the right ear lobe and the ground electrode was placed on the forehead. Signals were sampled at 256 Hz. Low pass filter is set to 1 Hz. and high pass filter is set to 40 Hz in BCI2000, additionally 50 Hz notch filter was also applied during the EEG signal acquisition. EEGlab plug-in with Matlab coding language was used to re-reference data with common average computation. EEGlab is also used to inspect and remove ocular and movement related artifacts. After additional filtering and ICA analysis with EEGlab, 45 s long epochs are extracted from where participants were performing the task under each background music condition. Mean theta, alpha, and beta power spectral density values are calculated for all 11 electrodes under each background music condition. Fast Fourier Transform is used to convert time domain data into frequency domain data to be able extract estimated power spectral density $\mu V^2/Hz$ values for alpha, beta, and theta waves.

### 2.3  Task

The main task in this study was Corsi Block tapping test which is a test to measure participants visual short-term memory, attention efficiency and attention capacity by Corsi in 1972 (Kessels et al. 2000). The tasks present 9 purple blocks on screen, and sequence of blocks lights up one at a time in yellow color (Shown in Fig. 1). Participants must memorize and repeat the correct box sequence in the same order which they were presented. The task difficult initially starts with only 2 boxes lightning up in order, with every successful attempt one additional box gets added to the sequential order up to 9 boxes. With one failed attempt, number of boxes presented decrease by one. If participants make two failed attempts in a row, task will be concluded, and it will present generated CBT score based on the maximum number of boxes each participant was able to memorize. PsyToolkit is used to present CBT task during the experiments. Participants selected 4 songs for each background music condition to hear in the background while performing the CBT task. Each condition had 4 trials, and experiment had total of 12 trials. 12 trials were fully randomized to avoid predictive learning and the whole experiment lasted from 30 to 40 min.

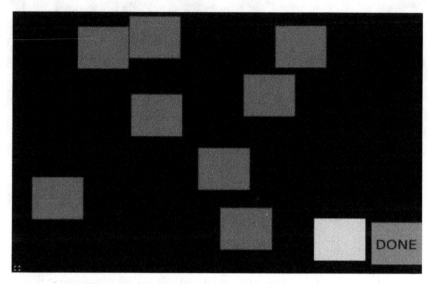

**Fig. 1.** Corsi task using PsyToolkit (Color figure online)

## 2.4 Procedure

Figure 2 below demonstrates the experiment environment where stimuli and task were presented through computer monitors and pair of headphones in a quiet room and an office setting. Before the experiment, participants filled out a demographic questionnaire and selected their song preference for each condition. 2 min of the selected songs were presented during the experiment. Initial 15 seconds of the experiment was resting, this followed by one of the three background music conditions randomly, after a minute into music listening the CBT test was presented for another additional minute. This was repeated for 12 times with 15 seconds rests in between. Participants filled out a post questionnaire to provide valuable feedback regarding the experiment.

**Fig. 2.** Experiment procedure

## 2.5  Independent Variables

Background music was the main stimuli and the only independent variable in this study. There were three different condition levels; no music, preferred relaxing music, and music choices that each participant dislikes. The songs for each independent variable condition were selected based on participants 'preferences and own selections.

## 2.6  Dependent Variables

**CBT Scores.** Task performance was measured using Corsi block tapping test (CBT) scores. CBT scores were gathered during the experiment by the experimenter. Each participant had total of 12 different CBT scores; Average of 3 different scores for each condition were calculated for final statistical analysis.

**Brain Activity.** Brain activity changes were measured in frequency domain; Theta (4 to 8 Hz), alpha (8 to 12 Hz) and beta (13 to 30 Hz) wave's relative power spectral density values.

## 2.7  Data Analysis

To observe the spectral power changes over whole brain montage, relative PSD is calculated for alpha, beta, and theta bands for each participant. Relative PSD value is a ratio of the selected band over the total frequency band. Relative PSD value is a ratio of the selected band over the total frequency band calculated with the following equation.

$$Relative\ PSD\ (\%) = \frac{Absolute\ Power\ of\ specific\ frequency\ range\ for\ theta,\ alpha\ or\ beta}{Total\ frequency\ band\ (4\ to\ 30\ Hz)}. \tag{1}$$

To observe the significant changes on alpha, beta, theta frequency bands, one way analysis of variance (ANOVA) test is conducted with significance level of 0.005.

## 3  Results

### 3.1  CBT Scores

The results showed a significant main effect of music condition on CBT scores ($F_2$, $_9$ = 3.66, p = 0.0463). The post hoc test showed the scores in relaxing music condition (M = 6.47, SD = 0.95) were significantly higher than that in no music condition (M = 6.05, SD = 0.82). However, the scores were not significantly different between relaxing music condition and disliked music condition (M = 6.20, SD = 1.11).

### 3.2  Beta Waves (13 to 30 Hz)

The results showed a significant main effect of music condition on relative beta power spectrum density values ($F_2$, $_9$ = 3.70, p = 0.0451). The post hoc test showed that the relative beta power spectral density values during relaxing music (M = 0.4077, SD = 0.08357) and disliked music (M = 0.4017, SD = 0.08468) were both significantly larger than that no music condition (M = 0.3804, SD = 0.07296). There was no significant difference between relaxing and disliked music conditions.

### 3.3  Theta Waves (4 to 8 Hz)

The results showed a significant main effect of music condition on relative theta power spectral density values ($F_2$, $_9$ = 4.45, p = 0.0270). The post hoc test showed that the relative theta power spectral density values during relaxing music (M = 0.3469, SD = 0.1052) were significantly larger than disliked music condition (M = 0.3280, SD = 0.1105).

### 3.4  Alpha Waves (8 to 12 Hz)

The results did not show a significant main effect of music condition on relative alpha power spectral density values ($F_2$, $_9$ = 3.52, p = 0.0513). However, p value was close to being significant. The post hoc test showed that the relative alpha power spectral density values during relaxing music (M = 0.2452, SD = 0.03763) were smaller compared to no music condition (M = 0.2744, SD = 0.0599) and disliked music condition (M = 0.27018, SD = 0.0623).

Topology results generated from alpha power spectral density values are demonstrated in Table 1.

**Table 1.** Topology results for alpha waves showing frontal and parietal asymmetry

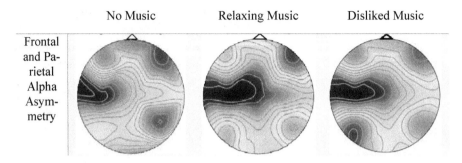

| | No Music | Relaxing Music | Disliked Music |
|---|---|---|---|
| Frontal and Parietal Alpha Asymmetry | | | |

## 4   Discussion

### 4.1   CBT Scores

Presented data supports that background music improves the task performance. Each participant showed their best performance while they were under preferred relaxing music, or disliked music. Some participants even performed best while they were listening to the disliked music stating that it helped them cancel out the outside distractions in the post questionnaire. All participants stated that background music enhanced their task performance. Seven out of ten participants had their best score during the relaxing music condition, three of the participants had their best score while listening to the disliked music condition (Fig. 3).

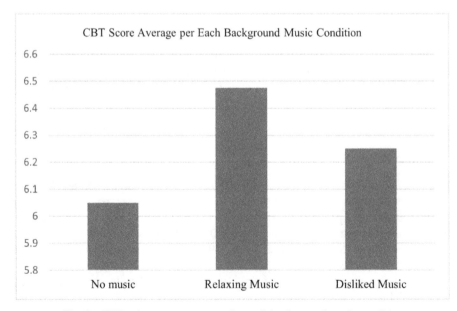

**Fig. 3.** CBT task score averages under each background music condition

## 4.2  Beta Waves (13 to 30 Hz)

In literature, it was observed that more beta power enhances cognitive task performance (Küssner et al. 2016). Fitzgibbon et al. (2004) concluded that participants who had larger beta power values achieved better scores on cognitive tests. Küssner et al. (2016) also detected that the beta power values predict the performance of participants in the word recall task since the individuals with higher beta power learnt more vocabulary words. Our study showed similar findings where highest scores were achieved during the relaxing music when relative beta PSD values were also the highest. Background music significantly increased the relative beta PSD. Beta activity was previously found to be more active during the music listening compared to the resting condition (Nakamura et al. 1999) which might be why our results also indicated a significant increase of beta power values with background music. It might be possible that music enhances beta power in human mind where higher beta power increases the cognitive processing, which then leads to higher task performance.

## 4.3  Alpha Waves (8 to 12 Hz)

It was observed that listening to pleasing music increased the EEG activity of the alpha waves (Tsang et al. 2001). Even though, our statistical analysis found no significant effect, the p value was close to being significant. Additionally, power spectral topology results shown in Table 1 demonstrated different patterns for each background music condition indicating physiological differences. Frontal alpha asymmetry is a commonly used topology measurement to draw meaningful conclusions however in this study it was not part of our statistical analysis. With the addition of more participants, this measurement will be considered in the future, since it can be a valuable indicator towards new findings.

## 4.4  Theta Waves (4 to 8 Hz)

Past research indicates a significant correlation between frontal theta power changes and capacity of working memory (Puma et al. 2018). Increased in theta power values have been often linked to attention (Sammler et al. 2007). Our results also demonstrated participants performing better while having the highest relative theta PSD. Correlation to background music our analysis indicated significant increase in relative theta power during relaxing music compered to disliked music which supports the previous findings of listening to pleasing music enhancing the theta power (Sakharov et al. 2005). Klimesch et al. (1994) also showed a theta power increase during tasks related to memory. It has been stated that listening to self-selected preferred music increased task focus states while reducing distraction (Kiss and Linnell 2020). Mori et al. (2014) also demonstrated participants achieving higher performance in visual search task while listening to music they enjoy. The task being used in our study; Corsi task uses visual memory, and we think our results also emphasize a significant correlation between visual memory, task performance, preferred pleasing music and theta waves.

Our analysis did not consider different lobes however, it has been previously stated that power value changes in different lobes can also indicate more meaningful conclusions. It has been previously shown that listening to pleasing music increased theta power values in frontal lobe (Balasubramanian et al. 2018). In the next phase of the research, spectral changes in different lobes can be a significant factor to consider.

## 5 Conclusion

In this preliminary study, relationship between background music, task performance and brain activity were investigated. It was concluded that background music had a significant effect on task performance, relative beta, and theta spectral power density values. Beta and theta power values were significantly larger under relaxing music condition. It was also found that background music had a significant effect on task performance. Participants performed significantly better during the relaxing music condition. Our statistical analysis did not show any significant relationship between background music, relative alpha power, and task performance.

Study offered preliminary initial results and it had a limited sample size. In the next phase, more participants will be recruited, findings regarding alpha, theta and beta waves will be analyzed even further. Current study only conducted an analysis over whole montage. Statistical analysis did not consider power changes from different lobes and did not consider alpha frontal and parietal asymmetry. Topology results displayed some significantly different patterns displayed in Table 1. Carrying this research further with more sample size while considering PSD changes in different lobes can be quite informative towards future research.

## References

Asada, H., Fukuda, Y., Tsunoda, S., Yamaguchi, M., Tonoike, M.: Frontal midline theta rhythms reflect alternative activation of prefrontal cortex and anterior cingulate cortex in humans. Neurosci. Lett. **274**(1), 29–32 (1999)

Almudena, G., Manuel, S., Julián Jesús, G.: EEG analysis during music perception. In: Electroencephalography-From Basic Research to Clinical Applications (2021)

Alley, T.R., Greene, M.E.: The relative and perceived impact of irrelevant speech, vocal music, and non-vocal music on working memory. Curr. Psychol. **27**(4), 277–289 (2008)

Avila, C., Furnham, A., McClelland, A.: The influence of distracting familiar vocal music on cognitive performance of introverts and extraverts. Psychol. Music **40**(1), 84–93 (2012)

Balasubramanian, G., Kanagasabai, A., Mohan, J., Seshadri, N.G.: Music induced emotion using wavelet packet decomposition—An EEG study. Biomed. Signal Process. Control **42**, 115–128 (2018)

Bishop, D.T., Wright, M.J., Karageorghis, C.I.: Tempo and intensity of pre-task music modulate neural activity during reactive task performance. Psychol. Music **42**(5), 714–727 (2014)

Chou, P.T.M.: Attention drainage effect: how background music effects concentration in Taiwanese college students. J. Sch. Teach. Learn. **10**(1), 36–46 (2010)

Corsi, P.: Memory and the medial temporal region of the brain. Unpublished Doctoral dissertation. McGill University, Montreal, QB (1972)

Crust, L., Clough, P.J., Robertson, C.: Influence of music and distraction on visual search performance of participants with high and low affect intensity. Percept. Motor Skills **98**(3), 888–896 (2004)

Fitzgibbon, S.P., Pope, K.J., Mackenzie, L., Clark, C.R., Willoughby, J.O.: Cognitive tasks augment gamma EEG power. Clin. Neurophysiol. **115**(8), 1802–1809 (2004)

Herrington, J.D., Capella, L.M.: Practical applications of music in service settings. J. Serv. Mark. **8**, 50–65 (1994)

Höller, Y., Thomschewski, A., Schmid, E.V., Höller, P., Crone, J.S., Trinka, E.: Individual brain-frequency responses to self-selected music. Int. J. Psychol. **86**, 206–213 (2012). Husain, G., Thompson, W.F., Schell

Jausovec, N., Jausovec, K., Gerlic, I.: The influence of Mozart's music on brain activity in the process of learning. Clin. Neurophysiol. **117**(12), 2703–2714 (2006). https://doi.org/10.1016/j.clinph.2006.08.010

Kessels, R.P., Van Zandvoort, M.J., Postma, A., Kappelle, L.J., De Haan, E.H.: The Corsi block-tapping task: standardization and normative data. Appl. Neuropsychol. **7**(4), 252–258 (2000)

Kiss, L., Linnell, K.J.: The effect of preferred background music on task-focus in sustained attention. Psychol. Res. **85**, 1–13 (2020)

Klimesch, W., Schimke, H., Schwaiger, J.: Episodic and semantic memory: an analysis in the EEG theta and alpha band. Electroencephalogr. Clin. Neurophysiol. **91**(6), 428–441 (1994)

Kristeva, R., Chakarov, V., Schulte-Mönting, J., Spreer, J.: Activation of cortical areas in music execution and imagining: a high-resolution EEG study. Neuroimage **20**(3), 1872–1883 (2003). https://doi.org/10.1016/s1053-8119(03)00422-1

Küssner, M.B., Groot, A.M., Hofman, W.F., Hillen, M.A.: EEG beta power but not background music predicts the recall scores in a foreign-vocabulary learning task. PLoS ONE **11**(8), e0161387 (2016). https://doi.org/10.1371/journal.pone.0161387

Mammarella, N., Fairfield, B., Cornoldi, C.: Does music enhance cognitive performance in healthy older adults? The Vivaldi effect. Aging Clin. Exp. Res. **19**(5), 394–399 (2007)

Molteni, E., Bianchi, A.M., Butti, M., Reni, G., Zucca, C.: Analysis of the dynamical behaviour of the EEG rhythms during a test of sustained attention. In: 2007 29th Annual International Conference of the IEEE Engineering in Medicine and Biology Society, pp. 1298–1301. IEEE (2007)

Mori, F., Naghsh, F.A., Tezuka, T.: The effect of music on the level of mental concentration and its temporal change. In: CSEDU (1), pp. 34–42 (2014)

Nakamura, S., Sadato, N., Oohashi, T., Nishina, E., Fuwamoto, Y., Yonekura, Y.: Analysis of music–brain interaction with simultaneous measurement of regional cerebral blood flow and electroencephalogram beta rhythm in human subjects. Neurosci. Lett. **275**(3), 222–226 (1999)

O'Hare, A.: The effect of vocal and instrumental background music on primary school pupils' verbal memory using a sentence recall task. Stud. Psychol. J. **2**, 1–11 (2011)

Rideout, B.E., Dougherty, S., Wernert, L.: Effect of music on spatial performance: a test of generality. Percept. Motor Skills **86**(2), 512–514 (1998)

Perham, N., Vizard, J.: Can preference for background music mediate the irrelevant sound effect? Appl. Cogn. Psychol. **25**(4), 625–631 (2011)

Sammler, D., Grigutsch, M., Fritz, T., Koelsch, S.: Music and emotion: electrophysiological correlates of the processing of pleasant and unpleasant music. Psychophysiology **44**(2), 293–304 (2007)

Sakharov, D.S., Davydov, V.I., Pavlygina, R.A.: Intercentral relations of the human EEG during listening to music. Hum. Physiol. **31**(4), 392–397 (2005)

Savan, A.: The effect of background music on learning. Psychol. Music **27**(2), 138–146 (1999)

Schaefer, R.S., Vlek, R.J., Desain, P.: Music perception and imagery in EEG: alpha band effects of task and stimulus. Int. J. Psychophysiol. **82**(3), 254–259 (2011)

Schellenberg, E.G., Nakata, T., Hunter, P.G., Tamoto, S.: Exposure to music and cognitive performance. Psychol. Music **35**(1), 5–19 (2007)

Steele, K.M., Ball, T.N., Runk, R.: Listening to Mozart does not enhance backwards digit span performance. Percept. Motor Skills **84**(3_Suppl), 1179–1184 (1997)

Thompson, W.F., Schellenberg, E.G., Letnic, A.K.: Fast and loud background music disrupts reading comprehension. Psychol. Music **40**(6), 700–708 (2012)

Tsang, C.D., Trainor, L.J., Santesso, D.L., Tasker, S.L., Schmidt, L.A.: Frontal EEG responses as a function of affective musical features. Ann. N. Y. Acad. Sci. **930**(1), 439–442 (2001)

Verrusio, W., Ettorre, E., Vicenzini, E., Vanacore, N., Cacciafesta, M., Mecarelli, O.: The Mozart effect: a quantitative EEG study. Conscious. Cogn. **35**, 150–155 (2015)

# Do Mathematical Typesetting Applications Affect User Manipulation of Fractions? Evidence from an Eye-Tracking Experiment

Francis Quinby[1]([✉]), Marco Pollanen[1], Wesley S. Burr[1],
and Michael G. Reynolds[2]

[1] Department of Mathematics, Trent University, Peterborough, ON, Canada
`francisquinby@trentu.ca`
[2] Department of Psychology, Trent University, Peterborough, ON, Canada

**Abstract.** What-you-see-is-what-you-get word processing editors that support the typesetting of mathematical content allow for direct manipulation of 2-dimensional mathematical notation within a 1-dimensional environment. The models used to represent mathematical structure generally fall into two categories: (1) free-form, in which symbols are placed and moved freely in the workspace and (2) structure-based, where 2-dimensional structures are inserted and then populated with other structures or symbols. To understand the consequences of these models for writing mathematical expressions we examined the sequential order of symbol insertion when transcribing fractions, and compare this to the natural order employed when handwritten. Markov transition matrices were created from recordings of fraction transcriptions to quantify the probability of inserting a symbol immediately following insertion of other symbols. The three writing techniques yielded different dominant transition patterns and also differed in their ability to tolerate differences from the dominant pattern. This study likely represents the first empirical assessment of symbol insertion order probabilities when handwriting fractions, while also identifying differences in insertion order during use of different types of digital editors for typesetting mathematical content. These results have important implications for the usability of mathematical typesetting software applications and should be considered in the future design of such programs.

**Keywords:** Mathematical software · Software user interfaces · Fractions · Mathematics education

## 1 Introduction

Mathematical notation often contains 2-dimensional structure which is challenging to effectively represent in the 1-dimensional inline typesetting environments of most word processing software applications. Fractions are a common form of

D. Harris and W.-C. Li (Eds.): HCII 2022, LNAI 13307, pp. 97–107, 2022.
https://doi.org/10.1007/978-3-031-06086-1_8

2-dimensional structural notation encountered in mathematics. The fraction is likely the first 2-dimensional structure students will encounter, and fractions are well known to present conceptual challenges for many learners [2,13,20]. Due to the 1-dimensional nature of most word processing applications, to effectively express a fraction the 2-dimensional notation must either be represented in a 1-dimensional format, or an alternative environment must be made available for the user. Some simple fractions can clearly be represented in one dimension without the risk of misinterpretation, by replacing the fraction bar, or *vinculum*, with a forward slash; $a/b$ is clearly equivalent to $\frac{a}{b}$.

However, when multiple terms appear in the numerator and/or the denominator, a 2-dimensional representation becomes increasingly important to preserve the meaning and facilitate the effective communication of the mathematical object. Consider the fraction $\frac{x}{a+b}$. If one were to simply replace the fraction bar with a forward slash the result would be $x/a+b$, which would be read and calculated as $\frac{x}{a}+b$ due to the standard order of mathematical operations (division is given higher priority than addition; the forward slash also represents the division operator). Thus, to effectively communicate the fraction in a 1-dimensional environment parentheses should be used in the following manner: $x/(a+b)$. In this example, only one set of parentheses are necessary which is not likely to overwhelm most users, though learners who have not acquired a full understanding of the order of mathematical operations may not realize their necessity. However, when transcribing a more complex expression in a 1-dimensional environment, say:

$$\frac{\frac{(x+3)(x+4)}{4x}}{\frac{5x(x-1)}{x-9}}$$

which could be represented as $(((x + 3)(x + 4)/4x)/(5x(x - 1)/(x - 9)))$, the requisite parentheses are more numerous and are thus likely to present more of a challenge to coordinate, especially for students who struggle with the comprehension of fractions.

Fractions can represent a variety of mathematical entities (a part-whole relationship, a quotient, a numeric value, an operator, or a ratio [1]) and the conversion of a 2-dimensional fraction to a 1-dimensional representation may require individuals to possess some level of fluid cognitive understanding of the fraction concept, and have the ability to easily transform a given fraction between registers. This is an ability which users who lack proficiency and/or experience in mathematics may be less likely to have. In the previous example, the forward slash is generally representative of the division operator while a fraction in 2-dimensional form usually represents a numeric value, though both are context dependent. Therefore, for many users an environment which allows for the direct insertion and manipulation of 2-dimensional structure in the user workspace is likely to provide increased efficiency and effectiveness for digitally transcribing and communicating mathematical expressions containing fraction notation (and other 2-dimensional mathematical notation).

There exist multiple ways to represent mathematical notation containing 2-dimensional structure in 1-dimensional word processing software environments.

WYSIWYG (what-you-see-is-what-you-get) editors which allow users to directly edit mathematical output [10,11], are used exclusively by many beginners, as opposed to editors such as LaTeX which require compilation of 1-dimensional strings encoding 2-dimensional output. WYSIWYG editors can be classified by the model used to represent 2-dimensional structure within the processing environment [4]. One such model is a structure-based model, notably featured in Microsoft Word Equation Editor (MWEE), in which 2-dimensional "shells" are inserted into the environment and can be subsequently populated with the desired symbols or structures, e.g., a fraction is inserted as a horizontal line with spaces above and below, into which the numerator and denominator are entered. However, it should be noted that the current iteration of MWEE does not feature a pure structure-based model and allows for users to enter certain characters or strings (including a subset of LaTeX code) which are automatically converted to structures or symbols (e.g., typing 4/5 followed by a space will convert the text to $\frac{4}{5}$; note that typing 4+x/5 followed by a space will convert to $4 + \frac{x}{5}$). Alternatives include free-form models in which users insert drag-droppable mathematical objects into 2-dimensional workspaces. In such models, not all structures require insertion, as some can be created by manipulation of the expression's spatial configuration, e.g., dragging a 2 into superscript position squares an element. As implied by the name, the free-form model allows users greater freedom when transcribing mathematical content and thus, is more consistent with the natural handwriting process where users are solely constrained by the dimensions of the writing surface (generally paper) and what has already been written therein.

WYSIWYG editors using different models for mathematical structure vary in how fractions are inserted into the workspace, which may affect user cognition, manipulation, and conceptualization of mathematical content. Differences have been found between models in the sequence of inserting fraction components (numerator, denominator, fraction bar), with users more likely to insert the fraction structure (fraction bar), followed by the numerator and denominator when using the structure-based model than when using the free-from model [16]. Analyzing this insertion order invites a comparison to the "natural" insertion order when handwriting fractions. To our knowledge, no baseline measure exists of symbol insertion order when writing fractions by hand, so any comparisons of digital models to handwriting must assume a natural sequence. A left-to-right, top-to-bottom order has been suggested when handwriting mathematical expressions in general [4], and it has been shown that mathematical expressions are read in a similar scanning order [3,6]; does the insertion of symbols during the writing of fractions follow this same sequence? Here we present Markov transition probability matrices, generated from transcription tasks which took place during an eye-tracking experiment designed to evaluate the performance of software applications for digitally typesetting mathematics [17]. Such matrices represent the probabilistic insertion order of fractions during digital transcription using WYSIWYG editors featuring free-form and structure-based models, as well as when writing by hand, allowing for meaningful comparisons between models and between digital models and a control. Such comparisons provide insight into how well the models contained within the tested mathematical typesetting software mimic the natural process of handwriting mathematical expressions. Furthermore, interpretation of these matrices in relation to previously reported cognitive measures derived from eye-tracking data [17] provides additional insight into the user-experience of these models which have been shown to cause interference with working memory and cognitive function [18]. Such comparisons are essential to increase understanding of how these interfaces affect users' conceptualization of fractions, and have important implications for mathematics education, especially when delivered in virtual format.

## 2    Methods

A detailed description of the experimental procedure can be found in Quinby *et al.* [17]. Briefly, during an eye-tracking experiment, participants (undergraduate and graduate students from Trent University in Ontario, Canada; $n = 26$) transcribed 12 mathematical expressions containing a fraction with multiple terms in either the numerator or denominator (such as in Fig. 1), using $MC^2$ (a mathematical communication application using the free-form model) [7,14], MWEE (structure-based model), and pen and paper as a control (4 fractions using each method). All experimental transcription tasks were video captured and symbol insertion events were classified based on the component of the fraction represented (components defined in Fig. 1), recorded, and time-stamped.

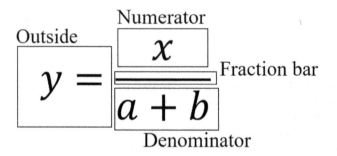

**Fig. 1.** Components of the fraction structure as included in Markov transition matrix model. The fraction displayed is similar to those used as experimental stimuli in the eye-tracking experiment.

The insertion sequence of fraction components was used to develop a Markov transition matrix $T$ for each trial, with an element $T_{i,j}$ representing the probability of a component in column $j$ being inserted into the workspace immediately following insertion of component in row $i$, i.e., a user "transition" from the component in row $i$ to that in column $j$. Mean transition probability matrices were then created for all participants for each of the 3 transcription methods by calculating the mean of the corresponding elements in the 4 trial transition matrices, and final mean transition probability matrices were calculated for each transcription method across all participants in a similar manner. Note that probabilities in rows do not always sum to 1 due to the fact that some components, most often the denominator, rarely had a component inserted after, i.e., the component was the final insertion. Therefore, the probability that the component represented in row $i$ of a transition matrix $T$ was the final component inserted can be calculated as:

$$1 - \sum_{j=1} T_{i,j}$$

## 3  Results

Final transition probability matrices for the three typesetting methods are shown in Table 1. The most common insertion order of fractions while using both the structure-based and the free-form models involves first inserting the fraction structure, and subsequently populating the numerator followed by the denominator with appropriate symbols (Fig. 2, top), though the probability of this insertion sequence is higher in the structure-based model than the free-form model (0.88 versus 0.41; $T_{1,3} * T_{3,2} * T_{2,4}$ in transition matrices). This is contrary to the most common insertion order when handwriting the expressions in which symbols are inserted in a left-to-right, top-to-bottom fashion (Fig. 2, middle), i.e., numerator, fraction bar, denominator. Interestingly, only with the free-form model was there a non-zero probability (0.11) of users inserting the fraction bar indicator *following* the denominator (probable overall insertion sequence displayed in Fig. 2, bottom). Note that probabilities closer to 0.5 indicate a greater level of uncertainty, or variability in the represented event as shown by the variance for a proportion $p$, calculated as $p(1 - p)$.

## 4  Discussion

The Markov transition matrices revealed clear differences between the order in which symbols are transcribed for handwriting and the two digital editors. When the fractions were handwritten, the dominant transcription order followed a left-to-right, top-to-bottom spatial approach analogous to the order in which the symbols would be read. This means that when transitioning from the left to the right side of the equation, the first symbol added was in the numerator. In contrast, the first symbol entered on the right side the equation was the fraction bar object for both digital models. The fraction bar was followed by the numerator and then denominator. The primacy of the fraction bar in the structure-based model is a consequence of the lack of flexibility offered by model (inserting the numerator followed by the fraction structure will result in an expression such as in Fig. 3). The primacy of the fraction bar when using the free-form model is surprising given its flexibility. One possibility is that it was used as a visual

**Table 1.** Fraction component mean transition probability matrices for expressions handwritten with pen and paper (top), and transcribed with MWEE (middle) and MC$^2$ (bottom). Each element $i, j$ represents the probability of inserting the component in column $j$ immediately following insertion of the component in row $i$. Variance of a probability $p$ can be calculated as $p(1-p)$. Fraction components represented in the rows and columns of matrices are consistent with the definitions established in Fig. 1. The size of the probabilities in matrices is determined by the magnitude of the probability, with those from 0.50–0.99 in the largest font, those from 0.10–0.49 in a large font, and those from 0.00–0.09 in a regular sized font.

| | | | To | | |
| From | | Outside | Numerator | Fraction bar | Denominator |
| --- | --- | --- | --- | --- | --- |
| Outside | | .00 | .75 | .25 | .00 |
| Numerator | | .00 | .00 | .75 | .25 |
| Fraction bar | | .00 | .26 | .00 | .74 |
| Denominator | | .00 | .00 | .00 | .00 |

| | | | To | | |
| From | | Outside | Numerator | Fraction bar | Denominator |
| --- | --- | --- | --- | --- | --- |
| Outside | | .00 | .05 | .94 | .01 |
| Numerator | | .01 | .00 | .03 | .97 |
| Fraction bar | | .02 | .97 | .00 | .01 |
| Denominator | | .02 | .00 | .00 | .00 |

| | | | To | | |
| From | | Outside | Numerator | Fraction bar | Denominator |
| --- | --- | --- | --- | --- | --- |
| Outside | | .00 | .29 | .70 | .00 |
| Numerator | | .00 | .00 | .18 | .82 |
| Fraction bar | | .01 | .71 | .00 | .17 |
| Denominator | | .01 | .00 | .11 | .00 |

spatial marker for the placement of symbols in the numerator and denominator and that this is not necessary for handwritten symbols. Performance across the writing methods differed in a second way. Although each writing method had a clearly dominant transition sequence, the mean probabilities for this sequence

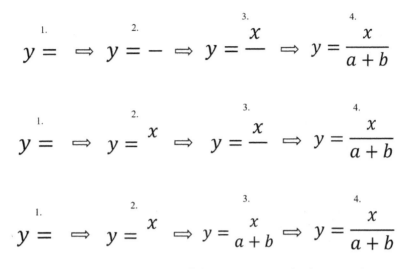

**Fig. 2.** Most probable insertion order of the components of a fraction when using the digital typesetting applications featuring both the free-form model and the structure-based model (top), and when handwriting mathematical expressions (middle, can be assumed as natural writing order), as well as an alternate insertion order of components displayed occasionally by users of $MC^2$ (free-form model, bottom)

was smaller in the handwriting (.75) and free-form model (.74) compared to the structure-based model (.96). This suggests that the sequence for symbol entry was more variable in the handwriting and free-form model conditions. In the handwriting condition the deviation from the dominant model resembled the structure-based model and in the free-form model condition the deviation from the dominant model resembled the left-to-right, top-to-bottom sequence observed in the handwriting condition.

Although the structure-based model seems to disrupt the natural writing order used for fractions, this does not mean that it is less efficient. Use of the structure-based model has been shown to be more efficient when transcribing fractions than the free-form model, with handwriting more efficient than both of the digital methods [17]. Overall, eye-tracking results also suggested a greater demand on cognitive resources for users while transcribing fractions with the free-form model compared to the structure-based model [17]. One possible explanation for the counter intuitive findings with regards to the structure-based model is that it is due to its lack of flexibility. One of the 10 usability heuristics for software interface design proposed by Nielson is consistency [5,12], which the lack of flexibility of the structure-based model may provide for users and thus be beneficial. However, another usability heuristic states that interfaces should prevent errors [5,12]. Past research has shown an increased number of user errors (e.g., Fig. 3) associated with the use of the structure-based model for transcribing fractions [15], and this criteria should also be taken into account when evaluating the usability of these tested models. The rigidity of the structure-based model

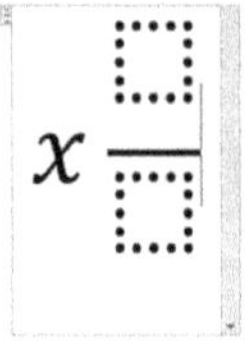

**Fig. 3.** Resulting output when attempting to insert the numerator of a fraction immediately prior to insertion of the fraction structure when using the structure-based model featured in Microsoft Word Equation Editor, highlighting the lack of flexibility offered by this model.

may become more problematic for users when faced with increasingly complex mathematical content to transcribe, or even more-likely, when the expression includes structures that are rarely used in the interface. An error in complex nested expression could require substantial re-writing or a re-conceptualization of the structure placing increased cognitive demands on the user. Furthermore, the desired order of insertion of different fraction components may change when users are performing calculations or solving problems, compared to when they are simply copying a presented expression and this must also be considered. When interpreting these results, a level of caution should be exhibited as the models for the representation of mathematical structure live inside of different interfaces. The results related to performance measures (efficiency, cognitive load, working memory) are likely more susceptible to being influenced by such interfaces compared to results relating to symbol insertion order, however, these should be considered when interpreting results.

The transition matrices for the relatively simple expressions reported in this study are notably different from those reported by Quinby et al. [16], derived from the transcription of more complex expressions using the same two software applications (MC$^2$ and MWEE); in that experiment, a handwritten control was not included. In that work, transition probabilities were more consistent with the natural reading order described in the current study, such that users were more likely to insert the numerator, followed by the fraction bar and the denominator. When using the structure-based model, a number of the transition probabilities were closer to 0.5 than in our results, indicating greater variability/uncertainty in insertion orders. Variability could become more prevalent when expressions to be transcribed increase in complexity, both vertically and horizontally, e.g.,

$$\frac{\sqrt{\frac{\sqrt{x^2+2x+2}}{x}}}{x^2+1} \quad \text{vs.} \quad j = \frac{4r}{2i+9o}.$$

Differences in the Markov transition matrices from the two studies could be a result of the increased number of symbols present in the expressions transcribed in Quinby et al. [16]; $n$ symbols give $n!$ possible insertion orders (though many are highly improbable) introducing greater room for variability, as well as increasing the likelihood of user error. Future research should focus on differentiating the variability which can be attributed to a greater number of symbols versus that which is the result of increasing complexity from nested structure.

Perhaps the most interesting finding from this research is that variation exists in the order in which individuals write fractions by hand, with participants in about 25% of handwritten trials inserting the fraction bar first followed by the insertion of the numerator and denominator. This finding raises a number of questions and ideas for future research on the topic. For example, do individuals with different levels of mathematical expertise show contrasting patterns of variation in the order of insertion when writing out mathematical expressions? Research has shown differences in the reading and processing of mathematical material based on experience level [8,9]; does this extend to the order of writing mathematics? Furthermore, are differences in the order of handwriting fractions attributed to conceptual differences or are they an artifact of some past educational experiences? Interestingly, learners from some different cultures may be more likely to transcribe fractions in contrasting sequential order; for example Koreans generally insert the denominator and fraction bar first, prior to the numerator when handwriting a fraction (S. Kim & M. Pollanen, personal communication, 2020), contrary to the insertion probabilities observed in our study with Canadian students. Korean students generally show better performance on fraction computation tasks than American students [19], which may indicate a connection between the order of inserting the components of fractions and the general understanding of the concept. Insertion of the denominator and fraction bar first may indicate that an individual shows greater recognition of the fraction as a whole, whereas insertion of the numerator first may indicate over-reliance on this numeral in the understanding of the overall fraction, but such an assertion would need to be tested empirically. It is interesting to note that the literal translation of the Korean word for denominator is "mother of the fraction" while numerator means "child of the fraction", perhaps suggesting a difference in perspective. At minimum, cultural differences in the mathematical writing process should be investigated and taken into account. Overall, the notable differences observed in insertion orders of fraction components when typesetting them digitally compared to the natural order when handwriting may indicate that users conceptualize fractions differently when typesetting them using the tested WYSIWYG models versus handwriting them, and future work should test this hypothesis.

## 5   Conclusion

In conclusion, through the use of Markov transition matrices to quantify symbol insertion order when transcribing fractions using two software applications featuring differing models to represent 2-dimensional mathematical notation as well as when handwriting, we were able to identify important differences between the methods. Matrices indicated that the most probable insertion order by users of the digital methods was to insert the fraction bar first, followed by the numerator and denominator, which deviates from the most probable natural order of insertion observed when handwriting: first inserting the numerator, followed by the fraction bar and denominator. Insertion probabilities of the structure-based model showed very little variability, while dominant transition probabilities derived from both the free-form model and the handwritten control displayed higher variability. These findings highlight important differences in user behaviour patterns when using these mathematical typesetting applications, which have important implications for the future design of software which allows for user input of mathematical content. Furthermore, differences observed between the digital and handwritten transcription of fractions could indicate differences in the cognition of the mathematical content which has implications for the education and learning of mathematics.

# References

1. Charalambous, C.Y., Pitta-Pantazi, D.: Drawing on a theoretical model to study students' understandings of fractions. Educ. Stud. Math. **64**(3), 293–316 (2007)
2. Davis, G., Hunting, R.P., Pearn, C.: What might a fraction mean to a child and how would a teacher know? J. Math. Behav. (1993)
3. Gillan, D.J., Barraza, P., Karshmer, A.I., Pazuchanics, S.: Cognitive analysis of equation reading: application to the development of the math genie. In: Miesenberger, K., Klaus, J., Zagler, W.L., Burger, D. (eds.) ICCHP 2004. LNCS, vol. 3118, pp. 630–637. Springer, Heidelberg (2004). https://doi.org/10.1007/978-3-540-27817-7_94
4. Gozli, D.G., Pollanen, M., Reynolds, M.: The characteristics of writing environments for mathematics: behavioral consequences and implications for software design and usability. In: Carette, J., Dixon, L., Coen, C.S., Watt, S.M. (eds.) CICM 2009. LNCS (LNAI), vol. 5625, pp. 310–324. Springer, Heidelberg (2009). https://doi.org/10.1007/978-3-642-02614-0_26
5. Hinze-Hoare, V.: The review and analysis of human computer interaction (HCI) principles. arXiv preprint arXiv:0707.3638 (2007)
6. Jansen, A.R., Marriott, K., Yelland, G.W.: Parsing of algebraic expressions by experienced users of mathematics. Eur. J. Cogn. Psychol. **19**(2), 286–320 (2007)
7. Kang, S., Pollanen, M., Damouras, S., Cater, B.: Mathematics classroom collaborator ($MC^2$): technology for democratizing the classroom. In: Davenport, J.H., Kauers, M., Labahn, G., Urban, J. (eds.) ICMS 2018. LNCS, vol. 10931, pp. 280–288. Springer, Cham (2018). https://doi.org/10.1007/978-3-319-96418-8_33
8. Kim, S., Pollanen, M., Reynolds, M.G., Burr, W.S.: Identification of errors in mathematical symbolism and notation: implications for software design. In: Davenport, J.H., Kauers, M., Labahn, G., Urban, J. (eds.) ICMS 2018. LNCS, vol. 10931, pp. 297–304. Springer, Cham (2018). https://doi.org/10.1007/978-3-319-96418-8_35
9. Kim, S., Pollanen, M., Reynolds, M.G., Burr, W.S.: Problem solving as a path to comprehension. Mathemat. Comput. Sci. **14**(3), 607–621 (2020)
10. Knauff, M., Nejasmic, J.: An efficiency comparison of document preparation systems used in academic research and development. PLoS ONE **9**(12), e115069 (2014)
11. Murphy, D., Kember, D.: Mathematical typesetting from an operator perspective. Educ. Technol. **29**(4), 40–44 (1989)
12. Nielsen, J.: Usability Engineering. Morgan Kaufmann, Burlington (1994)
13. Pantziara, M., Philippou, G.: Levels of students' "conception" of fractions. Educ. Stud. Math. **79**(1), 61–83 (2012)

14. Pollanen, M., Kang, S., Cater, B., Chen, Y., Lee, K.: MC$^2$: mathematics classroom collaborator. In: Proceedings of the Workshop on Mathematical User Interfaces (2017)

15. Quinby, F.: Characteristics of models for representation of mathematical structure in typesetting applications and the cognition of digitally transcribing mathematics. Master's thesis, Trent University, Canada (2020)

16. Quinby, F., Kim, S., Kang, S., Pollanen, M., Reynolds, M.G., Burr, W.S.: Markov transition matrix analysis of mathematical expression input models. In: Bigatti, A.M., Carette, J., Davenport, J.H., Joswig, M., de Wolff, T. (eds.) ICMS 2020. LNCS, vol. 12097, pp. 451–461. Springer, Cham (2020). https://doi.org/10.1007/978-3-030-52200-1_45

17. Quinby, F., Kim, S., Pollanen, M., Burr, W.S., Reynolds, M.G.: An evaluation of two-dimensional digital input models for mathematical structure: effects on working memory, cognitive load, and efficiency. In: Harris, D., Li, W.-C. (eds.) HCII 2021. LNCS (LNAI), vol. 12767, pp. 212–222. Springer, Cham (2021). https://doi.org/10.1007/978-3-030-77932-0_18

18. Quinby, F., Pollanen, M., Reynolds, M.G., Burr, W.S.: Effects of digitally typesetting mathematics on working memory. In: Harris, D., Li, W.-C. (eds.) HCII 2020. LNCS (LNAI), vol. 12186, pp. 69–80. Springer, Cham (2020). https://doi.org/10.1007/978-3-030-49044-7_7

19. Shin, J., Lee, S.J.: The alignment of student fraction learning with textbooks in Korea and the United States. J. Math. Behav. **51**, 129–149 (2018)

20. Tsai, T.-L., Li, H.-C.: Towards a framework for developing students' fraction proficiency. Int. J. Math. Educ. Sci. Technol. **48**(2), 244–255 (2017)

# Effects of a Robot Human-Machine Interface on Emergency Steering Control and Prefrontal Cortex Activation in Automatic Driving

Hiroko Tanabe[1][(✉)] ⓘ, Yuki Yoshihara[1] ⓘ, Nihan Karatas[1] ⓘ, Kazuhiro Fujikake[2] ⓘ, Takahiro Tanaka[1] ⓘ, Shuhei Takeuchi[3] ⓘ, Tsuneyuki Yamamoto[3] ⓘ, Makoto Harazawa[3] ⓘ, and Naoki Kamiya[3] ⓘ

[1] Nagoya University, Furo-cho, Chikusa-ku, Nagoya, Aichi 464-8601, Japan
h.tanabe@mirai.nagoya-u.ac.jp
[2] Chukyo University, 101-2, Yagotohonmachi, Showa-ku, Nagoya, Aichi 466-8666, Japan
[3] Tokai Rika, Co., Ltd., Oguchi-cho, Niwa-gun, Aichi 480-0195, Japan

**Abstract.** Advanced driver assistance systems (ADASs) support drivers in multiple ways, such as adaptive cruise control, lane tracking assistance (LTA), and blind spot monitoring, among other services. However, the use of ADAS cruise control has been reported to delay reaction to vehicle collisions. We created a robot human-machine interface (RHMI) to inform drivers of emergencies by means of movement, which would allow drivers to prepare for the disconnection of autonomous driving. This study investigated the effects of RHMI on response to the emergency disconnection of the LTA function of autonomous driving. We also examined drivers' fatigue and arousal using near-infrared spectroscopy (NIRS) on the prefrontal cortex. The participants in this study were 12 males and 15 females. We recorded steering torque and NIRS data in the prefrontal region across two channels during the manipulation of automatic driving with a driving simulator. The scenario included three events in the absence of LTA due to bad weather. All of the participants experienced emergencies with and without RHMI, implemented using two agents: RHMI prototype (RHMI-P) and RoBoHoN. Our RHMI allowed the drivers to respond earlier to emergency LTA disconnection. All drivers showed a gentle torque response for RoBoHoN, but some showed a steep response with RHMI-P and without RHMI. NIRS data showed significant prefrontal cortex activation in RHMI conditions (especially RHMI-P), which may indicate high arousal. Our RHMI helped drivers stay alert and respond to emergency LTA disconnection; however, some drivers showed a quick and large torque response only with RHMI-P.

**Keywords:** Human-machine interface (HMI) · Automated driving · Driving assistance system (ADAS) · Near-infrared spectroscopy (NIRS)

## 1 Introduction

Advanced driver assistance systems (ADASs) play a central role in level 2 automation, which is the current automation state of mainly released automated vehicles. An ADAS

D. Harris and W.-C. Li (Eds.): HCII 2022, LNAI 13307, pp. 108–123, 2022.
https://doi.org/10.1007/978-3-031-06086-1_9

provides various functions, such as lane tracking assistance (LTA), adaptive cruise control, blind spot monitoring, advanced parking assistance, driver monitoring, and traffic sign recognition, but the main operator of the vehicle remains the driver. This sharing of roles between human and machine could be responsible for the low usage of rate of ADAS, resting on a lack of system's perceived usefulness, ease of use, trustworthiness, and cost [1, 2]. In addition, ADAS cruise control has been reported to delay the reaction to impending vehicle collisions [3]. This could be ascribed to multiple factors, including the psychological (e.g., overconfidence that leads to reduced awareness), physiological, and/or biomechanical (e.g., stress, fatigue, and sleepiness). For this reason, ADAS should require a more highly receptive human-machine interface (HMI) to prompt drivers understand the state of ADAS better and to make the transfer of roles between drivers and ADAS smoother.

An HMI in an ADAS informs drivers of its operation state and/or mode: normal (in which the system works without any trouble), caution (where drivers should pay attention to an abnormal situation), and warning (where the driver must take over operation of the vehicle). The most recent commercially available HMI designs for ADAS operations and modes use pictograms on dashboard displays and mirrors [4]. However, this means of presenting information could be ambiguous for drivers due to the difficulties in recognizing small icons and their colors and understanding the states and modes of the ADAS. To improve the interaction quality between vehicles and drivers, voice-based HMIs, head-up displays (HUDs), and augmented reality-based HUDs have been reported to be useful [5–7]. In addition, robot HMIs (RHMIs) have the potential to make the interactions more engaging, familiar, acceptable, and enjoyable [8] and are also useful for changing drivers' behavior through increased self-awareness [9] and for prompting drivers to pay closer attention to the road, owing to their believable social presence [10]. This implies that RHMIs could also improve the quality of interaction between drivers and vehicles; however, the effects of RHMIs that support ADAS functions remain unclear. Therefore, in this study, we created a system to inform the drivers of ADAS states and modes that employs RHMIs, especially in emergency situations, and investigated its effects on drivers' response to the unexpected events and psychological/physiological states.

Human-like behaviors performed by humanoid robots, such as nodding, hand-waving, and eye gazing, function as social cues [11, 12]. Therefore, humanoid robots have the potential to provide improved social presence as driver agents [13]. A small humanoid robot, RoBoHoN (SHARP Co., Ltd.) showed greater acceptability as a driver agent than the audio and video agent forms [14]. However, when we use humanoid robots as driver agents, there are only restrictions to taking full advantage of their human-like appearance and behavior; that is, their physical expression should be moderate to prevent them from being eye-catching and disturbing the driver. On the other hand, non-humanoid robots are simple and inexpensive owing to their simpler mechanism and reduced degrees of freedom [15]. The designs of non-humanoid robots reduce unrealistic expectations [16], which makes their appearance and behavior intuitive. Thus, non-humanoid robots may be better suited for use as an RHMI in the in-car environment and have been used as driving agents in several studies [17–19]. However, the precise differences in usefulness between humanoid and non-humanoid RHMIs in supporting ADAS functions remain unclear.

In this study, to evaluate our RHMI systems, we focused on drivers' psychological and physiological states, such as sleepiness, aggression, and fatigue, as well as their response to emergency LTA disconnection. Emotions and physiological states can be estimated using cortical activation, which can be noninvasively measured with near-infrared spectroscopy (NIRS), which measures changes in oxygenated hemoglobin (oxy-Hb) and deoxygenated hemoglobin (deoxy-Hb) in the cerebral cortex [20]. This indicates cortical activation, as neural activation is associated with increased oxy-Hb and decreased deoxy-Hb [21–26]. Although NIRS does not measure activation deep inside of the brain, and unlike fMRI or positron emission tomography, its spatial resolution is relatively low (20–30 mm), it has the advantage that its measurement is fully noninvasive, relatively robust against motion artifacts [27], and less subject to the restriction of noisy conditions [28]. NIRS study is useful for evaluating activation in the prefrontal region associated with emotions [29]. Left-dominant activation in the frontal region reflects aggression [30, 31]; on the other hand, inactivation in left frontal cortex is related to fatigue [32]. In addition, sleepiness is negatively correlated with oxy-Hb in the bilateral frontal regions [33]. Guided by these conclusions, we investigated drivers' aggression, fatigue, and sleepiness with NIRS data.

This study investigated the effects of RHMI on drivers' steering operation (i.e., their response to unexpected events) and on drivers' aggression, fatigue, and sleepiness in emergency LTA disconnection. To compare the effects between humanoid and non-humanoid robots, we created two kinds of RHMIs, with humanoid and non-humanoid robots to provide physiological evidence for creating ameliorating and practical driving agents.

## 2 Methods

### 2.1 Experimental Protocols and Measurements

All procedures used in this study were in accordance with the Declaration of Helsinki and were approved by the Ethics Committee of Nagoya University. This approval was based on an appropriate risk/benefit ratio and a study design in which the risks were minimized. All procedures were conducted in accordance with the approved protocol. The individuals participating in this study provided written informed consent to partic-ipate in this study and for the case details to be published. Informed consent continued throughout the study via a dialog between the researcher and participants. No special collection permit was required for the study.

A total of 12 males and 15 females (mean age $50.04 \pm 8.39$ years) participated in this study. None of the participants had a significant medical history or any sign of a gait, postural, or neurological disorder. All participants had driver's licenses. The participants experienced a highway-driving scenario in a driving simulator (SCANeR™ studio, AV Simulation, France). They were instructed to hold the steering wheel at all times while driving. The driving scenario in this study simulated a level 2 automated driving along a 12.5-km-long highway with a speed of the self-vehicle at 80 km/h. The weather was set as foggy and drizzling (visibility distance was 1 km), which made it difficult for the LTA function to recognize the white lanes and position the vehicle between the lanes by maneuvering the steering wheel. The scenario included three emergency LTA disconnections: each start point was 3.00, 3.65, and 4.30 km at the start of the scenario.

All participants experienced three unexpected events with and without RHMI, implemented in two forms: (1) the NoRHMI condition, with C-HMI only; (2) the RHMI prototype (RHMI-P) condition; and (3) the RoBoHoN condition (see Sect. 2.2 and Fig. 3 for design information). We used two RHMIs to compare the effects of the degree of anthropomorphism on drivers' behavioral, physiological, and psychological factors. The order of experimental conditions was counterbalanced to reduce the order effects. Figure 1 illustrates the LTA off events during the scenario. Each emergency consisted of two ADAS states: an unstable state, in which we assumed the vehicle was entering an area where the LTA had difficulty detecting white lines (a 0–150 m area from each start of LTA off event), and a suspended state, in which the LTA function was disconnected, and manual operation was necessary (a 150–450 m area from the start of each LTA off event). In other sections, we set the ADAS condition in a normal state, where LTA was tracking the white lanes and arranged the position of the vehicle by maneuvering the steering wheel between the lanes. Along with LTA disconnection events, we changed the display contents of a conventional HMI (C-HMI), and the RHMIs changed their modes with different motions and/or coloring (see Sect. 2.2 for details).

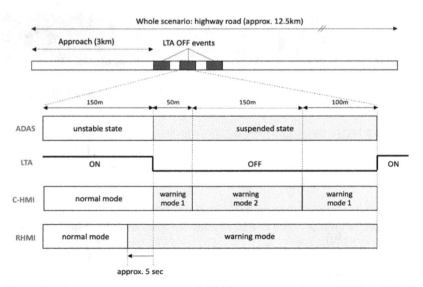

**Fig. 1.** Driving scenario, the transition of ADAS state, and modes of C-HMI and RHMI

To investigate the effects of our RHMIs on the response to an unexpected event and on drivers' physiological and psychological factors (in this study, we focused on sleepiness, aggression, and fatigue), we recorded steering torque and NIRS data for the prefrontal region in two channels. Steering torque was exported from the logged data of the driving simulator. For the NIRS recording, we used the Brain Activity Monitor Hb133 (Astem Co., Ltd., Japan), operated at two near-infrared wavelengths, 770 and 830 nm. Two channels were arranged at 85 mm apart, in the prefrontal region. Changes in the oxy-Hb and deoxygenated Hb (deoxy-Hb) concentrations were obtained for each channel. We recorded NIRS data for each condition separately (i.e., we obtained three recordings for each participant) because NIRS recording was frequently halted between conditions due to network disturbances. The sampling frequencies for steering torque and NIRS recording were 100 and 10 Hz, respectively.

## 2.2 Conventional HMI and Robot HMI Designs

A C-HMI was set on the dashboard display and presented information on the ADAS operations (Fig. 2). The design of our C-HMI was based on the specification of commercially available vehicles [34, 35]. In the normal and unstable states of the ADAS, both the green LTA icon and the blue line guard were lit (normal mode). When the vehicle entered the area of the suspended state of the ADAS suspended state, the LTA icon was turned gray, and the line guard was turned off (warning mode 1). Then, as the vehicle passed 50 m from LTA off, the takeover icon (an illustration of holding the wheel) appeared together with a beeping sound (warning mode 2). Then, at the point where the vehicle passed another 150 m, the C-HMI returned to warning mode 1.

**Fig. 2.** A conventional HMI (C-HMI) used in this study (Color figure online)

The two RHMIs, located on the left side of dashboard front, were used as an add-on to the C-HMI, intended at increasing the understandability of the ADAS operations and their states. Using the necessary cues for the expression of animacy [36], we created RHMI motions and appearance as follows:

**RHMI-P.** RHMI-P consists of the body, lid, and pedestal (Fig. 3a). The body was 40 mm tall when the lid was closed and was 54 mm tall when the lid was maximally opened (20°). The width of the body was 70 mm. The height and width of the pedestal were 62 and 150 mm, respectively. RHMI-P had two LED eyes, and a ring LED was embedded in the lid. Both body and lid had one DoF: rotation in the horizontal direction for the body and an opening-closing movement for the lid (from 0° to 20°). In accordance with the states of LTA function, we changed the modes of RHMI-P expression in relation to its eye color and lid and by body motions: turning angle, speed, and lid opening angle. As the degree of emergency increases, we increased its movement speed and altered its eye and eyelid color to ones that would prompt drivers to recognize the emergency.

*Normal Mode.* During the normal state of LTA function, RHMI-P moves peacefully and sluggishly with its eyes and eyelids having a bluish color, which has a calming effect [37]. The rotation angle and speed of the body were set to 135° and 5 rpm, respectively. The opening angle of the eyelid was 8°.

*Warning Mode.* We changed the RHMI-P behavior to the warning mode approximately 5 s before the vehicle entered the area of the suspended state of ADAS, in which the ADAS was not stable. Because high-frequency motion and intensity express danger and strong colors (especially red) induce neuronal excitement [38], we set RHMI-P's eye and eyelid color to red. We also set its rotation angle and body speed to 108° and 80 rpm, respectively. To increase its visibility, we opened the lid maximally, that is 20°.

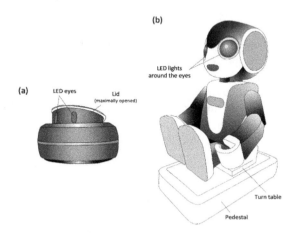

**Fig. 3.** Designs of (a) RHMI-P and (b) RoBoHoN (Color figure online)

**RoBoHoN.** RoBoHoN is a 19.5-cm-tall humanoid robot that can interactively talk, sing, and dance (Fig. 3b). Although RoBoHoN can inform drivers of an emergency situation by its utterances or physical expressions, we restricted its movement to rotation in the horizontal plane and turned off its utterance function. This is because we focused on differences in level of anthropomorphism between RHMI-P and RoBoHoN. Therefore, we made RoBoHoN's motion as similar as possible to that of RHMI-P. In this study, we placed RoBoHoN on a turntable that rotated in the horizontal plane in the same manner as RHMI-P: the sitting height of RoBoHoN and the height of pedestal were approximately 14.5 and 3.5 cm, respectively. The rotation angle and speed of the turntable were operated by a computer connected via Bluetooth. Although its eye contours were covered with LED lights, we were not able to change these colors in the API used. In this study, the eye contours were lit in yellow throughout the experiment. We set RoBoHoN's motion to alter in accordance with ADAS states as follows:

*Normal Mode.* In a similar manner to RHMI-P, RoBoHoN moved quietly during normal LTA functioning. Its rotation angle and speed were 45° and 5 rpm, respectively. We set RoBoHoN's rotation angle smaller than that of RHMI-P because RoBoHoN's motion has higher visibility than that of RHMI-P, whose body and lid had a round shape.

*Warning Mode.* Approximately 5 s before the vehicle entered the area of the ADAS suspended state, RoBoHoN began to rotate at 45° and 80 rpm.

### 2.3 Data Analysis

**Response to the Emergency Disconnection of LTA.** Using a steering torque profile, we detected response times and peak response torques against emergency LTA disconnection as follows: First, we obtained a steering torque profile in the absence of manual operation against the LTA disconnection events, which we called *baseline*. Because the vehicle gradually moved out of the lane if there was no manual operation during the ADAS suspended state, we connected the torque profiles of three LTA events to make a single *baseline* profile. Next, the time series data of the difference between torque profile and *baseline* was passed through a fourth-order butterworth low-pass filter with a cutoff frequency of 10 Hz. We named this low-pass filtered profile *manual torque*. Finally, we detected a response timing to be the time when *manual torque* exceeded the *threshold*. The *threshold* was defined as $1.5 \times MaxAmp$, where *MaxAmp* was the maximum amplitude of the *baseline* while LTA was disconnected: *MaxAmp* was equal to 0.0028 Nm. The response time was the period from the time of LTA disconnection to response timing. In addition, we identified a maximum value of *manual torque* in the period of 1.5 s from the response time, and we defined this value to be the peak response torque to the emergency LTA disconnection.

In human motor control, there is a tradeoff between the speed and accuracy of a movement [39, 40]. In this study, for smooth takeover against emergency LTA disconnection, the response torque should not be too large. That is, it is associated with the accuracy of driving movement. Because the time-accuracy relationship of human motor control is nonlinear [39, 40], we fit the response time-torque data for each condition to the exponential function. The approximation was conducted using the *fit* function in MATLAB. To investigate the effects of our RHMIs to the tradeoff between response time and smoothness, we focused on the degree of fit (i.e., the coefficients of determination) and the shape of the approximate curves for each condition.

**Fatigue and Arousal by NIRS Data Analysis.** We analyzed changes in oxy-Hb concentrations throughout the LTA disconnection events. First, we excluded the data of 15 participants due to measurement failures. The data of the remaining 12 participants was passed through bandpass filters: a 8.1 MHz high-pass filter to remove long-term drift artifacts and a 150 MHz low-pass filter to remove respiration, heartbeat, and high-frequency noise artifacts [41]. We excluded the data where the oxy-Hb and deoxy-Hb profile showed in-phase relationship, which was interpreted as an artifact. Among the 24 samples (2 channels of data for 12 participants), 19, 19, and 20 samples were obtained for the subsequent analysis for NoRHMI, RoBoHoN, and RHMI-P conditions, respectively.

Prefrontal cortex activation was evaluated using phase plot bias: a distribution rate across the first, second, and fourth quadrants of significantly more than 75% represented the activation of the prefrontal cortex, which may indicate wakefulness (Fig. 4). A left-dominant imbalance of activation is related to fatigue and stress [30, 31]. Before we focused on the rate distribution during emergency LTA events, we checked the distribution rate throughout the entire recording period: $75.25 \pm 1.86\%$, $75.25 \pm 1.24\%$, and $75.43 \pm 1.75\%$ for the NoRHMI, RoBoHoN, and RHMI-P conditions, respectively. This result indicates that there was no bias toward activation/deactivation throughout the entire recording period.

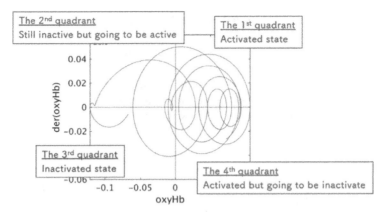

**Fig. 4.** Sample phase plot of oxy-Hb concentration during LTA disconnection events

**Statistical Analysis.** All signal processing to calculate response time, peak response torque, and distribution rate in the phase plot of oxy-Hb was implemented with MAT-LAB. All of the data in this study are expressed as mean ± standard deviation. The normality of the data was first assessed using the Lilliefors test with the *lillietest* function of MATLAB. The subsequent statistical analysis was performed with SPSS. Levene's test was used for the test for homogeneity of variance. When the variance was homogenous, the data were analyzed using one-way ANOVA, and the subsequent post hoc multiple comparisons were performed with Tukey's test. For the non-parametric test, an overall difference between the conditions was determined with the Kruskal–Wallis test. The significant level was set at $p < 0.05$.

## 3   Results

The following sections present the results of only the first trial for each participant, that is only one condition within NoRHMI, RoBoHoN, and RHMI-P per participant. This is because there were no differences between conditions for the second and third conditions. This could be due to the participants' familiarity with the emergency, allowing them to predict the events from the road environment and prepare for the events during the second and third trials. Ten, eight, and eight participants experienced the NoRHMI, RoBoHoN, and RHMI-P conditions, respectively.

### 3.1   Response to the Emergency Disconnection of LTA

The left figure in Fig. 5 shows the response time at the first emergency during the first trial. The data were not normally distributed, and the Kruskal-Wallis test showed no statistical difference between conditions ($p = 0.404$). Although there were no statistical differences between conditions, some participants who used RHMIs (especially RoBoHoN) were able to respond predictively earlier (sooner than 0.2 s) for the first emergency in the first condition. This implies that our RHMIs had the ability to inform drivers of the system malfunction earlier and allow them to prepare for it. In addition to the response time, the amplitude of the responses was crucial for avoidance. Therefore, we also investigated the peak response torque and the response time. The data were not normally distributed, and the subsequent Kruskal-Wallis test revealed that there was no statistical difference between the conditions ($p = 0.45$). Although there were no statistical differences between conditions, some participants, especially in the NoRHMI and RHMI-P conditions, responded to the event with a large steering torque.

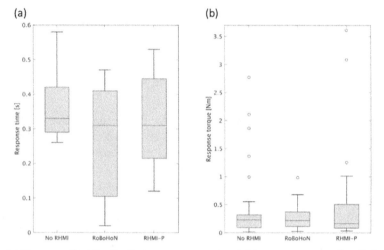

**Fig. 5.** (a) Response time for the first emergent event and (b) response torque for all the events during the first trial

To investigate the effects of our RHMIs on the tradeoff between response time and smoothness, we also examined the response time-torque relationship. Figure 6 shows the response time and torque relationship for all of the emergencies during the first trial. The blue, yellow, and red marks represent data for the NoRHMI, RoBoHoN, and RHMI-P conditions, respectively. The first, second, and third events are depicted separately using circle, triangle, and square marks, respectively. Some data from the NoRHMI and RHMI-P conditions showed quick but large steering responses (more than 1.5 Nm), which could be interpreted as the tradeoff between response time and accuracy in the torque control. The data for the NoRHMI and RHMI-P conditions were moderately well fitted to the exponential function. Their approximate curves and the coefficients of determination were as follows: $y = 3.255e^{-13.11x}$ and $R^2 = 0.39$ for the NoRHMI condition and $y = 5.099e^{-19.5x}$ and $R^2 = 0.43$ for the RHMI-P condition. On the other hand, the data for the RoBoHoN condition did not fit to the exponential function: $y = 0.3634e^{-1.01x}$ and $R^2 = 0.059$. These results imply that only RoBoHoN could soften the tradeoff between response time and torque control and allow drivers to respond quickly and gently for the unexpected emergency LTA disconnection.

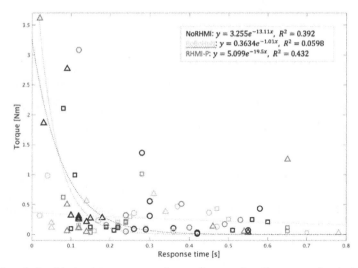

**Fig. 6.** The relationship between response time and torque for all emergencies during the first trial and approximate curves to exponential function (Color figure online)

### 3.2 Fatigue and Arousal from NIRS Study

We evaluated the activation of the prefrontal region during LTA disconnection events, using the bias of oxy-Hb signal in the phase plot, that is the distribution rate across the first, second, and fourth quadrants. The distribution rate for NRHMI, RoBoHoN, and RHMI-P conditions were $66.12 \pm 15.64$, $75.80 \pm 20.14$, and $89.16 \pm 13.28$, respectively. The data were normally distributed, and the homogeneity of variance was confirmed by Levene's test (p = 0.161). The one-way ANOVA test revealed that there were no statistical differences between conditions (F(2, 15) = 2.962, p = 0.082). In spite of this, the distribution rate of the RHMI-P condition tended to be larger than that of NRHMI condition (p = 0.073 by Tukey's test). The distribution rate of RHMI-P condition was larger than 75%. This implies that the prefrontal region was activated during emergency events with RHMI-P, which could be interpreted as high arousal [33].

Left-right imbalance in the activation of the prefrontal cortex is associated with aggression [30, 31] and fatigue [32]. Although there were only a small number of samples in this study (only one, three, and three left-right pairs of oxy-Hb signals for NRHMI, RoBoHoN, and RHMI-P conditions, respectively), one pair showed activity only in the left prefrontal cortex for the NRHMI and RoBoHoN conditions. This left dominance could be interpreted as aggression. Figure 7 presents one sample from the NRHMI condition that showed left-dominant activity. For the RHMI-P condition, there was no left-right pair that showed left-dominant activity. In addition, we did not observe left-dominant inactivity, which is associated with fatigue, for any condition.

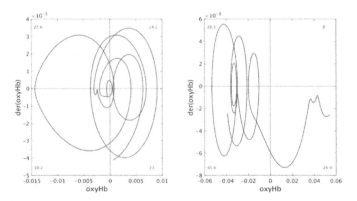

**Fig. 7.** A phase plot that showed left-dominant activity (a sample from NRHMI condition)

## 4 Discussion

In this study, we investigated the effects of RHMI on drivers' steering operation (i.e., their response to the emergencies) and on drivers' aggression, fatigue, and sleepiness at emergency LTA disconnection. To compare the effects between humanoid and non-humanoid robots, we created two kinds of RHMIs to assist the drivers with RoBoHoN and non-humanoid RHMI-P. Our RHMIs made it possible for drivers to respond predictively earlier (~300 ms) against emergencies even at the first event during the first trial, which was impossible for the NoRHMI condition (Fig. 5a). This could be because the drivers anticipated the emergency due to the change in visual/auditory information about the ADAS state from the robots. This result suggested that our RHMIs could induce a rapid response against unexpected situations where the drivers need to take control. Thus, our RHMIs could help overcome the challenges that current ADAS is confronted: the use of ADAS could delay the response to emergency vehicle collision [3]. However, not every participant driving with our RHMIs accelerated their response: some showed relatively slow (400–600 ms) takeover. This could be due to the tradeoff between speed and accuracy for human motor control [39, 40]. That is, in this study, drivers did not necessarily allocate resources only to the response speed, even though they recognized the upcoming emergencies in advance. Instead, of the speed, drivers could take time to take over controls smoothly and steadily.

The amplitude of the response torque is crucial for smooth takeover and subsequent steering control. A torque response that is too large could impede the smooth and safe transition to manual operation. In this study, some participants showed relatively large response torque, especially under the NoRHMI and RHMI-P conditions (Fig. 5b), most of which indicated a rapid response time (Fig. 6). Among these participants, the one with the NoRHMI condition responded with large torque in the subsequent two conditions, which implies that this participant would take the response speed rather than the torque amplitude, regardless of the presence of our RHMIs. Other participants showed a large response torque under either NoRHMI or RHMI-P conditions. They managed to avoid the emergency (i.e., they were able to keep the lane), but their takeover transitions were not smooth enough. The reason for this quick and large torque response could be as follows: those participants had the urge to respond as rapidly as possible to avoid lane deviation and were unable to manage the smooth torque control due to the tradeoff between time and accuracy. In addition, we also observed relatively large ($>1.0$ Nm) and slow ($>0.6$ s) responses for one sample in the RHMI-P condition (Fig. 6). This could be associated with the mechanism of surprise: because the emotion of surprise delays the required action [42], the recourses of response time and torque accuracy/smoothness decreased, and then the driver's response became slow and large. On the other hand, RoBoHoN allowed most of the participants to respond with mild torque (Fig. 5b), and the torque amplitude did not tend to increase exponentially as the response time grew in speed (Fig. 6). These results indicated that RoBoHoN would be the more effective for the quick and smooth takeover compared with RHMI-P and NoRHMI conditions. It has been reported that drivers tend to perform smoother takeover control as a vehicle approaches its operational design domain exits, where the drivers were informed of a request of intervene earlier, compared with the situation of sudden system failure, as in this study [43]. Thus, our RHMI with RoBoHoN could prompt drivers to intervene the system substantially earlier, soon enough for a smooth takeover.

To investigate the drivers' physiological and psychological factors during emergencies, we also focused on sleepiness, aggression, and fatigue through the NIRS study. During LTA disconnection, drivers' prefrontal region tended to be deactivated in the NoRHMI condition and activated in the RHMI-P condition. For the RoBoHoN condition, there tended to be no bias in activation level. These results imply that drivers' sleepiness during the emergencies tended to be higher without RHMIs and low with RHMI-P. Because sleepiness is an important issue for driving automated vehicles [44], our RHMIs (especially RHMI-P) would be beneficial for keeping drivers awake. In addition, one sample of the NoRHMI condition (out of one sample) and one sample of the RoBoHoN condition (out of three samples) showed left-dominant prefrontal activation, which could reflect aggression [30, 31]. This result shows the possibility that only RHMI-P could succeed in preventing aggression. Automated driving makes drivers feel tired more quickly than manual driving and also makes the transition from automated driving back to manual operation more difficult [45]. However, our data from the NIRS study (from approximately 11 min of driving with three emergency events) did not show deactivation on the left side of prefrontal region, which is associated with fatigue. The effect of our RHMIs on drivers' fatigue requires continued investigation. In addition, because the number of samples of NIRS data was small due to the design and due to measurement failure, it is necessary to perform further investigations to expand the data to understand the physiological and psychological effects of our RHMIs.

In overall summary, the behavioral, physiological, and psychological effects of our RHMIs on emergency LTA disconnection were as follows: our RHMIs allowed drivers to respond early and predictively to unexpected and unexperienced emergencies. Especially with RoBoHoN, the tradeoff between response time and torque control tended to be diminished; that is, RoBoHoN allowed the drivers to respond quickly and gently to the emergencies. On the other hand, RHMI-P tended to be effective for making drivers awake and suppressing their aggression. A questionnaire survey about the impression of our RHMIs identified that RHMI-P was evaluated to be more trustworthy and have higher competence and efficiency than RoBoHoN [46]. Those differences between RHMI-P and RoBoHoN are due to the difference in the gap between the experienced urgency and the urgency information that RHMI provides. That is, it could be speculated that the urgency information that RoBoHoN provides was weaker than actual urgency, and therefore, its awakening effect was less intense, which increased some drivers' aggression due to insufficient information, whereas in the other case, drivers could respond more easily and with a calm mind. On the other hand, it would be possible that the urgency information that RHMI-P provides exceeded actual urgency, and as a result, drivers were fully awake and had less aggression due to having sufficient information from RHMI-P, but some drivers showed quick and large torque response because surplus urgency information from RHMI-P caused impatience in response to the event. As a background to these differences between our RHMIs even though the behavior of RHMI-P and RoBoHoN was set to the similar level, drivers could have more expectations of RoBoHoN as an informant, as it was a humanoid robot that could express social cues through its rich body expression and utterance [11, 12]. This high expectation of RoBoHoN could lead to information asymmetry, which has been reported to affect the feeling of trust and aggression [47], between robots and drivers. Therefore, to reduce information asymmetry, RoBoHoN may need to provide the information about an impending emergency in more sophisticated manner due to its humanoid characteristics to make it physiologically and psychologically more effective. On the other hand, RHMI-P requires improvement in response to emergencies, some of which showed a large response torque. To resolve this problem in a future study, we could fill the gap between actual urgency and the urgency information that RHMI-P provides by making its information presentation expression gentler.

## 5   Conclusion

In this study, we created RHMIs to inform drivers of emergencies through robots' movements to allow drivers to prepare for the disconnection of autonomous driving. Our RHMI allowed drivers to respond earlier to impending LTA disconnection. All drivers showed a gentle torque response with RoBoHoN, but some showed a steep response with RHMI-P and without RHMI. NIRS data showed significant prefrontal cortex activation in RHMI conditions (especially RHMI-P), which could be interpreted as high arousal. In addition, under RoBoHoN and NoRHMI conditions, some participants showed left-dominant prefrontal activation, which may be associated with aggression. Our RHMI helped drivers remain alert and respond to emergency LTA disconnection; however, our results also suggested that it is necessary to improve the method of information presentation method in response to the robot's appearance (humanoid or non-humanoid).

## References

1. Trübswetter, N., Bengler, K.: Why should I use ADAS? Advanced driver assistance systems and the elderly: knowledge, experience and usage barriers. In: 7th International Driving Symposium on Human Factors in Driver Assessment, Training and Vehicle Design (2013)
2. Viktorová, L., Šucha, M.: Drivers' acceptance of advanced driver assistance systems–what to consider. Int. J. Traffic Transp. Eng. 8(3), 320–333 (2018)

3. Jammes, Y., Behr, M., Llari, M., Bonicel, S., Weber, J.P., Berdah, S.: Emergency braking is affected by the use of cruise control. Traffic Injury Prev. **18**(6), 636–641 (2017)
4. Bruyas, M.P., Le Breton, B., Pauzié, A.: Ergonomic guidelines for the design of pictorial information. Int. J. Ind. Ergon. **21**(5), 407–413 (1998)
5. Karatas, N., et al.: Evaluation of AR-HUD interface during an automated intervention in manual driving. In: 2020 IEEE Intelligent Vehicles Symposium (IV), pp. 2158–2164. IEEE (2020)
6. Langlois, S., Soualmi, B.: Augmented reality versus classical HUD to take over from automated driving: an aid to smooth reactions and to anticipate maneuvers. In: 2016 IEEE 19th International Conference on Intelligent Transportation Systems, ITSC, pp. 1571–1578. IEEE (2016)
7. Braun, M., Mainz, A., Chadowitz, R., Pfleging, B., Alt, F.: At your service: designing voice assistant personalities to improve automotive user interfaces. In: 2019 CHI Conference on Human Factors in Computing Systems, pp. 1–11 (2019)
8. Serpell, J.: Anthropomorphism and anthropomorphic selection—Beyond the "cute response." Soc. Anim. **11**(1), 83–100 (2003)
9. Tanaka, T., Fujikake, K., Yoshihara, Y., Karatas, N., Aoki, H., Kanamori, H.: Preliminary study for feasibility of driver agent in actual car environment—Driver agent for encouraging safe driving behavior. J. Transp. Technol. **10**(02), 128 (2020)
10. Biocca, F., Harms, C., Burgoon, J.K.: Toward a more robust theory and measure of social presence: Review and suggested criteria. Presence: Teleoper. Virtual Environ. **12**(5), 456–480 (2003)
11. Bartneck, C., Forlizzi, J.: A design-centred framework for social human-robot interaction. In: RO-MAN 2004. 13th IEEE International Workshop on Robot and Human Interactive Communication, IEEE Catalog No. 04TH8759, pp. 591–594. IEEE (2004)
12. Fong, T., Nourbakhsh, I., Dautenhahn, K.: A survey of socially interactive robots. Robot. Auton. Syst. **42**(3–4), 143–166 (2003)
13. Wang, M., Lee, S.C., Kamalesh Sanghavi, H., Eskew, M., Zhou, B., Jeon, M.: In-vehicle intelligent agents in fully autonomous driving: the effects of speech style and embodiment together and separately. In: 13th International Conference on Automotive User Interfaces and Interactive Vehicular Applications, pp. 247–254 (2021)
14. Tanaka, T., et al.: Effect of difference in form of driving support agent to driver's acceptability—Driver agent for encouraging safe driving behavior. J. Transp. Technol. **8**(03), 194 (2018)
15. Anderson-Bashan, L., et al.: The greeting machine: an abstract robotic object for opening encounters. In: 27th IEEE International Symposium on Robot and Human Interactive Communication (RO-MAN), pp. 595–602. IEEE (2018)
16. Parlitz, C., Hägele, M., Klein, P., Seifert, J., Dautenhahn, K.: Care-O-bot 3-rationale for human-robot interaction design. In: 39th International Symposium on Robotics, ISR, pp. 275–280 (2008)
17. Karatas, N., Yoshikawa, S., De Silva, P.R.S., Okada, M.: NAMIDA: multiparty conversation based driving agents in futuristic vehicle. In: Kurosu, M. (ed.) HCI 2015. LNCS, vol. 9171, pp. 198–207. Springer, Cham (2015). https://doi.org/10.1007/978-3-319-21006-3_20
18. Zihsler, J., et al.: Carvatar: increasing trust in highly-automated driving through social cues. In: Adjunct Proceedings of the 8th International Conference on Automotive User Interfaces and Interactive Vehicular Applications, pp. 9–14 (2016)
19. Williams, K., Breazeal, C.: Reducing driver task load and promoting sociability through an affective intelligent driving agent (AIDA). In: Kotzé, P., Marsden, G., Lindgaard, G., Wesson, J., Winckler, M. (eds.) INTERACT 2013. LNCS, vol. 8120, pp. 619–626. Springer, Heidelberg (2013). https://doi.org/10.1007/978-3-642-40498-6_53

20. Ferrari, M., Quaresima, V.: A brief review on the history of human functional near-infrared spectroscopy (fNIRS) development and fields of application. Neuroimage **63**(2), 921–935 (2012)
21. Hirth, C., et al.: Noninvasive functional mapping of the human motor cortex using near-infrared spectroscopy. NeuroReport **7**(12), 1977–1981 (1996)
22. Hock, C., Müller-Spahn, F., Schuh-Hofer, S., Hofmann, M., Dirnagl, U., Villringer, A.: Age dependency of changes in cerebral hemoglobin oxygenation during brain activation: a near-infrared spectroscopy study. J. Cereb. Blood Flow Metab. **15**(6), 1103–1108 (1995)
23. Hoshi, Y., Tamura, M.: Detection of dynamic changes in cerebral oxygenation coupled to neuronal function during mental work in man. Neurosci. Lett. **150**(1), 5–8 (1993)
24. Obrig, H., et al.: Near-infrared spectroscopy: does it function in functional activation studies of the adult brain? Int. J. Psychophysiol. **35**(2–3), 125–142 (2000)
25. Villringer, A., Planck, J., Hock, C., Schleinkofer, L., Dirnagl, U.: Near infrared spectroscopy (NIRS): a new tool to study hemodynamic changes during activation of brain function in human adults. Neurosci. Lett. **154**(1–2), 101–104 (1993)
26. Watanabe, A., Kato, T.: Cerebrovascular response to cognitive tasks in patients with schizophrenia measured by near-infrared spectroscopy. Schizophr. Bull. **30**(2), 435–444 (2004)
27. Miyai, I., et al.: Cortical mapping of gait in humans: a near-infrared spectroscopic topography study. Neuroimage **14**(5), 1186–1192 (2001)
28. Okamoto, M., et al.: Multimodal assessment of cortical activation during apple peeling by NIRS and fMRI. Neuroimage **21**(4), 1275–1288 (2004)
29. Doi, H., Nishitani, S., Shinohara, K.: NIRS as a tool for assaying emotional function in the prefrontal cortex. Front. Hum. Neurosci. **7**, 770 (2013)
30. Harmon-Jones, E., Allen, J.J.: Anger and frontal brain activity: EEG asymmetry consistent with approach motivation despite negative affective valence. J. Pers. Soc. Psychol. **74**(5), 1310 (1998)
31. Kubo, K., Okanoya, K., Kawai, N.: Apology isn't good enough: an apology suppresses an approach motivation but not the physiological and psychological anger. PLoS ONE **7**(3), e33006 (2012)
32. Nishikawa, T., Watanuki, K., Kaede, K., Muramatsu, K., Mashiko, N.: Effects of subjective visual fatigue on brain function during luminescent sentence reading task. In: 2020 IEEE/SICE International Symposium on System Integration (SII), pp. 390–394. IEEE (2020)
33. Suda, M., et al.: Decreased cortical reactivity underlies subjective daytime light sleepiness in healthy subjects: a multichannel near-infrared spectroscopy study. Neurosci. Res. **60**(3), 319–326 (2008)
34. Toyota Europe Homepage (2016). https://myportalcontent.toyota-europe.com/Manuals/toyota/C-HR_HV_OM_Europe_OM10538E.pdf
35. Toyota USA, Detailed System Overview Lane Tracing Assist (LTA) (2019). https://www.youtube.com/watch?v=COfzwGQ9r7w&ab_channel=ToyotaUSA
36. Tremoulet, P.D., Feldman, J.: Perception of animacy from the motion of a single object. Perception **29**(8), 943–951 (2000)
37. Goldstein, K.: Some experimental observations concerning the influence of colors on the function of the organism. Occup. Ther. **21**(3), 147–151 (1942)
38. Küller, R., Mikellides, B., Janssens, J.: Color, arousal, and performance—A comparison of three experiments. Color Res. Appl. **34**(2), 141–152 (2009)
39. Fitts, P.M.: The information capacity of the human motor system in controlling the amplitude of movement. J. Exp. Psychol. **47**(6), 381–391 (1954)
40. Woodworth, R.S.: The accuracy of voluntary movement. Psychol. Rev.: Monogr. Suppl. **3**(3), i–114 (1899)

41. Pinti, P., Cardone, D., Merla, A.: Simultaneous fNIRS and thermal infrared imaging during cognitive task reveal autonomic correlates of prefrontal cortex activity. Sci. Rep. **5**(1), 1–14 (2015)

42. Meyer, W.U., Niepel, M., Rudolph, U., Schützwohl, A.: An experimental analysis of surprise. Cogn. Emot. **5**(4), 295–311 (1991)

43. Yao, H., An, S., Zhou, H., Itoh, M.: Driver takeover performance in conditionally automated driving: sudden system failure situation versus ODD exit situation. SICE J. Control Meas. Syst. Integr. **14**(1), 89–96 (2021)

44. Vogelpohl, T., Kühn, M., Hummel, T., Vollrath, M.: Asleep at the automated wheel—Sleepiness and fatigue during highly automated driving. Accid. Anal. Prev. **126**, 70–84 (2019)

45. Schömig, N., Hargutt, V., Neukum, A., Petermann-Stock, I., Othersen, I.: The interaction between highly automated driving and the development of drowsiness. Proc. Manuf. **3**, 6652–6659 (2015)

46. Karatas, N., et al.: Effects of including a robotic-human-machine interface and its human-likeness level in advanced driver assistance systems. Front. Robot. AI. (in revision)

47. Xu, Y., He, W.: More information = less aggression? Impact of information asymmetry on Chinese patients' aggression. Front. Public Health **7**, 118 (2019)

# The Influence of Font Size, Contrast, and Weight on Text Legibility for Wearable Devices

Xiaoyu Wang[1,2], Huihui Zhang[1], Miao He[3], Yanfang Liu[3], and Liang Zhang[1,2(✉)]

[1] Institute of Psychology, Chinese Academy of Sciences, Beijing 100101, China
zhangl@psych.ac.cn
[2] Department of Psychology, University of Chinese Academy of Sciences, Beijing 100049, China
[3] Huawei Device Co., Ltd., Shenzhen 518129, Guangdong, China

**Abstract.** Wearable devices have a rapid development and popularity in the last decade, and the human-computer interaction issues in this field have become prominent. In general, the screen size of wearable devices is much smaller. Besides, the usage scenario is usually outdoors under the state of moving. Consequently, it is difficult to apply the existing standards of other devices, such as laptops, on them. In this study, we used a smartwatch as the interaction device, and 45 users participated in this study. Two experiments were designed to investigate the influence of the key factors (font size, contrast, and weight) that influenced legibility of text (numbers and characters) on behavioral performance and subjective experience for two age groups (people aged 18–40 vs. people aged over 40). The results showed that the font size had the greatest influence on legibility. For people over 40, the very small size and the small size text could not be clearly recognized. For the young people aged 18–40, the font size had a subtle influence on performance. However, too large font size reduced the preference for message reading. Contrast is another variable that influence legibility. Low contrast needs to be avoided in the design. The influence of weight is relatively small, and very thin weight is worse than medium and very thick weight. In general, the method used in this study had high ecological validity and we hope to provide useful suggestions for the design of smartwatch.

**Keywords:** Text-legibility · User experience · Wearable devices · Walking · Age

## 1 Introduction

Since the release of the first smartwatch in 2014, smart wearable devices (e.g., smartwatches, smart band) have grown rapidly in less than a decade with an astonishing speed of iteration and popularity. Wearable devices have been applied in various fields, becoming an essential gadget for more and more people [1].

Compared with other visual display terminals, wearable devices have their distinctive differences. First, the screen size is different. The interface of smart wearable devices (e.g., smartwatches, smart band) is evidently smaller than other devices, which substantially limits the font size and capacity of text. The second difference is the variability of using environment, which means users will not only use these devices in the static state (such as sitting condition), but also on moving condition; not only indoors, but also outdoors in natural light conditions. Studies have shown that the moving condition will reduce the user's operational performance compared with the static state. For example, Hayes et al. found that the accuracy and speed of target selection and reading tasks on tablets and mobile phones decreased significantly in the mobile state [2]. Dinger et al. found that reading performance dropped significantly when users read on smartwatches while walking [3]. Additionally, light also has an impact on word recognition [4]. Thus, it is unreasonable to directly apply the past research results and design specifications from large-screen devices to wearable devices with small screens.

Small-screen wearables also present different content from other devices. According to the surveys, the most used functions of smartwatch are, in order: time telling, timing, notification, activity detection, and short message viewing [5, 6]. The main needs of computers and mobile phones (e.g., complex operations or long article reading) are inconsistent with those of smartwatch users. Instead, the clarity, accuracy, and speed of short text recognition on the interface are primary concerns, including numbers (e.g., time, steps) and short texts (e.g., notifications, messages). Therefore, to ensure a quality user experience, the legibility of numbers and Chinese characters needs to be fully considered for Chinese smartwatch users.

Legibility, defined as whether users are able to recognize and distinguish the characters in the text, is the lowest-level consideration in content usability [7]. In text-legibility research, font (e.g., font size, weight, contrast, etc.), environment and user characteristics are all influential and meaningful factors that need to be involved [8, 9]. In terms of font factors, previous studies on traditional interfaces have shown that font size is the most dominant factor affecting the recognition of alphabetic and Chinese characters [10–12]. For example, Liu et al. found a positive correlation between the font size and the performance by conducting a visual search task [13]. Liu et al. found that improperly small font size was the major reason for fatigue in e-book reading [14]. In addition, weight and contrast are influential to legibility as well. Some studies have found that the higher the contrast was, the faster users could recognize characters in the text, and the better the performance in search task [15, 16]. However, other studies have found performance may decrease when the contrast reaches a critical value. For instance, two studies found medium contrast was a better choice for performance than extremely high or low one [17, 18]. Moreover, weight is also an important property of font. Currently, there are a variety of weight choices in the visual display terminals, and the application of thin font or ultra-thin font is very common [19, 20]. To our knowledge, few studies have investigated the effect of weight on legibility.

In addition, the users' characteristics also affect the legibility, among which the most important individual difference is age. Substantial studies have presented that visual function decreases with age. For example, Pitt et al. found that saccadic speed decreases by about 0.25% every year between the age of 20 and 68 [21]. Fozard (1990) proposed that visual problems may occur after 40 years old (e.g., difficulty in adjusting focus and decreased visual acuity when looking at a close target) [22]. Furthermore, this issue is more prominent on small-screen wearable devices that usually have smaller characters.

To conclude, this study aimed to investigate the effect of font size, contrast and weight on text-legibility, and to explore the differences between these effects in different age groups. In this study, two experiments were conducted to investigate the influence of font factors on the legibility of number and Chinese characters, respectively. Differences between two age groups of users were also investigated. The experiment tasks were designed according to the typical usage scenarios of smartwatches. Study 1 set up a number identification task according to the health monitoring scenario, and study 2 set up a message reading task according to the common reading scenario of smartwatches.

## 2 Study 1: The Legibility of Number

### 2.1 Method

**Participants.** A total of 45 participants were recruited, including 20 young participants aged 18–40, and 25 middle-aged and elderly participants aged above 40. The mean age of the young participants was 26.70 years (SD = 6.47), of which 50 percent were male. The mean age of middle-aged and older participants was 57.88 years (SD = 8.09), 12 of whom were male. All participants had experience with smart devices and subjectively reported no ocular diseases (e.g., cataract, glaucoma).

**Experiment Devices.** The experimental device is a HUAWEI WATCH 2 with a resolution of 390 × 390 and a 1.2 inches round screen size. The experimental program was developed by JavaScript. The experimental site was an outdoor open space in the Institute of Psychology, Chinese Academy of Sciences, and the range of surround lighting was 10klx–30klx. The brightness of the smartwatch changed adaptively according to the surround lighting, so that the participant's subjective perception of the screen brightness was similar.

**Experimental Design.** The study used a mixed design of 2 (age: people aged 18–40, people aged over 40) × 3 (contrast: low, medium, and high) × 3 (weight: standard, medium, and bold) × 4 (font size: small, medium, large, and ultra-large). Age was the between-participants variable. Contrast, weight, and font size were the within-participants variables. The dependent variables were correct rate, reading speed, and subjective evaluation (including clarity, comfort, and preference).

**Experimental Procedure.** The participants were asked to complete the number discrimination task under a simulated daily walking condition. The task procedure is illustrated in Fig. 1. When the watch vibrates, the participant raised the wrist (the sight distance is user's comfortable distance), and the watch appeared the unlock interface (the watch shows "Slide to continue the task<<<"). The task interface appeared after the slide, and the heart rate fluctuated randomly in the range of $[60, 75) \cup (75, 90]$. Participants needed to judge heart rate by swiping down with the index finger if the value was less than 75, otherwise swiping up. After the judgment, the screen returned to the 5–8 s waiting interface. The next vibration from the smartwatch would remind the participant to judge next heart rate value. Participants needed to complete each trial rapidly and accurately.

**Fig. 1.** Task schematic of the number discrimination task (The original characters on the interface were in Chinese and we translated for reading only in this article)

Each condition was repeated three times, and then the participant rated that condition subjectively on a five-point scale ranging from 1 to 5. The questions for clarity, comfort and preference were: 1) Can you see it clearly? (1 = Not legible at all, 5 = Very legible); 2) Is it comfortable to look at? (1 = Not comfortable at all, 5 = Very comfortable); 3) Do you like the size and style? (1 = Not at all, 5 = Very much). Participants can use their finger to evaluate, then they can swipe left to start the next question. There was also a 5–8 s waiting interval between each font condition. As weight and font size changed, the other text would be enlarged or reduced in the same proportion. The order of these conditions was balanced among participants.

## 2.2 Results

**The Effect of Font on Behavioral Performance Indicators.** Correct rate and reaction time were objective behavioral indicators, and the results were analyzed using repeated measured ANOVAs. The data of the wrong answer trials were removed from the calculation of RTs, and the results of multiple comparisons were corrected according to Bonferroni. The main effect of font size on correct rate was significant ($F(3, 108) = 10.06$, $p < 0.001$, $\eta_p^2 = 0.19$). The correct rate in the condition of small font size was significantly lower than medium ($p = 0.004$), large ($p = 0.004$), and ultra large sizes ($p = 0.008$), with no significant differences between other sizes. Meanwhile, the main effect of font size on RT was significant ($F(3, 108) = 33.11$, $p < 0.001$, $\eta_p^2 = 0.48$). The RT in small size condition was significantly longer than medium size ($p < 0.001$), the RT in medium size condition was significantly longer than large size ($p = 0.035$), and there was no statistically significant difference of RT between conditions of large and ultra-large size.

The main effect of weight on RT was significant ($F(2, 72) = 5.83$, $p = 0.004$, $\eta_p^2 = 0.14$). Standard weight had a significantly longer RT than medium weight ($p < 0.001$). There was no significant difference in the correct rate of each weight.

The main effect of contrast on correct rate was significant ($F(2, 72) = 3.41$, $p = 0.038$, $\eta_p^2 = 0.07$). The correct rate of low contrast was slightly less than high contrast ($p = 0.025$). Contrast had a significant main effect on RT ($F(2, 72) = 36.61$, $p < 0.001$, $\eta_p^2 = 0.50$). Low contrast differed significantly from medium and high contrast ($ps < 0.001$). However, there is no significant difference between medium and high contrast.

There was a second-order interaction effect between font size, contrast, and weight on RT. Specifically, the interaction effect between contrast and the font size was significant

($F(6, 216) = 5.08$, $p < 0.001$, $\eta_p^2 = 0.12$). Simple effect analysis revealed that the RT of small, medium and large font sizes decreased significantly at low contrast, and the RT reached the best at large font size. No significant difference between the RTs of large font size and ultra-large font size was observed. At medium and high contrast, the RT of the small font was significantly longer than other font sizes, but there was no significant difference between medium, large and ultra-large font sizes. The interaction effect between weight and contrast was significant ($F(4, 144) = 2.52$, $p = 0.044$, $\eta_p^2 = 0.066$); only at low contrast, the RT of standard weight was significantly longer than that of medium weight and bold ($p_1 = 0.012$, $p_2 = 0.044$); at medium and high contrast, the RTs of the three weights were not significantly different. There was no interaction effect between font size, contrast, and weight on correct rate.

**The Effect of Age on Behavioral Performance Indicators.** Age was a significant variable affecting behavioral performance. The correct rate for over-40 age group was significantly lower than that for 18–40 age group ($F(1, 36) = 13.05$, $p = 0.001$, $\eta_p^2 = 0.23$), and RT for over-40 age group was significantly slower than that for 18–40 age group ($F(1, 36) = 35.98$, $p < 0.001$, $\eta_p^2 = 0.50$). Font size and age had interaction effect on correct rate $F(3, 108) = 10.76$, $p < 0.001$, $\eta_p^2 = 0.20$, and RT ($F(3, 108) = 13.94$, $p < 0.001$, $\eta_p^2 = 0.28$). For the 18–40 age group, there were no significant differences in RT or correct rate for the four font sizes. For the over-40 age group, the correct rate of small font size judgment was only 75% (SD = 2.9%), which was significantly lower than the other font sizes. The RT decreased significantly with the increase of font size, and there was no significant difference between the RTs of large font size and ultra-large font size. Age and contrast interacted significantly on RT ($F(2, 72) = 7.22$, $p < 0.001$, $\eta_p^2 = 0.50$). RT was significantly longer for low contrast than for medium and high contrast ($p_1 = 0.023$, $p_2 = 0.014$) for people aged 18–40, while there was no significant difference between medium and high contrast. For people aged over 40, the RT declined significantly with the increase of contrast.

Contrast × font size × age third-order interaction effect was significant ($F(6, 216) = 2.58$, $p = 0.020$, $\eta_p^2 = 0.07$, presented in Fig. 2). Simple simple effects analysis found the interaction effect between contrast and font size is significant on both age groups. For participants aged 18–40, the RT for the small font size was significantly longer than the other font sizes at low contrast; at medium and high contrast, there was no significant difference between the font sizes. For participants aged over 40, the RT of small, medium, and large font sizes decreased significantly at low contrast, and there was no significant difference between the RT of large font size and ultra-large font size. At medium and high contrast, the RT of small font sizes was significantly longer than that of other font sizes, but there was no significant difference between medium, large, and ultra-large font sizes.

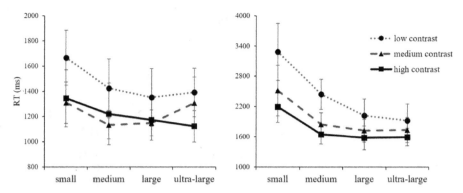

**Fig. 2.** RTs for each font size at low, medium, and high contrast for the young group (left) and the middle-aged and elderly group (right). The error bar in the figure indicates the 95% confidence interval.

**Subjective Evaluation Indicators.** Clarity, comfort, and preference were subjective evaluations of the participants. Repeated ANOVAs were conducted to analyze these three dependent variables, and the results of multiple comparisons were corrected according to Bonferroni. The results showed that the main effects of font size, contrast, and weight were all significant. Table 1 provides an overview of statistical values.

For font size, a positive correlation between the subjective evaluation and font size were found ($ps < 0.001$). Subjective evaluations at low contrast were significantly lower than medium and high contrast, while there was no significant difference between that of medium and high contrast.

Clarity and comfort were slightly lower for standard weights than for bold, with no significant differences for other weights; preference for standard weights was significantly lower than for medium weights and bold, with no significant differences for medium and bold. The interaction effect between contrast and font size was significant ($F(6, 216) = 3.34$, $p = 0.003$, $\eta_p^2 = 0.07$). For small font sizes, clarity was significantly higher for low, medium, and high contrast in that order; for medium font sizes, low contrast clarity ratings were significantly lower than high contrast, and the difference was not significant in other cases; for large and ultra-large font size, there was no significant difference between the three contrasts.

The interactions effect between weight and font size were significant for all three subjective evaluations. For small font size, there was no significant difference in the clarity ratings of each weight, and the mean values were all less than 3; for medium font size, the evaluation score of standard weight was significantly lower than bold; for large font size, the evaluation score of standard weight was significantly lower than medium weight and bold. In terms of comfort and preference, the subjective ratings of standard weights were significantly lower than bold at small and medium font sizes; at large font size, the subjective ratings of standard weights were significantly lower than medium weights. At ultra-large font sizes, there was no significant difference in the subjective ratings of each weight. The specific ratings of the subjective evaluation varied greatly among individuals, and the trends of ratings on each variable were similar across ages. Thus, the results of age-related subjective ratings were not shown in this section.

**Table 1.** Statistical values of main effects for subjective evaluation of digital discrimination tasks

| Independent variable | Clarity | | Comfort | | Preference | |
|---|---|---|---|---|---|---|
| | $F$ | $\eta_p^2$ | $F$ | $\eta_p^2$ | $F$ | $\eta_p^2$ |
| Font size | $98.18^{***}$ | 0.70 | $100.85^{***}$ | 0.70 | $82.26^{***}$ | 0.66 |
| Contrast | $11.64^{***}$ | 0.21 | $11.81^{***}$ | 0.22 | $10.53^{***}$ | 0.17 |
| Weight | $5.71^{**}$ | 0.12 | $6.79^{**}$ | 0.14 | $7.74^{**}$ | 0.15 |

*Note.* \*\*\* for significance $p < 0.001$, \*\* for significance $p < 0.01$, \* for significance $p < 0.05$

## 3   Study 2: The Legibility of Chinese Characters

### 3.1   Method

**Participants.** Participants in this study were the same as in Study 1, and the order of whether participate conducted study1 or 2 first was balanced.

**Devices and Materials.** The experimental equipment and site were the same as in Study 1.

The reading materials were compiled by the researchers and consisted of 90 messages (about 15 words) containing the sender, time, place, or event. For example, '<Liu\*\*>: Is the three o 'clock meeting this afternoon on the fifth floor?', '<Huang\*\*>: I'm going to Guangzhou on business for a few days, see you next week!', etc.

**Experimental Design.** The Chinese character legibility study used a mixed design of 2 (age: people aged 18–40, people aged over 40) × 3 (contrast: low, medium, and high) × 3 (weight: standard, medium, and bold) × 5 (font size: very small, small, medium, large, and ultra-large; Here, the naming is similar to that in Study 1, however, the actual size is not the same). Age was the between-participants variable; contrast, weight, and font size were the within-participants variables. The dependent variables were correct rate, reading speed, and subjective evaluation (including clarity, comfort, and preference).

**Experiment Procedure.** The participants were asked to complete the message reading under a simulated daily walking condition. The task procedure is illustrated in Fig. 3. When the watch vibrated, the participant raised wrist (the distance is as far as the user feels comfortable), and the watch appeared the unlock interface (the watch shows 'Slide to continue the task<<<'). After the participant swiped left, the task interface appeared. Participants needed to read the text message and swipe left to indicate the end of the reading. The experiment program would ask questions about the text message, and the participant would choose one answer. The participant would complete this task twice for the same condition. At the end of the two reading tasks, the participant would evaluate the font subjectively as same as Study 1.

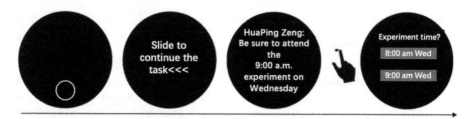

**Fig. 3.** Task schematic of Message Reading Task (The original characters on the interface were in Chinese and we translated for reading only in this article)

## 3.2  Results

**Behavioral Performance Indicators.** The correct rate and reading speed as two objective behavioral indicators were analyzed using repeated measured ANOVAs. Reading speed was calculated by the number of words in the message divided by the reading time. The incorrect trials were removed, and the results of multiple comparisons were Bonferroni corrected.

For correct rate, the main effect of contrast was significant ($F(2, 86) = 7.17$, $p = 0.001$, $\eta_p^2 = 0.14$); high contrast lead to a significantly higher correct rate than low and medium contrast ($p_1 = 0.004$, $p_2 = 0.007$), however, the effects of low and medium contrast were not significantly different. The main effect of weight was significant ($F(2, 86) = 5.42$, $p = 0.006$, $\eta_p^2 = 0.11$); the correct rate of standard weight was significantly lower than moderate weight, and moderate weight was not significantly different from bold. The main effect of font size was significant ($F(4, 172) = 18.57$, $p < 0.001$, $\eta_p^2 = 0.30$). The youth population had significantly higher correct rate than the middle-aged and elderly population ($p < 0.001$). The interaction between age and font size was significant ($F(4, 172) = 10.17$, $p < 0.001$, $\eta_p^2 = 0.19$). For the middle-aged and older cohorts, there was no significant difference in the correct rate of each font size; for the middle-aged and older cohorts, the mean correct rate of the very small font size was 61%, slightly higher than the random level. Both the very small and small font correct rate were significantly smaller than the medium font, with the medium font reaching the highest correct rate and no significant differences between the other font sizes. For the dependent variable of reading speed, the main effect of weight was significant ($F(2, 86) = 6.80$, $p = 0.002$, $\eta_p^2 = 0.14$); the reading speed of standard weight was lower than that of moderate weight ($p = 0.001$). The main effect of contrast was not significant. The main effect of font size on reading speed was significant ($F(4, 172) = 10.55$, $p < 0.001$, $\eta_p^2 = 0.20$). The interaction effect between font size and age was significant ($F(4, 172) = 7.84$, $p < 0.001$, $\eta_p^2 = 0.15$). For the young group, there was no significant difference in the correct rate of each font size. For the middle-aged and older groups, the reading speeds for very small and small font sizes were instead much greater than for other font sizes; there was no significant difference in reading speeds for medium, large, and ultra-large font sizes. Combined with the correct rate, this may be due to the inability of the elderly to recognize the message in the text with very small and small font sizes, which made them slide right directly. Meanwhile, because the option of this task is binary, participants had a high probability of getting the right answer by guessing. Deleting wrong trial data could not thoroughly eliminate this bias, thus, the reading speed of relatively small font size seemed very high.

**Subjective Evaluation Indicators.** We performed repeated measured ANOVAs on the three dependent variables of clarity, comfort, and preference. Results of the multiple comparisons were Bonferroni corrected. The main effect results are shown in Table 2. The main effects of contrast were all significant on subjective ratings. Low contrast has significantly lower subjective ratings than both medium and high contrast, and no significant differences between medium and high contrast. The clarity and comfort ratings of bold were slightly higher than those of medium weight, and the main effect of weight on preference was not significant. The main effect of font size on subjective ratings was significant, and there was an interaction effect between font size and age for clarity ($F(4, 172) = 5.72, p < 0.001, \eta_p^2 = 0.12$), comfort ($F(4, 172) = 5.72, p < 0.001, \eta_p^2 = 0.12$), and preference ($F(4, 172) = 5.72, p < 0.001, \eta_p^2 = 0.12$). For participants aged over 40, clarity, comfort, and preference ratings increased significantly with increasing font size, with no significant differences in subjective ratings between large and ultra-large font size, as shown in Fig. 4. For participants aged 18–40, clarity ratings showed an overall upward trend, with a significant increase in clarity for very small, small, and medium font sizes, but no significant differences between medium, large, and ultra-large font sizes, as shown in Fig. 4 (Left). The comfort rating of very small, small, and medium sizes increased significantly, and there was no significant difference between medium, large and ultra-large size. Ultra-large sizes decreased slightly in value than large sizes, see Fig. 4 (middle). For the young group, the preference level increased as the size rose, and there was no significant difference between medium and large size, and the rating of ultra-large size decreased significantly, see Fig. 4 (right).

**Table 2.** Statistical values of main effects for subjective evaluation of message reading task

| Independent variable | Clarity | | Comfort | | Preference | |
|---|---|---|---|---|---|---|
| | $F$ | $\eta_p^2$ | $F$ | $\eta_p^2$ | $F$ | $\eta_p^2$ |
| Font size | 73.14*** | 0.63 | 90.14*** | 0.68 | 72.09*** | 0.63 |
| Contrast | 6.13** | 0.13 | 7.66** | 0.15 | 5.57** | 0.12 |
| Weight | 5.28** | 0.11 | 4.39* | 0.09 | 1.08 | 0.34 |

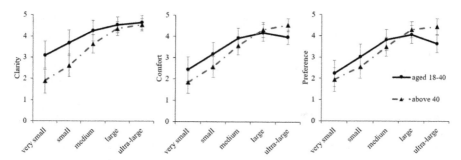

**Fig. 4.** Evaluation of clarity (left), comfort (middle) and preference (right) of each font size by age group. *Note.* The error bar in the figure indicates the 95% confidence interval.

## 4 Discussion

This study comprehensively examined the text-legibility effects of font factors (font size, contrast, and weight), as well as the user factor of age, on small-screen devices. It is found that font factors affected user behavioral performance and subjective evaluations most, for both numbers and Chinese characters. Meanwhile, these effects specifically vary across age groups.

Outdoor natural light conditions and walking conditions were used as the experiment environment to study the factors affecting text legibility. It was found that the most influential factor on legibility is still the font size, which is consistent with previous literature [11]. Sufficiently large font size is the basis for ensuring that users can receive the information in the text. In contrast, too low levels are not advisable, which will affect recognition and comfort. When the contrast was greater than a critical value, behavioral performance and subjective evaluation were better and did not differ much from any higher levels. However, former studies of legibility conducted indoor have found medium contrast to be optimal. When the contrast is raised above a certain value, performance may decline [17, 18]. The reason may be that the illuminance of outdoor environments is much higher than that indoor, and the contrast between high-contrast text and ambient light is diminished, thus, the performance level was not reduced. This stresses the necessity of thorough consideration of the specific practice environment of usability research. We found that weight had a subtle effect on legibility. In addition, the lowest level weight has a smaller effect than the other two. Thus, very thin font should be avoided in practice.

The interaction effects between font size, contrast, and weight are worthy to consider. When one design factor is at a lower level (such as, very small font size), the effects on the behavioral performance of other variables are more evident. For example, for small font size, low contrast reduced legibility, while the effect of contrast was not significant for large font size. In practice, when a small font size must be used for improving the utilization of small screen, increasing the contrast is an acceptable way to ensure text-legibility.

Age is a crucial factor affecting legibility. In general, people aged over 40 had a longer RT and relatively lower correct rate. The reason is the decrease in both cognitive ability and motor performance as getting older [23]. More importantly, the interaction effect of age and font factors were found. For the people aged 18–40, the font size did not affect behavioral performance. For people aged over 40, difficulties in recognizing numbers at small font sizes were manifested by an evident decrease in behavioral performance; in the case of Chinese characters, very small and small font sizes are almost impossible to read. In other words, Chinese characters that can be recognized by the young group may be hard to read for the elderly. Thus, the range of text specification design should be carefully adjusted according to the oriented users in practical applications. Although different age groups showed higher subjective evaluations of large font size and high contrast, the Chinese characters still showed differences in subjective evaluations among different groups. The subjective ratings for people aged over 40 increased linearly with increasing font size. However, for the younger people, the preference declined if the font size was too large. We believe these results will shed light on the design of elderly-oriented products and designs targeted at different age groups.

Moreover, there were differences in the relationships between different dependent variables and independent variables. Specifically, in the case of font size, for example, behavioral performance showed a curve that raised and then flattened out as the font size increased (i.e., behavioral performance reached stability when the text was clearly identified). On the contrary, subjective evaluations usually increased linearly with increasing font size, while there still were subtle differences in individual subjective evaluations of clarity, comfort, and preference. In addition, reading speed or accuracy are less sensitive to detect the effect of different factors in message reading task. Many human factors researchers have similarly found that reading tasks are not sufficiently sensitive as an objective indicator. This makes experiments to compare differences between conditions using subjective ratings only [9, 24]. This may be because reading is a complicated cognitive process whose factors mask the differences introduced by the font design. Moreover, low correlations between subjective evaluation and behavioral performance were found in several domains of psychology [25]. Legibility is a concept containing various meaning. Designers and researchers should use multi-assessment to choose suitable parameters for interface.

There are several limitations and some suggestions for future directions. In this study, we explored two age groups: young, middle-aged and elderly. Such a division can initially show the criteria that apply to users of different ages are inconsistent. Future studies can try to expand the sample size and make a more detailed classification by age to obtain more targeted design specifications. In this increasingly serious aging society, adopting the right parameters for wearable devices to meet the needs of the elderly has great significant. In addition, the most widely used wearable device, the smartwatch, was selected as the device in this study. However, there are variations in screen size and other aspects among various watches, which indicate the results obtained need to be re-considered in the application process in relation to the specific device.

## 5 Conclusion

This study investigated the effects of font size, contrast and weight on the text-legibility of wearable devices for different age groups. The following conclusions were obtained: (1) The effect of font size on legibility is the greatest. The interaction effect of age and font factors were found. For people aged over 40, the application of large font should be considered first. For people aged 18–40, the use of ultra-large font size of Chinese characters for reading should be avoided; (2) the proper increase of contrast can eliminate the negative effect from small font size on legibility (3) The impact of weight on legibility is subtle, and the use of very thin weight should be avoided.

**Acknowledgment.** This work was supported by National Natural Science Foundation of China (52072406). We are particularly grateful to the support of the Huawei & Chinese Academy of Sciences UX Design Human Factors joint Lab.

# References

1. Iqbal, S.M., Mahgoub, I., Du, E., Leavitt, M.A., Asghar, W.: Advances in healthcare wearable devices. npj Flexible Electron. **5**(1), 1–14 (2021)
2. Hayes, S.T., Hooten, E.R., Adams, J.A. (eds.) Tablet interaction accuracy and precision: seated vs. walking. In: Proceedings of the human factors and ergonomics society annual meeting. SAGE Publications Sage CA, Los Angeles, CA (2014)
3. Dingler, T., Rzayev, R., Schwind, V., Henze, N. (eds.) RSVP on the go: implicit reading support on smart watches through eye tracking. In: Proceedings of the 2016 ACM International Symposium on Wearable Computers (2016)
4. Ou, L.C., Sun, P.L., Huang, H.P., Ronnier, L.M.: Visual comfort as a function of lightness difference between text and background: a cross-age study using an LCD and a tablet computer. Color. Res. Appl. **40**(2), 125–134 (2015)
5. Pizza, S., Brown, B., McMillan, D., Lampinen, A. (eds.) Smartwatch in vivo. In: Proceedings of the 2016 CHI Conference on Human Factors in Computing Systems (2016)
6. Chun, J., Dey, A., Lee, K., Kim, S.: A qualitative study of smartwatch usage and its usability. Hum. Factors Ergon. Manuf. Serv. Indus. **28**(4), 186–199 (2018)
7. Nielsen, J.: Legibility, Readability and comprehension: making users read your words (2015). https://www.nngroup.com/articles/legibility-readability-comprehension. Accessed 30 Dec 2021
8. Zhao, Y., Ding, L., Li, Y., Ran, L. (eds.) The effect of font size, age and lighting environment on Chinese character legibility. In: 2016 9th International Congress on Image and Signal Processing, BioMedical Engineering and Informatics (CISP-BMEI), IEEE (2016)
9. Darroch, I., Goodman, J., Brewster, S., Gray, P.: The effect of age and font size on reading text on handheld computers. In: Costabile, M.F., Paternò, F. (eds.) Human-Computer Interaction - INTERACT 2005, pp. 253–266. Springer Berlin Heidelberg, Berlin, Heidelberg (2005). https://doi.org/10.1007/11555261_23
10. Bernard, M.L., Chaparro, B.S., Mills, M.M., Halcomb, C.G.: Comparing the effects of text size and format on the readability of computer-displayed Times New Roman and Arial text. Int. J. Hum Comput Stud. **59**(6), 823–835 (2003)
11. Dobres, J., Wolfe, B., Chahine, N., Reimer, B.: The effects of visual crowding, text size, and positional uncertainty on text legibility at a glance. Appl. Ergon. **70**, 240–246 (2018)
12. Chan, A., Lee, P.: Effect of display factors on Chinese reading times, comprehension scores and preferences. Behav. Inform. Technol. **24**(2), 81–91 (2005)
13. Liu, N., Yu, R., Zhang, Y.: Effects of font size, stroke width, and character complexity on the legibility of Chinese characters. Hum. Factors and Ergon. Manuf. Serv. Indus. **26**(3), 381–392 (2016)

14. Lin, H., Wu, F.-G., Cheng, Y.-Y.: Legibility and visual fatigue affected by text direction, screen size and character size on color LCD e-reader. Displays **34**(1), 49–58 (2013)
15. Ayama, M., Ujike, H., Iwai, W., Funakawa, M., Okajima, K.: Effects of contrast and character size upon legibility of Japanese text stimuli presented on visual display terminal. Opt. Rev. **14**(1), 48–56 (2007)
16. Lin, C.-C., Huang, K.-C.: Effects of color combination and ambient illumination on visual perception time with TFT-LCD. Percept. Mot. Skills **109**(2), 607–625 (2009)
17. Roufs, J.A., Boschman, M.C.: Text quality metrics for visual display units: I. Methodological aspects. Displays **18**(1), 37–43 (1997)
18. Zhu, Z., Wu, J.: On the standardization of VDT's proper and optimal contrast range. Ergonomics **33**(7), 925–932 (1990)
19. Burmistrov, I., Zlokazova, T., Ishmuratova, I., Semenova, M. (eds.) Legibility of light and ultra-light fonts: eyetracking study. In: Proceedings of the 9th Nordic conference on human-computer interaction (2016)
20. Dobres, J., Reimer, B., Chahine, N. (eds.) The effect of font weight and rendering system on glance-based text legibility. In: Proceedings of the 8th international conference on automotive user interfaces and interactive vehicular applications (2016)
21. Pitt, M., Rawles, J.: The effect of age on saccadic latency and velocity. Neuroophthalmology **8**(3), 123–129 (1988)
22. Fozard, J.L.: Vision and hearing in aging. Handbook Psychol. Aging **3**, 143–156 (1990)
23. Sleimen-Malkoun, R., Temprado, J.-J., Berton, E.: Age-related dedifferentiation of cognitive and motor slowing: insight from the comparison of Hick-Hyman and Fitts' laws. Front. Aging Neurosci. **5**, 62 (2013)
24. Heinz, M., et al.: Perceptions of technology among older adults. J. Gerontol. Nurs. **39**(1), 42–51 (2013)
25. Dang, J., King, K.M., Inzlicht, M.: Why are self-report and behavioral measures weakly correlated? Trends Cogn. Sci. **24**(4), 267–269 (2020)

# Aesthetic Preference in the Composition Ratios of Graphic Designs

Yao-Sheng Wu[✉]

Department of Industrial Design, National Cheng Kung University, Tainan, Taiwan, R.O.C.
neilwu0906@gmail.com

**Abstract.** For the golden ratio, there has been extensive development in design, aesthetics and fields. What is regarded as the "perfect ratio" is indeed found in many experiments and is not the most preferred ratio. But if you look at it from another point of view, perhaps this is the ratio that people are most accustomed to, because there are many relationships of the golden ratio hidden in nature, so the golden ratio still has its value in use. Therefore, it is assumed that the golden ratio is the favorite ratio of human beings, and by manipulating specific ratios in different presentation methods, the influence of the golden ratio on human preferences is discussed. The experimental design was divided into a two-factor within-subject design of 3 (ratio, 1.25, 1.618, and 2) × 3 (presentation, thumbnails of web pages, figures and backgrounds, and thumbnails of internal scales). It is divided into two stages. In the first stage, the aesthetic preference score of a single image is used as the dependent variable, and the second stage is based on the relative aesthetic preference score as the dependent variable. Experimental results in both stages, the effect of presentation method has a significant impact. While the effect of proportionality had no significant effect in the first stage, it had near-significant results in the second stage. This can indicate that evaluating an image does not seem to have much effect on manipulating proportions. However, if you compare images of different scales at a time, it seems to be better at distinguishing the difference in the degree of preference for different scales. Compared with previous studies, almost all experiments are designed in a similar way to the first stage, so such results have room for discussion. However, the data of this experiment are too small, so the presumption of the results cannot be reliable and valid.

**Keywords:** Display design · Aesthetic preference · Golden ratio · Composition · Graphic design

## 1 Introduction

The evolution of aesthetic concepts has been continuously updated with the needs and preferences of the times, and several of the aesthetic concepts that have continued from ancient times to the present seem to have become the "standards" of aesthetics. The principle of composition is an important aesthetic presentation technique. The application of compositional principles in aesthetics has long been quite common, and its application level has extended to many different fields. The most common technique is to present the main object to be emphasized at a specific position in the picture, and the specific position is based on the composition principle so that the distance and proportion between the main object and the border of the picture can have a more suitable relative relationship.

One of the most famous ratios in the composition principle is the Golden Section, or the Golden Ratio. The golden ratio was originally a proportional relationship from the Fibonacci sequence to the limit value, about 1.618. Then it was discovered that the golden ratio has many beautiful properties in mathematical principles, such as the golden rectangle, infinite series and so on. (Falbo 2005). Then such a ratio was used in the design of artistic aesthetics, and was euphemistically called "the most perfect ratio", thus opening the meaning of the golden ratio being widely used in various fields. Its principles can be seen not only in the aesthetic creation of painting, photography, architecture, etc., but also affect the aesthetics of many fields, such as: medicine, media image design and so on. Even in nature, many relationships that conform to the golden ratio can be found, such as the growth angle of plant stems and leaves, the division relationship of animal cells, or the growth base of spotted animals, etc.

In early psychological experiments, it was confirmed that the compositional ratio of the golden ratio is aesthetically preferred (Benjafield and Adams 1976). But such a result does not prove that the preference for composition is directly influenced by the composition principle of the golden ratio. (Boselie 1997). And when people judge the ratio, there is no special acuity to feel the golden ratio. It seems that the range close to this ratio can be evaluated by similar preferences (Tang Dalun 2004). The Implicit Association Test (IAT) was also used to explore the implicit liking of real works of art, and the results were also insignificant (Stieger and Swami 2015).

Although many studies have pointed out that the golden ratio may not be an absolutely perfect composition principle, but will vary according to individual differences. However, it still has a great influence on the proportion of use in various fields. I divide the possible reasons for this into two. First, it may be the influence of the "glorification of the golden ratio". Because such a ratio has existed in both aesthetics and various fields from ancient times to the present, and it has even been dubbed the "perfect ratio like gold". Because of the reputation of the golden ratio, we naturally associate the concept of the golden ratio with the perfect ratio. Another point of view, perhaps the golden ratio feels more like it, is because of the relationship we are more familiar with such a ratio. In nature, we often come into contact with structures or forms composed of the golden ratio, such as the human body, the proportions of teeth, the golden thread and so on. Therefore, our preference for the golden ratio may come from the fact that we are familiar with such ratios. For these two possible reasons, we believe that the golden ratio is still favored in most cases.

## 1.1  Purpose

Whether the influence of the golden ratio can really produce a preference for aesthetic feeling is the topic that this research wants to explore. Therefore, different design techniques are used to discuss the presentation of the ratio. This study wondered if the golden ratio could be subject to higher subjective aesthetic preference scores when the golden ratio was used as a benchmark for design ratios. And we use modern elements as the medium we want to present, which is more in line with the concepts and methods of modern design. For example, the presentation of web design, the design of app thumbnails, and the design of simple icons, etc., let the subjects rate the aesthetic preference of different presentation methods of specific proportions. We also expect designs based on the golden ratio to have higher aesthetic preference scores.

Therefore, this study aims to clarify the relationship between aesthetic preference and composition ratio, especially the golden ratio. It is assumed that the composition ratio of the golden ratio is aesthetically preferred, in advance, through the display of different graphic designs in the 3 composition ratios, it is possible to explore the influence of these ratios on people's preferences.

## 2   Method

The experimental design is divided into a two-factor within-subject design. It mixed 3 kinds of composition ratios (1.25, 1.618, and 2) with the 3 graphic designs (webpage layout, logo or symbol design using explicit ratios, and logo or symbol design using implicit ratios). There are 5 type graphic design in each condition, totally 45 stimulus materials in this study. It is divided into two stages. It is divided into two stages. The first stage uses the aesthetic preference score of a single picture as the dependent variable, and the second stage uses the relative aesthetic preference score as the dependent variable.

### 2.1   Participant

A total of 61 subjects (35 males, 26 females) were enrolled in this study, all of whom were students at National Chung Cheng University. Subjects participated in this experiment voluntarily and without any additional fee. Before the experiment, the proportion-related content of this experiment was not mentioned, and the informal research name "the differences in subjective aesthetic feelings of different people to different pictures" was used as the recruitment and explanation before the experiment.

### 2.2   Material

This experiment was a two-factor within-subject design of 3 (scale, 1.25, 1.618, and 2) × 3 (presentation, thumbnails of web pages, figures and backgrounds, and thumbnails of internal scales). It is divided into two stages. In the first stage, the aesthetic preference score of a single image is used as the dependent variable, and the second stage is based on the relative aesthetic preference score as the dependent variable.

### 2.3   Research Design

The experimental design is divided into a two-factor within-subject design. It mixed 3 kinds of composition ratios (1.25, 1.618, and 2) with the 3 graphic designs (webpage layout, logo or symbol design using explicit ratios, and logo or symbol design using implicit ratios). There are 5 type graphic design in each condition, totally 45 stimulus materials in this study. It is divided into two stages. It is divided into two stages. The first stage uses the aesthetic preference score of a single picture as the dependent variable, and the second stage uses the relative aesthetic preference score as the dependent variable.

## 2.4  Stimulus

The design concept of each stimulus: 1. thumbnails of web pages: the ratio between the reading blocks of the web page, or the ratio between the reading blocks and the blank area; 2. figures and backgrounds: the ratio with the background pattern; 3. thumbnails of internal scales: adjust the presentation of the ratio with different design concepts, such as angle ratio, area ratio, length ratio. As can see Fig. 1.

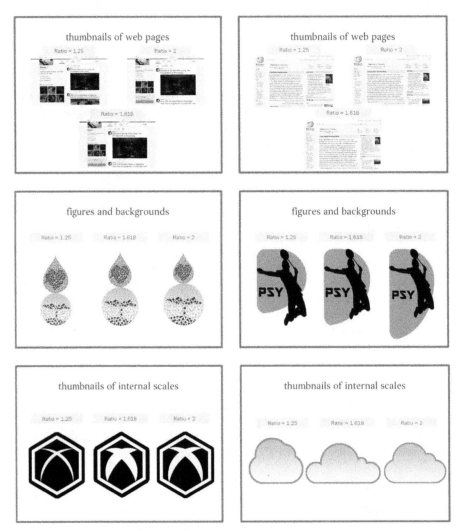

**Fig. 1.**  The stimulus examples by 3 × 3 research design

## 2.5  Procedure

In these two stages, a "+" symbol is displayed in the center of the screen (presentation time is 400 ms), which is the gaze point of the eyes. Next, in the first stage (Fig. 2), a picture had displayed in the center of the screen, and the participants were asked to drag the bar in response to their aesthetic preference score.

In the second stage (Fig. 3), two pictures randomly selected from 3 composition ratios are displayed on both sides of the screen, and participants are asked to drag the bar according to their relative relationship with aesthetics preference section. ISI = 500 ms. The scoring method is to move the mouse to control the cursor of the number line from 0

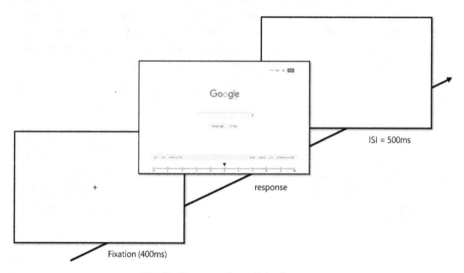

**Fig. 2.** The procedure of the first stage

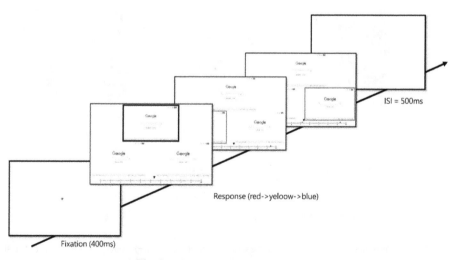

**Fig. 3.** The procedure of the first stage

to 10, and click the left button of the mouse to score the corresponding score. The order of trials was randomly arranged, and there were 12 practice questions before answering the two-stage experiment.

## 3  Result

After analyzing the obtained results, it was found that the effect of the first stage for each proportion was not significant ($p = 0.970$), but there was a significant difference in aesthetic preference for different presentation methods ($p = 0.002$). The interaction of the two independent variables was also not significant ($p = 0.989$). Such results seem to fall short of the expected assumptions, and the difference in proportions does not seem to have much of an effect when scoring a single image for subjective aesthetic preference. However, there are significant differences in the preferences of presentation methods, which means that different types of presentation methods seem to have higher or lower results due to their preferences for the pictures themselves. However, in the second stage, the effect for each scale was close to a significant effect ($p = 0.063$), and there was still a significant difference in preference ($p = 0.045$) across scale presentations. The interaction effect was also not significant ($p = 0.587$). Different from the first stage, the second stage is a relative aesthetic preference score, so when it can be directly compared with pictures of different scales, the results of the scale can be more obvious. Although the effect of the proportional variable is not significant, if the number of subjects increases and the amount of data is more complete, it may be able to achieve a significant effect. The assumption of homogeneity of variance in both stages was not significant ($p = 0.535$ and $p = 0.938$).

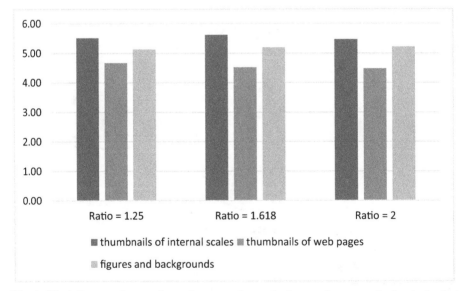

**Fig. 4.** The influence of proportion and presentation method on preference evaluation in the first stage

The descriptive statistics of each variable, stage 1 and stage 2, are attached to Tables 1 and 2 respectively (Fig. 4).

**Table 1.** Narrative statistics of the first stage

| Ratio | Layout Design | M | SD | N of items |
|---|---|---|---|---|
| 1.25 | Thumbnails of web pages | 4.65 | 0.941 | 5 |
| | Figures and backgrounds | 5.55 | 0.644 | 5 |
| | Thumbnails of internal scales | 5.08 | 0.508 | 5 |
| | SUM | 5.09 | 0.767 | 15 |
| 1.618 | Thumbnails of web pages | 4.51 | 0.933 | 5 |
| | Figures and backgrounds | 5.56 | 0.627 | 5 |
| | Thumbnails of internal scales | 5.24 | 0.391 | 5 |
| | SUM | 5.10 | 0.781 | 15 |
| 2 | Thumbnails of web pages | 4.47 | 0.826 | 5 |
| | Figures and backgrounds | 5.49 | 0.597 | 5 |
| | Thumbnails of internal scales | 5.18 | 0.593 | 5 |
| | SUM | 5.04 | 0.769 | 15 |
| SUM | Thumbnails of web pages | 4.54 | 0.838 | 15 |
| | Figures and backgrounds | 5.53 | 0.578 | 15 |
| | Thumbnails of internal scales | 5.16 | 0.472 | 15 |
| | SUM | 5.08 | 0.755 | 45 |

This result makes us wonder if the golden ratio is the most popular ratio if the manipulation of the ratio is very close to a significant effect in the second stage? We can see from Fig. 1 that the preference for the golden ratio is actually the lowest among the three different presentations. This is the opposite of what we originally expected. The same results can be obtained from descriptive statistics (means of proportions 1.25, 1.618 and 2 are: 5.144, 4.857, 5.203, respectively) (Fig. 5).

## 4   Discussion

From the results, it seems that the experimental design of the first stage, the same as that of many previous studies, is to score the aesthetic preference for pictures of different scales. And the result seems to be the same as ours, there is no particular aesthetic preference for the golden ratio. However, from the results of the second stage of the experiment, it seems that the experimental method of the first stage has a more relationship with the individual differences in the preference of the experimental method, that is, the manipulation of different presentation methods. Therefore, the results of many previous experiments on the aesthetic feeling of the golden ratio may still have a lot of room for discussion.

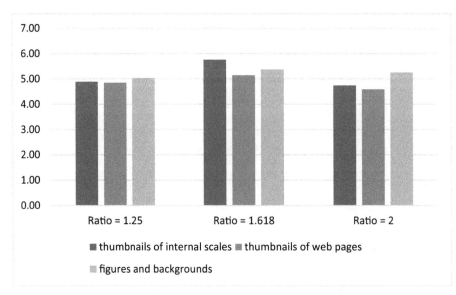

**Fig. 5.** The influence of proportion and presentation method on preference evaluation in the second stage

**Table 2.** Narrative statistics of the second stage

| Ratio | Layout Design | M | SD | N of items |
|---|---|---|---|---|
| 1.25 | Thumbnails of web pages | 5.03 | 0.541 | 5 |
| | Figures and backgrounds | 4.88 | 0.744 | 5 |
| | Thumbnails of internal scales | 4.84 | 0.268 | 5 |
| | SUM | 4.92 | 0.737 | 15 |
| 1.618 | Thumbnails of web pages | 5.37 | 0.833 | 5 |
| | Figures and backgrounds | 5.76 | 0.627 | 5 |
| | Thumbnails of internal scales | 5.15 | 0.441 | 5 |
| | SUM | 5.43 | 0.731 | 15 |
| 2 | Thumbnails of web pages | 5.58 | 0.846 | 5 |
| | Figures and backgrounds | 5.74 | 0.567 | 5 |
| | Thumbnails of internal scales | 4.74 | 0.523 | 5 |
| | SUM | 4.86 | 0.759 | 15 |
| SUM | Thumbnails of web pages | 4.54 | 0.838 | 15 |
| | Figures and backgrounds | 5.53 | 0.568 | 15 |
| | Thumbnails of internal scales | 5.16 | 0.422 | 15 |
| | SUM | 5.07 | 0.755 | 45 |

In the second stage, the comparison of images with different ratios makes the effect of ratios close to significant. However, the results obtained were the opposite of our expectations, with the lowest score on the golden ratio preference score. There are two possible reasons: First, the experiment stimulates the manipulation of materials in the golden ratio. There is no exquisite design of modern professional designers, so they are not liked. Second, there may be too little experimental data, because individual differences appear that specific data will affect the overall average. However, if the experiment can be made more certain in the future, this is still the result. That can also be explained, either when judging images at different scales individually, or when comparing designs at other scales simultaneously. There is no proof that the golden ratio is people's favorite ratio. Perhaps as long as the ratio is close to the golden ratio, it can still make people have more preferences for beauty. These can be discussed in future research.

In addition, this experiment is controlling the internal validity (internal validity), because the number of data is too small, so the result analysis is easily affected by a small number of extreme quality. And the interview after the experiment also asked about the data of the subjects who responded in line with the experiment. However, since the amount of data is too small, it is still processed with reservations. And in the experimental stage, it is easily affected by the expected effect of the subjects, and the scores made are not really what they like. This would make the results less inferentially valid. In the control of external validity (external validity), because the subjects are all students of the Department of Psychology of Chung Cheng University, there may be biases due to a non-representative sample. In terms of construct validity, perhaps the stimuli pictures we designed cannot represent the golden ratio method used in modern design. Therefore, the experimental manipulation may be very successful, and it cannot be analogized to modern design concepts. These are all areas that need to be noted and improved when conducting this experiment in the future.

# References

Dalun, T.: Exploring the psychological substance of golden ratio aesthetics by response variation. Chin. J. Advert. **9**, 134–142 (2004)

Boselie, F.: The golden section and the shape of objects. Empir. Stud. Arts **15**(2), 131–141 (1997)

Benjafield, J., Adams-Webber, J.: The golden section hypothesis. Br. J. Psychol. **67**(1), 11–15 (1976)

Falbo, C.: The golden ratio—a contrary viewpoint. Coll. Math. J. **36**(2), 123–134 (2005)

Stieger, S., Swami, V.: Time to let go? No automatic aesthetic preference for the golden ratio in art pictures. Psychol. Aesthet. Creat. Arts **9**(1), 91 (2015)

# Cognition at Work

# Influence of Technostress on Work Engagement and Job Performance During Remote Working

Michele Di Dalmazi⬛, Marco Mandolfo(⬛) ⬛, Chiara Stringhini⬛, and Debora Bettiga⬛

Department of Management, Economics and Industrial Engineering, Politecnico di Milano, Via Lambruschini 4/B, 20156 Milan, Italy
{michele.didalmazi,marco.mandolfo,debora.bettiga}@polimi.it,
chiara.stringhini@mail.polimi.it

**Abstract.** The Covid-19 pandemic forced millions of people worldwide to engage in remote working practices, and several organisations are expected to continue adopting work-from-home even in the post-pandemic scenario. This phenomenon has highlighted the importance of human-technology interaction in enabling telework, but it has also increased awareness about the potential adverse effects of information and communication technologies (ICTs) on employees' wellbeing. Even if recent literature has delved into these consequences in terms of technostress, there has been little quantitative analysis within the telework literature. The present study aims to fill this gap by introducing and testing an empirical model grounding on a transactional-based model of stress. We assess the influence of three techno-stressors (i.e., techno-overload, techno-complexity, and techno-invasion), two typologies of individual psychological responses as mediator variables (i.e., affective and cognitive strain), and individuals' work outcomes (i.e., work engagement and job performance). We collected self-reports through survey research involving a sample of 135 remote workers. Data was analysed using Partial Least Square – Structural Equation Modeling. The results show that techno-overload positively influences affective strain, techno-invasion positively influences both affective and cognitive strain, while techno-complexity positively influences cognitive strain. Further, we show that cognitive strain negatively affects both work engagement and job performance, while affective strain negatively influences only job performance. Possible stress coping strategies based on the redesign of the working environment and mindfulness practices to inhibit techno-stressors are discussed. Also, we discuss how adaptive systems tracking individual behavioral and cognitive strain can create positive feedback loops to enhance individual wellbeing.

**Keywords:** Technostress · Stress · Remote working · Home office · Personal wellbeing · Technology

## 1 Introduction

The evolution of technology has impacted a plethora of fields without neglecting the professional one. Over the last decades, information and communication technologies

(ICTs) have allowed telework to constantly evolve and diversify, providing organisations with manifold possibilities in terms of where, when, and how work can be performed. Moreover, during 2020 and early 2021, the outbreak of the Covid-19 pandemic forced a sizable portion of organisations to introduce mandatory remote working practices, permanently modifying the perception of the physical and temporal dimensions of the workplace by the employees. This phenomenon has underscored the relevance of human-technology interaction to enable work-from-home, but it has also raised awareness about the side effects that ICT-mediated telework could have on employees' wellbeing. Transitioning to home offices and employing ICTs to cooperate with colleagues has reportedly led to a fragmentation of work and influenced individuals' emotional stability, fatigue, and stress [1, 2].

In 1984, Brod defined technostress for the first time as "a modern disease of adaptation caused by an inability to cope with the new computer technologies in a healthy manner" [3]. So far, different studies have investigated technology-driven stressors which might induce strain and produce job-related outcomes in the workplace (e.g., [4, 5]) but less attention has been paid to remote-working settings. The unprecedented change that emerged from the pandemic offered the unique opportunity to study technology-human relationship. Research has shown that in nearly the 50% of organisations, the 81% of the employees had worked remotely during the coronavirus pandemic [6]. Interestingly, the same study revealed that about 40% of employees estimated to work remotely even in the post-emergency scenario. Hence, to see remote working as a viable alternative for the foreseeable future, it is essential to evaluate the long-term impacts of technology-driven stressors on individuals' wellbeing and organizational performance. To the best of our knowledge, there has been little quantitative analysis within the telework literature investigating the relationship between techno-stressors, individual psychological responses, and outcomes in terms of employees' work engagement and performance in the workplace.

The present study aims to fill this gap by assessing the influence of three techno-stressors (i.e., techno-overload, techno-complexity, and techno-invasion), two typologies of individual psychological responses as mediator variables (i.e., cognitive and affective strain), and individuals' work outcomes (i.e., work engagement and job performance).

## 2   Background

Even if remote working has become popular in recent years due to COVID-19 emergency, the practice is older in time. The first conceptualisation dates back to 1970s, when Jack Nilles shaped the notion of "telecommuting network" as the assembly of "computational and telecommunications components which enable employees of large organisations to work in offices close to (but generally not in) their homes, rather than commute long distances to a central office" [7]. During the COVID-19 pandemic, internet-based services became the primary mean to communicate, interact, and accomplish job task. However, prior research has described that certain processes may be accountable for delivering adverse reactions to ICTs. These processes can be summarised under the wide concept of "technostress". Technostress is an IT user's experience of stress when using technologies [5]. Hence, investigations on technostress are rooted in previous studies on general work stress. In the present paper we investigate such a construct following a transactional-based conceptualisation of stress [8]. With this end, we formulate a conceptual framework that encompasses three layers, namely techno-stressors, psychological strain, and organisational outcomes. These are illustrated in Fig. 1 and discussed in the following.

## 2.1 Techno-Stressors

Techno-stressors are those technology-related factors that may create strain [5]. In 2007, Tarafdar and colleagues identified five techno-stressors that have been widely discussed by the majority of cross-sectional studies [4]. Those factors are techno-overload, techno-invasion, techno-complexity, techno-insecurity, and techno-uncertainty. Since the present study aims at investigating the effect of technostress caused by telework practices during the COVID-19 period, three techno-stressors are considered: techno-overload, techno-complexity, and techno-invasion. Indeed, techno-insecurity and techno-uncertainty relate most directly to the organisation's workplace, resulting in less suitable items to be investigated in the remote working environment.

First, techno-overload can be defined as ICTs' potential to force users to work more, faster, and longer. This situation may elicit a change in work habits through the imposition of more work to be handled within very tight time schedules [9]. Second, techno-invasion is the ICTs' effect of invading users' personal lives through constant connectivity. The continuous exposure to information conveyed by ICTs leads workers to be constantly accessible, resulting in individual's losing control of time and space [4]. This situation presents many adverse effects on the individuals. For instance, a study noted that workers' perception of being constantly "on-call" negatively affects their sense of security and job satisfaction [10]. Finally, techno-complexity describes the situations in which ICTs' features and complexity make users feel inadequate concerning their skills [4]. Since ICTs are subject to constant changes and updates, the hard skills needed - including technical capabilities and terminology - become more and more complex. This situation introduces anxiety and fear in all the employees who find new technologies intimidating and difficult to understand [11]. As mentioned before, these conditions may cause a series of adverse psychological, behavioural, and physical reactions known as individual strain.

## 2.2 Strain

Strain is defined as the individual's response to techno-stressors. Tarafdar et al. [9] proposed that techno-stressors can influence both the extent to which individuals are satisfied with the ICT applications they use and the job performed. Hence, there is a distinction between adverse job-related outcomes and adverse ICT-use related outcomes. Job-related outcomes include psychological strains, namely emotional reactions to stressor conditions such as dissatisfaction with the job, depression, and negative self-evaluation [9]. In psychology, this kind of strain occurs when organisational stress lead to ineffective cognitive functioning or disturbed affective states [12]. Consequently, we theorise it is further possible to distinguish between two components of technostress-induced psychological strain: the cognitive and affective components.

From one side, cognitive strain depicts the negative effect on individual cognitive functioning, namely the mental processes involved in information processing such as attention, working memory, decision-making, and learning [13]. On the other side, the term "affect" refers to the mental counterpart of internal bodily representations associated with emotions [14]. Affective strain is a significant outcome in stress research because it is inherently linked to the experience of stressful situations [15]. Hence, the construct is widely used in occupational stress research. In this study, the affective component of psychological strain is conceptualised as an individual state characterised by high arousal and displeasure, reflecting the anxious condition of affective wellbeing [16]. This decision is intended to mirror the stress impact on the affective component theorised by Pejetersen et al. [17].

Prior research has described various affective dimensions of strain (such as anxiety [18], and tension [19]) as well as negative cognitive experiences (e.g., fatigue and exhaustion [20]) due to the use of technologies. For instance, Lewis underlined that the use of ICT may lead to poor decision-making, difficulty in memorising and remembering, and a reduced attention span [21]. For these reasons, we suppose that the techno-stressors has an influence on an individual's cognitive and affective reactions. Specifically, remote working may force users to work more and fulfil multiple demands within very tight time schedules. This simultaneous exposure to multiple stimuli creates a gap between what they are demanded to do and what they can efficiently handle [22]. Hence, we hypothesise that this exhausting condition may deliver negative consequences both from a cognitive and affective viewpoint. Namely:

H1a: Techno-overload has a positive influence on affective strain.
H1b: Techno-overload has a positive influence on cognitive strain.

Moreover, the invasion of private life due to technology may create pressures of constant connectivity (techno-invasion). This scenario may lead employees to manifest symptoms like fatigue, burnout, tension, and dissatisfaction, thus influencing cognitive and affective response. Consequently, we propose the following hypothesis:

H2a: Techno-invasion has a positive influence on affective strain.
H2b: Techno-invasion has a positive influence on cognitive strain.

Finally, techno-complexity forces workers to spend resources learning and understanding ICTs, to not feel unskilled [9, 23]. This condition may raise negative affective states such as anxiety in all those employees who find new technologies intimidating [11], making ICT learning processes difficult [24], and thus requiring higher cognitive efforts. Formally:

H3a: Techno-complexity has a positive influence on affective strain.
H3b: Techno-complexity has a positive influence on cognitive strain.

## 2.3   Job-Related Outcomes

The consequences of technostress are not limited to individuals' wellbeing since strain can lead to organisational outcomes too. Several studies have investigated the unfavourable effect of techno-stressors on companies' performance such as organisational commitment [5] and productivity [23]. However, very few studies have addressed the topic of job engagement within telework practice and none have investigated the relationship between techno-stressors, strain, and work engagement. According to Khan's definition of work engagement, employees are engaged when they are physically, cognitively, and emotionally connected with their work [25]. Work engagement has been discussed in the "off-line" job context because of its direct impact on organisational results. Indeed, engaged employees experience positive feelings like gratitude, joy, enthusiasm, and better health [26], resulting in readiness to dedicate their full resources to accomplish work goals and, as a consequence, to work more [4]. To be engaged, employees should present a significant involvement both from a cognitive and emotional point of view. Hence, it is expected that psychological strain shows a negative relationship with work engagement. Hence, the following hypotheses are theorised:

H4a: Affective strain has a negative influence on work engagement.
H4b: Cognitive strain has a negative influence on work engagement.

Campbell described individual work performance as "behaviours or actions that are relevant to the goals of the organisation" [27], entailing that: (i) individual work performance should be defined in terms of behaviours rather than results, and (ii) it includes only those behaviours that are relevant to the organisation's goals [28]. As a consequence, individual work performance is not output-oriented (as productivity); rather it can be measured through quality of outputs, job knowledge, and leadership, to name three [29]. Individual work performance is a multidimensional, abstract, and latent construct that cannot be pointed to or measured directly. For this reason, it should be distinguished from other constructs, even if different concepts often seem to be used interchangeably in the literature. Individual work performance is a very relevant construct for organisations since it represents an early signal of team and company performance, both factors that raise organisation competitiveness [28]. Even if in literature the impact of technostress on task [30] and end-user performance [9] has been deeply investigated, to the best of our knowledge, there is a lack in the study of the relationship between psychological strain and individual work performance in the remote working environment. Hence, we investigate the impact of strain on individual work performance by testing the following hypotheses:

H5a: Affective strain has a negative influence on work performance.
H5b: Cognitive strain has a negative influence on work performance.

## 3   Materials and Methods

We developed our questionnaire relying upon already-validated constructs. Techno-stressors were measured with the short version of the scale developed by Molino and

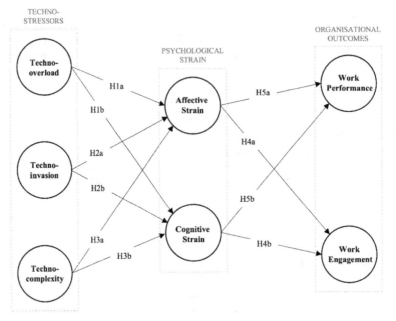

**Fig. 1.** Conceptual model and related hypotheses

colleagues [31]: we took into account three items for techno-overload, three items for techno-invasion, and four items for techno-complexity. Psychological strain constructs were measured employing the Copenhagen psychosocial questionnaire II [17], using four items for each strain (cognitive and affective). Items to measure work engagement has been taken and adapted from the Short version of the Utrecht Work Engagement Scale [32]: three items were selected from the vigour and dedication class, while one item was employed to investigate the absorption dimension. Finally, individual work performance has been measured through a 3-items construct taken from the Individual Work Performance Questionnaire [28]. All items were measured with Likert scales (from 1 = strongly disagree/never to 7 = strongly agree/always to answer) and translated into Italian. A full copy of the items investigated is provided in Table 1 in Appendix A.

The questionnaire was delivered in the form of a digital survey delivered to a sample of 171 Italian workers experiencing work-from-home from January 2020 to June 2021. Overall, 135 responses have been usable for analysis purposes, representing the 79% of the overall collected questionnaires (57% female, $M_{age} = 32.1$, $SD_{age} = 9.8$, age-range = 21–61). Participants have been contacted asking them to fill in a self-reported questionnaire on a voluntary basis. After the collection of the responses, a construct reliability check was performed. Overall, 57% of the respondents worked remotely for more than 5 months, 26% resorted to remote working for 3–5 months, while the remaining part worked remotely for two months or less. The majority of the sample (77%) proved to be full-time workers, and 76% of the total respondents worked from home more than four days a week. Most of the participants were married or cohabited with friends/roommates (84%), while 80% did not have children.

A data analysis was carried out using Partial Least Square – Structural Equation Modeling (PLS–SEM) to test the relationships among techno-stressors, psychological strain, and organisational outcomes. PLS-SEM is a second-generation multivariate data analysis method that tests linear and additive models. It can be considered a valid alternative to canonical correlation or covariance-based structural equation modelling since it can relate a set of independent variables to multiple independent dependent variables. We opted for PLS-SEM due to the explorative type of research. Our sample size was satisfactory, being more than 10-times the largest number of structural paths directed to a particular latent construct in the structural model [33]. The estimations and data manipulations were performed using SmartPLS3.

## 4   Results

The number of iterations to find convergence was 8, suggesting the goodness of the model [34]. The reliability and validity measures, as well as the descriptive statistics for the model constructs are available in Table 2 in Appendix A. We assessed composite reliability and Cronbach's alpha to test internal consistency. CR index is above 0.70, and Cronbach's alpha values range from 0.709 to 0.921 and are greater than the recommended minimum value of 0.7, thus confirming the validity of our model [35]. We employed AVE to test of both convergent and divergent validity. AVE values were above 0.5, a threshold indicating convergent validity [36]. We establish discriminant validity by the Fornell–Larcker criterion [37]. All our AVE square roots were satisfying this condition. As a measure of fit of the model, we evaluated the standardized root mean square residual (SRMR). Our model has a saturated model SRMR of 0.076, that is below the suggested maximum value of 0.08 [38], thus confirming the good fit. Finally, our model does not present critical collinearity issues among the measured constructs indicators since structural Variance Inflation Factor (VIF) coefficients are all lower than 5 [39].

After the model had been validated, the hypothesised relationships among the constructs of the structural model were tested. A bootstrapping with 5,000 samples was conducted [40]. Then, determination coefficients, path coefficients, and significance levels were examined. As shown in Fig. 2, the majority of the hypotheses are supported. Indeed, excluding H1b, H3a, and H4a, all the path coefficients are significant at the 0.05 significance level and below. The coefficients of determination $R2$ are 0.335 for affective strain, 0.271 for cognitive strain, 0.158 for work engagement, and 0.247 for work performance, representing adequate effects for our model [41]. Blindfolding technique was used as a measure of predictive relevance of the model. The $Q2$ values of cross-validated redundancy are 0.257, 0.151, 0.083, and 0.144 for affective strain, cognitive strain, work engagement, and individual work performance, respectively. Since all the $Q2$ values are above zero, the observed values are adequately reconstructed, and the model has predictive relevance [42].

The results show that, through the mediation of affective and cognitive strain, techno-stressors tend to reduce both the work engagement and job performances of remote workers. In particular, we show that techno-overload positively influences affective strain, techno-invasion positively influences both affective and cognitive strain, while techno-complexity positively influences cognitive strain. Further, we show that cognitive strain affects negatively both work engagement and job performance, while affective strain influences negatively only the job performance.

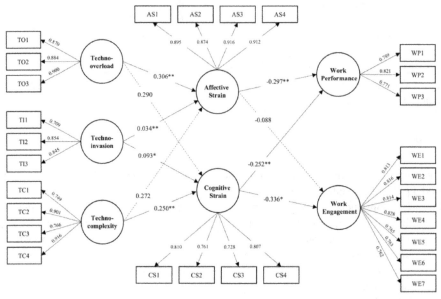

Note: *p-value <0.05; **p-value < 0.01

**Fig. 2.** Structural model results

## 5  Discussion and Conclusion

This study carries meaningful insights on the relationships among the main techno-stressors involved in telework practices and work outcomes, also evaluating the mediating role of individual psychological response. In our model, techno-invasion presents a more extensive effect with respect to techno-overload and techno-complexity, since it is the only stressor to influence both the psychological strains. These results underline that constant connectivity, which causes techno-invasion, may require a higher employee effort to concentrate on working activities rather than domestic ones, consequently manifesting significant effects on individual wellbeing. Moreover, techno-complexity seems to significantly affect the cognitive resources of the workers. This result is not surprising since the tendency of workers to spend time and effort in learning and understanding complex ICT, as well the prolonged hours spent in understanding something considered out of their capabilities, may induce employees to be mentally strained. Finally, since techno-overload positively influences the affective strain, it can be safe to assume that the negative feelings raised by working faster and longer may increase pressure on employees. If not properly managed, this pressure might be translated into high arousal and displeasure, introducing the employee to a condition of anxiety, ultimately impacting his/her performance.

Even if we proved that affective strain negatively influences individual work performance (underlining the importance of a positive state of mind in approaching job-related tasks), no significant relations between affective strain and work engagement have been found. This result is unexpected since the definition of engagement includes an emotional component, too [25]. Further studies may focus on this relationship, considering the impact of individual inhibitors (e.g., mindfulness) on secondary appraisal process. The significance of cognitive strain is underlined by its effects on both work engagement and individual work performance, confirming the implication of the attentional dimension on job performance. Even if this result is not new to traditional working literature, few studies addressed the topic in remote working research. Since other seminal papers in stress coping research state that the ability to effectively cope with an external stressor is determined by a specific cognitive appraisal process [43], it may be possible that cognitive burnout caused by techno-stressors could influence the individual's attitude toward the negative stimulus' extent, creating negative feedback loops.

The present study raises several relevant implications for academicians, practitioners, and policymakers. First and foremost, it contributes to extant literature concerning technostress in remote working settings by highlighting how specific techno-stressors influence work engagement and job performance. Moreover, it emphasises the mediating effect of individual psychological responses both from a cognitive and affective viewpoint, providing a three-step framework that can be adopted in future research. These findings are in line with previous literature in psychology about reasoned-action approach, stating that attitudes toward technology are based on a person's beliefs about that topic and those beliefs - cognitive and affective - can influence their behaviour [44]. Under this light, our results suggest that the adoption of remote working practices may influence users' attitude towards the technological facility, affecting employees' behaviour and the organisation's results.

Second, extant literature suggests practitioners to exploit three levels of action to contrast the loss of individual performance caused by techno-stressors: (i) primary interventions (acting on the factor creating stress), (ii) secondary interventions (influencing the individual's coping response to such conditions), and (iii) tertiary interventions (namely leveraging on the outcomes that the individual experiences) [4]. To reduce the impact of techno-stressors at its source, our study suggests minimising the negative effect of techno-overload, invasion, and complexity. For instance, managers may employ workers' task load reduction in order to improve job performance in the long term and to working environment redesign with the aim to reduce ICT-related complexity.

Regarding secondary interventions, managers should correctly identify efficient inhibitors to reduce technostress impact on the individual strain. A consistent literature stream has already investigated the elements that can reduce strain caused by technostress in "offline" contexts, but these inhibitors may demonstrate less efficacy in the domestic environment because of the context-specificity of technostress. Hence, we suggest practitioners to focus on those inhibitors that are more concentrated on individuals rather than organisations. Given the importance of affective strain in the technostress process, mindfulness [45] may lead employees to increase their capacity for objectivity in relation to an internal or external experience, reducing, in turn, negative thoughts and feelings like anxiety and worry. For these reasons, we suggest practitioners to find effective ways to foster mindfulness practices among employees, such as meditation routines and stress reduction programs during working hours.

Finally, our results suggest leveraging both affective and cognitive components to monitor employees' psychological strain conditions. Indeed, affective computers equipped with cameras, microphones, and sensors may recognise physiological components of emotions. Moreover, monitoring individual real-time performance such as time of task accomplishment and quality of the work produced may contribute to indirectly assessment of mental fatigue and exhaustion. Then, the measure of these two dimensions may result in the deduction of a real-time individual psychological condition allowing the determination of real-time adaptive responses. For instance, after identifying an increasing worker's strain condition, the computer can interact with the user, suggesting quick breaks or providing encouraging feedback or advice. In this regard, wearable devices may offer a twofold contribution since they can measure many physiological responses over time and they can draw user's attention through haptic or sound notifications, creating positive feedback loops to enhance individual wellbeing [46].

This study proposes interesting outcomes for policymakers too. Indeed, given the significant effect of working conditions on individual psychological health, governments should regulate on working time and workload of employees adopting remote-working practices. For example, considering the influential effect of techno-invasion, it may be beneficial in terms of workers' wellbeing to consolidate the debate on the right to disconnect, by guaranteeing a clear, juridical distinction between private and professional life.

## 6  Limitations and Future Research

The discussed results might be subjected to some limitations. First, work performance has been measured with a validated scale reflecting respondents' perception of their performance while working at home, thus not considering independent assessments made by peers or supervisors. Hence, employees' perceptions and supervisors' valuation might differ. Furthermore, even if the pandemic has provided a unique chance to conduct the present study during the highest pick of work-from-home adoption, it may have had consequences on individuals' work and stress processes. Indeed, the emotional distress directly related to the emergency situation has not been investigated separately in the study. Finally, since some studies have theorised that stressors may lead to positive outcomes at the individual and organisational level [47], future investigations may adopt our framework to evaluate how positive stress (namely, eustress) may enhance specific job performance by investigating the possible mediator positive effect of affective and cognitive strain.

# Appendix A

**Table 1.** List of all items employed in the survey

| Construct | Indicator | Item |
|---|---|---|
| Techno-overload *(Molino et al., 2020)* | TO1 | *I am forced by this technology to work much faster* |
| | TO2 | *I am forced by this technology to do more work than I can handle* |
| | TO3 | *I am forced by this technology to work with very tight time schedules* |
| Techno-invasion *(Molino et al., 2020)* | TI1 | *I spend less time with my family due to this technology* |
| | TI2 | *I have to be in touch with my work even during my vacation and weekend time due to this technology* |
| | TI3 | *I feel my personal life is being invaded by this technology* |
| Techno-complexity *(Molino et al., 2020)* | TC1 | *I do not know enough about this technology to handle my job satisfactorily* |
| | TC2 | *I need a long time to understand and use new technologies* |
| | TC3 | *I do not find enough time to study and upgrade my technology skills* |
| | TC4 | *I often find it too complex for me to understand and use new technologies* |
| Affective strain *(Pejtersen et al., 2010)* | AS1 | *How often have you had problems relaxing?* |
| | AS2 | *How often have you been irritable?* |
| | AS3 | *How often have you been tense?* |
| | AS4 | *How often have you been stressed?* |
| Cognitive strain *(Pejtersen et al., 2010)* | CS1 | *How often have you had problems concentrating?* |
| | CS2 | *How often have you found it difficult to think clearly?* |
| | CS3 | *How often have you had difficulty in taking decisions?* |
| | CS4 | *How often have you had difficulty with remembering?* |

*(continued)*

**Table 1.**  (*continued*)

| Construct | Indicator | Item |
|---|---|---|
| Work performance *(Koopmans et al., 2012)* | WP1 | *I managed to plan my work so that it was done on time* |
| | WP2 | *I was able to separate main issues from side issues at work* |
| | WP3 | *I was able to perform my work well with minimal time and effort* |
| Work engagement *(Seppälä et al., 2009)* | WE1 | *At my work, I feel bursting with energy* |
| | WE1 | *At my job, I feel strong and vigorous* |
| | WE3 | *When I get up in the morning, I feel like going to work* |
| | WE4 | *I am enthusiastic about my job* |
| | WE5 | *My job inspires me* |
| | WE6 | *I am proud on the work that I do* |
| | WE7 | *I feel happy when I am working intensely* |

**Table 2.**  Descriptive statistics, reliability, and validity measures for the model constructs

| Construct | Estimates | | | | Indicators | Final model | | |
|---|---|---|---|---|---|---|---|---|
| | Cronbach α | rho_A | CR | AVE | | Loadings | Mean | Std. Dev |
| *Techno-overload* | 0.861 | 0.863 | 0.915 | 0.783 | TO1 | 0.870 | 3.289 | 1.761 |
| | | | | | TO2 | 0.884 | 3.689 | 1.930 |
| | | | | | TO3 | 0.900 | 3.363 | 1.810 |
| *Techno-invasion* | 0.729 | 0.754 | 0.846 | 0.649 | TI1 | 0.709 | 3.363 | 1.810 |
| | | | | | TI2 | 0.854 | 3.807 | 2.053 |
| | | | | | TI3 | 0.845 | 4.222 | 1.984 |
| *Techno-complexity* | 0.856 | 0.885 | 0.902 | 0.699 | TC1 | 0.766 | 2.156 | 1.414 |
| | | | | | TC2 | 0.916 | 2.156 | 1.530 |
| | | | | | TC3 | 0.749 | 2.822 | 1.634 |
| | | | | | TC4 | 0.901 | 2.074 | 1.449 |
| *Affective strain* | 0.921 | 0.925 | 0.944 | 0.809 | AS1 | 0.895 | 4.037 | 1.641 |
| | | | | | AS2 | 0.874 | 3.933 | 1.441 |
| | | | | | AS3 | 0.916 | 4.119 | 1.502 |
| | | | | | AS4 | 0.912 | 4.237 | 1.551 |

(*continued*)

**Table 2.** (*continued*)

| Construct | Estimates | | | | Indicators | Final model | | |
|---|---|---|---|---|---|---|---|---|
| | *Cronbach α* | *rho_A* | *CR* | *AVE* | | *Loadings* | *Mean* | *Std. Dev* |
| *Cognitive strain* | 0.781 | 0.786 | 0.859 | 0.604 | CS1 | 0.810 | 3.622 | 1.520 |
| | | | | | CS2 | 0.761 | 2.785 | 1.307 |
| | | | | | CS3 | 0.728 | 2.896 | 1.378 |
| | | | | | CS4 | 0.807 | 2.733 | 1.339 |
| *Work performance* | 0.709 | 0.716 | 0.837 | 0.631 | WP1 | 0.789 | 3.844 | 1.365 |
| | | | | | WP2 | 0.821 | 3.756 | 1.438 |
| | | | | | WP3 | 0.771 | 3.800 | 1.505 |
| *Work engagement* | 0.905 | 0.948 | 0.923 | 0.632 | WE1 | 0.813 | 4.296 | 1.388 |
| | | | | | WE1 | 0.816 | 4.074 | 1.364 |
| | | | | | WE3 | 0.814 | 4.585 | 1.230 |
| | | | | | WE4 | 0.828 | 4.037 | 1.374 |
| | | | | | WE5 | 0.765 | 5.281 | 1.331 |
| | | | | | WE6 | 0.763 | 4.578 | 1.368 |
| | | | | | WE7 | 0.762 | 3.978 | 1.432 |

# References

1. Tarafdar, M., Pirkkalainen, H., Salo, M., Makkonen, M.: Taking on the "dark side" - coping with technostress. IT Prof. **22**, 82–89 (2020). https://doi.org/10.1109/MITP.2020.2977343
2. Oksanen, A., Oksa, R., Savela, N., Mantere, E., Savolainen, I., Kaakinen, M.: COVID-19 crisis and digital stressors at work: a longitudinal study on the Finnish working population. Comput. Human Behav. **122**, 106853 (2021). https://doi.org/10.1016/j.chb.2021.106853
3. Brod, C.: Technostress - The Human Cost of the Computer Revolution. Addison-Wesley Publishing Company, Reading, USA (1984)
4. Tarafdar, M., Tu, Q., Ragu-Nathan, B.S., Ragu-Nathan, T.S.: The impact of technostress on role stress and productivity. J. Manag. Inf. Syst. **24**, 301–328 (2007). https://doi.org/10.2753/MIS0742-1222240109
5. Ragu-Nathan, T.S., Tarafdar, M., Ragu-Nathan, B.S., Tu, Q.: The consequences of technostress for end users in organizations: conceptual development and validation. Inf. Syst. Res. **19**, 417–433 (2008). https://doi.org/10.1287/isre.1070.0165
6. Gartner Statistics (2020). https://www.gartner.com/en/newsroom/press-releases/2020-04-14-gartner-hr-survey-reveals-41--of-employees-likely-to-. Accessed 23 Apr 2022
7. Nilles, J.M.: Telecommunications and organizational decentralization. IEEE Trans. Commun. **23**, 1142–1147 (1975). https://doi.org/10.1109/TCOM.1975.1092687
8. Cooper, C.L., Dewe, P.J., O'Driscoll, M.P.: Organizational Stress: A Review and Critique of Theory, Research, and Applications. Sage Publ. Inc. (2001)
9. Tarafdar, M., Tu, Q., Ragu-Nathan, T.: Impact of technostress on end-user satisfaction and performance. J. Manag. Inf. Syst. **27**, 303–334 (2010). https://doi.org/10.2753/MIS0742-1222270311

10. Weil, M.M., Rosen, L.D.: TechnoStress: Coping with Technology. John Wiley Sons, New York (1997)
11. Yaverbaum, G.J.: Critical factors in the user environment: an experimental study of users, organizations and tasks. MIS Q. Manag. Inf. Syst. **12**, 75–88 (1988). https://doi.org/10.2307/248807
12. Bhagat, R.S., Krishnan, B., Nelson, T.A., Leonard, K.M., Moustafa, K., Billing, T.K.: Organizational stress, psychological strain, and work outcomes in six national contexts: a closer look at the moderating influences of coping styles and decision latitude. Cross Cult. Manag. **17**, 10–29 (2010). https://doi.org/10.1108/13527601011016880
13. Kalakoski, V., et al.: Effects of a cognitive ergonomics workplace intervention (CogErg) on cognitive strain and well-being: a cluster-randomized controlled trial. A study protocol. BMC Psychol. **8**, 1–16 (2020). https://doi.org/10.1186/s40359-019-0349-1
14. Feldman Barrett, L., Bliss-Moreau, E.: Affect as a psychological primative. Adv. Exp. Soc. Psychol. **41**, 167–218 (2009). https://doi.org/10.1016/S0065-2601(08)00404-8.Affect
15. Lazarus, R.S.: Stress and Emotion: A New Synthesis. Springer Publishing Co, New York, NY, US (1999)
16. Ommen, N.O., Heußler, T., Backhaus, C., Michaelis, M., Ahlert, D.: The impact of country-of-origin and joy on product evaluation: a comparison of Chinese and German intimate apparel. J. Glob. Fash. Mark. **1**, 89–99 (2010). https://doi.org/10.1080/20932685.2010.10593061
17. Pejtersen, J.H., Kristensen, T.S., Borg, V., Bjorner, J.B.: The second version of the Copenhagen psychosocial questionnaire. Scand. J. Public Health. **38**, 8–24 (2010). https://doi.org/10.1177/1403494809349858
18. Salanova Soria, M., Psicología, D., Llorens, S., Cifre, E., De Investigación, E., Psicosocial, W.: Tecnoestrés: concepto, medida e intervención psicosocial [Technostress: Concept, Measurement and Prevention]. https://www.insst.es/documents/94886/327446/ntp_730.pdf/55c1d085-13e9-4a24-9fae-349d98deeb8a (2007)
19. Heinssen, R.K., Glass, C.R., Knight, L.A.: Assessing computer anxiety: development and validation of the computer anxiety rating scale. Comput. Human Behav. **3**(1), 49–59 (1987). https://doi.org/10.1016/0747-5632(87)90010-0
20. Ayyagari, R., Grover, V., Purvis, R.: Technostress: technological antecedents and implications. MIS Q. **35**, 831–858 (2011)
21. Lewis, C.: Dying for Information?: An Investigation into the Effects of Information Overload in the UK and Worldwide. Reuters, London (1996)
22. Fisher, W., Wesolkowski, S.: Tempering technostress. IEEE Technol. Soc. Mag. **18**, 28–42 (1999). https://doi.org/10.1109/44.752243
23. Tarafdar, M., Tu, Q., Ragu-Nathan, T.S.: The impact of technostress on role stress and productivity. J. Manag. Inform. Syst. **24**, 301–328 (2007)
24. Nimrod, G.: Technostress: measuring a new threat to well-being in later life. Aging Ment. Health. **22**, 1–8 (2017). https://doi.org/10.1080/13607863.2017.1334037
25. Kahn, W.A.: Psychological conditions of personal engagement and disengagement at work. Acad. Manag. J. **33**, 692–724 (1990). https://doi.org/10.2307/256287
26. Fredrickson, B.L.: The role of positive emotions in positive psychology: the broaden-and-build theory of positive emotions. Am. Psychol. **56**, 218–226 (2001). https://doi.org/10.1037/0003-066X.56.3.218
27. Campbell, J.P.: Modeling the performance prediction problem in industrial and organizational psychology. In: Dunnette, M.D., Hough, L.M. (eds.) Handbook of Industrial and Organizational Psychology, pp. 687–732. Consulting Psychologists Press (1990)
28. Koopmans, L., Bernaards, C., Hildebrandt, V., Van Buuren, S., Van Der Beek, A.J., de Vet, H.: Development of an individual work performance questionnaire. Int. J. Product. Perform. Manag. **62**, 6–28 (2012). https://doi.org/10.1108/17410401311285273

29. Bélanger, F.: Workers' propensity to telecommute: an empirical study. Inf. Manag. **35**, 139–153 (1999). https://doi.org/10.1016/S0378-7206(98)00091-3

30. Hackman, J.R., Vidmar, N.: Effects of size and task type on group performance and member reactions. Sociometry **33**, 37 (1970). https://doi.org/10.2307/2786271

31. Molino, M., et al.: Wellbeing costs of technology use during Covid-19 remote working: An investigation using the Italian translation of the technostress creators scale. Sustain **12**, 1–20 (2020). https://doi.org/10.3390/SU12155911

32. Seppälä, P., et al.: The construct validity of the utrecht work engagement scale: multisample and longitudinal evidence. J. Happiness Stud. **10**, 459–481 (2009). https://doi.org/10.1007/s10902-008-9100-y

33. Barclay, D., Thompson, R., Higgins, C.: The partial least squares (PLS) approach to causal modeling: personal computer adoption and use an illustration. Technol. Stud. **2**, 285–309 (1995)

34. Wong, K.K.K.-K.: 28/05 - partial least squares structural equation modeling (PLS-SEM) techniques using SmartPLS. Mark. Bull. **24**, 1–32 (2013)

35. Hundleby, J.D., Nunnally, J.: Psychometric theory. Am. Educ. Res. J. **5**, 431 (1968). https://doi.org/10.2307/1161962

36. Chin, W.W.: The partial least squares approach to structural equation modelling. In: Marcoulides, G.A. (ed.) Mod. Methods Bus. Res., vol. 295, pp. 295–336 (1998)

37. Fornell, C., Larcker, D.F.: Evaluating structural equation models with unobservable variables and measurement error. J. Mark. Res. **18**, 39 (1981). https://doi.org/10.2307/3151312

38. Hu, L.T., Bentler, P.M.: Cutoff criteria for fit indexes in covariance structure analysis: conventional criteria versus new alternatives. Struct. Equ. Model. **6**, 1–55 (1999). https://doi.org/10.1080/10705519909540118

39. Hair, J.F., Risher, J.J., Sarstedt, M., Ringle, C.M.: When to use and how to report the results of PLS-SEM. Eur. Bus. Rev. **31**, 2–24 (2019). https://doi.org/10.1108/EBR-11-2018-0203

40. Hair, J.F., Ringle, C.M., Sarstedt, M.: PLS-SEM: indeed a silver bullet. J. Mark. Theory Pract. **19**, 139–152 (2011). https://doi.org/10.2753/MTP1069-6679190202

41. Falk, R.F., Miller, N.B.: A primer for soft modeling. Open J. Bus. Manag., University of Akron Press, Akron, OH, vol. 2, p. 103 (1992)

42. Henselar, J., Fassott, G.: Testing moderating effects in PLS path models: an illustration of available procedures. In: Vinzi, V.E., Chin, W.W., Henselar, J., Wang, H. (eds.) Handbook of Partial Least Squares, pp. 713–735. Springer Berlin Heidelberg, Berlin, Heidelberg (2010). https://doi.org/10.1007/978-3-540-32827-8_31

43. Lazarus, R.S.: The role of coping in the emotions and how coping changes over the life course. In: Handbook of Emotion, Adult Development, and Aging, pp. 289–306 (1996)

44. Hill, R.J., Fishbein, M., Ajzen, I.: Belief, attitude, intention and behavior: an introduction to theory and research. Contemp. Sociol. **6**, 244 (1977). https://doi.org/10.2307/2065853

45. Cardaciotto, L., Herbert, J.D., Forman, E.M., Moitra, E., Farrow, V.: The assessment of present-moment awareness and acceptance: the Philadelphia mindfulness scale. Assessment **15**, 204–223 (2008). https://doi.org/10.1177/1073191107311467

46. Chianella, R., Mandolfo, M., Lolatto, R., Pillan, M.: Designing for self-awareness: Evidence-based explorations of multimodal stress-tracking wearables. In: Kurosu, M. (ed.) HCII 2021. LNCS, vol. 12763, pp. 357–371. Springer, Cham (2021). https://doi.org/10.1007/978-3-030-78465-2_27

47. Tarafdar, M., Cooper, C.L., Stich, J.F.: The technostress trifecta - techno eustress, techno distress and design: theoretical directions and an agenda for research. Inf. Syst. J. **29**, 6–42 (2019). https://doi.org/10.1111/isj.12169

# Applying Hierarchical Task Analysis to Identify the Needs of Intelligent Equipment for Traffic Police in China

Wenxuan Duan[1], Yan Shang[1,2,3], Jingyu Zhang[1,2(✉)], Huiyun Wang[1,2], and Xiangying Zou[4]

[1] Institute of Psychology, Chinese Academy of Sciences, Beijing, China
zhangjingyu@psych.ac.cn
[2] Department of Psychology, University of Chinese Academy of Sciences, Beijing, China
[3] TD Tech Limited, Beijing, China
[4] Department of Industrial Engineering, Tsinghua University, Beijing, China

**Abstract.** Due to the increasing of traffic and the introduction of new technologies, the way to perform tasks by modern traffic police have been changed. However, few studies have systematically analyzed the tasks of modern traffic police, a major force in enhancing the efficiency and safety of the transportation network. Based on Hierarchical Task Analysis (HTA), this study investigated the major tasks of front-line traffic policemen in China with a focus on how new technology are implemented. Overall, the results suggested that 135 Fast response to incidents, Drunk driving inspection, Routine patrol and road guidance, serious accident disposal, and AVI checkpoint interception are the key tasks, while body-worn cameras, police terminals and hand-held radios are the main intelligent equipment for policing. This HTA provided insight into key traffic police workflows and laid the foundation for improving the traffic policemen performance, as well as producing and developing more effective smart equipment for police use.

**Keywords:** Hierarchical task analysis · Traffic policemen · Policing equipment · Intelligent equipment

## 1 Introduction

Transportation is a typical complex system involving infrastructure, vehicle, human, environmental and social factors (Wang 2003). As a major force in urban governance to manage the complex transportation system, the traffic police is responsible to enforce road safety regulations, deter traffic violations and prevent driving offenses (Adler et al. 2014; Liu and Liu 2020). Effective policing deployment is key to reduce crime and road accidents and increase transportation efficiency (Adler et al. 2014). To do so, the traffic police should come to the right location promptly, making right judgment and using right procedures. Therefore, understating how traffic police work is an important research question to enhance the smoothing running of the complex transportation system.

D. Harris and W.-C. Li (Eds.): HCII 2022, LNAI 13307, pp. 164–178, 2022.
https://doi.org/10.1007/978-3-031-06086-1_13

The duties of traffic police officers in China have become significantly more complex and challenging due to the fast development of transportation system (Chen 2018; Fayard 2019). Numerous administrative tasks have placed a heavy workload on front-line police officers, and the situation further worsened the shortage of manpower (Wang 2011; Zhou 2013; Scoggins and O'Brien 2016). In addition, the modern citizen movement has created new challenges for the police as it strives to increase the transparency of policing practices (Jiang et al. 2021; Backman and Löfstrand 2021). For example, Body-Worn Cameras (BWCs) were required to be worn by all Chinese police officers, as their counterparts in the USA, from year 2016 (Ministry of Public Security, PRC 2016). Other source of workload includes unpredictable conditions at incident scenes, community relations, and shortages of appropriate equipment (Abdollahi 2002).

As job-related workload can have an impact on police satisfaction and job performance, many attempts have been made to reduce the burden on police officers mentioned above. Training is an effective way to reduce the operational risk by targeted repeat practice, such as simulations that facilitate realistic decisions to reduce anxiety (Bennell et al. 2007; Oudejans and Pijpers 2009), physical training to develop strength and endurance capabilities (Irving et al. 2019; Zwingmann 2021), social interaction training to mitigate controversial incidents between police and citizens (Wolfe et al. 2020), cognitive training to assist the novel skill acquisition and promote complex motor skills of policemen (Di Nota and Huhta 2019). The development of training programs usually arises from a focus on the requirements associated with the specific tasks performed by the policemen, for instance, the heavy loads imparted by their personal protective equipment (Grani et al. 2021).

To improve the task performance of policemen, modern technologies have been rapidly introduced and equipped by the police. For example, the satellite positioning technology and location-based services (LBS) offered more possibilities for wireless communication (Peng et al. 2015). Moreover, modern miniaturization technologies have made many necessary devices smaller in size and weight. For example, compared with the mobile computer terminal (MCT), which is a computer installed in a police vehicle that carries functions such as internal communications and notifications, GPS data, case-related information, video recording and other task-specific module (Zahabi et al. 2020), the new generation of such terminal can be integrated in a mobile phone which has already been widely equipped in Chinese police workforce (Mu 2021).

Whereas the functions of these equipment have substantially evolved, whether these smart devices have good usability remains an important and not yet fully answered question. Usability refers to "the extent to which a product can be used by specified users to achieve specified goals with effectiveness, efficiency and satisfaction in a specified context of use" (ISO 9241-11 1998). Without good usability, the users may find the equipment hard to use, feel confusion, or make errors and delays in completing certain tasks (ISTQB 2016). Many studies have suggested that new products or features can only be acceptable and effective if the usability of the product is good (Marcus and Gasperini 2006; Van Velsen et al. 2008).

For this purpose, some studies have been conducted to explore the user demands and evaluate the usability of new equipment for the police. For example, Marcus and Gasperini (2006), Zahabi and Kaber (2018) and Shahini et al. (2020) have investigated the in-vehicle technologies; Pfeil et al. (2019) and Miranda (2020) have suggested that the BWC should be designed with greater accessibility, a more comfortable wearing experience, a better system to use and a simpler way to operate in the daily police work. However, the reality of usability remains an issue. A survey of Chinese police officers revealed that BWC's main concerns are technical issues related to product reliability and usability, such as higher expectations for battery life and camera performance (Jiang et al. 2021).

In order to ameliorate the usability of these policing products, a thorough understanding of their tasks is needed. The usability issues of a device could be identified during a task analysis process (Hong et al. 2011). While broad job descriptions are available to describe what police officers do in the United States (e.g., Oliver 2020; MCOLES 2018), there is no targeted research that has been conducted on Chinese police officers, to understand their tasks and problems in using different equipment.

Hierarchical task analysis (HTA) is a well-established and systematic framework for identifying the behaviors that occur during a task (Annett 2003; Phipps et al. 2011). The task is explored through a hierarchy of *goals* (indicating what a person is expect to do) and broken down into *sub-goals*, each of which has a series of specific *operations* that together form *plans* for successful task performance (Shepherd 1998). Using HTA to conduct usability evaluation is a widely accepted approach in complex systems such as development of medical equipment (Liljegren 2006), pilot operations (Li et al. 2021), rail driver operations (Naweed et al. 2018) and high-speed railway events (Wang et al. 2021). On the application of HTA to usability, potential needs and user scenarios could be identified during the decomposition of goals, sub-goals and specific operations for tasks to create testable design hypotheses with performance levers (Lim and Sato 2003; Crystal and Ellington 2004). However, little research has been done to describe the tasks of traffic police officers in China.

Given the above, this study aims to produce a comprehensive HTA of front-line traffic police's major tasks with the objective to recognize how equipment was currently being used for policing in China. The hierarchical description of the tasks illustrated the performance of front-line traffic police officers to achieve work goals and the interaction of policing equipment in the task completion process. As the first job-specific task analysis for traffic policemen, this could be used as a basis for task evaluation, risk assessment and police equipment development to assist in current road safety supervision and law enforcement. Correspondingly, the two research questions of this study were:

1. What are key tasks of front-line traffic police? and
2. What equipment do they need to perform each task?

## 2 Methods

### 2.1 Study Design

All of the task analysis guides emphasized the importance of multiple sources of information to guide, check, and verify the accuracy of the HTA (Stanton 2006). Consistent with key methods in constructing the HTA, this study incorporated a combination of document analysis, observations, walkthroughs and focus groups (Annett 2003; Stanton

2006). Firstly, literature and documents related to previous task analysis of police in general and traffic police in particular has been collected. Secondly, we conducted interviews and focus group discussion with experienced and senior police officers to gain overall knowledge of their tasks. Thirdly, we conducted observations to understand how they perform their work and use walkthroughs to understand how they use of certain equipment in reality. Lastly, critical tasks were identified and the relevant HTA diagram were drawn and validated.

## 2.2   Procedure

**Interviews and Focus Group Discussion.**  To collect rich data for the construction of the HTA, interviews and focus group discussions were chosen for this study because of the flexibility and immediacy of its methodology (Morgan et al. 1988; Stewart et al. 2007; Tremblay et al. 2010; Stewart and Shamdasani 2014; Krueger 2014). Seven focus groups and two one-to-one interviews were conducted online or offline over the course of two months (March to May, 2021). A total of 29 participants were included, 12 of whom were current front-line traffic police officers, including 5 district-level commanders (all males, ranging from 21 to 38 years of age), 5 municipal commanders (1 female and 4 males, aged between 30 and 49 years), 2 dispatchers, and 10 others from traffic police administrations (males only, aged between 21 and 36 years). The remaining 7 participants were technicians or designers of police equipment (2 females and 5 males, between the ages of 23 and 43). Participant numbers were allocated to asynchronous focus groups based on place and time constraints.

**Direct Observation and Walkthroughs.**  In addition to the self-reported tasks of traffic police officers, direct observation and walkthrough sessions were carried out to confirm the procedure in action performing their tasks. Data collected from the interviews and focus group discussions provided supporting information for the observations and vice versa. During the observations and walkthroughs, the researcher continually noted items of interest and collected on-site information to generate the HTA, by observing the policing activities, note-taking, responding and engaging with the participant if they initiated a discussion. A 2-week period field study with several interactive sessions was conducted to investigate the routine and demand-specific tasks of front-line traffic officers in a central province of China and its capital city. Each session lasted for 1–5 h depending on participant availability, task complexity, the volume of feedback and rostering schedule.

## 2.3   Data analysis

All data were analyzed according to the steps described by Stanton (2006) for constructing the HTA. In preparation for analysis, we had defined the purpose of the analysis (step 1) and collected data in various means (step 2). Areas of technology, team member interaction and decision making were focused on during the data collection process. The overall goal of the task was determined primarily based on the administrative roles of front-line traffic police, and the major tasks were identified during the study process (step 3). The overall goal was broken down into corresponding sub-goals, which together constituted the tasks required to accomplish the overall goal (step 4). Subsequently, sub-goals were further broken down into additional sub-goals and operations (step 5). Then plans were added to show how the goals were achieved (step 6). Finally, we identified the key equipment in police use (step 7). The HTA compilation was carried out by three researchers together.

## 3 Results

### 3.1 Overview of Goals

Table 1 gives a summary the goals generated by HTA of traffic police performing tasks. Five major high-level goals were extracted from the analysis, each with its own sub-goals. In general, the tasks of front-line traffic policemen can be divided into two categories, one is fixed routine mission including Routine patrol and road guidance, Drunk driving inspection. This type of task is usually completed without time constraint, mainly by the police who independently identify task needs and arrange the corresponding personnel and materials. The other type of task is the urgent goals included in the regular mission, including Serious Accident Disposal, 135 Fast Response to incidents and AVI Checkpoint Interception. This type of task has more stringent time requirements and is usually ordered by the command center, requiring fast mobility and high efficiency of the personnel to perform the task. The actual working scenarios of the above five tasks are shown in Fig. 1, all images are from publicly available materials on the web.

**Table 1.** Goals of traffic policing in HTA

| Task scenarios (high-level goals) | | Task steps (sub-goals) | |
| --- | --- | --- | --- |
| 1 | 135 Fast response to incidents | (1) | 1 min: Accept the task |
| | | (2) | 3 min: Arrive at the scene |
| | | (3) | 5 min: Handling the incident |
| 2 | Drunk driving inspection | (1) | Preparedness |
| | | (2) | Primary inspection |
| | | (3) | Impose penalties |
| 3 | Routine patrol and road guidance | (1) | Routine patrol |
| | | (2) | Road guidance |
| 4 | Serious accident disposal | (1) | Accept the alarm message |
| | | (2) | On-site disposal |
| | | (3) | Impose penalties |
| 5 | AVI checkpoint interception | (1) | Accept the task |
| | | (2) | Intercept the vehicle |
| | | (3) | Imposing administrative penalties |

**Fig. 1.** Five major tasks of front-line traffic policemen identified in this study.

## 3.2  Tasks in the HTA

HTA diagrams detailing the task steps for each task scenario are provided separately below, followed by explanations of portable police equipment used. If not specifically explicated, the objective of the task scenario is operated by the front-line police officer in the related district. Generally, the frequently used equipment are Body-Worn Camera (BWC), which is a portable camera providing an unalterable audio and visual record of interactions that capture empirical evidence in law enforcement (BJA 2020); intelligent mobile terminal (i.e. police terminal shown in HTA, differentiate from phone that indicates the personal phone of policemen without policing systems) that embedding the police mobile wireless system, which is an information management system required for mobile policing; and the hand-held radio (i.e. walkie-talkie), a two-way radio transceiver used among policemen or between the police and the command center (examples of these equipment see Fig. 2). Other equipment used for specific tasks will be indicated in the corresponding task.

1. an example for Body-worn Camera     2. an example for Police Terminal     3. an example for Hand-held Radio

**Fig. 2.** Three main equipment identified in this study.

The HTA compilation was produced by two researchers and subsequently checked by two subject matter experts. The symbols that used in HTA were listed in Fig. 3.

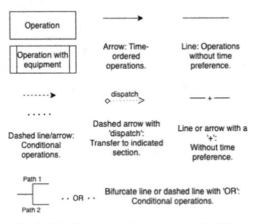

**Fig. 3.** The illustration of symbols used in HTA.

**Fast Response to Incidents.** The "135" ("1 min rapid response, 3 min to reach the disposal, 5 min to restore traffic") rapid response disposal mechanism is a specialized police task set up to minimize the impact of traffic incidents and vehicle breakdowns on urban road travel.

This task is one of the urgent goals included in the mission routine of traffic police officers (see Table 1). As shown in Fig. 4, the signal received from the command center starts the overall action of fast response, which is different from tasks that could be handled by front-line police only. Operations practiced in this task were commonly related with incidents and other units collaborated with the front-line traffic police officers such as Accident Section and medical institutions who participated in the task with dispatch.

In the goal of 135 fast response to incidents, the traffic police officer assigned to the task will be equipped with the necessary police information equipment, including the police terminal (installed on smart phones), the hand-held radios (walkie-talkie) and the BWC. The hand-held radios are primarily used as communication tools that receiving instruction from the command center. The BWC provides evidence of the incident for both the officer and the subject, especially in assigning responsibility for traffic law (from operation 3.1 to 3.8).

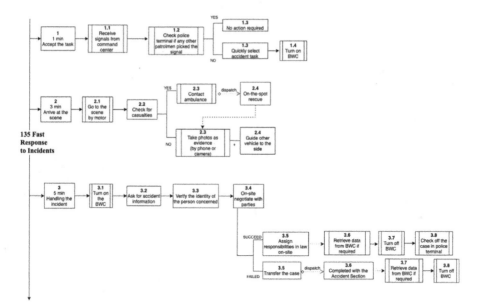

**Fig. 4.** HTA for goal of "135 Fast response to incidents".

**Drunk Driving Inspection.** Inspecting drunk driving behavior is a core component of traffic police's mission provisions. The risk of the illegal behavior has critical impact on maintaining the road traffic order, preventing and reducing traffic accidents. As shown in Fig. 5, sub-goals involved preparedness of personnel and equipment; primary inspection of the passing vehicles; disposal of intercepted vehicles and drunk drivers (impose penalties or not).

Several equipment were used in this task to complete a regular drunk-driving inspection (prepared in operation 1.3), including communication tools to deliver message and photos, such as police terminal and the walkie-talkie; portable devices to collect evidence, such as BWC; test instruments to detect alcohol level, such as the breathalyzer; medical vessels to measure alcohol concentration on blood, saliva or urine, such as gas chromatography, the saliva or urine alcohol test strip; and also vehicles to transport all the equipment and personnel related to the deployment (police car in usual).

**Routine Patrol and Road Guidance.** This task is a regular mission for front-line traffic police officers, and the events to be processed in the scenario are random in nature. The HTA focuses on presenting the operations of the task observed in investigating police officers deployed on roads to perform patrol duty tasks. As shown in Fig. 6, sub-tasks involved routine patrol within assigned duty area and road guidance (support for traffic in morning and evening rush-hour in the investigation).

In routine patrol and road guidance, the traffic police officer's police terminal and walkie-talkie are always kept open for communication, data collecting and message delivering, while in the event of an incident that needs to be handled, the BWC will be used to record the event (from operation 1.6 to 2.10). For police officers who rotate their posts over long distances, a police motor may also be a necessity.

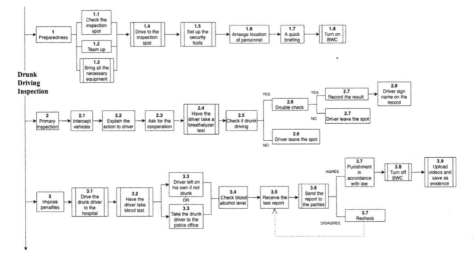

**Fig. 5.** HTA for goal of "Drunk driving inspection".

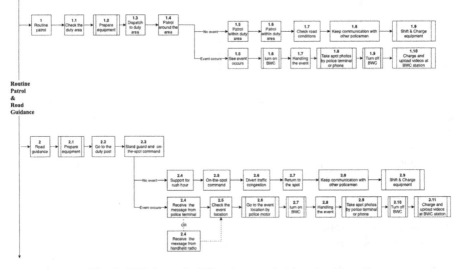

**Fig. 6.** HTA for goal of "Routine patrol and road guidance".

**Serious Accident Disposal.** In comparison to responding to 135 command channel, performing the urgent task of serious accident disposal involved more contact with other departments, such as medical institutions and accident section. This task is the most complicated scenario for the front-line traffic police officers, including these steps: receive an alarm message and verify information about the scene after accepting the task; confirm casualties at the scene and rescue the injured to complete the on-site disposal;

investigate into parties in interest of the traffic accident and define legal liabilities to impose penalties (see Fig. 7).

Despite the emergency of this task, required equipment remain complicated. All tools in task of 135 fast response to incidents must be used. Due to the need for more detailed scene information collection and quick direction of the traffic flow, barricades and flash equipment will also be needed to protect the scene and warn other vehicles to detour during the process of accident disposal (in operation 2.8: protect the scene with tools). In addition, a higher precision SLR camera will be provided to take pictures of the scene, although the graph of accident environment is still mainly based on hand-drawn paper (in operation 2.7).

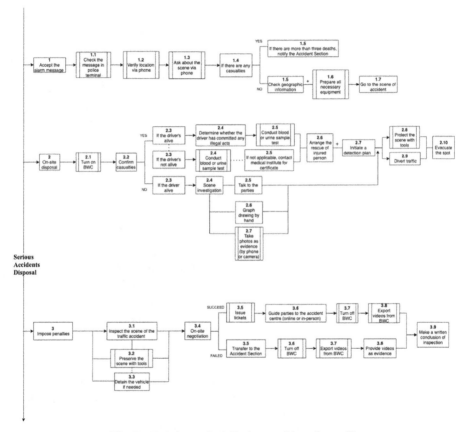

**Fig. 7.** HTA for goal of "Serious accident disposal".

**AVI Checkpoint Interception.** The interception checkpoint system set fixed poles and integrated capture cameras in both directions to capture passing motor vehicles, to take automatic picture capture of passing checkpoint vehicles, to get automatic identification of license plate numbers, traffic statistics, comparison/alarm/processing of illegal and controlled information.

When the access surveillance on Automatic Vehicle Identification (AVI) checkpoint detected a suspected or illegal vehicle, the traffic police officer near the checkpoint will receive the task and go to the corresponding checkpoint to intercept the vehicle and then give the penalty according to the specific situation (see Fig. 8).

Similar to other urgent tasks, the police terminal will receive signals from the interception checkpoint system (installed in the police terminal), prompting the police should go to the monitoring checkpoint to check the relevant vehicles, the whole process from accepting the assignment to closing the case will be operated on the policing platform of the police terminal (from operation 1.1 to 3.9). BWC needs to keep recording throughout (from operation 3.1 to 3.10).

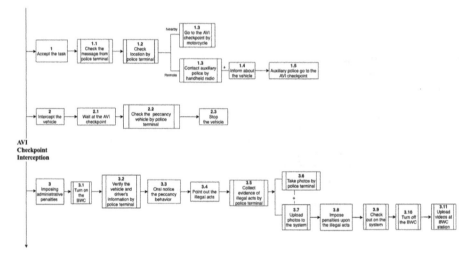

**Fig. 8.** HTA for goal of "AVI checkpoint interception".

## 4 Discussion

Regarding the lack of domestic research in specialist police, a construct is needed to better define the task scenarios of traffic police and identify the corresponding equipment in police use. The job-specific tasks of police have been investigated during this study, with the evaluation of modern equipment in policing. The HTA presented in this study is the first complete task analysis of front-line traffic police officers in their daily work featuring multiple intelligent equipment. This study provided the academic community with more information about the tasks of traffic police officers, laid foundations for assessing their task load, fatigue level, performance assessment and management in the future. For industry, the user journeys formed by task analysis can also be used to conduct more usability evaluations and user experience surveys of police equipment.

The analysis in this study highlighted the complexity of policing by traffic police. Our results showed that serious accident disposal is the most complicated work of traffic police, which is in line with the importance of road safety and the research focus of road traffic fatalities/injuries (for example, see Hu et al. 2011; Zhang et al. 2011; Zhang et al. 2013). The complexity of the task is a combination of long operation times, different departments involved, and a variety of operations of handling accidents, while the use of multiple smart devices also increases the workload of the task. Besides, other urgent tasks including 135 fast response to incidents and AVI checkpoint interception required officers to travel quickly to the appropriate locations, and operating smart devices while riding motorcycles could pose a threat to their safety, bringing the need for police vehicles and devices to be linked to deal with the problem.

Another need that emerged from the task analysis was to consolidate the photo functions of multiple devices and streamline unnecessary equipment. The police terminal is equipped with two systems, one system is designed for police work which was installed in policing platforms, and the system does not share the same photo album with another system available for personal use (installed with SNS application for communication with parties outside the police department), thus leads to the need for police officers to take photos with their own cell phones and upload photos to the SNS application in order to share information on the scene, rather than operating directly with the police terminal (without SNS application due to safety considerations). In addition, since using a SLR camera to photograph the accident scene is one of the police regulations, there are four tools available to take photos at the scene at the same time. Creating shared albums in both systems of police terminals or enhancing the photo function of BWC to replace SLR camera are possible solutions.

For specific tasks, the functionality of some equipment can be optimized to fit the actual needs. For example, since the video recorded by BWC needs to be transmitted to other departments for administrative penalty determination in tasks, adding the function of automatically identifying scene features for tagging when recording video may reduce unnecessary workload for subsequent archiving and exporting. Meanwhile, it takes time and effort in surveying the scene and drawing the scene map, and the inaccurate data will affect the result of the disposal, a pre-processed scene investigation by the cooperation between the AVI near the spot and the command center (with a more comprehensive GPS) will reduce the workload of the front-line traffic police officers and increase the accuracy of the scene identification.

However, there were a few of limitations in this study. Firstly, the method chosen for this study was based on HTA, which aimed to explore the task structure and process of traffic police. We did not investigate the cognitive resources of traffic police to a deeper extent; subsequent studies on traffic police could set experiments for cognitive analysis. Secondly, this study selected a group of traffic police in a central region of China for investigation, which may have some limitations in terms of subjects. Thirdly, this study selected key traffic police tasks, i.e., tasks that occur more frequently and are more difficult, other rare or less difficult tasks are not included in this investigation, such as the community education mission. For further research in this area, the number of subjects and the range of selected tasks can be expanded.

In conclusion, our study showed that there are five major tasks of front-line traffic police officers. Two of them are regular missions, including drunk driving inspection and routine patrol and road guidance. Three of them are urgent tasks within the regular missions, including 135 fast response to incidents, serious accident disposal and AVI checkpoint interception. Further decomposition of the primary task into sub-tasks revealed that a variety of intelligent equipment were used to accomplish policing tasks, including BWC, police terminal and hand-held radio. Taken together, findings of this HTA study demonstrated the characteristics of policing with operational complexity, cross-departmental interaction, and highly demand on certain equipment. These findings can also be used as a foundation for police management, training, and supervision.

**Acknowledgments.** This study was supported by the National Natural Science Foundation of China [T2192932]. The authors gratefully acknowledge assistance from Ruojia Sun in the early work. Wenxuan Duan and Yan Shang contributed equally to the writing of this paper.

# References

Abdollahi, M.K.: Understanding police stress research. J. Forensic Psychol. Pract. **2**(2), 1–24 (2002)

Adler, N., Hakkert, A.S., Raviv, T., Sher, M.: The traffic police location and schedule assignment problem. J. Multi-Criteria Decis. Anal. **21**(5–6), 315–333 (2014)

Annett, J.: Hierarchical task analysis. In: Hollnagel, E. (ed.) Handbook of Cognitive Task Design, pp. 17–35. CRC Press (2003)

Backman, C., Löfstrand, C.H.: Representations of policing problems and body-worn cameras in existing research. Int. Crim. Justice Rev. (2021). https://doi.org/10.1177/10575677211020813

Bennell, C., Jones, N.J., Corey, S.: Does use-of-force simulation training in Canadian police agencies incorporate principles of effective training? Psychol. Public Policy Law **13**(1), 35–58 (2007)

Chen, Z.: Job satisfaction among frontline police officers in China: the role of demographic, work-related, organizational and social factors. Psychol. Crime Law **24**(9), 895–914 (2018)

Crystal, A., Ellington, B.: Task analysis and human-computer interaction: approaches, techniques, and levels of analysis. In: AMCIS 2004 Proceedings, p. 391 (2004)

Di Nota, P.M., Huhta, J.-M.: Complex motor learning and police training: applied, cognitive, and clinical perspectives. Front. Psychol. **10**, 1797 (2019)

Fayard, G.: Road injury prevention in China: current state and future challenges. J. Public Health Policy **40**(3), 292–307 (2019)

Grani, G., et al.: Can training trunk musculature influence musculoskeletal pain and physical performance in military police officers? Ergonomics **65**(2), 265–275 (2021)

Hong, S., Kim, S.C.: Mobile web usability: developing guidelines for mobile web via smart phones. In: Marcus, A. (ed.) DUXU 2011. LNCS, vol. 6769, pp. 564–572. Springer, Heidelberg (2011). https://doi.org/10.1007/978-3-642-21675-6_65

Hu, G., Baker, T., Baker, S.P.: Comparing road traffic mortality rates from police-reported data and death registration data in China. Bull. World Health Organ. **89**, 41–45 (2011)

ISO 9241-11: Ergonomic requirements for office work with visual display terminals (VDTs) - Part 11 Guidance on usability (1998)

Irving, S., Orr, R., Pope, R.: Profiling the occupational tasks and physical conditioning of specialist police. Int. J. Exerc. Sci. **12**(3), 173 (2019)

ISTQB: International software testing qualifications board, advanced level syllabus usability tester (2016). https://www.istqb.org/

Jiang, F., Xie, C., Ellis, T.: Police officers' perceptions of body-worn video cameras in Beijing. Int. Crim. Justice Rev. **31**(3), 286–303 (2021)

Krueger, R.A.: Focus Groups: A Practical Guide for Applied Research. Sage Publications (2014)

Marcus, A., Gasperini, J.: Almost dead on arrival: a case study of non-user-centered design for a police emergency-response system. Interactions **13**(5), 12–18 (2006)

Ministry of Public Security of the People's Republic of China:《公安机关现场执法视音频记录工作规定》(Regulations on audio and video recording of onsite law enforcement for public security units). Retrieved February 13, 2022, from https://www.mps.gov.cn/n2255079/n4876594/n4974590/n4974593/c5445275/content.html (2016)

Miranda, D.: Body-worn cameras 'on the move': exploring the contextual, technical and ethical challenges in policing practice. Polic. Soc. **32**(1), 18–34 (2022). https://doi.org/10.1080/10439463.2021.1879074

Mu, X.: The platform construction of the traffic management smart police center under the background of "Internet+". In: 2021 Fifth International Conference on I-SMAC (IoT in Social, Mobile, Analytics and Cloud) (I-SMAC), pp. 929–932 (2021)

Naweed, A., Balakrishnan, G., Dorrian, J.: Going solo: hierarchical task analysis of the second driver in "two-up" (multi-person) freight rail operations. Appl. Ergon. **70**, 202–231 (2018). https://doi.org/10.1016/j.apergo.2018.01.002

Oliver, P.: Why conduct a job task analysis? Ohio Police Chief **68**(1), 52 (2020)

Oudejans, R.R., Pijpers, J.R.: Training with anxiety has a positive effect on expert perceptual–motor performance under pressure. Q. J. Exp. Psychol. **62**(8), 1631–1647 (2009)

Peng, H., Qin, Y., Yang, Y., Zhang, Z., Chariete, A.: Study on individual traffic police on-duty behavior analysis method with time series scheduling. Math. Probl. Eng. **2015**, e832426 (2015). https://doi.org/10.1155/2015/832426

Phipps, D.L., Meakin, G.H., Beatty, P.C.W.: Extending hierarchical task analysis to identify cognitive demands and information design requirements. Appl. Ergon. **42**(5), 741–748 (2011). https://doi.org/10.1016/j.apergo.2010.11.009

Pfeil, K., Wisniewski, P., LaViola, J.J., Jr.: An analysis of user perception regarding body-worn 360°camera placements and heights for telepresence. ACM Symp. Appl. Percept. **2019**, 1–10 (2019)

Lim, Y., Sato, K.: Scenarios for usability evaluation: using design information framework and a task analysis approach. In: The Proceedings of the International Ergonomics Association 15th Technical Congress (2003)

Li, M., Ding, D., Wang, M., Wang, G., Xiao, G., Ye, X.: Going SPO: hierarchical task analysis of pilot flying and pilot monitoring in two-crew operations. In: 2021 IEEE/AIAA 40th Digital Avionics Systems Conference (DASC), pp. 1–5 (2021)

Liljegren, E.: Usability in a medical technology context assessment of methods for usability evaluation of medical equipment. Int. J. Ind. Ergon. **36**(4), 345–352 (2006)

Liu, Q., Liu, C.: The theoretical model of the administrative power of the traffic police in China. China Legal Sci. **8**, 27 (2020)

Scoggins, S.E., O'Brien, K.J.: China's unhappy police. Asian Surv. **56**(2), 225–242 (2016)

Shahini, F., Zahabi, M., Patranella, B., Mohammed Abdul Razak, A.: Police officer interactions with in-vehicle technologies: an on-road investigation. In: Proceedings of the Human Factors and Ergonomics Society Annual Meeting, vol. 64, No. 1, pp. 1976–1980. SAGE Publications, Sage CA, Los Angeles, CA (2020)

Shepherd, A.: HTA as a framework for task analysis. Ergonomics **41**(11), 1537–1552 (1998)

Stanton, N.A.: Hierarchical task analysis: Developments, applications, and extensions. Appl. Ergon. **37**(1), 55–79 (2006). https://doi.org/10.1016/j.apergo.2005.06.003

Stewart, D.W., Shamdasani, P.N.: Focus Groups: Theory and Practice (20). Sage publications (2014)

Tremblay, M.C., Hevner, A.R., Berndt, D.J.: Focus groups for artifact refinement and evaluation in design research. Commun. Assoc. Inf. Syst. **26**, 600–618 (2010). https://doi.org/10.17705/1CAIS.02627

Van Velsen, L., Van Der Geest, T., Klaassen, R., Steehouder, M.: User-centered evaluation of adaptive and adaptable systems: a literature review. The Knowl. Eng. Rev. **23**(3), 261–281 (2008)

Wang, F.-Y.: Integrated intelligent control and management for urban traffic systems. In: Proceedings of the 2003 IEEE International Conference on Intelligent Transportation Systems, vol. 2, pp. 1313–1317 (2003) https://doi.org/10.1109/ITSC.2003.1252696

Wang, N.: A survey study on police involvement in non-policing activities among street-level police officers [guanyugonganjiguan jicengpaichusuo canyufeijingwuhuodongqingkuangde diaochayanjiu]. J. Jiangxi Police College **5**, 71–77 (2011)

Wang, Z., Zhang, J., Sun, X., Guo, Z.: Applying hierarchical task analysis to improve the safety of high-speed railway: how dispatchers can better handle the breakdown of rail-switch. In: Stephanidis, C., Antona, M., Ntoa, S. (eds.) HCII 2021. CCIS, vol. 1421, pp. 528–536. Springer, Cham (2021). https://doi.org/10.1007/978-3-030-78645-8_67

Wolfe, S., Rojek, J., McLean, K., Alpert, G.: Social interaction training to reduce police use of force. Ann. Am. Acad. Pol. Soc. Sci. **687**(1), 124–145 (2020)

Zahabi, M., Kaber, D.: Identification of task demands and usability issues in police use of mobile computing terminals. Appl. Ergon. **66**, 161–171 (2018)

Zahabi, M., Pankok, C., Jr., Park, J.: Human factors in police mobile computer terminals: a systematic review and survey of recent literature, guideline formulation, and future research directions. Appl. Ergon. **84**, 103041 (2020)

Zhang, X., Hongyan, Y.A.O., Guoqing, H.U., Mengjing, C.U.I., Yue, G.U., Xiang, H.: Basic characteristics of road traffic deaths in China. Iran. J. Public Health **42**(1), 7 (2013)

Zhang, X., Xiang, H., Jing, R., Tu, Z.: Road traffic injuries in the People's Republic of China, 1951–2008. Traffic Inj. Prev. **12**(6), 614–620 (2011)

Zhou, J.: Jicengminjing mianlin zuidadekunnan shi jinglibuzu [The biggest difficulty that frontline officers face is police manpower shortage] (2022). http://lianghui.people.com.cn/2013npc/n/2013/0309/c357320-20734430.html

Zwingmann, L., Hoppstock, M., Goldmann, J.-P., Wahl, P.: The effect of physical training modality on exercise performance with police-related personal protective equipment. Appl. Ergon. **93**, 103371 (2021)

# Social Exposure and Burnout During the Pandemic: An Investigation on Three Different Positions of Frontline Metro Staffs

Yao Fu[1], Ranran Li[4], Jingyu Zhang[2,3]([✉]), Zizheng Guo[1,5,6], and Guo Feng[7]

[1] School of Transportation and Logistics, Southwest Jiaotong University, Chengdu, China
[2] Institute of Psychology, Chinese Academy of Sciences, Beijing, China
1741555301@qq.com
[3] Department of Psychology, University of Chinese Academy of Sciences, Beijing, China
[4] Chengdu Rail Transit Group Co., Ltd., Chengdu, China
[5] Comprehensive Transportation Key Laboratory of Sichuan Province, Chengdu, China
[6] National Engineering Laboratory of Integrated Transportation Big Data Application Technology, Chengdu, China
[7] Psychological Research and Counseling Center, Southwest Jiaotong University, Chengdu, China

**Abstract.** Besides being a threat to public physical health, COVID-19 may also bring harm to peoples' mental health as well. This preliminary study aimed to explore how different levels of social exposure might result in different mental health outcomes (e.g., burnout) on frontline metro staff, who guarantee the efficiency and safety of urban transportation. Three positions of frontline metro staff with different levels of social exposure, namely station attendants, train drivers, and maintenance workers. Two waves of cross-sectional studies were conducted at two time points, one was shortly after the lockdown in 2020, the other was 5 months later in July 2020. Results showed that there is no significant difference between stress levels after the lockdown. However, a significant difference was observed in the burnout levels after several months of operation. Staff with more contact with passengers (i.e., station attendants) reported the highest level of burnout. Staff with less contact with passengers (i.e., maintenance workers) reported the lowest level of burnout. A possible explanation of such phenomenon was that higher social exposure during the pandemic may cause more anxiety and fear to be infected as well as more emotional labor to deal with people wearing masks. We also discussed possible methods to improve the well-being of metro staff.

**Keywords:** Metro staff · COVID-19 · Burnout · Stress · Social exposure

## 1 Introduction

The novel coronavirus (COVID-19) outbreak at the beginning of 2020 has caused widespread impact on work and life worldwide [1]. In response to the pandemic, governments around the world initiated different levels of social distancing policies and encourage work-at-home to avoid contract the virus [2]. However, the personnel in important public sectors have to maintain normal, if not more stressed, operations. For example, doctors have to be in close contact with patients or suspected infected people [3]. The police need to maintain order and protect the safety of the population [4]. Staff in the transportation department were also required to provide their service.

Studies have pointed out that the mental health of these workers might be undermined. A survey of resident physicians found that COVID-19 presented a threat to the mental health of the medical staff [5]. There has been a clear surge of pandemic-related psychological distress including fear, anxiety, perceived threat, depression, and stress [6]. The psychological and social effects of the COVID-19 pandemic are pervasive, and there is potential for a long-lasting impact on mental health [7].

Feeling burnout is a severe but common experience for the public sector workers in the pandemic. Burnout refers to kinds of attitude symptoms of job pressure situation characterized by high emotional exhaustion, high levels of cynicism and reduced personal accomplishment [8]. It could not only damage the physical and mental health of employees, but also have negative impact on staffs' job performance [9]. The Economist (UK) reported that the COVID-19 pandemic had led to burnout and a wave of turnover among restaurant and hospitality staffs in the US. In 2021, an average of about 700,000 hotel staffs will leave every month. A study on the COVID-19 Burnout Scale showed that COVID-19 burnout experienced during the later stages of the pandemic might be a permanent risk factor for mental health problems [10]. Because of the importance of burnout, many studies are looking for the causes of burnout.

Social exposure might be one important factor that can influence people's burnout. Social exposure refers to frequent and intensive contact with people. One study demonstrated that people in jobs with frequent and intensive contact with people usually suffer from burnout syndrome [11]. During the pandemic, staff with high social exposure levels could worry about the safety of themselves and their colleagues [12]. We suggested that there are machismos that may cause people with higher level of social exposure to have more severe burnout. On the one hand, emotional labor could cause burnout. A study proved that nurses' emotional labor exacerbated their burnout, which increased turnover intervention [13]. It was also found that public health nurses' burnout was positively associated with emotional labor during the pandemic [14]. On the other hand, staff could fear exposure to infection, which could lead to burnout. A study about nurses, physicians and allied health staffs mentioned that respondents were most concerned about contracting COVID-19, infecting family members and caring for patients with COVID-19 [12]. Faced with COVID-19, the police plays a special role and had to stand psychological pressure as an organization that provides security services to the general public [4]. In addition, the study on health care staffs found that radiologic technicians (RTs) in isolation centers who would be directly involved in the diagnosis and treatment of COVID-19 patients were more anxious than radiologic technicians who work indirectly [15]. All of these stressors could cause them to suffer mixed emotional and psychological pain, bringing negative emotions and attitudes to themselves or their organizations, such as burnout [16].

Although many studies have been conducted on staffs in the healthcare industry, the influence on staffs in transportation department have not been fully examined. The study of Tehran metro operators found that metro operators scored high on job burnout [17]. The first serious consequence of burnout is turnover. A study found that emotional exhaustion among burnout significantly increased the staffs' turnover intention [18]. Turnover is more damaging to the transportation industry during the pandemic. More-over, feeling burnout may result in higher likelihood of traffic accidents. Past studies have found that burnout could affect drivers' behavioral performance, leading to an increase in the frequency of bad driving behavior, thus endangering road safety [19]. A case study on traffic accidents that occurred on the expressway found that the burnout problem of freeway traffic police was one of the factors that lead to highway traffic accidents [20]. But the issue has not been adequately studied. Existing researches have focused too little on burnout in the transportation industry. Current researches have focused on highways as well as road transportation such as buses. Few studies have focused on burnout in subway transportation. Most of the previous studies are case studies, with few empir-ical studies. Even in the empirical studies, the sample sizes are not large. In addition, previous studies have focused only on the serious consequences of burnout. Few studies have examined the factors influencing burnout in the transportation industry and how to reduce burnout.

In this study, we proposed to examine how the pandemic may cause burnout on metro workers. The metro industry is an important part of the transportation system with a complex structure, featuring, safety, high capacity, punctuality, efficiency and conve-nience [21]. But Metro staffs have a heavy workload. The front-line staff of metro face huge work challenges, including managing operations, supervision, and safety accident prevention. More specifically, we would attempt to investigate whether different levels of social exposure may result in different levels of burnout. To do so, we compared workers at three different positions after the resumption of work after the lockdown. These workers were different in their social exposure levels. The division of the three positions of the frontline subway staffs are divided as follows.

**Station Attendants:** Station attendants have the highest level of social exposure. They are responsible for maintaining order on the platform, proactively providing service to passengers in need, and assisting customers to ensure comfort or safety. In related occupational interviews, 70% of staffs identified contact with passengers as very close.

**Train Drivers:** Train drivers have the moderate level of social exposure. They are required to drive passenger vehicles to transport passengers and to monitor their sur-roundings for potential hazards. In case of emergency, they need to notify others first. In occupational interviews, 68% of employees responded that they need to be in constant contact with others.

**Maintenance Workers:** Maintenance workers have the lowest level of social exposure. They are responsible for diagnosing, adjusting, and repairing rail vehicles on a daily basis. In the occupational interview, 56% of employees answered that they need to have contact with other people. But most of they come in contact with during work hours are colleague (Fig. 1).

**Fig. 1.** Position of subway station attendants, train drivers and maintenance workers

## 2 Materials and Methods

### 2.1 Research Design

Two waves of cross-sectional data were collected for this study. The two waves of data were used to analyze how different positions in the subway changed after restarting to work for a period of time during COVID-19. The first wave of data was collected in February 2020, shortly after the lockdown. The second wave of data was collected in July 2020, during which the pandemic was still a threat and no vaccine was available.

### 2.2 Subjects

At stage 1, a total of 1335 participants working at the Chengdu Metro company finished the online surveys. In this sample, 67.42% were male and the average age of this sample was 24.35 (SD = 3.49). The ratio of station attendants, train drivers and maintenance workers were 40.90%, 37.83%, 21.27%, respectively.

At stage 2, a total of 805 participants working at the same company finished the online surveys. In this sample, 64.10% of the sample were male and the average age of this sample was 24.61 (SD = 3.50). The ratio of station attendants, train drivers and maintenance workers were 44.10%, 27.33%, 28.57%, respectively.

### 2.3 Measurement

**Perceived Stress:** The perceived stress was measured using the revised Chinese version of the Perceived Stress Scale (CPSS) [22, 23] at stage 1. The scale consists of 14 items (e.g., "During the pandemic, you felt tense and stressed"). The participants rated each item on a 5-point Likert scale ranging from 1 ("never") to 5 ("a lot") based on their feelings during the period since the outbreak. The higher the composite score, the greater the perceived pressure. The Cronbach's alpha for the scale was 0.76.

**Burnout:** The Chinese version of the Maslach Burnout Inventory General Survey (MBI-GS) was used to measure job burnout [8, 24] at stage 2. The scale consists of 15 items which can be divided into three dimensions: five times for emotional exhaustion (e.g., "My work left me exhausted both physically and mentally"); four times for cynicism (e.g., "I'm not as enthusiastic about my work as I used to be"); and six items for reduced personal accomplishment (e.g., "I can solve problems at work effectively"). Participants were asked to answer each question on a 7-point Likert scale, 0 ("never") to 6 ("everyday"). The Cronbach's alphas were 0.94, 0.92, 0.92, and 0.78 for the emotional exhaustion, cynicism, reduced personal accomplishment, and the overall scale of burnout, respectively.

## 2.4 Procedure

To investigate the changes that occurred in metro staffs during COVID-19 at the beginning of their work and after a period of work, online questionnaires were collected in two separate surveys. Both of which included demographic variables: the first survey focused on stress levels, and the second survey concerned about their burnout.

# 3 Results

## 3.1 Descriptive Statistics for All Variables

The basic demographic variables of the two samples were showed in Table 1. A series of non-parameters chi-square tests suggests that the two samples did not different in the composition of gender ($\chi 2 = 2.47$, $p > 0.1$), age ($\chi 2 = 5.11$, $p > 0.05$), and work experience ($\chi 2 = 2.84$, $p > 0.1$). Thus, the two samples were comparable.

**Table 1.** Demographic characteristics of the sample at stage 1

| Characteristics | Variable | Stage 1 | | Stage 2 | |
|---|---|---|---|---|---|
| | | N | % | N | % |
| Gender | Female | 435 | 32.58 | 289 | 35.90 |
| | Male | 900 | 67.42 | 516 | 64.10 |
| Age | 19–25 | 1032 | 77.30 | 588 | 73.04 |
| | 26–30 | 223 | 16.70 | 163 | 20.24 |
| | 31–46 | 80 | 6.00 | 54 | 6.72 |
| Work experience | 0–3 year | 1016 | 76.10 | 595 | 73.91 |
| | 4–6 year | 226 | 16.93 | 159 | 19.75 |
| | >6 years | 93 | 6.97 | 51 | 6.34 |
| Job category | Station attendants | 546 | 40.90 | 355 | 44.10 |
| | Train drivers | 505 | 37.83 | 220 | 27.33 |
| | Maintenance workers | 284 | 21.27 | 230 | 28.57 |

## 3.2   One-Way Analysis of Variance

To explore what kind of changes had occurred across different positions from the restart of work to working for a period of time during the pandemic, this study conducted a series of One-way ANOVAs to investigate the effects of positions on stress at stage 1, and burnout at stage 2.

**Stress Across Different Positions at the First Stage:** In this first sample, we found a significant main effect of position on stress levels, $F_{(2,1334)} = 3.72$, $p < 0.05$, but post-hoc analysis suggests that there were no significant differences for between any of the two positions (see Fig. 2).

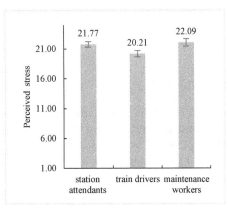

**Fig. 2.**   Stress levels of three different metro staffs

**Burnout Across Different Positions at the Second Stage:** For the sample collected at stage 2 data, we conducted a series of ANOVAs on the scores of the three sub-dimensions and the overall burnout scale (see Fig. 3).

The main effect of position on emotional exhaustion was significant, $F_{(2, 805)} = 7.34$, $p < 0.001$. The post hoc analysis showed that emotional exhaustion for station attendants higher than overhaulers ($p < 0.001$), train drivers higher than maintenance workers ($p < 0.05$).

The main effect of position on reduced personal accomplishment was significant, $F_{(2, 805)} = 5.71$, $p < 0.05$. The post hoc analysis indicated that reduced personal accomplishment for station attendants higher than maintenance workers ($p < 0.01$).

The main effect of position on burnout scores was also significant, $F_{(2,805)} = 8.93$, $p < 0.001$. The post hoc analysis revealed that total burnout score for station attendants higher than maintenance workers ($p < 0.001$), train drivers higher than maintenance workers ($p < 0.001$).

Generally, in terms of score ranking, maintenance workers for pressure level higher than station attendants and train drivers; and in terms of burnout score ranking, station attendants higher than train drivers and maintenance workers (see Fig. 4).

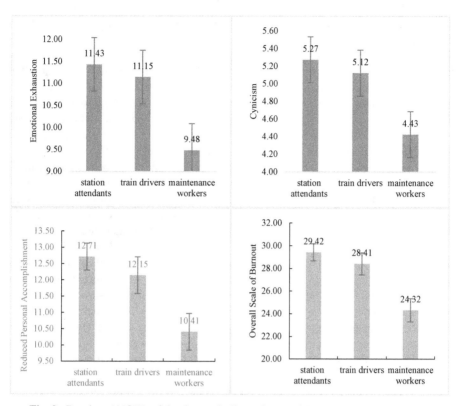

**Fig. 3.** Post hoc ANOVA of the three sub-dimensions and the overall scale of burnout

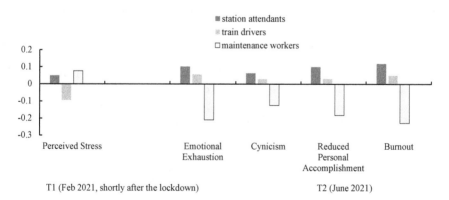

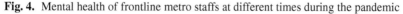

**Fig. 4.** Mental health of frontline metro staffs at different times during the pandemic

## 4   Discussion

In order to understand whether the social exposure may result in higher level of burnout among metro staffs during the pandemic, the present conducted a study by comparing the stress and burnout levels at two different stages across three positions different in their social exposure.

The study found that while no significant differences were observed across different job positions on the initial stress levels after the lockdown, there were significant differences on burnout levels after three months of work in the pandemic. More specifically, burnout reached the highest level in the position that required the highest level of social interaction with people (station attendants) and reached the lowest level in maintenance workers, who had the least amount of exposure to people. Train drivers, with a moderate level of social exposure, also had a medium level of burnout.

To note, during the lockdown, most public transportation has been suspended. As a result, the metro personnel did not differ in their perceived stress shortly after the restart of their work because they did not have much work stress. However, after several months of work during the pandemic, the difference in burnout levels occurred, and the direction lied in according to our prediction. Station attendants had the highest level of contact with people during the pandemic, followed by the train drivers. This exposes them to great anxiety and stress when serving passengers [15]. Although the present studies did not identify the specific sources of such anxiety, several recent studies have shown that during COVID-19, workers who require significant exposure to people (i.e., physicians, nursing staff) would be fearful to get infected [12]. In addition, they may also experience increased burden of emotional labor because of the social distancing policies and masking wearing [14]. A recent study suggested that wearing masks may reduce the capability to detect others' emotion [25], which might cause tensions for those who need to provide services.

We found people working at different positions may have different level of burnout and the possible cause might be related to the degree of social exposure.

Burnout was not only a mental health problem but may also threat safety performance of metro staffs. As a result, certain action is needed to improve the situation of frontline subway employees. In our study, we help identify that social exposure might be an important risk factor during the pandemic. As a result, certain support should be provided to those who need to have frequent contact with people.

Several measures might be useful in these circumstances. First, the employees might need certain counseling to deal with fear to the covid. Second, they may need training to cope with emotional unstable passengers and colleagues. Finally, they may need more organizational support such as reduction of work and more positive.

Some limitations should be mentioned before making a final conclusion. Frist, we conducted two cross-sectional studies and measured two different variables at each stage rather using a longitudinal design due to difficulty to track the original participants. Although the compositions of the two samples were similar, readers must be aware that other difference between the two samples might confound the results. Second, we did not measure and controlled the actual workload of the three positions. One alternative explanation might be that the cause behind the job differences was not social exposure but actual workload. It is possible that maintenance workers may happen to have few works to do during this period. Future studies may benefit from using better controls to improve our understanding of such phenomenon.

# 5  Conclusions

In summary, this study focused on the effects of the COVID-19 pandemic on burnout among frontline metro staffs in different positions. As the pandemic continues, burnout occurs among staffs in frontline subway positions. In addition, burnout is more severe in positions with higher levels of social exposure. This study provides preliminary valuable information for the study of mental health as well as burnout among staffs in frontline subway positions. However, these results should be considered in light of limitations. The study did not consistently collect data on staff stress levels. The follow-up study design should be optimized to allow for the tracking and collection of staff stress levels and burnout levels. Further, the veracity of this finding should be argued.

**Acknowledgements.** Yao Fu and Ranran Li contributed equally to the writing of this paper. This study was supported by the National Natural Science Foundation of China (Grant NO. 52072320)

# References

1. Wang, C., Horby, P.W., Hayden, F.G., Gao, G.F.: A novel coronavirus outbreak of global health concern. Lancet **395**(10223), 470–473 (2020)
2. Toscano, F., Zappalà, S.: Social isolation and stress as predictors of productivity perception and remote work satisfaction during the COVID-19 pandemic: the role of concern about the virus in a moderated double mediation. Sustainability **12** (2020)
3. Xiao, C.: A novel approach of consultation on 2019 novel coronavirus (COVID-19)-related psychological and mental problems: structured letter therapy. Psychiatry Invest. **17**(2), 175–176 (2020)
4. Andraszak, N.: Engagement of the police during the COVID-19 crisis: how did the pandemic change the work of police officers? E-Mentor **3**, 32–40 (2020)
5. Roman, M., Pea, A., Rajko, M., Trukelj, T.: Building organisational sustainability during the COVID-19 pandemic with an inspiring work environment. Sustainability **13** (2021)
6. Albery, I.P., Spada, M.M., Nikcevic, A.V.: The COVID-19 anxiety syndrome and selective attentional bias towards COVID-19-related stimuli in UK residents during the 2020–2021 pandemic. Clin. Psychol. Psychother. **28**(6), 1367–1378 (2021)
7. Holmes, E.A., et al.: Multidisciplinary research priorities for the COVID-19 pandemic: a call for action for mental health science. Lancet Psychiatry **7**(6), 547–560 (2020)
8. Maslach, C., Schaufeli, W.B., Leiter, M.P.: Job burnout. Ann. Rev. Psychol. **52**(1), 397–422 (2001)
9. Schaufeli, W.B., Bakker, A.B.: Job demands, job resources, and their relationship with burnout and engagement: a multi-sample study. J. Organ. Behav. **25**(3), 293–315 (2004)
10. Moron, M., Yildirim, M., Jach, L., Nowakowska, J., Atlas, K.: Exhausted due to the pandemic: validation of coronavirus stress measure and COVID-19 burnout scale in a Polish sample. Curr. Psychol. (2021)
11. Friganovi, A., Seli, P.: Levels of burnout syndrome in Croatian critical care nurses: a cross-sectional study. Psychiatria Danubina **32**(Suppl. 4), 478–483 (2020)
12. Sara, H., et al.: Immediate impact of the COVID-19 pandemic on the work and personal lives of Australian hospital clinical staff. Australian Health Review: A Publication of the Australian Hospital Association (2021)

13. Back, C.Y., Hyun, E.S., Jeung, Y., Chang, S.J.: Mediating effects of burnout in the association between emotional labor and turnover intention in Korean clinical nurses. Saf. Health Work **11**(1), 88–96 (2020)

14. Kim, M.-N., Yoo, Y.-S., Cho, O.-H., Hwang, K.-H.: Emotional labor and burnout of public health nurses during the COVID-19 pandemic: mediating effects of perceived health status and perceived organizational support. Int. J. Environ. Res. Public Health **19**(1) (2022)

15. Omar, R., Hussein, A.: Stress-induced cognition among radiologic technologists in COVID-19 quarantine centers in Palestine. Clin. Psychol. Psychother. **28**(6) (2021)

16. Zare, S., Kazemi, R., Izadi, A., Smith, A.: Beyond the outbreak of COVID-19: factors affecting burnout in nurses in Iran. Annals Global Health **87**(1) (2021)

17. Khani, M.H., Nia, A.A.A.: The relationship between equity-perception and job burnout among Tehran urban rail operators (metro). Life Sci. J. Acta Zhengzhou University Overseas Ed. **10**(1), 874–881 (2013)

18. Na, S.Y., Park, H.: The effect of nurse's emotional labor on turnover intention: mediation effect of burnout and moderated mediation effect of authentic leadership. J. Korean Acad. Nurs. **49**(3), 286–297 (2019)

19. Ma, X., et al.: Effect of organizational identity and job burnout on aberrant driving behavior of bus drivers. J. Highway Transport **33**(6), 224–234 (2020). (in Chinese)

20. Li, B., Liu, J.X.: Research on preventive management of freeway traffic accident. In: Paper presented at the International Conference on Materials, Transportation and Environmental Engineering (CMTEE 2013), Taichung, Taiwan, 21–23 Aug 2013

21. Peng, M., Cheng, X., Cong, W., Yang, H., Zhang, H.: Experimental investigation on the characteristics and propagation of fire inside subway train. Tunnel. Underground Space Technol. **107**, 103632 (2021)

22. Cohen, M.R., Pickar, D., Dubois, M.: The role of the endogenous opioid system in the human stress response. Psychiatric Clin. North Am. **6**(3), 457–471 (1983)

23. Yang, T.-z., Huang, H.-t.: An epidemiological study on stress among urban residents in social transition period. Chin. J. Epidemiol. (9), 11–15 (2003)

24. Li, C., Shi, K., Luo, Z.: Work-family conflict and job burnout of doctors and nurses. Chin. Mental Health J. (2003)

25. Carbon, C.C.: Wearing face masks strongly confuses counterparts in reading emotions. Front. Psychol. **11** (2020)

# User-Centered Interface Design and Evaluation for Teleoperated Cranes with Boom Tip Control

Lorenz Prasch[1], Felix Top[2(✉)], Jonas Schmidtler[1], Klaus Bengler[1], and Johannes Fottner[2]

[1] Chair of Ergonomics, Technical University of Munich, Munich, Germany
`lorenz.prasch@tum.de`
[2] Chair of Material Handling, Material Flow, Logistics, Technical University of Munich, Munich, Germany
`felix.top@tum.de`

**Abstract.** Several human-centered remote control systems for cranes that track the operator's position were developed and evaluated. Current HMI solutions are hard to master as they are not in accordance with the users' mental models. A series of two empirical studies investigated the potential, first in an online questionnaire, and second using a crane operated by expert users as well as novices. Usability in terms of effectiveness, efficiency and satisfaction was the central dependent variable. Results show potential for the newly developed solutions, mainly in terms of satisfaction. Effectiveness and efficiency were on the same level with the newly developed systems as with the conventional control system. Despite no clear indication that performance in terms of effectiveness and efficiency increased, the advantages in applicability of the new control systems as well as participant preference suggest that further development of user-centered teleoperation controls is worthwhile. The results provide insight into human remote control operation, general perspectives toward human orientation changes, and a fundament for future development of teleoperation interfaces.

**Keywords:** Human-machine interaction · User-centered design · Crane control · Teleoperation · Boom tip control

## 1 Problem Statement

Cranes are important tools in numerous industrial sectors. Except for a few special applications, all cranes—regardless of their field of application—are controlled by a human operator ("crane operator") who essentially has two core tasks [1]: to monitor the crane, the load and the environment and, by exercising due care and taking appropriate precautions, to ensure that dangerous situations and damage of all kinds are avoided. Additionally, it is the operator's job to control the crane drives and thus determine the load's movement in such a way that the operator moves the load safely from the starting point to its destination.

© The Author(s), under exclusive license to Springer Nature Switzerland AG 2022
D. Harris and W.-C. Li (Eds.): HCII 2022, LNAI 13307, pp. 189–211, 2022.
https://doi.org/10.1007/978-3-031-06086-1_15

According to experts, operator error is the main source for all kind of risks during crane operation [42]. Research shows for example that 43% of all examined crane accidents between 2004 and 2010 originate in operator failure [25]. Recent studies show that human factors play a crucial role in up to one third of all crane accidents [45]. Therefore, a closer look at current crane control seems appropriate. Crane loads are usually moved by directly controlling individual drives inside the crane, such as slewing gears, trolleys and hydraulic cylinders via a haptic user interface. The most common user interfaces are joysticks, levers or buttons [32]. Total load movement is the sum of all the crane's translatory and rotary drive movements. Determining the required direction of control actuation requires the operator to mentally convert the desired load movement to the individual degree of freedom (DOF) of the system, whereby both the DOF's characteristics (possible movements and accelerations) and the direction of movement must be correctly assessed.

Additionally, many cranes are equipped with a radio control system that allows the operator to move freely relative to the crane during the load movement. The advantages of radio control systems over operation from a fixed operator position (e.g., cabin) are numerous [32]. In addition to flexibility, using radio control systems can result in considerable safety gains. The operator can freely select his position in order to have an optimum view of the load and the transport environment, allowing him to perform the monitoring function properly. While this flexibility in operator location does often complicate mentally computing the correct control inputs, the advantages of teleoperation over a fixed operating station have made remote crane control an indispensable tool in many cases [32]. The fact that the radio control's input actuators are linked to the crane's DOF and thus to the cranes' coordinate system means that the operator must consider several facts to move a load safely. Variables include the crane's current position, the crane's kinematics and operator's current position relative to the crane.

As all crane movements are controlled by the operator, the design of the human-machine interface becomes a critical component in process and operator safety. Especially with the frequent simultaneous movements of several DOFs, the associated cognitive load for the operator complicates manipulating the load. From a human factors point of view, operating problems occur mainly because the user and machine coordinate systems do not match, which is a violation of the *compatibility postulate* by [7]. The consequence is an increase of the conversion effort for the operator, which—due to the increased cognitive load—can be reflected in longer execution times and increased error rates. Consequently, the current design of radio remote control leaves great potential for improvement. The stated problems occur in teleoperated cranes regardless of the operating environment and are also the subject of research in related domains such as telerobotics.

## 2    State of the Art

### 2.1    Current Crane Control

In accordance with DIN EN 13557 [11], manual crane control can—amongst others—be performed either from a driver's cab that is permanently installed on the crane or from a floor-mounted, i.e., portable control panel. In general, control elements based on the crane coordinate system are used, which are referred to as *axis-based* controls. This means that the movement of a particular control element results in movement of the assigned single DOF (i.e., drive) on the crane. Assignment of individual control elements to corresponding crane drives is visualized via icons, which are placed next to the respective control elements on the radio control. The icons are uniformly specified for each crane type (see e.g., [12]; icon examples are displayed in Fig. 1). The main differences between existing crane radio controls from the operator's point of view are the design of the transmitter and the control elements. The most frequently used control devices for drive movements are linear levers and joysticks [32], as shown in Fig. 1. Additionally, remote controls with push buttons also exist [32]. Generally, any type of crane can be controlled with any type of control, as long as the control has the same number of degrees of freedom as the crane has drives.

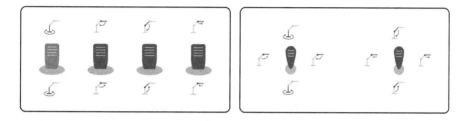

**Fig. 1.** Schematics of the two archetypical control solutions for loader cranes. Linear lever control *(left)* and dual joystick control *(right)*.

## 2.2   Research Approaches

Research related to improving crane control focuses on two areas:

- Resolving incompatibility between the control element input and the hook's movement, to simplify the mapping between control elements and the crane movements. This is mainly done by introducing *boom tip control*.
- Improving the usability of the remote crane control (i.e., the human-machine interface) by using alternative, optimized interaction paradigms.

**Boom Tip Control.** In order to resolve the incompatibility between user input and load movement, *boom tip control* is a promising approach. When using boom tip control, the desired movement of the hook is specified directly, instead of controlling the movements of several individual DOF independently in order for all joint movements to accumulate to the desired hook or load movement. A computer calculates the necessary directions and speeds of all individual crane drives by using inverse kinematics so that the desired hook movement emerges.

Research regarding boom tip control is primarily found in the areas of forest machinery and loader cranes, as seen for example in [2,15,28,29,46–49]. Apart from research, a few commercial cranes already exist that can be equipped with boom tip control, showing that it is of great interest for machine manufacturers, too [20,21]. In particular, [28] shows that boom tip control leads to shorter learning times and less mental stress for the operator, especially when working with forestry machines. [31] confirm the promising potential of boom tip controls in hydraulic cranes for forest operations in a study with novices: Cycle times and error rates are significantly lower with boom tip controls than with conventional degree-of-freedom controls. Consequently, boom tip control is considered an appropriate concept for improving crane control with regard to usability and operator acceptance.

While boom tip control proves a viable concept for crane control, in order to unfold its full potential, it needs to be accompanied by an adequate humanmachine interface (HMI). Only this combination can ensure a solid system usability as well as a fast learning curve.

**Improving the Crane Control's Usability.** Different works by Peng et al. show the potential of alternative input possibilities for boom tip control. The Magic Wand [37] uses a camera above the hook on a bridge crane. Using image processing, the system can locate a reflective marker mounted at the end of a wand and follow the marker movement along with the hook movement. Another approach, which is also based on motion tracking, is described in [38,39]: Instead of a marker on a stick, the hook follows an active RFID tag, which is either held in the operator's hand or worn directly by the operator as part of a glove. For this purpose the crane and its surroundings are equipped with RFID receivers. The studies by Peng et al. [36] show a saving potential of up to 40% (depending on environment and sequence of movements) in operating time when lifting devices using both the "Magic Wand" and the RFID tag as well as considerable improvement in the cognitive load when using ergonomically optimized input possibilities. In addition, an ergonomically designed operator interface and the resulting elimination of conversion between the operator and machine coordinate system significantly reduce the number of errors, since the probability of operating errors is reduced by improved compatibility between the user and the machine. However, controlling the hook movement using optical or electromagnetic tracking is not possible without problems in all applications: camera-based tracking may react relatively sensitively to changing light conditions or long ranges, while RFID tracking requires spatially distributed RFID receivers and thus corresponding infrastructure in the vicinity of the crane to be controlled.

Furthermore, the works of [26,43,44] investigate boom tip control with the aid of touch-sensitive input devices (touch screens). Results show that if the input modality on the screen is optimized for input mode (touch operation), and a machine control system suitable for touch input is implemented at the same time, there is significant potential for improvement compared with existing crane control systems.

[27] additionally investigate the potential of control coordinate systems that rotate with the user, allowing the operator to control the hook directly from the operator's perspective. They show that the possibility of direct hook control from the operator's perspective leads to significantly lower travel times and error rates for inexperienced operators as well as increased operator satisfaction. The results thus confirm the relationship between compatibility, user orientation and usability, especially in the context of crane operation, supporting similar findings that are known from other areas such as computer mouse control (see e.g., [14,51]).

[8,10,24] present assistance systems for load handling where the operator manipulates the load by touch. For this purpose, the forces applied by the operator are measured in amount and direction, and the crane hook follows the direction of the applied force. This is done either via sensors attached to the crane or, as in [24], via a glove equipped with sensors (referred to as Magic Glove). The disadvantage of these concepts using direct physical manipulation is that the hook must be accessible to the operator at all times. They are therefore primarily suitable for supporting employees in very limited areas, for example, when handling heavy loads in production.

In summary, it can be said that improving conventional degree of freedom controls for lifting equipment has been and is the subject of numerous research projects. The investigated approaches are thematically very broad. In contrast to the industrial application examples, however, the research focuses not primarily on hook movement and control in the form of boom tip control, but also focuses on the type and design of user input. In this context, interaction paradigms are also examined that go beyond the conventional input means, i.e., beyond the known coordinate-giving input means involving common haptic user interfaces such as linear levers, joysticks and push buttons, to enter the user's request.

## 2.3  Weaknesses of Current Controls

Current crane controls are either designed as individual drive controls or—less common—as boom tip controls. In both cases, moving a load using a manual control system requires the operator to perform several steps.

With the existing axis-based control, the desired hook movement must first be converted into movements of the crane joints. Then these movements must be assigned to the control elements by means of icons or the experience of the crane operator before they can finally be operated in the required sequence. To increase efficiency, several control elements can be moved simultaneously. Such a multidimensional control task, in which the joints are actuated separately—often simultaneously—not only contradicts the mental model of wanting to move an object [23], but consequently represents a considerable mental burden for the operator. As it is essentially multiple single tasks requiring the same resources, this increase in complexity can be explained by the multiple resources theory [33,50]. Thus, operation can lead to frustration, as can every system that does not behave in a way expected by the users [3]. This multidimensionality reduces performance and efficiency [16] of the decision-making processes during use, which in turn affects the safety in handling the system. Conventional, axis-based crane control systems represent the system model of a crane and contradict the mental model of the human operator, which focuses on the movement of the load and not on the movement of individual crane drives.

If radio control is used instead, the operator can move freely relative to the crane, but the operator coordinate system is usually not congruent with the crane coordinate system. In this case, a mental conversion is necessary. This is mainly due to the lack of compatibility between user input and machine output [7]. Despite the potential for improvement through boom tip control, the conversion problem remains. There is currently no concept known to the authors that combines the advantages of boom tip control and also solves the compatibility problem between user and machine coordinate system for use on a lifting gear in an industrially suitable manner.

### 2.4   Research Gap and Proposed Solution

Nevertheless, the boom tip control systems with innovative input paradigms show promising approaches for improving the current control situation for cranes [28,31]. However, the solutions presented so far all require either additional infrastructure in the operating environment (complete or partial illumination of the working area with cameras [37], RFID readers [36,38,39] etc.), constant physical access to the load [8,10,24], a fixed operator position, for example, in the cab [20,21,28,30,31], or lack the fulfillment of basic industrial control standards (i.e., haptic feedback [26,43,44]). So far, none of the concepts have been able to combine industrial teleoperation of the corresponding cranes and thus the direct, direction-oriented specification of the desired direction of movement from the user's point of view with the numerous advantages of radio control.

Hence, the following basic requirements for a user-centered, intuitive control system for load-lifting machines using radio control can be derived from the state of the art:

1. Direct specification of the hook movement, i.e., compatibility between user input and hook movement through an ergonomically favorable and technically robust interaction paradigm.
2. Control with free operator movement, i.e., by using a radio control.
3. Bridging inaccessible areas, i.e., no necessity for permanent hook or machine contact by the operator in order to be applicable to cranes with long ranges and lifting heights.
4. Compatibility between internal user reference and hook coordinate system, i.e., "front" of the user is at all times "front" of the crane.
5. No complex infrastructure in the vicinity of the crane, i.e., no large-scale camera or RFID reader illumination of the entire working area or other external equipment.

It appears that as of yet, there is no intuitive, radio-based input option in combination with a boom tip control that meets all basic requirements.

We developed an ergonomic load control concept that enables operators to directly manipulate the load instead of the singular degrees of freedom of a given crane by using a remote control. Considering the main objective, to move a load from point A to point B, the new concept relies on inverse kinematics and positional tracking of the operator to calculate crane movements based on user input. The user concentrates solely on the load and directs it toward its destination as if directly controlling the trajectory of the load. At the same time, operators use remote control to adjust their position freely in the crane's environment.

# 3   Intuitive Load Control

The challenge of how exactly this can be achieved was tackled in two consecutive studies that aimed to answer the following research questions.

## 3.1   Research Questions

1. **Input modality:** Which types of controls and interaction paradigms are suitable for an intuitive, goal-oriented specification of a desired load movement?
   Intuitive in this context describes a control system that is as learner-friendly as possible, so that an operator—regardless of previous experience—can discover full system functionality through trial-and-error with minimal errors. This is in line with the [4], who describe intuition as a fast and non-concious process that utilizes knowledge gained through prior experience. Additionally, we assume a cartesian space as the basis of an operator's mental model for movements [22].
2. **Compatibility:** How and when does the internal reference system for the user (groups) change?
3. **Evaluation:** How do new control concepts differ from conventional radio control systems with regard to objective (efficiency and effectiveness) and subjective (user satisfaction and acceptance) criteria?

# 4   Study 1

As described above, the two most common types of crane control units within commercial loader cranes are the linear lever control and dual joystick control. Since the general movement of the load corresponds to a two-dimensional movement in a two-dimensional cartesian space (x-y plane, parallel to the ground), in terms of primary compatibility [7] the dual joystick control was chosen as the basis for the new intuitive control. We therefore call this system the intuitive dual joystick control. It allows the operator to manipulate the load's movement so that its movement in the x-y plane is always parallel to the joystick's movement. Additionally, the load's speed corresponds to the joystick's angle of deflection. We assume that this corresponds to a novice's initial mental model [23] when wanting to move a load (not the crane) and should minimize the recoding effort extensively [19].

## 4.1   Methods

Since the goal of the first study is to provide an exploratory insight into how much potential the new, intuitive control provides, and the mental model is difficult to measure [34], we conducted a closed-question video simulation study to cover a wide range of users. In order to investigate the usability of the new control system as compared to the conventional linear lever control, we investigated usability in terms of effectiveness, efficiency and satisfaction [13]. Effectiveness was measured using the number of errors made during input. Efficiency was operationalized using the time-on-task as well as certainty of users' answers. Finally, we measured satisfaction using the system usability scale (SUS) according to [6]. We conducted a mixed $2 \times 2$ factor study with the between-subject factor experience (novices vs. experts) and the within-subjects factor control system (conventional single lever vs. intuitive dual joystick control).

We investigated the influence of the different control systems using videos of load movements animated in Blender. They showed a simulated crane with a moving load in the x-y plane from different perspectives on the ground as well as a picture-in-picture representation of the movement from a birds-eye view (see Fig. 2). The camera was placed at a height of 169.1 cm or the eyes of the 50th percentile (German) male [41] 12 m from the crane. Participants watched a video of a movement (see Fig. 2 *top*) and had to reconstruct the input necessary on the respective control type via the questionnaire (c.f. Fig. 2 *bottom*). For ease of execution, we divided the dual joystick control into eight discrete levels. Since the first study only focuses on the general usability of intuitive dual joystick control, only movements in the x-y plane were investigated. Hook movements in z-direction were not part of the initial investigation. Therefore, the videos showed load movements that only took place within the same x-y plane.

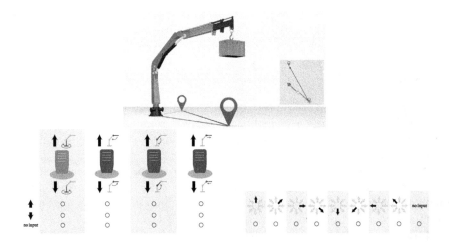

**Fig. 2.** Video of the load movement *(top)* and input options of the online questionnaire, single lever *(bottom left)* or intuitive dual joystick *(bottom right)*.

Depending on the answer to a self-assessment question on previous experience with crane control, participants were either categorized as novice or expert. From the two control systems, one was chosen at random to start with. Participants had to reconstruct three movements from a random perspective in permutated order and answer the SUS afterward. After participants finished working on the first control system, the second system was presented in the same manner. In order for participants to understand the control systems as well as the questionnaire including crane movements, explanatory videos for the questionnaire as well as both control types were included before beginning the respective trials.

## 4.2    Results

During a four-week period a total of $N = 200$ participants answered the questionnaire. 150 of these answers were complete and one additional set of answers was excluded, since the time for completing them was shorter than the length of the videos displayed. $n = 149$ participants were considered in analysis. The sample consisted of 45 experts and 104 novices ranging in age from of 16–66 ($M = 31.62$, $SD = 11.93$).

**Correctness.** A participant's correctness is calculated using the number of correct answers divided by the total amount of answers (three) per control system. This consequently means, that a participant can be 0%, 33%, 67% or 100% correct. Figure 3 shows that the correctness of participants using the linear lever control is rather equally distributed. Using the intuitive dual joystick control, participants are observed to be correct more often among both experience levels.

**Table 1.** Means and standard deviations of the correctness of the respective groups.

|  | Linear lever | | Dual joysick | |
|---|---|---|---|---|
|  | M | SD | M | SD |
| Experts | 0.48 | 0.39 | 0.61 | 0.45 |
| Novices | 0.46 | 0.36 | 0.78 | 0.33 |

A multifactorial analysis of variance (ANOVA) with the factors experience and control system shows a significant effect of the control system on the correctness ($F(1,147) = 26.98$, $p < .001$, $\eta^2 = .114$). A comparison of the means (see Table 1) shows that users were more often correct when using the intuitive dual joystick control as compared to the linear lever control. Experience does not have a significant influence. There is a significant interaction of correctness between control system and experience ($F(1,147) = 4.68$, $p < .05$, $\eta^2 = .012$). A comparison of the means (see Table 1) shows that both groups are similar in their correctness with the single lever control. Using the intuitive dual joystick control, both groups produce correct results more often. In the latter case, novices, however, are correct significantly more often than experts.

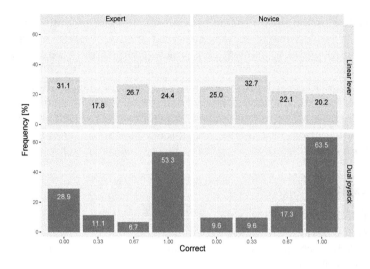

**Fig. 3.** Histogram of the percentage of correct answers for each group and control system. Since there were three inputs per participant, each participant could either get a correctness of 0%, 33%, 67% or 100%. Corresponding data can be found in Table 1.

**Time.** The time needed by participants to complete every page of the questionnaire with a single movement includes the time needed to play the video, understand the task and select the appropriate response. This corresponds to reality, where participants also need to imagine the movement, understand the necessary action and apply the appropriate control input. Figure 4 illustrates the times needed.

A multifactorial ANOVA with the factors experience and control system shows a significant effect of the control system on the time to complete $(F(1,147) = 117.74, p < .001, \eta^2 = .107)$. A comparison of the means (see Table 2) shows that users were quicker when using the intuitive dual joystick control as compared to the linear lever control. Experience does not have a significant influence. There is also no significant interaction of experience and control system.

A multifactorial ANOVA with the factors control system and trial number shows a significant effect of the control system $(F(1,148) = 118.5, p < .001, \eta^2 = .107)$ and the trial number $(F(2,592) = 9.88, p < .001, \eta^2 = .016)$ on the time to complete. A comparison of the means (see Table 2) shows that users were quicker when using the intuitive dual joystick control as compared to the linear lever control. Also, a gradual decline in time needed to complete with advancing trials can be observed, regardless of the control system used. There is no significant interaction of control system and trial number.

**Usability.** The usability of the two control systems was recorded using the SUS questionnaire. Figure 5 gives an overview of the obtained results. We also asked the participants to rate the certainty of their answers on a scale ranging from 0 to 100.

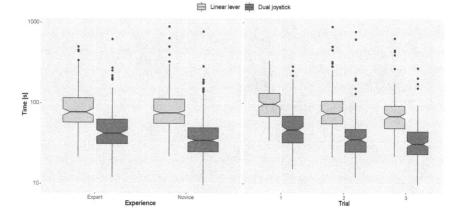

**Fig. 4.** Boxplots of the time to complete, divided in experience and control system *(left)* as well as trial number and control system *(right)*. The corresponding data can be found in Table 2. The boxplot shows the median with a 95-% confidence interval (notches) and the box from the 25.-75. quartile with the whiskers including all values within the 1.5 interquartile range. Note that the y-axis is logarithmic.

**Table 2.** Means and standard deviations of the time of the respective groups.

|  | Trial | Control system | | | |
|---|---|---|---|---|---|
|  |  | Linear lever | | Dual joystick | |
|  |  | M | SD | M | SD |
| Experts | 1 | 121.0 | 72.7 | 71.2 | 52.7 |
|  | 2 | 110.0 | 98.4 | 60.7 | 92.0 |
|  | 3 | 89.8 | 90.0 | 50.0 | 48.7 |
| Novices | 1 | 106.0 | 50.7 | 56.3 | 41.0 |
|  | 2 | 96.6 | 101 | 45.6 | 76.3 |
|  | 3 | 83.8 | 72.3 | 36.0 | 22.8 |

A multifactorial ANOVA with the factors experience and control system shows a significant effect of the control system on the SUS score $(F(1,147) = 202.68, p < .001, \eta^2 = .387)$ and the certainty toward the own answer $(F(1,147) = 40.03, p < .001, \eta^2 = .055)$. A comparison of the means (see Table 3) shows that users rated the intuitive dual joystick control more highly on its usability and were more certain of their own answers. Experience does not have a significant influence. Neither is there a significant interaction of experience and control system.

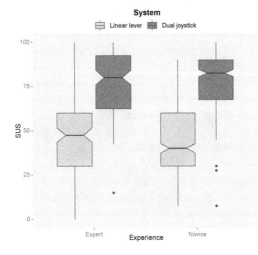

**Fig. 5.** Boxplot of the SUS scores divided into experience and control systems. The boxplot shows the median with a 95-% confidence interval (notches) and the box from the 25.-75. quartile with the whiskers including all values within the 1.5 interquartile range.

**Table 3.** Means and standard deviations of the SUS scores and the certainty of the respective groups.

|  |  | Control system | | | |
|  |  | Linear lever | | Dual joystick | |
|  |  | M | SD | M | SD |
|---|---|---|---|---|---|
| Experts | SUS | 47.3 | 25.3 | 76.4 | 19.4 |
|  | Certainty | 69.8 | 27.3 | 82.5 | 20.8 |
| Novices | SUS | 44.8 | 20.5 | 78.3 | 17.8 |
|  | Certainty | 65.0 | 26.1 | 77.2 | 26.1 |

### 4.3 Discussion

Based on the analysis presented, we can conclude that the intuitive dual joystick control has higher effectiveness, efficiency and satisfaction, or more generally speaking, higher anticipated usability than the conventional single lever control. It therefore should be more closely tailored to the user's mental model [35].

To some extent, the learning effect might seem surprising (see Fig. 4 right) because both systems, the linear lever control and the dual joystick control, show a similar decrease of time-on-task across both groups. In particular, the fact that novice users show a decent learning curve in the linear lever control condition is to some extent unexpected. We assume the reason behind this to be the study format as an online study. Since the learning effect is persistent over all control systems and experience groups, while especially control systems exhibit significant differences across other dependent variables, we hypothesize that the learning effect is—at this stage—merely an effect of the online questionnaire. Participants simply got quicker in using the questionnaire during the course of the experiment.

This study shows promising results, confirming the inherent potential of a new intuitive load control with a wide range of users. However, the environment in which the experiment was carried out was very artificial and did not allow for visual feedback (and thus recognition as well as correction of errors), nor did it provide the opportunity for participants to alter their position toward the load, hence obliterating the advantages of remote control in the first place. Since a moving operator is one pivotal advantage of teleoperation however, the consequences of changing operator positions and orientations should be subject of further investigation. Observations have shown that users tend to walk and adjust their body and head posture whilst controlling a load. Two options could be implemented, either continuous or discrete change of the trajectory. Those two will be elaborated and investigated within the second study.

## 5   Study 2

In the newly developed approach for intuitive crane control, the positions of the load, the machine and the orientation of the user are considered. This approach includes implementing inverse kinematics, which allows the automatic transformation of a desired, three-dimensional load movement (x-y-z coordinates) to the respective input controls of the four degrees of freedom (slewing gear, main boom cylinder, jib cylinder and telescopic system) of the crane. Consequently, users are able to determine the resulting direction of movement for the load from their perspective, without having to first perform a mental rotation and having to break down the desired trajectory into control inputs of the individual degrees of freedom. The user controls the desired direction of movement of the load using a dual joystick control (see Fig. 1 bottom). With one joystick, the movement in the x-y plane (horizontally) can be controlled, with the other one, it is possible to move in the z-direction (vertically).

We included the point of reference within the controller and continuously capture its orientation toward the load. This is taking into account several limitations and their expected consequences within a real crane environment. As the only viable alternative would be to place the origin within an additional head-mounted device, but construction sites are usually highly dynamic and uncontrollable environments, a sudden head movement (e.g. as response to an unexpected stimulus) could have dire consequences. This is why the movement of the load was implemented to be in line with the input vector entered on the joystick. By measuring and live tracking the remote control's orientation using inertial measurement unit (IMU) sensors, we produce an alignment between the hook's direction of movement and the tilting direction of the joystick: regardless of the remote control's orientation, the hook movement is always parallel to the joystick's deviation direction. This allows for the operator to move the load without any internal conversions between his/her (and the remote control's) current orientation, the internal reference coordinate system, the crane's position, the crane's joints and the desired load movement.

Building on the results achieved thus far, the evaluation will focus on the possibility of changing the user's location during movement and the consequences this has on usability.

### 5.1   Methods

For this purpose two systems with different characteristics regarding the change of perspective when the user rotates were implemented:

- **Discrete**
  The system only changes the rotation of the user (or the radio control) at zero crossings of the joystick. So—once a movement has been started—it is continued in the exact same direction (provided the joystick position stays consistent), regardless of whether the user changes orientation toward the load or not.
- **Continuous**
  The system continuously adapts to the rotation of the user (i.e. the radio control). This enables the change of the trajectory of the load during a movement by changing the rotation of the user. For example, with this system, it is possible to "shoo the load away from you" by rotating a user's perspective toward the load, while keeping the joystick position consistent.

We conducted a $2 \times 3$ study in mixed design. The between-subjects factor experience (*experts* vs. *novices*) was tested with the within-subjects factor control system with the specifications *conventional* (the state-of-the-art crane control system with specific degrees of freedom control as a baseline), *discrete* and *continuous*. The study was conducted on an open space at the TUM campus in Garching near Munich (Germany). A loader crane (Palfinger PK 7.501) was mounted on the ground and fitted with a foam cube as substitute for a heavy load (see Fig. 6). The foam cube had a marker on its bottom to accurately determine precision. Laid out on the ground were three targets (1–3) with concentric circles spaced 8 cm apart as well as three starting positions. The starting positions were chosen to correspond to a 45°, 90° and 180° rotation between user and crane coordinate system. In order to force participants to move during the experiment, a visual obstruction was positioned between target two and three.

At the beginning of the experiment, participants filled out a demographic questionnaire that included questions regarding their experience with crane control. Similar to the first experiment, the answer to this subjective question determined whether a participant was deemed a novice or an expert. Next, the tasks to be completed were introduced. Participants were then given adequate safety gear (hard hat and safety shoes) and had the opportunity to test all three control systems in an open setting without targets or fixed positioning. As soon as participants stated that they had grasped the concept of each of the three control systems, experimental trials started. Starting with one control system, participants had to perform three different movements while standing in one of three

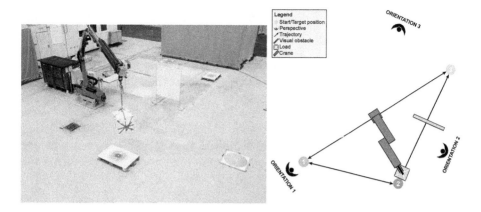

**Fig. 6.** Picture *left* and schematics *right* of the setup for the evaluation. The image shows the loader crane, including a foam load, two targets in blue and green, two orientation positions (blue-green and green-red) and the visual obstruction. Not in the picture are the third target (red) and orientation position. The orientation positions were chosen to correspond to a 45°, 90° and 180° rotation between user and crane coordinate system. (Color figure online)

different orientation positions at the beginning of the movement (see Fig. 6). Each movement started with the load in one of the target positions and the participant in the corresponding orientation position. Participants were then tasked with moving the load to one of the other targets. During the load movement, participants could move around at will. The order of movements was permutated. After completing all three trials, participants were asked to complete the SUS questionnaire while the experimenter prepared the next control system. The order of control systems was permutated as well. This research complied with the American Psychological Association Code of Ethics and was approved by the Institutional Review Board at TUM. Informed consent was obtained from each participant.

Since the degree of assistance increases with the different control systems (conventional: no assistance; discrete: inverse kinematics + discrete orientation tracking; continuous: inverse kinematics + continuous orientation tracking), our alternative hypotheses were:

$H_1$ Independent of experience, using the continuous system is more effective than the two other systems.

$H_2$ Novices are most efficient while using the continuous control system.

$H_3$ Both intuitive control systems (discrete and continuous) are more satisfying than the conventional control system.

We operationalized the three usability criteria of effectiveness, efficiency and satisfaction comparable to the previous study. For effectiveness, we recorded the precision with which participants were able to place the load on the desired target. The marker mounted at the bottom of the load indicated one of nine concentric circles. Each circle was assigned a numeric value ranging from 1 (center, perfect) to 10 (target missed entirely). Additionally, we counted the number of errors participants made. An error was recorded every time a steering input moved the load farther away from the target rather than closer to it. Distance was calculated using the 3D coordinates of the hook and the respective target. Efficiency was measured using the time participants needed from starting the movement to hitting the target. We assessed satisfaction via the SUS questionnaire, which showed values ranging from 0 to 100 and the preference rating after the experiment. The preference rating is reported in percentages of participants favoring a system.

## 5.2   Results

A total of $N = 60$ participants took part in the experiment. Four of these had to be excluded from analysis because of technical difficulties, resulting in $n = 56$ (6 female) datasets from 28 experts and 28 novices ranging in age from of 20–62 ($M = 35.46$, $SD = 12.15$). The data analyzed is depicted in Fig. 7.

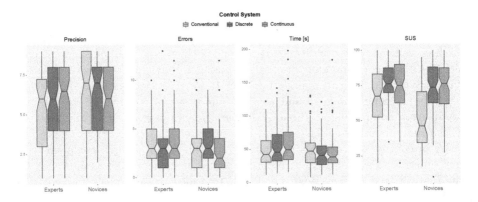

**Fig. 7.** Boxplot of the time, the precision of load placement, the number of errors and the SUS scores produced with the three different control systems (*conventional, discrete* or *continuous*). All data is divided into the two experience levels experts and novices. The boxplots show the median with a 95-% confidence interval (notches) and the box from the 25.-75. quartile with the whiskers including all values within the 1.5 interquartile range.

**Effectiveness.** A multifactorial ANOVA with the factors experience and control system shows no significant effect of the experience ($F(1,54) = 3.48$, $p = .068$, $\eta^2 = .010$) or the control system ($F(2,108) = 0.47$, $p = .626$, $\eta^2 = .002$) on the precision. There is also no interaction effect between experience and control system ($F(2,108) = 1.70$, $p = .187$, $\eta^2 = .008$). There is, however the tendency for experts to show greater precision (i.e., lower values) than novices ($M_{exp} = 5.78$, $SD_{exp} = 2.37$, $M_{nov} = 6.26$, $SD_{nov} = 2.33$), see Fig. 7.

A multifactorial ANOVA with the factors experience and control system shows no significant effect of the experience ($F(1,54) = 2.36$, $p = .130$, $\eta^2 = .009$) or the control system ($F(2,108) = 1.17$, $p = .314$, $\eta^2 = .005$) on the number of errors. The findings did reveal a significant interaction effect between experience and control system ($F(2,108) = 3.53$, $p = .033$, $\eta^2 = .014$). A post-hoc Tukey test showed a significant difference between experts using the conventional control system and novices using the continuous control system. A means comparison (see Table 4) shows that experts using the conventional control system make more mistakes than novices using the continuous control system.

**Table 4.** Means and standard deviations of the precision, the errors, the time in seconds, and the SUS score produced by the two groups for all three control systems.

| | | Precision | | Errors | | Time [s] | | SUS | | Preference [%] |
|---|---|---|---|---|---|---|---|---|---|---|
| | | M | SD | M | SD | M | SD | M | SD | |
| Experts | Conventional | 5.42 | 2.45 | 3.77 | 2.22 | 48.0 | 24.1 | 66.6 | 21.1 | 17.9% |
| | Discrete | 5.86 | 2.34 | 3.13 | 2.31 | 55.0 | 29.9 | 75.5 | 14.5 | 32.1% |
| | Continuous | 6.06 | 2.29 | 3.55 | 2.42 | 61.5 | 37.3 | 72.3 | 19.8 | 50.0% |
| Novices | Conventional | 6.35 | 2.46 | 3.12 | 2.35 | 50.4 | 26.8 | 50.7 | 21.7 | 7.1% |
| | Discrete | 6.43 | 2.18 | 3.43 | 2.06 | 45.7 | 25.0 | 70.8 | 21.0 | 35.7% |
| | Continuous | 6.00 | 2.35 | 2.60 | 2.08 | 45.3 | 27.1 | 73.1 | 18.5 | 57.1% |

**Efficiency.** A multifactorial ANOVA with the factors experience and control system shows no significant effect of the experience ($F(1,54) = 3.00$, $p = .089$, $\eta^2 = .018$) on the time-on-task. One trend suggests that experts show a longer time-on-task than novices ($M_{exp} = 54.9$, $SD_{exp} = 31.3$, $M_{nov} = 47.1$, $SD_{nov} = 26.3$, see Fig. 7). The control system did not exert any significant effect ($F(2,108) = 1.32$, $p = .272$, $\eta^2 = .004$). It did reveal a significant interaction effect between experience and control system ($F(2,108) = 6.192$, $p = .003$, $\eta^2 = .017$). A post-hoc Tukey test showed significant differences between:

- experts using the conventional control system and experts using the continuous control system
- experts using the continuous system and novices using the discrete system
- experts using the continuous system and novices using the continuous system

Comparing the means (see Table 4) shows that experts using the conventional control system are faster than experts using the continuous control system, whereas experts using the continuous system are slower than novices using both the discrete and the continuous system.

**Satisfaction.** A multifactorial ANOVA with the factors experience and control system shows a significant effect of the experience ($F(1,54) = 4.13$, $p = .047$, $\eta^2 = .024$) on the SUS score. Comparing the means reveals that experts generally rate all systems higher than novices. It also showed a significant effect of the control system on the SUS ($F(2,108) = 10.35$, $p < .001$, $\eta^2 = .101$). Comparing the means reveals that the two intuitive control systems were generally rated higher than the conventional control system. The ANOVA did not reveal a significant interaction effect between experience and control system. A post-hoc Tukey test showed a significant difference between novices using the conventional control system and all other groups as well as a significant difference between experts using the conventional and the discrete control system. Comparing the means (see Table 4) shows that novices rate the conventional control system worse than both groups rate any other system and experts rate the discrete control system higher than the conventional control system.

The question regarding which control system participants would prefer to work with in the future revealed that 30 participants would prefer the continuous system (14 experts, 16 novices), 19 would prefer the discrete system (9 experts, 10 novices) and 7 would prefer the conventional system (5 experts, 2 novices).

## 5.3   Discussion

Our first alternative hypothesis, which states that independent of experience, using the continuous system is more effective than the two other systems has to be rejected. Results have shown that there are no main effects in terms of time-on-task and errors. While precision does gradually increase with increasing level of assistance for experts, novices actually show the worst precision levels when using the continuous system. Since the continuous system is the best solution for novices in all other metrics, we assume this drop in precision occurs because participants were told to move the load to its target position as swiftly as possible without focusing on the exact positioning (speed-accuracy trade-off). This drop in precision could mean that, when working with the system they were most comfortable with, novices concentrated less on the specific movements and just positioned the load intuitively. This would result in a lower mental workload and also explain the better rating in the SUS.

Our second hypothesis, which states that novices are most efficient when using the continuous control system, must be rejected as well. Although our subjects did show the lowest time-on-task when using the continuous system, results did not significantly differ between control systems in novices. Visual comparisons (see Fig. 7 and small effect of $\eta^2 = .017$) do suggest, however, that there is a stable trend that shows that experts need more time with an increasing level of assistance, whereas novices need less. In absolute numbers, novices need an average of 10% less time using one of the new intuitive control systems when compared to the conventional control, whereas experts show a 10% to 20% increase in time-on-task with the intuitive control solutions. This discrepancy should be further investigated with more participants in order to verify the trend, and it would be interesting to determine how fast experts can adjust their mental model in order to perform on the same level as novices.

Still, the results—especially in terms of temporal advantages—do not show the expected clarity. There are several possible causes for this observation: First, we hypothesize the lack of clarity is due to the fact that the small difficulty of the tasks in combination with a long exploration phase of all three control systems lead to an overall low cognitive workload. When designing the experiment, the tasks were chosen so that they closely approximated actual crane operations but not to be particularly difficult. This is due to the fact that it was our main goal to evaluate participant interaction with the system instead of their problem-solving capacity. Consequently, the realistic tasks that were chosen provided both experts and novices the opportunity to carry them out properly, but—in combination with the long exploration phase—lead to generally low cognitive workload values in all tasks with all control systems. Consequently, this had the effect that the recoding effort did not create a bottleneck for performance.

Second, our sample—especially the two distinctive groups of experts and novices—might not prove to be representative of the general user population. Experts were significantly older than novices ($M_{exp} = 40.5$, $SD_{exp} = 12.2$; $M_{nov} = 30.4$, $SD_{nov} = 10.1$; $t(52.21) = 3.35$, $p = .001$), suggesting that cognitive capabilities—and therefore performance—might be skewed in favor of novices. This would mean that while experts have already peaked in their skill using the conventional control system, novices were quick learners and had plenty of room to improve. All the while, experts are not significantly worse using the two intuitive control modes as compared to the conventional mode that they are used to.

The third hypothesis can be accepted. Both intuitive control systems are rated more highly in the SUS and preferred by the majority of our participants when posed the question.

No clear recommendation can be made when comparing the two intuitive control concepts. The intuitive control concepts do not differ significantly in terms of effectiveness, efficiency or satisfaction. Due to the slightly better performance by novices when using the continuous control system (e.g., regarding the number of errors), however, continuous position adjustment would be preferable. Generally, it can be observed that both systems are extremely fast to be adopted by novices and experts. The user's mental model is therefore quickly adjusted to using both systems, which makes the intuitive dual joystick controls favorable compared to conventional joint-based control.

## 6  Discussion

Some of the limitations are stated in the sections above and more specific toward each study or result. This discussion is intended to be more holistic in discussing the initial motivation and introduction of the paper.

This article provides two empirical studies investigating incompatibility in control element inputs and simplifying mapping between control elements and manipulator movements. Doing so, the initially anticipated improvements in the usability of remote controlled cranes by using an alternative, optimized interaction paradigm could not be shown. The user's mental model of an interaction coordinate system in the input device is accepted. No clear difference between a continuously or discretely adapting coordinate system was identified.

Simultaneously, the newly developed systems showed distinct advantages in subjective preference while being equivalent in performance to the conventional control system. This proved true in both the expert and novice populations. Combined with the fact that these control systems enable steering of any load bearing device (i.e., different types of cranes, robots, support devices for elderly or disabled people) is a strong point in favor of adaptive coordinate mapping and direct load control.

These results, especially in light of promising previous research as well as the motivation of improved usability in load manipulation, provide substantial arguments for adapting current crane control devices with regard to compatibility and mental models. At the same time, the results underline the strong need for further investigation. In particular, questions involving input devices and user research for load manipulating devices remain open. That said, leading questions for further investigations could be:

- Input devices: What are the influences of movement type? From direct manipulation using specific input devices for large-scale (sometimes even repeatable) remote movements [18] to haptic collaboration for precise positioning at a target [40].
- User research: What do users really need for load manipulation? Including investigation of environment, products being used and uncovering additional interaction of requirements.

Bearing all this in mind, we must look beyond a product-oriented perspective to developing technologically feasible products and to developing research that focuses on actual user-centric approaches. The latter may change drastically with the advent of new systems and expiration of traditional systems. The depiction of a crane may change and could be ousted by novel robotic concepts, for instance at construction sites [5], on assembly lines [17], or when used to assist disabled users in their homes and care facilities [9]. Further research should help design future systems that are also outside of classical work realms and in the private and personal realm. The presented research provides a substantial basis for tackling this field in future work.

# References

1. Abdel-Rahman, E.M., Nayfeh, A.H., Masoud, Z.N.: Dynamics and control of cranes: a review. J. Vib. Control **9**(7), 863–908 (2003). https://doi.org/10.1177/1077546303009007007
2. Bak, M.K., Hansen, M.R., Karimi, H.R.: Robust tool point control for offshore knuckle boom crane. In: Bittanti, S. (ed.) 18th IFAC World Congress. vol. 44, pp. 4594–4599. Curran, Red Hook (2011)

3. Bessiere, K., Newhagen, J.E., Robinson, J.P., Shneiderman, B.: A model for computer frustration: the role of instrumental and dispositional factors on incident, session, and post-session frustration and mood. Comput. Hum. Behav. **22**(6), 941–961 (2006)
4. Blackler, A., Popovic, V., Mahar, D.: Investigating users' intuitive interaction with complex artefacts. Appl. Ergon. **41**(1), 72–92 (2010). https://doi.org/10.1016/j.apergo.2009.04.010, https://www.sciencedirect.com/science/article/abs/pii/S0003687009000593
5. Bock, T., Linner, T.: Robot oriented design. Cambridge University Press (2015)
6. Brooke, J.: SUS: a 'quick and dirty' usability scale. In: Jordan, P.W., Thomas, B., McClelland, I.L. (eds.) Usability Evaluation in Industry, pp. 4–7. Taylor & Francis, London (1996)
7. Bubb, H.: Systemergonomische Gestaltung. In: Schmidtke, H. (ed.) Ergonomie, pp. 390–419. Carl Hanser-Verlag, München and Wien (1993)
8. Campeau-Lecours, A., Foucault, S., Laliberté, T., Mayer-St-Onge, B., Gosselin, B.: A cable-suspended intelligent crane assist device for the intuitive manipulation of large payloads. IEEE/ASME Trans. Mechatron. **21**(4), 2073–2084 (2016). https://doi.org/10.1109/TMECH.2016.2531626
9. Campeau-Lecours, A., et al.: Kinova modular robot arms for service robotics applications. In: Rapid Automation: Concepts, Methodologies, Tools, and Applications, pp. 693–719. IGI Global (2019)
10. Colgate, J.E., Peshkin, M., Klostermeyer, S.: Intelligent assist devices in industrial applications: a review. In: IEEE Institute of Electrical and Electronics Engineers (ed.) 2003 IEEE/RSJ International Conference on Intelligent Robots and Systems, pp. 2516–2521. IEEE, Piscataway (2003)
11. Deutsches Institut für Normung e.V.: Cranes - controls and control stations. DIN EN 13557, Berlin (2009)
12. Deutsches Institut für Normung e.V.: Cranes - loader cranes. DIN EN 12999, Berlin (2013)
13. Deutsches Institut für Normung e.V.: Ergonomics of human-system interaction - Part 11: Usability: Definitions and concepts. Standard, International Organization for Standardization, Geneva (2018)
14. Fitts, P.M., Seeger, C.M.: S-R compatibility: spatial characteristics of stimulus and response codes. J. Exp. Psychol. **46**(3), 199–210 (1953)
15. Fodor, S., Vázquez, C., Freidovich, L.: Interactive on-line trajectories for semi-automation: case study of a forwarder crane. In: IEEE Institute of Electrical and Electronics Engineers (ed.) 2016 IEEE International Conference on Automation Science and Engineering (CASE), pp. 928–933. IEEE, Piscataway (2016)
16. Garner, W.R., Felfoldy, G.L.: Integrality of stimulus dimensions in various types of information processing. Cogn. Psychol. **1**(3), 225–241 (1970)
17. Gosselin, C., et al.: A friendly beast of burden: a human-assistive robot for handling large payloads. IEEE Rob. Autom. Mag. **20**(4), 139–147 (2013)
18. Herbst, U.: Gestaltung eines ergonomischen Interaktionskonzeptes für flexibel einsetzbare und transportable Roboterzellen. Dissertation, Technische Universität München (2015)
19. Herbst, U., Rühl, S., Hermann, A., Xue, Z., Bengler, K.: Ergonomic 6D interaction technologies for a flexible and transportable robot system: a comparison. IFAC Proc. Volumes **46**(15), 58–63 (2013)
20. HIAB: Ctc - crane tip control (2018), https://www.hiab.com/en/company/newsroom/news/hiab-crane-tip-control/

21. John Deere: Intelligente Kransteuerung ibc (2013), https://www.deere.de/de/forstmaschinen/ibc/
22. Johnson-Laird, P.N.: Mental models, deductive reasoning, and the brain. Cogn. Neurosci. **65**, 999–1008 (1995)
23. Johnson-Laird, P.N.: Mental models: towards a cognitive science of language, inference, and consciousness. No. 6, Harvard University Press (1983)
24. Kazerooni, H., Fairbanks, D., Chen, A., Shin, G.: The magic glove. In: IEEE Institute of Electrical and Electronics Engineers (ed.) 2004 IEEE International Conference on Robotics and Automation, pp. 757–763. IEEE, Piscataway (2004)
25. King, R.A.: Analysis of Crane and Lifting Accidents in North America from 2004 to 2010. Masterarbeit, Massachusetts Institute of Technology, Cambridge (2012). https://dspace.mit.edu/handle/1721.1/73792
26. Kivila, A., Porter, C., Singhose, W.: Human operator studies of portable touchscreen crane control interfaces. In: IEEE Institute of Electrical and Electronics Engineers (ed.) IEEE International Conference on Industrial Technology (ICIT), pp. 88–93. IEEE, Piscataway (2013). https://doi.org/10.1109/ICIT.2013.6505653
27. Kivila, A., Singhose, W.: The effect of operator orientation in crane control. In: Berg, J.M. (ed.) Proceedings of the ASME 7th Annual Dynamic Systems and Control Conference, pp. 1–7. ASME, NY (2014)
28. Löfgren, B.: Kinematic control of redundant knuckle booms with automatic path-following functions. Dissertation, Royal Institute of Technology, Stockholm (2009)
29. Majewski, M., Kacalak, W.: Innovative intelligent interaction systems of loader cranes and their human operators. In: Silhavy, R., Senkerik, R., Kominkova Oplatkova, Z., Prokopova, Z., Silhavy, P. (eds.) Artificial Intelligence Trends in Intelligent Systems, vol. 573, pp. 474–485. Springer, Cham (2017). https://doi.org/10.1007/978-3-319-57261-1_47
30. Manner, J., Mörk, A., Englund, M.: Comparing forwarder boom-control systems based on an automatically recorded follow-up dataset. Silva Fennica 53(2) (2019). https://doi.org/10.14214/sf.10161
31. Manner, J., Gelin, O., Mörk, A., Englund, M.: Forwarder crane's boom tip control system and beginner-level operators. Silva Fennica **51**(2), 1717 (2017)
32. Miadlicki, K., Pajor, M.: Overview of user interfaces used in load lifting devices. Int. J. Sci. Eng. Res. **6**(9), 1215–1220 (2015)
33. Navon, D., Gopher, D.: On the economy of the human-processing system. Psychol. Rev. **86**(3), 214 (1979)
34. Nielsen, J.: Let's ask the users [user interfaces]. IEEE Softw. **14**(3), 110–111 (1997)
35. Norman, D.A.: Some observations on mental models. In: Mental Models, pp. 15–22. Psychology Press (2014)
36. Peng, K.: Methods for improving crane performance and ease of use. Dissertation, Georgia Institute of Technology, Atlanta (2013)
37. Peng, K., Singhose, W.: Crane control using machine vision and wand following. In: IEEE Institute of Electrical and Electronics Engineers (ed.) IEEE International Conference on Mechatronics. IEEE, Piscataway (2009). http://ieeexplore.ieee.org/servlet/opac?punumber=4914928
38. Peng, K., Singhose, W., Gessesse, S., Frakes, D.: Crane operation using hand-motion and rfid tags: radio frequency identification. In: IEEE Institute of Electrical and Electronics Engineers (ed.) IEEE International Conference on Control and Automation, pp. 1110–1115. IEEE, Piscataway (2009)
39. Peng, K., Singhose, W., Frakes, D.H.: Hand-motion crane control using radio-frequency real-time location systems. IEEE/ASME Trans. Mechatron. **17**(3), 464–471 (2012). https://doi.org/10.1109/TMECH.2012.2184768

40. Schmidtler, J.A.: Optimizing haptic human-robot collaboration considering human perception and idiosyncrasies. Dissertation, Technische Universität München (2018)
41. Seidl, A., Trieb, R., Wirsching, H.J.: Sizegermany-the new german anthropometric survey conceptual design, implementation and results. In: Proceedings of 17th World Congress on Ergonomics, Beijing (2009)
42. Shapiro, L.K., Shapiro, J.P.: Cranes and Derricks. 4 edn., McGraw-Hill, NY (2011)
43. Sorensen, K., Spiers, J., Singhose, W.: Operational effects of crane interface devices. In: IEEE Institute of Electrical and Electronics Engineers (ed.) 2nd IEEE Conference on Industrial Electronics and Applications, pp. 1073–1078. IEEE Operations Center, Piscataway (2007). https://doi.org/10.1109/ICIEA.2007.4318573
44. Suter, J., Kim, D., Singhose, W., Sorensen, K., Glauser, U.: Evaluation and integration of a wireless touchscreen into a bridge crane control system. In: IEEE Institute of Electrical and Electronics Engineers (ed.) IEEE/ASME International Conference on Advanced Intelligent Mechatronics, pp. 1–6. IEEE Service Center, Piscataway (2007). https://doi.org/10.1109/AIM.2007.4412586
45. Tomakov, I., Tomakov, V., Pahomova, G., Semicheva, E., Bredihina, V.: A study on the causes and consequences of accidents with cranes for lifting and moving loads in industrial plants and construction sites of the russian federation. J. Appl. Eng. Sci. **16**(1), 95–98 (2018). https://doi.org/10.5937/jaes16-16478
46. Top, F., Krottenthaler, J., Fottner, J.: Evaluation of remote crane operation with an intuitive tablet interface and boom tip control. In: IEEE Institute of Electrical and Electronics Engineers (ed.) IEEE International Conference on Systems, Man and Cybernetics (SMC). Conference Proceedings, pp. 3275–3282. IEEE, Piscataway (2020)
47. Top, F., Pütz, S., Fottner, J.: Human-centered HMI for crane teleoperation: empirical study on the operators' mental workload. In: Proceedings of the IEEE International Conference on Electrical, Computer, Communications and Mechatronics Engineering, pp. 01–13 (2021)
48. Top, F., Pütz, S., Fottner, J.: Human-centered HMI for crane teleoperation: intuitive concepts based on mental models, compatibility and mental workload. In: Harris, D., Li, WC. (eds) Engineering Psychology and Cognitive Ergonomics. HCII 2021. LNCS, vol. 12767, pp. 438–456. Springer, Cham
49. Top, F., Wagner, M., Fottner, J.: How to increase crane control usability: an intuitive HMI for remotely operated cranes in industry and construction. In: Karwowski, W., Ahram, T. (eds.) Intelligent Human Systems Integration, pp. 293–299. Advances in Intelligent Systems and Computing, Springer, Cham (2019). https://doi.org/10.1007/978-3-030-11051-2_45
50. Wickens, C.D.: Multiple resources and mental workload. Hum. Factors **50**(3), 449–455 (2008)
51. Worringham, C.J., Beringer, D.B.: Operator orientation and compatibility in visual-motor task performance. Ergonomics **32**(4), 387–399 (1989)

# A Study on the Influence of Personality on the Performance of Teleoperation Tasks in Different Situations

Kuo Qin[1], Yijing Zhang[1,2], and Jingyu Zhang[3(✉)]

[1] School of Mechanical-Electronic, Beijing University of Civil Engineering and Architecture, Beijing, China
[2] Department of Industrial Engineering, Tsinghua University, Beijing, China
[3] Institute of Psychology, Chinese Academy of Sciences, Beijing, China
zhangjingyu@psych.ac.cn

**Abstract.** Personality is considered as one of the internal potential influencing factors of performance and an effective index to predict job performance. Past literature reveals the relationship between personality and task performance, and there is evidence that personality can effectively predict teleoperation task performance. In this study, we aim to explore the impact of personality on teleoperation performance under different situations, and to provide theoretical reference for operator selection. In this study, 96 male participants with no teleoperation experience were recruited. Their personalities were evaluated by the Big Five Inventory. The experimental task is to remotely operate a virtual machine car to complete the designated task, each task will have different levels of latency and clearance. Completion time, distance, collisions, and workload were used as indicators of teleoperation performance. Hierarchical Linear Model was used to test the relationship between personality and teleoperation performance. The results showed that with more clearance and longer latency, the number of collisions in higher extroversion participants significantly increased, while in higher negative emotionality participants, the scores decreased significantly. With more clearance, the workload of participants with higher extroversion scores decreased significantly. Further analysis found that energy level and depression were the main sub-dimensions leading to the increase in the number of collisions among the subjects with high score of extroversion and negative emotionality. With longer latency, the completion time of the participants with higher degree of anxiety increased significantly. The results showed that personality have different predictive effects on teleoperation task performance in different situations. These results may be helpful to the selection of operators.

**Keywords:** Teleoperation · Personality · Big five · Task performance · HLM

## 1 Introduction

When the working environment and intensity exceed human's normal ability, the robot can replace human for completing the task. However, due to the limitation of the level of automation and intelligence of the robot, the efficiency and quality of its individual work cannot be compared with that of human beings in some special circumstances. This contradiction can be solved by teleoperation [1], a form of operation that remotely controls a robot or system to complete a given task [2].

In recent years, teleoperation is more and more widely used, and it has a good development in the fields of surgery, disaster rescue, military mission and space exploration [3]. By teleoperating the surgical robot, surgeons can stay in a specific position for longer time, thus a series of problems caused by slight tremors of hands can be reduced, and accuracy and flexibility can also be improved [4, 5]. Search and rescue personnel can remotely operate the robot and conduct safety assessment at the scene of the disaster [6]. Teleoperation of the space roaming robot can prevent astronauts from encountering danger during planetary exploration and improve the safety of space exploration [7].

With the increasing distance, the communication latency between the operator and the robot also increases [8, 9], resulting in performance deterioration, longer completion time, and more mistakes [10–12]. In addition, due to the complexity of the environment, the space clearance in which robot can move is limited and changeable. For example, when natural cavity endoscopic surgery is performed by teleoperation, the limited space in the cavity and the diversity of the patient's cavity size makes the fault tolerance rate in the teleoperation process very small. If the patient's cavity is narrow, it will not only reduce the doctor's operational performance, but also bring great safety risks to patients [13]. Scholover (2021) also found that the smaller the horizontal distance between the environmental boundaries of the robot, the more operation errors would happen [14]. Therefore, how to improve the performance of teleoperation with latency and limited space clearance is an urgent problem to be solved.

In the most of the existing studies, teleoperation performance was improved by escalating display technology and automation level of robots [11, 15, 16]. In addition to hardware technology, human-related factors are also equally important in the process of teleoperation [17], Scholover (2018) found that temporal sensitivity of individuals can affect the performance of teleoperation tasks [18]. Personality is also considered to be one of the important potential factors influencing performance [19, 20]. For example, responsibility and emotional stability significantly affect the driver's task performance [21]. Extroverts performed faster in teleoperation tasks of robotic arms, but perform poorly in terms of safety [17]. So far, only a small number of teleoperation studies take personality into account, and there are no studies to explore the effects of personality on teleoperation performance in different situations of latency and space clearance.

To explore the effect of personality on teleoperation task performance in different situations, we built a teleoperation experimental platform, in which we set different latency and space clearance of the environment, and conducted the experiment with large samples (N > 80). Task performance is evaluated in terms of task completion time, number of collisions, and distance, and the operator's workload is also measured.

## 2 Method

### 2.1 Participants

A total of 96 participants were recruited in this study. The participants were all males and were all right-handed with no color blindness or weakness and no experience of teleoperation. Before the experiment, participants were told the details of the experimental scheme and gave informed consent orally. They went through an experiment that lasted about three hours and finally awarded ¥180 for their participation.

### 2.2 Teleoperation Experiment Platform

The experimental platform was robot simulation modeling software Coppeliasim 4.2.0 developed by CoppeliaRobotics Company. With reference to the research of Scholcover (2021) [14], the experimental situation is improved and the virtual environment of teleoperation is constructed. As shown in Fig. 1, to reduce the learning effect, three maps are constructed according to the setting principles similar to those of Upham-Ellis (2008) [22], in which the route was designed to have an equal number of left and right turns. In order to set up different space clearance, to express the horizontal distance between the environmental boundaries of the robot, the wall thickness of each map is adjusted proportionally, so that the 4 possibilities for clearance is ranged from 0.36 to 0.9 m in 0.18 m steps. Additionally, there are 6 possibilities for latency with a step size of 0.2 s, which varies from 0 to 1 s. 3 maps, 4 levels of space clearances and 6 levels of latency constitute 72 different experimental scenes ($3 \times 4 \times 6$). The latency is set in the system background and is combined with the map and clearance through coordinates. For example, if the scene consists of map 1 with a clearance of 0.9m and a latency of 0.2 s, then it will be defined as (1, 0.9, 0.2). Thus, there are 72 different coordinates. To avoid fatigue effects, we divided 72 coordinates into 6 groups, each containing 12 coordinates. The 12 coordinates contain 3 maps, 6 levels of latency and 2 levels of space clearance (0.9 m and 0.54 m, 0.9 m and 0.36 m, 0.72 m and 0.54 m, or 0.72 m and 0.36 m), which are the experimental scenes that each participant needs to experience. The 72 experimental scenes were traversed for every 6 participants. Finally, 96 participants traversed all the situations 16 times. The manipulated object is a robot car with a width of 0.108 m, and the participants see the image presented by the camera behind the car from the perspective of the first person, as shown in Fig. 2. Participants operate a three-degree-of-freedom joystick (LitestarPNX-2113) to control the forward, backward, turning or waiting of the car.

### 2.3 Independent Variables

First, we would discuss the teleoperation performance in different situations that were made up of different latency and clearance. Thus, different levels of latency and clearance are independent variables of task situation. Then, personality was the independent variable of individual. We used The Big five Inventory revised by Soto (2017) [23], which evaluate personality in five dimensions: extroversion (E), agreeableness (A), sense of responsibility (C), neuroticism (N) and openness of experience (O) and their

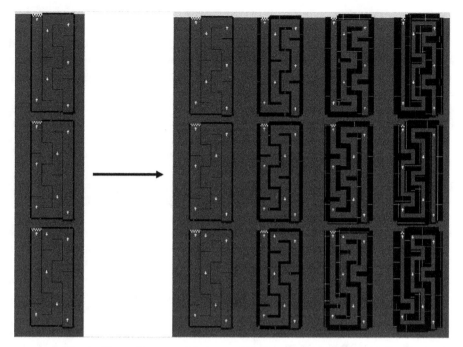

**Fig. 1.** Three of maps and their corresponding roads of different widths

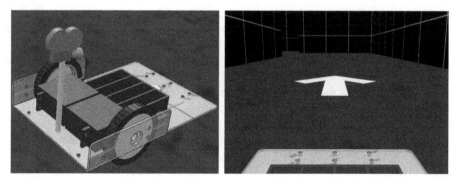

**Fig. 2.** The car operated and the perspective of the participants

sub-dimensions: Sociability, Assertiveness, and Energy Level for Extraversion; Compassion, Respectfulness, and Trust for Agreeableness; Organization, Productiveness, and Responsibility for Conscientiousness and Anxiety, Depression, Emotional Volatility for Negative Emotionality. The questionnaire introduces a strong hierarchical structure and has better prediction ability, which still retaining the conceptual focus, simplicity, and understandability of the original measurement, consists of 60 items, and each item has five options, from "1-very disagree" to "5-very agree". The score of each dimension is the sum of related items and reverse scores.

## 2.4  Dependent Variables

Teleoperation performance was evaluated from the perspectives of task performance and workload. Task performance reflects operational efficiency and effectiveness through the number of collisions, completion time and driving distance. Workload was measured by the total score of NASA-TLX. The details are as follows:

1. collisions: when the car left the wall after contact with the wall, it was regarded as a collision. If the car keeps rubbing against the wall, the number of collisions would increase at the rate of one per second. The fewer collisions, the better the task completion.
2. completion time: the time taken by the participant to run the car from the starting point to the end point. The completion time reflects the work efficiency, and the shorter time indicates the better performance of the task.
3. distance: according to the change of the coordinates of the car, the moving distance of the car was calculated in real time, and the sum of all the calculated results can be obtained after reaching the end point.
4. workload: mental needs, physical needs, time needs, performance level, effort level and frustration were used to evaluate the mental load of participants when completing each task. The higher the total score, the greater the workload [24].

## 2.5  Experimental Task and Procedure

All the experiments were done in front of a 13.6-in. laptop. Participants were asked to operate the robotic car through a joystick to complete the driving task from the starting point to the end as fast as possible, and minimize collision with the wall. They were first instructed by the experimental procedure and completed the Big five Personality Test, and then trained with and without latency to familiarize themselves with the control of the joystick for about 30 min. After a five-minute break, the formal experiment began. Before starting the operation, they were told that the latency and clearance of all subsequent experiments were random and were not told the actual latency. At the beginning of each experiment, participants were informed of the latency they would experience ("no delay", "moderate delay" or "high delay") through the prompt window in front of the screen. Every time they completed the task of a scene, they would ask to complete the NASA-TLX test. Each participant finished NASA-TLX tests 12 times.

## 2.6  Data Analysis

Because the performance of teleoperation is affected by both the task situation and the individual operator, the variables at the individual level are embedded in the variables at the task context level. In order to ensure the scientific nature of the research, this study uses the multi-layer linear model (HLM) developed and popularized by American statisticians Bryk and Raudenbush [25]. Through the hierarchical establishment of the regression equation, the intercept and slope of the individual level regression equation are set as the functions of the group level variables. Thus, different levels of data are linked together to deal with hierarchical nested data. In this study, spss 20.0 was used to sort out experimental data into two levels, and HLM6.0 is used to analyze the data.

# 3 Results

## 3.1 Null Model

First of all, in order to test the differences between groups of independent variables, the zero model test of each dependent variable is carried out according to the method of Hofmann (1997) [26]. The zero model of task performance is as follows:

$$\text{Level 1}: \quad \text{Performance} = \beta_{0j} + r_{ij} \tag{1}$$

$$\text{Level 2}: \quad \beta_{0j} = Y_{00} + \mu_{0j} \tag{2}$$

where $\beta_{0j}$ is the average performance level of the individual in the j situation; $r_{ij}$ is the total average of the performance level in each situation, indicating the random error of the task situation level; $Y_{00}$ is the difference of the average performance level of the individual i in the j situation; $\mu_{0j}$ is the difference between the j situation and the total average $Y_{00}$, which is a random error at the individual level. The analysis results of the zero model are shown in Table 1, where ICC shows the proportion of changes in dependent variables in the context level and individual level. According to Cohen, $0.01 \leq$ ICC $\leq 0.059$ is low association, $0.059 \leq$ ICC $\leq 0.138$ is medium association, and $0.138 \leq$ ICC is high correlation [27]. According to the standard, the collision times, driving distance and workload of teleoperation can be analyzed by two-layer linear model. The completion time is not suitable for HLM analysis. However, due to the hierarchical nesting structure of the data, using a single-layer linear regression model to deal with the completion time alone will make the results more complex, so the researchers still include the completion time into the results.

**Table 1.** Null model analysis results

| Variable name | df | σ | $\chi^2$ | p | ICC |
|---|---|---|---|---|---|
| Completion time | 95 | 0.051 | 110.203 | 0.137 | 0.000 |
| Collisions | 95 | 25.454 | 231.275 | < 0.001 | 0.107 |
| Distance | 95 | 2.183 | 203.302 | < 0.001 | 0.087 |
| Workload | 95 | 6320.641 | 808.841 | < 0.001 | 0.385 |

## 3.2 Random Coefficient Model

In order to test the influence of different situations on task performance, taking the number of collisions, driving distance and workload as performance evaluation indicators, the latency, clearance and their interaction terms (multiplying respectively after decentralization) were introduced into the Level1 equation to investigate the impact of task situation on performance. The model is as follows:

$$\text{Level:}\quad \text{Performance} = \beta_{0j} + \beta_{1j}(\text{latency}) + \beta_{2j}(\text{clearance}) + \beta_{3j}(\text{latency} \times \text{clearance}) + r_{ij} \tag{3}$$

$$\text{Level 2:}\quad \beta_{oj} = Y_{00} + \mu_{0j} \tag{4}$$

$$\beta_{1j} = Y_{10} + \mu_{1j} \tag{5}$$

$$\beta_{2j} = Y_{20} + \mu_{2j} \tag{6}$$

$$\beta_{3j} = Y_{30} + \mu_{3j} \tag{7}$$

where $\beta_{1j}$, $\beta_{2j}$ and $\beta_{3j}$ are the partial regression coefficients of the influence of independent variable latency, clearance, and their interaction on teleoperation task performance, respectively. The results of the random coefficient regression model are shown in Table 2, which shows that latency, clearance and the interaction between them can significantly predict the performance of teleoperation tasks. The higher the latency, the longer the completion time, the more the number of collisions, the longer the driving distance, the greater the workload. The larger the clearance, the shorter the completion time, the less the number of collisions, the shorter the driving distance, and the smaller the workload. With the increase of clearance, the negative effect of latency on completion time and collision times is getting smaller and smaller, the negative effect on driving distance is increasing, and there is no significant predictive effect on workload.

**Table 2.** Analysis results of random coefficient regression model

| Variable name | Collision | Distance | Workload | Completion time |
|---|---|---|---|---|
| Intercept | 13.412*** | 33.707*** | 261.216*** | 3.048*** |
| Latency | 27.309*** | 9.809*** | 197.503*** | 4.289*** |
| Clearance | −33.367*** | −6.175*** | −92.414*** | −2.570*** |
| Latency × clearance | −50.926*** | 8.022*** | 21.125 | −2.607*** |

NOTE. * $p < 0.05$; ** $p < 0.01$; *** $p < 0.001$. The value of the first row in the table is the intercept of the regression equation, and the other rows are the regression coefficients of independent variables to dependent variables.

### 3.3 Intercept as Outcome Model

Based on the null model, the scores of participants under five personality dimensions were introduced into the Level2 equation to investigate the influence of individual personality on teleoperation task performance in different situations. The model is as follows:

$$\text{Level 1:}\quad \text{Performance} = \beta_{0j} + r_{ij} \tag{8}$$

$$\text{Level 2}: \quad \beta_{oj} = Y_{0i}X_i + \mu_{0j} \tag{9}$$

where $X_i$ is the score of each individual dimension, and $Y_{0i}$ is the partial regression coefficient of each personality dimension to the teleoperation task performance. As shown in Table 3, it can be seen that most personality have no significant predictive effect on teleoperation performance ($p > 0.1$). The predictive effects of extroversion, agreeableness, neuroticism on completion time and agreeableness on driving distance only reached the marginal significant level ($p < 0.1$).

**Table 3.** Analysis results of intercept prediction model 1

| Variable name | Collision | Distance | Workload | Completion time |
|---|---|---|---|---|
| E | 0.055 | −0.003 | −9.356 | −0.111+ |
| A | −0.100 | −0.312+ | 0.279 | 0.060* |
| C | −0.714 | −0.207 | −3.056 | 0.029 |
| N | −0.487 | −0.162 | 9.679 | 0.116+ |
| O | 0.104 | −0.100 | 2.530 | 0.027 |

+$p < 0.1$; *$p < 0.05$; **$p < 0.01$; ***$p < 0.001$. The value in the table are the regression coefficients of independent variables to dependent variables.

In order to further investigate the influence of personality on teleoperation performance, researchers extracted the scores of participants in each sub-dimension of the five personalities and introduced them to Level2's equation. Because of the large amount of data, only significant results are listed, as shown in Table 4. The results show that the degree of anxiety has a significant positive predictive effect on the completion time and a significant negative predictive effect on the number of collisions. The higher the degree of anxiety, the longer the completion time, the less the number of collisions. The level of trust has a significant negative predictive effect on the number of collisions. The higher the level of trust is, the less the number of collisions is, and the predictive effect on driving distance and workload only reaches the marginal significant level. Compassion has a significant positive predictive effect on completion time. The stronger the compassion is, the longer the completion time is, and the predictive effect on workload only reaches the marginal significant level ($p = 0.068$). The degree of decisiveness and curiosity only reached the marginal significant level in predicting the completion time ($p = 0.08$; $p = 0.07$).

### 3.4 Slope as Outcome Model

Through the random coefficient regression model and intercept model, this study examines the effects of task context and individual variables on teleoperation performance, and continues to investigate whether the variables at the task context level affect the slope between independent variables and dependent variables at the individual level, based on which the slope prediction model, namely the whole model, is obtained. In this study,

**Table 4.** Analysis results of intercept prediction model 2

| Variable name | Collision | Distance | Workload | Completion time |
|---|---|---|---|---|
| Agreeableness | 0.349 | −0.087 | −3.818 | −0.105+ |
| Compassion | −0.386 | −0.139 | 15.849+ | 0.117* |
| Trust | −1.207* | −0.351+ | −14.303+ | 0.019 |
| Anxiety | −0.733* | −0.207 | 7.330 | 0.186** |
| Curiosity | −0.542 | −0.183 | −1.486 | 0.101+ |

Note. +p < 0.1; *p < 0.05; **p < 0.01; ***p < 0.001. The value in the table are the regression coefficients of independent variables to dependent variables.

through the previous analysis, it has been found that several elements of personality have a significant effect on the operational performance, and the interaction between the personality and the slope of task performance has been investigated in the whole model. The model is as follows:

Level 1 :  Performance $= \beta_{0j} + \beta_{1j}(\text{latency}) + \beta_{2j}(\text{clearance}) + \beta_{3j}(\text{latency} \times \text{clearance}) + r_{ij}$ (10)

$$\text{Level 2}:\quad \beta_{oj} = Y_{00} + Y_{01}X_i + \mu_{0j} \tag{11}$$

$$\beta_{1j} = Y_{10} + Y_{01}X_i + \mu_{1j} \tag{12}$$

$$\beta_{2j} = Y_{20} + Y_{01}X_i + \mu_{2j} \tag{13}$$

$$\beta_{3j} = Y_{30} + Y_{01}X_i + \mu_{3j} \tag{14}$$

where $X_i$ is a personality trait that can predict the performance of teleoperation (p < 0.1). In order to prevent the collinearity problem, the researchers centralize the latency and clearance of the adjustment test. The significant results are shown in Table 5.

For individuals with high extroversion scores, the increase of clearance will significantly increase the negative effect of latency on the number of collisions. Further analysis shows that the level of vitality is the main factor leading to this result. In terms of workload, the higher the score of extroversion, the positive effect of the increase of clearance on the workload will be significantly enhanced. Further analysis shows that sociability interaction is the main factor leading to this result.

For individuals with high score of agreeableness, the increase of clearance will significantly increase the number of collisions of teleoperation. Further analysis shows that trust is the main factor leading to this result. On the other hand, the increase of clearance will significantly reduce the negative effect of latency on distance.

For individuals with high scores of negative emotionality, the increase of latency will significantly reduce the collisions of teleoperation. Further analysis shows that anxiety is the main factor leading to this result. Individuals with high anxiety score will significantly enhance the negative effect of latency on completion time, while individuals with high degree of depression will significantly enhance the positive effect of clearance on the number of collisions in the case of high latency.

For individuals with a strong sense of responsibility, no significant effect on performance was found. However, in the sub-dimension of responsibility, the workload of individuals with high degree of responsibility will increase significantly with the increase of latency. For individuals with a high level of organization, the driving distance and completion time will be significantly reduced with the increase of latency.

**Table 5.** Analysis results of slope prediction model

| Variable name | Collision | Distance | Workload | Completion time |
|---|---|---|---|---|
| E × clearance | 6.822 | 0.728+ | −22.288* | 0.130 |
| Sociability × clearance | 2.163 | 0.613 | −28.636** | 0.067 |
| E × latency × clearance | 6.823* | 1.179 | −2.167 | 0.018 |
| Energy × latency × clearance | 7.126** | 0.720+ | 32.030 | −0.257 |
| N × latency × clearance | −8.658** | −0.437 | 12.805 | 0.140 |
| Anxiety × latency | −1.990+ | −0.256 | 1.340 | 0.304* |
| Anxiety × latency × clearance | −6.506+ | −0.548 | 6.449 | −0.148 |
| Depression × latency × clearance | −7.772* | −0.306 | 22.160 | 0.417 |
| Responsibility × latency | −0.034 | −0.400 | 24.044* | −0.004 |
| Organization × latency | −1.427 | −0.835* | 2.748 | −0.835* |
| A × latency | −0.872 | −0.743+ | 19.965+ | 0.160 |
| A × clearance | 3.692** | −0.339 | 8.864 | 0.010 |
| A × latency × clearance | 3.454 | −2.335* | −32.828 | −0.134 |

Note. +p < 0.1; *p < 0.05; **p < 0.01; ***p < 0.001. The value in the table are the regression coefficients of independent variables to dependent variables.

## 4   Discussion

Personality plays an important role in the way people react to the environment. In this study, it is found that personality have different effects on teleoperation task performance in different situations. Extroverted individuals have less workload in the context of large clearance, and social ability is the main influencing factor. Individuals with strong sociability are more likely to think positively [28]. Are more likely to be positively affected. However, in the situation of high latency and large clearance, extroverted individuals are also more likely to have more collisions, and the level of vitality is the main influencing factor. This is similar to the results of [16]. The level of energy mainly reflects the degree of nerve excitement [29], and individuals with high level of energy level prefer to pursue stimulation [30]. We speculate that the increase of latency will stimulate the individuals with high level of vitality to a certain extent, which leads them to satisfy their emotions through more collisions in the case of large clearance. Therefore, according to the different task situations, when selecting teleoperation operators, people with strong sociability are more suitable to work in such situations if the environment in which the robot is located is more mobile. If the environment of the robot is far away from the operator, there is a higher latency and a large clearance, it is not suitable to select individuals with a high level of energy.

Individuals with high scores of neuroticism had less collisions in situations with higher latency and more clearance, depression level was the main influencing factor, and anxiety degree also had a certain influence ($p = 0.06$). This is contrary to the results of [17]. Depression levels are usually accompanied by low energy and low arousal levels [23], and anxiety levels reflect an individual's fear of future events [31]. We speculate that the increase in latency reduces the behavior of individuals with these two traits and increases their fear of collisions. Although the reduction of the number of collisions improves the safety of teleoperation, individuals with high degree of anxiety will spend more time to complete the task with the increase of latency ($p = 0.02$). Therefore, when the latency is high and the clearance is large in the task situation of teleoperation, if safety is the main concern, operators with high neurotic scores can be considered to participate. If the completion time is given priority to, it is not suitable to choose operators with high neurotic scores.

Although there is no significant effect of individuals with high score of responsibility on the performance of teleoperation tasks, individuals with high scores of responsibility in the sub-dimension of responsibility will produce higher workload with the increase of latency, and individuals with high organizational level can complete tasks faster and travel shorter distances in the case of high latency.

Despite individuals with high scores of conscientiousness have no significant influence on the performance of teleoperation tasks, individuals with high score of responsibility will have higher workload with the increase of latency. Individuals with high degree of responsibility to persevere in order to pursue their goals [31]. The requirements of high-quality tasks bring them a greater workload, while individuals with high organizational levels have a clearer understanding of the order and structure of work [32]. When the latency increases, they can operate in real time more reasonably to achieve the highest performance. Therefore, when the latency is higher in the task situation of teleoperation, the operator with higher organizational score can complete the task better. In addition, this study found that individuals with higher scores of agreeableness drove shorter distances to complete tasks in the context of larger clearance and higher latency, which was similar to (Pan et al., 2016) [17], but did not find a proper reason to explain the results. In a word, personality have different predictive effects on teleoperation task performance in different situations. It is beneficial to select teleoperation operators according to the suitability of personality and specific task situations, which is helpful to start from the aspect of personnel. Improve the task performance of teleoperation.

## 5   Conclusion

In this study, in order to explore the influence of personality on teleoperation task performance in different situations, a teleoperation experimental platform was built, and different task situations were set up with different latency and clearance. The personality of individuals were measured by the Big five Inventory, and an empirical study of 96 samples was completed. The results showed that personality have different effects on teleoperation task performance in different situations. This finding supports the consideration of the influence of personality in teleoperation tasks with different situations. Future research should further set up specific task situations according to the actual situation, in order to investigate the role of personality in specific situations, so as to effectively select operators. At the same time, as more and more women participate in teleoperation, future research should also collect data from female operators to investigate the impact of gender differences on teleoperation tasks in different situations.

# References

1. Bacocco, R., Melchiorri, C.: LQ control design of cooperative teleoperation systems. In: 14th International Conference on Advanced Robotics, pp. 1–6. Germany (2009)
2. Park, S.H., Woldstad, J.C.: Design of visual displays for teleoperation. In: Karwowski, W. (ed.) International Encyclopedia of Ergonomics and Human Factors. CRC Press, Boca Raton (2000)
3. Boboc, R.G., Moga, H., Talabă, D.: A review of current applications in teleoperation of mobile robots. Bull. Transilvania Univ. Brasov, Ser. I: Eng. Sci. **5**(2), 9–16 (2012)
4. Marescaux, J., et al.: Transcontinental robot-assisted remote telesurgery: feasibility and potential applications. Ann. Surg. **235**, 487–492 (2002)
5. Spinoglio, G., Marano, A., Priora, F., Melandro, F., Formisano, G.: History of robotic surgery. Robot. Surg., 1–12 (2015)
6. Murphy, R., et al.: Search and rescue robotics. Springer Handbook of Robotics, pp. 1151–1173. Springer, Heidelberg (2008)
7. Schmidt, G.R., Landis, G.A., Oleson, S.R.: HERRO missions to Mars and Venus using telerobotic surface exploration from orbit (2011)
8. Haidegger, T., Benyo, Z.: Surgical robotic support for long duration space missions. Acta Astronaut. **63**, 996–1005 (2008)
9. Lester, D., Thronson, H.: Human space exploration and human spaceflight: latency and the cognitive scale of the universe. Space Policy **27**, 89–93 (2011)
10. MacKenzie, I.S., Ware, C.: Lag as a determinant of human performance in interactive systems. In: Proceedings of the INTERACT' 1993 and CHI' 1993 Conference on Human Factors in Computing Systems, pp. 488–493 (1993)
11. Sheridan, T.B.: Space teleoperation through time latency: review and prognosis. IEEE Trans. Robot. Autom. **9**, 592–606 (1993)
12. Sheridan, T.B., Ferrell, W.R.: Remote manipulative control with transmission latency. IEEE Trans. Hum. Factors Electron. **HFE-4**, 25–29 (1963)
13. Haidegger, T., Rudas, I.J.: From concept to market: surgical robot development. Human-Computer Interaction: Concepts, Methodologies, Tools, and Applications. IGI Global (2016)
14. Scholcover, F., Gillan, D.J.: Temporal sensitivity and latency during teleoperation: using track clearance to understand errors in future projection. Hum. Factors, 187208211011842 (2021)
15. Dybvik, H., et al.: A low-cost predictive display for teleoperation: investigating effects on human performance and workload. Int. J. Hum. Comput. Stud. **145**, 102536 (2021)
16. Kok, L.: Singapore expertise pioneers quick and scarless surgery. Press release of the Nanyang Technological University (2011)
17. Pan, D., et al.: Association of individual characteristics with teleoperation performance. Aerospace Med. Hum. Perform. **87**(9), 772–780 (2016)

18. Scholcover, F., Gillan, D.J.: Using temporal sensitivity to predict performance under latency in teleoperation. Hum. Factors **60**, 80–91 (2018)

19. Poropat, A.E.: A meta-analysis of the five-factor model of personality and academic performance. Psychol. Bull. **135**(2), 322–338 (2009)

20. Hough, L.M., Furnham, A.: Use of personality variables in work settings. In: Borman, W.C., Ilgen, D.R., Klimoski, R.J. (Eds.) Handbook of Psychology, vol. 12, pp. 131–170 (2003)

21. Sommer, M., Herle, M., Häusler, J., Risser, R., Schützhofer, B., Chaloupka, C.: Cognitive and personality determinants of fitness to drive. Transport. Res. F: Traffic Psychol. Behav. **11**(5), 362–375 (2008)

22. Upham-Ellis, L.: Perception and displays for teleoperated robots. Doctoral dissertation. Retrieved from UCF Electronic Thesis and Dissertation Digital Collections Database (2008)

23. Soto, C.J., John, O.P.: The next big five inventory (BFI-2): developing and assessing a hierarchical model with 15 facets to enhance bandwidth, fidelity, and predictive power. J. Pers. Soc. Psychol. **113**(1), 117–143 (2017)

24. Hart, S.G., Staveland, L.E.: Development of NASA-TLX (task load index): results of empirical and theoretical research. Adv. Psychol. **52**, 139–183 (1988)

25. Davidian, M.: Hierarchical linear models: applications and data analysis methods. Publ. Am. Stat. Assoc. **98**(463), 767–768 (2002)

26. Hofmann, D.: An overview of the logic and rationale of hierarchical linear models. J. Manag. **23**(6), 723–744 (1997)

27. Cohen, J.: Statistical power analysis for the behavioral sciences. J. Am. Stat. Assoc. **2**(334) (1988)

28. Lucas, R.E., Le, K., Dyrenforth, P.S.: Explaining the extraversion/positive affect relation: sociability cannot account for extraverts' greater happiness. J. Pers. **76**, 385–414 (2008)

29. Watson, D., Clark, L.A.: Extraversion and its positive emotional core. In: Hogan, R., Johnson, J.A., Briggs, S. (eds.) Handbook of Personality Psychology, pp. 767–793. Academic Press, San Diego, CA (1997)

30. Eaves, L., Eysenck, H.: The nature of extraversion: a genetical analysis. J. Pers. Soc. Psychol. **32**(1), 102–112 (1975)

31. McCrae, R.R., Costa, P.T.: NEO Inventories Professional Manual. Psychological Assessment Resources, Lutz, FL (2010)

32. Saucier, G., Ostendorf, F.: Hierarchical subcomponents of the big five personality factors: a cross-language replication. J. Pers. Soc. Psychol. **76**, 613–627 (1999)

# An Emergency Centre Call Taker Task Analysis

Norman G. Vinson[1]([✉]) [ID], Jean-François Lapointe[1] [ID], and Noémie Lemaire[2]

[1] National Research Council Canada, Digital Technologies Research Centre, Ottawa, Canada
{norman.vinson,jean-francois.lapointe}@nrc-cnrc.gc.ca
[2] Thales Digital Solutions, Montréal, Canada
noemie.lemaire2@thalesdigitalsolutions.ca
https://nrc-cnrc.canada.ca, https://www.thalesgroup.com

**Abstract.** In the context of a project on the roll-out of the Next Generation 911 (NG911) emergency call system, we conducted a task analysis of call takers at an emergency call centre. Much of the emergency response literature focuses on *disaster response*. In contrast, our article is focused on *day-to-day emergencies*. To map out the call takers' tasks, we analyzed training documents and conducted semi-structured interviews. We found that call takers send high priority incidents to dispatch with just enough information for dispatchers to send first responders to the incident. Call takers then enter the remaining required information. Regarding the roll-out of NG911, we identified risks relating to the operational impact of multimedia with disturbing content, and the localization of smart phones. We also touch on artificial intelligence approaches that could be employed to increase call taker efficiency and protect centre staff from disturbing multimedia content.

**Keywords:** Emergency call centre · 911 call taking · Task analysis · Next generation 911 · NG911

## 1 Introduction

Much of the emergency response literature focuses on disaster response [8,9,22,23]. In contrast, the focus of this article is primarily on day-to-day emergencies (such as automobile accidents) rather than disasters (such as a hurricane). There are several differences between emergency response and disaster response that affect tasks, workflows, and roles. These differences make it difficult to generalize findings from disaster response to emergency response. This study of day-to-day operations of an emergency call centre therefore contributes to an underrepresented literature.

This project was supported by the Canadian Safety and Security Program, a federal program led by Defence Research and Development Canada's Centre for Security Science, in partnership with Public Safety Canada. Project partners include Thales Digital Solutions and Service de police de la Ville de Québec (SPVQ).

D. Harris and W.-C. Li (Eds.): HCII 2022, LNAI 13307, pp. 225–241, 2022.
https://doi.org/10.1007/978-3-031-06086-1_17

Emergency call centres (ECCs) receive phone calls from members of the public in need of, or witnessing a need for, first responders. These first responders could be police officers, firefighters or paramedics. ECC staff members who receive calls from the public are *call takers*, while staff members who direct first responders to the location of the incident are *dispatchers*.

ECC staff performance is critical since a delay of a few seconds can mean the difference between life and death [33]. The first step in improving the call takers' performance is to understand their tasks. Once the tasks are well described and understood, we can determine where technology can increase the call takers' efficiency. In this article, we describe the call takers' tasks in a particular ECC, namely Québec City's ECC, which is managed by the Québec City Police Service (SPVQ).[1]

This task analysis was conducted in the context of a research project on the roll out of Next Generation 911 (NG911). NG911 is a migration of the US and Canada's emergency calling system from the landline (switched voice data) telephony network to an internet (IP) network. This migration will provide new capabilities, such as the ability to process multimedia and Internet of Things sensor data [4].[2]

## 2  Method

We employed two data collection techniques: we reviewed documentation from the ECC and we conducted semi-structured interviews of ECC staff.

For documentation review, we were provided with three documents, all of which are training manuals. The first was the centre's call-taking training manual. The second one was for computer assisted call dispatching. Finally, the third training guide provided alternatives to police response (e.g. municipal services calls, precinct police station, etc.).

For the semi-structured interviews, a set of questions was prepared ahead of the interviews and additional questions were asked as needed during the interviews, in order to help refine our understanding of the work practices of the Québec City 911 centre.

For data representation, we used a hierarchical task analysis [10] method inspired by MAD [29] and its enhanced version, MAD* [28].

The constructors ALT, LOOP, PAR and SEQ explain the links between activities and sub-activities shown in Figs. 2 and 3. Their meaning is as follows:

- ALT = alternative tasks: different ways to execute a same task.
- LOOP = cyclical tasks: tasks that must be repeated several times.
- PAR = parallel tasks: executed simultaneously or in any order.
- SEQ = sequential tasks: which must be executed in order (left to right).

---

[1] In Canada and the United States, ECCs are typically refereed to as Public Safety Answering Points or PSAPs [4,17].

[2] While the 911 system in both the US and Canada is being transitioned to an IP network, national and local agencies in each country maintain final approval and control of over the roll-out timelines [6,17].

## 2.1  Participants

For this analysis of the call centre, we were able to conduct seven one-hour semi-structured interviews, with a total of five different consenting operators of the call centre. All the participants were interviewed during their normal work hours and were thus being paid to participate in the study. This study, which involves human subjects has been approved both by the SPVQ and the Research Ethics Board of the National Research Council Canada (protocol 2020-116), which follows the Tri-Council Policy Statement [3].

## 2.2  Recruitment

The names, roles and email addresses of potential recruits were provided by SPVQ management. Email invitations were then sent to them in several rounds along with information about the project and the consent form. Since all the process was online, participants returned a signed consent form via email. Five participants consented to participate in the study, out of 69 invitations.

## 2.3  Procedure

Our objective was to map out the tasks performed by the call takers, including the conditions under which, and the order in which, they performed them. Essentially, our main objective was to construct Figs. 2 and 3. In addition, a secondary objective was to determine the call takers' difficulties.

In keeping with our objectives, we analysed the three training documents [30, 31, 36] and conducted the interviews in search of the steps taken by the call takers. Once we identified a step, we documented it, confirmed it through other interviews and by relating it to the documentation. Finally, the information presented both in the flowcharts and in the figures of this report was validated by a supervisor of the 911 centre to ensure its accuracy.

All the interviews were conducted by using the Microsoft Teams video-conference application. Nothing was electronically recorded and a team of two or three people interviewed the participant during each session, generally with one or two asking questions and the other one taking notes.

Because of the COVID-19 pandemic, all the data collection, recruitment and interviewing activities were conducted remotely and online.

# 3  Results and Discussion

## 3.1  Organizational Context

The ECC's organizational structure and workflow (Fig. 1) provide a context to situate the call takers' tasks in the broader ecosystem.

Citizens dial 911 to reach the centre. These calls are received by the call taker. Most of these calls are about emergencies requiring an immediate response. Some calls require police or firefighter response, but are not considered urgent (reporting a break-in that occurred earlier, for example). Some calls relate to other municipal services (parks and recreation, for example).

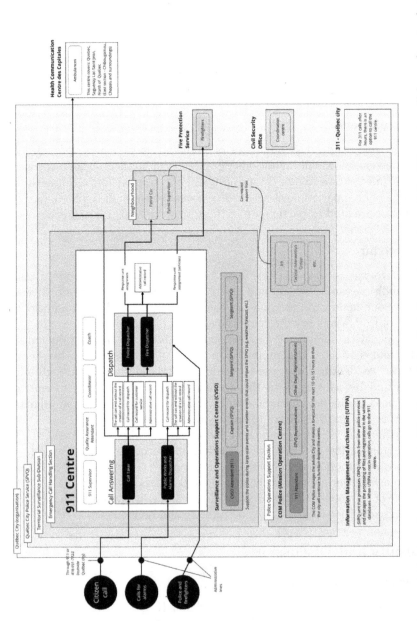

**Fig. 1.** Emergency call centre broad context. The figure shows that the various actors of the 911 centre all have direct relationships through the call record.

The centre also receives calls (and instant messaging texts) from police and firefighters who need additional information about an incident to which they are responding, and calls regarding alarms. These calls come in through special administrative lines rather than through 911. They are handled by police and fire dispatchers or the public works and alarms dispatcher instead of the call taker.

Inside the ECC, communication regarding incidents between people in the roles mentioned above occurs primarily through the call record—a computer-based record containing important and relevant information about an incident. However, they also use Microsoft Teams as a secondary system.

In addition to roles that are directly involved in communications about an incident, call centre staff also have management and training roles: supervisor and coordinator, quality assurance attendant, and coach. These roles are not directly involved in incident processing. Most ECC staff perform several roles depending on their experience. Only those with the least training are exclusively call takers.

The ECC as an entity communicates with several other units and organizations:

- Police units.
- The Surveillance and Operation Support Centre (CVSO) for police operations requiring coordination.
- Firefighters.
- Ambulance dispatch (Health Communication Centre des Capitales).
- External services (like utility companies).

## 3.2   Call Taker

Call Taker is the entry-level role that every staff member of the call-centre can perform. As indicated in Fig. 1, a call taker's main responsibility is to interactively process a 911 call.

The call taker's main tasks are:

1. Answering the call.
2. Identifying the ECC, to notify the caller in case the 911 call was routed to the wrong ECC.
3. Identifying the incident type.
4. Locating the incident.
5. Determining which type of response is required.
6. For police and firefighter response,
   (a) Assigning a response type and priority code to the incident.
   (b) Entering the code and any relevant information into the digital call record.
   (c) Submitting the call record, which is then sent automatically to the appropriate dispatcher (police or fire).
7. For paramedic/ambulance response,
   (a) Transferring the call to the Health Communication Centre whose catchment area includes the incident location.
   (b) Monitoring the call to determine whether a police/firefighter response is also needed.

8. For municipal service requests, referring the caller to the relevant municipal department.

The call taker workflow shown in Figs. 2 and 3 and the following description provide more detail as well as the relationships between these tasks.

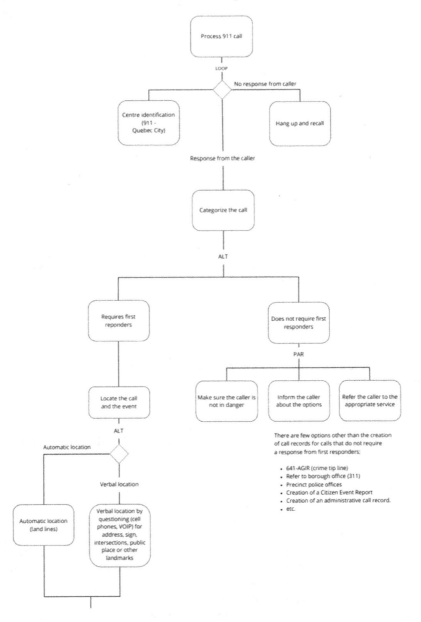

**Fig. 2.** Call taker workflow, Part 1. The first part of the call taker's workflow. The second part is displayed in Fig. 3. ALT = alternative tasks: different ways to execute a same task. LOOP = cyclical tasks: tasks that must be repeated several times. PAR = parallel tasks: executed simultaneously or in any order. SEQ = sequential tasks: which must be executed in order (left to right).

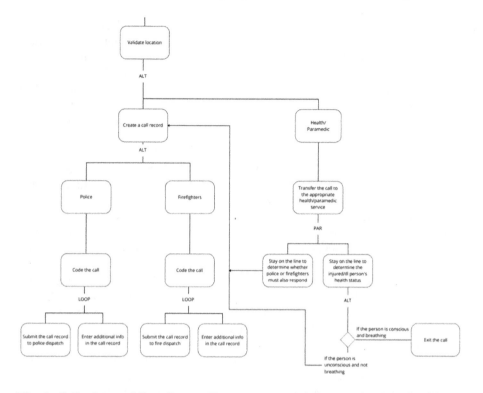

**Fig. 3.** Call taker workflow, Part 2. The second part of the call taker's workflow. The first part is displayed in the Fig. 2 above. ALT = alternative tasks: different ways to execute a same task. LOOP = cyclical tasks: tasks that must be repeated several times. PAR = parallel tasks: executed simultaneously or in any order. SEQ = sequential tasks: which must be executed in order (left to right)

As such, the first thing a call-taker does when answering a call is to identify the service. The call taker says "911, Québec City". It is necessary to alert callers about which ECC they have reached because calls are sometimes routed to the wrong ECC. This could happen if, for example, a cell phone caller is in a neighbouring catchment area near the border of Québec City's catchment area and her call is picked up by a cell tower *inside Québec City's area*. Similar problems can occur with both static and mobile IP-based (VoIP) calls and multi-line telephone systems. Technological enhancements to increase the precision of location information have already been deployed in many areas in North America. Additional enhancements are being deployed within the current 9-1-1 framework, and will continue in the NG911 framework [5].

The caller is then questioned to collect all the required information to categorize the incident type. The incident type will determine which service should respond. There are also codes to be used when multiple services are required. Identifying the service type is a common call taker task across ECCs [15,22].

As in other ECCs, not every call is an emergency [15]. For example a report of a stolen car is not an emergency. The call taker must collect sufficient information to determine whether the call relates to an emergency and more generally, determine the call's response priority [15,32]. For calls that do not involve an emergency, the call taker may refer callers to a crime tip line or the local police station. In some cases, the police wants a record of the call, but there is no need to dispatch officers. The call taker then creates a *administrative* call record that is *not* routed to dispatch upon submission.

It is not always easy for call takers to obtain the required information as callers may be, for example, mentally ill, very young, or witnesses calling from a location away from the incident. Of course, this problem is not unique to this ECC [15].

Incident type and priority are embedded in the incident type code assigned by the call taker. This code can be revised later. In the Québec City's ECC, this revision is often performed by dispatchers rather than the call takers themselves. Each code is composed of three to six letters, with the exception of a *COVID-19* code. There are 100 codes in total to be memorised by the call taker. Fire-related incident have only two levels of priority which are 1 (high - visible fire or smoke) or 2 (low), while police codes have seven priority levels.

For the type of calls that require police or firefighters call takers locate the emergency, enter the collected information in a call record and submit it to the system so that it is automatically sent to the appropriate dispatcher (police or fire) for further validation and eventual dispatch of the first responder unit(s). It is important to note that for emergencies, as soon as the call takers have the location and the incident type code they submit the call record to enable dispatchers to send units quickly. Further information is added to the call record after submission.

In case of health-related calls, they are transferred directly to the appropriate Health Communication Centre, but call takers stay on the line to ensure that the person is conscious and breathing and determine whether there is a need for police and/or firefighters. If the person is not breathing and/or is unconscious, a call record is created and a police unit is sent immediately to perform resuscitation. If police and/or firefighters are required (for traffic accidents for example), a corresponding call record is created.

When both firefighters and police are required to respond to an incident, the call taker enters a multi-service incident code. The system then automatically creates linked call records: one for police and one for firefighters. Moreover, the information entered by the call taker in one of these linked call records is automatically added to the other call record. If paramedics are also required, the call is then transferred to the Health Communication Centre.

Multiple call records can also arise when several callers are reporting the same incident. This has become more common with the advent of mobile phones. Now, several witnesses to an incident can all report it to 911 at about the same time. Fortunately, the software automatically notifies call takers of other recently submitted call records with the same or nearby location information. This allows call takers to delete the record they are creating and switch to a previously created record for the same incident. The call takers can then add information to the original call record. Similarly, several related incidents (for example, someone committing multiple assaults across different locations) will result in several call records. However, call takers can link these records manually through a (virtual) button.

Each call taker has five computer displays, four of them for the RAO (computer assisted dispatching) and one for the phone-related data. Figure 4 below illustrates an instance of a call record with fictitious information. The location information and the incident code is in the top left corner. Information about the caller is below. Most of the left half of the display is for comments from the call taker or dispatcher to provide additional contextual information to the first responders who have access to the call record. The right side of the displays holds button for certain situations that may arise, such as the need to link several call records. The police and fire assistance buttons are used primarily by the dispatcher when first responders at the scene request assistance.

The alarm buttons relate to the fire response. The greater the number of alarms, the more fire response units are needed. Moreover, a large response will typically require the distribution of fire response units throughout the city so that no area is left without units nearby. Typically, the call taker will enter an alarm value of 1. It is the dispatcher who adjusts the number of alarms in consultation with the firefighters on the scene and the dispatcher also initiates and oversees the redistribution of fire response units when required.

Finally, ECC staff, first responders and some allied staff (see Fig. 1) have the ability to add attachments to the call record. The attachments could be documents, images, audio or video files. In the call record user interface, the button for adding attachments is located on the far right.

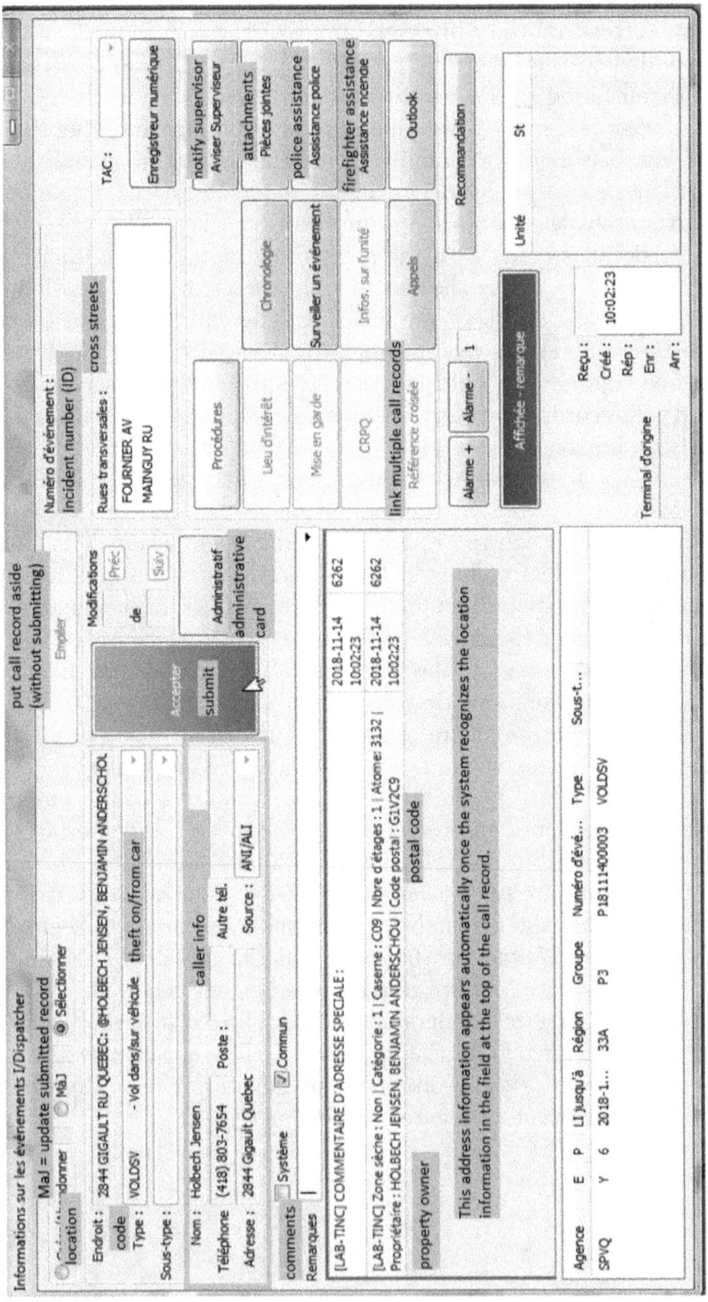

**Fig. 4.** Call record as displayed on the call taker's computer screen. English translations are provided in black text on a teal background. They are *not* part of the call taker's display.

# 4   Performance Metrics

For the call taker, there are two important performance metrics: time to submit the call record to the system, and quality of the information entered into the call record. Keep in mind that the call taker may submit the call record *before* entering all the mandated information. If so, the rest of the information would be entered *after* the record is submitted. Call takers follow this workflow so the dispatcher can send first responders to the scene as quickly as possible.

Indeed, in the case of a fire emergency, no more than 90 s must elapse between the call reception and the moment at which the units are dispatched, in accordance with North American National Fire Protection Association standards [25]. In the case of a police dispatch, the target dispatch time depends of the priority of the incident. For a priority 1 incident, the target dispatch time is 1 min. For a priority 2 call, the target dispatch time is 3 min. Of course, these metrics conflate the call taker's response time with the dispatcher's response time.

The call taker must also transfer medical emergency calls to the Health Communication Centre des Capitales within 1 min [19].

In addition, regulations specify the types of information that the SPVQ ECC must enter into into each call record [19].

To assess call taker performance changes following a change in their computer system, we would measure the time between call reception and the submission of a call record that has sufficient information for the dispatcher to send first responders to the scene. For more accurate diagnosis of performance problems we would also measure the proportion of times the call record information is insufficient for dispatch. In addition to that, we would have to measure the proportion of incomplete call records.

# 5   Call Taking Challenges

Our task analysis revealed some of the challenges faced by call takers. These challenges provide opportunities to develop software that will better support call takers. Below, psycho-social issues, location information, computer assisted coding, and question support are discussed.

## 5.1   Psycho-social Issues

One of their difficulties is obtaining relevant information from callers who are having difficulty providing it, because they are too young, they are too upset, or they are suffering from mental issues (also reported in [15]).

Similarly, call takers reported that 911 call taking can be psychologically taxing (also reported in [15,37]). In addition to dealing with emergencies involving injuries and severe property damage, ECC staff can be exposed to disturbing images, audio or video. In the SPVQ ECC's system, first responders, ECC staff, and some allied staff have the ability to append files to the call record (see Figs. 1 and 4). There have been a few instances of staff seeing disturbing images appended to the call record and having to take time off as a result. The increased prevalence of camera-enabled smartphones, web-accessible CCTV surveillance, and social media simply increases these risks. Moreover, the coming NG911 system is intended to transmit images and video [4,34], making exposure to troubling images and video even more likely.

## 5.2    Reliable Location Data

The 911 system typically provides ECC call takers with accurate caller location data. This saves time because it is much faster to simply confirm a location than to first obtain the location from the caller and then confirm it. Before the advent of the cell phone, location data was provided automatically through landlines. Obviously, cell phone location could not be provided in the same way. At first, there was simply no location provided. Later, the location of the cell tower receiving the call was provided, but this was often inaccurate to the point of the call being routed to the wrong ECC.

For several years now, the enhanced 911 system has been providing ECCs with the GPS coordinates of the cell phone making the 911 call. The regulations have required the coordinates to be increasingly more accurate. However, the Québec City ECC still experiences difficulties will cell call localization. In some cases, especially in urban areas, the GPS coordinates are still not sufficiently precise (having an error of up to 800 m) to support an efficient response. Buildings with several floors are even more problematic since localization data does not indicate the floor from which the call originates. In response, service providers are beginning to provide the height of the cell phone to make it easier to identify the floor [5,12,13,35].

However, even if all calls provided an accurate caller location automatically, the call taker would still have to confirm the location of the incident with the caller. The reason for this confirmation is that the caller is not necessarily located at the same place as the incident. For example, someone could be calling from a car about an incident they saw while driving, or someone from a high rise could be calling about a fire in another building.

In the NG911 context, location would again become a problem if social media (twitter, messenger, for example) were used to contact the ECC. Smartphone users can turn off location tracking both in general and for specific apps [2,24]. Consequently, the location of a user who turned off his location tracking would be unavailable to the ECC. Remedying this problem would require software changes in the mobile device operating system, the social media app, and some coordination with the ECCs so that the mobile device software can recognize the recipient of a message as a legitimate ECC.

The multimedia roll-out for NG911 appears to centre on Real Time Text (RTT) [7]. RTT is similar to the text message service we currently use on mobile phones except that, with RTT, the recipient can see every character the sender types in *as it is typed*, as opposed to having to wait for the sender to send the message. In addition, RTT allows voice communication on the same call as text messaging. Eventually, RTT may also allow callers to send video [11]. RTT is currently available on iPhones through the accessibility settings [1], and on some android phones [18].

## 5.3   Computer Assisted Coding

When people are required to generate and enter a code for an event, a natural assumption is that coding can be supported by software, either through automatic coding or Computer Assisted Coding (CAC). With CAC, the system generates one or more codes and the coder validates or selects the appropriate code. Automatic coding generates and enters the code automatically without requiring user validation.

A few features of 911 coding make it difficult for any automated system to improve coding performance.

First, there are only 100 codes, 51 of which are high priority (priority 1 or 2). Consequently, it is fairly easy for call takers to learn, memorize, and recall the codes.

Second, for high priority incidents, especially fires, call takers will often enter the code and send the call record to dispatch before entering any additional information besides location. This allows first responders to get under way as quickly as possible. After additional information is added to the call record, the dispatcher updates the firefighters over the radio, while police typically access the call record on their computers. In such cases, the incident code is entered before any information that could be used to determine the code is entered into the call record. Consequently, a CAC or automatic coding system that depends on information in the call record would be unable to generate a code for such high priority events. The incident responses that are the most important to speed up would therefore not benefit from CAC or automated coding. As a result, it would therefore be challenging to develop a *useful* automated coding or CAC system.

## 5.4   Question Support

In our NG911 project, we are attempting to support the call taker's collection of *relevant* information from the caller. We intend to combine a knowledge base of the incident codes with speech recognition and Natural Language Processing (NLP) to suggest questions for the call taker to ask the caller to more quickly and more accurately determine the incident code. For high priority incidents question guidance is unlikely to be helpful for submitting the call record to dispatch because the call record is submitted with so little information. However, in such cases, the call taker remains on the call to collect the additional information required by government regulations [19]. This additional information may also result in a modification to the incident code. Question guidance, if successful, would be useful in this context.

# 6   Conclusion

A few descriptions of call takers' and dispatchers' tasks can be found in the literature, even though these publications focused on another topic [14–16]. In general, our findings regarding the call takers' tasks are very consistent with the tasks reported in those articles, though more details are provided here.

One important observation is that high priority incidents are submitted to dispatch as quickly as possible so that first responders can be sent to the scene as quickly as possible. Call takers then update the call record with additional information from the caller, and this new information is conveyed to the first responders. As discussed earlier, this workflow has design implications for building an efficient and effective ECC computer system.

Another issue that should considered in ECC system design is regulations and standards. The SPVQ centre is regulated by the province and the 911 infrastructure by the Canadian federal government. The centre also follows North American National Fire Protection Association standards [25]. Centres in other areas will be subject to different regulations and may follow different standards such as the National Emergency Number Association (NENA) standards [26].

Note also that organizational structures differ markedly across ECCs. In Québec City, the ECC handles all incoming calls but transfers health-related calls to the ambulance service (but may still dispatch police to the incident). In contrast, for example, some centres may answer all 911 calls, but then transfer each call to the appropriate agency for call taking [27]. A variety of other arrangements are also possible [14, 22, 27].

To support the call taker we will explore the use Artificial Intelligence (AI) to suggest questions for the call taker to ask the caller to obtain all the required information as efficiently as possible. This could help the call taker fill in the calling record more efficiently *after dispatch* in high priority incidents, and *before dispatch* in lower priority incidents.

We will also explore the use of AI to support the ECC with the roll-out of the next generation 911 network (NG911). NG911 is expected to increase multimedia communications to the ECC. This could disrupt ECC operations by exposing staff to disturbing images and videos. We intend to explore the use of AI-based image analysis to detect such media and provide users with a trigger warning before displaying the media.

One design method we did not discuss above but may prove useful is the GOMS (Goals Operators Methods Selection) approach. GOMS is a method for analyzing user goals and behavior often in the context of using a computer system. The GOMS method can be used to evaluate computer user interface designs to optimize certain performance metrics [21]. If the case of an ECC, some relevant metrics would be time to submit a call record, quality of the information entered into the call record, time to dispatch. Since the GOMS approach has been found to accurately predict user performance times with different user interface designs [20] and response time is quite important in ECC operations, GOMS could prove useful to design an ECC user interface that reduces performance times.

# References

1. Apple: set up and use RTT and TTY on iPhone. https://support.apple.com/en-ca/guide/iphone/iph3e2e47fe/ios
2. Apple: turn location services and GPS on or off on your iPhone, iPad, or iPod touch (2021). https://support.apple.com/en-ca/HT207092
3. Canadian institutes of health research, natural sciences and engineering research council of canada, and social sciences and humanities research council: tri-council policy statement: ethical conduct for research involving humans. Secretariat on Responsible Conduct of Research, Government of Canada (2018). https://ethics.gc.ca/eng/documents/tcps2-2018-en-interactive-final.pdf
4. Canadian radio-television and telecommunications commission: next-generation 9-1-1 – modernizing 9-1-1 networks to meet the public safety needs of canadians, telecom regulatory policy CRTC 2017–182, File numbers: 1011-NOC2016-0116 and 8665–C12-201507008. Canadian Radio-Television and Telecommunications Commission, Government of Canada (2017). https://crtc.gc.ca/eng/archive/2017/2017-182.pdf
5. Canadian radio-television and telecommunications commission: 9-1-1 services for traditional wireline, VoIP and wireless phone services. Canadian Radio-Television and Telecommunications Commission, Government of Canada (2020). https://crtc.gc.ca/eng/phone/911/can.htm
6. Canadian radio-television and telecommunications commission: next-generation 9-1-1. Canadian Radio-Television and Telecommunications Commission, Government of Canada (2021). https://crtc.gc.ca/eng/phone/911/gen.htm
7. Canadian radio-television and telecommunications commission: telecom decision CRTC 2021–199 : establishment of new deadlines for Canada's transition to next-generation 9-1-1. Canadian Radio-Television and Telecommunications Commission, Government of Canada (2021). https://crtc.gc.ca/eng/archive/2021/2021-199.htm
8. Chatfield, A.T., Scholl, H.J., Brajawidagda, U.: Sandy tweets: citizens' co-production of time-critical information during an unfolding catastrophe. In: Proceedings of the Annual Hawaii International Conference on System Sciences. IEEE, pp. 1947–1957 (2014)
9. Dearstyne, B.: The FDNY on 9/11: information and decision making in crisis. Gov. Inf. Quart. **24**(1), 29–46 (2007)
10. Diaper, D., Stanton, N.: The Handbook of Task Analysis for Human-Computer Interaction. Lawrence Erlbaum Associates (2004)
11. Emergency Services Working Group (ESWG): RTT-based NG9-1-1 text messaging specifications. Canadian Radio-Television and Telecommunications Commission, Government of Canada (2018). https://crtc.gc.ca/public/cisc/e-docs/ESRE0083.pdf
12. Federal Communications Commission: 911 and E911 services. Federal Communications Commission, Federal Government of the United States of America (2021). https://www.fcc.gov/general/9-1-1-and-e9-1-1-services
13. Federal communications commission: indoor location accuracy timeline and live call data reporting template. Federal Communications Commission, Federal Government of the United States of America (2021). https://www.fcc.gov/public-safety-and-homeland-security/policy-and-licensing-division/911-services/general/location-accuracy-indoor-benchmarks

14. Feufel, M.A., Lippa, K.D., Klein, H.A.: Calling 911: emergency medical services in need of human factors. Ergonomics Des. Q. Hum. Factors Appl. **17**(2), 15–19 (2009)

15. Forslund, K., Kihlgren, A., Kihlgren, M.: Operators' experiences of emergency calls. J. Telemedicine Telecare **10**(5), 290–297 (2004)

16. Franklin, A.L., Hunt, E.: An emergency situation simulator for examining time-pressured decision making. Behav. Res. Methods Instrum. Comput. **25**(2), 143–147 (1993). https://doi.org/10.3758/BF03204487

17. Gallagher, J.C.: Next generation 911 technologies: select issues for congress (R45253 - Version: 4). Congressional Research Service, United States Congress (2018). https://crsreports.congress.gov/product/details?prodcode=R45253

18. Google: use real-time text (RTT) with calls. https://support.google.com/accessibility/android/answer/9042284?hl=en

19. Government of Quebec: regulation respecting standards, specifications and quality criteria applicable to 9-1-1 emergency centres and to certain secondary emergency call centres (2021). http://www.legisquebec.gouv.qc.ca/fr/ShowDoc/cr/S-2.3,%20r.%202%20/

20. Gray, W.D., John, B.E., Atwood, M.E.: Project ernestine: validating a GOMS analysis for predicting and explaining real-world task performance. Hum. Comput. Interact. **8**(3), 237–309 (1993). https://www.tandfonline.com/doi/abs/10.1207/s15327051hci0803_3

21. John, B.: Why GOMS? Interactions **2**(4), 80–89 (1995). https://doi.org/10.1145/225362.225374

22. Kim, J.K., Sharman, R., Rao, H.R., Upadhyaya, S.: Framework for analyzing critical incident management systems (CIMS). In: Proceedings of the Annual Hawaii International Conference on System Sciences. vol. 4, pp. 1–8 (2006)

23. Kim, J.K., Sharman, R., Rao, H.R., Upadhyaya, S.: Efficiency of critical incident management systems: instrument development and validation. Decis. Support Syst. **44**(1), 235–250 (2007)

24. Krasnoff, B.: Android 101: how to stop location tracking. The Verge (2021). https://www.theverge.com/21401280/android-101-location-tracking-history-stop-how-to

25. National Fire Protection Association. https://www.nfpa.org

26. NENA - The 9-1-1 association: NENA standard for 9-1-1 call processing. https://cdn.ymaws.com/www.nena.org/resource/resmgr/standards/nena-sta-020.1-2020_911_call.pdf

27. POMAX Consulting: a review of fire and police communications and dispatch in Waterloo Region (2021). https://www.kitchener.ca/en/resourcesGeneral/Documents/COR_CAO_Waterloo_Region_Fire_and_Police_Communications.pdf

28. Scapin, D.L., Bastien, J.M.C.: Analyse des tâches et aide ergonomique á la conception : i'approche MAD*. In: Kolski, C., pp. 85–116. Analyse et conception de l'IHM Hermès (2001)

29. Scapin, D.L., Pierret-Golbreich, C.: MAD: une méthode de description de tâche. In: Colloque sur l'ingénierie des interfaces homme-machine. pp. 131–148 (May 1989)

30. Service de Police de la Ville de Québec: Guide Prise D'appels - Apprenant Juillet 2020. Ville de Québec, Canada (2020)

31. Service de Police de la Ville de Québec: Options alternatives au déplacement policier; Formation prise d'appel. Ville de Québec, Canada (nd)

32. Shively, R.J.: Emergency (911) dispatcher decision making: ecological display development. Proc. Hum. Factors Ergon. Soc. Ann. Meet. **39**(9), 506–510 (1995)

33. Terrell, I.S., McNeese, M.D., Jefferson, T.: Exploring cognitive work within a 911 dispatch center: using complementary knowledge elicitation techniques. Proc. Hum. Factors Ergon. Soc. Ann. Meet. **48**(3), 605–609 (2004). http://journals.sagepub.com/doi/10.1177/154193120404800370
34. U.S. Government: next generation 911. https://www.911.gov/issue_nextgeneration911.html
35. U.S. Government: 911 service, 47 C.F.R. §9.10 (2022). https://www.ecfr.gov/current/title-47/chapter-I/subchapter-A/part-9/subpart-C/section-9.10#p-9.10(i)(2)(i)
36. Service de Police de la Ville de Québec: Opérations - Centrale 9-1-1, Guide De Formation. Ville de Québec, Canada (2020)
37. Weibel, L., Gabrion, I., Aussedat, M., Kreutz, G.: Work-related stress in an emergency medical dispatch center. Ann. Emerg. Med. **41**(4), 500–506 (2003). https://www.sciencedirect.com/science/article/pii/S0196064403000052

# Cognition in Aviation and Space

# Cultural Effects on the Selection of Aviation Safety Management Strategies

Wesley Tsz-Kin Chan$^{(\boxtimes)}$ and Wen-Chin Li

Safety and Accident Investigation Centre, Cranfield University, Cranfield, UK
`wesley.chan@cranfield.ac.uk`

**Abstract.** The link between culture and the classification of causal factors contributory to human deficiencies are well-established, but attempts to actively create Safety Cultures, such as through mandatory Safety Management System (SMS) programs, retain a narrow view in which the values of the workforce are considered homogenously. The effects of diverse national cultures on the design and application of human factors interventions have been less examined. The present research compares aviation professionals' cultural backgrounds with their preference towards the five intervention approach categories in the Human Factors Intervention Matrix (HFIX) framework, with a goal to understand how the cultural profile of the workforce and target users of intervention strategies may affect how these strategies are perceived, judged, and received. Whilst the results found non-significant association between national culture and preferences for intervention approach categories, this study complements previous research on the categorisation of human factors, proposing that professional experiences can concurrently moderate both the categorisation of causal factors and the consequential recommendations of safety interventions. Present findings can benefit the development of safety management programs by providing an awareness of how cultural biases on the attribution of faults can carry forward to biases in the formulation and application of safety management strategies.

**Keywords:** Safety culture · National culture · Human factors intervention

## 1 Introduction

Safety Culture is defined as the way that "safety is perceived, valued and prioritized in an organization" [1], and culture is represented by shared beliefs and behaviours [2]. As the culture of organisations are reflective of the values held by its employees [3], from a philosophical point of view Safety Culture can thus be considered as an outcome of safety values [2–4]. The relationship between safety values and the cultural values carried by employees as part of their personal national cultural backgrounds have been extensively studied [5–7], and noteworthy differences in patterns of human factors attributable to culture were strongest between Eastern (Asian) and Western (North American/European) perspectives [8, 9]. Although the International Civil Aviation Organisation (ICAO) has made it mandatory for industry to implement organisational-level Safety Management

Systems (SMS) to systematically manage safety and establish Safety Cultures [2], current SMS processes reflect the ICAO's "myopic" view of culture in which the values of people in the workforce were viewed as homogenous [10]. In practice, safety management approaches are not one-size-fits-all solutions. The wide range of cultural values held by the globalised aviation workforce means that safety interventions, strategies, and training programs are unlikely to concurrently suit every possible user of the system.

## 1.1  National Cultural Values

Culture provides the cognitive tools that are employed by the workforce to construct strategies and actions [11]. In relation to SMS goals to create organisational Safety Cultures, it was recognised that cockpit crew members' national cultural values toward leadership, the maintenance of harmony, and attitudes towards the sharing of knowledge exerted a strong level of influence on their trust and satisfaction with the implementation of management strategies [4]. National cultural tendencies for uncertainty avoidance amongst air traffic management professionals were found to be negatively associated with Safety Culture [3]; and aviation accident investigators' cultural preconceptions in relation to power gradients and time orientation were known to affect their interpretation of human factors issues [12, 13]. More recent studies extended these conceptualisations of culture to include social interactions, with negative interactions in cross-cultural teams found to degrade safety performance in aviation settings [10].

Overall, differences in cultural values create varying individual experiences which in turn affects personal preferences towards Safety Culture and human factors intervention strategies. People from Asian cultures, who tend to have higher power distance and collectivism, were found to have a greater preference for supervisory or administrative interventions to correct for human factors deficiencies as they were comparatively more dependent on the directions of superiors [14]. This illustrates that the same human factors intervention, management strategy, or training program may be perceived, judged, and received differently by people from different cultural backgrounds.

## 1.2  Professional and Occupational Influences

In addition to differences in national culture, dissimilarities in the operational land-scape and professional culture environments may also alter workforce preferences in relation to human factors interventions. Exposure to professional and occupational cultural experiences were found to mitigate and alter nationally-determined traits [15], and even amongst geographically and culturally similar nations, dissimilarities in the operational landscape and regulatory environments can modify the acceptance of risk [16]. Industrial organisations such as commercial airlines are also unlikely to have sufficient resources to simultaneously carry out different a large assortment of safety management methods to suit everyone [17]. Given these limitations, a risk is that SMS practitioners may choose to implement inappropriate intervention approaches, the consequences of which can manifest negatively into the Safety Culture through workforce disengagement [18]. Therefore, it is necessary to deliberately select safety interventions based on their success potential. In the design and development of human factors interventions, safety management strategies, or training programs, it is necessary to first analyse and understand the cultural profile of the target learners and workforce.

### 1.3  Categorisation of Human Factors Intervention Approaches

The Human Factors Intervention Matrix (HFIX) provides a practical framework where human factors interventions and error mitigation strategies can be categorised into five general approaches (see Table 1) [19]. These include organisational or administrative changes ("organisational/administrative"); amendments to the task and mission environment ("task/mission"); alterations to the hardware ("technology/engineering"); changing the operational or physical environment ("operational/physical environment"); and interventions involving human-centred developments ("human/crew training"). The goal of this study was to evaluate whether aviation professionals' national cultural backgrounds had an influence on their preference levels for interventions related to the five different approaches.

**Table 1.** Examples of HFIX categories of intervention approaches

| Human factors intervention approaches | Examples |
| --- | --- |
| Organisational/administrative | • Human resource management evaluations<br>• Reviewing and issuing rules, regulations, and policies<br>• Improving information management and communication<br>• Conduct research and studies |
| Task/mission | • Amending, reviewing, and modifying procedures and manuals |
| Technology/engineering | • Design, repair, or inspect parts and equipment |
| Operational/ Physical Environment | • Modifications to the operational or ambient environment (e.g. weather, altitude, terrain, heat, vibration, lighting) |
| Human/crew | • Reviewing, developing, and implementing training programs |

## 2  Method

### 2.1  Participants

In total, 101 valid responses were included in the analysis, of which 24 participants were of Asian backgrounds and 77 participants were categorised into the Western group (North American, European, Anglo-Oceania). The participants were all aviation industry professionals, including engineering (n = 7), air traffic control (n = 2), cabin crew (n =

26), pilots (n = 17), ground services (n = 8), training providers (n = 10), executive and administration (n = 18), safety specialists (n = 8), and others (n = 5). The age range was from 19 to 70 years (m = 40.2, s.d. = 10.0), and occupational experience in the aviation industry ranged from less than one year to 44 years (m = 14.8, s.d. = 9.9).

Participation was voluntary, no identifying information was collected, and ethics approval was provided by the Cranfield University Research Ethics System (CURES/12950/2021).

## 2.2 Research Design

An online survey hosted on the Qualtrics platform was used for data collection. Recruitment of participants was by chain referral sampling, and initial requests for participation were sent through contacts established with an aviation safety consortium and two aviation universities as part of a wider investigation on cultural diversity. Survey items relevant to the present paper included demographic information on age, occupation, and years of experience. An item which allowed participants to self-select their national cultural background enabled the categorisation of responses into Asian and Western groups. These were followed by an evaluation exercise, based on the five intervention approach categories within HFIX, in which participants were asked to choose what they thought was the most suitable human factors intervention category to improve cultural diversity in technical aviation occupations. Responses were collected from March to April 2021 and was analysed using SPSS (version 28).

## 3   Results and Discussions

### 3.1   Intervention Preferences Not Significantly Associated with National Culture

The frequency of participants indicating that a human factors intervention approach category was most suitable by cultural background (Asian or Western) is presented in Fig. 1.

Statistical analysis revealed that there was not a significant association between participants' national cultural background and their first choice amongst the five human factors intervention categories (two-tailed $p = .555$, Fisher's exact test, see Table 2).

The finding of non-significant association between national cultural background and preferences towards human factors intervention categories corresponds with existing research. It was known that professional experiences can bring about detectable changes in traits such as attitudes towards hierarchy, work values related to career advancement and high earnings, and levels of concern towards automation usage [15]. These practical traits are reflective of national cultural values of power distance, individualism, and uncertainty avoidance, which in turn were recognised to be influential to the identification of human factors hazards in previous accident investigation research [12, 13]. As the identification of casual factors during accident investigations is the precursor to the recommendation and assessment of potential human factors interventions [19], it is perhaps unsurprising that as the participants were all aviation professionals, their professional background may have moderated their evaluation of human factors recommendations

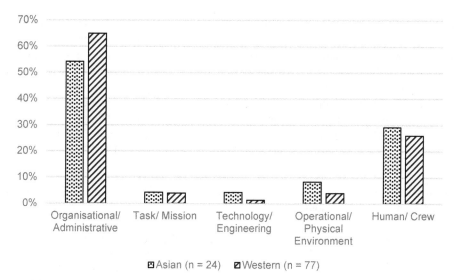

**Fig. 1.** Intervention category considered most suitable by Asian and Western groups.

**Table 2.** Preference for HFIX intervention approaches by national culture group.

| Human factors intervention approaches | Asian (n = 24) | Western (n = 77) | Overall (N = 101) |
|---|---|---|---|
| Organisational/administrative | 54.2% (n = 13) | 64.9% (n = 50) | 62.4% (n = 63) |
| Task/mission | 4.2% (n = 1) | 3.9% (n = 3) | 4.0% (n = 4) |
| Technology/engineering | 4.2% (n = 1) | 1.3% (n = 1) | 2.0% (n = 2) |
| Operational/physical environment | 8.3% (n = 2) | 3.9% (n = 3) | 5.0% (n = 5) |
| Human/crew | 29.2% (n = 7) | 26.0% (n = 27) | 26.7% (n = 27) |

and interventions in the same way as it has moderated their investigative identification of causal factors.

Another possible explanation for this finding highlights a limitation of this study. The participants were recruited by chain-referral sampling, with the initial points-of-contact being a North American aviation safety consortium and researchers from aviation universities in Australia and Canada, all of which are in the Western cultural sphere. It is therefore probable that the participants, regardless of their personal national cultural background, may have been acculturated in the Western context through occupational or academic exposure.

## 3.2  Workforce Preferences Reflect Frequency of Recommendation

Another interesting observation was that the present findings of the aviation workforce's preferences for each of the five intervention approaches was closely coordinated with the safety recommendations proposed by previous aviation accident and incident investigation reports. Table 3 presents the current data on individual preferences compared with existing aviation safety recommendations from incident and accident reports from two different databases. The first database included 614 recommendations made by the Federal Aviation Administration's Joint Safety Analysis and Implementation Teams (JSAT/JSIT), classified into the HFIX intervention approach categories by Shappell, Wiegmann, and their research team in 2006 [20]. The second database, classified by Chen, Chi, and Li (2013), included 182 unique safety recommendations from 31 incident reports of commercial airline occurrences between 2009 and 2011 [14].

**Table 3.** Percentage of human factors intervention approaches preferred by the workforce and in current safety recommendations.

| Human factors intervention approaches | Overall workforce preference | Safety recommendations from accident/incident report databases | |
|---|---|---|---|
| | Current study | JSAT/JSIT [20] | 31 airline occurrences [14] |
| Organisational/administrative | 62.4% | 36.6% | 41.1% |
| Task/mission | 4.0% | 7.3% | 11.4% |
| Technology/engineering | 2.0% | 22.2% | 11.0% |
| Operational/physical environment | 5.0% | 1.3% | 1.1% |
| Human/crew | 26.7% | 32.6% | 35.2% |

Results of the present study found that for both Asian and Western groups, the greatest preference was for 'Organisational/Administrative' approaches, followed by 'Human/Crew' changes (see Fig. 1). The pattern was similar in the previous research teams' classification of human factors interventions, with both databases having the highest ratio of recommendations falling into the 'Organisational/Administrative' category, followed secondly by 'Human/Crew'. This observation demonstrates that the development of human factors interventions, management strategies, or training programs may be subject to cultural "mitigation myopia", as in the fixes suggested by investigators may be biased to their own beliefs of what happened and what can be done about it [20]. Whilst this notion was conventionally considered to be a by-product of professional acculturation, wherein engineers tended to recommend 'Technology/Engineering' interventions, and psychologists tended to suggest 'Human/Crew' fixes, findings from the present study which included participants from a wide plethora of aviation professions would suggest that "mitigation myopia" may also be caused by cultural effects. Cultural biases on the attribution of faults at the investigation stage have the potential to be carried forward to biases in the creation and application of safety management strategies, as what strategies are considered to be accomplishable in a given situation will be subject to individual philosophical interpretations. Thus, a more global consideration and awareness of one's cultural or philosophical beliefs will be desirable when formulating safety recommendations in the future.

# 4 Conclusion

The relationship between employee national culture and safety values of the workforce have been widely studied, and their effects on the categorisation of human factors hazards and deficiencies have also been widely examined. However, there was little empirical research on how these attitudes which are determined by national culture can lead to variations in how human factors intervention strategies are perceived, judged, and received differently by people from different cultural backgrounds. By comparing aviation professionals' self-reported cultural background with their preference for the different types of human factors interventions based on the five categories provided within the HFIX framework, results of the present study confirm previous findings that cultural traits associated with national culture can be moderated by professional experience, and possibly suggests that acculturation to a professional environment may override personal cultural contexts in the evaluation of intervention approaches. It was also discovered that workforce preferences for the five HFIX approaches was coordinated with the types of safety recommendations provided in currently available accident and incident reports. Whilst these findings would suggest that current recommendations towards establishing Safety Cultures match perfectly with cultural preferences of the aviation workforce, the link between the categorisation of human factors deficiencies and the preference for human factors interventions highlights that safety recommendations are possibly affected by biases in earlier interpretations of events. Biases in the investigation stage may carry forward to the recommendations and intervention stage by altering internal evaluations of what is accomplishable. Thus, when designing organisational SMS programs, it will be desirable to avoid "myopic" viewpoints by actively considering how wider cultural contexts may be affecting investigation stages which precede the interventions and recommendations. It will also be advantageous to consider the interactive linkages between various cultural influences, such as professional experience, and take into account their moderating effects on the overall cultural values of the workforce.

# References

1. Skybrary.: Safety Culture. Available at: https://skybrary.aero/articles/safety-culture. Accessed 24 Feb 2022
2. ICAO.: ICAO Doc 9859, Safety Management Manual (SMM), 4th edn. Doc 9859 AN/474 (2018)
3. Noort, M.C., Reader, T.W., Shorrock, S., Kirwan, B.: The relationship between national culture and safety culture: implications for international safety culture assessments. J. Occup. Organ. Psychol. (2016). https://doi.org/10.1111/joop.12139
4. Liao, M.Y.: Safety culture in commercial aviation: differences in perspective between Chinese and western pilots. Saf. Sci. (2015). https://doi.org/10.1016/j.ssci.2015.05.011
5. Helmreich, R.L., Merritt, A.C.: Culture at Work in Aviation and Medicine. Routledge, New York, NY (1998)
6. Merritt, A., Maurino, D.: Cross-cultural factors in aviation safety. In: Advances in Human Performance and Cognitive Engineering Research (2004). https://doi.org/10.1016/S1479-3601(03)04005-0

7. Chan, W.T.-K., Harris, D.: Third-culture kid pilots and multi-cultural identity effects on pilots' attitudes. Aerosp. Med. Hum. Perform. **90**(12), 1026–1033. https://doi.org/10.3357/AMHP. 5397.2019. 1 Dec 2019

8. Li, W.-C., Harris, D., Chen, A.: Eastern minds in western cockpits: meta-analysis of human factors in mishaps from three nations. Aviat. Space Environ. Med. (2007)

9. Li, W.C., Harris, D., Li, L.W., Wang, T.: The differences of aviation human factors between individualism and collectivism culture. In: Lecture Notes in Computer Science (including subseries Lecture Notes in Artificial Intelligence and Lecture Notes in Bioinformatics) (2009). https://doi.org/10.1007/978-3-642-02583-9_78

10. Ram, A.: Degrading human factors through the invisible 'Freaky 13th' element. In: Engineering Psychology and Cognitive Ergonomics. HCII (2022)

11. Hofstede, G., Hofstede, G.J., Minkov, M.: Cultures and Organizations: Software of the Mind, Intercultural Cooperation and Its Importance for Survival. Cultures and Organizations (2010). https://doi.org/10.1007/s11569-007-0005-8

12. Li, W.-C., Young, H.-T., Wang, T., Harris, D.: International cooperation and challenges: understanding cross-cultural issues. ISASI Forum – Air Saf. Through Investig. **40**(4), 16–21 (2007)

13. Chan, W.T.-K., Li, W.-C.: Culture's consequences on the categorisation of causal factors in aviation accident reports. In: Proceedings of the 22nd HCI International Conference (2021)

14. Chen, J.C., Chi, C.F., Li, W.C.: The analysis of safety recommendation and human error prevention strategies in flight operations. In: Lecture Notes in Computer Science (including subseries Lecture Notes in Artificial Intelligence and Lecture Notes in Bioinformatics) (2013). https://doi.org/10.1007/978-3-642-39354-9_9

15. Chan, W.T.-K., Li, W.-C.: Assessing professional cultural differences between airline pilots and air traffic controllers. In: Proceedings of the 22nd HCI International Conference (2020)

16. Dona, C.M., Pignata, S.: Content and context analysis of fatigue management regulations for flight crew in the South Asian region. In: Engineering Psychology and Cognitive Ergonomics. HCII (2022)

17. Chen, J.C., Lin, S.C., Yu, V.F.: Structuring an effective human error intervention strategy selection model for commercial aviation. J. Air Transp. Manage. (2017). https://doi.org/10. 1016/j.jairtraman.2017.01.008

18. Mizzi, A., Lohmann, G., Carim, Jr.G.: Clipped wings: the impact of the covid-19 pandemic on airline pilots and influence on safety climate. In: Engineering Psychology and Cognitive Ergonomics. HCII (2022)

19. Shappell, S., Wiegmann, D.: Closing the loop on the system safety process: the human factors intervention matrix (HFIX). In: ISASI 2009 Proceedings, pp. 62–67 (2009)

20. Shappell, S., Wiegmann, D.: Developing a methodology for assessing safety programs targeting human error in aviation. In: Proceedings of the Human Factors and Ergonomics Society (2007). https://doi.org/10.1177/154193120705100208

# Improved Spectral Subtraction Method for Civil Aircraft Approach and Landing Crew Interactive Voice Enhancement

Nongtian Chen$^{(\boxtimes)}$, Weifeng Ning, Yongzheng Man, and Junhui Li

College of Aviation Engineering, Civil Aviation Flight University of China, Guanghan, Sichuan, China
chennongtian@hotmail.com

**Abstract.** Aiming at the situation that traditional spectral subtraction will produce "music noise" in the enhanced speech and the complex background noise of the cockpit is difficult to completely removed, this paper proposes an improved spectral subtraction method. Firstly, the over-subtraction factor α and the compensation factor β are introduced on the basis of spectral subtraction to reduce "music noise". Secondly, on the basis of the introduction of the two factors, we introduce a smoothing mechanism to improve the intelligibility of enhanced speech. Finally, aiming at the special background noise of the cockpit, we add a low-pass filter is added to filter the periodic and high-frequency noise on the basis of the above, and the improved method is evaluated and verified by experimental tests. Experimental results show that the final improved method can handle cockpit background noise well, maintain enhanced speech intelligibility and completeness, and improve subjective perception quality by 1.000 points compared with traditional spectral subtraction.

**Keywords:** Crew dialogue · Spectral subtraction · Over-subtraction factor · Smoothing mechanism · Low-pass filter

## 1 Introduction

With the booming development of the air transportation industry, aviation safety has become the focus of people's attention. In flight accidents, unsafe accidents caused by human factors account for about 70%. Flight accidents accounted for 67.16% [1]. For civil aircraft, the approach and landing phase is one of the most critical phases in the entire flight phase. Flight accidents in this phase account for more than 70% of the total flight accidents worldwide, of which 50% are caused by crew (dialog) errors [2]. However, the complex noise components of the aircraft cockpit include engine noise, air-conditioning noise and so on [3], which adversely affect the dialogue between crew members. So, separating clean voice from cockpit noise is of great significance to ensure the safety of aviation operations.

At present, traditional speech enhancement algorithms mainly include spectral subtraction [4], wiener filtering method [5], wavelet decomposition speech enhancement algorithm [6], subspace algorithm [7, 8], phase compensation algorithm [9], auditory masking effect algorithm [10] etc. As the earliest proposed method of speech enhancement, spectral subtraction has quickly become a popular algorithm due to its simple operation, excellent denoising and de-reverberation effects. On the contrary, the algorithm will produce "music noise" and reduce its performance. Scholars at China and abroad have optimized it from many aspects and the algorithm has been proposed many improvements. In 2008, Hamid Reza Abutalebi et al. artificially reduced the "music noise" produced by spectral subtraction. They applied image processing technology to the spectral output of spectral subtraction and proposed a symmetry based on adjacent music noise blocks. The results showed that the method could significantly reduce the "music noise" without affecting the enhanced speech intelligibility [11]. The same year, Sheng Li et al. proposed an iterative spectral subtraction method for radar speech that was severely weakened by additive combined noise. This method reduced the music noise retained during the pre-spectral subtraction process in each iteration. Simulation results showed this method could effectively reduce music noise [12]. In 2010, Kuldip Paliwal et al. used the modulation domain as an alternative acoustic domain for speech enhancement and used the analysis-correction-comprehensive framework in the modulation domain, finally, spectral subtraction was used to modulate the additive noise. The results showed this method could effectively suppress noise and improve voice quality [13]. In 2014, Kaladharan N proposed a signal-to-noise ratio value to measure the performance of spectral subtraction and studied the noise removal method of spectral subtraction, equally, he realized the noise reduction effect of spectral subtraction and reached the expected goal [14]. In 2017, Wu Lifu et al. used masking method to calculate the masking factors after spectral subtraction dereverberation in order to reduce the music noise, finally they applied the masking factors to process the reverberation signal. The results showed that this method was significantly less than the traditional spectral subtraction method to obtain music noise [15]. In 2018, Peng Jianxin and others used a combination of spectral subtraction and Wiener filtering to process the noise in the snoring signal in order to improve the signal-to-noise ratio of the snoring signal. The experiment result showed that the combination of the two methods results in a higher signal-to-noise ratio [16]. The same year, Jin Xuedong and others introduced a noise reduction model based on spectral subtraction and proposed a controlled recursive algorithm to adapt to non-stationary noise. Experimental results show that the improved method can increase the signal-to-noise ratio and improve the speech quality [17]. In 2019, Peng Peng and his partners combined spectral subtraction and wavelet decomposition to deal with transformer noise when testing outdoor transformer noise, which was susceptible to external environment. The results showed that this method can reduce the impact of external environment on transformer noise testing effectively [18]. In 2020, Tusar Kanti Dash et al. tried to obtain better speech enhancement results under the condition of low signal-to-noise ratio, they combined deep neural network and adaptive multi-band spectral subtraction to train the signal and used a hybrid algorithm to optimize the results finally. The results showed that this method can achieve better results under a lower signal-to-noise ratio [19]. Last year, Yadava G. Thimmaraja combined linear predictive coding (LPC) and voice activity detection (SS-VAD) spectral subtraction to propose a speech data enhancement coding algorithm, which could reduce noise of different types of noise and has been proved by experiments. The enhanced coded speech data obtained by this method has a higher quality [20]. Md Shohidul Islam et al. proposed a speech enhancement method based on dual-tree complex wavelet transform (DTCWT) and non-negative matrix factorization (NMF), which utilizes subband smoothing ratio masks (SSRM) through a joint learning process [21]. Lujun Li et al. proposed an end-to-end speech enhancement system by applying a self-attention mechanism to GANs, thereby realizing a system that can flexibly model long-range and local interactions and can be computationally efficient at the same time [22].

In summary, many scholars around the world have carried out a series of in-depth research on speech enhancement, and have achieved fruitful results, but less focus on the application of cockpit speech in the aviation field, especially the approach and landing segment. Considering the complex working environment of civil aircraft cockpit and the noise environment of special working conditions, there is still in-depth research on voice recognition and enhancement methods for crew dialogue communication. Aiming at the situation that traditional spectral subtraction will produce "musical noise" in the enhanced speech, and it is difficult to deal with the complex background noise of the cockpit, this paper proposes an improved spectral subtraction to improve and introduces a smoothing mechanism and a low-pass filter to improve the enhanced Speech intelligibility. On the basis of spectral subtraction, an over-subtraction factor $\alpha$ and a compensation factor $\beta$ are introduced to reduce "musical noise", and then a smoothing mechanism is further introduced on the basis of the introduction of the two factors to improve the intelligibility of the enhanced speech. On the basis of the above background noise, a low-pass filter is added to filter periodic and high-frequency noise for experimental test evaluation and verification. The research conclusions can provide the basis for the subsequent research on the risk identification and control technology of civil aircraft approach and landing based on the voice dialogue of the cockpit crew.

## 2   Principle of Spectral Subtraction

The basic principle of spectral subtraction assumes that additive noise is uncorrelated with the short-term stationary noisy speech signal. First, the amplitude spectrum of the noise signal is subtracted from the amplitude spectrum of the noisy speech signal to obtain the amplitude spectrum estimate of the clean speech signal, then combine the phase of the noisy speech signal to do the inverse transformation of the short-time Fourier transform to obtain the enhanced speech signal.

Supposing the time-domain sampling signal of pure speech is, and the time-domain sampling signal of noise is, then the time-domain signal of noisy speech can be expressed as:

$$y(n) = x(n) + d(n) \tag{1}$$

After performing discrete Fourier transform on both ends of the equation, we can get:

$$Y(\omega) = X(\omega) + D(\omega) \tag{2}$$

In addition, there is a polar coordinate representation for $Y(\omega)$:

$$Y(\omega) = e^{j\theta_{y(\omega)}}|Y(\omega)| \tag{3}$$

$|Y(\omega)|$ is the amplitude spectrum, $\theta_{y(\omega)}$ is the phase spectrum of the original noisy signal, similarly, we can get:

$$D(\omega) = e^{j\theta_{d(\omega)}}|Y(\omega)| \tag{4}$$

Under the premise of not affecting the speech intelligibility, use phase spectrum $\theta_{y(\omega)}$ instead of $\theta_{d(\omega)}$, and put formulas (3) and (4) into formula (2) to obtain an estimated form of clean speech spectrum:

$$|\widetilde{X}(\omega)| = \Big[|Y(\omega)| - |\widetilde{D}(\omega)|\Big]e^{j\theta_{y(\omega)}} \tag{5}$$

Among them, is the amplitude spectrum estimation of the noise when no voice activity is generated. Simplify formula (5) to get the basic form of amplitude spectrum subtraction:

$$|\widetilde{X}(\omega)| = |Y(\omega)| - |\widetilde{D}(\omega)| \tag{6}$$

In the real frequency domain, cannot be less than zero, or it may be due to non-stationary noise signals or deviations in the noise estimation process. Generally, when is less than zero, we set it to zero:

$$|\widetilde{X}(\omega)| = \begin{cases} 0 & |\widetilde{X}(\omega)| < 0 \\ |\widetilde{X}(\omega)| & |\widetilde{X}(\omega)| \geq 0 \end{cases} \tag{7}$$

The power spectrum can be derived from the amplitude spectrum subtraction algorithm and the effects of two algorithms are different in diverse environments. The power spectrum estimation of pure speech is expressed as:

$$|\widetilde{X}(\omega)|^2 = |Y(\omega)|^2 - |\widetilde{D}(\omega)|^2 \tag{8}$$

As same as the amplitude spectrum subtraction, $|\widetilde{X}(\omega)|^2$ cannot be less than zero. Refer to the method of formula (7), the form is as follows:

$$|\widetilde{X}(\omega)|^2 = |Y(\omega)|^2 - |\widetilde{D}(\omega)|^2 \tag{9}$$

Finally, the estimated spectrum $|\widetilde{X}(\omega)|$ is subjected to the inverse transform of the short-time Fourier transform and the phase of the original noisy speech is reused to obtain an enhanced speech signal. The basic process of spectral subtraction is as shown below (Fig. 1):

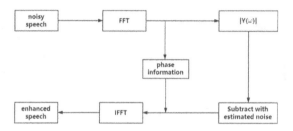

**Fig. 1.** Spectral subtraction process.

## 3  Improved Spectral Subtraction

The traditional spectrum subtraction method is to subtract the estimated value of the noise amplitude spectrum of the same degree from the entire speech segment to obtain an enhanced pure speech signal. However, this method has many shortcomings. Firstly, the energy distribution of the speech signal is uneven and the energy in the frequency spectrum is mostly concentrated in a certain frequency band. Therefore, only using a single standard to process noise components cannot highlight the components of pure speech. Secondly, the composition of noise in the cabin is complex, resulting in a large difference between the noise estimation value in the no-speech segment and the actual frequency domain value of the noise then the overestimation problem occurs. If only set the negative value to 0 (Eq. 7), it will cause small, independent peaks to appear at random positions in the signal frame spectrum, which is called music noise. In order to avoid this situation, we introduce an over-subtraction factor $\alpha$ to control it artificially. The improved method is as follows:

$$|\tilde{X}(\omega)| = \left(|Y(\omega)|^{\Upsilon} - \alpha|\tilde{D}(\omega)|^{\Upsilon}\right)^{\frac{1}{\Upsilon}} \tag{10}$$

When $|\tilde{X}(\omega)|$ is less than 0, set threshold $\beta|\tilde{D}(\omega)|$ to control its size, where $\beta$ is the compensation factor. The specific formula is as follows:

$$|\tilde{X}(\omega)| = \begin{cases} \beta|\tilde{D}(\omega)| & |\tilde{X}(\omega)| < \beta|\tilde{D}(\omega)| \\ |\tilde{X}(\omega)| & |\tilde{X}(\omega)| \geq \beta|\tilde{D}(\omega)| \end{cases} \tag{11}$$

When $\alpha = 1$ and $\beta = 0$, it is the traditional spectral subtraction method. Increasing the over-subtraction factor and compensation factor can suppress noise, highlight pure voice components and improve the human ear's acceptance of noise. However, this method will cause the amplitude spectrum line Discontinuity affects the intelligibility of speech, as shown in Fig. 2.

To solve this problem, a smoothing mechanism is introduced. Smoothing is an important operation of digital signal processing. Smoothing technology is widely used in video traffic prediction, digital image processing and other fields and has achieved excellent results [23, 24]. Application of smoothing processing in speech enhancement: The speech data has $T_{noise}$ frames. First, take the first several frames and do the average processing to get $E(\omega)$, then subtract each frame from the mean $E(\omega)$, then take it in each dimension

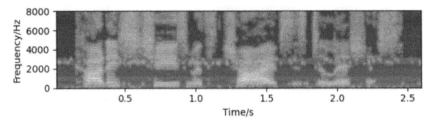

**Fig. 2.** Spectrogram generated after the introduction of the subtraction factor and the compensation factor

the maximum value gives the maximum noise residual. If the pure speech amplitude spectrum obtained by spectral subtraction is smaller than the maximum noise residual, the estimated amplitude spectrum is considered to be small. At this time, the minimum value of several adjacent frames is replaced for the part that is too small, and then it has a smoothing effect. The specific formula is as follows:

$$\max(\omega) = \arg\max \sum_{t=0}^{T_{noise}} E_t(\omega) - E(\omega) \cdot \tag{12}$$

$$|\tilde{X}(\omega)| = \begin{cases} \arg\min \sum_{t-k}^{t+k} |\tilde{X}(\omega)| & |\tilde{X}(\omega)| < \max(\omega) \\ |\tilde{X}(\omega)| & |\tilde{X}(\omega)| \geq \max(\omega) \end{cases} \tag{13}$$

Spectral subtraction introduces over-subtraction factors and compensation factors and uses a smoothing mechanism. The spectrogram is shown in Fig. 3. From Figs. 2 and 3 and the enhanced speech, it can be concluded that the spectral line of the spectral subtraction with smoothing mechanism is more continuous and the enhanced speech intelligibility after the introduction of the smoothing mechanism is significantly higher.

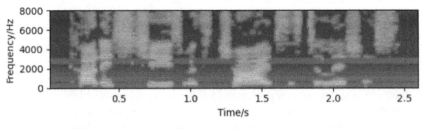

**Fig. 3.** Spectrogram generated with smoothing mechanism

In view of the periodic and high-frequency noise in the cockpit of an aircraft, such as exhaust noise, compressor noise, and mechanical vibration [25], a low-pass filter is added on the basis of the above improvements, which can suppress noise above a certain frequency, while allowing voice signals below that frequency to pass through [26].

# 4  Experiment and Result Analysis

## 4.1  Data Sources

The speech processed in the experiment is the speech of the crew during the approach and landing phase of a civil aircraft polluted by cabin noise. The file format is .wav, the sampling rate is 16 kHz, and the bit rate is 16 bit. The compilation software used in the speech enhancement experiment is pycharm, the virtual environment is python3.7 and the over-subtraction factor $\alpha$ and the compensation factor $\beta$ take values 4 and 0.0001 respectively after multiple verifications.

## 4.2  Experimental Results

The experiment evaluated the performance of traditional spectral subtraction, spectral subtraction with over subtraction factor, spectral subtraction with smoothing mechanism, and low-pass filter based on the spectrogram, subjective evaluation method MOS, and analyzed and compared the experimental results. The following figures are comparison between the spectrogram of noisy speech and the spectrogram of traditional and improved spectral subtraction (Fig. 4, Fig. 5, Fig. 6, Fig. 7).

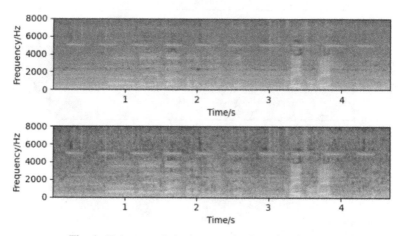

**Fig. 4.** Noisy speech (top), spectral subtraction (bottom)

It can be seen from the figures that the spectral subtraction performance after the introduction of the subtraction factor is better than the traditional spectral subtraction; although the spectral subtraction with the smoothing mechanism can remove most of the background noise, it highlights the high-frequency noise. Although this method can maintain voice integrity outstandingly, long-term high-frequency noise will be uncomfortable; after adding a low-pass filter, high-frequency noise can be significantly reduced, while maintaining good voice integrity.

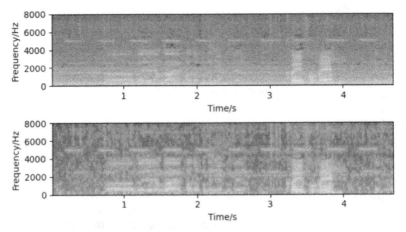

**Fig. 5.** Noisy speech (top), introducing over-subtraction factor spectral subtraction (bottom)

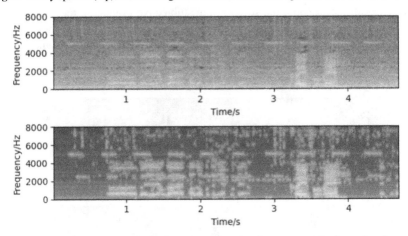

**Fig. 6.** Noisy speech (top), introducing over-subtraction factor spectral subtraction (bottom)

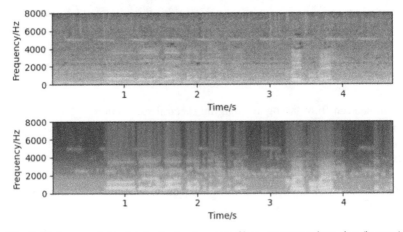

**Fig. 7.** Noisy speech (top), introducing low-pass filter spectrum subtraction (bottom)

## 4.3  MOS Scoring Standards

Due to the lack of clean voice for the crew dialogue during the approach and landing phase of the civil aircraft, the Mean Opinion Score (MOS) was used to further evaluate and compare the effects of several enhancement methods. The average opinion scoring method is a subjective evaluation method, in which people subjectively evaluate the enhanced speech. The specific evaluation method is that the participants listen to the fully enhanced speech and give a score according to the scoring standard (Table 1), and then the score perform a weighted average, and the final score is the MOS score [27]. The weighted average formula is:

$$MOS = \frac{1}{M} \sum_{K=1}^{5} S_K M_K \tag{14}$$

Among them, M represents the number of testers, K represents the voice quality level, SK represents the number of Kth values, and MK is the MOS score corresponding to the voice quality level.

**Table 1.** MOS scoring standards

| MOS score | Example | Participants feel |
|---|---|---|
| 5 | Very excellent | Can't hear the noise |
| 4 | Excellent | Just can hear a little noise |
| 3 | Good | Can hear the noise and get a little bored |
| 2 | Bad | Bored but tolerable |
| 1 | Very bad | Can not stand |

The experiment selected 23 non-professionals aged 19–45 in a quiet environment using the same equipment to listen to the voice enhanced by the above method. Each person listened to each sentence four times and followed the same evaluation criteria (Table 2).

**Table 2.** Participants' scoring situation

| MOS score | 1 | 2 | 3 | 4 | 5 | Total |
|---|---|---|---|---|---|---|
| Spectral subtraction | 0 | 0 | 12 | 11 | 0 | 23 |
| Introducing an over-subtraction factor | 0 | 0 | 10 | 13 | 0 | 23 |
| Introduce smoothing mechanism | 0 | 0 | 1 | 20 | 2 | 23 |
| Introduce low-pass filtering | 0 | 0 | 0 | 12 | 11 | 23 |

Finally, according to the participant's scoring situation and formula (14), the results are shown in Fig. 8. The figure is easy to understand: the traditional spectral subtraction, the addition of the over-subtraction factor, the introduction of smoothing mechanism, and the introduction of low pass filtering methods obtain MOS scores of 3.478, 3.565, 4.040, 4.478, it can be seen from the experimental results that the performance of the method proposed in this paper is better than the traditional spectral subtraction method on the MOS index. suitable.

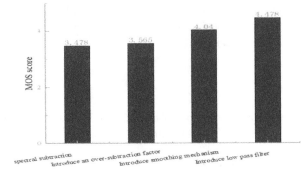

**Fig. 8.** MOS score

## 5    Conclusions

In view of the situation that traditional spectral subtraction will leave "music noise" in the enhanced speech, we introduce an over-subtraction factor $\alpha$ and a compensation factor $\beta$ and a smoothing mechanism to further suppress the reduction of speech intelligibility caused by this method. At the same time, according to the background noise of the aircraft cockpit we introduce a low-pass filter to filter out some periodic and high-frequency noise and carry out the experimental test evaluation and verification. Experiments show that under the background of cockpit noise, the final optimization method can handle noise well and maintain speech intelligibility and obtain stronger denoising ability than traditional spectral subtraction. The final improved method is more subjective than traditional spectral subtraction. The perceived quality has been improved by 1.000, which can better deal with the complex noise of the aircraft cockpit. The research conclusions can provide a basis for the subsequent research on human error recognition and risk management and control technology for civil aircraft approach and landing based on the voice dialogue of the cockpit crew.

**Funding.** This research was funded by National Natural Science Foundation of China, grant number U2033202; Key R&D Program of Sichuan Provincial Department of Science and Technology (22ZDYF2942); Safety Capability Fund Project of Civil Aviation Administration of China (2022J026).

# References

1. Civil Aviation Administration of China.: Annual Report on Aviation Safety in China, 2018. Civil Aviation Administration of China, Beijing (2019)
2. Li, F.H., Xie, Z.N.: Analysis on the law of flight accidents and incidents during the approach and landing phase of China's civil aircraft and research on preventive measures. J. Civil Aviation Flight Univ. China **19**(2), 3–7 (2008)
3. Benyassine, A., et al.: ITU-T Recommendation G. 729 annex B: a silence compression scheme for use with G. 729 optimized for V. 70 digital simultaneous voice and data applications. IEEE Commun. Mag. **35**(9), 64–73 (1997)
4. Boll, S.F.: Suppression of acoustic noise in speech using spectral subtraction. IEEE Trans. Acoust. Speech Signal Process. **27**(2), 113–120 (1979)
5. Chen, J.D., et al.: New insights into the noise reduction wiener filter. IEEE T Audio Speech **14**(4), 1218–1234 (2006)
6. Martin, R.: Speech enhancement based on minimum meansquare error estimation and supergaussian priors. IEEE Trans. Speech Audio Process. **13**(5), 845–856 (2005)
7. Ephraim, Y., Van Trees, H.L.: A signal subspace approach for speech enhancement. IEEE Trans. Speech Audio Process. **3**(4), 251–266 (1995)
8. Jensen, S.H., et al.: Reduction of broad-band noise in speech by truncated QSVD. IEEE Trans. Speech Audio Process. **3**(6), 439–448 (1995)
9. Donoho, D.L.: De-noising by soft-thresholding. IEEE Trans. Inform. Theory **21**(3), 613–627 (1995)
10. Virag, N.: Single channel speech enhancement based on masking properties of the human auditory system. IEEE Trans. Speech Audio Process. **7**(2), 126–137 (1999)
11. Abutalebi, H.R., Dashtbozorg, B.: Signal processing: musical noise reduction by processing spectrogram of spectral subtraction output. Renew. Sust. Energ. Rev. **6**(10), 2979–2986 (2008)
12. Sheng, L.: Iterative spectral subtraction method for millimeter-wave conducted speech enhancement. J. Biomed. Sci. Eng. **3**(2), 187–192 (2010)
13. Paliwal, K., Kamil, W., Schwerin, B.: Single-channel speech enhancement using spectral subtraction in the short-time modulation domain. Speech Commun. **52**(5), 450–475 (2010)
14. Kaladharan, N.: Speech enhancement by spectral subtraction method. Int. J. Comput. Appl. **96**(13), 45–48 (2014)
15. Wu, L.F., Shen, H.: Reducing musical noise in dereverberation of spectral subtraction based on masking method. J. Electron. Meas. Instrum. **31**(11), 1855–1859 (2017)
16. Peng, J.X., Tang, Y.F.: Sleep snoring noise reduction processing combined with spectral subtraction and Wiener filtering. J. South China Univ. Technol. Nat. Sci. Ed. **46**(3), 103–107 (2018)
17. Jin, X.D., Li, D.X.: Improved algorithm for voice signal noise reduction based on spectral subtraction. Foreign Electron. Meas. Technol. **37**(5), 63–67 (2018)
18. Peng, P., et al.: Preprocessing method for transformer noise measurement based on wavelet packet decomposition and spectral subtraction algorithm. High Volt. Appar. **55**(11), 177–183 (2019)
19. Dash, T.K., Solanki, S.S.: Speech intelligibility based enhancement system using modified deep neural network and adaptive multi-band spectral subtraction. Wireless Pers. Commun. **111**(2), 1073–1087 (2020)
20. Thimmaraja, Y.G., Nagaraja, B.G., Jayanna, H.S.: Speech enhancement and encoding by combining SS-VAD and LPC. Int. J. Speech Technol. **24**(6), 1–8 (2021)
21. Islam, M.S., et al.: Supervised single channel speech enhancement based on dual-tree complex wavelet transforms and nonnegative matrix factorization using the joint learning process and subband smooth ratio mask. Electronics **3**, 1–18 (2019)

22. Li, L.J., et al.: Light-weight self-attention augmented generative adversarial networks for speech enhancement. Electronics **10**(13), 1–16 (2021)
23. Li, Y., et al.: Smoothing-aided support vector machine based nonstationary video traffic prediction towards B5G networks. IEEE Trans. Veh. Technol. **69**(7), 7493–7502 (2020)
24. Sharma, V., Srivastava, D., Mathur, P.: A Daubechies DWT based image steganography using smoothing operation. Int. Arab J. Inf. Technol. **17**(2), 154–161 (2020)
25. Bao, J.P.: Research on the Influence of Cockpit Noise on Pilot Situation Awareness. Nanjing University of Aeronautics and Astronautics, Nanjing (2019)
26. Wang, P., Zhang, D., Lu, B.: Robust fuzzy sliding mode control based on low pass filter for the welding robot with dynamic uncertainty. Ind. Robot **47**(1), 111–120 (2020)
27. Bahadur, I.N., Kumar, S., Agarwal, P.: Performance measurement of a hybrid speech enhancement technique. Int. J. Speech Technol. **24**(7), 665–677 (2021)

# Active Supervision in a Remote Tower Center: Rethinking of a New Position in the ATC Domain

Maik Friedrich$^{(\boxtimes)}$ ⓘ, Felix Timmermann, and Jörn Jakobi

German Aerospace Center, Lilienthalplatz 7, 38108 Braunschweig, Germany
Maik.Friedrich@dlr.de

**Abstract.** Air Traffic Control Officers are the most valuable resource in the Air Traffic Control Domain. They devote their full capacities into safe and efficient traffic control. The Remote Tower Center is the next step to use this resource as efficient as possible, optimizing the existing methodologies and procedures. The initial concept for the Remote Tower Center contains a supervisor. Therefore, this paper focusses on the supervisor and how the supervisor workplace is defined as a coordinating and support position for all Multiple Remote Tower Modules in the center. Based on the existing concept of multiple remote tower operations and the supervisor workplace, two research questions were proposed to analyze the supervisor working position in combination with the multiple remote tower workplaces. A real time simulation study was conducted and a total of 15 air traffic control officers from two air navigation service providers participated. Due to the difficulty of comparing two different workplaces, the data analysis is based on descriptive data collected from the questionnaires. The study analyzed the application and handling of use cases as a reference for realistic task descriptions during a multi workplace real time simulation. The results show that the selected use cases represent the task of the supervisor and can help to validate the workplace. This study also shows the different perceptions of task handling within the remote tower center.

**Keywords:** Multiple remote tower · Supervisor · Real-time simulation · Cooper-Harper scale

## 1 Introduction

The most valuable resource in the Air Traffic Control (ATC) Domain are the Air Traffic Control Officers (ATCO) that fully devote their capacities into safe and efficient traffic control. To use this resource as efficient as possible, a steady process of developing and optimizing the existing methodologies and procedures is needed. As an alternative for the traditional tower control operations, remote tower has been researched for the last two decades. Remote Tower Operations (RTO) in general are a solution for airports with a low amount of traffic to efficiently distribute their resources. The concept is based on single Remote Tower Operation, which is the control of one airport from a distant location. Weber [1] presents the first German remote tower operation of Saarbrücken

D. Harris and W.-C. Li (Eds.): HCII 2022, LNAI 13307, pp. 265–278, 2022.
https://doi.org/10.1007/978-3-031-06086-1_20

airport from Leipzig center. Saarbrücken is 450 km away from Leipzig, but RTO allows a safe and efficient monitoring of the airport. In the next years, the number of airports remotely controlled from Remote Tower Center Leipzig will increase.

With single remote tower operations proven to be operational, further research focuses on the Multiple Remote Tower Operations (MRTO). MRTO is the provision of ATC for more than two airports at the same time from one workplace. These concepts enable the air navigation service (ANS) providers to rethink their existing workplaces and role assignments and open up new working positions in the ATC domain. Besides an efficient use of ATCOs, MRTO has a positive influence on the hazard of boredom [2, 3]. Even so MRTO have their advantages, Möhlenbrink, Friedrich and Papenfuss [4] claim that one of the major challenges for MRTO is to keep a separate mental picture for each remote-controlled airport and safely switch between those. Generating and keeping a mental picture can be difficult especially in high workload situations [5]. Workload can increase depending on the traffic situation on each individual airport and the resulting traffic mixture.

Following this connection between high workload traffic mixtures and performance [for a summary see 6], methodologies that reduce the occurrence of those situations are needed to ensure a successful transition from single to multiple remote tower. Based on the tower supervisor position, a remote tower center supervisor is considered as a first approach to coordinate the traffic in advance to monitor current and anticipated task load and to balance workload for the individual ATCOs. This paper supports the MRTO concept by analyzing the remote tower center supervisor position.

## 2  Remote Tower Center with Supervisor

The initial concept for the Remote Tower Center (RTC) supervisor (SUP) is still research in progress [7]. For the purpose of this paper, the supervisor is defined as a coordinator and support position for all Multiple Remote Tower Modules (MRTM) in the center. Each MRTM is considered to have one active ATCO and up to three Airports that are controlled remotely at the same time. Figure 1 shows an overview of the RTC and the main interaction of the SUP with MRTM and airports. The main task of the SUP workplace is to gather pre-tactical data from all airports, plan a distribution of airports onto workplaces that reduce the traffic load for each individual MRTM and implement this plan. The implementation is done with split & merge operations, which means the supervision of an airport is split from one MRTM and merged into another one. The method of communication between SUP and MRTM should be directly via voice or telephone. The tactical information from the airport to the SUP workplace should be transferred automatically and can include e.g. weather and amount of traffic.

Secondary tasks of the SUP are to support each individual MRTM with additional coordination, if requested. Therefore, additional ways of communication are required, especially in connection to each airport, e.g. telephone of the approach control. Additional information for each individual airport, like out-of-the-window view or radar are only available on the MRTMs. Derived from both aspects of the task, the SUP workplace should include ATC functionalities, e.g. weather information and traffic distribution for each airport and radio communication to each ATCO.

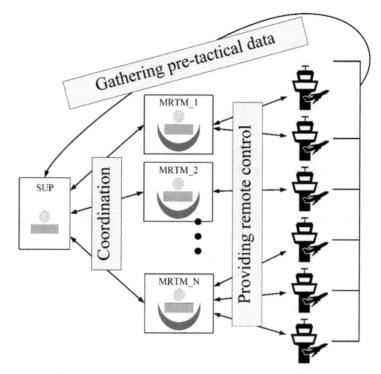

**Fig. 1.** Set-up for remote tower center supervisor, from [7]

In accordance to the EUROCONTROL/FAA [8] white paper for human performance, the majority of operational procedures can be measured by use cases. Therefore, three design workshops with the focus on general requirements for the remote center supervisor workplace, main use cases and additional use cases were conducted. Friedrich, Timmermann and Jakobi [7] used a user-centered design approach to develop the operational procedures and identified use cases that are relevant for the SUP. Following the MRTO concept, these use cases represent tasks that are expected from the SUP to handle multiple times throughout a shift. For this paper, we focus on the following nine use cases (Table 1), selected from [7]. Each use case requires a mix of information, from the airports and the MRTM directly, that need to be processed by the SUP and transferred into a planning for the near future.

In the context of the use cases (Table 1), two trigger directions for activation were identified. The first is bottom up, which, in this context means, the ATCO of one of the MRTM starts the use case by requesting support. The second is top down, when the SUP initiates the use case by gathering information from airports or asking ATCOs about their availability. Because the SUP is supporting up to 15 MRTM positions, there is a strong connection between his/her workload and the workload of the ATCOs. The general dynamic between the SUP and the ATCOs is an important factor of the concept and needs to be considered for the analysis.

**Table 1.** Nine use cases that represent the SUP tasks, from [7]

| Use Cases | Description |
| --- | --- |
| Daily planning | Due to an unexpected event an ATCO is not available for his/her shift that starts in a couple of hours |
| Handling SUP/ATCO request | Due to unforeseen increased traffic volume on a specific airport, either the ATCO on a MRTM or the SUP requests the split & merge of a specific airport away from the MRTM to another position |
| Scheduled workload increase | Due to expected increased traffic volume on a specific airport, the SUP requests the split & merge of a specific airport away from the MRTM to another position |
| Scheduled airport closing | The scheduled closing of an airport begins and the airport needs to be closed |
| Scheduled airport opening | The scheduled opening of an airport needs to be handled |
| Unplanned airport closing | Due to severe weather events in the near future (e.g. low visibility) a specific airport has to be closed |
| Unplanned airport opening | An aircraft requests landing for an airport that is closed |
| Unplanned runway closing | Due to a technical failure an aircraft blocks the runway on a specific airport |
| Unscheduled ATCO replacement | Due to unexpected circumstances, an ATCO has to be relieved and replaced for some time by another ATCO (Ex. health issues) from his/her MRTM |

## 3   Research Questions

Based on the existing concept of multiple remote tower operations and the introduction literature to the workplace SUP [7], the following research questions (RQ) are proposed. RQ1: How realistic is this SUP workplace in terms of operational feasibility for MRTO? Due to the current level of the concept this RQ is important to understand if further investigation into the topic is sensible. RQ2: How does the handling differ between a traditional supervisor role and a SUP in an RTC?

With regard to RQ1 we hypothesize that, due to the close relation to an existing supervisor position workplace in a traditional tower, the ATCOs have no difficulties in understanding the purpose and the necessity of the SUP working position. We also hypothesize (RQ2) that workload for the SUP as well as the ATCOs at the MRTM will always be well-balanced, without under- and overload situations and without situations with impaired safety. As an extension to RQ2, it is important to consider that SUP and MRTM are exposed to the same use cases but from a different perspective.

## 4   Method

A real time simulation study was conducted to create an environment that allows to simulate the selected use cases and analyze the SUP's behavior in a realistic environment.

The selected 9 use cases and the implication for a validation from Friedrich, Timmermann and Jakobi [7] were the basis for the experimental set-up and design of the study.

## 4.1 Participants

The sample consists of a total of 15 ATCOs (14 male/1 female) from two ANS providers. Eight were recruited from Oro navigacija (Lithuania) and seven from PANSA (Poland) and participated voluntarily during their working hours. Therefore, all participants were active ATCOs. Table 2 shows an overview of the demographic information and the work experience as tower ATCO and tower supervisor. It has to be noted that not all participants have supervisor experience, but due to their training, they all had knowledge of the supervisor working position. The study was performed in accordance with the General Data Protection Regulation (EU) 2016/679.

**Table 2.** Democratic overview of age and work experience (in years)

|     | Age   | ATCO experience | Supervisor experience |
|-----|-------|-----------------|-----------------------|
| M   | 39,20 | 12,80           | 3,20                  |
| SD  | 5,36  | 6,83            | 4,09                  |
| Min | 32    | 4               | 0                     |
| Max | 46    | 22              | 15                    |

## 4.2 Design and Material

For this study, the set-up of a Remote Tower Center (RTC) was simulated in a high fidelity setting. One SUP, two real MRTM (Module 1 and 2) and 4 virtual MRTM (Module 3 to 6) were simulated to create a RTC. Authentic traffic patterns and flight information were simulated by the NARSIM [9]. The MRTM had the possibility to provide air traffic service via radio communication. The radio communication between the airports was coupled and each ATCO had a headset. In addition, radar, out-the-window view, weather and flight strips for up to three airports could be activated on each MRTM. A detailed description for the MRTM is available by [10].

A within-subject design was used for the factor working position. In order to minimize the learning effect two almost similar scenarios were used. The difference between scenario 1 and 2 was the order of the emerging use cases and scenario 2 had 4 additional use cases with coordination phone calls. These use cases had a duration of approximately 30 s and only required an additional phone call. The amount of traffic was kept similar. The scenarios represent normal workday situations within a RTC. The planned duration for each scenario was approximately 60 min. The traffic volume on each MRTM had a maximum of 7 movements in parallel independent from the airports. The supervisor position overlooked a total of 15 airports. Even though the focus of the validation was the SUP, data of handling qualities and performance during the use cases was collected from every working position.

Each use case (Table 1) depended on traffic situations. Use cases could be activated either by time (opening of an airport) or by traffic situation, e.g., the amount of parallel movements was expected to exceed 8 at a single MRTM (use case "Scheduled workload increase"). The traffic load for a single airport was derived from its usual amount of traffic. For example, a mid-sized airport had around 12 movements per hour, whereas a small airport had approximately 4 to 6 movements. Important for the scenario and the use cases was the traffic distribution generated by combining different airports on one MRTM. In general, the use cases were planned to happen at least once per scenario. Only "scheduled airport opening" and "scheduled workload" were planed with an average of two, because they are the common use cases for the SUP task.

Figure 2 shows the experimental set-up in the TowerLab [3] at the Institute of Flight Guidance, German Aerospace Center (DLR). For this study it was assumed that one ATCO can only hold 4 endorsements at a time. The ATCO on MRTM 1 always held the endorsements for Aalborg Airport, Aarhus Airport, Billund Airport and Budapest Ferenc Liszt International Airport. The ATCO on MRTM 2 always held the endorsements for Billund Airport, Budapest Ferenc Liszt International Airport, Debrecen International Airport, and Pápa Air Base. This allowed for a possible handover of either Billund or Budapest airport, because these endorsements were available by both ATCOs. The virtual ATCOs were available via telephone.

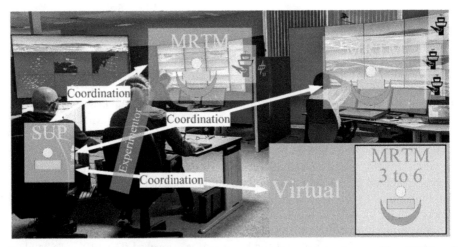

**Fig. 2.** RTC real-time simulation set-up with one remote tower supervisor position (SUP) and two multiple remote tower module (MRTM_1 and MRTM_2)

Derived from the use cases, system requirements were identified for a tool to support the SUP in his/her tasks. The tool provided the SUP with an overview of the 15 airports and their opening and closing times. Weather, traffic density and technical status were also indicated for each airport. In addition, a pool of 10 available ATCOs was provided, including a list of their individual endorsements. The SUP tool also provided an overview of 6 MRTM, that the SUP could use to assign airports and ATCOs and thereby keep track of the current configuration within the RTC. The SUP tool also provided warnings if the expected traffic load for a MRTM was to increase above the number of 8 movements in parallel.

### 4.3  Procedure

The study was conducted from the 15$^{th}$ of November to the 1$^{st}$ of December in 2021. The 15 participants were assigned to 5 groups of three participants. Each group was scheduled for two days. Each group received a briefing describing the MRTO concept, the SUP and MRTM workplaces, and the MRTO procedure. Written consent for the recording of personal data was gathered from each participant. Then, a training session with a duration of approximately 40 min per person started. The participants used this time to familiarize themselves with the two workplaces, and the procedures to handle the traffic. After the training, the participants were randomly assigned to either SUP, MRTM 1 or MRTM 2. The positions were changed after each run.

A total of 6 runs (2 scenarios, twice per participant) were performed, three on day one and three on day two. The duration of each run varied between 55 and 60 min, depending on the decisions each SUP made during the run. The participants on either MRTM controlled up to three aerodromes in parallel. During each run, only the SUP answered questions after finishing a use case. After each run all participants completed a standard and a tailor-made questionnaire for the workplace they previously worked at. Each group of participants was debriefed together.

### 4.4  Data Analysis

Due to the comparability of the two workplaces, the data analysis is based on descriptive data collected from the questionnaires. Dependent on the SUP or the MRTM the participants have to act and react differently in each use case. On the one hand this increases the realism of the experimental set-up, and on the other it allows only for comparison of workload and safety level on a subjective level. It also allows for realistic feedback on the general MRTO concept, which is especially important for RQ1.

A tailor-made questionnaire was developed to identify the feasibility of the SUP workplace and its operational practicability within the MRTO. The questionnaire consisted of 6 statements that the participants could agree or disagree on a 5-point scale ("Strongly disagree", "Disagree", "Neither disagree nor agree", "Agree", "Strongly agree"). The participants completed the questionnaire after each run they worked at the SUP workplace (scenario 1 and 2). The 6 statements are available in Fig. 3.

The subjective handling and perceived safety from both workplaces were collected with the cooper-harper scale [11]. To account for the specifics of the work environment the cooper-harper scale was adapted for the SUP and MRTM. The adapted cooper-harper scale had 10 steps that allows to evaluate if the use case was controllable, impairments in situational awareness could be expected, or safety critical situations would arise. The scale value 1 to 3 indicated efficient and smooth workflow. The scale values from 4 to 6 indicated adequate situation awareness. The scale values from 6 to 9 indicated safe controllability of the situation and 10 indicated an unsafe situation.

At the SUP workplace the ATCOs were questioned directly after each completed use case during the scenario. The MRTM were questioned with the post run questionnaire. Therefore, the results from the SUP workplace were summarized for each run. Even so, the influence between the workplaces cannot be distinguished and therefore they have to be evaluated separately. The same applies to our interpretation of the results in the Discussion and Conclusion sections.

## 5   Results

Following the research questions, the result section is divided into two sub sections. The data collection worked properly without any technical issues. A restriction of the results is, that due to the degree of realism and the structure of the scenarios, not all needed use cases could be simulated during each run.

### 5.1  SUP Workplace in General

The first analysis concerns the feasibility of the concept for a supervisor workplace with regards to MRTO (RQ1). Figure 3 presents the agreement or disagreement for each statement supporting RQ1. Each statement was presented once per scenario to each participant. The analysis shows that the majority of the participants agreed that the SUP workplace provides an appropriate addition to the RTC. They even agreed by taking the complexity of the task itself or the traffic volume presented in the scenarios into account. The participants also agreed that the provided SUP tool supported them during the split and merging procedures. The answers of the participants suggest that they did in general neither disagree nor agree with the procedures used to split & merge the aerodromes between the MRTM, nor did they feel supported by the SUP tool to prepare for those operations.

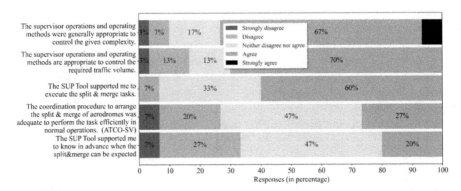

**Fig. 3.** Agreement or disagreement to the tailor-made questions twice per scenario for each participant

## 5.2  Handling of SUP and ATCOs

The second analysis concerns the perceived quality of handling for each workplace. This analysis is separated into two steps. First, the amount of answers per use case, scenario and working position is analyzed to identify the comparability of the results. Second, the analysis focuses on the subjective rating to each workplace and the use cases with direct interaction between the workplaces.

**Quantity of the Use Cases.** All participants at the MRTM completed the tailor-made questionnaire twice but not all experienced the same use cases in their exercises and therefore were not always able to provide answers regarding the requested use cases. This is similar for the SUP workplace if not all use cases could be handled during a run, and the questioning was always done directly after each use case. Therefore, the amount of responses to the use cases varies between the scenarios and the workplaces. another difference is the unbalanced workplace distribution per run. While one participant worked as SUP, two participants worked on the MRTM. This means that every time the adapted cooper-harper scale is completed for a use case by the SUP, it is completed twice from the MRTM perspective after the run.

In preparation for the understanding of the later analysis and to get an overview of the frequency of use cases, the amount of answers collected was evaluated. Table 3 presents the amount of answers collected for both workplaces separated per use case and scenario. The use cases "Daily planning", "Scheduled airport closing", "Unplanned airport closing", "Unplanned airport opening", "Unplanned runway closing", "Unplanned airport closing", and "Unscheduled ATCO replacement" together occurred with an average of 1 per scenario for all SUPs. Only the use cases "Scheduled airport opening" and "Scheduled Workload" occurred 2.45 times per scenario for the SUP. Since the ATCOs on the MRTM were only questioned at the end of each run, their maximum of answers is 30. The ATCOs were instructed to not answer the question if they did not experience the use case during the last run. This leads to an average of 24.6 answers per scenario and MRTM.

**Table 3.** Amount of answers to each use case per scenario for SUPs and MRTM

| Use Cases | Amount of Answers | | | |
|---|---|---|---|---|
| | Scenario 1 | | Scenario 2 | |
| | SUP | MRTM | SUP | MRTM |
| Daily planning | 14 | | 17 | |
| Handling SUP/ATCO request | 19 | 24 | 23 | 25 |
| Scheduled airport closing | 15 | 25 | 17 | 26 |
| Scheduled airport opening | 39 | 27 | 40 | 27 |
| Scheduled Workload increase | 38 | 26 | 30 | 27 |

(continued)

**Table 3.** (*continued*)

| Use Cases | Amount of Answers | | | |
|---|---|---|---|---|
| | Scenario 1 | | Scenario 2 | |
| | SUP | MRTM | SUP | MRTM |
| Unplanned airport closing | 17 | 21 | 19 | 25 |
| Unplanned airport opening | 14 | | 16 | |
| Unplanned runway closing | 13 | | 13 | |
| Unscheduled ATCO replacement | 13 | 21 | 13 | 22 |

**Handling Use Cases for Each Workplace.** The next analysis focused on the distribution of workload per use case and scenario. Figure 4 presents the answers to the adapted cooper-harper scale per use case and scenario for the SUP. From an overall of 370 answers, the results show that only 1 use case was classified as safely controllable and 328 use cases were classified with 3 or less. Even though scenario 2 had an increased number of use cases in total, no difference was found in the adapted cooper-harper scale for the single use cases.

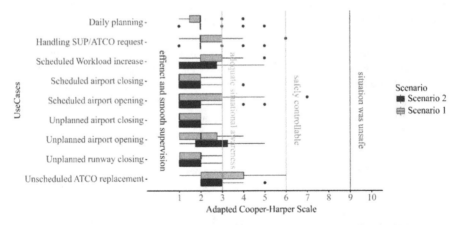

**Fig. 4.** Answer from the adapted cooper-harper scale per use case for the SUP

Figure 5 presents the answers to the adapted cooper-harper scale per use case and scenario for the ATCO workplace. From a total of 360 possible answers only 296 use case answers were given. The results show that 32 use case were classified as safely controllable and 233 use cases were classified with 3 or less on the adapted cooper-harper scale. As with the SUP, there is no influence or tendency of the factor scenario.

**Interaction of Use Cases.** The final analysis shows the direct comparison in handling the workplace. For this analysis the data for each scenario was combined, because the

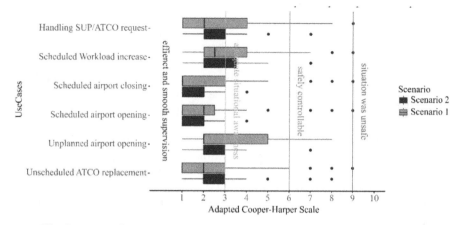

**Fig. 5.** Answer from the adapted cooper-harper scale per use case for the MRTM

previous analysis showed no influence. Also, the analysis only takes the use cases into account that were experienced at both workplaces. Figure 6 shows the adapted cooper-harper scale results for both workplaces and their interactive use cases. The results show that the average adapted cooper-harper scale was higher for each use case at the MRTM. The use case with the biggest difference is "Scheduled Workload increase".

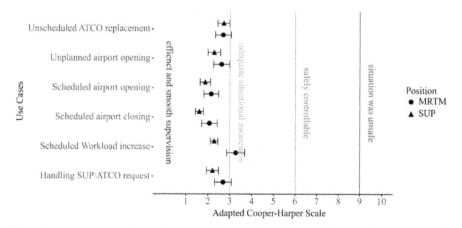

**Fig. 6.** Average answer with standard error from the adapted cooper-harper scale per use case for both workplaces.

## 6  Summary for the MRTO Concept

The following chapter summarizes the results individually for each RQ. The sample size of 15 ATCOs is relatively high for an expert sample size in aeronautical research domain, however, still low for inference statistics. The experimental set-up and the approach to compare two different working positions in one environment with unequal number of workplaces (one SUP and two MRTM) could only be covered with an explorative approach that provides a realistic environment to quantify the procedures with use cases. Because the requirements for inferential statistical analysis have not been met, the results are restricted to descriptive analysis. In the context of the development of a new working position and with a focus on RQs, a discussion about the results is essential.

**Operational Feasibility of the SUP.** As we expected from RQ1, the results for operation feasibility of the SUP shows general approval about the workplace itself. The idea of the workplace is derived from the tower supervisor, which is good for understanding the necessity and the benefits of such a workplace. An influential factor is the SUP tool and its quality to support the task. The SUP tool should provide needed information at the best time. The results suggest that the SUP tool was not as supportive as expected. Another challenge for the SUP is that the procedures were not defined clearly enough. Due to the explorative character of the study the participants were encouraged to explore different approaches for the split & merge procedures. This might have led to a reevaluation process during the split & merge situation and therefore to the results of the questionnaire.

**Handling Different Workplaces.** RQ 2 investigated how the handling of the different workplaces is perceived during normal operations. Normal operations were implemented as use cases that both workplaces had to complete at the same time. The analysis showed that the planning of the scenarios was successful and that all use cases were handled during the runs. The use cases could be implemented and performed as often as planned and, for some use cases, even more often. This increases the amount of data collected and thereby the quality of the study.

Even though scenario 2 had 4 additional use cases to scenario 1, the workload increase had no influence on the average adapted cooper-harper scale results. This leads to the assumption that either workload does not directly influence the perceived handling of a workplace or that the questioning after each use case, as it was for the SUP, minimized the effect of the general increased workload. Since there is no effect measured for the MRTM by applying the adapted cooper-harper scale after each run, based on this data, the first assumption would be the more plausible. This suggests that the adapted cooper-harper scale is independent from workload, which increases its explanatory power for the RQ2.

The ATCOs on each workplace subjectively identified problems with their own performance during the runs. The results for the interaction on use cases showed that the MRTM handling was more challenging. The results in general support the concept of the SUP workplace as a supporter for the MRTM. Even though the MRTM handling was rated as more intense, the rating on both workplaces expressed efficient and smooth supervision. Only for the use case "scheduled workload increase" the ATCOs on the MRTM stated that smooth and efficient supervision was not possible on average. The increased handling at the MRTM in relation to the SUP raises the idea to redefine the SUP even more as a supporter than a supervisor. Of course, the long-term planning is still only possible at the SUP workplace, but additional tasks could be found, e.g. supporting the split & merge process. Even so, the general handling of both workplaces seemed to be manageable.

## 7  Conclusion

In summary, this study aimed for the validation of a new workplace within the MRTO concept. Two RQs were postulated to evaluate the influence of the SUP to the RTC. The study analyzed the application and handling of use cases as reference for realistic task description during a multi workplace real time simulation. The results show that the selected use cases represent the task of the supervisor and can help to validate the workplace. RQ 1 is answered and the focus of the further development should be an improvement to the SUP tool and related new operational procedures. The results also show that a rethinking of the workplace is necessary and that the role of a an RTC SUP is more one of a strategical and tactical planner and dispatcher position than a the traditional Tower supervisor or back up ATCO as it is today. This is especially important for further development of the multiple remote center supervisor position.

**Acknowledgements.** The authors thank SESAR Joint Undertaking for funding this project as well as their project partners PANSA, Oro Navigacija and Frequentis for their collaboration. This project has received funding from the SESAR Joint Undertaking under the European Union's Horizon 2020 research and innovation programme under grant agreement No 874470.

## References

1. Weber, E.: Remote Tower Control Centre in Leipzig. https://www.smartinfrastructurehub.com//blog//flexa-0 (2021) 14 Nov 2021
2. Fisherl, C.D.: Boredom at work: a neglected concept. Human Relations **46**(3), 395–417 (1993)
3. Hagl, M., Friedrich, M., Jakobi, J., Schier-Morgenthal, S., Stockdale, C.: Impact of Simultaneous Movements on the Perception of Safety, Workload and Task Difficulty in a Multiple Remote Tower Environment, pp. 1–9
4. Möhlenbrink, C., Friedrich, M., Papenfuss, A.: RemoteCenter: Eine Mikrowelt zur Analyse der mentalen Repräsentation von zwei Flughäfen während einer Lotsentätigkeitsaufgabe [RemoteCenter: A microworld for analysing the mental representation of two airports during the air traffic control task.], pp. 65–72
5. Kontogiannis, T., Malakis, S.: Strategies in controlling, coordinating and adapting performance in air traffic control: modelling 'loss of control' events. Cogn. Technol. Work **15**(2), 153–169 (2013)
6. Young, M.S., Brookhuis, K.A., Wickens, C.D., Hancock, P.A.: State of science: mental workload in ergonomics. Ergonomics **58**(1), 1–17 (2015)
7. Friedrich, M., Timmermann, F., Jakobi, J.: Supervising Multiple Remote Tower Operations: How to develop and test a new workplace in the ATC Domain?, In: HCI International 2021, Washington DC, USA (2021)
8. EUROCONTROL/FAA: Human Performance in Air Traffic Management Safety: A White Paper, Action Plan 15 Safety (2010)

9. Teutsch, J., Postma-Kurlanc, A.: Enhanced Virtual Block Control for Milan Malpensa Airport in Low Visibility, pp. E1–1 – E1–13

10. Friedrich, M., Hamann, A., Jakobi, J.: An eye catcher in the ATC domain: Influence of Multiple Remote Tower Operations on distribution of eye movements

11. Mansikka, H., Virtanen, K., Harris, D.: Comparison of NASA-TLX scale, modified Cooper–Harper scale and mean inter-beat interval as measures of pilot mental workload during simulated flight tasks, Ergonomics, 1–9 (2018)

# Effects of Intensity of Short-Wavelength Light on the EEG and Performance of Astronauts During Target Tracking

Yang Gong[1], Ao Jiang[2(✉)], ZiJian Wu[1], Xinyun Fu[1], Xiang Yao[1], Caroline Hemingray[2], Stephen Westland[2], and WenKai Li[1]

[1] Xiangtan University, Xiangtan, Hunan, China
[2] School of Design, University of Leeds, Leeds, UK
aojohn928@gmail.com

**Abstract.** In complex human-machine systems such as spacecraft, poor astronaut performance leads to dangerous accidents, and assessing the functional state of astronauts during a mission has positive impacts on risk reduction and efficiency. This paper aimed to assess the functional state of astronauts in performing target tracking tasks of different difficulty at three different short-wavelength light intensities (40 lx, 80 lx, and 160 lx) in a simulated space station module with a head-mounted display (HMD) and electroencephalogram (EEG) equipment, and collect EEG and task performance changes as well, aiming to better understand the cognitive behavior of astronauts during spacecraft operations. Thirty healthy participants were recruited for this experiment and their EEG physiological signals were collected during simulated astronauts in conducting target tracking tasks. Meanwhile, all participants wore a head-mounted display (HMD) to perform target tracking tasks of low, medium, and high difficulty in three intensities (40 lx, 80 lx, and 160 lx) of short-wavelength light ($\lambda_{max} = 475$ nm), while remaining in the darkness ($<1$ lx). All the participants' EEG power in the beta range after exposure to 160 lx light was significantly higher than that to 40 lx and 80 lx light, or it kept in the darkness. In addition, alpha and theta power were significantly lower in 160 lx light than in darkness. This study provides some evidence that nighttime short-wavelength light exposure can improve the astronaut task performance in performing target tracking.

**Keywords:** Short-wavelength light · Target tracking · EEG · Task performance

## 1 Introduction

Most tasks performed by astronauts during manned space missions require high levels of brain activity. Moreover, cosmic radiation, microgravity, and light exposure have impacts on the astronaut's brain [1–4]. Therefore, it is particularly important to explore the factors that affect the brain load of astronauts [2]. The National Aeronautics and Space Administration (NASA) is focusing its space exploration on the Moon in the coming years, and other countries are also pursuing more interplanetary exploration programs [5]. As various human space exploration missions advance and humans spend more time in space, understanding the challenges faced by astronauts who live and work in the space environment and knowing how to address them are important for the development and planning of future human space missions [6].

Long-term adaptation to the space environment is critical to the health, safety and productivity of all astronauts [6, 7]. When astronauts go to the Moon, Mars and other planets to carry out complex and diverse space missions, they are susceptible to disturbances in the spaceflight environment, thus resulting in increased mental fatigue and impairing the human ability to process information, which has impacts on the efficiency of the mission [6, 8]. Similar to other human spaceflight activities, as an important spaceflight operation task, target tracking requires astronauts' rich experience and precise operation. Furthermore, due to the reduced concentration, slow thinking or sluggish movements of astronauts during operations, the target tracking task is performed less efficiently and may result in in-flight accidents [2].

Some researches on date have revealed that light is not limited to influencing human physiological parameters and circadian rhythms but also has impacts on neurobehavioural performance [1, 9, 10]. In Lin et al.'s study, all participants were irradiated with three intensities of short-wavelength light and darkness, all of which revealed significant changes in electroencephalogram (EEG) power at different frequencies [11]. Other studies have proved that higher illumination levels can speed up cognitive responses in humans and improve task performance [12]. What's more, Sunde et al.'s study exposed healthy participants to different wavelengths of light for the assessment of work performance, and it was found that participants' productivity was significantly improved by using short-wavelength light exposure compared with long-wavelength light [13]. However, as the effects of different wavelengths of illumination on humans when performing target tracking tasks were still not discovered at this stage, more researches are clearly needed to discover the effects of intensity of short-wavelength light on brain activity and task performance.

To better understand the effects of different intensities of short-wavelength light on astronaut EEG and task performance, this study used a head-mounted display (HMD) and EEG equipment to investigate the effects of different intensities of short-wavelength light on participants' EEG and task performance, while performing target tracking tasks of various difficulties in a simulated space station module. Thus, (Q1) does the exposure to short-wavelength light affect the EEG power and task performance? (Q2) Are there differences in the effects of different short-wavelength light intensities on EEG power and task performance?

## 2  Methods

### 2.1  Participants

Thirty healthy male participants were enrolled for this trial to participate in the study at the age of 18–28 years (M = 23.5, SD = 1.9). All participants were non-smokers without the history of cardiovascular or cerebrovascular disease or psychiatric disorders. During the experiment, all participants were required to be in good psychological condition and avoid smoking, alcohol, and caffeine intake. On the other hand, all participants had participated in a course on the use of head-mounted displays (HMD). The participants were briefed on the procedure and precautions before the experiment, and all participants signed an informed consent form. The experiment was approved by the local ethics review board.

## 2.2  Scene Building

Researchers used a joint Rhino and Unity platform to develop the interior scenes of the crew module of the International Space Station. The program was set up in C# and a 3D computer rendering program was used to simulate the space station module scene with various color surroundings. The panoramic view is shown in Fig. 1. Reference to the International Space Station environment, the ceiling, floor, walls are covered with a primary color, while cabinets, and the processors are decorated with secondary colors. This method has been used in previous studies [14]. All participants were required to wear an HMD for viewing, and the handle controller is represented as a virtual hand in the scene. The virtual hand can be used to perform tasks in the scene.

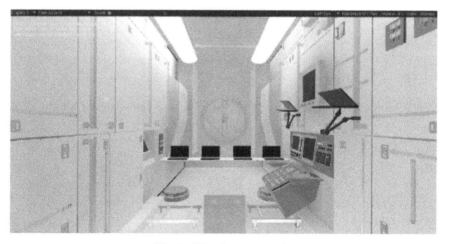

**Fig. 1.** Virtual space capsule

## 2.3  Lighting Conditions

This experiment adjusted the lighting parameters in the control interface in Unity, and the lighting system in this environment provided spectrally tunable illumination. All participants were asked to wear an HMD to experiment in the virtual environment.

Four light settings were used for the experiments, including a dim (CCT2000 K, <1 lx) and three short-wavelength lighting conditions. The short-wavelength condition had a peak at about 480 nm and was approximately Gaussian with a half-width half-height of 35 nm. Three intensities were 40 lx, 80 lx and 160 lux ($\pm$1 lx). The spectra of the three test lighting conditions were measured with an X-Rite i1Pro spectro-photometer

(Fig. 2). According to the new CIE S 026/E: 201818, the a-opic irradiance for each lighting was calculated (Table 1).

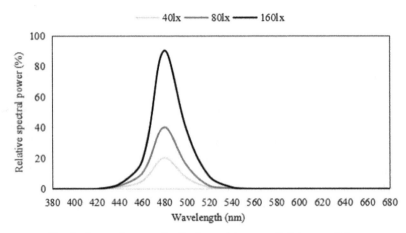

**Fig. 2.** Spectral power distributions of three test lighting conditions

**Table 1.** $\alpha$-Opic irradiance (mW/m$^2$) for three lighting conditions and 1 lx daylight (for reference).

| α-opic irradiance for | S-cone-opic | M-cone-opic | L-cone-opic | Rhodopic | Melanopic |
| --- | --- | --- | --- | --- | --- |
| 40 lx | 157.98 | 131.44 | 80.48 | 277.64 | 324.25 |
| 80 lx | 340.38 | 273.25 | 167.00 | 580.18 | 678.81 |
| 160 lx | 716.54 | 557.33 | 340.56 | 1187.21 | 1389.97 |
| 1 lx D65 | 0.82 | 1.46 | 1.63 | 1.45 | 1.33 |

## 2.4  Procedures

From November to December 2021, all participants were brought to the lab after 20:00 and each participant completed four sessions over four nights. At the same time, all participants were fitted with EEG electrodes before starting the experiment. The order of the conditions (Dim, Blue 40 lx, 80 lx, and 160 lx) was selected randomly for each participant to avoid potential sequence effects. To avoid potential carry-over effects, the interval between light experiments of different intensities was at least 72 h, and each light intensity environment was equipped with low, medium, and high difficulty target tracking tasks.

In the target tracking mission, the tracking target appeared randomly at any location in the space station and moved randomly in any way. The higher the difficulty was, the faster the tracking target moved. The tracking target was a white ball of 65 pixels ×

20 pixels and the tracker was a rectangular target of the same shape of 130 pixels × 40 pixels (Fig. 3). The participant controlled the joystick so that the on-screen tracker covered the tracking target until the tracking target was in the center of the tracker and the tracking target stops moving (Fig. 4).

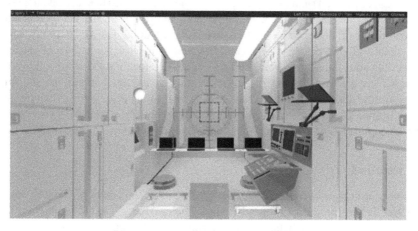

**Fig. 3.** Rectangular target and white ball

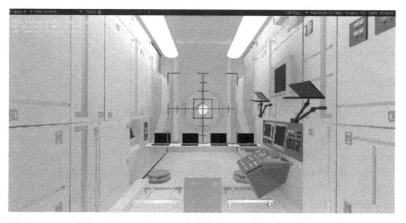

**Fig. 4.** One target tracking test completed

After the experiment started, the first 5 min were used to collect the resting-state signal of the participants, in which the participants were recommended to sit still and minimize their mental activity. To avoid potential sequence effects, the difficulty of the target tracking task was randomly selected, and all participants were required to perform 35 tests at each difficulty. The program automatically recorded the time for each test and took the last 20 test times for calculation, and the average tracking time was used to measure the participants' performance.

## 2.5  Signal Acquisition

EEG data were collected using Brain Vision Analyzer 2.2 Live Software with wireless advanced brain monitoring (ABM) EEG device (X10 headset with standard sensor strips). The recordings consisted of EEG with nine electrode positions (Fz, Cz, Poz, F3, F4, C3, C4, P3, and P4) and two reference mastoid electrodes. The electrode impedance test was conducted each time before the experiment to ensure the good conductivity between the scalp and electrodes, thus obtaining the good quality of the signal. The EEG signal was band-passed to 1–40 Hz and decontaminated using ABM's validated artifact identification and decontamination algorithms that identify and remove five artifact types, namely electromyogram, electrooculogram, excursions, saturations, and spikes. Power spectral density (PSD) was computed by performing Fast Fourier Transform with the application of a Kaiser window, and the PSD of selected 1-Hz bins was averaged after the application of a 50% over-lapping window across three one-second overlays.

## 2.6  Statistical

All statistical analyses were performed using SPSS 25.0, and one-way ANOVA was used to explore differences in EEG power between short-wavelength light and the three brainwave frequencies of alpha, beta, and theta during target tracking missions, and determine statistical significance. The Alpha values of 0.05 were considered to be significant. After testing the static distributivity of the data, HSD post hoc tests of statistical significance ($p < 0.05$) on these data was performed.

# 3  Results

## 3.1  Electroencephalogram (EEG)

A one-way ANOVA on the EEG power data was performed under different intensities of short-wavelength light and the data displayed significant differences in EEG power between the three different intensities of short-wavelength light (40 lx, 80 lx, 160 lx) and the dim condition under alpha, beta, and theta waves ($F(1, 1836) = 6.24$, $p = 0.002$, $\eta^2 = 0.007$). The analysis illustrated that EEG power was more significant ($p < 0.05$) under light conditions, with more significant ($p < 0.05$) EEG power under short-wavelength light conditions at 160 lx than at 80 lx and 40 lx, and more significant ($p < 0.05$) EEG efficiency under 80 lx than under 40 lx. Post hoc tests showing that the higher the intensity is, the more significant the EEG power is generated by performing target tracking ($p < 0.05$) (Fig. 5).

## 3.2  Defferent Frequencies

A one-way ANOVA indicated that the three short-wavelength light intensities at different frequencies differed significantly ($p < 0.05$) from the EEG power in the dim condition. There were significant differences between the short-wavelength light intensities of 160 lx, 80 lx, and 40 lx and the dim condition at the alpha wave ($F(1, 1044) = 54.42$, $p = 0.000$, $\eta^2 = 0.141$). At the beta wave, there were significant differences between the

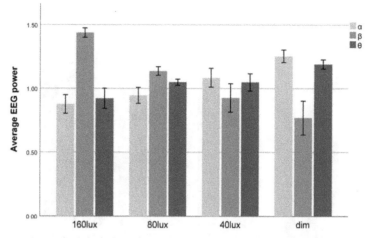

**Fig. 5.** Mean ± standard deviation of mean normalized EEG power for four light intensities at different frequencies of brain waves

short-wavelength light intensities of 160 lx and 80 lx, and 40 lx and the dim condition ($F(1, 1044) = 54.244$, $p = 0.000$, $\eta^2 = 0.116$); at theta waves, short-wavelength light with the intensities of 160 lx, 80 lx, and 40 lx were significantly different from the dim condition ($F(1, 1044) = 130.85$, $p = 0.000$, $\eta^2 = 0.261$). According to post hoc tests, EEG power was more significant in the light condition than that in the dim condition ($p < 0.05$). Under alpha and theta waves, low-intensity light was more significant ($p < 0.05$) than high-intensity light, and EEG power was higher under dim conditions than that under 40 lx, 80 lx, and 160 lx conditions. In beta waves, high-intensity light was more significant than low-intensity light ($p < 0.05$), and EEG power was obviously higher in light conditions than in dim conditions ($p < 0.05$).

### 3.3  Various Difficulties

Analysis of the data for subjective performance displayed significant differences in task performance between the three short-wavelength light intensities and the dim conditions ($F(1, 1836) = 4.133$, $p = 0.016$, $\eta^2 = 0.006$). The data indicated that the task performance under 160 lx light was more significant ($p < 0.05$) than that under 80 lx and 40 lx light, and 80 lx was more significant ($p < 0.05$) than 40 lx light ($p < 0.05$) for task performance. The results indicated that high-intensity light improved task efficiency more significantly ($p < 0.05$) compared with low-intensity light. There were significant differences in performance for different difficulty tasks in the three short-wavelength light conditions ($F(1, 1836) = 3.053$, $p = 0.048$, $\eta^2 = 0.004$), with more significant performance for tasks of lower difficulty ($p < 0.05$). The post-hoc tests showed that EEG power was significantly higher in the light condition than that in the dim condition for the three different difficulty tasks ($p = 0.02 < 0.05$). The task performance was significantly higher under 160 lx light than that under 80 lx and 40 lx ($p = 0.026 < 0.05$), and the task performance was significantly higher under 80 lx light than under 40 lx light (Fig. 6).

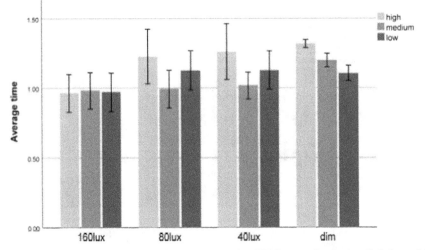

**Fig. 6.** Mean ± standard deviation of the mean normalized EEG power for the four light intensities at different levels of difficulties

## 4  Discussion

The results of this study proved that high-intensity short-wavelength light is a more effective stimulus than low-intensity short-wavelength light and that it can make the brains of astronauts on missions more active. In contrast to previous studies that short-wavelength light could not significantly alter EEG activity in theta waves [15], the present experiment remarkably increased the EEG power in the alpha and theta bands in all the three short-wavelength light conditions compared with dim light conditions, where the lower the intensity of the short-wavelength light was, the higher the EEG power was. Given that a new study suggested that individual differences at different time periods have effects on EEG activity following short-wave blue light exposure [16]. Thus, our choice of experimental time may also have inadvertently interfered with the power of the alpha and theta EEG bands, and these differences could explain our differences from previous findings. In the β-band, all the three short-wavelength light conditions remarkably increased the EEG power compared with the dim light conditions. Different from under the alpha and theta waves, the higher intensity short-wavelength light in the beta band was more effective in increasing the EEG power, which could provide findings that are consistent with the effects of short-wavelength light on EEG in the beta wave range in the study conducted by Lin et al. [11].

While most previous studies focused on the effects of different short-wavelength light intensities on EEG and circadian rhythms [10, 16], this paper centered on exploring the effects of different intensities of short-wavelength light exposure on task performance. The results for the subjective performance were as expected, with efficiency in performing different and difficult target tracking tasks correlated with light intensity. Participants could effectively reduce target tracking task time and improve task performance on the three difficult target tracking tasks with high intensity short-wavelength light (160 lx) compared with dim light conditions and lower intensity short-wavelength light. The lower intensity short-wavelength light (40 lx, 80 lx) can improve performance on the medium and high difficulty target tracking tasks compared with the dim light, while it was not effective in improving performance on the low difficulty target tracking task, which was significantly different from the high intensity short-wavelength light (160 lx). Therefore, high-intensity short-wavelength light is a more correct choice than low-intensity short-wavelength light in improving target tracking task performance. It was also found that high-intensity light could improve task performance in Smolders' study, and use the light intensities of 200 lx and 1000 lx for comparison [12].

A limitation of this study is that the experimental environment is somewhat different from the actual situation, but even small differences may significantly affect EEG and task performance. This study was conducted on the ground, whereas the microgravity environment in which the astronauts were exposed during the actual space task in the real space environment could impair the astronauts' tracking task performance [17]. It has been proved that the subjective perception and visual comfort of the operator is also a potential factor affecting task performance [18–21]. Therefore, task performance may not be optimized under the influence of the stressors of long-term space, even with the use of high-intensity short-wavelength light exposure. Furthermore, the space light environment was created by the combination of natural light and lighting systems, so if the equipment capable of simulating the effects of natural light was incorporated and the subjective measurements of current short-wavelength light conditions were made, the experimental measurements could be more closely aligned to accurate values [18].

The function of current space lighting equipment was limited to supporting astronaut vision, and it is critical to provide an illuminated environment that can work efficiently and awaken the EEG [1, 22, 23] Therefore, the data from this study can still be used as a potential countermeasure to improve the space lighting system, which could offer effective support for further in-depth studies on astronaut EEG assessment during missions and future long-term space exploration. From other perspectives, the improvements in space lighting systems could also be applied on Earth, which could provide a valuable reference for the design of optimized home environments and workplaces.

## 5  Conclusion

The analysis on the results of this study led to the following conclusions: Short-wavelength light exposure significantly enhanced EEG activity and can improve task performance. Higher intensity short-wavelength light has better effects than lower intensity short-wavelength light. Future researches on the effects of short-wavelength light intensity on astronauts may be extended to explore the changes in EEG and mission performance of astronauts during missions due to short-wavelength light exposure. Most importantly, future extensions are necessary to validate the conclusions drawn from this study and provide the right direction for optimizing astronaut performance during human spaceflight missions.

**Acknowledgements.** We thank the team of IMA, HI-SEAs, Blue Planet Energy Lab, ILEWG at ESA for support in the preparation of the experiment. This work is supported by a research project of a research project of the National Social Science Fund of China (No. 20BG115), a scholarship from the China Scholarship Council and the University of Leeds (No. 201908430166).

# References

1. Fucci, R.L., et al.: Optimizing lighting as a countermeasure to sleep and circadian disruption in space flight. Acta Astronaut. **56**(9–12), 1017–1024 (2005)
2. Li, Y., Zhou, Q., Zu, X.: The assessment and analysis of astronaut mental fatigue in long-duration spaceflight. 39th COSPAR Scientific Assembly **39**, 1074 (2012)
3. Roberts, D.R., et al.: Prolonged microgravity affects the structure and function of human brain. Am. J. Neuroradiol. **40**(11), 1878–1885 (2019)
4. Davis, C.M., Allen, A.R., Bowles, D.E.: Consequences of space radiation on the brain and cardiovascular system. J. Environ. Sci. Health C **39**(2), 180–218 (2021)
5. Roberts, D.R., Stahn, A.C., Seidler, R.D., Wuyts, F.L.: Understanding the effects of spaceflight on the brain. The Lancet Neuro. **19**(10), 808 (2020)
6. Mhatre, S.D., et al.: Neuro-consequences of the spaceflight environment. Neuroscience & Biobehavioral Reviews (2021)
7. Jiang, A., Yao, X., Schlacht, I.L., Musso, G., Tang, T., Westland, S.: Habitability study on space station colour design. In: International Conference on Applied Human Factors and Ergonomics, pp. 507–514. Springer, Cham (July 2020)
8. Manzey, D., Lorenz, B., Schiewe, A., Finell, G., Thiele, G.: Dual-task performance in space: The results from a single-case study during a short-term space mission. Hum. Factors **37**(4), 667–681 (1995)
9. Ruger, M., Gordijn, M.C., Beersma, D.G., de Vries, B., Daan, S.: Time-of-day-dependent effects of bright light exposure on human psychophysiology: Comparison of daytime and nighttime exposure. American J. Physio.-Regul. Integra. Compara. Physio. **290**(5), R1413–R1420 (2006)
10. Warman, V.L., Dijk, D.J., Warman, G.R., Arendt, J., Skene, D.J.: Phase advancing human circadian rhythms with short wavelength light. Neurosci. Lett. **342**(1–2), 37–40 (2003)
11. Lin, J., Westland, S., Cheung, V.: Effects of intensity of short-wavelength light on electroencephalogram and subjective alertness. Light. Res. Technol. **52**(3), 413–422 (2020)
12. Smolders, K.C., De Kort, Y.A., Cluitmans, P.J.M.: A higher illuminance induces alertness during office hours: Findings on subjective measures, task performance and heart rate measures. Physiol. Behav. **107**(1), 7–16 (2012)
13. Sunde, E., et al.: Alerting and circadian effects of short-wavelength vs. long-wavelength narrow-bandwidth light during a simulated night shift. Clocks & sleep **2**(4), 502–522 (2020)
14. Jiang, A., Yao, X., Hemingray, C., Westland, S.: Young people's colour preference and the arousal level of small apartments. Color Research & Application (2021)
15. Okamoto, Y., Rea, M.S., Figueiro, M.G.: Temporal dynamics of EEG activity during short-and long-wavelength light exposures in the early morning. BMC. Res. Notes **7**(1), 1–6 (2014)
16. Siemiginowska, P., Iskra-Golec, I.: Blue light effects on EEG activity: The role of exposure timing and chronotype. Light. Res. Technol. **52**(4), 472–484 (2020)
17. Yang, J.J., Shen, Z.: Effects of microgravity on human cognitive function in space flight. Hang Tian yi xue yu yi xue Gong Cheng= Space Medicine & Medical Engineering **16**(6), 463–467 (2003)
18. Lu, M., Hu, S., Mao, Z., Liang, P., Xin, S., Guan, H.: Researches on work efficiency and light comfort based on the EEG evaluation method. Build. Environ. **183**, 107122 (2020)

19. Jiang, A., Foing, B.H., Schlacht, I.L., Yao, X., Cheung, V., Rhodes, P.A.: Colour schemes to reduce stress response in the hygiene area of a space station: a Delphi study. Appl. Ergon. **98**, 103573 (2022)
20. Yu, K., Jiang, A., Wang, J., Zeng, X., Yao, X., Chen, Y.: Construction of crew visual behaviour mechanism in ship centralized control cabin. In: International Conference on Applied Human Factors and Ergonomics, pp. 503–510. Springer, Cham (July 2021)
21. Yu, K., Jiang, A., Zeng, X., Wang, J., Yao, X., Chen, Y.: Colour design method of ship centralized control cabin. In: International Conference on Applied Human Factors and Ergonomics, pp. 495–502. Springer, Cham (July 2021)
22. Lu, S., et al.: Effects and challenges of operational lighting illuminance in spacecraft on human visual acuity. In: International Conference on Applied Human Factors and Ergonomics, pp. 582–588. Springer, Cham (July 2021)
23. Lu, S., et al.: The effect on subjective alertness and fatigue of three colour temperatures in the spacecraft crew cabin. In: International Conference on Applied Human Factors and Ergonomics, pp. 632–639. Springer, Cham (July 2021)

# The Effect of Pilots' Expertise on Eye Movement and Scan Patterns During Simulated Flight Tasks

Yue Hua, Shan Fu, and Yanyu Lu[✉]

School of Electronic Information and Electrical Engineering, Shanghai Jiao Tong University,
No. 800 Dongchuan Road, Minhang District, Shanghai, China
luyanyu@sjtu.edu.cn

**Abstract.** In aviation safety nowadays, pilot errors are responsible for most accidents, instead of the failure of aircrafts. Human factors aims at reducing pilot-related errors and improving safety. Eye movement has been proven to be a useful tool when studying human factors in human-computer interaction (HCI). This paper takes an insight into the effect of pilots' expertise on eye movement during different flight phases and then analyze the pilots' scan patterns according to various situations. Three eye metrics are studied in detail: fixation duration, saccade frequency and entropy. The statistical analysis result of the metrics shows that pilots' expertise has significant effect on all the three metrics in specific task phases and the scan patterns of pilots in the "expert" group are more systematic and efficient compared to the "medium" and "novice" group. These findings help identify various types of scan patterns during flight phases and provides better comprehensive of efficient pilots' scan patterns.

**Keywords:** Eye movement · Human factors · Entropy · Saccade frequency · Fixation duration

## 1 Introduction

As people have already benefitted a lot from automated systems, the role of human factors in aviation is more and more emphasized. In aviation accidents, human errors account for the majority causes instead of the technical factors like the system failure. Especially, almost all critical incidents are aroused by pilot-related errors. Human factors utilizes the theory of human psychology and physiology and focuses on improving the system, intended to reduce human errors, increase efficiency and ensure safety and comfort.

A number of efforts have been made to modify the design and automated systems of the airplanes and optimize pilot training based on human factors. The main methods comprise three kinds: subjective assessment like NASA Task Load Index, performance evaluation and physiological measurement including EEG, eye movement, heart rate, breath and so on. Compared to subjective assessment and performance evaluation, physiological measurement is more objective and accurate. In physiological signals, eye movement data is easy to collect and obtained. What's more, eye-tracking is an essential technique in human-computer interaction area and the eye-tracking technology is invasiveness.

Eye movement has been taken into consideration in diverse fields concerning human-computer interaction for the last few decades. For example, in medical science, eye movement helps understand the behavior of patients with different diseases, contributing to the comprehensive of pathogenesis. In computer science, eye movement could evaluate the interaction of human and computer [1]. In-depth study is also conducted on the drivers' visual attention [2], which offers great referential to the researches on the eye movement of pilots.

Researches regarding with pilot eye movement have been carried out in many directions. For example, the effect of different variables on eye movement is studied to find out whether eye movement can be a reliable measurement. The variables include working experience of pilots [1], the cockpit design [3], the flight complexity [4] and so on. In addition, the scan patterns, which are able to describe pilots' search strategies and attention allocation, have attracted great attention in recent years. The pilots' scan patterns are quite complicated to analyze during flight but can indicate pilot performance, cognitive workload and the efficiency of automatic systems. Researches also suggested that there is significant difference in pilots' scan patterns during different flight phases and eye movement is a valid tool to capture pilots' situation awareness [5]. Eye movement can also be an indicator to predict pilots' cognitive workload [6] and can be applied to the classification models to identify high cognitive load.

Although there are quite a few analytic techniques of scan patterns on the basis of eye movement, the study of pilots' scan patterns should be distinguished from that in other fields because of the particularity of the aviation domain. It is ambiguous sometimes which eye metrics be utilized and the application of the eye metrics need to be standardized [7].

This study aims to discover the inferred information about pilots' scan patterns from eye metrics. Certified pilots executed flying tasks containing diverse kinds of failure and their eye movement is collected. Depending on the eye data, pilots' scan patterns are analyzed considering pilots' expertise and different flight phases.

## 2 Methodology

### 2.1 Participants

Nineteen male pilots with professional license aged 30–50 years participated in the study. They formed 11 crews and each crew included a pilot flying (pf) and a pilot monitoring (pm). All the participants are healthy and were able to complete the flying tasks. They all knew the design of the study and agreed to wear physiological measurement equipment.

The participants are separated into three groups according to their flying experience regarding with the airbus A320. Among them, five are familiar with A320 and classified as the "expert" group. Four haven't flown A320 before, group as "novice". The left have flown A320 before but are not experienced enough and they are categorized as "medium". In this study, considering only pilots monitoring, three crews belong to the "expert" group and three belong to the "novice". The remaining five crews are classified as the "medium" group.

## 2.2  Procedure

The simulator simulated five failure scenarios: aborted takeoff, engine fire warning, horizontal stabilizer jam, smoke on board and emergency electrical configuration. In each scenario, participants performed approach and landing tasks and dealt with failure at the same time.

There were pre-experiments for each crew. When tasks began, the simulator put the airplane at the initial position and speed and set the initial altitude. Then, pilots started to execute an approach task. When the failure occurred, there would be alarm sounds and a warning light. After handling the failure, pilots continued to approaching and landing until the landing is completed.

## 2.3  Apparatus

A full flight A320 simulator is applied to the study, which passed the D-level certification of the Civil Aviation Administration of China (CAAC) (see Fig. 1). The simulator system data is collected, consisting of the altitude, aircraft parameters, airplane situations, runway conditions of each airport, and so on.

**Fig. 1.**  Flight simulator cockpit environment

Participants all wear Tobii Pro Glasses 3, a wearable eye-tracker. It is easy and comfortable to wear and is made up of an eyeglasses with two units: one for eye tracking and one for recording the video. This instrument can provide a series of accurate gaze data sampled at 100 Hz.

### 2.4 Eye Metrics

The following eye metrics are analyzed in our study: fixation duration, saccade frequency and entropy.

Fixations and saccades are two basic metrics in the analysis of eye movement [7]. Fixations are defined as stationary eye movement located in one area within a period of time while saccades refer to quick eye movement between two fixations. The eye-tracker in this study applies the Velocity-Threshold Identification (I-VT) fixation classification algorithm to identify fixations and saccades and the velocity threshold is set to 30° per second. In other word, when the gaze velocity is more than 30° per second, the eye movement is regarded as a saccade. Otherwise, the eye movement is considered as a fixation.

Entropy is a concept borrowed from the information theory. Applied to study the eye behavior, entropy represents the randomness of one's gaze pattern. Given a sequence $x$ with $n$ states, the entropy of $x$ is calculated as follows [8]:

$$H(x) = -\sum_{i=1}^{n} p_i \sum_{j=1}^{n} p(i,j) \log_2 p(i,j) \qquad (1)$$

Here $p_i$ is the proportion of the sequence $x$ in state $i$ and $p(i,j)$ represents the probability of the transition from state $i$ to state $j$. The minimum value of the entropy is zero. In this case, the eye movement only locates in one area and the scan pattern is totally predictable and systematic. The larger the value is, the scan pattern is more complex and harder to predict. When the proportion of each transition from state $i$ to state $j$ is equal under the condition where the transitions are unobserved, the value is the largest, or $H_{max} = \log_2(n-1)$.

In order to calculate the entropy, the cockpit display is divided into seven areas of interest (AoI, see Fig. 2): primary flight display (PFD), mode control panel (MCP), electronic centralized aircraft monitoring (ECAM), control display unit (CDU), flight control panel (FCP), standby (STANDBY) and the area out of the windows (OTW). All the areas that pilots mainly paid attention to during the tasks are included in the above seven AoIs. Thus, the number of states is eight (the area other than the above seven AoIs is also regarded as a state).

## 3  Results

Kruskal–Wallis H test [9], a non-parametric test method, is applied to study the effect of pilots' expertise on the three eye metrics: entropy, fixation duration and saccade frequency.

**Fig. 2.** Division of AoIs. Each color block represents a certain area of interest. The corresponding label on the color block suggests the name and function of the area. The remaining area that is not marked is seen as a whole.

### 3.1 Fixation Duration

It can be seen from Table 1 that there is significant difference among the three groups at both task phases ($p = 0.006$ before alerting, $p = 0.007$ after alerting). This implies that the fixation duration differs greatly among pilots with different familiarity and experience. The fixation duration of the "expert" group is the longest ($M = 573.12$ before alerting, $M = 657.84$ after alerting) while that of the "medium" group is the shortest ($M = 573.12$ before alerting, $M = 657.84$ after alerting). Additionally, the standard deviation of the fixation duration of the "expert" group is the smallest ($SD = 130.34$ before alerting, $SD = 183.73$ after alerting). The above results illustrate that compared to the other two groups, pilots in the "expert" group spent more time during each fixation and their gaze patterns are more consistent within the group.

Comparing the two phases, the fixation duration of the three groups all increases after alerting. It proves that pilots demanded more time to encode information when the task were complex.

### 3.2 Saccade Frequency

It can be observed from Table 2 that there is significant difference on the saccade frequency among the three groups before alerting ($p = 0.021$) but no significant difference after alerting ($p = 0.458$). This could indicate that when pilots deal with simple tasks, the

**Table 1.** The effect of pilots' expertise on the mean fixation duration in different task phases.

| Task phases | Expertise | $M$(ms) | $SD$(ms) | $p$ |
|---|---|---|---|---|
| Before alerting | Expert | 573.12 | 130.34 | **.006** |
| | Medium | 397.28 | 208.34 | |
| | Novice | 495.77 | 137.52 | |
| After alerting | Expert | 657.84 | 183.73 | **.007** |
| | Medium | 432.90 | 190.84 | |
| | Novice | 541.23 | 226.75 | |

M: mean; SD: standard deviation; p: probability. $p \leq .05$ means that there is significant difference between variables. The bold values indicate significant difference.

saccade frequency can make a clearer distinction among various scan patterns. Before alerting, the saccade frequency of pilots in the "expert" group is the smallest ($M = 65.73$) and that of the "novice" group is the largest ($M = 73.48$). The standard deviation of the saccade frequency of the "expert" group is the smallest compared to the other two groups ($SD = 6.24$). After alerting, no matter the mean or the standard deviation of the three groups is both similar. As a result, the saccade frequency can evaluate pilots' scan patterns only when the tasks are simple and the effect will fail once the flight tasks are complicated.

Furthermore, there is an increase in the saccade frequency after alerting among all the three groups and the "expert" group has the largest increase ($M = 65.73$ before alerting, $M = 74.27$ after alerting). It shows that the saccade frequency is proportional to the complexity of flight phases, which means more searches are in demand to deal with urgent situations.

**Table 2.** The effect of pilots' expertise on the mean saccade frequency in different task phases.

| Task phases | Expertise | $M$(min$^{-1}$) | $SD$(min$^{-1}$) | $p$ |
|---|---|---|---|---|
| Before alerting | Expert | 65.73 | 6.24 | **.021** |
| | Medium | 68.15 | 9.24 | |
| | Novice | 73.48 | 7.10 | |
| After alerting | Expert | 74.27 | 8.20 | .458 |
| | Medium | 71.12 | 7.73 | |
| | Novice | 74.41 | 8.81 | |

M: mean; SD: standard deviation; p: probability. $p \leq .05$ means that there is significant difference between variables. The bold values indicate significant difference.

## 3.3 Entropy

As is shown in Table 3, there is no significant difference among the three groups before alerting ($p = 0.304$). However, there is significant difference among the three groups after alerting ($p = 0.009$), proving that the entropy could reflect the scan patterns better during complicated flight phases.

The entropy of the "expert" group is the highest ($M = 0.156$) and the entropy of the "novice" group is the lowest ($M = 0.120$) before alerting while the entropy of the "expert" group is the lowest ($M = 0.074$) and the entropy of the "novice" group is the highest ($M = 0.141$) after alerting. It suggests that the scan patterns of pilots in the "novice" group are more systematic before alerting whereas pilots in the "expert" group tend to scan more systematically after alerting.

As for the "expert" group, the entropy is quite low after alerting but high before alerting. Meanwhile, the standard deviation of the entropy of the "expert" group is the smallest after alerting ($SD = 0.042$). It can be shown that the scan patterns of the expert is much more systematic after alerting and there was a quick transition of pilots' scan patterns when the alerting occurred. The "medium" group has the same trend as the "expert" group ($M = 0.146$ before alerting, $M = 0.123$ after alerting) whereas the "novice" group has the opposite trend.

**Table 3.** The effect of pilots' expertise on the entropy in different task phases.

| Task phases | Expertise | M | SD | p |
|---|---|---|---|---|
| Before alerting | Expert | 0.156 | 0.060 | .304 |
| | Medium | 0.146 | 0.066 | |
| | Novice | 0.120 | 0.053 | |
| After alerting | Expert | 0.074 | 0.042 | **.009** |
| | Medium | 0.123 | 0.054 | |
| | Novice | 0.141 | 0.065 | |

M: mean; SD: standard deviation; p: probability. $p \leq .05$ means that there is significant difference between variables. The bold values indicate significant difference.

## 4   Discussion

The above results demonstrate that fixation duration, saccade frequency and entropy all can indicate the difference of scan patterns of pilots with various expertise. However, it only works in certain flight phases, or different metrics are meaningful only in certain situations.

### 4.1   The Effect of Pilots' Expertise on Eye Metrics

The results of the fixation duration of different groups during the two phases are consistent. It reveals significant difference on the fixation duration among the three groups and the fixation duration of the "expert" group is the longest. This is contrary to the previous researches, which show that longer fixation duration represents that longer time is demanded to deal with the information [7]. One explanation could be that the information presented by the cockpit display is understandable and even those who are unfamiliar with it could get started quickly. Pilots in the "expert" group are more familiar with the cockpit display and the problem-solving procedure. Thus, their scan patterns have high efficiency. Conversely, pilots in the "medium" and "novice" group have to seek for the location where the information needed is. The time for this process is much shorter than the process of dealing with the information. In other words, pilots in the "expert" group fixate in the intention of processing information instead of checking information.

Saccade frequency is another eye metric that can show the efficiency of pilots' scan patterns as saccades illustrate the process of searching [7]. The result suggests that significant difference can be observed on the saccade frequency among the three groups before alerting but no significant difference can be observed after alerting. In addition, all the pilots in the three groups scanned more frequently after alerting. During complex tasks, more searches are demanded and the percentage of invalid searches increases largely leading to the decrease in search efficiency. No matter how experienced the pilot is, it is inevitable to make more efforts to seek for useful information under complex circumstances. As a result, the search efficiency differs significantly during the simple flight phases and the saccade frequency is hard to predict in complex tasks.

No significant difference on the entropy among the three groups is observed before alerting. It is probably because pilots' scan patterns are more casual due to the low workload during simple task phases (before alerting). However, there is significant difference on entropy among the three groups after alerting. Furthermore, before alerting, pilots in the "expert" group have the lowest entropy and pilots in the "novice" have the highest entropy while after alerting the result is the exact opposite. Previous work points out that the novice tend to have lower entropy than the expert because they could be more cautious during the task [10]. However, faced with the system failure or complex situations, pilots are more concentrated and careful no matter how experienced they are. Thereby, the former conclusion is only appropriate for the simple flight tasks. Comparing the entropy before and after alerting, the expert can transform their scan patterns quickly to adapt to various situations and guarantee the efficiency of information processing at the same time. In addition, the "novice" group, with decreased entropy after alerting, is the most special group as the entropy of the "expert" and "medium" group both increase. Since the novice are in high tension throughout the flight, there may be other factors that could slightly influence the entropy, such as the duration. To conclude, the entropy does make sense when studying the effect of the pilots' expertise.

## 4.2 Pilots' Scan Patterns

All the three metrics of the "expert" group have the smallest standard deviation along with the smallest entropy during the phases where the effect of pilots' expertise has significant difference on the metric. It suggests that experienced pilots' scan patterns are more systematic and consistent. Due to professional training and experience accumulation, their search and information-acquisition strategies are optimized and of great efficiency.

With longer fixation duration and lower saccade frequency, the pilots in the "expert" group can quickly find the target information and follow the optimized scan path.

Given the entropy of the "expert" group, pilots' scan patterns can be well described by entropy as pilots have to strictly follow the steps of the checklists when performing tasks [4]. Pilots retrieve relevant resources from memory, react quickly and make decisions fast. All of the behavior is closely related to the expertise. The changing trend of entropy of the "expert" group is relatively clear, so it is possible to apply the entropy to examine cognitive workload, evaluate pilots' performance, measure the training strategies and so on [11]. As an eye metric, the entropy has not yet been taken full advantage of. More attention should be paid to think about how the entropy reveals the implicit pilots' visual behavior and scan patterns.

The results obtained above are not exactly the same as the previous researches on eye movement for that the conclusion derived from the study of analysis of eye movement in other fields cannot be applied directly to the aviation domain. The pilot training is standardized and each operation during the flight is normalized. Thus, the pilots' scan patterns could be different from those in other fields of human-computer interaction. Furthermore, the failure pilots are faced with used to be urgent and severe. Under such circumstances, the pilots' scan patterns are stable and relatively easy to predict.

## 5 Conclusion

The objective of this study is to analyze pilots' scan patterns and explore how efficient scan strategies work by examining the effect of pilots' expertise and flight complexity on eye movement. Results show that there is a significant effect of pilots' expertise on eye movement metrics and eye movement could reveal pilots' scan patterns. According to the statistical analysis of the metrics, the fixation duration differs greatly among different groups, the saccade frequency differs before alerting and the entropy differs after alerting. Obviously, the complexity of the flight tasks is essential in the application of eye movement. Moreover, the expert and the novice show quite different scan patterns. The expert would search for information and make decision more efficiently. Due to the standardized process during flight, the scan patterns of pilots tend to be systematic. Thereby, the scan patterns of the experienced pilots are more worthy of studying. These findings can be further applied to the pilot training, the role of pilots during the flight, the interface design and the automation.

Future work is expected to concentrate on the visualization and quantification of scan patterns in order to better understand the visual strategies of the pilots. What's more, the entropy could be a basis for further study of human factors in human-computer interaction.

## References

1. Wang, Y., et al.: Effect of working experience on air traffic controller eye movement. Engineering 7, 488–494 (2021)
2. Wang, Y., et al.: Examining drivers' eye glance patterns during distracted driving: insights from scanning randomness and glance transition matrix. J. Saf. Res. 63, 149–155 (2017)

3. Dill, E.T., Young, S.D.: Analysis of eye-tracking data with regards to the complexity of flight deck information automation and management - inattentional blindness, system state awareness, and EFB usage (2015)
4. Diaz-Piedra, C., et al.: The effects of flight complexity on gaze entropy: an experimental study with fighter pilots. Appl. Ergon. **77**, 92–99 (2019)
5. Yu, C.S., et al.: Pilots' visual scan pattern and situation awareness in flight operations. Aviat. Space Environ. Med. **85**(7), 708–714 (2014)
6. Han, S.Y., Kim, J.W., Lee, S.W.: Recognition of pilot's cognitive states based on combination of physiological signals. In: 2019 7th International Winter Conference on Brain-Computer Interface (BCI) (2019)
7. Poole, A., Ball, L.J.: Eye tracking in human-computer interaction and usability research: current status and future (2005)
8. Ciuperca, G., Girardin, V.: On the estimation of the entropy rate of finite Markov chains (2005)
9. Kruskal, W.H., Wallis, W.W.: Use of ranks in one-criterion variance analysis. J. Am. Stat. Assoc. **47**(260), 583–621 (1952)
10. Harris, R.L., Glover, B.J.: Analytical techniques of pilot scanning behavior and their application. Measurement (1986)
11. Shiferaw, B.A., Downey, L.A., Westlake, J., et al.: Stationary gaze entropy predicts lane departure events in sleep-deprived drivers. Sci. Rep. **8**, 2220 (2018)

# The Effect of the COVID-19 Pandemic on Air Traffic Controllers' Performance: Addressing Skill Fade Concerns in Preparation for the Return to Normal Operations

Shane Kenny[(✉)] and Wen-Chin Li

Safety and Accident Investigation Centre, Cranfield University, Cranfield, UK
S.Kenny@cranfield.ac.uk

**Abstract.** This research aims to provide insight regarding the impact of the COVID-19 pandemic on ATCO (Air Traffic Control Officer) skill performance and to identify the effectiveness of methods for reducing skill fade, as perceived by controllers. A questionnaire was administered to fifty-six air traffic controllers from three airports within a European state and an independent sample t-test was then performed on the data output. 78% of controllers agreed to some degree that their skill levels may have reduced since the beginning of the COVID-19 pandemic. A significant difference was recorded in the response scores for controllers at a large airport and controllers at smaller airports for six pandemic-related attitude statements. Simulation sessions, checklists and face-to-face briefings recorded the highest scores among methods for addressing controller skill fade. ATCO responses suggest that controllers operating at large international airports perceive higher levels of skill decay and may be more susceptible to the effects of skill fade after prolonged exposure to low traffic levels. Skills associated with the implementation of declarative knowledge are most susceptible to decay, particularly if these skills are performed in isolation and without 'integration complexity'. Controller skill fade is a significant concern after the COVID-19 pandemic. As the aviation industry begins to recover, ANSPs must assess the influence of sustained low traffic levels on ATCO performance at a unit level and implement tools which most suitably addresses the effects of skill decay.

**Keywords:** Air traffic control · Skill fade · COVID-19

## 1 Introduction

### 1.1 Background

The COVID-19 pandemic had a lasting effect on aircraft traffic levels across the globe. In Europe, forecasts predict that it will not be until 2024 before traffic levels reach 95% of 2019 levels again [1], with this prediction being heavily dependent on the easing of travel restrictions and widespread adoption of COVID-19 vaccines. Airlines, airports, and air navigation service providers (ANSPs) have all experienced periods of sustained low

D. Harris and W.-C. Li (Eds.): HCII 2022, LNAI 13307, pp. 300–313, 2022.
https://doi.org/10.1007/978-3-031-06086-1_23

traffic levels during 2020 and 2021, leading to rising concerns that aviation professionals may succumb to the effects of skill fade [2]. This skill fade, or skill decay, is associated with "the loss or decay of trained or acquired skills (or knowledge) after periods of non-use" [3] and has been identified as a significant hazard for ATCOs as traffic levels return towards pre-pandemic levels. Thus, in anticipation of these increased traffic volumes, busier ATC sectors, and higher levels of workload for controllers, ANSPs are required to address any potential skill performance issues among ATCOs.

In collaboration with ANSPs, aviation safety organisations have published documents which aim to identify potential skill fade issues for ATCOs as the industry returns to 'normal operations' [4, 5]. The output of this research therefore considers the effect of the pandemic on ATCO skill performance, based on the feedback of controllers from three airports within a European state. One of these airports is a large international airport, which handled more than 30 million passengers a year before the onset of the pandemic, while the other two airports operate lower levels of traffic, with pre-pandemic traffic at both aerodromes ranging between 1.5–3 million yearly passengers. From April to December 2020, passenger numbers for the larger airport dropped to below 4 million, while less than 150,000 passengers flew through either of the other two airports during the same period. By exploring controllers' perceptions of skill fade at these units, this study aims to provide information to allow ANSPs to consider any potential skill-related issues arising from the COVID-19 pandemic.

## 1.2 Influence of Skill Fade on ATCO Skills

Before identifying which skills are most susceptible to decay, it first becomes necessary to consider how declarative and procedural knowledge facilitate the learning and performance of skills. Declarative knowledge encompasses factual information, while procedural knowledge concerns the knowledge required to carry out a given task [6]. Henik et al. [7] found that procedural knowledge decays slower than declarative knowledge and proposed that, as an individual develops expertise at a given task, procedural memory is used increasingly more.

Lower levels of skill proficiency can result in a skill being more sensitive to skill decay [8], as the individual must refer to stored declarative knowledge and cannot rely on the 'automated' performance of a task associated with higher levels of expertise. As explained by Stothard and Nicholson [9], developing expertise facilitates the conversion of declarative knowledge to procedural knowledge (which is characterised by 'autonomous' learning) and reduces the potential for skill fade to occur when performing a 'routine' task. Evidence for this concept was presented by Numminen et al. [10], who found that there is a positive correlation between one's own perception of competence for a given skill and the frequency by which that skill is performed. Prospective memory (which is associated with procedural knowledge) was also found to be superior when individuals are presented with regularly occurring scenarios [11].

Although the performance of tasks can become 'automated', the associated skill(s) can still be susceptible to skill decay if the task is learned to a high degree of automation, but not routinely practiced [12]. Kim et al. [6] discuss the consequences of such scenarios, whereby a lack of skill implementation leads to decreased accuracy and increased response times (as the operator considers previously learned declarative knowledge) when performing the task. The authors also advise that declarative knowledge can be susceptible to degradation over time, but the operator may still be capable of performing the task if new declarative knowledge is not required to accurately complete the task, or if the knowledge cannot be forgotten (i.e., it is accessible in the environment). Thus, "steps that are forgotten tend to be those that are not suggested by the previous sequence of steps or by the equipment" [13]. In this case, skills which rely on "knowledge-in-the-world" are more likely to be remembered and easier to re-learn after an extended period of non-use, when compared to skills which are supported by knowledge stored in memory [14]. For skills which rely on recalling knowledge from memory, Volz and Dorneich [12] propose that workload levels increase as the individual attempts to revert to the declarative knowledge when performance of a skill is reduced due to lack of implementation. Procedural memory was also found to be superior when measured against declarative knowledge for the visual position of cues [15], which could have significant implications for ATC operations. Ultimately, if controllers are task-saturated and relying on declarative knowledge (due to inexperience or skill fade) to complete certain tasks, this may inhibit their ability to read environmental cues and instigate tasks which do not benefit from external cues. This is a risk that is reduced with operational currency, as one study observed that task saturation was reduced for experienced helicopter pilots who were capable of monitoring 'the big picture' of their operational environment [16].

Eißfeldt [17] identified that controllers consult previous knowledge and real-time information when establishing situational awareness. The author refers to Endsley's [18] model for establishing situational awareness and describes that the three levels of Endsley's model (perception of environmental elements, comprehension of current situation and projection of future status) are "supported or impaired by limited supply of attention and/or working memory, by poor or incorrect mental models or by inadequate goals." Should the skills that facilitate controller tasks become decayed, effective processing of information will therefore be delayed or obstructed as the operator reverts to declared knowledge to perform the required task(s). This hazard was identified by Eurocontrol [19], who warned that such a scenario could lead to a controller being "unable to maintain full situational awareness for timely conflict detection and resolution in the entire area of responsibility, in particular in traffic spike periods." Since declarative knowledge is more susceptible to skill decay [2], the inputs for establishing situational awareness become limited if the skill which supports the task has not been activated in a substantial period. Childs and Spears [20] summarise this occurrence as being a result of inadequate "cognitive monitoring", whereby the automatic element of performing the task is limited by the "rapid" decay of the cognitive components (declarative knowledge) which facilitate the process.

Having been exposed to consistently low traffic levels during the pandemic, it is possible that ATCO skills have decayed due to lack of use, although all skills may not be subject to the same rate of decay. Vlasbom et al. [21] suggest that "a complex cognitive task, and the associated required competences, are generally better retained over time than tasks that only require simple, univocal skills such as applying a certain procedure." EASA [2] refer to this as 'integration complexity', whereby the more integrated a set of skills are, the higher the resistance of those skills to decay. Tasks of higher complexity can provide cues which allude to the steps to be taken when performing the task, provided that the associated skills were highly familiar to the ATCO before the risk of skill fade was introduced [9]. Skill retention can be measured by recall and recognition, and Stothard and Nicholson [9] point to a study by Semb and Ellis [22] which demonstrates that recognition tasks are retained better than recall tasks. If ATCO tasks follow a clear sequence of steps, therefore, recollection of the process may be superior when compared to the ability to recall the steps to a task. Additionally, controller skills which are low in complexity and are rarely performed during periods of low traffic are highly susceptible to skill decay, particularly if they are associated with 'recalling' knowledge.

### 1.3   Methods for Reducing Skill Fade

Simulation tools are the most effective method of creating a realistic ATC environment and by using this type of training "controllers are expected to build up an inventory of technical skills and revive procedural knowledge during short courses on high-fidelity simulators" [23]. For students with no previous ATC experience, exposure to ATC simulator sessions also increased their own self-perceived knowledge and [24]. Once an initial base of technical ATC skills has been developed for an ATCO, however, simulations may not be the only effective method available for reducing skill fade. Sanders et al. [25] report that "after initial instruction and a session of monitored physical practice, mental imagery rehearsal was as effective as physical practice in learning surgical skills." This suggests that ATCOs can benefit from training methods which sufficiently facilitate mental rehearsal of practices without the aid of a simulator, if skills were initially learned to an expert level. For ATCOs, this type of training method could include face-to-face briefings, presentations and information packages which provide the individual with the resources that are necessary to engage in mental imagery rehearsal.

Research on skill fade was also conducted in the aviation domain before the onset of the pandemic. Sitterly et al. [26] considered the effectiveness of various training methods for reducing skill fade in pilots. After four months of no practice, pilot performance was found to have reduced for operation of the flight controls and for tasks which involved implementing procedures (which are associated with the application of declarative knowledge). Three methods were assessed to reduce this degradation: "static rehearsal (checklists and briefings), dynamic rehearsal (briefings and videotaped flight presentations), [and] dynamic warmup practice (closed loop simulator practice)". Static rehearsal methods demonstrated the highest value and cost benefit advantages when addressing issues associated with skill fade, meaning that these training methods could be highly effective for providing ATCOs with 'reminder' information ahead of a 'ramp-up' in traffic levels. By largely focusing on the declarative knowledge required to carry out tasks which have been rarely performed since the onset of the pandemic (e.g., implementing arrival spacings during low-vis operations which are dependent on the 'category' of the preceding aircraft), results from the study suggests that static rehearsal methods could be used effectively to counteract ATCO skill fade. As described by Childs and Spears [20], the method of training should be dependent on the type of skills that required addressing, as "it would make little sense, for example, to employ computer-generated image displays in conjunction with a simulator having low control fidelity for upgrading complex control skills." It is important, therefore, that the ATC training methods which are implemented are fit for purpose and are allocated based on their suitability for adequately addressing the type of skill(s) in question.

## 2  Method

### 2.1  Participants

Fifty-six Air Traffic Control Officers from three separate terminal control units took part in the research. Forty-eight of the participants were male, seven participants were female, and one participant elected not to submit gender information. Participants advised the age category (prescribed in five-year segments) in which they belonged, and submissions were received ranging from the '21–25' to '56–60' years-old age categories. Similar categories were prescribed for recording years of controllers' work experience, and responses were collected ranging from the '1–5' to '31–35' years of experience categories. All participants exercised air traffic control ratings at the time of the research and were based at one of three airports in the same European Country. 'Unit A' is a large international airport, while 'Unit B' and 'Unit C' provide an ATC service to smaller airports. Due to the similar operational characteristics of 'Unit B' and 'Unit C', the results from these two units were grouped together when analysing the data.

### 2.2  Research Design

Data collection took place over a two-week period, from 14th–27th July 2021. A URL link to the questionnaire was sent to each of the participants, which included a briefing on the background to the research and how the research data would be collected. The average time taken to complete the questionnaire was 12 min and 55 s.

An Independent sample t-test was performed using IBM SPSS Statistics (Version 26) to ascertain if there was a significant difference in the recorded scores for 'Gender', 'Age', 'Experience', 'Unit' and 'Rating'. Q-Q plots were produced and assessed to verify the assumption of normality for the data, and Levine's test was used to understand if data samples in each group complied with the assumptions of homogeneity of variances ($p > 0.05$). A Cohen's d value was also calculated to ascertain the independent sample effect sizes for each of the examined groups.

## 3  Results

### 3.1  Operational Concepts

Eight statements which related to operational concepts were presented, and participants were required to indicate their level of agreement to each statement. The eight statements are displayed in Table 1 below.

**Table 1.** Operational concepts

| Code | Statement |
|------|-----------|
| O1 | "I feel that my overall skill when performing controller tasks may have reduced since the onset of the pandemic" |
| O2 | "I am motivated by the thought of operating under busy traffic levels again" |
| O3 | "I will add an extra 'buffer' between aircraft spacings, separation standards, etc., while I get re-accustomed to busy traffic levels" |
| O4 | "I felt that my skill level significantly increased after my most recent simulation refresher day" |
| O5 | "My general knowledge of procedures has reduced throughout the pandemic" |
| O6 | "I am confident in my ability to recall and apply any new procedures that have been introduced over the last year, without error" |
| O7 | "I believe that general adherence to procedures has NOT declined as a result of the pandemic" |
| O8 | "When traffic returns to busy levels, I will be more likely to arrive at my workplace early, in order to take extra time to prepare for my duty, read notices, etc." |

O2 recorded the highest mean score response for any statement (M = 4.05, SD = 0.862), with 80.3% of participants indicating that they were motivated by working under increased levels of traffic once more. This statement was also the only statement not to record a 'Strongly Disagree' response, and it maintained the lowest overall frequency of disagree-type responses (7.1%). The second-highest response score was recorded for O1 (M = 3.86, SD = 1.017), whereby 78% of controllers agreed to some degree that their skill levels may have reduced since the beginning of the pandemic. 10.8% of controllers disagreed that their skill levels may have decreased, with half of these participants selecting 'Strongly Disagree' and the remaining participants selecting 'Disagree'. When asked to consider if they would add an 'extra-buffer' between separation standards as they get reaccustomed to busy traffic levels, 67.9% of participants indicated that they would. This statement therefore recorded the third highest level of combined agreeing responses (M = 3.62, SD = 1.037). O6 (M = 2.93, SD = 0.931) and O7 (M = 3.13, SD = 1.08) relate to the recollection and application of procedures and recorded the highest frequency of disagreeing responses, with 39.3% of controllers disagreeing to some degree with both statements.

An independent sample t-test was implemented to identify any significant difference between demographics' responses to each of the eight operational statements. No significant difference was identified in the scores for years of experience or age. One set of responses was identified to have significant difference for gender groups, with a significant difference in scores identified between males (M = 2.85, SD = 0.97) and females (M = 4.43, SD = 0.79) for statement O8; $t = -4.792$, $p < 0.05$, $d = -1.64$. A significant difference in the response scores for O8 was also detected for Radar (M = 2.74, SD = 1.06) and Tower (M = 3.48, SD = 0.96) controllers; $t = -2.69$, $p < 0.05$, d

$= -0.72$ with this statement yielding the only significant difference in response scores attributable to 'Rating' for the ten operational statements.

A significant difference was also identified in the scores of Unit groups for five of the operational statements. Response scores for both unit groups exhibited a significant difference for O1, O3, O4, O5 and O6. 'Unit A' recorded a higher mean score for four of the operational statements, with 'Units B and C' only recording a higher mean score for O6.

## 3.2  Controller Skills

Although all seventeen skills were applicable to Radar controllers, only ten were applicable to the role of a Tower controller. Based on participants' responses, the ability to recall procedures was identified as being the skill that the group believed was most likely to have reduced by some degree (M = 2.23, SD = 0.572). 67.9% of ATCOs indicated that they believed their ability to recall procedures was 'Slightly Reduced' compared to pre-pandemic operations, with an additional 5.4% of controllers indicating that this skill has 'Greatly Reduced'. This skill also recorded the lowest 'Unchanged' value (25%), thereby indicating that the sample population believe that this skill was the most susceptible to some form of change after the COVID- 19 pandemic.

Coordinating with other sectors (M = 2.54, SD = 0.602) and maintaining situational awareness (M = 2.54, SD = 0.631) recorded the second-lowest mean scores, while receiving a handover recorded a mean score of M = 2.61 (SD = 0.652). The efficient handling of VFR flights (M = 3.2, SD = 0.724) recorded the highest overall mean score for any of the assessed skills, with the skill receiving the greatest number of combined 'Slightly Increased'/'Greatly Increased' responses (32.2%). Handling VFR flights was also the only skill included in this study which recorded a mean score above M = 3. Resolving conflicts received the largest number of 'Unchanged' responses, with 66.1% of participants indicating that this skill has been unaffected by the low traffic levels experienced during the pandemic.

A significant difference in scores between 'Age' groups was recorded for delivering a handover and resolving conflicts. For delivering a handover, ages 21–40 recorded a mean score of M = 2.45 (SD = 0.87), while ages 41–60 recorded a mean score of M = 2.89 (SD = 0.42); t = −2.44, p < 0.05, d = −0.2. The mean score for the younger age group was lower for resolving conflicts, however, with ages 21–40 recording a score of M = 2.83 (SD = 0.38) and ages 41–60 recording a score of M = 2.5 (SD = 0.64); t = 2.16, p < 0.05, d = 0.59.

Observation of the independent sample t-test results for 'Experience' groups also revealed a significant difference in scores for delivering a handover and receiving a handover. For delivering a handover, the less-experienced group recorded a score of M = 2.42 (SD = 0.81), while the higher-experienced group recorded a score of M = 2.96 (SD = 0.46); t = −3.16, p < 0.05, d = −0.80. Receiving a handover results were similar, with the less-experienced group recording the same mean value of M = 2.42 (SD = 0.72) and the higher-experienced group recording a slightly lower mean value of M = 2.84 (SD = 0.47); t = −2.63, p < 0.05, d = −0.67.

Skills which were specific to radar controllers (N = 33) recorded mean scores in the range of M = 2.12–2.42, and so ATCO responses indicate that the seven skills have reduced when compared to skill performance before the onset of the COVID-19 pandemic. Vectoring traffic (M = 2.42, SD = 0.663), sequencing aircraft for presentation to next sector (M = 2.42, SD = 0.561) and implementing correct departure/arrival spacings (M = 2.42, SD = 0.708) all recorded the highest mean scores. Managing aircraft in a hold recorded the lowest mean score of all radar-specific skills, with M = 2.12 (SD = 0.82).

Although appropriate application of speed control did not record the lowest mean score (M = 2.15, SD = 0.566), participants' responses indicate that radar controllers believe that it is the most susceptible to some form of decline, with over half of radar controllers (53.6%) indicating that this skill has reduced. It did not record the highest 'Greatly Reduced' response rate, however, which was recorded by managing aircraft in the hold (16.1%). The highest recorded 'Unchanged' value among radar skills was associated with sequencing aircraft to a hold, which recorded an 'Unchanged' response frequency of 62.5%.

## 3.3  Reducing Skill Fade

Simulation exercises recorded the highest mean value (M = 3.71, SD = 0.91) of all methods, while emails containing information resources recorded the lowest mean value (M = 1.79, SD = 0.825). Checklists (M = 3.5, SD = 0.915) and face-to-face briefings (M = 3.32, SD = 0.855) recorded the second and third highest mean values respectively, and these were the only methods which did not receive a 'Not at all Effective' response. Both methods also recorded the same frequency of 'Highly Effective' responses (35.7%), although checklists recorded a higher number of 'Extremely Effective' responses (14.3%), compared to 7.1% for face-to-face briefings. Electronic briefings which display 'reminder' information (M = 2.48, SD = 0.738) and procedures from the previous fifteen months (M = 2.52, SD = 0.786) scored similar mean values. Neither of these two methods recorded an 'extremely effective' response from a participant. Face-to-face briefings and checklists were the only methods which did not receive a 'Not at all Effective' response.

The scores associated with simulation exercises demonstrated a significant difference for males (M = 3.58, SD = 0.9) and females (M = 4.43, SD = 0.79); t = −2.4, p < 0.05, d = −0.98, while scores for checklists, copies of procedures and safety information were also significantly different for males (M = 3.38, SD = 0.87) and females (M = 4.14, SD = 0.9); t = −2.18, p < 0.05, d = −0.88. No significant difference was observed for either of the groups within the 'Age' or 'Experience' demographics.

Rating groups recorded significantly different values for two of the listed methods. A significant difference in values was recorded between Radar (M = 3.06, SD = 0.89) and Tower (M = 3.64, SD = 0.7) controllers for face-to-face briefings (t = −2.64, p < 0.05, d = −0.71), and between Radar (M = 1.48, SD = 0.724) and Tower (M = 2.16, SD = 0.8) controllers for emails which contain links (t = −3.31, p < 0.05, −0.89).

The only method responses to have significantly different values for the Unit groups were attributable to simulation exercises, whereby Unit A responses recorded a mean value of M = 3.87 (SD = 0.82) and Unit B and C recorded a mean value of M = 3.09 (SD = 1.04); t = 2.68, p < 0.05, d = 0.90.

## 4   Discussion

The topics examined in this paper concern the influence of skill fade on ATCOs after the COVID-19 pandemic. By analysing the feedback of current air traffic controllers, this research attempts to identify how ATCOs perceive the pandemic's influence on skill performance. In addition to this, the study also aims to consider how various training methods can be employed to reduce the effect of skill decay. Based on the data collected from the research, it is proposed that skill fade arising from the pandemic is a significant concern for ATCOs in 2021, as traffic levels begin to return towards 2019 levels. Despite this, the data collected suggests that controllers are largely motivated to return to operate control busy levels of traffic once more, as the industry recovers from the pandemic's influence.

It should first be noted that ATCOs' perceptions of experienced skill fade are significantly different for 'Unit B and C', when compared to their colleagues in 'Unit A'. Thus, based on the feedback from controllers, it is suggested that ATC staff providing a service at busier aerodromes may be more susceptible to the effects of skill fade after the pandemic. This is likely due to the relatively large change in operational tasks performed by ATCOs at busy airports which occurred during the pandemic, in comparison to the changes in operational tasks performed at smaller terminal units. Crucially, Numminen et al. [10] outline that a positive correlation exists between the frequency by which a skill is implemented and an individual's own perception of their competence for performing that skill. This potentially explains the significant difference in results between units, as the relative change in types of tasks performed at busier units is likely to be significantly greater than the change in tasks typically performed at smaller units. ATCOs providing a service to a busy aerodrome before 2020, for example, may have performed daily tasks which were rarely experienced during the pandemic (e.g., control traffic on a Standard Terminal Arrival Route, implement holding procedures, sequence multiple aircraft to provide specific 'gaps', etc.). In comparison, the daily tasks for ATCOs at smaller units will not have changed to the same degree, as the influence on variation of tasks during lower traffic numbers is considerably less than that of busier airports. Further support for this theory is based on the significant difference in responses between 'Unit' A and the two other units, when ATCOs were asked to consider if they would apply an extra "buffer" between aircraft as traffic levels increase. 'Unit A's substantially higher score for this dynamic implies a self- awareness of reduced ability among these ATCOs, while the tendency to implement additional precautions was not reflected in the responses of 'Unit B and C'. It is likely that this self-awareness for 'Unit A' ATCOs also stems from participants' most recent experience in a simulator, where controllers were occasionally assigned to handle busy artificial traffic while real-life traffic levels remained low. This is also represented by the significant difference between unit groups for O4, whereby 'Unit A' controllers recorded a considerably higher score when asked to consider if their skill level had increased after the most recent simulator session. Once again, it is proposed that the relative difference in variation of operational tasks performed, in comparison to routine tasks performed during pre-pandemic and/or simulator operations, is responsible for the higher scores generated by 'Unit A' in response to the operational concepts.

As advised by Stothard and Nicholson [9], lower levels of expertise can result in an individual being more susceptible to skill decay, since the required expertise to convert declarative information to procedural information is absent. Based on this concept, one might therefore expect to observe a significant difference between the response scores of controllers with '1–15 years' and '16–35 years' experience. It is possible that this is a consequence of measuring 'perceived' skill fade from the perspective of the controller, however, as opposed to measuring 'actual' skill fade. Thus, it could be argued that controllers with lower operational experience may not realise the degree to which they are susceptible to skill fade (i.e., unconscious incompetence), while controllers of greater experience may appreciate the implications of prolonged periods of low operational intensity to a greater degree. This concept is consistent with the theories presented by Kim et al. [6], who proposed that the operator can still perform a task if relying on declarative knowledge, provided that accurate completion of the task is not required. In the case of an ATCO with low levels of operational experience, therefore, it may not be until the controller is required to complete a time-sensitive task under high levels of workload before a vulnerability to skill fade is recognised. As mentioned above, this is a hazard which has also been recognised by Eurocontrol [19]. Thus, although no significant difference was observed in the data output, this is still a hazard that should be monitored carefully by ANSPs to ensure that ATCOs with lower levels of experience are appropriately supported.

While ANSPs can implement methods to reduce the effect of skill decay among staff, responsibility also lies with the individual for ensuring that they are suitably prepared to provide a safe and efficient ATC service. ATCOs should observe warnings from the reviewed literature, which suggests that controllers are likely to operate at reduced performance levels, as they revert to increased observation of declarative knowledge when workload levels increase [6, 20]. While ATCOs are required to allow sufficient time for briefings before each duty, it could be proposed that extra time should be allocated before a shift to facilitate the review of procedures/notices (associated with declarative knowledge) and mentally prepare for the duty ahead. Although this tendency was reflected in the O8 responses of 'Tower' controllers, 'Radar' controllers' responses were observed to be significantly different for this dynamic. When assessed alongside the responses to skill fade for the list of individual skills, this attitude may present a hazard in the context of receiving/delivering handovers. Mean score results for 'receiving a handover' and 'delivering a handover' suggest an awareness of degradation for these skills, which is likely due to the low operational complexity associated with handovers since the pandemic began. Interestingly, the group with '1–15 years' experience recorded a score for delivering and receiving a handover considerably lower than their more experienced colleagues. Since Pounds and Ferrante [27] report that 35% of operational errors in ATC occur within twenty minutes of receiving a handover, reduced performance when delivering/receiving handovers for lesser- experienced controllers could present a significant hazard as sectors become busier. This hazard becomes greater if the controller operates a radar position, as it is less likely that the ATCO will have taken extra time to arrive early and prepare for the duty. As mentioned above, EASA [28] have recognised the importance of mental preparation for all aviation workers to reduce the potential for hazards such as this to occur. It is therefore recommended that ANSPs promote the themes covered in EASA's 'Ramp Up – Be Ready, Stay Safe' campaign to all staff, with particular focus on 'Radar' controllers.

As proposed by Numminen et al. [10] and Soldatov et al. [29], there appears to be a positive correlation between ATCOs' perceptions of experienced skill fade and the rate for which the associated skill is implemented. It is unsurprising, therefore, that providing a Flight Information Service (FIS) to aircraft was the only skill included in this research that was not suggested to have decreased among controllers. Although local travel restrictions limited Visual Flight Rules (VFR) traffic for a number of months after the onset of the pandemic, VFR traffic levels were observed to closely represent levels for 2019 in the weeks which preceded the data collection for this research. Since the service provided to commercial traffic is typically prioritised over VFR traffic, reductions in airline movements over the pandemic has facilitated ATCOs in providing high levels of service to VFR flights. This increased interaction with VFR aircraft is therefore likely to have contributed to the skill recording the highest mean score among ATCO participants. The reduction in airline traffic was also represented in the response scores for skills which are most associated with the handling of busy levels of commercial traffic, with the ability to recall procedures quickly recording the lowest score for all skills within the combined 'Radar' and 'Tower' group. Lower scores were recorded for 'Radar' specific skills and almost all of these skills require recalling declarative knowledge regarding procedures. 'Managing aircraft in a hold' recorded the lowest mean score among 'Radar' controllers and is an example of such a skill, as it requires the application of a procedure which has rarely been implemented by ATCOs over the course of the pandemic. Sequencing to/from a hold and implementing the correct spacings between aircraft are other examples of skills which were performed infrequently over the pandemic and require the recollection of declarative knowledge. It is reasonable, therefore, that the mean scores for these skills was also recorded to be low. As outlined in the reviewed literature [13, 20], delays will occur when ATCOs attempt to access the declarative information required to implement these skills under busy traffic levels.

It is well recognised that ANSPs implement simulators as a primary training tool, since they are the most effective method for creating a realistic ATC environment [23]. Simulators provide a method for training and assessing ATCO skills in a true-to-life manner and can be adjusted to focus on the use of specific skills or operation of specific scenarios. Cant et al. [3] highlight the value in this characteristic by stressing that an operator should be exposed to a training method which best simulates a busy operational environment, particularly if the operator has not experienced the high workload levels within the real-world environment for a prolonged period of time. It is little surprise, therefore, that simulators recorded the highest mean score among participants for effectiveness when addressing skill fade. Additionally, 'Radar' controllers perceive the effectiveness of simulator tools methods to be significantly higher compared to 'Tower' controllers, which is likely a result of the relative extent by which simulators can represent a real-life environment. Where radar displays can visually represent an operational scenario to highly accurate degree, the components of tower simulators lack the same realism that can only be experienced by controlling aircraft in a real-life visual control tower.

While it is acknowledged that simulators can address a wide range of ATCO skills, the literature suggests that other tools may be equally as effective for skill fade, depending on the type of skill to be addressed [25, 30]. In addition to this, the resources required to operate simulators can mean that they are costly tools to implement on a large scale. Given that the lowest recorded mean scores in this study related to the recollection and implementation of procedures, skill fade influencing these abilities may be best addressed by introducing the static rehearsal promoted by Sitterly et al. [26]. Results from this study support this concept, based on checklists near operational positions and face-to-face briefings recording the second and third highest scores among all methods. Since these methods facilitate the review of declarative knowledge that may not have been frequently applied during the pandemic, both of these tools are a cost-effective method for addressing skill fade among controllers. Most importantly, these static rehearsal tools have the added benefit of specifically addressing an ATCO's declarative knowledge stores, which may have been subjected to effects of skill fade during the pandemic. The significant difference in recorded scores between 'Rating' types for face- to-face briefings is also likely to be a result of the interactive element of the training tool. 'Tower' environments are dynamic and may be subjected to large numbers of daily operational notices, including details of airport infrastructure works or temporary changes in operational procedures. Thus, by providing an ability to interact with an 'expert' during face-to-face briefings, ATCOs' questions and concerns can be directly addressed.

## 5    Conclusion

This research provides insight into ATCOs' perceptions of the effect of the COVID-19 pandemic on skill performance and considers the effectiveness of various tools for limiting the harmful effect of skill decay. Controller skill fade is a significant concern as traffic levels begin to increase after the pandemic. This research demonstrates that controllers operating at large international airports perceive higher levels of skill decay and may be more susceptible to the effects of skill fade after prolonged exposure to low traffic levels. Skills associated with the implementation of declarative knowledge are most susceptible to decay, particularly if these skills are characterised by low levels of 'integration complexity'. If the influence of skill decay is not suitably addressed before controllers operate in a busy sector, there is a risk that performance of tasks will take longer, and accuracy will decrease. While simulators are an effective method of addressing ATCO skill fade by replicating busy real-world scenarios, they are not the only effective method for addressing skill fade issues arising from the pandemic. Static rehearsal methods, such as checklists and briefings, are effective and inexpensive methods of addressing ATCO skill fade. These tools can also be modified to present declarative knowledge based on the requirements of the applicable unit. ANSPs must therefore monitor the areas of skill performance which require attention and implement the most suitable tool to address potential skill fade issues.

## References

1. Eurocontrol: Eurocontrol Forecast Update 2021–2024 (2021). https://www.eurocontrol.int/publication/eurocontrol-forecast-update-2021-2024. Accessed 25 Aug 2021

2. EASA: Safety Issue Report – Skills and Knowledge Degradation due to Lack of Recent Practice, 4 August 2021. https://www.easa.europa.eu/community/sytem/files/202108/Safety%20Issue%20Report%20%20%20Skills%20and%20Knowledge%20Degradation_REV2%20Clean_0.pdf. Accessed 24 Aug 2021

3. Arthur, W., Bennett, W., Stanush, P., McNelly, T.: Factors that influence skill decay and retention: a quantitative review and analysis. Hum. Perform. **11**(1), 57–101 (1998)

4. EASA: Maintenance of ATCO Skills: Guildelines in Relation to the COVID-19 Pandemic (2021). https://www.easa.europa.eu/sites/default/files/dfu/maintenance_of_atco_skills_-_easa_guidelines_in_relation_to_the_covid-19_pandemic_issue_1.pdf. Accessed 6 June 2021

5. Civil Aviation Authority: Awareness of Skill Fade and Suggested Mitigations (2021). https://publicapps.caa.co.uk/docs/33/SafetyNotice2021011.pdf. Accessed 15 May 2021

6. Kim, J.W., Ritter, F.E., Koubek, R.J.: An integrated theory for improved skill acquisition and retention in the three stages of learning. Theor. Issues Ergon. Sci. **14**, 22–37 (2013)

7. Henik, A., Brainin, E., Schwarz, D.: The Preservation and the Decay of Military Skills. Ben Gurion University of the Negev, Israel (1999)

8. Prophet, W.W.: Long-Term Retention of Flying Skills: An Annotated Bibliography. Human Resources Research Organisation, Virginia (1976)

9. Stothard, C., Nicholson, R.: Skill acquisition and retention in training: DSTO support to the army ammunition study. DTSO Electronics and Surveillance Research Laboratory, Australia (2001)

10. Numminen, O., Meretoja, R., Isoaho, H., Leino-Kilpi, H.: Professional competence of practicing nurses. J. Clin. Nurs. **22**(9–10), 1411–1423 (2013)

11. Andrzejewski, S.J., Moore, C.M., Corvette, M., Herrmann, D.: Prospective memory skill. Bull. Psychon. Soc. **29**(4), 304–306 (1991)

12. Volz, K.M., Dorneich, M.C.: Evaluation of cognitive skill degradation in flight planning. J. Cogn. Eng. Decis. Making **14**(4), 263–328 (2020)

13. Shields, J.L., Goldberg, S.L., Dressel, J.D.: Retention of Basic Soldiering Skills. U.S. Army Institute for the Behavioural and Social Sciences, Virginia (1979)

14. Cahillane, M., MacLean, P., Smy, V.: Novel application of a predictive skill retention model to technical VLE content production skills among Higher Education teachers: a case study. Interact. Learn. Environ. **27**(3), 336–348 (2019)

15. Posner, M.I.: Cognition: An Introduction. Scott Foresman, Illinois (1973)

16. Minotra, D., Feigh, K.: Eliciting knowledge from helicopter pilots: recommendations for revising the ACTA method for helicopter landing tasks. In: Proceedings of the Human Factors and Ergonomics Society Annual Meeting, Austin, Texas, 9–13 October 2017, vol. 61, pp. 242–246 (2017)

17. Eißfeldt, H.: Ability requirements for air traffic controllers - review and integration. In: The 24th EAAP Conference, Crieff Hydro, Scotland, 4–8 September 2000, pp. 1–22 (2000)

18. Endsley, M.R.: Situation awareness in aviation systems. In: Garland, D.J., Wise, J.A., Hopkin, V.D. (eds.) Handbook of Aviation Human Factors, pp. 257–276. Lawrence Erlbaum Associates Publishers, New Jersey (1999)

19. Eurocontrol: Safety Argument for return to normal ops (2021). https://www.skybrary.aero/bookshelf/books/5741.pdf. Accessed 23 June 2021

20. Childs, J.M., Spears, W.D.: Flight skill decay and recurrent training. Percept. Mot. Skills **62**, 235–242 (1986)

21. Vlasbom, J., Pennings, H., Van der Pal, J., Oprins, E.: Competence retention in safety-critical professions: a systematic literature review. Educ. Res. Rev. **30**, 1–14 (2020)

22. Semb, G.B., Ellis, J.A.: Knowledge taught in school: what is remembered? Rev. Educ. Res. **64**(2), 253–286 (1994)

23. Malakis, S., Kontogiannis, T.: Refresher training for air traffic controllers: is it adequate to meet the challenges of emergencies and abnormal situations? Int. J. Aviat. Psychol. **22**, 59–77 (2012)
24. Lindenfeld, M., Radigan, J., Figuccio, M.: Does the use of simulation significantly impact students' perceptions of their air traffic control knowledge and skill? J. Aviat. Technol. Eng. **9**, 32–40 (2020)
25. Sanders, C.W., Sadoski, M., Bramson, R., Wiprud, R., Van Walsum, K.: Comparing the effects of physical practice ad mental imagery rehearsal on learning basic surgical skills by medical students. Am. J. Obstet. Gynecol. **191**(5), 1811–1814 (2004)
26. Sitterley, T.E., Zaitzeff, L.P., Berge, W.A.: Degradation of Learned Skills: Effectiveness of practice Methods on Visual Approach and Landing Skill Retention. NASA, Seattle (1972)
27. Pounds, J., Ferrante, A.S.: FAA strategies for reducing operational error causal factors. In: Kirwan, B., Rodgers, M., Schafer, D. (eds.) Human Factors in Air Traffic Management. Ashgate, Vermont (2005)
28. EASA: Ramp Up Campaign Master (2021). https://www.easa.europa.eu/community/system/files/202105/Ramp%20Up%20Campaign%20ATM.pdf. Accessed 15 June 2021
29. Soldatov, S.K., Zasyad'ko, K.I., Bogomolov, A.V., Vonarshenko, A.P., Solomka, A.V.: Professionally important skills of air traffic controllers. Hum. Physiol. **44**(7), 775–778 (2018)
30. Kelc, R., Vogrin, M., Kelc, J.: Cognitive training for the prevention of skill decay in temporarily non-performing orthopedic surgeons. Acta Orthop. **91**(5), 523–526 (2020)

# Investigating Pilots' Operational Behaviours While Interacting with Different Types of Inceptors

Wojciech Tomasz Korek[1,2(✉)], Wen-Chin Li[3], Linghai Lu[4], and Mudassir Lone[2]

[1] Faculty of Automatic Control, Electronics and Computer Science,
Silesian University of Technology, Gliwice, Poland
[2] Dynamics, Simulation and Control Group, Cranfield University, Cranfield, UK
{w.t.korek,m.m.lone}@cranfield.ac.uk
[3] Safety and Accident Investigation Centre, Cranfield University, Cranfield, UK
wenchin.li@cranfield.ac.uk
[4] Centre for Aeronautics, Cranfield University, Cranfield, UK
l.lu@cranfield.ac.uk

**Abstract.** There are different designs of inceptors applied in the modern flight deck. How do pilots define how to precisely control the aircraft as their intention? Ten pilots have been asked to take part in the flight simulation trials. They were given tasks to execute using sidestick, Xbox gamepad and touchscreen controller and provide feedback using the System Usability Scale. The aim was to investigate the feasibility of replacing conventional inceptors in aircraft. The results have shown that there is a potential in introducing alternate Human-Computer Interaction (HCI) methods in the flight deck, especially in terms of learnability, however there is still a lot of work before it happens. This paper summarises the 'pilot study' results and shows the potential for further research.

**Keywords:** Flight simulation · Control inputs · Human-computer interactions · System usability · Touchscreen · Inceptors

## 1 Introduction

Handling qualities as an engineering field has developed hand in hand with the discipline of flight control engineering since the beginning of aviation. This is evident from the stability and control focus of the Wright Brothers [15] and the work of Norton on roll damping in 1923 [12]. Methods and tools for handling qualities assessment have had to evolve with every significant advancement in flight control design. This is exemplified by the works of McRuer [11], Hodgkinson [4] and Klyde [6] that effectively chart Western evolution in the study of handling qualities targeting problems specific to each new flight control technology. Moreover, methods for collecting qualitative pilot feedback and commentary (such as that of Cooper and Harper [3]) have also been a fundamental aspect of

D. Harris and W.-C. Li (Eds.): HCII 2022, LNAI 13307, pp. 314–325, 2022.
https://doi.org/10.1007/978-3-031-06086-1_24

handling qualities. Pilot workload and overall experience can also be collected using metrics such as the System Usability Scale (SUS) [8,10] (used in the work presented here). A traditional handling qualities engineer has so far focused on flight control architecture, stick feel systems and experimental testing (design, execution and analysis) for demonstrating performance, while at the same time, interacting with various engineers from all disciplines to ensure the aircraft can satisfactorily perform all mission task elements. An interaction that has seen very limited change is the interface with human factors engineers in the design of inceptors. Not much has changed from the pilot's perspective with regards to inceptors found in the cockpit of large commercial transport aircraft. What was found for manual control on the Airbus A300 and the Boeing 707 can be found replicated on the Airbus A350 and the Boeing 787, albeit with significant 'back-end' changes in the flight control system. Today, the advancement in cockpit automation together with the envisioned changes in the role of the pilot has led to researchers questioning the suitability of existing inceptors and wondering whether better alternatives exist.

Recent work in the field has explored designing a control system that helps pilots with limited experience to fly safely [13] with emphasis on aspects of learnability and safety. Experimental research done by Efremov et al. has shown that type of the inceptor is a key variable shaping the dynamics of the pilot-vehicle system and its design parameters (such as its position in the cockpit, or whether it senses displacement or force, its stiffness and damping) can significantly influence pilot performance. For example, sidesticks were found to increase time delay in scenarios focusing on lateral channel movement (roll tracking) as compared to longitudinal channel (pitch tracking). Furthermore, choosing either force sensing or displacement sensing inceptors can significantly effect the phase delay introduced by the pilot and therefore, overall performance when executing specific tracking or compensatory tasks. [1,2,16] However, to date much of this exploration has been limited to traditional inceptors such as sidesticks and control columns. The work presented here is a first step towards exploring the suitability of radically different alternatives. The aim of this research is to test the feasilibity of designing a new replacement control inceptor based on gamepads and touchscreens, as suggested in the authors' previous work [7]. The study aims to test the following hypotheses, using data collected from piloted flight simulator trials:

$H_1$: "There is a significant difference in pilot's feedback on system usability among three control inputs".
$H_2$: "There is a significant difference in pilot's variance of error among three control inputs".

## 2   Experimental Setup

This section presents the methodology used in this research. The data was gathered using a 'pilot study' method [5]. Ten licensed pilots were invited to participate in a flight simulator experiment, involving executing tasks using different types of aircraft control inceptors.

## 2.1  Participants

Ten participants holding a valid piloting license, aged from 24 to 63 (M = 39.60, SD[1] = 12.19) with fixed-wing total flight hours experience ranging from 800 to 13300 (M = 5810, SD = 3847) took part in this research. Majority of them have an airliner-type rating (Airbus A320 family or Boeing B737-400/B747-400) and 8 of them were flight instructors. All of them were right-handed.

## 2.2  Environment

The trials were conducted in an engineering flight simulator called Future Systems Simulator (FSS), shown in Fig. 1. It was developed by Cranfield University and Rolls-Royce in order to test various aerospace technologies, from the engine systems to Human-Machine Interface (HMI). For the purpose of this research, it was modified to accommodate the trials involving different inceptors. Tests were conducted using an aircraft model of a generic long-range business jet based on Gulfstream G550.

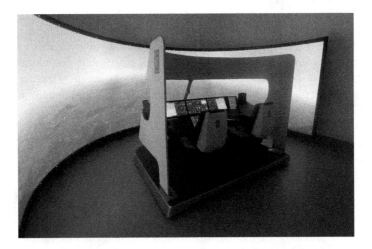

**Fig. 1.** Future Systems Simulator (FSS), located at Cranfield University. The flight deck consists of touchscreen monitors and the cockpit is modular and fully reconfigurable; the shroud can also be taken away to accommodate simulation of drone flight or air traffic management.

## 2.3  Trial Procedure

Each participant had to fill in a demographic questionnaire, followed by a video briefing explaining the aims and objectives of the study. After that they were seated in the flight simulator cockpit and shown the inceptor briefing. The order

---

[1] Standard Deviation.

of inceptors was randomised. For each inceptor, the pilot had been given 1 min of a test flight to get accustomed to the inceptor and aircraft dynamics. Four tasks followed after that, described in Subsect. 2.5. After completing the tasks, they were given a SUS questionnaire. When they tested the three inceptors, they were given a final feedback questionnaire to fill in. The trial procedure is shown in Fig. 2.

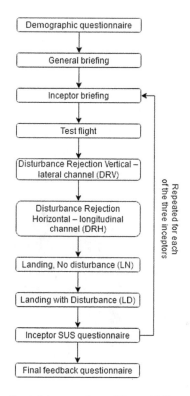

**Fig. 2.** Diagram showing the trial procedure. The middle part from Inceptor briefing to SUS questionnaire is repeated three times, each for different inceptor explored in this study.

## 2.4   Inceptors

The study uses the following inceptors:

**Sidestick:** The default FSS controller is a sidestick, shown in Fig. 3. It is a passive displacement sidestick with a custom-made handle, mounted on a base of Thrustmaster HOTAS WARTHOG™. Passive sidesticks are used in Airbus A320, among other aircraft and the total number of cockpits equipped with passive sidesticks have increased significantly over the period of 2007 to 2017. [14]

**Gamepad:** Xbox gamepad controller was chosen to investigate how pilots with different backgrounds in using the gamepad for video games will adapt and perform the various tasks. Participants were asked to hold the controller in both hands but only use their right thumb to move the right stick, while resting both hands on the extendable tray in front of them, as presented in Fig. 4.

**Touchscreen:** The touchscreen controller is a modified mobile touchscreen displacement stick. It is located in the centre of PFD, as shown in Fig. 5. The Y-axis is reversed in order to allow the aircraft to go in the direction pointed by the subject. Participants were asked to use their right index finger to interact with the inceptor.

None of the controller types are active inceptors, and therefore no tactile feedback is provided to the pilots.

**Fig. 3.** FSS sidestick.          **Fig. 4.** Xbox gamepad.

## 2.5   Tasks

Four tasks were developed for the purpose of this study: two main scenarios, each divided into two sub-scenarios:

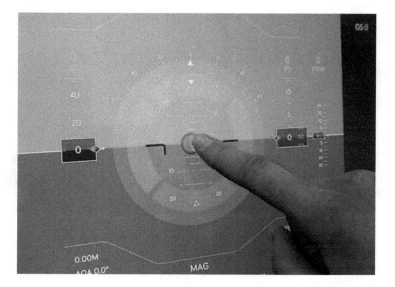

**Fig. 5.** Touchscreen controller.

**Disturbance Rejection Task - (1) Vertical/(2) Horizontal Axis:** Depending on the axis, the pilot was required to (a) keep the flight path vector indicator on the horizon line of the attitude indicator (Vertical Axis, Fig. 6) or (b) keep the roll indicator on the centre position of the indicator (Horizontal Axis, Fig. 7). The task started with 5 s of no disturbance, then the disturbance signal was injected to the inceptor signal for 45 s, followed by 10 s for a cooldown. For each of the sub-scenarios, the other control channel was disabled, so the pilot was only able to move up and down or left and right, for respective vertical/horizontal tasks.

**Landing Task - (1) Without Disturbance/(2) with Disturbance:** The pilot was required to perform a landing. The starting position of the aircraft was 5 min away and in 54.5° offset angle to the runway. Initial speed was 150 knots (0.25 Mach), altitude was 1400 ft and heading was 90°. Desired glide slope was 3°. (a) First sub-scenario did not have any disturbance. (b) In the second sub-scenario, 5 s after start, the disturbance was introduced to both inceptor channels - vertical and horizontal and it lasted for 90 s. This is how long it took for the aircraft to reach the runway.

For all types of tasks, weather conditions were clear and there was no wind (only simulated turbulence as a disturbance). There was no other air or airport traffic. The disturbance tasks were chosen to familiarise the pilot with control in only one channel, and then to put both channels to the test in a landing scenario (harder and easier - with and without added disturbance). The disturbance signal was pre-generated using a sum-of-sines forcing function [9]. The disturbance signal is different for each task, but kept consistent between participants. The following data was collected from each session:

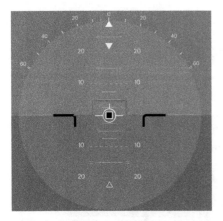

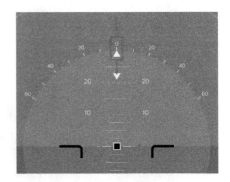

**Fig. 6.** Disturbance Rejection Vertical task objective - keep the flight path vector indicator on the horizon line of the attitude indicator.

**Fig. 7.** Disturbance rejection horizontal task objective - keep the roll indicator on the centre position of the indicator.

1. Demographic information, experience with piloting aircraft and attitude towards introduction of touchscreen technology in aircraft;
2. Pilot's control input data - raw and with added disturbance;
3. Flight simulation data - aircraft aerodynamics.

As this study focuses exclusively on pilots' behaviour while interacting with control surface inceptors, all other cockpit elements such as engine throttle, landing gear, flaps and spoiler levers, brakes and autopilot control were automated to minimise pilot's workload. Moreover, participants were told to minimise usage of the rudder pedals while in flight.

## 3   Results and Analysis

Preliminary data recorded by the authors before the trials have shown differences in root mean square (RMS) error in sidestick and touchscreen controller deflection and performance in keeping the disturbance rejection task's target. Interestingly, sidestick and gamepad results had similar RMS error values, as seen in Table 1.

The 'pilot study' trials have shown that, throughout the experiment, pilots would give highest SUS scores for the sidestick, however according to findings of Mclellan et al., users tend to put 15—16% higher scores for systems they already know [10]. With that in mind, it can be assumed that the scores for gamepad and touchscreen would be greater if participants had previous experience with them. This phenomenon can also be seen in the case of gamepad - two of the pilots who had previous experience in playing video games using gamepad (around 50%—75% of time spent playing) gave a SUS Total score much higher than average:

**Table 1.** Preliminary results of RMS error values (variance of error) (in degrees) using different inceptors in disturbance rejection vertical task, with researcher acting as a pilot.

| Inceptor | RMS |
|---|---|
| Sidestick | 1.61 |
| Gamepad | 1.48 |
| Touchscreen | 2.27 |

92.50/71.25 between all four tasks, when the mean gamepad SUS Total score among all participants was 59.00. Since there is no previous research involving replacement of the physical sidestick with touchscreen controller, one can assume that the scores would be 15% higher if pilots had any experience with piloting the aircraft using the touchscreen technology.

SUS analysis has also shown that Disturbance Rejection - Vertical axis task was easiest to perform (with mean SUS Total score across the participants of 45.94 (SD = 29.35) for touchscreen, 67.19 (SD = 37.03) for gamepad and 78.44 (SD = 36.10) for sidestick), while the hardest one was the landing task with disturbance (with mean SUS Total score of 20.94 (SD = 19.44) for touchscreen, 48.75 (SD = 33.77) for gamepad and 66.88 (SD = 32.51) for sidestick). Boxplots showing the distribution of SUS results can be seen in Fig. 8 for Usability, Fig. 9 for Learnability and Fig. 10 for Total Score.

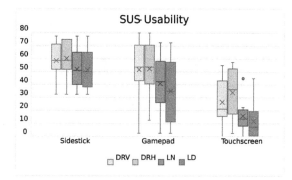

**Fig. 8.** System usability scale - usability.

Pilots have ranked the sidestick as highest Usability controller, followed by gamepad and touchscreen. The main reason of this is the familiarity - they already had previous experience with sidestick. Gamepad results were lower than those of sidestick, but there is much bigger standard deviation - this is because some pilots already experienced using this type of controller in video games. Touchscreen inceptor scored the lowest because none of the participants have experienced this type of controller in the past.

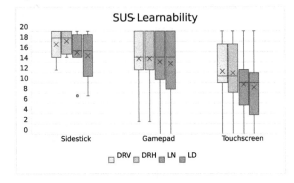

**Fig. 9.** System usability scale - learnability.

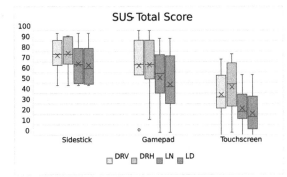

**Fig. 10.** System usability scale - total score.

There's also a tendency in significantly higher SUS scores among pilots who indicated an interest in touchscreen technology being introduced in aircraft cockpits - 40.00 (SD = 10.51) for people who liked the idea and 26.46 (SD = 23.51) for people who did not.

It can be seen that for the majority of participants, learnability for all three inceptors, especially for Disturbance Rejection tasks, was at least satisfactory. Landing tasks, being more challenging, especially using the novel touchscreen controller, was somehow lower than the rest. Interestingly, the learnability for gamepad was high, especially for subjects with previous gaming experience.

Randomising the order of the inceptors did not have a significant change in pilots' behaviour: SUS score for gamepad was slightly higher (4.5 points on average) than sidestick from participants with sidestick as a first inceptor, however participants who tested gamepad and touchscreen first had the same trend for scoring: sidestick > gamepad > touchscreen. An interesting observation can be made here: in Disturbance Rejection tasks, the RMS error was lower for gamepad than sidestick across all the participants, which means that they performed the best using the gamepad (and they did not realise that, because it is on the contrary to majority of the SUS scores). The RMS values can be found in Table 2 and the distribution of RMS between subject is shown in Fig. 11.

**Table 2.** Root Mean Square (RMS) of error (deviation from the task objective) (in degrees) averaged across all pilots for Disturbance Rejection Vertical (DRV) and Disturbance Rejection Horizontal (DRH).

|  | Sidestick | | Gamepad | | Touchscreen | |
| --- | --- | --- | --- | --- | --- | --- |
|  | Mean | SD | Mean | SD | Mean | SD |
| DRV | 2.19 | 1.28 | 1.41 | 0.40 | 4.87 | 2.18 |
| DRH | 2.49 | 0.98 | 1.65 | 0.22 | 2.88 | 0.54 |

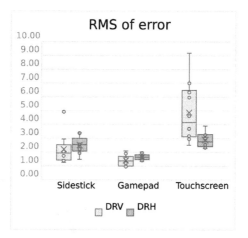

**Fig. 11.** Root Mean Square (RMS) of error (deviation from the task objective) (in degrees).

Interesting point was raised by one of the participant, who said that landing tasks were easier for them using gamepad than sidestick, which is reflected in SUS Usability score being higher by 3 points for both landings and their after-trial inceptor preference choice of gamepad. It is worth to note that according to the demographic questionnaire, he/she has never or hardly ever played video games nor used this type of controller.

Analysis of the results has shown that the hypothesis $H_1$: "There is a significant difference on pilot's feedback on system usability among three control inputs" applies for comparison of sidestick with touchscreen and gamepad with touchscreen, however comparison of SUS scores from sidestick and gamepad have not shown significant differences. Hypothesis $H_2$: "There is a significant difference on pilot's variance of error among three control inputs" is true when comparing the Disturbance Rejection Vertical task results among the three studied inceptors (RMS Mean equal to 2.19, 1.41 and 4.87, respectively for sidestick, gamepad and touchscreen), however RMS error Mean from Disturbance Rejection Horizontal task has shown that gamepad was more accurate inceptor than the rest (RMS Mean equal to 2.49, 1.65 and 2.88, respectively for sidestick, gamepad and touchscreen).

## 4    Conclusions and Future Work

The purpose of the study was to compare pilot's behaviour using three different inceptors - conventional sidestick, Xbox gamepad and novel touchscreen controller. The two formed hypotheses were checked against the results and confirmed to be true in most cases. While there is still a lot of work in touchscreen technology in flight decks and there is a long way before replacing the physical inceptors with digital ones, this research shows that even though the touchscreen controller scored the lowest on a SUS, majority of pilots were able to put the aircraft on the ground in this challenging circumstances. As this was only a 'pilot study', the conclusions made based on the experimental results were mostly applicable to airline pilots who have already had training and experience with conventional inceptors. This could have introduced bias in the statistical metrics because they lacked the same training on the other alternative inceptors. Future tests will include comparison of pilots with non-pilots to see the effect of learnability: non-pilots will not have any experience in using the sidestick, hence they won't be biased by the habits learned in flying schools. Further research will be conducted to find participants with no experience in neither of the controllers.

**Acknowledgements.** Co-financed by the European Union through the European Social Fund (grant POWR.03.02.00-00-I029) and E-PILOTS project (Clean Sky 2 Joint Undertaking (JU) under grant agreement No 831993) and Powerplant Integration of Novel Engine Systems (PINES) project, UKRI project reference 113263.

## References

1. Efremov, A.V., Efremov, E.V., MbiKayi, Z., Irgaleev, I.K.: Influence of inceptors on pilot-aircraft system characteristics and flying qualities. IOP Conf. Ser.: Mater. Sci. Eng. **476**, 012010 (2019). https://doi.org/10.1088/1757-899X/476/1/012010
2. Efremov, A., Aleksandrov, V., Efremov, E., Vukolov, M.: The influence of different types of inceptors and their characteristics on the pilot-aircraft system. IFAC-PapersOnLine **51**(34), 372–377 (2019). https://doi.org/10.1016/j.ifacol.2019.01.013
3. Harper, R.P., Cooper, G.E.: Handling qualities and pilot evaluation. J. Guidance Control Dyn. **9**(5), 515–529 (1986). https://doi.org/10.2514/3.20142
4. Hodgkinson, J.: History of low-order equivalent systems for aircraft flying qualities. J. Guidance Control Dyn. **28**(4), 577–583 (2005). https://doi.org/10.2514/1.3787
5. In, J.: Introduction of a pilot study. Korean J. Anesthesiol. **70**(6), 601 (2017). https://doi.org/10.4097/kjae.2017.70.6.601

6. Klyde, D.H., Schulze, P.C., Mitchell, D., Alexandrov, N.: Development of a process to define unmanned aircraft systems handling qualities Reston, Virginia. In: 2018 AIAA Atmospheric Flight Mechanics Conference. American Institute of Aeronautics and Astronautics (2018). https://doi.org/10.2514/6.2018-0299

7. Korek, W.T., Mendez, A., Asad, H.U., Li, W.-C., Lone, M.: Understanding human behaviour in flight operation using eye-tracking technology. In: Harris, D., Li, W.-C. (eds.) HCII 2020. LNCS (LNAI), vol. 12187, pp. 304–320. Springer, Cham (2020). https://doi.org/10.1007/978-3-030-49183-3_24

8. Li, W.C., Bord, T., Zhang, J., Braithwaite, G., Lone, M.: Evaluating system usability of augmented reality in flight operations. In: Contemporary Ergonomics and Human Factors (2020)

9. Lone, M.: Pilot modelling for airframe loads analysis. Ph.D. thesis. Cranfield University (2013)

10. McLellan, S., Muddimer, A., Peres, S.: The effect of experience on system usability scale ratings. J. Usability Stud. **7**(2), 56–67 (2012)

11. McRuer, D., Jex, H.: A review of quasi-linear pilot models. IEEE Trans. Hum. Factors Electron. **HFE–8**(3), 231–249 (1967). https://doi.org/10.1109/THFE.1967.234304

12. Norton, F.H.: The measurement of the damping in roll on a JN4h in flight. Technical report, US Government Printing Office (1923)

13. Tomczyk, A.: Experimental fly-by-wire control system for general aviation aircraft. In: AIAA Guidance, Navigation, and Control Conference and Exhibition (2003). https://doi.org/10.2514/6.2003-5776

14. Wolfert, F., Bromfield, M.A., Stedmon, A., Scott, S.: Passive sidesticks and hard landings - is there a link? In: AIAA Aviation 2019 Forum, pp. 1–10 (2019). https://doi.org/10.2514/6.2019-3611

15. Wright, O., Wright, W.: The Wright brothers' aeroplane. Aeronaut. J.(London, England: 1897) **20**(79), 100–106 (1916). https://doi.org/10.1017/S2398187300142525

16. Zaychik, L.E., Grinev, K.N., Yashin, Y.P., Sorokin, S.A.: Effect of feel system characteristics on pilot model parameters. IFAC-PapersOnLine **49**(32), 165–170 (2016). https://doi.org/10.1016/j.ifacol.2016.12.208

# Assessments on Human-Computer Interaction Using Touchscreen as Control Inputs in Flight Operations

Wen-Chin Li[1(✉)], Yung-Hsiang Liang[1], Wojciech Tomasz Korek[2,3],
and John J. H. Lin[4]

[1] Safety and Accident Investigation Centre, Cranfield University, Cranfield, UK
Wenchin.li@cranfield.ac.uk
[2] Dynamics, Simulation and Control Group, Cranfield University, Cranfield, UK
[3] Faculty of Automatic Control, Electronics and Computer Science, Silesian University of
Technology, Gliwice, Poland
[4] Institute of Science Education, National Taiwan Normal University, Taipei, Republic of China

**Abstract.** The developing technology on innovative touchscreen applied in the cockpit can integrate control inputs and outputs on the same display in flight operations. Flight systems could be updated by modifying the touchscreen user interface without the complicated processes on reconfiguring cockpit panels. There is a potential risk on touchscreen components constrained by the issues associated with inadvertent touch, which may be defined as any system detectable touch issued to the touch sensors without the pilot's operational consent. Pilots' visual behaviours can be explored by using eye trackers to analyze the relationship between eye scan patterns and attention shifts while conducting monitoring tasks in flight operations. This research aims to evaluate human-computer interactions using eye tracker to investigate the safety concerns on implementation of touchscreen in flight operations. The scenario was set to conduct an instrument landing on the final approach using future system simulator. Participants were required to interact with all the control surfaces and checklists using the touchscreens located on different areas in the cockpit. Each participant performed landing scenario as pilot-flying (PF) and pilot-monitoring (PM) in random sequence. Currently PF and PM perform different tasks related to control inputs and control outputs monitoring in the flight deck. The PF's primary obligation is to fly the aircraft's flight path, and the PM's main responsibility is to monitor the aircraft's flight path and cross-check to the PF's operational behaviours. By analyzing participants' visual behaviours and scanning patterns, the findings on HCI related to applying touchscreen for future flight deck design would be applicable. There are some benefits on the implementation touchscreen for future flight deck design if the human-centred design principle can be integrated in the early stage.

**Keywords:** Attention distribution · Flight deck touchscreen · Human-computer interactions · System usability · Visual behaviours

# 1   Introduction

The applicability of touchscreen in modern flight deck has been investigated for a long time. There is a potential risk on touchscreen components constrained by the issues associated with inadvertent touch, which may be defined as any system detectable touch issued to the touch sensors without the pilot's operational consent. That is, a pilot may activate touchscreen control buttons inadvertently because of turbulence, vibrations, or aspects of the pilot's physical and cognitive workload which may have serious consequence of operational error and incidents [1]. The developing technology on innovative touchscreen applied in the cockpit can integrate control inputs and outputs in the same display on flight operations. Flight systems could be updated by modifying the touchscreen user interface without the complicated processes on reconfiguring cockpit panels. Other advantages of touchscreen including reduced space and weight, improved operational efficiency and accessibility [2, 3]. However, air turbulence and factors caused to aircraft vibration are the challenges for the potential use of touchscreen in flight operations. Previous research revealed that moderate levels of simulated turbulence could increase data entry times on touchscreen, error rates, fatigue, and perceived workload while compared with no turbulence scenario [4]. Previous research demonstrated that an effective method for determining if a control button on a touch screen device has been inadvertently touched using eye tracking technology [5].

Visual behaviours can be explored by using eye trackers to analyze the relationship between eye scan patterns and attention shifts while conducting monitoring tasks in flight operations [6]. Eye scan pattern is one of the methods for assessing a pilot's cognitive process and situation awareness (SA) in the cockpit based on physiological measures [7]. Furthermore, eye movements are a sensitive and automatic response that may serve as a window into the process of pilots' mechanism of situational awareness (SA) and reflect their mental state [8]. Fixation is defined as the eye movement pausing over informative stimulus for the purposes of interpreting the information [9]. The patterns of fixations on the areas of interest (AOIs) can reveal a pilot's visual trajectory of attention on the processing tasks [10]. Fixation duration is the total time fixating on an instrument that can reflect the level of importance or difficulty in extracting information [11]. The nature of human beings is such that they tend to distribute longer fixation duration to relevant AOIs than to those irrelevant areas [12]. Attention blurring is characterized by small number of fixations and increased number of transitions between instruments and not able to actually interpret the information [13]. Pilot's scan patterns and visual parameters have been successfully applied to evaluate the performance of situational awareness during flight operations. Eye tracking technology has been applied to evaluate pilot's situation awareness and human-computer interactions to validate the effectiveness of aviation training and flight deck design. Visual characteristics can reveal pilots' attentional distributions and provide scientific evidence to assess pilots' cognitive process. Figure 1 demonstrated while interacted with augmented design, pilots' pupil dilations are smaller and fixation duration are shorter compared with traditional design [14].

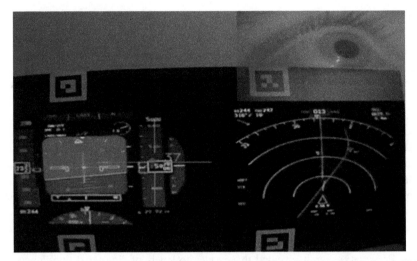

**Fig. 1.** Pilot's fixation at the altitude indicator (red-cross) and pupil dilation (right-hand side) on augmented design of PFD recorded by Pupil Eye Tracker (from [14]) (Color figure online)

Visual parameters are objective data reflected to cognitive costs on task performance which are relevant to the HCI issues on applications of touchscreen in the flight deck design. Attention distorting is described by small number of fixations and increased number of transitions between instruments and not able to actually interpret the information [13]. Pilot's scan patterns and visual parameters have been successfully applied to evaluate the performance of situational awareness during flight operations. Eye tracking technology has been applied to evaluate pilot's situation awareness and human-computer interactions to validate the effectiveness of flight deck design [10]. The evaluating HCI issues on touchscreen applications should be covered the finger and hand occlusion in the flight deck setting using eye tracking technology. Some of the errors observed in previous studies were likely due to the finger and hand occluding targets, and in the safety critical cockpit environment it is important to know whether bracing postures increases susceptibility to this type of error [1]. Furthermore, prior findings show that humans adapt their hand postures as they move towards targets, in preparation for a suitable grip once contact is obtained [15]. In a similar manner, the principle on HCI research may have to explore how pilots manipulating their fingers towards target buttons in the complicated operational environments while a braced touch posture is aimed. To ensure operational safety, the pilot-flying (PF) and the pilot-monitoring (PM) must conduct cross checks by moving their head and eyes to the levers and displays on different positions in the flight deck. The application of touchscreen technology in this area can reduce pilots' head-down time and to increase SA, which is a significant advantage of using touch screens. However, the application of touchscreen in the flight deck may inadvertently create some safety concerns during hazardous situations including turbulence and vibration scenarios which are stressful for pilots on precisely controlling the aircraft [16]. Therefore, implementation of touchscreen on the flight deck must demonstrate high usability and safety requirements with regards to human-centered design.

## 2   Method

### 2.1   Participants

There are 12 participants aged from 21 to 53 years old (M = 29.92, SD = 10.97) with varying levels of flight experience (M = 1150, SD = 4019.9) attended in this research. The research proposal was submitted to Research Ethics System for ethical approval before conducting data collection. As stated in the consent form, participants are anonymous and have the right to terminate the experiment at any time and to withdraw their provided data at any moment even after the data collection.

### 2.2   Research Apparatus

Future Systems Simulator (FSS): research apparatus has applied the Rolls-Royce award-winning FSS, which provided the ability to quickly model current and future aircraft configurations [17]. The FSS is a highly reconfigurable modular flight simulator, in which seat positions, displays, side sticks, thrust levers and touchscreens can be repositioned (Fig. 2). The FSS builds reassuringly on familiar aircraft controls, with information presented on up to four large reconfigurable touchscreens and two smaller side screens. This allows pilots to explore the potential impact on future flight decks design for single pilot operations including smarter, more autonomous engines, as well as revolutionary new technologies.

**Fig. 2.** Participant wears eye tracker performing landing scenario as pilot-flying interacting with touchscreen on Future Systems Simulator

Pupil Labs core: A light-weight eye tracker which consists of a headset and two cameras for participant's visual behaviours and pupil dilation data. The eye camera is connected to the eye camera via the ball joint allowing six degrees of rotation to get a good image of the eye. The world camera can rotate up and down to align with participant's field of view (FOV). There are four areas of interests (AOIs) identified as follows: Primary Flight Display (PFD), Navigation Display (ND), Checklist Display (CD) and Central Upper Display (CUD), containing mode control panel for autopilot control, engine display and digital levers for flaps, Landing Gear and spoilers. The 'world-camera' is mounted on the right top of the headset showing the orientation and view of participant's FOV and the eye-camera is mounted offset right and low and is adjustable to suit different facial layout and track their pupil parameters accordingly [18]. Data recorded by two cameras can be synchronized after calibration.

### 2.3  Scenario

The scenario used in the trail is an instrument landing which participants were required to interact with flaps, landing gears and spoilers and checklists using touchscreen located on different areas in the flight deck. Based on the standard operational procedures (SOPs). Pilot-flying is expected to coordinate with pilot-monitoring to perform cross-check. Therefore, each participant has to conduct two landing scenarios randomly to eliminate practice effects.

### 2.4  Research Design

This research involved in assessing HCI in flight operations using innovative touchscreen in the FSS and eye tracking device. All participants undertook the following procedures; (1) complete the demographical data including age, gender, working experience and total flight hours (5 min); (2) briefing the purpose of the study and familiarized with touchscreen layouts (15 min); (3) seat in simulator for calibration on eye tracker (5–10 min); (4) perform the scenario on instrument landing as pilot-flying or pilot-monitoring randomly to eliminate practice effects (10–15 min); (5) debriefing and answering participants' questions (5 min). It took around 50 min for each participant to complete the experiments.

### 2.5  Data Analysis

The fixation counts (FC) and fixation duration (FD) were used to measure pilots' visual behaviours on HCI in the flight deck. Both FC and FD were adopted in other studies focused on flight deck design and the results suggested these two visual parameters were effective on detecting pilots' visual attention and evaluating SA in flight operations [10, 19]. For each participant, eye movement parameters on both fixation duration and fixation counts were collected for data analysis using Pupil Player. These two measures are sensitive to the visual responses when a participant was synchronously performing the instrument landing on both PM's or PF's positions. Participants consecutive gaze points that fall into a circle with a radius with 1.5 degree and a duration longer than 150 ms is defined as a fixation point in current study. Specifically, there are three research questions as followings:

RQ1. What is the difference between PFs and PMs on fixation counts for four AOIs?
RQ2. What is the difference between PFs and PMs on fixation duration for four AOIs?
RQ3. What are the correlations among AOIs?

## 3  Results

### 3.1  Sample Characteristics

Given each participant performed both roles on PF and PM randomly, repeated measure-based analysis was conducted throughout this study. In addition, Pearson's correlation analysis is applied to evaluate eye movement parameters among Primary Flight Display, Navigation Display, Checklist Display and Central Upper Display between PFs and PMs. Furthermore, repeated measure analysis of variance (RM-ANOVA) was conducted to compare the difference between PFs and PMs on the fixation duration and fixation counts among four AOIs. The assumption of sphericity was examined in terms of the Mauchly's test. Suppose the assumption of sphericity is violated, the results of multivariate tests would be used. Post-hoc analysis was performed using the Bonferroni correction after a significant effect is confirmed [20]. The effect size of RM-ANOVA was evaluated by partial eta-square [21]. Table 1 shows the descriptive statistics of FC and FD among four AOIs between PF and PM.

**Table 1.** Descriptive statistics of mean and standard deviation for online and offline measures.

| Measures | PF | | | PM | | |
|---|---|---|---|---|---|---|
| | N | Mean | STD | N | Mean | STD |
| CD_FC | 12 | 3.83 | 6.87 | 11 | 54.18 | 15.37 |
| CD_FD | 12 | 171.02 | 137.14 | 11 | 252.21 | 32.44 |
| CUD_FC | 12 | 19.58 | 22.56 | 11 | 50.27 | 11.87 |
| CUD_FD | 12 | 248.10 | 44.90 | 11 | 245.36 | 48.76 |
| ND_FC | 12 | 21.17 | 13.19 | 11 | 59.64 | 71.89 |
| ND_FD | 12 | 244.37 | 36.82 | 11 | 249.57 | 59.82 |
| PFD_FC | 12 | 120.75 | 75.47 | 11 | 119.64 | 65.40 |
| PFD_FD | 12 | 302.79 | 76.39 | 11 | 302.62 | 61.71 |
| Total_FC | 12 | 388.92 | 106.93 | 11 | 388.09 | 146.82 |

### 3.2  Visual Parameters Among AOIs

To evaluate the visual attention and scanning patterns between PFs and PMs, it is suitable to apply RM_ANOVA with AOIs as the factor was computed. The main research interest is whether participants spent more time fixating on a specific AOI. The results suggested

FC on AOIs were different for PFs, F(3, 9) = 10.58, $p = .003$, $\eta_p^2 = .78$. Post-hoc analysis suggested PFs focused on PFD more frequently than Checklist Display (CD), Central Upper Display (CUD) and Navigation Display (ND). In addition, PFs focused on ND more frequently than CD. For PMs, results suggested FC on AOIs were different, F(3, 8) = 8.69, $p = .007$, $\eta_p^2 = .77$. Post-hoc analysis suggested PMs focused on PFD more frequently than CD and ND. Figure 3 illustrates FC on the four AOIs for PFs and PMs.

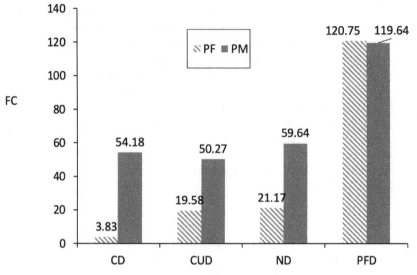

**Fig. 3.** An illustration of FC on the four AOIs for PFs and PMs.

Regarding FD, results suggested FD on AOIs were different for PFs, F(3, 9) = 10.10, $p = .003$, $\eta_p^2 = .77$. Post-hoc analysis suggested PFs focused on PFD longer than CD. For PMs, results suggested FD on AOIs were different, F(3, 8) = 5.57, $p = .023$, $\eta_p^2 = .68$. Post-hoc analysis suggested PMs focused on PFD longer than CD. Figure 4 illustrates FD on the four AOIs for PFs and PMs.

### 3.3 Correlations Between PM and PF's Visual Parameters Among AOIs

The results suggested significant positive correlations among eye movements. For examples fixation counts on between PM and PF, $\gamma = .65$, p < .05. There is a negative correlation between fixation count and fixation duration on CUD, $\gamma = -.68$, p < .05. Furthermore, there is significant correlations among eye movement measures. To avoid redundancy, please refer to Table 2 which shows the correlations on PM and PF's visual parameters among AOIs. In addition, the number of significant correlation coefficients for PFs are smaller than that of PMs.

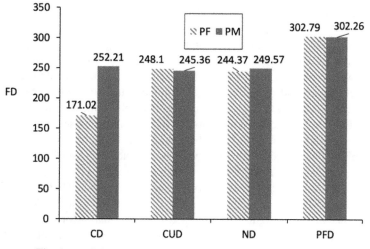

**Fig. 4.** An illustration of FD on the four AOIs for PFs and PMs

**Table 2.** Correlation coefficients and p values for eye movement measures among AOIs

| PF | PM | | | | | | | | |
|---|---|---|---|---|---|---|---|---|---|
| | 1 | 2 | 3 | 4 | 5 | 6 | 7 | 8 | 9 |
| 1. CD_FC | 1 | −0.18 | 0.04 | −0.54 | 0.23 | −0.54 | 0.57 | −0.01 | 0.51 |
| 2. CD_FD | 0.36 | 1 | .774** | .687* | −0.60 | 0.56 | −0.58 | .631* | −.798** |
| 3. CUD_FC | .647* | .632* | 1 | 0.39 | −.606* | 0.23 | −.648* | .611* | −.621* |
| 4. CUD_FD | 0.16 | 0.17 | 0.39 | 1 | −0.20 | .777** | −.656* | 0.47 | −.641* |
| 5. ND_FC | −0.18 | 0.16 | 0.28 | 0.11 | 1 | 0.03 | .632* | −0.54 | .765** |
| 6. ND_FD | −0.24 | −0.06 | 0.16 | 0.17 | .640* | 1 | −0.43 | 0.10 | −0.42 |
| 7. PFD_FC | 0.07 | 0.20 | 0.14 | −.684* | 0.31 | 0.09 | 1 | −0.36 | .768** |
| 8. PFD_FD | 0.04 | 0.54 | 0.52 | 0.21 | 0.34 | 0.56 | 0.28 | 1 | −.655* |
| 9. Total_FC | 0.39 | −0.03 | 0.42 | −0.05 | 0.38 | −0.15 | 0.24 | −0.33 | 1 |

Note: 1. Lower triangle show correlations for PFs; upper triangle show correlations for PMs.
2. $p < .05^*, p < .01^{**}$.

## 4  Discussion

Touchscreen could be an innovative design for improving human performance in the flight deck if it followed human-centered design principles. Modern technologies have paved the way to recreate high fidelity flight scenarios in the safe simulated environment. Developments and research in flight simulation technology have resulted in the Future Systems Simulator (FSS) with touch-screen display which can model all types of advanced aircraft. While advanced technology shows many promises, one must consider HCI challenges and pilots' operational behaviours and limitations [22]. This research assessed PF and PM's visual behaviours while using touchscreen on the FSS. Moreover, practical applications from a HCI standpoint are discussed.

The difference among four AOIs on fixation count is significant between PF and PM. PFs focused on PFD more frequently than CD, CUD and ND (Table 1 and Fig. 3). The result suggested that PFD might be the main source of information for instrument landing, since all the flight data that correlated with maintaining the aircraft attitude (angle of attack, air speed, altitude, vertical speed) are all displayed on the PFD. Additionally, PFs focused on ND more frequently than CD. Similarly, PMs focused on PFD more frequently than CD and ND. Another finding is that PMs had more FC on CD, CUD, and ND, except on PFD. This could be due to the fact that PMs required evaluating whether the operations of PFs were following the standard operating procedures (SOPs) by cross-checking the aircraft configuration with checklist display. Therefore, PMs needed to validate by checking CD, CUD, and ND more often than PFs to ensure the aircraft configuration is correct on final approach which may lead to more FC on the three AOIs for PM. In contrast, PFs need to perform landing in a limited time frame. Therefore, the FC of PFs is fewer than that of PMs on those three AOIs in the flight deck but more FC on the runway and precision approach path indicators (PAPIs) shown in Fig. 5.

**Fig. 5.** PF's fixations switching between the centre of runway and cockpit displays demonstrated the attention distributions to maintain SA (left); PM's scanning patterns and fixations moving around AOIs to conduct cross-check with PF's operational procedures for instrument landing (right)

The results also demonstrated that there is a significant difference among four AOIs on fixation duration between PF and PM. PFs focused on PFD longer than on CD (Table 1) demonstrate that PFD might be the main source of information for instrument landing, whereas all the critical information related flight operation are presented on this AOI. Similarly, PMs focused on PFD with longer fixation duration than CD. Furthermore, the results reveal that fixation duration at each AOI for PFs are roughly equal to PMs, except CD, in which PMs had longer fixation duration than that that for PFs. Such findings provided valuable information regarding minimal fixation duration that were necessary for PFs and PMs to extract information from CUD, ND, and PFD are roughly equal. On the other hand, as a PM, the fixation duration required to extract information and validated cross-check to PFs' operational behaviours from CD taken longer time.

There are significant correlations among four AOIs on visual parameters between PM and PF. The numbers of significant correlation coefficients for PFs are smaller than PMs. In other words, PFs inclined to make a decision after cross-checking 1–2 AOIs; while PMs inclined to cross-check more AOIs to confirm PFs' operational responses and decision-making following SOPs. Such differences might result from different tasks to be done between PFs and PMs inherently on the current design principles for two-pilots flight deck design. As a PF, the main task is to perform a safe landing task; in contrast, a PM is expected to validate the operations of PFs operational behaviours and providing necessary support to maintain safety in flight operations, which could lead to more cross-checking than PFs. Another finding is that PMs switched the attention among AOIs more frequently, and the durations tend to be longer as well. In summary, for a PMs to complete their task, more cross-checking and fixation counts with longer fixation duration are required.

To understand PM and PF' experience, there was a feedback session after the experiment was completed for the de-briefing. Both PF and PM expressed that information was clearly presented on the touchscreens, but important control buttons were initially difficult to find. Especially the layout of the flight-deck changed between PF and PM set-ups and looked different with current flight deck layout. However, as the experiment progressed, PF and PM found these touchscreen controls easier to locate after becoming familiar with the layout of displays. They also felt that selecting flaps and gear requires more cognitive attention when using touchscreens compared to conventional levers, hence monitoring performance of the PM may temporarily be compromised. Therefore, extra time was required to ensure the correct selection was made as PM conducting cross-check to PF's flight operations and control inputs alongside with checklists. This phenomenon may detract PM's attention and require extra time to confirm the SOPs during critical phases of landing. It should also be noted that the experiment was performed in a normal operational environment, yet turbulence could exacerbate the problems on the above scenario.

Currently PF and PM perform different tasks related to control inputs and control outputs monitoring in the flight deck. The PF's primary obligation is to fly the aircraft's flight path including managing the automated flight systems, and the PM's main responsibility is to monitor the aircraft's flight path and to immediately bring any concern to the PF's attention including radio communications, aircraft systems, other operational activities. Therefore, there are differences on the attention distributions among AOIs in the flight deck between PF and PM (Fig. 6). The system usability of touchscreen has been proved as beneficial to pilots' situation awareness on flight operations in normal operational environment [23] their visual behaviours associated with task executions and monitoring while interacting with touchscreen were analyzed using eye tracking technology in current study. The application of touchscreens in the flight deck may have the potential for single pilot operations in the future, but the design of touchscreen must be consistent with human factors principles on cross-monitoring and integrated information to improve usability and pilots' situation awareness in flight operations.

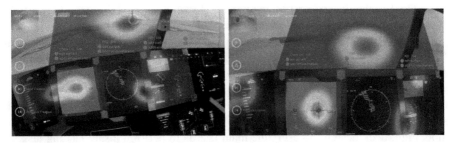

**Fig. 6.** Attention distributions among different displays on the flight deck shown as heatmap between PF (left) and PM (right)

## 5   Conclusion

By analyzing participants' visual behaviours and scanning patterns, the findings on HCI related to applying touchscreen for future flight deck design would be applicable. There are some benefits on the implementation of touchscreen for future flight deck design if the human-centered design principle can be integrated in the early stage. Furthermore, there are different requirements for PF and PM's tasks in the current flight deck, whereby the cognitive workload and the attention distributions on monitoring performance are different. The significant differences of FC between PFs and PMs have been demonstrated in the heatmap (Fig. 6) and the illustration above (Fig. 2). Task for PMs was mainly concentrating on monitoring the flight data, conducting the checklist, and manipulating the control for PFs, whereas PFs were relatively focused on controlling the aircraft attitude and the altitude in the landing scenario. The potential limitations should be taken into account on current research, first limitation is the small sample size, which could lead to small effect sizes. To validate the findings, a large sample size would suffice for future study; the second limitation would be the difficulty of defining an AOI for outside view, which is one of the most common areas that pilots are fixating on outside cockpit. Various attention distributions between PFs and PMs could be identified by using eye tracking technology. Despite these limitations might have impacts to the contributions on current research, the innovative FSS touchscreen is an effective testbed for future flight deck design.

**Acknowledgements.** Co-financed by the European Union through the European Social Fund (grant POWR.03.02.00-00-I029).

# References

1. Cockburn, A., et al.: Design and evaluation of braced touch for touchscreen input stabilisation. Int. J. Hum Comput Stud. **122**, 21–37 (2019). https://doi.org/10.1016/j.ijhcs.2018.08.005
2. Zammit-Mangion, D., Becouarn, L., Aymeric, B., Fabbri, M., Bader, J.: A single interactive display concept for commercial and business jet cockpits (2011). https://doi.org/10.2514/6.2011-7062
3. Komer, J.L., Gepner, J.E., Hogan, R.K., Mabie, T.D.: Avionics control and display unit having cursor control mode of operation. US Patent App. 13/438,613. US Patent App. 13/438,613 (2013)
4. Dodd, S., Lancaster, J., Miranda, A., Grothe, S., DeMers, B., Rogers, B.: Touch screens on the flight deck: the impact of touch target size, spacing, touch technology and turbulence on pilot performance. In: Proceedings of the Human Factors and Ergonomics Society Annual Meeting, vol. 58, pp. 6–10 (2014). https://doi.org/10.1177/1541931214581002
5. Kawalkar, A.N.: Touch screen and method for providing stable touches. US Patent App. 13/162,679 (2012)
6. Ahlstrom, U., Friedman-Berg, F.J.: Using eye movement activity as a correlate of cognitive workload. Int. J. Ind. Ergon. **36**, 623–636 (2006). https://doi.org/10.1016/j.ergon.2006.04.002
7. Yu, C.-S., Wang, E., Li, W.-C., Braithwaite, G.: Pilots' visual scan patterns and situation awareness in flight operations. Aviation **85** (2014). https://doi.org/10.3357/ASEM.3847.2014
8. Kuo, F.-Y., Hsu, C.-W., Day, R.-F.: An exploratory study of cognitive effort involved in decision under framing—an application of the eye-tracking technology. Decis. Support Syst. **48**, 81–91 (2009). https://doi.org/10.1016/j.dss.2009.06.011
9. Salvucci, D., Goldberg, J.: Identifying fixations and saccades in eye-tracking protocols (2000). https://doi.org/10.1145/355017.355028
10. Li, W.-C., Zhang, J., Le Minh, T., Cao, J., Wang, L.: Visual scan patterns reflect to human-computer interactions on processing different types of messages in the flight deck. Int. J. Ind. Ergon. **72**, 54–60 (2019). https://doi.org/10.1016/j.ergon.2019.04.003
11. Durso, F., Sethumadhavan, A.: Situation awareness: understanding dynamic environments. Hum. Factors **50**, 442–448 (2008). https://doi.org/10.1518/001872008X288448
12. McColeman, C.M., Blair, M.R.: The relationship between saccade velocity, fixation duration, and salience in category learning. Vis. Cogn. **21**, 701–703 (2013). https://doi.org/10.1080/13506285.2013.844965
13. Kilingaru, K., Tweedale, J., Thatcher, S., Jain, L.: Monitoring pilot "Situation Awareness." J. Intell. Fuzzy Syst. Appl. Eng. Technol. **24**, 457–466 (2013). https://doi.org/10.3233/IFS-2012-0566
14. Li, W.-C., Horn, A., Sun, Z., Zhang, J., Braithwaite, G.: Augmented visualization cues on primary flight display facilitating pilot's monitoring performance. Int. J. Hum Comput Stud. **135**, 102377 (2020). https://doi.org/10.1016/j.ijhcs.2019.102377
15. Klatzky, R.L., Lederman, S.J.: Touch. In: Weiner, I., Healy, A., Proctor, R. (eds.) Handbook of Psychology, vol. Experimental Psychology, pp. 152-176. Wiley, Hoboken (2013)
16. Cockburn, A., et al.: Turbulent touch: touchscreen input for cockpit flight displays. In: Proceedings of the 2017 CHI Conference on Human Factors in Computing Systems, Denver, Colorado, USA, pp. 6742–6753. Association for Computing Machinery (2017). https://doi.org/10.1145/3025453.3025584
17. Korek, W.T., Mendez, A., Asad, H.U., Li, W.-C., Lone, M.: Understanding human behaviour in flight operation using eye-tracking technology. In: Harris, D., Li, W.-C. (eds.) HCII 2020. LNCS (LNAI), vol. 12187, pp. 304–320. Springer, Cham (2020). https://doi.org/10.1007/978-3-030-49183-3_24

18. Kassner, M., Patera, W., Bulling, A.: Pupil: an open source platform for pervasive eye tracking and mobile gaze-based interaction. In: Proceedings of the 2014 ACM International Joint Conference on Pervasive and Ubiquitous Computing: Adjunct Publication, Seattle, Washington, pp. 1151–1160. Association for Computing Machinery (2014). https://doi.org/10.1145/263 8728.2641695

19. Li, W.-C., Yu, C.-S., Braithwaite, G., Greaves, M.: Pilots' attention distributions between chasing a moving target and a stationary target. Aerosp. Med. Hum. Perform. **87**, 989–995 (2016). https://doi.org/10.3357/AMHP.4617.2016

20. Barrett, K.C., Morgan, J., George, A.: SPSS for Intermediate Statistics: Use and Interpretation. Psychology Press (2005)

21. Haase, R.F.: Classical and partial eta square in multifactor ANOVA designs. Educ. Psychol. Measur. **43**, 35–39 (1983). https://doi.org/10.1177/001316448304300105

22. Carroll, M., Dahlstrom, N.: Human computer interaction on the modern flight deck. Int. J. Hum.-Comput. Interact. **37**, 585–587 (2021). https://doi.org/10.1080/10447318.2021.189 0495

23. Coutts, L.V., et al.: Future technology on the flight deck: assessing the use of touchscreens in vibration environments. Ergonomics **62**, 286–304 (2019). https://doi.org/10.1080/00140139. 2018.1552013

# Establishment of a Situation Awareness Analysis Model for Flight Crew Alerting

Xianxue Li[✉]

Shanghai Aircraft Design and Research Institute, No. 5188 JinKe Road, PuDong New District, Shanghai 201210, China
lixianxue@comac.cc

**Abstract.** Flight crew should maintain a sufficient situation awareness during flight especially during abnormal and emergency situation. In order to analyze the situation awareness requirement, this study combines the GDTA method proposed by Endsley (goal-oriented task analysis) and FCM (fuzzy cognitive map) to establish a situation awareness model. It is more scientific to obtain the critical factors related to situation awareness in the process of handling the flight crew alerting.

**Keywords:** Civil aircraft · Situation awareness · Model

## 1 Introduction

When some parts of an aircraft are fault or in abnormal flight status, flight crew alerting information will be prompted to the flight crew to help them acknowledge the malfunction and timely perform appropriate procedure to eliminate the influence of malfunction to ensure the flight safety during all the flight phase.

If the flight crew fails to obtain sufficient situation awareness, the flight crew may incorrectly judge the situation, and take inappropriate operations to deal with the abnormal status in time which may result in some flight accident. According to accident statistics, 88% of flight accidents are caused due to flight crew's failure to establish sufficient situation awareness. It can be seen that establishing a good situation awareness during flight is very important for the flight crew to quickly and accurately take appropriate procedure to eliminate the malfunction. Therefore, when designing the HMI of flight crew alerting system, it is important to ensure that the flight crew can obtain the required information. In order to know which information is needed to establish situation awareness and which factors affect situation awareness, we have analyzed the factors related to situation awareness and a situation awareness model is established.

This study combines the GDTA method proposed by Endsley (goal-oriented task analysis) and FCM (fuzzy cognitive map) [1] to establish a situation awareness model. It is more scientific to obtain the critical factors related to situation awareness in the process of handling the flight crew alerting.

© The Author(s), under exclusive license to Springer Nature Switzerland AG 2022
D. Harris and W.-C. Li (Eds.): HCII 2022, LNAI 13307, pp. 339–348, 2022.
https://doi.org/10.1007/978-3-031-06086-1_26

## 2  Methods

The GDTA model contains the following steps: Objective (Goals), Decision-making (Decisions), and Scenario Awareness Needs (SA Requirement).

The specific steps of GDTA are shown in Fig. 1.

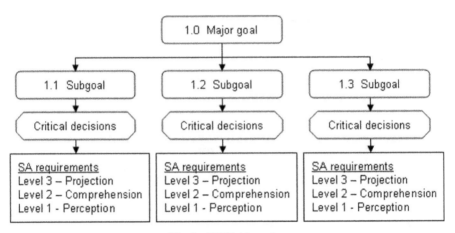

**Fig. 1.**  GDTA hierarchy

Bart Kosko introduced a fuzzy set theory on the basis of Robert Axelrod cognitive graph in 1980s and put forward the concept of fuzzy cognitive graph (FCM). The Fuzzy cognitive graph is a kind of causality expression based on people's experience. FCM method is simple and intuitive, It can directly reflect the process of the system's dynamic change and is used in the fields of accident analysis and risk assessment.

The following is the introduction of methods of establishing situation awareness model by combining GDTA and FCM.

First of all, we need to establish a GDTA model to obtain the critical factors related to situation awareness.

Firstly, the main tasks are divided into sub-tasks. Secondly, for each sub-task, the critical decisions needed to complete the sub-task are analyzed. Thirdly, according to the three steps of situation awareness analyze proposed by Endsley, it is necessary to carry out situation awareness analyze layer by layer for sub-tasks. The factors related to situation awareness and the critical information needed to establish situation awareness are obtained.

After that, each factor's influence weight on the situation awareness is analyzed through FCM method. Assume each factor is regarded as a node in the FCM, there are n nodes $C_1, C_2 \ldots\ldots C_n$ which represent n factors related to situation awareness. $A_i^t$ is the influence weight value of the ith node $C_i$ at $t$ time, then the influence weight value at next moment can be expressed as $A_i^{t+1}$,

$$A_i^{t+1} = f(A_i^t + \sum\nolimits_{j=1, j\neq i}^{n} A_j^t \omega_{ji})$$

According to the above formula, the state value of a node at the next moment is related to two factors, one is the current state value of the node, the other is the influence of other nodes on the node. $\omega_{ji}$ is the influence coefficient of the jth node on the ith node, and its value is obtained by expert evaluation. Assuming that there are n experts, the $k$ th expert's influence coefficient is $\omega_{ij}$, then the final value is of $\omega_{ij}$ is:

$$\omega_{ij} = \frac{\sum_{k=1}^{n} \omega_{ij}^k}{n}$$

The following causality matrices can be constructed:

$$W = \begin{bmatrix} 1, \omega_{12}, \omega_{13} \ldots \ldots \ldots \omega_{1n} \\ \omega_{21}, 1, \omega_{23} \ldots \ldots \ldots \omega_{2n} \\ \omega_{31}, \omega_{32}, 1 \ldots \ldots \ldots \omega_{3n} \\ \ldots \ldots \ldots \ldots \ldots \ldots \ldots \\ \ldots \ldots \ldots \ldots \ldots \ldots \ldots \\ \omega_{n1}, \omega_{n2} \ldots \ldots \ldots \ldots .1 \end{bmatrix} \quad W_{ij} = \begin{cases} \omega_{ij}, i \neq j \\ 1, i = j \end{cases}$$

Assuming $A^t = \left[A_1^t, A_2^t \ldots \ldots A_n^t\right]$ represent the state of each node at t time, then $A^{t+1} = f(A^t * W)$, which $f(x)$ is conversion function, where the variable of any numerical value is converted to the interval [0, 1]. There are many types for $f(x)$, and which type of function is used depends on the actual situation. There are several common used functions:

$$f(x) = \begin{cases} 0, x \leq 0.5 \\ 1, x > 0.5 \end{cases} \tag{1}$$

$$f(x) = \begin{cases} -1, x \leq -0.5 \\ 0, -0.5 < x < 0.5 \\ 1, x \geq 0.5 \end{cases} \tag{2}$$

$$f(x) = \frac{1}{1 + e^{-\lambda x}} \tag{3}$$

First, set the initial state values for each node: $A^0 = \left[A_1^0, A_2^0, A_3^0 \ldots A_n^0\right]$;
Then $A^1 = f(A^0 * W)$, $A^2 = f(A^1 * W) \ldots \ldots \ldots A^{t+1} = f(A^n * W)$, it iterates until the state value matrix A reaches a stable state. A stable state means that the value of each corresponding element in the matrix should be equal between $A^t$ and $A^{t+1}$ if it is a discrete function such as (1) (2), or the difference between the value of each corresponding element in the matrix should be less than 0.001 between $A^t$ and $A^{t+1}$ if it is a continuous function, for example (3). After reaching a stable state, the state value of each node corresponds to the influence weight of the influencing factors related to situation awareness.

For some tasks, after sub-task division, we need to determine the order of each sub-task, this can also be solved by FCM method which we can set $f(x)$ as a discrete function, taking each sub-task as a node, analyzing the change of the state value of each node after each iteration, then we can find out the order of each task.

Finally, though the situation awareness model we can obtain the influence factors related to situation awareness and their influence weight coefficient.

## 3   Model Application and Analysis

Based on the situation awareness model, we can study the influence factors during flight crew alerting processing. A case is used to show how the model is performed.

### 3.1   Main Steps

The main steps of situation awareness model are as follows:

- Set the flight crew alerting processing as general task, and divide it into several sub-tasks through GDTA method;
- Determine the sequence of sub-tasks by FCM method;
- Obtain the key factors required to complete each sub-task by GDTA method;
- Determine the influence weight coefficient of each key factor by FCM method.

### 3.2   Task Decomposition

Refer to the procedure during abnormal situation, the general task of flight crew alerting processing is divided into the following sub-tasks through GDTA method (Table 1).

**Table 1.** Task decomposition of flight crew alerting processing

| General task | Sub-tasks |
|---|---|
| Flight crew alerting processing during flight | Get informed of the meaning of alerting |
| | Make sure the causes of abnormal situation |
| | Make sure the flight phase and essential flight information such as location, speed, altitude and attitude |
| | Make sure the procedure to be performed |
| | Confirm whether the alerting is eliminated |

### 3.3   Operational Procedure

Firstly, the sequence of each sub-task is determined by FCM method. Set the 5 sub-tasks as key nodes to establish the FCM network which is shown in Fig. 2. Then the causality matrix $W$ is obtained by expert evaluation.

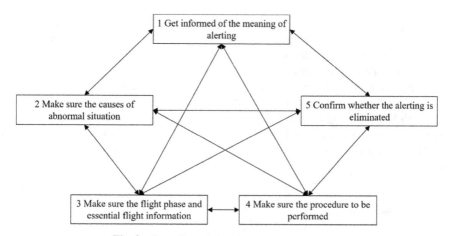

**Fig. 2.** Causality relationship between sub-tasks

$$W = \begin{bmatrix} 1.00, 0.92, 0.92, 0.33, 0.50 \\ 0.83, 1.00, 0.55, 0.91, 0.58 \\ 0.92, 0.92, 1.00, 0.92, 0.55 \\ 0.75, 0.58, 0.58, 1.00, 0.50 \\ 0.33, 0.33, 0.42, 0.67, 1.00 \end{bmatrix}$$

Then the initial value of state matrix A should be determined which means which sub-task starts first to process the alerting. By expert survey, sub-task 1 'Get informed of the meaning of alerting' should be performed first, then the initial valve of matrix A is [1, 0, 0, 0, 0]. Node 1 related with sub-task 1 equals 1 means this sub-task is completed while other nodes equal 0 means the sub-tasks are not completed yet.

The following value of matrix A after 4 iterations is shown as follows.

$$A^1 = f(1.00, 0.92, 0.92, 0.33, 0.50) = [1, 1, 1, 0, 0]$$

$$A^2 = f(2.75, 2.83, 2.46, 2.16, 1.63) = [1, 1, 1, 1, 1]$$

$$A^3 = f(3.83, 3.75, 3.47, 3.83, 3.13) = [1, 1, 1, 1, 1]$$

$$A^4 = f(3.83, 3.75, 3.47, 3.83, 3.13) = [1, 1, 1, 1, 1]$$

After 4 iterations, we can see that the state value of matrix A reaches stable. In $A^1$, state value equals 1 related with sub-tasks 2 and 3, and state value equals 0 related with sub-tasks 4 and 5, it means that sub-tasks 2 and 3 need to be performed after sub-task 1, however the state valve of sub-tasks 2 and 3 changes to 1 at the same time after 1 iteration, their sequence needs to be judged according to experience. After discussion, sub-task 2 is considered to be carried out first, followed by sub-task 3. Similarly, sub-tasks 4 and 5 need to be performed after sub-tasks 2 and 3 are completed. After discussion with experts, it is considered that task 4 should be carried out before task 5.

After all, the operational sequence of flight crew alerting processing is shown as in Fig. 3.

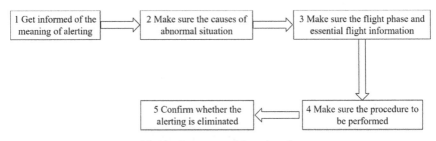

**Fig. 3.** Sequence of the sub-tasks

### 3.4 Influence Factors of Situation Awareness

The essential influence factors required to complete the sub-tasks is listed in Table 2 based on GDTA analysis.

**Table 2.** Key influence factors decomposition

| General | Order | Sub-tasks | Key influence factors | Order |
|---|---|---|---|---|
| Flight crew alerting processing | 1 | Get informed of the meaning of alerting | Alerting message received | 1 |
| | | | Understand the alerting message | 2 |
| | | | Check related display interface | 3 |
| | | | Check related indicator lights | 4 |

(*continued*)

**Table 2.** (*continued*)

| General | Order | Sub-tasks | Key influence factors | Order |
|---------|-------|-----------|-----------------------|-------|
| | 2 | Make sure the causes of abnormal situation | Aircraft's current status | 5 |
| | | | Status during abnormal condition | 6 |
| | | | Status during normal condition | 7 |
| | | | Information on the display interface | 8 |
| | 3 | Make sure the flight phase and essential flight information | Information on the display or instrument | 9 |
| | | | Get information from ground controls | 10 |
| | 4 | Make sure the procedure to be performed | Identify the alerting level and cause | 11 |
| | | | Check the procedure on the manual | 12 |
| | | | Refer to previous experience | 13 |
| | | | Related equipment and system's status | 14 |
| | | | Internal and external environment | 15 |
| | | | Flight condition and relative flight information | 16 |
| | 5 | Confirm whether the alerting is eliminated | Whether the flight status and relative flight parameter is normal | 17 |
| | | | Whether relative system and equipment is normal | 18 |
| | | | Whether alerting message disappears | 19 |
| | | | Whether fault indicator light goes off | 20 |

### 3.5 Influence Weight Coefficient

Since the information provided by the cockpit interface to the pilot is basically obtained through perception and direct acquisition, the impact of interface design on the pilot's situational awareness is mainly concentrated in the first level (i.e. perception level). Therefore, this paper mainly analyzes the influence degree of the first level (perception level) on the completion of tasks.

Take sub-task 1 'Get informed of the meaning of alerting' as an example. This sub-task has 4 key influence factors, which is shown in Fig. 4.

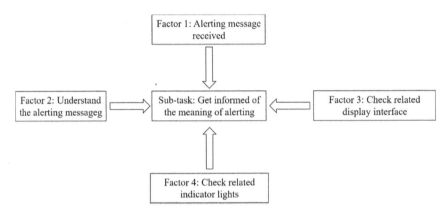

**Fig. 4.** Key influence factors of sub-task 1

Set each key influence factor as a node, there causality matrix is:

$$W = \begin{bmatrix} 1.00, 0.70, 0.92, 0.67 \\ 0.75, 1.00, 0.78, 0.75 \\ 0.75, 0.45, 1.00, 0.53 \\ 0.75, 0.60, 0.33, 1.00 \end{bmatrix}$$

Where the initial state value of the matrix A is $A = [0.97, 0.52, 1, 0.63]$ which is based on expert's experience. The larger the value, the more important the factor is to complete the task, and 1 indicates the factor is essential, 0 indicates the factor has no impact on completing the task.

Transformation function $f(x) = \frac{1}{1+e^{-0.5x}}$ is selected for multiple iterations, and the results is shown in Table 3.

According to the influence of various factors, the key information that the pilot needs to obtain to complete the task can be obtained, which has significant reference significance for designing the cockpit interface. For example, in sub-task 1, 'alerting message received' has the largest weight coefficient, therefore, when designing the cockpit interface, it is necessary to arrange the interface or indicator light relative with flight crew alerting in pilot's primary field of view to ensure that the pilot can notice the alerting information in time. It is also important to "check related display interface", so it is necessary to ensure that the pilot can obtain abnormal information on the display interface at any time.

**Table 3.** Weight coefficient of key influence factors

| Sub-task | Key influence factors | Weight coefficient |
|---|---|---|
| Get informed of the meaning of alerting | Alerting message received | 0.7740 |
| | Understand the alerting message | 0.7382 |
| | Check related display interface | 0.7593 |
| | Check related indicator lights | 0.7528 |

Similarly, the weight coefficients of the remaining sub-tasks can be obtained and is shown in Table 4.

**Table 4.** Weight coefficient of key influence factors for the remaining sub-tasks

| Sub-tasks | Key influence factors | Weight coefficient |
|---|---|---|
| Make sure the causes of abnormal situation | Aircraft's current status | 0.7655 |
| | Status during abnormal condition | 0.8150 |
| | Status during normal condition | 0.8147 |
| | Information on the display interface | 0.7655 |
| Make sure the flight phase and essential flight information | Information on the display or instrument | 0.7925 |
| | Get information from ground controls | 0.7299 |
| Make sure the procedure to be performed | Identify the alerting level and cause | 0.8490 |
| | Check the procedure on the manual | 0.8764 |
| | Refer to previous experience | 0.8256 |
| | Related equipment and system's status | 0.8383 |
| | Internal and external environment | 0.8020 |
| | Flight condition and relative flight information | 0.8511 |
| Confirm whether the alerting is eliminated | Whether the flight status and relative flight parameter is normal | 0.7814 |
| | Whether relative system and equipment is normal | 0.7814 |
| | Whether alerting message disappears | 0.7394 |
| | Whether fault indicator light goes off | 0.7292 |

Based on the above analysis, for the task 'flight crew alerting processing', the important information to be obtained includes: receiving the alerting message, abnormal instrument reading or interface display information, important flight parameters related to alerting, alerting related equipment and system's status, etc. When designing the cockpit interface, it is necessary to ensure that the pilot can obtain these information at any time, so as to help the pilot better maintain situational awareness, process alerting and ensure flight safety.

## 4  Conclusions

This study combines the GDTA method proposed by Endsley (goal-oriented task analysis) and FCM (fuzzy cognitive map) to establish a situation awareness model. It is more scientific to obtain the critical factors related to situation awareness in the process of handling the flight crew alerting and the results can be used to modify the cockpit interface to provide sufficient information for the pilot to maintain situational awareness, process alerting and ensure flight safety.

## Reference

1. Liu, J., et al.: Index weight algorithm based on the weight ratio for civil aviation pilot safety behaviors. Math. Pract. Theory 47(6), 163–169 (2017)

# Ergonomic Evaluation of the Touch Screen in the Cockpit Under Stationary and Vibration Conditions

Ang Liu, Zhen Wang$^{(\boxtimes)}$, and Shan Fu

Department of Automation, Shanghai Jiao Tong University, Shanghai, China
b2wz@sjtu.edu.cn

**Abstract.** Compared with the traditional input mode, the touch screen has the advantages of convenient operation and saving cockpit space. As the touch screen began to appear in the aircraft cockpit, the impact of turbulence on touch screen operation has become a major challenge for touch screen application. In order to explore the influence of turbulence on touch screen operation, we designed touch screen input experiments, simulated the cockpit vibration and static environment, and studied the touch screen input mode. We compared the effects of different button sizes and button spacing on completing the input task. The results show that appropriate button layout is helpful to reduce the adverse effect of vibration on touch screen operation, and the reason is studied combined with the analysis of eye movement data.

**Keywords:** Touch screen · Ergonomics · Vibration · Aviation

## 1  Introduction

In recent years, touch screen has been applied to aircraft cockpit. Compared with traditional buttons, the interaction mode of touch screen is more intuitive and natural, which makes it easier to operate. Since there is no need for physical buttons, the range and content displayed on the screen can be switched freely to provide more flexible information for the pilots. Pilots do not need to go through a specific intermediate device. They only need to reach out and touch the module on the touch screen to complete the operation [1]. In addition, when iterating and upgrading flight equipment, it is not necessary to change the physical buttons, but only need to update the software, which greatly reduces the maintenance cost [2].

Benefiting from the popularity of electronic products with touch screen in daily life, the training cost for pilots to operate touch screens has become lower. Today, many pilots have used iPad or other touchscreen devices to perform some flight tasks, such as checking electronic documents, viewing electronic charts, confirming maps and so on. As a new form of human-computer interaction, the touch screen has good application prospects in the aircraft cockpit.

D. Harris and W.-C. Li (Eds.): HCII 2022, LNAI 13307, pp. 349–357, 2022.
https://doi.org/10.1007/978-3-031-06086-1_27

At the same time, the touch screen also brings many ergonomic problems, the most prominent of which is the impact of turbulence on the operation of the touch screen. Dobie mentioned in his research in 2003 that vibration during the flight causes the collapse of human perception system, and human visual acuity, self perception and vestibular system will be damaged, resulting in the decline of pilot performance, and adverse symptoms such as fatigue and dizziness [3]. When flying an aircraft with a touch screen, the display screen and the pilot's body will vibrate in the flight environment [4]. Therefore, with the gradual introduction of touch technology into the aircraft cockpit, the vibration caused by turbulence has become a major challenge of touch screen technology. Under vibration conditions, the interaction between the pilot and the touch screen may be severely impaired, resulting in reduced touch efficiency, which makes the mistouch of the touch screen more likely to occur. On the other hand, due to the lack of relevant design standards, touch screens lack a convincing feedback mechanism compared to traditional physical buttons. In order to achieve accurate control of the touch screen, it undoubtedly increases the workload of the pilots. Matthes, 1988 pointed out that the increased physical and mental workload of pilots affected the ability of pilots to safely maneuver the aircraft. When perception deteriorated, touch screens became unreadable, making it more difficult for pilots to accurately operate the system [5]. Guerard [7] studied the simulation of turbulence on Hexapod, and preliminarily explored the operation of touch screen in combination with the subjective score of subjects. Dodd [2] designed a data entry experiment to study the effects of touch technology, touch target size, touch target spacing and turbulence on pilot mission performance and analyzed the effects of different workloads. Cockburn [6] carried out experiments and studied three input modes: touch, trackball and touch screen mask. Their experiment results show that the touch interaction performance decreases with the increase of vibration.

More generally, the pilot cannot guarantee the control accuracy when interacting with the touch screens in vibration environments, which may cause wrong operations and longer operation time. When operating the touch screen, the pilots often need to allocate more attention resources to locate position to be clicked in the screen in order to improve the operation accuracy, which leads to additional attention occupation. Therefore, the ergonomic evaluation of touch screens in vibration environment is of great significance to the application of touch screens and the design of man-machine interface.

## 2   Experiment

### 2.1   Subjects

Five subjects were evaluated in the experiment. All subjects were in good health and had good vision after correction. All the subjects were well trained and familiar with the operation process of the experiment.

## 2.2   Equipment

The experiment was carried out on a flight simulator (see Fig. 1). The central control area of the simulator is composed of a touch screen. Data acquisition equipment is Tobii Glasses 3 eye trackers developed by Tobii Technology. The whole experimental process was recorded by the front camera of the eye tracker.

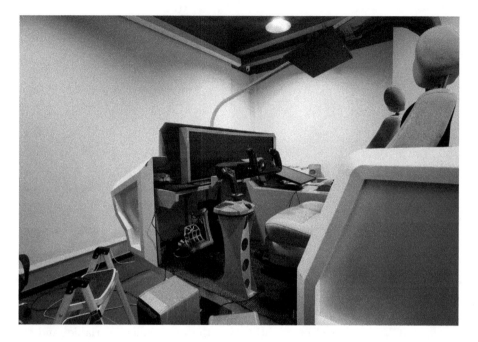

**Fig. 1.** Six degree of freedom flight simulator with central control touch screen.

## 2.3   Experimental Design

We simulate the cockpit vibration under turbulent conditions through a six degree of freedom motion platform. The motion platform performs periodic motion with an amplitude of 1mm and a frequency 10 Hz. Subjects were asked to fasten their seat belts to ensure a constant distance from the touch screen throughout the experiment. The task interface is shown in the Fig. 2.

The task required the subjects to complete the input of the given string as much as possible in ten minutes. Whenever the subject completes and submits the current string, the program regenerates and displays a new target string. During the task, the entered characters are displayed in the text box, and the subjects can click the "Delete" button to clear the last characters for modification. The program will record the key value entered and the operation time of each string group for subsequent analysis. The whole process of the experiment needs to wear an eye tracker.

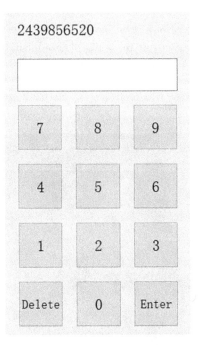

**Fig. 2.** Task interface.

## 3   Experimental Results

We used ANOVA to analyze the differences in the data obtained. In the analysis of ANOVA, the level of vibration was the independent variable, and the participants' operation time and average fixation duration were the dependent variables. The analysis program is run in Matlab under Windows system.

### 3.1   Operation Time

In the experiment, we recorded the operation time of the subjects under the static and vibration conditions. Figure 3 shows the boxplot of the subjects' operation time. From the distribution of the operation time in the figure, it can be concluded that under the vibration condition, the average time for the subjects to complete the input task becomes longer. In order to further explore the influence of button layout on input operation, we chose different button sizes and spacing to repeat this experiment. The results show that although the button size and button spacing are adjusted, the operation time under vibration is still greater than that without vibration. With the adjustment of the button size, the number of errors increased. Figure 2 shows the operation time difference caused by gradually increasing the button spacing when the button size is fixed to 70".

We used one-way ANOVA to test the influence of vibration on operation time. The analysis results show that: When the button spacing is 0.1", the presence of vibration had a significantly effect on operation time ($F = 22.63, P-value < 0.01$). When the button spacing is changed to 0.2", the influence of vibration on operation time begins to weaken ($F = 4.17, P-value < 0.05$). Increase the button spacing to 0.3", and the effect of vibration on operation time is no longer significant ($F = 2.51, P-value > 0.05$).

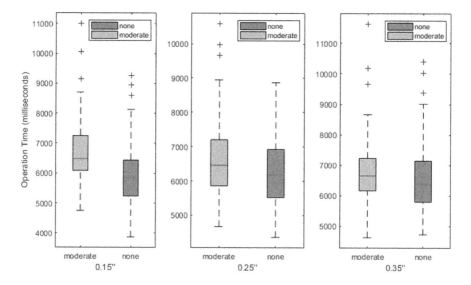

**Fig. 3.** The boxplot of participants' operation time under different button spacing. The y-axis represents the operation time, and the x-axis shows the presence or absence of vibration in the simulator during the task. The three pictures adopt different button spacing.

During the experiment, the cumulative number of errors also showed certain characteristics. Figure 4 illustrates the average number of errors of subjects in each turn. With the increase of button spacing, the difference in the number of operation errors caused by vibration decreases significantly.

We still conducted one-way ANOVA on the above data, and the results show that under the three button sizes, whether there is vibration or not has a significant impact on the operation time. When the button size is 0.6", the presence of vibration had a significantly effect on operation time ($F = 3.99, P-value < 0.05$). When the button spacing is changed to 0.7", the influence of vibration on operation time is statistically ($F = 4.46, P-value < 0.05$). Increase the button size to 0.8", and the result shows that the effect of vibration on operation time is still significant ($F = 4.49, P-value < 0.05$).

The above experimental results show that vibration has many adverse effects on subjects performing input tasks, which will prolong the operation time and increase the number of errors. The influence of vibration on the task process is closely related to the button layout. Figure 2, Fig. 3 show that increasing the

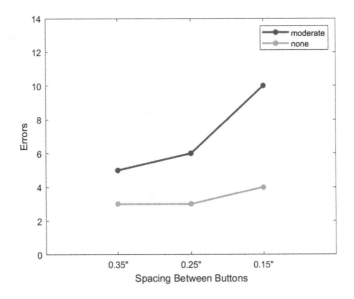

**Fig. 4.** Figure of average error times of experiment under different button spacing. The size of the buttons is 70".

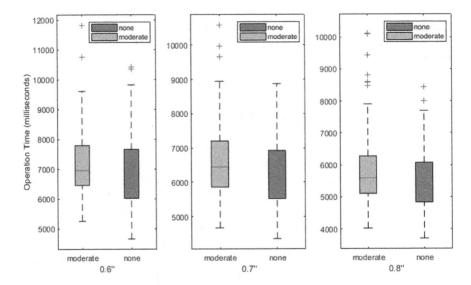

**Fig. 5.** The boxplot of participants' operation time under different button sizes. The y-axis represents the operation time, and the x-axis shows the presence or absence of vibration in the simulator during the task. The three pictures adopt different button sizes.

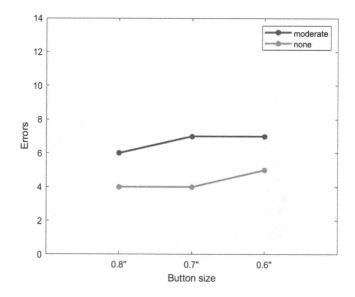

**Fig. 6.** Figure of average error times of experiment under different button sizes. The spacing between the buttons is 0.2".

button spacing can effectively alleviate the adverse impact of vibration on touch screen operation. With the increase of button spacing, the operation time of subjects completing character input task under vibration and static conditions gradually becomes consistent. At the same time, the number of input errors under vibration conditions is greatly reduced. It can be concluded that vibration may have a more serious impact on the scenario with closer button spacing. Therefore, moderately increasing the button spacing may facilitate the subject's touch screen interaction. Button size also has an important impact on operation time. Figure 5, Fig. 6 shows that the reduction of button size also leads to the increase in operation time and the number of errors.

## 3.2   Average Fixation Duration

In this experiment, we also recorded the subjects' eye movement data through the eye trackers (Figs. 7 and 8).

It can be intuitively concluded that the average fixation time under vibration condition is longer than that under static condition. To some extent, it shows that vibration will have an adverse impact on the subject's fixation process, and then prolong the operation time.

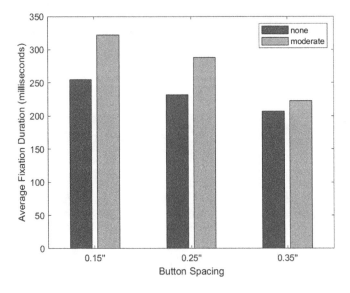

**Fig. 7.** Figure of average fixation duration under different button spacing. The button size is 0.7".

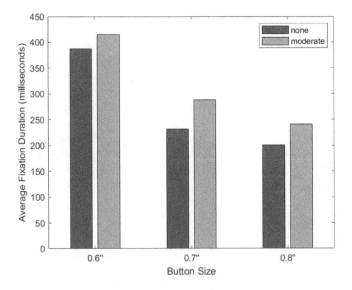

**Fig. 8.** Figure of average fixation duration under different button size. The button spacing is 0.25"

## 4    Discusstion

This experiment recorded the operation time of the subjects' touch screen input task under vibration and static conditions. After experimental comparison, it is concluded that vibration has an adverse effect on operation time. In order to further explain the influence of vibration on touch screen operation, we selected different specifications of button size and button spacing and repeat the experiment. The results show that the appropriate button layout strategy can reduce the impact of vibration. Choosing a larger button interval and a larger button size is helpful to reduce the impact of vibration on operation time. Button spacing has a more significant impact on the number of errors than button size. Choosing a larger button spacing helps to control the number of errors. In addition, we recorded subject's average fixation duration during the task. The results show that the average fixation time of subjects will be prolonged under vibration, which partly explains why it takes longer operation time under vibration.

## 5   Conclusion

The touch screen has a good application prospect in the field of aviation, and it also puts forward many new problems for ergonomic analysis. Under vibration conditions, pilots need to spend more resources to avoid wrong operation and maintain operation accuracy, which will cause additional occupation of attention. The ergonomic evaluation of touch screen under vibration and static conditions has important reference significance for designing more reasonable touch screen interaction interface and interaction mode.

## References

1. Dong, L., Xiang, C.Y., Zhang, C.X., et al.: Comprehensive evaluation of ergonomics of civil aircraft cockpit display touch control system. Acta Aeronautica et Astronautica Sinica **42**(6), 624053 (2021). (in Chinese). https://doi.org/10.7527/S1000-6893.2020.24053
2. Dodd, S., Lancaster, J., Miranda, A., et al.: Touch screens on the flight deck: the impact of touch target size, spacing, touch technology and turbulence on pilot performance. Proc. Hum. Factors Ergon. Soc. Ann. Meet. **58**(1), 6–10 (2014). https://doi.org/10.1177/1541931214581002
3. Dobie, T.G.: Critical significance of human factors in ship design. In: Proceedings of the 2003 RVOC Meeting, Large Lakes Observatory, University of Minnesota, 9 October 2003
4. Lancaster, J., et al.: The effect of touch screen hand stability method on performance and subjective preference in turbulence. In: Proceedings of the SID/SID Symposium Digest, vol. 42, no. 1, pp. 841–844 (2011)
5. Matthes, G.W.: Mission planning and proper design: the long range connection. In: Proceedings of the Joint GCP/FMP Symposium on Man Machine Interface in Tactical Aircraft Design and Combat Automation, pp. 3-1–3-4. AGARD (1988)
6. Cockburn A., Gutwin C., Palanque P., et al.: Turbulent touch: touchscreen input for cockpit flight displays. In: Proceedings of the 2017 CHI Conference on Human Factors in Computing Systems (CHI 2017), pp. 6742–6753. Association for Computing Machinery, New York. https://doi.org/10.1145/3025453.3025584
7. Guerard, S., et al.: Testing touch screens in realistic aeronautic turbulent conditions (light to severe). SAE Int. J. Aerosp. **8**(2), 243 (2015)

# Content and Context Analysis of Fatigue Management Regulations for Flight Crew in the South Asian Region

Chanika Mannawaduge Dona[(⊠)] [iD] and Silvia Pignata[iD]

University of South Australia, STEM Unit, Mawson Lakes Blvd, Mawson Lakes, SA 5095, Australia
chanika.mannawaduge_dona@mymail.unisa.edu.au

**Abstract.** For decades, fatigue has been identified as a significant risk factor in commercial air transport. The two main approaches to manage the fatigue risk in aviation are prescriptive and risk-based (performance-based). Countries' aviation authorities mandate either of these approaches or a combination of both through their national regulatory frameworks. This study investigated the content, context and implementation of International Civil Aviation Organization (ICAO) Standards and their recommended practices to manage flight crew fatigue risk in eight South Asian countries. The research design tabulated the fatigue-related regulations and conducted a comparative analysis of the approaches by assessing published standards, recommended practices, and regulations.

The findings show a considerable variability among these South Asian countries on the limits imposed for flight time, flight duty periods, duty periods, and rest periods. Notably, no country had implemented all three types of limitations (flight time, flight duty period and duty period) in their regulations. Most countries use a combination of two limitations as a minimum however, Bhutan, Sri Lanka and the Maldives only using flight duty periods in their regulations. All eight South Asian countries impose minimum rest limits. Additionally, the regulations vary with regard to crew composition, the start time of flight time/flight duty periods, and in-flight rest requirements.

The results highlight the varying limitations imposed in these South Asian countries on flight time, flight duty period, duty period and rest periods. It is hoped that these findings will be considered by regulatory bodies for aviation and airlines in the South Asia region in order to enhance existing regulatory frameworks.

**Keywords:** Fatigue · Prescriptive · Limitations · Flight duty period

## 1 Introduction

Managing the fatigue risk experienced by flight crew is essential to establishing a safe air transport system. Research indicates that 15 to 20 per cent of fatal accidents and incidents in commercial air transport are attributable to fatigue [1]. Flight crew have reported fatigue associated with the following three causation factors: (1) Sleep factors (i.e., early duty start times, late night and early morning flights, crossing multiple time zones); (2) work factors (i.e., high or low workloads in the cockpit, long duty periods, the intensity of job functions, the availability of resources, confined working environments); and (3) health factors (i.e., sleep apnea, insomnia, the consumption of alcohol, use of caffeine and medication) [2–4]. The International Civil Aviation Organization (ICAO), the specialized agency that specifies Standards and Recommended Practices (SARPs) to the aviation industry recommends two distinct approaches to address the fatigue risk experienced by flight crew. The SARPs specified by ICAO are adopted by the Member States and are enforced at the national level through each country's domestic legal framework. The two fatigue management approaches recommended by ICAO in Annex 6 are prescriptive and performance-based (risk-based) approaches. Each national Civil Aviation Authority prescribes the maximum flight time, flight duty period (FDP), and duty period limitations with the minimum rest requirements based on scientific knowledge and experience in the prescriptive approach [4, 5]. Air operators develop and obtain approval to implement a fatigue risk management system (FRMS) by the National Civil Aviation Authority in a performance-based approach. The FRMS is based on the principles of risk management and considers elements such as an individual's varying capacity (i.e., productivity, decision-making, problem-solving), sleep, and circadian levels relative to flight time/flight duty period, and the start and end times of each crew member's flights [3, 5].

Additional fatigue mitigation methods are identified in scholarly articles and include in-flight napping, the crew composition, flight duty period/flight time/duty start time, and the number of time zones crossed which are considered when formulating fatigue regulations [6–11]. Research confirms that in-flight sleep for flight crew is a primary fatigue mitigation strategy effective in long-range flights that provide an environment favorable to sleep [7, 10–12]. However, most commercial flights are operated with two flight crew on duty, which limits their opportunity to rest in flight. Research demonstrates that medium-range flights with two flight crew, may develop a pattern of building up fatigue while operating within the flight duty/flight time limits [9, 13, 14]. For example, evidence shows that significant risk is observed in flights that commence in the early morning (e.g., 0000–0559) rather than flights scheduled for later in the morning or the afternoon or at night, especially if the flight time/flight duty period starts in the window of circadian low (WOCL) (0200–0600). The WOCL is defined by ICAO as the time in the circadian body clock when the subjective fatigue and sleepiness is at a peak and individuals are least able to do mental and physical tasks [4]. Furthermore, in terms of risk, research has also identified a relationship between the time of the day and the level of error [6, 8]. For example, a study analyzed the records of 155,327 flight hours of Brazilian airlines from 1st April to 30th September 2005 by categorizing a 24 h day into the four periods of: (1) early morning; (2) morning; (3) afternoon; and (4) night. The results revealed that risk increases by 50 per cent during the early morning compared to the morning, and neither afternoon nor night flights were associated with significant risk [8].

Although extensive research has been conducted on the causes of fatigue, its impairments, and methods to measure fatigue, research that investigates flight crew fatigue regulations related to flight time, FDP, duty period, and rest is limited to a few studies. Wegmann et al. [15], for example, compared the flight crew fatigue regulations of nine countries and identified a considerable difference in the scope and applicability of regulations in these countries. Subsequently, Cabon et al. [16] and Missoni et al. [17] updated and expanded this area of research to 35 countries in five geographical regions (Europe, America, Asia, Africa, and Oceania). Together, these studies have compared flight time, FDP, and rest and work schedules, finding both similarities and differences in how these countries implemented ICAO principles and whether these regulations can prevent fatigue [16, 17]. These studies reveal that different geographical regions have varied flight times, FDPs, and duty period limitations and that different countries use a combination of traditional and flexible regulations (prescriptive and risk-based).

It is also noteworthy that the above-mentioned studies analyzed aviation fatigue management regulations for flight crews in Europe, the Middle East, and countries including Australia, New Zealand and the United States. However, no studies have focused on implementing SARPs for fatigue management in the South Asian region. Therefore, this research aims to examine this area and address this gap by examining the content, context and implementation of ICAO Standards in eight South Asian countries by tabulating and conducting a comparative analysis of their fatigue-related regulations. The present study will assess published standards, recommended practices, and regulations in order to investigate the overarching fatigue management regulatory framework in the South Asian region.

## 2 Materials and Methods

### 2.1 Documents and Selection

The present study examines 12 documents from ICAO and eight South Asian countries (Afghanistan, Bangladesh, Bhutan, India, Maldives, Nepal, Pakistan, Sri Lanka). For each country, these documents include the Standards and Recommended Practices (SARPs), Regulations and the Implementation Guidance for fatigue risk management in the aviation industry. As publicly available documents, ICAO Annex 6 and Doc 9966 were downloaded from the official website of ICAO and the regulations of each of the eight countries were downloaded from the official websites of the respective national aviation authorities. Table 1 lists all the documents used in the analysis.

### 2.2 Method of Analysis

The SARPs and regulations regarding flight crew fatigue were extracted and recorded in two tables that contain both text and numerical data. The key terms of duty, duty time, duty period, flight time, FDP, and flight deck duty time as included in ICAO Annexes and the regulations of eight South Asian countries are detailed in Table 2. This table also records the limits on flight time (FT), FDP, duty (D) and the rest periods (RP) of the eight countries. The data recorded in the tables were analyzed using a comparative analysis framework that focused on: (1) factors considered when defining flight crew fatigue; (2) the maximum limits for the FT, FDP, D, and RP with varying complements of flight crew;

**Table 1.** List of SARPs, regulations and documents.

| Organisation/ Country | SARP/Implementation Guidance/Regulation |
|---|---|
| ICAO | 1. Annex 6 to the Convention on International Civil Aviation Operation of Aircraft, Part I - International Commercial Air Transport – Aeroplanes<br>2. Manual for the Oversight of Fatigue Management Approaches Document 9966 |
| Afghanistan | Afghanistan Civil Aviation Regulations - Operations - Part 8 |
| Bangladesh | Air Navigation Order ANO (OPS) A.10 - Flight Operations Requirements<br>Part A - Flight crew training, licensing and authorisation |
| Bhutan | Bhutan Civil Aviation Requirements - BCAR OPS 1, Commercial Air Transport – Aeroplanes |
| India | Civil Aviation Requirement, Section 7 - Flight crew standards training and licensing, Series J Part III |
| Maldives | Maldivian Civil Aviation Regulations MCAR - Air Operations |
| Nepal | Flight Operations Requirements - Aeroplane FOR-A |
| Pakistan | Air Navigation Order - ANO-012-FSXX-6.0 |
| Sri Lanka | Implementing Standard - SLCAIS 054<br>Guidance Material SLCAP 4210 |

and (3) the rest period prior/after long-range, extended long-range and ultra-long-range operations [16, 17]. This comparative analysis framework uses a combination of models published by Cabon et al. [16] and Missoni et al. [17] to analyze the fatigue management regulations of flight crew.

Finally, eight graphs were plotted to show the flight times, flight duty periods, duty periods and rest periods in the eight countries.

## 3  Results and Discussion

The study reveals that not all eight South Asian countries incorporated flight time, FDP, and duty period limits into their regulations. There is extensive variability in the regulations among the eight countries in this geographical region, including the definitions related to flight crew fatigue (flight time, FDP, duty period, and rest period). The results of the analyses are presented and discussed in the following section.

### 3.1  ICAO SARPs and Guidance Material

ICAO has prescribed the standards and recommended practices related to flight crew fatigue in commercial aviation in Annex 6, Part I and the additional implementation guidance in Document 9966 (Doc 9966). ICAO SARPs urge its Member States to implement limitations on flight time, FDP, duty period, and rest periods in order to manage the fatigue risk in air transport [18]. ICAO Annex 6, Part I and Doc 9966 state that fatigue management regulations should be based on scientific principles, knowledge, and operational experience. ICAO further recommends that countries promulgate regulations to establish a fatigue management approach (prescriptive or performance-based or a combination) [4, 18]. A performance-based approach can take the form of a FRMS and should include a method to identify fatigue-related safety hazards and the resulting risk(s), remedial action to mitigate risk(s) and associated hazard(s), and a continuous improvement of the overall performance [19]. Doc 9966 provides further guidance to establish flight time, flight duty and duty period limitations, rest periods, an extension of duty time, positioning, split duty and standby requirements applicable for flight crews.

## 3.2   Definitions Related to Flight Crew Fatigue

The following seven definitions used in the context of flight crew fatigue are identified in the present study: (1) duty; (2) duty time; (3) duty period; (4) flight time; (5) FDP; (6) flight deck duty period; and (7) rest period. Table 2 lists the definitions for these seven terms as per ICAO Annex 6. If any South Asian country defined the term differently to Annex 6, this information is also included in the table for comparison. ICAO regulations do not define duty time and flight deck duty time, but the aviation authorities in Afghanistan and Bangladesh use these two terms in their regulations. The majority of the South Asian countries define the other terms similarly to ICAO Annex 6 if those terms are included in the respective regulations as indicated in the third column of the below table.

**Table 2.** Definitions in the context of flight crew fatigue

| Definition | ICAO | Status of South Asian Countries |
| --- | --- | --- |
| Duty | Any task that flight or cabin crew members are required by the operator to perform, including flight duty, administrative work, training, positioning and standby when it is likely to induce fatigue. | Not defined by BH, IN, MA, NE, PK and SL |
| Duty time | No ICAO definition | AF - The total time from the moment a person identified in these regulations begins, immediately after a rest period, any work on behalf of the certificate holder until that person is free from all restraint associated with that work. |
| Duty period | A period which starts when a flight- or cabin-crew member is required by an operator to report for or to commence a duty and ends when that person is free from all duties. | BA - the period of elapsed time beginning from 1 hour before the scheduled departure time (Blocks off) of all International flights and 45 minutes for Domestic flights; and ending at 30 minutes after actual arrival time (Blocks on) of all flights in connection with assigned duty of a flight crew. |
| Flight time | The total time from the moment an aeroplane first moves for the purpose of taking off until the moment it finally comes to rest at the end of the flight. | Not defined by IN and MA |
| Flight duty period | A period which commences when a flight or cabin crew member is required to report for duty that includes a flight or a series of flights and which finishes when the aircraft finally comes to rest and the engines are shut down at the end of the last flight on which he is a crew member | Not defined by AF and BA |
| Flight deck duty time | No ICAO definition | BA - any portion of flight time spent at a position for which a flight crewmember is required. |
| Rest | A continuous and defined period of time, subsequent to and/or prior to duty, during which flight or cabin crew members are free of all duties | BA - elapsed time between two consecutive duty periods (i.e. from the end of one duty period until the beginning of next duty period, when crewmembers are free of all restraint or any kind of duty and are free of all responsibility for work or duty should the occasion arise.) A horizontal resting period must be availed by the concerned flight crew. BH and IN defines defined rest period similar to ICAO but provide examples for duties (standby and reserve) |

Note: Afghanistan (AF), Bangladesh (BA), Bhutan (BH), India (IN), Maldives (MA), Nepal (NE), Pakistan (PK), Sri Lanka (SL)

### 3.3  Maximum Flight Time and FDP

**Maximum Flight Time.** ICAO defines flight time as 'the total time from the moment an aeroplane first moves for the purpose of taking off until the moment it finally comes to rest at the end of the flight' [4]. Afghanistan, Bangladesh, India, Nepal and Pakistan have imposed limitations on flight time to regulate flight crew fatigue (see Figs. 1, 2 and 3). Afghanistan has mandated a limit of 8 flight hours in the Afghanistan Civil Aviation Regulations - Operations - Part 8-8.12 and does not specify the number of flight crew required for the flight [19]. Bangladesh imposes a limitation of 11 h, which the air operator can extend to 14 h with three flight crew and two flight engineers, and 16 h with four flight crew and two flight engineers as shown in Figs. 1, 2 and 3 [20]. India has a diverse range of flight times from 8 to 14 h as the following two factors influence the wide range of flight times: (1) the crew complement (i.e., the number of crew members operating the flight); and (2) the number of landings/sectors performed within the flight time [21].

**Fig. 1.**  Maximum flight time

Nepal has a flight time limitation of 10 h (see Fig. 1) for two flight crew operations which increases to 12 h for three and four flight crew member operations; (see Figs. 2 and 3 for extended flight time limitations) [22]. The regulations in Pakistan have a minimum flight time of 9 h and a maximum of 18 h [23]. A two flight crew complement allows airlines to operate a flight time of 9 h (Fig. 1), and with three flight crew, it is extended to 10 h (see Fig. 2) [23]. A three flight crew complement can include two flight crew and a flight engineer. An augmented crew complement of three flight crew and one flight engineer allows a flight time of 11 h, and three flight crew with two flight engineers can operate up to 12 h, as shown in Fig. 2 [23]. A further increase of up to 16 flying hours is allowed for a double crew complement (see Fig. 3). Pakistan also specifies flights of long-range (16 h) duration, extended long-range (17 h), and ultra-long-range (18 h) duration for two and three sets of flight crew, respectively (see Fig. 3) [23].

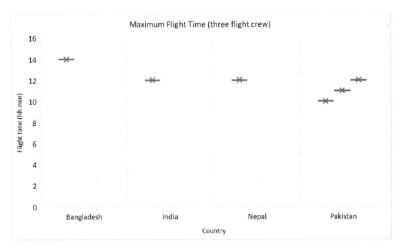

**Fig. 2.** Maximum flight time (three flight crew)

The results presented in the analysis show that the maximum flight time within the eight countries can range from 8 to 18 h and can also depend on the number of crew operating the flight. Countries such as Afghanistan and India allow a flight time of 8 h, which is the minimum flight time in the eight countries, whereas Pakistan allows a flight time of up to 18 h as a maximum flight time among the eight countries [19, 23]. Afghanistan Civil Aviation Regulations - Operations - Part 8 does not include any information on the number of flight crew members when mandating the maximum flight time [21]. It is of interest that India associates the flight time with the number of landings performed [19] and India and Pakistan are the only two countries that classify long-range, extended, and ultra-long-range flights. According to the results, some South Asian countries consider various aspects (i.e., crew complement, sectors performed, flight distance) in stipulating the maximum flight time. In contrast, certain countries only impose a limitation on flight time and provide little information on the rationale/evidence for their limits.

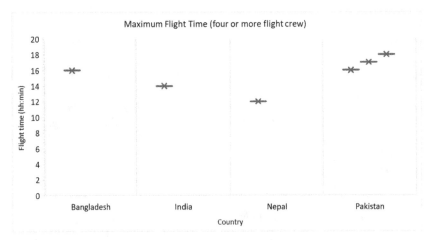

**Fig. 3.** Maximum flight time (four or more flight crew members)

**Maximum FDP.** Six out of the eight countries in the South Asian region impose a limitation on FDP for flight crew. ICAO defines a flight duty period as 'a period that commences when a flight or cabin crew member is required to report for duty that includes a flight or a series of flights and which finishes when an aircraft finally comes to rest and the engines are shut down at the end of the last flight on which he is a crew member' [4]. Sri Lanka and the Maldives have multiple FDPs, as shown in Fig. 4. These FDPs are established in reference to: (1) FDP start time; and (2) the sectors flight crew can operate within the FDP [24, 25]. The first FDP reference time commences at 0600 until 1329, then there are seven FDP reference time clusters with an interval of 29 min between the start and end times until 1659. The next time cluster starts at 1700 and runs until 0459. Finally, there are four time clusters with an interval of 14 min between the start and end time finishing at 0559. According to this criteria, there are 104 FDPs in the Maldives regulations. Figure 4 shows only the maximum FDPs out of the 104 for acclimatized flight crew in the Maldives. Furthermore, the Maldives has established a separate FDP for operators under a FRMS.

The FDP limitations in Sri Lanka take a similar form to the regulations in the Maldives however, only five FDP start time clusters are in the Sri Lankan Regulations [24]. The first period starts at 0600 and ends at 0759, thus the lapse time between the first cluster is one hour and 59 min. Each of the two subsequent time clusters have a lapse time of four hours and 59 min, the next cluster is three hours 59 min, and the last cluster is seven hours and 59 min (2200 to 0559). If the flight duty commences between 0800 to 1259 flight crew can work the maximum FDP according to the number of sectors they perform, as depicted in Fig. 4.

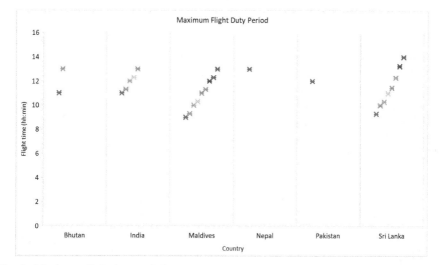

**Fig. 4.** Maximum flight duty period.
Note: Different color shadings are used to mark the FDPs in Bhutan, India, Maldives, and Sri Lanka for clarity as multiple FDPs are illustrated in the graph

Sri Lanka specifies the FDP is applicable for two or more acclimatized flight crew and the Guidance Material Sri Lanka Civil Aviation Procedure (SLCAP) 4210 also mandates a separate FDP for two or more flight crew who are not acclimatized to the sector. Furthermore, in India, the FDPs also consider the maximum number of landings that the flight crew can perform. The maximum applicable FDPs for two flight crew operations across six countries are shown in Fig. 4. The maximum FDP is 13 h with one landing, and if the landings are increased to six, it allows the flight crew to operate up to 11 h. From Fig. 4, it is evident that there are five FDPs, each with an addition of 30 min to the previous FDP (i.e., 1100, 1130, 1200, 1230, 1300). As the FDPs in India are associated with number of landings each 30 min extended in the FDP results in reducing one landing that flight crew can perform. The maximum FDP in Bhutan is 13 h, and if more than two sectors are performed the FDP reduces by 30 min for each sector from the third sector onwards for a maximum total reduction of two hours [26]. Pakistan allows a 12 h FDP period for two flight crew operations and 13 h in Nepal with three or four flight crew complement.

With regard to three crew member operations, India allows the FDP to be extended to 14 h (see Fig. 5), and with four or more flight crew, it can be extended to 18 or 22 h (see Fig. 6) [21]. These flights are considered long-range and ultra-long-range operations, respectively. Unlike the other countries in the region, Nepal has a higher maximum FDP limitation of 13 h. Three flight crew operations with a class 2 (e.g., seat in an aircraft cabin with flat or near flat sleeping position) or class 3 rest facility (e.g., seat in an aircraft cabin or flight deck with at least 40 degree recline capability and leg and foot support) can operate up to a FDP limit of 15 h (see Fig. 5) [22] which can be increased to 16 h with a class 2 or 3 rest facility, and 18 h with a class 1 rest facility (i.e. bunk or other surface with flat sleeping position separate from flight deck and passenger cabin) if four or more flight crew are engaged in operations (see Fig. 6). Pakistan allows a FDP of 13 h for three crew operations, including two flight crew and a flight engineer or with two captains and a first officer (see Fig. 5).

In Pakistan, the FDP can be increased to 15 h if three flight crew and 2 flight engineers are involved in flight operations, and a double crew complement allows a further increase of 18 h (see Fig. 6). Pakistan regulations permit long-range flights with a duration of up to 18 h with two sets of cockpit crew and extended long-range flights with two groups of cockpit crew and a cruise relief flight crew can fly for up to 20 h [23]. Three sets of flight crew can operate a maximum FDP of up to 21 h for ultra-long-range flights (see Fig. 6).

The results reveal that the Maldives and Sri Lanka are the only two countries that combine the FDP with duty start time and the sectors travelled. When mandating the maximum FDP, India, Nepal, Pakistan, and also Sri Lanka take into consideration the number of flight crew members required for the prescribed operation. Only two countries (India, Pakistan) in the region classify different FDPs for flights identified as long-range, extended, and ultra-long-range flights. Across all eight countries, Nepal is the only country that identifies in-flight rest as an essential aspect to extend the FDP. Overall, the results indicate that some South Asian countries formulate their FDP regulations based on: (1) FDP start time; (2) the number of sectors travelled /aircraft landings; (3) crew complement; (4) the duration of the flight; and (5) the period of in-flight rest. However, it

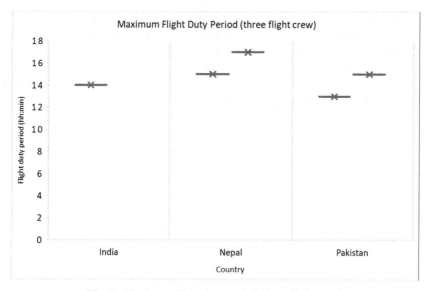

**Fig. 5.** Maximum flight duty period (three flight crew)

is noteworthy that only Nepal identifies the importance of in-flight rest in their in-flight crew fatigue management approach. Furthermore, only two countries base the flight crew FDP on when the duty period commences (see next section).

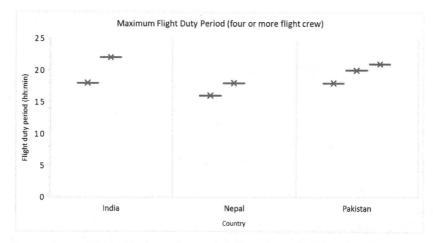

**Fig. 6.** Maximum duty period (four or more flight crew)

## 3.4  Duty Period

Duty period is 'a period which starts when a flight or cabin crew member is required by an operator to report for or to commence a duty and ends when that person is free from all duties' [4]. Afghanistan and Bangladesh impose a duty period limitation of 14 h for flight crew, as shown in Fig. 7 [19, 20]. Bangladesh regulations allow this limitation to increase to 16 h, when at least one flight crew member is added to the minimum crew complement. Furthermore, this can be expanded to 20 h if two more flight crew are assigned to the minimum crew complement. Other South Asian countries do not include a duty period limitation in their regulations.

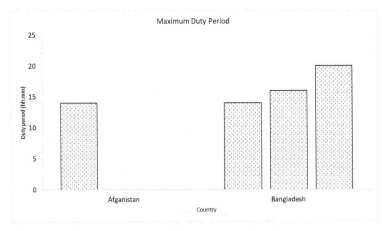

**Fig. 7.** Maximum duty period

### 3.5   Rest Period

All eight South Asian countries impose a minimum rest period for flight crew in their regulations, as shown in Fig. 8. ICAO defines rest as 'a continuous and defined period of time, subsequent to and/or prior to duty, during which flight or cabin crew members are free of all duties' [4]. For example, in Bangladesh, flight crew are allowed to rest for nine consecutive hours on the ground if a duty period is 14 h or less [20]. Air operators can reduce this rest period to eight hours by providing a subsequent rest period of 10 consecutive hours, and if the duty period is between 14 to 20 h, the flight crew must rest for 12 h. The regulations allow this rest to be 10 h, with a subsequent rest period of 14 consecutive hours. Before undertaking a FDP in Bhutan, India, Maldives, and Sri Lanka, the minimum rest period for flight crew is 12 h or a duration equivalent to the preceding duty period, whichever is greater (see Fig. 8) [4, 17, 21, 26]. However, for the FDP that starts away from the home base, a rest period of 10 h or equivalent to the preceding duty period should be provided in Bhutan and the Maldives and this period should include 8 h of sleep opportunity. In India, the minimum rest period can be extended to 18 h if crossing three to seven time zones and 36 h if crossing more than seven time zones. Nepal is the only country that mandates one rest period of a minimum of 9 h before commencing a FDP; see Fig. 8.

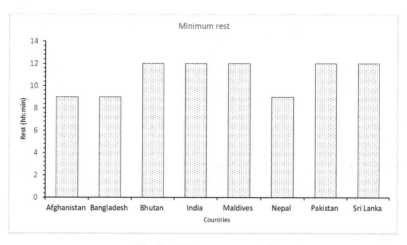

**Fig. 8.** Minimum rest period

In Pakistan, the minimum rest period is 12 h or twice the duration of the preceding FDP, whichever is greater [23]. For long-range (LR), and extended long-range (ELR) flights, the rest period should be 24 h before the flight, including one local night. This period is extended to 48 h for ultra-long-range (ULR) flights, including two local nights. The regulations also require a minimum rest period of double the duty time at the home base after operating LR, ELR or ULR flights. After returning to the home base from one of these flights, 48 h or double the FDP is the allowed minimum rest period for the flight crew. In Sri Lanka, if a rest period of 12 h is earned by flight crew away from the home base, the rest period can be reduced by one hour if the operator provides suitable accommodation. However, if the travelling time between the aerodrome and the accommodation is more than 30 min each way, the rest period must be increased by the total time spent travelling and one additional hour.

In summary, Afghanistan, Bangladesh and Nepal allow a minimum rest period of nine hours, whereas Bhutan, India, Maldives, Pakistan and Sri Lanka permit a minimum of 12 h rest. Three (Bhutan, Maldives, Sri Lanka) of the eight countries in the region also specify a rest requirement for rest away from the home base. Furthermore, India and Pakistan have mandated an extended rest period based on time zones crossed and the length of flight (LR, ELR, ULR). The results reveal that minimum rest criteria differ in the South Asian region and that some countries consider aspects including: (1) rest away from the home base; (2) the number of time zones crossed; and (3) the length/type of the flight operated.

## 4   Conclusion

This study reports on significant variability in the aviation regulations of eight countries and their implementation of ICAO SARPs. The majority of the South Asian countries have established regulations that consider key aspects of fatigue that can impact flight crew. However, some countries only impose limits on flight time, FDP, duty or rest periods. Although in-flight napping is regarded as an effective fatigue mitigation strategy by many scholarly articles [7, 10–12, 27], the results of the present study reveal that only Nepal incorporates it with the flight time and FDP. Aviation regulations in Nepal also consider the condition of the rest facility and environment in the provision of in-flight napping. Another frequently cited strategy for mitigating fatigue in flight crew is duty start times and the number of time zones crossed in flight time/FDPs. Sri Lanka and the Maldives combine duty start time with FDP, and together with these two countries, India also couples the flight time and FDP with the number of landings [6, 8, 13].

However, in addition to considering limitations on flight time, FDP and duty periods as a method to minimize the fatigue experienced by flight crew, regulations should also consider the crew complement, the in-flight rest facilities onboard and away from the crew member's home base, flights across a number of time zones, and duty start times as these factors have been identified as effective fatigue mitigation strategies in the extant literature [6, 8, 10, 13, 27].

A key strength of this study is the ease of access to the data, as the researcher used data and information that is publicly available on the official websites of ICAO and the national regulatory authorities. Therefore, there were no shortcomings to accessing current data about the standards, recommended practices, and regulations. However, it should be noted that in some cases, there is a need for the respective authorities to provide more and clearer information about the intended meaning of some of the regulatory provisions.

The present study evaluated the fatigue management regulations published by international organizations and the regulators in eight South Asian countries. This analysis provides a better understanding of ICAO's standards and recommended practices and the fatigue management regulatory framework of South Asia's eight civil aviation authorities. These research findings will provide international organizations, regulators, and airlines with a better understanding of the commonalities and differences in flight time, FDP, duty, and rest period limitations across these eight countries. It is hoped that the region's national civil aviation authorities will consider and incorporate these findings when reviewing and updating their existing regulatory frameworks and operational procedures.

## References

1. Dillard, M.B., Orhan, U., Letsu-Dake, E.: Nonintrusive pilot fatigue monitoring. In: 2016 IEEE/AIAA 35th Digital Avionics Systems Conference (DASC), 25–29 September 2016
2. Davidović, J., Pešić, D., Antić, B.: Professional drivers' fatigue as a problem of the modern era. Transport. Res. F: Traffic Psychol. Behav. **55**, 199–209 (2018). https://doi.org/10.1016/j.trf.2018.03.010
3. Efthymiou, M., Whiston, S., O'Connell, J.F., Brown, G.D.: Flight crew evaluation of the flight time limitations regulation. Case Stud. Transp. Policy **9**(1), 280–290 (2021). https://doi.org/10.1016/j.cstp.2021.01.002
4. International Civil Aviation Organisation, I.: Manual for the Oversight of Fatigue Management Approaches (2016). https://www.icao.int/safety/fatiguemanagement/FRMS%20Tools/Doc%209966.FRMS.2016%20Edition.en.pdf
5. Jerman, A., Meško, M.: How to measure fatigue among pilots? J. Polytech. Rijeka **6**, 13–21 (2018). https://doi.org/10.31784/zvr.6.1.7

6. Bourgeois-Bougrine, S., Carbon, P., Gounelle, C., Mollard, R., Coblentz, A.: Perceived fatigue for short- and long-haul flights: a survey of 739 airline pilots. Aviat. Space Environ. Med. **74**(10), 1072–1077 (2003)

7. Caldwell, J.A.: Fatigue in aviation. Travel Med. Infect. Dis. **3**(2), 85–96 (2005). https://doi.org/10.1016/j.tmaid.2004.07.008

8. de Mello, M.T., et al.: Relationship between Brazilian airline pilot errors and time of day. Braz. J. Med. Biol. Res. **41**, 1129–1131 (2008). http://www.scielo.br/scielo.php?script=sci_arttext&pid=S0100879X2008001200014&nrm=iso

9. Drury, D.A., Ferguson, S.A., Thomas, M.J.: Restricted sleep and negative affective states in commercial pilots during short haul operations. Accident Analysis Prevention **45**(Suppl), 80–84 (2012). https://doi.org/10.1016/j.aap.2011.09.031

10. Holmes, A., Al-Bayat, S., Hilditch, C., Bourgeois-Bougrine, S.: Sleep and sleepiness during an ultra long-range flight operation between the Middle East and United States. Accid. Anal. Prev. **45**(Supplement), 27–31 (2012). https://doi.org/10.1016/j.aap.2011.09.021

11. Roach, G.D., Darwent, D., Sletten, T.L., Dawson, D.: Long-haul pilots use in-flight napping as a countermeasure to fatigue. Appl. Ergon. **42**(2), 214–218 (2011). https://doi.org/10.1016/j.apergo.2010.06.016

12. Zaslona, J.L., O'Keeffe, K.M., Signal, T.L., Gander, P.H.: Shared responsibility for managing fatigue: Hearing the pilots. PLoS ONE **13**(5), e0195530 (2018). https://doi.org/10.1371/journal.pone.0195530

13. Powell, D., Spencer, M.B., Holland, D., Petrie, K.J.: Fatigue in two-pilot operations: implications for flight and duty time limitations. Aviat. Space Environ. Med. **79**(11), 1047–1050 (2008). https://doi.org/10.3357/asem.2362.2008

14. Schmid, D., Stanton, N.A.: Considering single-piloted airliners for different flight durations: an issue of fatigue management. In: Stanton, N. (ed.) AHFE 2019. AISC, vol. 964, pp. 683–694. Springer, Cham (2020). https://doi.org/10.1007/978-3-030-20503-4_61

15. Wegmann, H.M., Klein, K.E., Conrad, B., Esser, P.: A model for prediction of resynchronization after time-zone flights. Aviat. Space Environ. Med. **54**(6), 524–527 (1983)

16. Cabon, P., Bourgeois-Bougrine, S., Mollard, R., Coblentz, A., Speyer, J.-J.: Flight and duty time limitations in civil aviation and their impact on fatigue: a comparative analysis of 26 national regulations. Hum. Factors Aerosp. Saf. **2**, 379–393 (2002)

17. Missoni, E., Nikolic, N., Missoni, I.: Civil aviation rules on crew flight time, flight duty, and rest: comparison of 10 ICAO member states. Aviat. Space Environ. Med. **80**, 135–138 (2009). https://doi.org/10.3357/ASEM.1960.2009

18. Annex 6 to the Convention on International Civil Aviation, Part I (2016)

19. Afghanistan Civil Aviation Regulations ACAR - Operations (2015). http://acaa.gov.af/wp-content/uploads/2017/10/ACAR-Part-08-Rev_-3_0_1510143.pdf

20. Air Navigation Order (2002). http://www.caab.gov.bd/ano/anoopsa10.pdf

21. Civil Aviation Requirement Section 7- Flight Crew Standards Training and Licensing (2019). http://164.100.60.133/cars/D7J-J3(Issue3_April2019).pdf

22. Flight Operations Requirements (Aeroplane) (2020). https://flightsafety.caanepal.gov.np/storage/app/media/Flight%20Operations/flight%20operation%20requirement/fora-6th-edition-consolidated.pdf

23. Air Navigation Order (2020). https://caapakistan.com.pk/upload/documents/ANO-012-FSXX-6.0.pdf

24. Guidance Material SLCAP 4210 (2015). https://www.caa.lk/images/pdf/guidance_material/subject_specific/slcap_4210_limitations_on_flight_time_and_flight_duty_periods_and_rest_periods_2nd_edition.pdf

25. Maldivian Civil Aviation Regulation (2020). https://www.caa.gov.mv/rules-and-regulations/maldivian-civil-aviation-regulations-(mcar)#:~:text=MCAR%2C%20introduced%20in%20July%20'07,aviation%20regulations%20in%20the%20Maldives

26. Bhutan Civil Aviation Requirements BCAR OPS 1 (2017). https://www.bcaa.gov.bt/wp-con
tent/uploads/2017/04/BCAR-OPS-1-Issue-2-Aug-2017.pdf
27. Dawson, D., McCulloch, K.: Managing fatigue: it's about sleep. Sleep Med. Rev. **9**(5), 365–
380 (2005). https://doi.org/10.1016/j.smrv.2005.03.002

# Stabilise, Solve, Execute Creating a Management Model for Resilient Flight Deck Operations

Pete McCarthy[✉], Gregory Benichou, and Peter Hudson

Centre for Safety and Accident Investigation, Cranfield University, Cranfield, UK
pete_mccarthy@cathaypacific.com

**Abstract.** This paper details the project methodology undertaken to create a Flight Deck Management Model (FDMM), which aims to reflect the complexity of modern commercial flight deck operations in the 21$^{st}$ century. A comprehensive literature review, which included Decision Making, Situational Awareness (SA), complexity and resilience, was combined with a review of high-profile (well-known) air accident reports, in order to identify the main characteristics of the model. A series of focus groups followed this review, with the aim being to propose an initial structure for the FDMM. These focus groups consisted of Subject Matter Experts (SME's) who are current training captains and Flying Training Standards Team (FTST) pilots (representing Boeing and Airbus flying operations), Human Factors (HF) specialists, risk management specialists, training department managers and Flight Operations (FOP) management pilots. The focus groups were led by the Flying Standards Team (FST), FOP risk managers and the airline group Head of Human Factors (HF). Observations of flight and simulator operations, informal interviews with flight-crew and regular reviews of the progress of the FDMM activity was carried out over a 6 -month period.

The model, "Stabilise, Solve, Execute" (SSE) was accepted by both the Boeing and Airbus philosophy of flight deck management within the airline conducting the study. The model structure encourages pilot fast appraisal and response (stabilise), then and only if required, pilot slow appraisal and response (solve), and in either case, pilot action (execute). Each of these top levels of the model have subsequent actions and considerations which if followed aim to encourage and guide resilient behaviours and actions on behalf of the flight crew.

SSE is designed to aid Aeronautical Decision Making (ADM) and Flight Deck Management (FDM) – the research and development thus far has led the study team to explore wider application across other High Reliability Organisations (HROs) and any complex operations where managers may need to take actions and make decision within uncertain environments with competing goals.

**Keywords:** Decision making · Task management · Resilience · Complexity · Flight Deck management model · Systems thinking

## 1 Introduction

Safe operation within a modern flight deck environment has become ever more complex, as technology and sources of information across the aviation system continue to develop

D. Harris and W.-C. Li (Eds.): HCII 2022, LNAI 13307, pp. 373–383, 2022.
https://doi.org/10.1007/978-3-031-06086-1_29

and become widely distributed. When dealing with normal or non-normal flight operations, the traditional or generic flight-crew default fallback position of "Aviate (fly), Navigate, Communicate" may no longer be a sufficient mantra (or model) for our pilots to follow in order to manage dynamic situations – Aviate (fly) may be too simplistic, as this flying task is now more about flight path management and monitoring than traditional "stick and rudder skills" - and this requires knowledge of the flight management modes and effective Task Management (TM) of the automation.

Flight operations, training, testing and checking methods all require that the flight crew maintain and communicate a Shared Situational Awareness (SSA). Situational Awareness (SA) refers to the perception of the elements within their environment, the comprehension of their meaning and the projection of their status in the near future (Endsley 1988), according to Endsley (2003), SSA is further defined as "the degree to which team members have the same SA. In addition, the flight crew must have knowledge of the philosophy, procedures and processes which govern their particular operation, this information can be presented in many forms and is often specific to the airline, the aircraft type and the airspace they will operate within. In order to facilitate TM and FDM, flight crew must also be equipped with tools which will guide resilient behaviours such as, anticipation, monitoring, accurate response, continuous learning and synthesis.

FDM is conducted in an overall complex systems environment (although some elements may also be described as complicated or even simple). Complex systems, unlike simple or complicated systems, requires sensemaking to be applied across the system components in order to learn and develop - this sense making requires the pilots to actively seek information and solutions, and not to be passive in this capacity - therefore the characteristics of the methods employed by the flight crew will need to direct behaviour which will best cope with the complexity. We can classify system types ranging from simple, complicated to complex (see Table 1).

System complexity requires that flight crew make wide use of all of the sources of information and knowledge provided to them within the aviation system in order to make sense of their environment. They must make sense, and then make decisions based upon the feedback and knowledge gained from the technology, other human operators and the environment – a distributed system providing for Distributed Situational Awareness (DSA). This DSA theory (Stanton et al. 2006) purports that the knowledge that underlies DSA is distributed across the system and that there is an implicit communication of information rather than a detailed sharing of mental models between the human operators, with the aim of achieving SSA. With its roots in Cognitive Information Processing (CIP) theory, the Flight Deck Management Model (FDMM) proposed in this research aligns well with the theory of System 1 and 2 thinking (Kahneman 2011). When solving novel or complex problems which arise in this distributed environment, there are many Aeronautical Decision Making (ADM) mnemonics to aid the crew, a selection of these have been evaluated for their utility (Li and Harris 2005). SSE proposes a new ADM mnemonic "DOGAM" (see Sect. 3.2 below), a separate study will be undertaken to evaluate this mnemonic based method. FDMM is designed to provide structure to the TM and ADM required of the crew!

**Table 1.** Simple, complicated and complex systems - Pupilidy (2017)

| System name | Components | Frame | Pathway | Characteristic |
|---|---|---|---|---|
| Complex | The parts are interconnected, inter-active, diverse and adaptive (they adapt often predictably) | Organic - these systems cannot be bro-ken down without losing the ability to understand the interactions | Sense making, improvi-sation and learning - developing adaptations in real time | Unlimited number of questions with an equally unlimited number of answers - requires sensemaking |
| Complicated | The parts are interconnected, inter-active and di-verse | Systemic - These systems are composed of nested sub-systems | Directional flow relationships - cause and effect connections exist with a limited set of outcomes | Each question has a limited number of discreet answers. Reacts well to analysis |
| Simple | The parts are interconnected and interactive | Mechanical | Cause and effect connections are strong - problems can be solved | Each question has one discreet answer. Reacts well to analysis |

## 2  Background

Following detailed discussion at the FDMM Focus Groups, there was consensus that existing Flight Deck Management practices although having produced some satisfactory results in their current form might not be as reliable, efficient, and effective as they perhaps could be in the current environment. With the advent of Systems Thinking in mainstream organisational management practices, it is now assumed that the discretion of Flight Crews (based upon knowledge, experience and a thorough understanding of rules, regulations and procedures) should be the linchpin of Safety Management practices, as the complexity faced by flight crews in performing their duties may require a high degree of adaptability and mental agility. This discretion or performance variability must occur in the dynamic operating environment, but that variability must not unknowingly violate the system design assumptions (safety, operational, legal).

Accepting that Flight Safety is one emergent property of a system fostered around sound Flight Deck Management practices, we then accept that this can be improved by providing Flight Deck operators with a model which, despite the misgivings inherent to any such models, could help increase their adaptive capacity when faced with normal high workload tasks, or abnormal complex events. Notwithstanding the systemic challenges! This research has identified three key barriers to Flight Safety at operator level with regard to FDM:

The emotional and cognitive demands brought about by startle and surprise.

The difficulty of reducing complexity and make decisions in a time compressed environment.

The challenge of planning and executing a strategy while limiting any risk to violating the safety assumptions of the system.

## 2.1 SSE - A Model or Abstraction

In Modelling Command and Control, Stanton et al. (2008) direct that "a model is an abstraction of reality (Wainwright and Mulligan 2004), or 'a representation that mirrors, duplicates, imitates or in some way illustrates a pattern of relationships observed in data or in nature" (Reber 1995, p. 465)". A model is also a kind of theory, 'a characterisation of a process and, as such, its value and usefulness derive from the predictions one can make from it and its role in guiding and developing theory and research' (Reber 1995, p. 465).

The primary purpose of the current generic model of SSE is to reduce complexity and particularly when partnered with additional modelling techniques, to offer outcome metrics that can detect and describe non-random emergent properties.

The optimal Flight Deck Management Model can be defined as one that is malleable enough to detect and capture potent emergent properties, whilst containing merely 'sufficient' complexity to explain (and predict) these 'widely observed properties and behaviours in terms of more fundamental, or concepts' (Wainwright and Mulligan 2004).

**Constraints and Assumptions.** A critical component of any modelling initiative is the quality of the constraints and assumptions within the model. For instance, our Flight Crew Team will be faced with time constraints, noisy flight decks, task overload, possible cognitive – and in more extreme cases physiological – impairments, as well as other constraints that office staff would not have to contend with (eg inability to have face-to-face interactions). Therefore a FDMM cannot be reduced to merely Problem Solving and Classical Decision Making, rather it should integrate with other aspects of flight deck management, from a compliance and airmanship perspective.

**Aeronautical Decision Making (ADM).** There have been many models and approaches developed in order aid ADM, this study reviewed a selection of the most well-known and well utilised when designing the mne- monic aid which underpins the "Solve" element in the SSE FDMM.

Decision-Making for Risk Mitigation

Many years ago, the FAA published the DECIDE model in Advisory Circular 60-22, with a view to provide pilots with a decision-making tool for dealing with abnormal situations. DECIDE stands for:

- Detect the fact that change has occurred
- Estimate the need to counter or react to the change
- Choose a desirable outcome (in terms of success) for the flight
- Identify actions which could successfully control the change
- Do take the necessary action
- Evaluate the effect(s) of the action countering the change.

This demonstrates that there has always been a perceived need in the aviation industry for tools to help pilots in their problem solving and decision-making Journey.

ADM aids commonly follow Classical Decision-Making logic if a step by step linear thinking approach is the aim – some however follow more Naturalistic Decision paths in order to allow for complexity and the real-world issues around decision making within a dynamic environment. In a study in 2005, Li and Harris tasked 60 military pilots with assessing and reviewing 5 of the most common ADM mnemonic aids, this study reported that the pilots rated two of the five under review as most helpful, (SHOR (Stimuli, Hypotheses, Options, Response) and DESIDE (Detect, Estimate, Set Safety Objectives, Identify, Do, Evaluate), they chose these for very different reasons – one being helpful when quick decisions needed to be made in dynamic situations (aligned to NDM principles), the other allowing for a more thorough and deliberate decision making process (aligned to CDM principles).

The ADM mnemonic DOGAM, has been developed to allow for both dynamic flexibility in complex situations and for more deliberate linear complicated or simple decision making, problem solving scenarios.

## 2.2  Classical Decision Making (CDM)

Historically decision making was examined from a point where the factors impacting on them being made, such as ambiguity, time constraints, incomplete information, limited resource capacity were not captured and was referred to as Classical (normative) Decision Making. CDM environments could best be described as sterile laboratory settings. The real or 'large world' that Binmore (2009) describes, is a place of uncertainty and unknown probabilities.

## 2.3  Naturalistic Decision Making, Heuristics and Pattern Matching

Decisions made within aviation are no different to those taken in other high stakes and demanding surroundings. They exist in highly dynamic and often badly-structured environments that are coupled with bounded rationality. With these decision constraints in mind, Simon (1955) introduced the concept of Maximisers and Satisficers - Maximizers attempt to examine every single option before choosing the best one, whereas satisficers tend to consider a more limited range of options to find an option that is satisfactory or "good enough".

Whether NDM's foundation is experience or context driven, operating in such demanding environments offers the potential for cognitive overload (Baddeley 2000) and our limits of cognitive capacity requires support. In his seminal paper in 1956, Herbert Simon said that, '*it was often impossible to optimise decisions taken in the real world, but we should gear ourselves more towards satisficing decisions*'. Over half a century later in their investigation into pilot response to safety events, Clewley and Nixon (2019) concur and conclude, that even to experienced pilots, the world can be a poorly structured and confusing place, further suggesting the requirement for satisficing decisions.

Pilots learn quickly through the careful use of training and experiential learning to match patterns that support rapidly taken decisions (Klein 2008; Clewley and Nixon 2019). In "The Power of Intuition", Klien (2003) describes a pattern as, '*a set of cues that usually chunk together so that if you see a few of the cues you can expect to find others*'. He goes on to describe this further as an accumulation of experiences and building a reservoir of recognised patterns that strengthen our tacit knowledge.

However, pattern matching and heuristics in isolation are not without their weaknesses. Pattern matching can generate flawed options and slow down the decision-making process as the individuals have to go through a series of mental simulations before they can initiate or adapt a plan. The application of an incorrect pattern potentially adds to the complexity of the situation and can in fact magnify it to a point of no return.

### 2.4  Management and Risk

Not being able to manage normal as well as abnormal situations carries an inherent risk. Risk and Threat and Error Management (TEM) is the process in which we assess the actual and potential hazards that exist and decide which ones we are or are not willing to accept. The failure to be aware of the risks that exist could be due to complacency, but will most likely be due to a complex or complicated environment, therefore the failure to provide appropriate tools to assist the pilots could be construed as an organisational shortcoming in the quest for Operational Resilience.

When pilots are operating an aircraft, when fire-fighters are controlling a fire, when an operator is trying to find a fault in a production process, or when a physician is diagnosing a patient, decisions must be made in an inherently unstable environment. In such situations the system (the undesirable aircraft state, the fire, the production process or the patient) changes over time (less fuel, less time available, degrading patient condition), a factor the decision maker has to take into consideration.

## 3  Methodology - Designing the Flight Deck Management Model – Stabilise, Solve, Execute (SSE)

What are we trying to achieve with a FDMM:

- Aid the pilot in the process of flight deck management
- Provide a standardised process for ensuring the flight deck is correctly configured, the flight path is managed and there is correct individual/shared/distributed SA.
- The FDMM can be run even with degraded psychological or physiological condition (needs to be simplified and easily applied)
- Convenient for Task Management (TM)
- Optimum crew coordination and workload management
- Provide an ADM mnemonic for dynamic decision making
- To ensure "buy in" the model must reflect the complexity of the present-day operational task – it must not just be a nuisance change!
- Enhance co-ordination during high workloads and stressful conditions.

If we address all of the above, then the FDMM becomes a useful interface between the human/machine/environment.

## 3.1 Focus Groups

This research project used Focus Groups in order to allow for a free flow of information and expertise from Subject Matter Experts (SME's) across the disciplines involved in flight deck operations, training, checking, standardisation and fleet (aircraft type) specific philosophy. This representation was from:

Human Factors Specialist

Aviation Risk Managers - Flight Operations - current pilots

Flight Training – Course design and implementation – current pilots Training Standards – current pilots

Senior Flight Operations Managers and Training Managers - current pilots Simulator Training

Boeing and Airbus philosophy representation – current pilots

It was crucial to involve current pilots throughout the process as we then had a level of assurance that we were considering how the model may be applied in the "real world" and be reflective of "work as done"!

Work-as-done v work-as-imagined. There has been much literature addressing the difference between work as imagined and work as done. Some of the earliest references from a safety perspective were centred on a distinction between the system task description (work-as-imagined) and the cognitive tasks (work-as-done) (Hollnagel and Woods 1983), this distinction is now more broad and from an applied perspective work-as-imagined refers to work as seen from a management or organisation perspective (blunt end), it is work in strict adherence to the rules, regulations, guidance and procedures which direct that work. Work-as-done refers to the real work taking place at the sharp end. The individuals engaged in this activity are subject to a broad range of performance shaping influences, environmental, social and technical. The human operators have to adapt to these influences, shaping their performance in order to meet a range of sometimes competing goals. Tradeoffs are always occurring; this is described by Hollnagel when he outlines the "ETTO principle". ETTO refers to the Efficiency Thoroughness Trade Off we often see in action on the front line. Further to this, Safetyis also at risk of being traded for efficiency or thoroughness if those competing goals are considered to be of more value than the safety goal!

## 3.2 Flight Deck Management Model – Stabilise, Solve, Execute

**Stabilise.** From a Human Factors perspective this term is more reflective of modern flight deck management than the more traditional descriptor "aviate". Task management on a modern flight deck needs to reflect the additional complexity. Effective flight management depends on effective task management and an in depth understanding of operational flight systems. The traditional term "Aviate" or the act of flying the aeroplane is some- what superseded by the need to manage the flight path and monitor systems. Simply stating "aviate" may be an over simplification – pilot knowledge of the flight management modes and how they control, or protect the aircraft may not be accurate or complete at the time – therefore they may not be able to simply Aviate. Stabilise infers that a number of tasks may need to be managed in order to achieve the goal (Fig. 1).

| Primary Task | Sub-Task | Objectives |
|---|---|---|
| **Stabilize** | Control | **Maintain flight path control**: Make maximum use of automation tools, ensuring Lateral and Navigation Performance are adequate |
| | Operate | **Establish referential integrity**: Ensure compliance with normal and contingency procedures as far as practicable |
| | Manage | **Review collaboration requirements**: Brief stakeholders with their local tasks and objectives |
| **Solve** | Diagnose | **Analyse factual elements of the situation**: Establish a clear Problem statement, what, when, how, which one etc. |
| | Objective | **Set ambitious objective**: What the team would like to do first whilst remaining legal, what the team could, should, must do. Each objective will have to be screened for threats |
| | Generate | **Produce several options**: Brainstorm possible courses of actions that would allow the outcome to meet the objective |
| | Anticipate | **Anticipate threats**: Review options obtained above, register threats associated, consider mitigation strategies and their feasibility. If threats cannot be mitigated, a less ambitious objective must be set. |
| | Manage | **Review the Option Finding process**: Brief stakeholders on the option finding team rationale and update impact on local tasks and objectives |
| **Execute** | Plan | **Share plan**: Make individuals, teams and system(s) aware of the plan, program strategy into digital tools |
| | Brief | **Review and share**: Certify the plan, align mental models, review expected execution scenario and context, anticipate relevant contingencies |
| | Execute | **Perform tasks as briefed**: Act as was agreed, monitor stability of environment and precision of execution, challenge divergences, respond accordingly |
| | Debrief | **Capture scenario**: Record work-as-done vs work-as-imagined, clarify local rationale with participants, review feedback |
| | Learn | **Extract**: Nurture participants' engagement, extract bite-sized learning points, develop further training on the basis of lessons learned |

**Fig. 1.** SSE flight deck management model

Control the flight path – Automation (use highest level of appropriate automation), Lateral (confirm aircraft trajectory will remain satisfactory), Vertical (confirm modes, configuration and thrust are satisfactory).

Operate/procedures and systems – Non normal procedures (perform recommended non normal/abnormal procedures as needed). Normal procedures (perform normal and supplementary procedures as needed.

Manage outcomes – Review the situation (actions and information as required). Task sharing (assign tasks as required). Communicate (Air Traffic Control, Cabin Crew etc.).

**C-O -M** supports the stabilise TM.

### 3.3 Solve

We are attempting to achieve structure and accuracy in the team problem solving, through ADM depth of cognition and enhance individual and shared Situational Awareness (SA):

Accurate SA is the first step in effective decision making that can be lost, and arguably the last step that we actually recognise losing (Endsley 1995). Breakdowns at any of the three hierarchical levels of perception, comprehension and projection can lead to inaccurate situation assessment and to decision errors (Strauch 2016). Endsley (1997) suggests that 'human errors that are attributed to poor decision making actually involve problems with the SA portion of the decision-making process'.

**Solve - to Aid SA and Decision Making.** After stabilising the situation, if no clear procedures exist or the outcome of stabilise remains uncertain, and time pressure is not critical, flight crew may elect to problem solve using the DOGAM model. The solve function has been deconstructed to aid SA and decision making, the following guidance is designed to maximise cognitive task management:

**D**iagnose – What do you think happened, in what sequence, do we know the cause?

**O**bjective – Set the most ambitious viable objective e.g. continue, divert, fix!

**G**enerate – (options based upon the objective) – how can we make this objective work, is it safe, is it legal, is it efficient?

Anticipate – What are the possible threats, how can we mitigate threats.

**M**anage – Review the situation, actions and information as needed. Task sharing (assign as required), Communicate (Air Traffic Control, Cabin crew, Passengers etc.).

Though labelled "Solve" this ADM mnemonic tool is designed primarily for option generation and option finding, as opposed to problem solving. When faced with a problem, we may not be able to solve the problem or make it go away – we can generate options to manage the situation.

DOGAM can be used across the spectrum of complexity. Easy scenario: choosing which runway/approach configuration depending on weather conditions; complex: AFT cargo FIRE followed by FWD cargo FIRE: there is no checklist for that. The ability to deploy DOGAM routinely will help the team come up with a plan more effectively.

**Execute.** This phase utilises the language and behaviours of resilience.

Once a safe course of action has been determined, either from the completion of nonnormal checklists (Stabilise) or problem solving (DOGAM) the following priorities are recommended:

PLAN

Outline the tasks required to implement the agreed course of action. Anticipate contingencies.

BRIEF

Communicate crew plan to relevant agencies as needed.

EXECUTE

Complete tasks in accordance with established policies and procedures. Monitor outcomes satisfy the plan. Respond with contingencies as needed.

DEBRIEF

Facilitated discussion using local rationale to identify and analyze deviations to enhance the scope for learning.

LEARN

Understand what has happened and take away key learning points.

### 3.4  The Flight Deck Management Model – The Flow

(See Fig. 2).

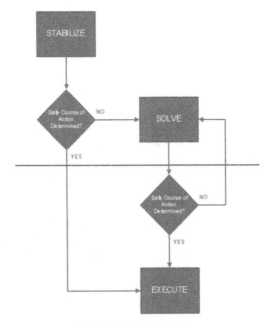

**Fig. 2.** FDMM flow chart

## 4   Conclusion and Recommendations

This model, SSE is designed to aid Aeronautical Decision Making (ADM) and Flight Deck Management (FDM) – the research and development thus far has led the study team to explore wider application across other High Reliability Organisations (HROs) and any complex operations where managers may need to take actions and make decision within uncertain environments with competing goals.

FDMM can be used routinely in both normal and abnormal situation. In fact, the continual use of the FDMM in low stakes environment helps to perfect mastery of the model, thereby reinforcing system integrity.

The model has been delivered and taught to training captains in order to be em bedded within their training practice – an online training package has also been developed in order to fully explain the rationale and application of the model in action.

### 4.1   Recommendations

Once the FDMM is fully established and widely utilised, a follow up study will be undertaken in order to gauge the efficacy of the model in real world application.

## References

Batty, M., Torrens, P.M.: Modelling and prediction in a complex world. Futures (2005). https://doi.org/10.1016/j.futures.2004.11.003

Binmore, K.: Rational Decisions. Princeton University Press, Princeton (2009)

Clewley, R., Nixon, J.: Understanding pilot response to flight safety events using categorisation theory. Theor. Issues Ergon. Sci. **20**, 572–589 (2019). https://doi.org/10.1080/1463922x.2019.1574929

Endsley, M.R.: Design and evaluation for situation awareness enhancement. In: Proceedings of the Human Factors Society Annual Meeting (1988). https://doi.org/10.1177/154193128803200221

Kahneman, D.: Thinking fast, thinking slow. Interpretation, Tavistock, London (2011)

Klein, G.: Naturalistic decision making. Hum. Factors **50**(3), 456–460 (2008)

Roscoe, S.N.: Concepts and definitions. In: Roscoe, S.N. (ed.) Aviation Psychology, 1st edn., pp. 3–10. Iowa State University Press, Ames (1980)

Klein, G.: The Power of Intuition. Penguin, New York (2003)

Klein, G.A., Orasanu, J., Calderwood, R., Zsambok, C.E. (eds.): Decision Making in Action: Models and Methods. Ablex Publishing Corporation, Norwood (1993)

Hollnagel, E.: Safety-I and safety-II: the past and future of safety management. In: Safety-I and safety-II: The Past and Future of Safety Management (2014). https://doi.org/10.1080/00140139.2015.1093290

Hollnagel, E.: The ETTO principle: efficiency-thoroughness trade-off: Why things that go right sometimes go wrong. In: The ETTO Principle: Efficiency-Thoroughness Trade- Off: Why Things That Go Right Sometimes Go Wrong (2012)

Hollnagel, E., Woods, D.D.: Cognitive systems engineering: new wine in new bottles. Int. J. Man-Mach. Stud. (1983). https://doi.org/10.1016/S0020-7373(83)80034-0

Li, W.C., Harris, D.: Aeronautical decision making: instructor-pilot evaluation of five Mnemonic methods. Aviat. Space Environ. Med. **76**, 1156–1161 (2005)

Pupilidy, I.: The Transformation of Accident Investigation: from finding cause to sensemaking (2015). https://pure.uvt.nl/ws/files/7737432/Pupilidy. The Transformation 01 09 2015.pdf

Reber, A.S.: Dictionary of Psychology. Penguin, London (1995)

Simon, H.A.: A behavioral model of rational choice. Q. J. Econ. **59**, 99–118 (1955)

Stanton, N.A., et al.: Distributed situation awareness in dynamic systems: theoretical development and application of an ergonomics methodology. Ergonomics **49**, 1288–1311 (2006)

Wainwright, J., Mulligan, M. (eds.): Environmental Modelling: Finding Simplicity in Complexity. Wiley, London (2004)

# Clipped Wings: The Impact of the COVID-19 Pandemic on Airline Pilots and Influence on Safety Climate

Andrew Mizzi[✉], Gui Lohmann, and Guido Carim Junior

Griffith University, Nathan, QLD, Australia
andrew.mizzi@griffithuni.edu.au

**Abstract.** COVID-19 has led to thousands of pilots being grounded, significantly impacting airline training and safety during operational recovery. Previous research has suggested that the airline safety climate has been negatively impacted during the COVID-19 pandemic, mostly because of borders closure and a sudden loss of revenue. This context led to thousands of pilots being furloughed or dismissed, increasing their stress and anxiety due to financial hardship and resource constraints. However, the influence of the pandemic on how pilots maintained their proficiency while stood down and how they kept engaged with the airline, and therefore the safety climate, has not yet been researched. Hence, this study sought to evaluate the impact that the COVID-19 pandemic had on grounded pilots. We evaluated the operational distractions caused by the pandemic, external stressors influencing motivation and morale towards work, and how this affected safety climate. A questionnaire study was conducted with 105 airline pilots who were grounded for longer than three months, requiring refresher training and then returned to operational flying. The research found that approximately half of the participants did not engage in any skill and knowledge upkeeping whilst grounded. COVID-19 measures restricted the access to training facilities for many participants, negatively influencing their motivation to skill-upkeeping. Uncertainty with sudden and indefinite grounding periods made it challenging to maintain engagement and motivation. Job-reattachment was further aggravated by the additional financial and personal stress. The pandemic led to distractions in effectively applying their skills to the job. Physical and mental health concerns were mentioned by many participants as a factor influencing their job performance. The study proposes recommendations for airlines to improve engagement of grounded pilots and pilots in isolation.

**Keywords:** Flight proficiency · Flight safety · Safety culture · Skill retention · COVID-19

## 1 Introduction

The COVID-19 pandemic has impacted the airline industry globally, causing domestic and international borders to be closed and an unprecedented drop in passenger numbers.

In Europe alone, Albers found that at least half the airlines went into a 'retrenchment mode', with several airlines such as Air Italy, Flybe and Norwegian Air Shuttle ceasing operations, entering administration or filing for bankruptcy [1]. By April 2020, 66% of the world's commercial air transport fleet was grounded [2], and by a year later, only 64% of the airlines had more than 80% of their pilots back on duty [3]. The reduction in flying led to many pilots being stood down, made redundant or furloughed, leading to a loss of proficiency and recent operational experience. The organisational engagement of these pilots while they are 'grounded' has varied from airline to airline. While some airlines have retained their employees on full pay, others have ceased paying their salaries or relied on government payments to support their staff during the pandemic. The impact of redundancies on organisational culture, morale and motivation is well known [4]. However, the pandemic's effect on airlines' safety climate is unknown.

Provan defines safety as "the ability of a system to perform its intended purpose, whilst preventing harm to persons" [5]. As a derivative of organisational culture, safety culture is understood by Turner as "the set of beliefs, norms, attitudes, roles, and social and technical practices that are concerned with minimising the exposure of employees, managers, customers and members of the public to conditions considered dangerous or injurious" [6]. It is crucial to define its relationship with safety climate when discussing safety culture. Safety climate is considered a 'snapshot' of safety culture [7], which focuses on employees beliefs about management commitment to safety. In this context, safety climate is a more appropriate discussion point concerning the COVID-19 pandemic [8–10]. Five safety climate themes were identified by O'Connor [7], which were designed upon research by Flin [11], and include management and supervision, safety systems, risk, work pressure and training and education. These themes provide the categorical basis to examine the pandemic's impact on the safety climate in flight operations.

Aviation safety regulators have relaxed pilots' recent experience requirements to assist airline operations due to a reduction in available training sectors and access to ground training facilities. Whilst airlines and regulators conduct risk assessments into these practices, the result of a lack of recency can still result in safety incidents [12, 13]. The impact of these factors on safe flight operations and safety climate is not yet fully understood.

As the pandemic continues, the purpose of this study was to understand the influences it has made on the safety climate within an airlines' flight operations, which is essential for the safe recovery to normal operations. Grounded airline pilots have endured the brunt of operational changes and associated stress of being stood down, making worthy research subjects understand the full impact on safety climate.

An online survey with pilots who have been stood down and have returned to the flying duties aimed to answer the following specific research questions:

1. How did external stressors manifest in airline pilots during the COVID-19 pandemic?
2. What operational distractions exist associated with the COVID-19 pandemic?
3. How can this influence the safety climate within airlines?

## 2 Literature Review

As a result of the pandemic, quieter air traffic, airports closing runways for maintenance, portions of airports closed for aircraft parking and routing shortcuts offered
by air traffic control, complexity in the environment airline pilots operate within has
increased [14]. These changes in the environment have influenced the safety of flight
operations. Research into atypical approaches into Charles de Gaulle airport in Paris
found an increase in riskier landing approaches, such as steeper vertical glide path inter-
cepts and final approach track shortening [15]. Adding to this, Olaganathan and Amihan
[16] found that a lack of practice affected pilots' proficiency during the COVID-19 pandemic. They analysed pilots' reports submitted to NASA's Aviation Safety Reporting
System (ASRS), finding that some incidents were attributed to this lack of proficiency.
This early research indicates that the operational nature of an airline pilot's work has
changed during the pandemic and increased safety risk.

Significant assistance for airlines has come from industry organisations providing
recommendations in managing operational recovery. IATA [17] published risk assessments to guide airlines in managing operational risk and pilot training during the pandemic. Recommendations included mitigations such as raising operational thresholds,
rejecting voluntary route shortcuts, and management of COVID related PPE and social
distancing measures. Whilst operational conservatism was recommended, the resulting
impact on departure and arrival delays was minimised, potentially due to decreased
overall air traffic [18].

Research into a flight training organisation impacted during the COVID-19 pandemic suggests that various safety culture and safety climate variables were negatively
affected [19]. For instance, 'production versus protection' variables showed decreased
worker agreement. Some of the decreases in employee engagement were attributed to
the pressure the flight training organisation faced with the pandemic, particularly in its
management of social distancing. However, this management of pandemic related issues
results in the prevailing safety climate associated with flight operations changing. Work
led stress from the pandemic has been found to influence safety culture. Saleem [20]
found that the pandemic harmed task and contextual performance. They found that a
positive safety culture would provide the foundation to moderate adaptive performance
and resilience.

Conversely, Schwarz [21] found that psychological stress positively influences
resilient behaviour but has a negative effect on safety culture development. When this
stress is combined with inconsistencies or changes in policies, procedures, and practices
that govern an airline pilot's role, research shows that it can lead to weaker safety climates [22]. There is limited research conducted into the influence on the safety climate
of airline pilots because of a grounded or furloughed workforce, particularly during a
pandemic. For airlines battling financial difficulty due to the pandemic, financial and
resource constraints increase pilots' stress, negatively impacting the organisation and
safety culture. Job reattachment can also be challenging when airline pilots return to
face operational policy and procedure changes, along with demanding practices related
directly to the pandemic [23].

The pandemic has led many pilots to face personal and financial stressors that influence their motivation towards work whilst grounded. Peyrat-Guillard and Grefe [24]

found that whilst pilots idealise their employing airline, this bond is fragile, particularly in the face of grounding or furlough. Majuarsa [25] found that the work environment positively affects pilot professionalism and that this profession seeks to create and improve its professional quality continually. Leveraging this trait, airlines may expect their pilots to study, even though they were stood down without pay in many cases. For airlines battling financial difficulties, an expectation to work without full remuneration can impact their organisational culture [26, 27]. Airline downsizing, a frequent consequence of the pandemic [1], has been directly linked to negatively impacting performance. Fraher [28] found an increase in stress, distraction, and mistakes, which led to a decrease in trust, morale and organisational commitment. Shore [29] found evidence of a 'post-downsizing stress syndrome' typified by impacting health, personal life, and attitude towards work, fostering a sense of desperation. The effect on safety climate can be significant if not corrected [30].

## 3   Research Methodology

An online survey was conducted to gather data from the participants. The survey method allowed access to a large participant group from many countries, which was particularly useful given border closures and travel restrictions at the time. Participants conducted the survey anonymously. The questionnaire consisted of two parts which focused on different pilots' operational status and roles within the airline.

The questionnaire was completed with other research seeking to understand aspects of competency decay and training activities on grounded pilots during the pandemic [31].

### 3.1   Questionnaire Design

Demographic data were collected on the participant and an understanding of their time grounded and expectations on a return to operation. The impact of COVID-19 related restrictions, such as social distancing and its impact on airline training resources, was questioned, gauging the airlines' engagement with their grounded pilots. Participants were asked to describe how the pandemic has increased distractions to their everyday work and how social distancing, border closures and related pandemic measures required them to modify their actions.

### 3.2   Data Collection

The survey hyperlink was shared through the authors' LinkedIn network, in addition to industry-specific groups in the platform, such as the Royal Aeronautical Society's Human Factors Group, Flight Safety Foundation, and Human Factors in Aviation. Several pilot unions, safety organisations, and airlines were contacted to share the survey link with pilots via email. The questionnaire remained available for participation throughout August 2021.

The inclusion criteria of a grounded pilot are defined as an airline pilot who, during the COVID-19 pandemic, lost recent experience requirements and are required to undergo training before returning to active operational status. This provides a reasonable classification to capture participants who had not flown for at least 90 days as per ICAO [32] requirements and, most likely, who also had other training requirements lapse.

A total of 391 individuals participated in the research study. Those participants who did not meet the inclusion criteria were excluded via a zero-quota option within the questionnaire logic, and incomplete surveys were also excluded from the sample. This research used 105 valid results (286 excluded surveys) specific to these research questions.

### 3.3  Respondents Profile

Of the 105 participants, there were one Training/Check Captain, 49 Captains, one Check/Training Officer, 37 First Officers, five Second Officers, and two Management Pilots. Most participants usually operate passenger flights (81%, n = 86), while a small number typically operate both passenger and cargo flights (9%, n = 9) or cargo-only flights (10%, n = 10). Most participants hold Air Transport Pilot Licences (92%, n = 97). Australian participants represented the highest proportion of pilots within the sample (47%, n = 49), likely due to the promotion of the survey by the Australian and International Pilots Association (AIPA) and the Australian Airline Pilots' Association (AusALPA). Many participants were also from Hong Kong (19%, n = 20) due to the internal circulation of the questionnaire by a Hong Kong airline.

The participant sample mainly was experienced pilots with an average total flying experience of 11,471 h (SD = 5,852). Participants were grounded on average eight months (SD = 5), with a minimum of one month and a maximum of 35 months, even though the expectation of grounding was four months (SD = 7), with most participants (30%, n = 32) expecting not to be grounded at all, as shown in Fig. 1. Participants grounded for longer than 18 months (5%, n = 5) include those on annual or medical leave before the pandemic.

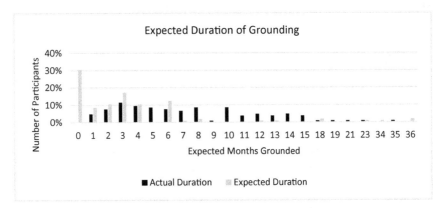

**Fig. 1.** Expected duration and duration of grounding.

### 3.4 Data Analysis

The questionnaire data was cleaned and organised with OpenRefine and analysed with Tableau, Excel, and SPSS. Open-ended questions were thematically analysed through NVivo into categories related to employee engagement (e.g., culture and climate), external stressors and operational distractions.

## 4 Results

### 4.1 Work Activities Whilst Grounded

Almost half of the participants (47%, n = 49) had not completed any work preparation study whilst they were grounded. We assume this happened in part because a third of them (30%, n = 32) were not expecting to be grounded in the first place. The second was the uncertainty created by the situation, which ended up being longer than expected, as suggested in the other of one of the respondents:

> *"Fatigue and demotivation from consistent negative news in both my local community, and worldwide gave little motivation to continue studying when the following thought was constantly at the forefront of my mind - Why should I study if I'm nowhere near getting back into a flight deck? Why waste my mental energy and time trying to commit the following to memory again when I can't even step foot in a simulator or aircraft yet to solidify the content I am studying?"*

Participants were asked whether their airlines set any explicit or implicit study expectations while they were grounded; however, the majority (63%, n = 66) said no expectation was placed upon them. For some participants, intrinsic professionalism traits influenced study habits. As explained by one participant, *"regardless of the company providing training opportunities, the pilots are required to demonstrate a high level of self-discipline and pursue the self-study on their initiative. Sort of like a professional ethos"*. However, social distancing and border closures measures influenced how participants studied. These measures restricted 21% of participants (n = 22) from conducting self-study activities they otherwise wished to accomplish because of closed or limited access to training facilities.

A small number of participants said they were expected to complete online training (6%, n = 6) and remain up to date with notices to crew/procedure changes (5%, n = 5). The majority (70%, n = 73) of participants did not receive any study programs or voluntary training opportunities from their airline. The lack of training investment in grounded pilots resulted in a more significant effort to return them to proficiency. If coupled with experienced pilots leaving the industry due to groundings, the resulting 'brain drain' can lead to a reduction in safety, as feared by one participant *"I fear there will be a massive skill deficit when we return requiring much more training than the industry is currently planning. This could lead to poor safety outcomes in the long run"*.

Upon the return to flying, the majority of participants (64%, n = 64) received some training from their airline, supplementary to the regulatory requirements of ICAO [32], with most (n = 33) explaining that specific simulator training designed for the return to operations was beneficial in re-developing their confidence. However, 15% (n = 15) of the pilot participants who had returned to operations reported that training programs insufficiently prepared them for regaining confidence. Participants mentioned that airlines were only training to the minimum required by their state regulator; *"Trained minimum competence, not confidence"* and *"there was very little scope to let me develop confidence"*. Classroom or ground-school training was provided to 13 participants (12%) and most commonly involved human factors or mental health welfare training and familiarisation with revised company procedures.

## 4.2   External Stressors Impacting Airline Pilots

Whilst some had undertaken other employment, 84% (n = 89) still sourced their primary income from their work as an airline pilot, waiting to return to operational status. Pilots' motivation has varied significantly. As one participant described, *"during the first 6–12 months of stand down, I felt zero interest in study or preparation for my eventual return to flying. I felt [a] disconnect and disengaged from the airline and felt frustrated"*. Other stressors have influenced grounded pilots during the pandemic. *"Mental and financial stress, uncertainty over [the] tenure of employment"* was a standard narrative described by the pilots. The disconnection those grounded pilots felt with their airline and the stressors they have been subject to will only continue to grow as pilots remain grounded. As a participant summarises:

> *"My main concern is for the mental health of professionals who may be stood down for a period greater than two years, and how to deal with the return to work. Many have lost houses, marriages and moved their children from school. Minimal assistance has been provided by the company they work for, yet they spend millions every month maintaining the grounded aircraft. The long-term damage done to the employer-employee relationship may never be recovered, and how that, in turn, reflects upon professional standards is of great concern"*.

The majority (61%, n = 62) of participants believe the pandemic-induced safety protocols impose extra demands on pilots, with around 22% of participants (n = 23) mentioning health screening measures as one of the most demanding. For participants who returned to work, *"on top of the return-to-duty-stress, there were all these new COVID regulations to comply with"*. New requirements included *"the constant changing of government rules and regulations dealing with crew of international aircraft"* and *"hygiene procedures (masks, social distancing, etc.) [which] were distractions, mainly on ground - i.e., meeting crew, planning, pre-flight, turnarounds"*. As one of the pilots explained, some *"airfields [are] taking the opportunity to conduct repairs and upgrades"* in their runways, taxiways and facilities due to the reduced air traffic. Consequentially pilots have to deal with *"many more NOTAMS"*, increasing their workload and risks to the operation. Two pilots summarise the sentiment of the participants by stating that *"flying has almost become secondary to the COVID stuff"* and *"the flying itself, from pushback to on blocks, has not changed too much; it is all the other things around it that are making things difficult or unpredictable"*.

### 4.3 Operational Distractions

Perhaps for some airlines, the concern of skill retention on grounded pilots is secondary to trying to maintain a viable business. It prompted comments such as *"the airline is stretched so tight they can't invest in training to return to work, so relying on pilots to prepare at home the best they can individually"*. Utilising a core group of Training Captains to operate much of the flying schedule was reported as a frequent method to ensure that this crucial group is ready to assist in the recovery of line pilots to operational status. However, prioritising groups has left many other pilots on the fringe or outside of this group with uncertainty on when (or if) they will return to work. It has been frustrating for some participants who stood down with no pay because *"my fleet manager said it was up to us to keep revising or risk losing our professional knowledge...he was on full pay"*. This sentiment reflects that crew engagement in voluntary training programs is one of the most significant hurdles airlines face whilst pilots are grounded. Some participants reported the introduction of a 'Pilot Preservation Program', which provided a non-jeopardy simulator session and ground training every few months. However, these efforts were flanked by domestic border closures making it difficult for pilots to participate.

According to the participants, mitigation to reduce the complexity and risk in flight operations as recommended by IATA were not adopted by their airlines. Instead, operational normality was being encouraged by airlines, as described in the pilots' narratives such as *"it has been a year of introducing new things just at a time when it would be helpful to fall back on familiar and established procedures"*. Some participants reported changes to procedures, the introduction of new tools such as Electronic Flight Bags (EFB), changes to fuel policies, aircraft performance calculations, and departure and approach briefing standards. As described by one participant:

> *"[Airline] expected crew to remain up to date with all of the regulatory and manual amendments. Despite long periods away from flying, there was no reduction in the number of manual/procedural changes made. A sensible approach, in my opinion, would have been to provide crew returning to work with an up to date document detailing the changes made over the last 3, 6, 9, 12 months etc. and why the changes were made, where to find the new procedures etc. This was not and is not being done."*

This type of situation was a catalyst of stress for some participants, one of which stated, *"after a long period away, I found the sheer volume of information to re-familiarise myself with was overwhelming and contributed to a lot of stress and anxiety before the refresher course began"*. More than being overwhelmed by information overload, the participants believe that reducing the flying schedule subsequently impacted organisational culture. *"Erosion of culture, loss of familiarity with other crew members, [and] loss of confidence to exert command authority which is already a challenge under Airbus operational philosophy"*, as stated by one of the respondents.

## 5 Impact on Safety Climate

This discussion is broken down into safety climate themes [7, 11], which are broad common themes developed by Gibbons [33] in the context of airline flight operations.

Their creation of these themes was important in recognising the need to account for an atypical employee-employer relationship in flight operations departments and its influence on safety climate.

## 5.1  Management/Supervision

Management and supervision are essential within the context of the safety climate. It drives the perceptions and beliefs of safety from a top-down perspective, particularly concerning the trade-off between production and protection. Stemming from the COVID-19 pandemic, this research found that the disconnect between grounded pilots and airline management significantly influences employee engagement. While some airlines have tried to motivate and engage their grounded pilots, the impact of the pandemic both personally and financially has hampered efforts. These stressors have played a prominent role in demotivating grounded pilots to prioritise skill and knowledge retention. Whilst airlines have focused on providing mental health support to pilots who have returned to operations via classroom training, pilots who are not actively engaged in training with their airline may not be receiving the support they require.

Primarily related to pilots' psychological stress, airline management needs an emphatic approach to personnel and performance management and ensure that well-being programs are in place for all crew. The research found that wellbeing programs were not commonly offered to grounded pilots until they returned to work, leaving them on the fringe without adequate support. These actions can leave those pilots feeling abandoned by their managers, negatively influencing their attitude towards management commitment to work and safety. Research has already identified a growing divide in pilots' professional standing and long-term career aspirations [27, 34], and the pandemic is likely bringing a further decline to the occupation to the forefront. It is particularly relevant as many grounded pilots have already left the industry to reskill and find alternative employment and careers. For those who intend to return to their profession, without airlines investing early and regularly in skill retention, the resultant cost of an extensive training volume will hamper airlines from recovering already decimated profit.

## 5.2  Safety Systems

Participants' perception of the state of the safety system was not frequently captured in this research and reflects that operational and industrial matters of their continued employment received a higher emphasis in participant responses than engagement with the safety management system.

## 5.3  Risk

IATA [2] provided extensive risk assessments and guidance into flight operations, personnel management, human factors and crew resource management, and aircraft cleanliness. Whilst participants did not mention any of the flight operation mitigations being utilised, such as increasing operational thresholds, each airline likely conducted risk assessments where appropriate, particularly in collaboration with their state regulator.

Several human factor items foreseen by IATA are congruent with this research findings. Increased distraction in tasks was found amongst participants, along with a breakdown in crew communication and alignment due to procedural and operational changes. These were mainly considered tolerable risks by IATA, with existing controls and mitigations utilised to manage. However, it is noted that IATA and participants pointed out reliance upon their check and trainers to provide some or all the necessary support for pilots return-to-operations journey. Risk assessments must ensure that personnel are also duly supported and protected from the resulting stressors of the pandemic to ensure that they can adequately provide their expertise.

## 5.4  Work Pressure

Work pressure is the balance maintained between production pressure and safety. Work pressure is regulated and managed through stringent standard operating procedures and highly regulated procedures in aviation. During the COVID-19 pandemic, airlines faced difficulties needing to remain competitive by adapting their operations with new technologies. Airlines introduced new electronic flight bags, performance optimisation, fuel policies and aircraft operation changes. However, the researchers discovered that pilots found it difficult to keep up with procedure and policy changes whilst grounded and upon their return. The drive for returning to 'Ops-normal' whilst still managing a workforce with diminished proficiency due to a lack of flying has a subsequent negative effect on safety climate [11].

## 5.5  Training/Education (Competence)

The workforces' general perception of the competence of its fellow employees is the essence of this safety climate theme. For pilots grounded, inadequate opportunities to retain competencies in their skills, knowledge and attitude can lead to increased difficulties for airlines to return their pilots to operational flying quickly. Personal and financial stressors have played a significant role in engaging pilots to remain engaged in study whilst grounded. Given that close to half of the participants did not study whilst grounded indicates that an impact to safety climate may occur when they return to operational flying, and that confidence in the pilot workforce's competence may linger for some time, particularly until regular flying schedules return to pre-pandemic levels. The competency level of high-performing crews who were previously grounded was also noted to have declined during the pandemic [31].

## 5.6  Recommendations

Airline management should recognise the significant mental and physical stress pilots have endured during the pandemic. Internal and external stressors' influence on flight operations will impact the safety climate. Operational distractions, such as avoiding numerous changes to the operational procedures and issuing constant internal memos, should be minimised until a significant level of pre-pandemic operations has been regained, and pilots are adequately prepared to manage their competency and work pressure. Also, providing ways to keep the pilots informed about the organisation and the operational environment, particularly those who are still grounded, can reduce disengagement and anxiety. Meetings with the pilots, updates on the operational setting and topics of training are all suggestions that require minimal effort and will keep the group informed and engaged.

## 6 Conclusion

The purpose of this study was to evaluate what stressors and distractions airline pilots have faced during the COVID-19 pandemic and how these can influence safety climate. Many participants explained a disconnect between them and their employing airlines, and this disengagement can manifest into the safety climate, particularly around work pressure and competency. Mental and financial stress upon grounded pilots negatively influenced motivation and engagement towards work, and for some, they felt disengaged and frustrated.

This research had several limitations. The study focused on pilots who had been grounded for longer than 90 days, which subsequently excluded pilots who faced stressors and distractions throughout the pandemic whilst remaining operational. This also limited the survey to airline pilots who suffered more protracted periods of groundings than some who retained a large percentage of their existing flying schedule. Additionally, as found in this research, motivation varied between participants, influencing participation in employment-related research.

As the COVID-19 pandemic continues, with many pilots still operationally grounded, additional studies should consider the measurement within flight operation departments and how the various airline and regulator interventions impact safety climate, consider the consequence of pilots leaving the industry and the detrimental impact on both the profession's future and impact on pilot shortage. It may provide influences that can be reversed.

## References

1. Albers, S., Rundshagen, V.: European airlines' strategic responses to the COVID-19 pandemic. J. Air Transp. Manage. **87**, 101863 (2020). https://doi.org/10.1016/j.jairtraman.2020.101863
2. IATA, Airline Industry Statistics Confirm 2020 Was Worst Year on Record. Montreal, Canada (2021). https://www.iata.org/en/pressroom/pr/2021-08-03-01/
3. IATA, 2nd IATA Survey – Report (2021). https://www.iata.org/contentassets/c0f61fc821dc4f62bb6441d7abedb076/report_2nd_iata_survey_status_of_pilot_population_training_currency_1st-april-2021.pdf
4. Thornhill, A., Gibbons, A.: The positive management of redundancy survivors: issues and lessons. Empl. Counc. Today (1995). https://doi.org/10.1108/13656529510091060
5. Provan, D.J., Woods, D.D., Dekker, S.W., Rae, A.J.: Safety II professionals: How resilience engineering can transform safety practice. Reliab. Eng. Syst. Saf. **195**, 106740 (2020). https://doi.org/10.1016/j.ress.2019.106740
6. Turner, B.A., Pidgeon, N., Blockley, D., Toft, B.: Safety culture: its importance in future risk management. In: Position Paper for the Second World Bank Workshop on Safety Control and Risk Management. Karlstad, Sweden (1989). https://doi.org/10.1016/j.ssci.2010.10.001

7. O'Connor, P., O'Dea, A., Kennedy, Q., Buttrey, S.E.: Measuring safety climate in aviation: a review and recommendations for the future. Saf. Sci. **49**(2), 128–138 (2011). https://doi.org/10.1016/j.ssci.2010.10.001

8. DeJoy, D.M.: Behavior change versus culture change: divergent approaches to managing workplace safety. Saf. Sci. **43**(2), 105–129 (2005). https://doi.org/10.1016/j.ssci.2005.02.001

9. Guldenmund, F.W.: The nature of safety culture: a review of theory and research. Saf. Sci. **34**(1–3), 215–257 (2000). https://doi.org/10.1016/S0925-7535(00)00014-X

10. Zohar, D.: Thirty years of safety climate research: reflections and future directions. Accid. Anal. Prev. **42**(5), 1517–1522 (2010). https://doi.org/10.1016/j.aap.2009.12.019

11. Flin, R., Mearns, K., O'Connor, P., Bryden, R.: Measuring safety climate: identifying the common features. Saf. Sci. **34**(1–3), 177–192 (2000). https://doi.org/10.1016/S0925-7535(00)00012-6

12. Honourable Company of Air Pilots, Commercial Air Transport Safety Briefing Note 01 - Pilot Recency when Normal Rating Validity Requirements are Relaxed (2021). https://www.airpilots.org/file/dd91e200f27482462d763d1209d41e1d/safety-briefing-note-01-pilot-recency-when-normal-rating-validity-requirememts-are-relaxed.pdf

13. EASA, Safety Issue Report – Skills and Knowledge Degradation due to Lack of Recent Practice (2021). https://www.easa.europa.eu/community/system/files/2021-08/Safety%20Issue%20Report%20-%20%20Skills%20and%20Knowledge%20Degradation_REV2%20Clean_0.pdf

14. Adrienne, N., Budd, L., Ison, S.: Grounded aircraft: an airfield operations perspective of the challenges of resuming flights post COVID. J. Air Transp. Manag. **89**, 101921 (2020). https://doi.org/10.1016/j.jairtraman.2020.101921

15. Jarry, G., Delahaye, D., Feron, E.: Flight safety during Covid-19: a study of Charles de Gaulle airport atypical energy approaches. Transp. Res. Interdisc. Perspect. **9**, 100327 (2021). https://doi.org/10.1016/j.trip.2021.100327

16. Olaganathan, R., Amihan, R.A.H.: Impact of COVID-19 on Pilot Proficiency–A Risk Analysis. Glob. J. Eng. Technol. Adv. **6**(03), 1 (2021). https://doi.org/10.30574/gjeta.2021.6.3.0023

17. IATA, Guidance for Managing Pilot Training and Licensing During COVID-19 Operations. International Air Transport Association (2020). https://www.iata.org/contentassets/c0f61fc821dc4f62bb6441d7abedb076/iata-guidance-for-managing-pilot-training-licensing-during-covid19-ed-2.pdf

18. Yimga, J.: The airline on-time performance impacts of the COVID-19 pandemic. Transp. Res. Interdisc. Perspect. **10**, 100386 (2021). https://doi.org/10.1016/j.trip.2021.100386

19. Byrnes, K.P., Rhoades, D.L., Williams, M.J., Arnaud, A.U., Schneider, A.H.: The effect of a safety crisis on safety culture and safety climate: the resilience of a flight training organization during COVID-19. Transp. Policy **117**, 181–191 (2021). https://doi.org/10.1016/j.tranpol.2021.11.009

20. Saleem, F., Malik, M.I., Qureshi, S.S.: Work stress hampering employee performance during COVID-19: is safety culture needed? Front. Psychol. **12** (2021). https://doi.org/10.3389/fpsyg.2021.655839

21. Schwarz, M., Kallus, K.W., Gaisbachgrabner, K.: Safety culture, resilient behavior, and stress in air traffic management. Aviat. Psychol. Appl. Hum. Factors **6**(1), 12–23 (2016). https://doi.org/10.1027/2192-0923/a000091

22. Zohar, D., Luria, G.: A multilevel model of safety climate: cross-level relationships between organization and group-level climates. J. Appl. Psychol. **90**(4), 616 (2005). https://doi.org/10.1037/0021-9010.90.4.616

23. Yuan, Z., Ye, Z., Zhong, M.: Plug back into work, safely: Job reattachment, leader safety commitment, and job engagement in the COVID-19 pandemic. J. Appl. Psychol. **106**(1), 62 (2021). https://doi.org/10.1037/apl0000860

24. Peyrat-Guillard, D., Grefe, G.: The psychological bonds between airline pilots and their work: from passion to reason. Shapes Tour. Employ.: HRM Worlds Hotels Air Transp. **4**, 173–186 (2020). https://doi.org/10.1002/9781119751342.ch11

25. Majuarsa, I.: The effect of work environment and individual characteristics on pilot performance with professionalism as an intervening variable. Management Science Letters **11**(6), 1855–1860 (2021). https://doi.org/10.5267/j.msl.2021.1.018

26. Fraher, A.L.: Invisibilised dirty work: The multiple realities of US airline pilots' work. Cult. Organ. **23**(2), 131–148 (2017). https://doi.org/10.1080/14759551.2016.1244825

27. Fraher, A.L.: The vulnerability of quasi-professional experts: a study of the changing character of US airline pilots' work. Econ. Ind. Democr. **40**(4), 867–889 (2019). https://doi.org/10.1177/0143831X16668580

28. Fraher, A.L.: Airline downsizing and its impact on team performance. Team Perform. Manage. **19**(1/2), 109–126 (2013). https://doi.org/10.1108/13527591311312123

29. Shore, B.: The legacy of downsizing: putting the pieces back together. In: Business Forum. Los Angeles, California. p. 5 (1996)

30. Didla, S., Mearns, K., Flin, R.: Safety citizenship behaviour: a proactive approach to risk management. J. Risk Res. **12**(3–4), 475–483 (2009). https://doi.org/10.1080/13669870903041433

31. Mizzi, A.: Pilot proficiency during the COVID-19 pandemic: skill retention methods to counter competency decline. Master's thesis, Griffith University (2021). https://doi.org/10.13140/RG.2.2.18074.11202

32. ICAO, Annex 6 to the Convention: Operation of Aircraft Part 1. 9th edn. International Civil Aviation Organization, Montreal, Quebec, Canada (2010)

33. Gibbons, A.M., von Thaden, T.L., Wiegmann, D.A.: Development and initial validation of a survey for assessing safety culture within commercial flight operations. Int. J. Aviat. Psychol. **16**(2), 215–238 (2006). https://doi.org/10.1207/s15327108ijap1602_6

34. Maxwell, G., Grant, K.: Commercial airline pilots' declining professional standing and increasing precarious employment. Int. J. Hum. Resour. Manage. **32**(7), 1486–1508 (2021). https://doi.org/10.1080/09585192.2018.1528473

# Degrading Human Factors Through the Invisible 'Freaky 13th' Element

Angeline Ram[(✉)] [iD]

University of Waterloo, Waterloo, ON N2L 3G1, Canada
a7ram@uwaterloo.ca

**Abstract.** The purpose of this paper is to explore how everyday experiences of the Aircraft Maintenance Engineers (AMEs) affects human factors by first understanding what experiences adversely affect the AMEs. This study uses qualitative methods to answer the question, how do negative experiences in the workplace degrade the human performance of AMEs in Ontario, Canada's air transportation sector? The preliminary findings suggest that an organisational culture that tolerates negative intra-employee and management to employee interactions degrades workers' safety. The findings of this study show that psychosocial risks, like negative interactions, degrade a workers' safety performance in a safety critical sociotechnical environment by creating distractions, increasing stress, and reducing communication. Keeping in line with the Dirty Dozen framework: organisational culture is the 'Freaky 13th' element. The findings of this study first show that culture is perceived differently by workers in the same occupation, and negative experiences with peers and management degrade HFs. When these findings are compared to how the International Civil Aviation Authority currently frames aviation safety, aviation safety culture and practices fall short in acknowledging safety risks.

**Keywords:** Human factors · Organisational safety culture · Aircraft maintenance

## 1 Introduction

Aviation Maintenance Engineers (AMEs), like doctors, carry the responsibility and liability for safeguarding human life [1]. AMEs face a unique set of human factors (HFs) that differ from pilots. Human Factors (HFs) include "what we know about human beings as it relates to their characteristics, limitations and abilities, to the design of the equipment they use, the environments in which they function and the jobs they perform [2]." HFs influences how humans perform within their working environments. Some HFs specific to AMEs include hazardous working conditions (working at heights), physically strenuous environments, physical exposure to extreme weather conditions, planning technical tasks, completing associated clerical duties, and problem-solving for long periods under time pressure [1]. Workers are also influenced by their organizational culture [3].

Although HFs in aviation is most commonly associated with pilots through Crew Resource Management (CRM) [4], HF's multidisciplinary approach combines many insights from psychology, engineering, and health [4]. In Canada, the Dirty Dozen HFs program informs maintenance personnel of human error that results from 12 common safety traps [4–6]. Human errors result from the human condition and limitations [4–6]. In general, aviation personnel recognize their safety responsibility in upholding safe practices [7] and their vulnerability to human limitations that can result in error [8–10]. However, HFs programs rarely acknowledge hazards resulting from an organisation's culture. Workers are both the solution to enhancing organisational safety culture and a source of risk. Risks that degrade workers' HFs must be mitigated through a worker-centred organisational safety culture.

This paper is part of a larger project that explores the everyday experiences of workers in Ontario, Canada's air transportation sector. The purpose and originality of this paper explores how every day experiences of the AMEs affects HFs by first understanding what experiences adversely affect the AMEs. The paper then explores how the experiences degrade human factors. This study builds on Dupont's 12 preconditions for HFs errors: fatigue, stress, complacency, communication, awareness, distraction, lack of knowledge, teamwork, lack of resources, pressure, lack of assertiveness, and norms [4]. Although the Dirty Dozen framework is under-researched, it mirrors the flight operation's Crew Resource Management (CRM) HFs framework that has been adopted for over 40 years and is influenced by Hofstede's [11] work on national culture and Helmreich's [12] insight on the Three Cultures of Aviation. Most importantly, the Dirty Dozen's framework is accepted as an applied human error framework for the aircraft maintenance sector in Canada.

The first section of this article positions workers within the heartland of safety culture and explores a limitation of aviation safety. Section two explains the methods, justifying why a qualitative approach is more suitable for understanding lived experiences in the workplace. Section three outlines the results, drawing attention to intra-employee interactions that degrade human performance. Section four discusses the findings, and the paper concludes in section five by providing recommendations and suggestions for future research.

## 1.1 Reframing Safety Culture

Organisational safety culture's influence is observed through the policies/controls that are upheld and how the organization views and approaches safety [3]. Investigations of organisational accidents like the 1989 Air Ontario crash in Dryden Ontario [13], academic insight through Reason's [14] accident causation model, and the Human Factors Analysis Classification System [15] show the gravity and role of organisational influences on human error. However, one limitation of culture is that it is viewed ubiquitously within an organisation. ICAO [16] defines culture as shared beliefs and behaviours. ICAO's myopic view of culture assumes the homogeneity of the workforce and fails to capture the different views and opinions of people. Organisational psychologists acknowledge that workplaces are enhanced through culture, supervisors, workers, and occupational hierarchy [4]. However, social determinants of wellbeing like discrimination and intra-employee relations [17] may adversely affect some workers and not others.

Extending beyond aviation's limited definition of culture to the field of social psychology, Schein [18, 19] describes organizational culture as a complex phenomenon composed of three levels; artifacts, espoused beliefs and values, and basic assumptions. Through Schein's [18, 19] description of the culture, workers are positioned in a complex ecosystem influenced by personal beliefs, occupational norms, and organizational factors.

The first level, artifacts, are visible or feelable structures and observed behaviours' [18, 19] within an organization. Often artifacts include posters that declare safety as a number one priority. The next level, espoused beliefs and values, are associated with the ideas, goals, values, aspirations, ideologies, and rationalizations that permeate an organization [19]. These espoused beliefs and values may not be congruent with observed behaviours and artifacts [19]. An example is overlooked policies prohibiting bullying because of cultural norms [20, 21]. The third level is the basic underlying assumptions [19]. These are unconscious, taken-for-granted beliefs and values [22]. An example is a belief that women should only work in feminine jobs rather than masculine occupations.

How workers engage with their workplace is a combination of their basic assumptions, and their organisation's espoused beliefs and artifacts. However, workers are confused when misalignments between espoused beliefs and artifacts exist. For example, an occupational culture that does not prioritize safety despite the organisation's safety promotion campaigns.

Overall, aviation recognizes the importance of an individual's action in aviation safety. Decades of research on HFs and safety culture show how pilot inter-employee relations adversely affect safety through hierarchy, national cultural norms, and, most recently, cross-cultural power gradients [23]. However, not all risks facing the workforce are given equal value. Despite two decades of research describing aviation's culture of discrimination [20, 21, 24, 25], it is not recognized as a risk to safe aircraft operations. Aviation safety's definition relates to "[the] functions related to or in direct support of the safe operation of aircraft [16, pp.1–4]." ICAO [16] separates aviation safety from the workers in that employee issues are an occupational health and safety (OHS) issue that does not handle aviation matters [16].

Although the worker continuously interfaces with technology, peers and the organisation, how workplace factors affect socio-technical environments remain underexplored. Emerging trends outside aviation show that certain people are more vulnerable to discrimination; however, organisational factors cause incident underreporting [26–28]. As a result, these events are not identified and therefore unrecognized. When an individual's sense of safety is compromised, they prioritize survival [30] over a collective safety culture.

## 2    Method

This section discusses the methods and research design for this article. This study uses qualitative methods to answer the question, how do negative experiences in the workplace degrade the human performance of AMEs in Ontario, Canada's air transportation sector? A qualitative approach provides context for the Research Participants' (RPs) lived experiences in the workplace [31]. This study provides insights into how everyday experiences in the workplace pose a risk to aviation safety. This study was reviewed and received ethics clearance through a University of Waterloo Research Ethics Board (ORE #43066).

Interviews were conducted from May until July 2021. The interview process took approximately 60–90 min, with the shortest interview lasting 60 min and the longest two hours and 34 min. The interviews were conducted until saturation.

Data was analyzed using a code set with an inter-rater reliability agreement level of 88%. Codes were applied to interview transcripts noting the number of mentions per code. The information was further analyzed based on a generic identity characteristic: licensed AME (n = 14) and apprentice (n = 4), and critically reviewed emerging themes.

### 2.1 Research Design

Due to the research question's context-dependent nature, this study draws on Stratford and Bradshaw [31] to design rigorous semi-structured interviews. Semi-structured interviews bridge empirical data by investigating complex behaviours by collecting a range of beliefs, opinions, and experiences [32] of all AMEs (n = 18) RPs. For this study, all RPs (apprentices and licensed AMEs) were given an indicator alphanumeric code prefaced with AME.

A sampling framework was designed to represent Canadian aviation's diverse workforce. RPs recruitment was conducted through the researcher's professional contacts, the Aircraft Maintenance Association of Ontario, and LinkedIn through recruitment posters and letters. Maximum variation and snowball sampling were used.

Interviews were conducted through the approved online platform and recorded to ensure accurate transcription following the RPs' informed consent. All interviews were transcribed verbatim. Drawing on Miles, Huberman, and Saldana's [33], interviews were analyzed deductively and inductively through content analysis using a computer-aided qualitative data analysis software, NVIVO 12.

## 3    Results

### 3.1 Preliminary Findings

In order to understand how workplace experiences degrade human performance, RPs were asked to describe their occupational culture and share their workplace experiences. RPs were also asked to reflect on an experience where they were required to work on an aircraft following an event where they felt that an aspect of their identity (race, gender, ethnicity, sexual orientation, physique, personality) was threatened or disrespected in the workplace. RPs then described how their negative social interactions degraded their human factors using the Dirty Dozen framework.

The data in this section is organized into three sections. The first set of data compares and contrasts the different perceptions of culture in the AME occupation through the lens of the licensed AMEs and apprentices. Next, two overarching categories of negative interactions that degrade HFs are presented. The last data set shows that HFs are degraded because of negative interactions.

**Perception of Occupational Culture.** AME occupational culture descriptors differ when comparing and contrasting the perception of licensed AMEs to apprentices. The top six occupational culture indicators of the licensed AME group shown in Table 1 differ from the top 5 indicators of the apprentice group. Table 1 shows that licensed AMEs list trust, competing priorities (time, money, customer service), liability, masculine/macho, responsibility and safety as their top six occupational culture indicators. Most licensed AMEs and half of the apprentice group mentioned trust as a cultural descriptor. Although competing priorities are mentioned more than trust and liability by licensed AMEs, safety is mentioned the same number of times as liability. Less than half the group identifies the culture as masculine/macho; however, the masculine nature of the culture is mentioned as many times as trust.

For the most part, the apprentices do not share the same view on the AME culture as the licensed AMEs. Although half of the apprentice group recognize the importance of trust, the Apprentice RPs do not view liability, masculinity/macho, responsibility, or safety as descriptors of the AME occupational culture.

**Table 1.** Top 6 number occupational culture descriptors comparison – licensed AMEs

| Cultural descriptor | % licensed AMEs (n = 14) | Number of mentions | Apprentice % (n = 4) | Number of mentions |
|---|---|---|---|---|
| Trust | 57% | 11 | 50% | 2 |
| Competing priorities | 50% | 12 | 25% | 1 |
| Liability | 50% | 9 | 0% | 0 |
| Masculine/macho | 36% | 11 | 0% | 0 |
| Responsibility | 36% | 7 | 0% | 0 |
| Safety | 36% | 9 | 0% | 0 |

AME 10 (Licensed AME, Woman) contextualizes the importance of trust within her business aviation Aircraft Maintenance Organisation (AMO).

*"I do hear a lot of racist stuff going around, but it is like everyone seems okay with it. If I speak up, I would be ousted, and I feel like it would affect promotions because now nobody will trust me. A lot of this job has to do with trust."*

Table 2 compares and contrasts the top five cultural descriptors mentioned by apprentices and licensed AMEs. The apprentices perceive their culture more relationally than a culture of responsibility. Most of the apprentices indicate toxicity as the number one cultural descriptor. The Apprentice RPs recognize the influence of workplace interaction because the subsequent top four descriptors described by half of the group are politics, nepotism, banter and trust.

AME 15 (Apprentice, Man) describes his experiences as an apprentice in an aircraft maintenance organization for a commercial airline. Although AME 15's describes his tasks as menial work in a hangar, his statement may explain why safety and HFs management are not part of their cultural perception.

> *"Yeah,[the culture of AMES] very much is you to do whatever, I mean, it is pretty much just menial labour. That's pretty much what I figured out as an apprentice. That's what I've been doing."*

**Table 2.** Top 5 number occupational culture descriptors comparison – apprentices

| Cultural descriptor | Apprentice % (n = 4) | Number of mentions | % licensed AMEs (n = 14) | Number of mentions |
|---|---|---|---|---|
| Toxic | 75% | 6 | 29% | 6 |
| Political | 50% | 4 | 29% | 9 |
| Nepotism | 50% | 3 | 29% | 9 |
| Banter | 50% | 2 | 21% | 3 |
| Trust | 50% | 2 | 21% | 0 |

**Experiences That Degrade Human Factors.** Although licensed AMEs and apprentices view their occupational culture differently, they are aligned with factors degrading their HFs in the workplace – negative social interactions. Licensed AMEs and apprentices identified two overarching categories that degrade their HFs, negative interactions with peers, and negative interactions with management, refer to Table 3.

**Table 3.** Experiences in the workplace that degrade human factors

| Negative interaction | % licensed AMEs (n = 14) | Number of mentions | Apprentice % (n = 4) | Number of mentions |
|---|---|---|---|---|
| With peers | 64% | 19 | 100% | 10 |
| With management | 64% | 22 | 75% | 13 |

**Table 4.** Top 3 dirty dozen human factors degraded

| Human factor | % licensed AMEs (n = 14) | Number of mentions | Apprentice % (n = 4) | Number of mentions |
|---|---|---|---|---|
| Distraction | 64% | 11 | 75% | 3 |
| Stress | 50% | 8 | 75% | 5 |
| Communication | 50% | 7 | 50% | 2 |

The interactions were further coded into nano codes capturing racism, sexism, bullying and verbal harassment, xenophobia, nuanced aggressions and exclusion. RPs described their negative social interactions with peers that occurred socially or off the hangar floor. Ironically, most of the negative social interactions between management and apprentices occurred while apprentices worked on aircraft.

All the apprentices described negative interactions as racism, sexism, xenophobia, bullying, or compounded forms of negative interactions. All the apprentices were racialized people. Except for AME 09, who immigrated to Canada with over 20 years of AME experience, the three others averaged five years of experience in their role.

Participant AME 18 (Apprentice, Woman) described her lived experience in aviation manufacturing by connecting culture, negative interactions, and exclusion.

*"Because I was an apprentice. I didn't know what I was allowed to do, and I wasn't allowed to do, or what I could say and what I couldn't say. [...] I had a manager; he waited to pick on me in front of everyone. When he thought nobody was around to defend me, he would tell me I was stupid or, like, I didn't have a future in aviation. I kept my mouth shut because there was nobody I could talk to because he was the manager."*

**Human Factors Degraded Through Negative Interaction.** RPs described how some or all Dirty Dozen factors (fatigue, stress, complacency, communication, awareness, distraction, lack of knowledge, teamwork, lack of resources, pressure, lack of assertiveness, or norms) were degraded due to negative social interactions. Table 4 shows that most licensed AMEs and apprentices identified degraded HFs through distractions. The apprentice group mentioned stress more than distractions, while licensed AMEs identified stress as a second factor that degraded their HFs. The third most degraded HFs resulting from negative interactions is communication, a crucial aspect of teamwork and HFs management.

AME 03 (Licensed AME, 2SLGBTQ+) shared how a homophobic comment by his boss caused a distraction and resulted in a missed step.

*"I remember being extremely frustrated marking all of the wires I was working on. I got up out of the airplane, used a walk to clear my head, then went back to work, I double-checked my work from my marking. Most of them are right, but I fixed the ones I missed."*

## 4   Discussion

The preliminary findings suggest that an organisational culture that tolerates negative intra-employee and management to employee interactions within an occupation degrades workers' safety. Degraded safety compromises public safety. During the interviews, RPs described that they found themselves fixated on the interaction and distracted while working on the aircraft following a negative interaction. Many RPs, regardless of race or gender, became emotional describing their experience. Many of the RPs were not aware that racism, discrimination, sexism, bullying and violence in the workplace are reportable into the organisation's Occupational Health and Safety System under the Human Rights Code of Canada [34] and Canada Labour Code [35].

## 4.1  Occupational Culture

Although the literature examines the role of an organisation in shaping safety culture [3, 36–38], very little aviation literature examines the link between occupational culture, workers' experiences, and how those experiences affect human performance. The findings of this study shows that licensed AMEs describe their occupational culture through trust, competing priorities, and machoism. This aligns with Warren's [40] social science research on masculinized manual craftwork of surfboard shapers who rely on their intimate knowledge of tools, haptic skills, and close personal interaction. This study's findings show that the AME culture is less aligned with how the pilot culture is conceptualized. Helmreich's [12] widely accepted Three Cultures of Aviation model influences how aviation culture is understood and trained. However, the limitation of this model is that the three cultures: organisational, professional and national, only describe the pilot culture. Helmreich [12] describes the pilot's professional culture as a sense of pride, a desire to help the organization, focusing on safety and efficiency, and a misplaced sense of invulnerability. Helmreich [12] describes a shared pilot culture across the globe. The findings indicate that all people within an occupation do not share the same cultural views.

People have different experiences and perceive their occupational culture differently within an occupation. ICAO's [16] simplified definition of organizational culture does not capture the variation of Canadian aviation's diverse labour markets. The findings indicate that licensed AMEs are aware of their role related to liability, responsibility and safety, but apprentices are not. All four apprentices who worked for different organizations from northern to southern Ontario (AME 18 worked in manufacturing, AME 16 worked in private aviation, AME 15 worked for a commercial airline aircraft maintenance organization (AMO), and AME 09 worked for an AMO in business aviation) do not see safety as a descriptor of the AME culture. The lack of safety recognition further supports Ram's [7] previous work exploring a misalignment of safety as a stated priority in Canadian aviation. The apprentice RPs perception of culture confirms a variation in how people view their occupational culture based on occupational hierarchy.

## 4.2  Organisational Safety Risk Through Occupational Culture

Over 20 years of aviation literature describes the mistreatment of pilots through machoism and sexism [21, 22, 24, 25]. Although the Three Cultures of Aviation model and Crew Resource Management acknowledge the risks associated with machismo behaviours [41], the results of this behaviour, like sexism and the people impacted, are dissociated from aviation safety.

Despite ICAO's HFs oversight in acknowledging human rights violations and workplace bullying (sexism, racism, xenophobia, bullying and exclusion) as a risk to aviation safety, the RPs are cognizant that interactions can create a culture of trust and that negative social interactions diminish their ability to focus on safety-critical tasks.

The Canadian Standard Associations standard CAN/CSA-Z1003-13 Psychological Health and Safety in the Workplace identifies negative interactions and organisational culture as psychosocial risk factors. Psychosocial risk factors are hazards including elements of the work environment, management practices, and organizational dimensions that increase the risk to health [42]. Revisiting ICAO's HFs description, HFs informs human performance and contribution within the operating systems [2]. The findings of this study show that psychosocial risks, like negative interactions, degrade workers' safety performance by causing distraction, increasing stress and reducing communication in safety critical socio-technical environments. Psychosocial risks are a hazard to HFs. The article shows that the Dirty Dozen's 12 factors are shaped by an unseen element that allows for psychosocial risks and a toxic occupational culture: organisational culture. Keeping in line with the Dirty Dozens, organisational culture is the 'Freaky 13th' element.

## 5 Conclusion

This paper aimed to explore how negative workplace interactions affect HFs. It is now possible to state organisational culture; the 'Freaky 13th' element degrades human performance through HFs. The findings of this study first show that culture is perceived differently by workers in the same occupation. Next, the findings show that negative experiences with peers and management degrade HFs. Finally, the findings show that HFs are degraded when AMEs face negative interaction in a socio-technical environment. Taken together with ICAO's definition of aviation safety and deliberate dissociation of workers psychosocial hazards from the aviation safety system, aviation safety culture and its practices fall short in acknowledging risks.

Despite the sector's reliance on humans, it appears that a safety emphasis is placed on safeguarding the machines and public safety rather than the individuals working on them. In recent years psychological health and safety in the workplace has become a focus. However, the sector's focus on flight safety as defined by ICAO may continue to overshadow normalized risks and psychosocial hazards facing the workforce. Workers are central to achieving organisational safety culture. If organisation's care about their safety culture, they also need to prioritize all aspects of workers' safety through their organisation's safety culture.

The limitation of this study is that women and members of the LGBTQ+ are underrepresented. Additionally, inquiry about RPs' perception of their organisation's safety culture was not within this study's scope. HFs already recognizes organisational safety risks; however, the aviation sector has yet to critically investigate how intra-employee interactions outside of the flight deck impact safety. Although safety improvements are a reiterative process, HFs frameworks have marginally evolved since their inception in the 1990 s. This stagnation opens the door for future transdisciplinary HFs research that examines the worker's role in shaping organisational safety culture, the changing demographic of workers in socio-technical environments, barriers to optimized human performance and ICAOs reconceptualization of aviation safety and culture.

## References

1. Hobbs, A.: An overview of human factors in aviation maintenance. ATSB Safety Report, Aviation Research and Analysis Report AR (2008)

2. ICAO Operational Safety Homepage, https://www.icao.int/safety/OPS/OPS-Section/Pages/HP.aspx. Accessed 16 Dec 2021
3. Wiegmann, D.A., Shappell, S.A.: A Human Error Approach to Aviation Accident Analysis: The Human Factors Analysis and Classification System, 1st edn. Routledge, London (2017)
4. FAA Human Factors, https://www.faasafety.gov/files/gslac/courses/content/258/1097/AMT_Handbook_Addendum_Human_Factors.pdf. Accessed 16 Dec 2021
5. Transport Canada Human Factors, https://tc.canada.ca/sites/default/files/migrated/hpf_ele mentary.pdf. Accessed 16 Dec 2021
6. Yilmaz, A.K.: Strategic approach to managing human factors risk in aircraft maintenance organization: risk mapping. Aircr. Eng. Aerosp. Technol. **91**(4), 654–668 (2019). https://doi.org/10.1108/AEAT-06-2018-0160
7. Helmreich, R.L.: On error management: lessons from aviation. Br. Med. J. **320**(7237), 781–688 (2000). https://doi.org/10.1136/bmj.320.7237.781
8. Ram, A., O'Connell, J., Efthymiou, M., Njoya, E.T.: How safe is safe? A Canadian air carriers (CAC) safety behavior investigation. J. Air Transp. Stud. **10**(2), 1–31 (2019)
9. Ludmila, M.: European Conference on Knowledge Management, Academic Conferences International Limited. Industry 4.0: Human-Technology Interaction: Experience Learned From the Aviation Industry. 571–XXIII (2018)
10. Dumitru, I.M., Boşcoianu, M.: Human factors contribution to aviation safety. International Scientific Committee **49** (2015)
11. Hofstede, G.: Attitudes, values and organizational culture: disentangling the concepts. Organ. Stud. **19**(3), 477–493 (1998). https://doi.org/10.1177/017084069801900305
12. Helmreich, R.L., et al.: The evolution of crew resource management training in commercial aviation. Int. J. Aviat. Psychol. **9**(1), 19–32 (1999). https://doi.org/10.1207/s15327108ijap0901_2
13. Helmreich, R.L.: On error management: lessons from aviation. Br. Med. J. **320**(7237), 781–785 (2000)
14. Reason, J.T.: Human Error. Cambridge University Press, Cambridge (1990)
15. Wiegmann, D.A., Shappell, S.A.: Human error analysis of commercial aviation accidents using the human factors analysis and classification system (HFACS) (No. DOT/FAA/AM-01/3). United States. Office of Aviation Medicine (2001)
16. ICAO. ICAO Safety Management Manual (SMM) Doc 9859 AN/474 (2018)
17. Liu, X., et al.: The relationship between perceived discrimination and wellbeing in impoverished college students: a moderated mediation model of self-esteem and belief in a just world. Curr. Psychol. 1–11 (2021). https://doi.org/10.1007/s12144-021-01981-4
18. Schein, E.H.: Organizational culture. Am. Psychol. Assoc. **45**(2), 109 (1990)
19. Schein, E.H.: Organizational Culture and Leadership, vol. 2. Wiley, New Jersey (2010)
20. Neal-Smith, S., Cockburn, T.: Cultural sexism in the UK airline industry. Gend. Manag. Int. J. (2009)
21. Ferla, M., Graham, A.: Women slowly taking off: an investigation into female underrepresentation in commercial aviation. Res. Transp. Bus. Manag. **31**, 100378 (2019). https://doi.org/10.1016/j.rtbm.2019.100378
22. Barnett, C.: Culture, geography, and the arts of government. Environ. Plann. D: Soc. Space **19**, 7–24 (2001). https://doi.org/10.1068/d236
23. Chan, W.-K., Li, W.-C.: Culture's consequences on the categorisation of causal factors in aviation accident reports. In: Harris, D., Li, W.-C. (eds.) Engineering Psychology and Cognitive Ergonomics. LNCS (LNAI), vol. 12767, pp. 19–27. Springer, Cham (2021). https://doi.org/10.1007/978-3-030-77932-0_2
24. Davey, C.L., Davidson, M.J.: The right of passage? The experiences of female pilots in commercial aviation. Fem. Psychol. **10**(2), 195–225 (2000). https://doi.org/10.1177/0959353500010002002

25. Germain, M.L., Herzog, M.J.R., Hamilton, P.R.: Women employed in male-dominated indus-tries: lessons learned from female aircraft pilots, pilots-in-training and mixed-gender flight instructors. Hum. Resour. Dev. Int. **15**(4), 435–453 (2012). https://doi.org/10.1080/13678868. 2012.707528

26. Eurofound and International Labour Organization: Working conditions in a global perspec-tive. Publications Office of the European Union, Luxembourg, and International Labour Organization, Geneva (2019)

27. Petitta, L., Probst, T.M., Barbaranelli, C.: Safety culture, moral disengagement, and accident underreporting. J. Bus. Ethics **141**(3), 489–504 (2015). https://doi.org/10.1007/s10551-015-2694-1

28. Banerjee, R.: An examination of factors affecting perception of workplace discrimination. J. Lab. Res. **29**(4), 380–401 (2008). https://doi.org/10.1007/s12122-008-9047-0

29. Tseng, E.S., et al.: Perceptions of equity and inclusion in acute care surgery: from the #EAST4ALL survey. Ann. Surg. **272**(6), 906–910 (2020). https://doi.org/10.1097/SLA.000 0000000004435

30. Herod, A.: From a geography of labor to a labor geography: labor's spatial fix and the geography of capitalism. Antipode **29**(1), 1–31 (1997)

31. Stratford, E., Bradshaw, M.: Qualitative research design and rigour. Qualitative Research Methods in Human Geography I. (Ed), Oxford University Press, Don Mills (2016)

32. Dunn, K.: Interviewing. Qualitative Research Methods in Human Geography, I. (Ed), Qualitative Research Methods in Human Geography. Oxford University Press, Don Mills (2016)

33. Miles, M.B., Huberman, A.M., Saldaña, J.: Qualitative Data Analysis. A Methods Source-books. Edition 3, SAGE, Los Angeles (2016)

34. The Occupational Health and Safety Act: FAQs | Ministry of Labour. The Occupational Health and Safety Act. https://www.labour.gov.on.ca/english/hs/faqs/ohsa.php. Accessed 13 Jan 2021

35. The Ontario Human Rights Code. Ontario Human Rights Commission. http://www.ohrc.on. ca/en/ontario-human-rights-code. Accessed 13 Jan 2021

36. Bosak, J., Coetsee, W.J., Cullinane, S.J.: Safety climate dimensions as predictors for risk behavior. Accid. Anal. Prev. **55**, 256–264 (2013). https://doi.org/10.1016/j.aap.2013.02.022

37. Cohen, T.N., Wiegmann, D.A., Shappell, S.A.: Evaluating the reliability of the human factors analysis and classification system. Aerosp. Med. Hum. Perform. **86**(8), 728–735 (2015). https://doi.org/10.3357/AMHP.4218.2015

38. Moshanskey, V., von Veh, F.R., Mc Bey, R.J.: Commission of inquiry into the air Ontario crash at Dryden, Ontario. Final Report Volume I (1992). Available at: https://reports.aviation-saf ety.net/1989/19890310-1_F28_C-FONF.pdf. Accessed 18 Sept 2020

39. Wiegmann, D.A., Shappell, S.A.: A human error approach to aviation accident analysis: the human factors analysis and classification system. 1$^{st}$ edn, Routledge, London (2003). https:// doi.org/10.4324/9781315263878

40. Warren, A.: Crafting masculinities: gender, culture and emotion at work in the surfboard industry. Gend. Place Cult. **23**(1), 36–54 (2016)

41. Gross, B.: Crew resource management–a concept for teams in critical situations. In: Proceed-ings of 5th International Conference on Integrated Natural Disaster Management at: Tehran 9 (2014)

42. Canadian Standards Association (CSA) CAN/CSA-Z1003-13/BNQ 9700-803/2013 Psycho-logical Health and Safety in the Workplace (2013)

# Experimental Assessment of Fixation-Based Attention Measurement in an Aircraft Cockpit

Simon Schwerd(✉) ⓘ and Axel Schulte ⓘ

Insititute of Flight Systems, Universität der Bundeswehr, 85577 Munich, Germany
{simon.schwerd,axel.schulte}@unibw.de

**Abstract.** Goal of this study was to improve eye-tracking-based attention measurement by fixation-based classification in an aircraft cockpit simulator. Most eye-tracking studies measure attention with averaging metrics which is not suitable for application in adaptive systems. Alternatively, attention classification based on fixation on AoI is a reasonable method but sometimes fails to correctly classify visual attention in modern HMIs. To find the cause of these problems, we conducted an aircraft simulator experiment with 10 pilots and collected baseline data for visual attention on different cockpit instruments. With this data, we evaluated fixation durations, fixation vicinity and the relationship between interaction and fixation position. The results showed that, graphical or moving display elements can be perceived with shorter fixations and near-peripheral perception compared to displays of text and numbers. Also, control input is often aligned with visual attention to associated information. With these results, visual attention measurement can be improved by adapting minimum fixation durations and areas of interest to the displayed content and using interaction as a proxy for attention.

**Keywords:** Visual attention · Eye tracking · Aircraft cockpit

## 1 Introduction

Measuring attention in real-world work environments enables new methods to train and support users pursuing their tasks. Applications such as adaptive interfaces [1, 2], adaptive support [3] or intelligent tutoring systems [4] change their behavior according to their user's attention. These applications often rely on near-real-time measurement of user attention to determine *what* the user is attending to *at the very moment*. In these applications, measurement of attention is a classification problem. For this, eye-tracking based fixation classification is an established approach especially when used in a multi-task environment such as the aircraft cockpit. But this method fails to reliably classify attention and often produces many false positives and negatives. In this contribution, we investigate the cause of these problems by collecting baseline attentional data in a cockpit simulator experiment. Based on the results of the experiment, we propose measures to improve attention measurement by fixation classification.

D. Harris and W.-C. Li (Eds.): HCII 2022, LNAI 13307, pp. 408–419, 2022.
https://doi.org/10.1007/978-3-031-06086-1_32

## 2  Background

Attention describes the involved cognitive mechanisms, that filter the great amount of sensory input for information that is subsequently processed by the human cognitive system. The term often covers two different forms of attention: selective and divided attention. The former being responsible for selection of information and the latter for allocating cognitive resources to semantic analysis, response selection and action execution [5, 6]. In a work environment, both, selective and divided attention are modulated by the user's expectations and goals. For example, information is sampled more often when it is relevant to a current task and information changes are expected with high frequency. This goal-driven distribution of attention can be interrupted by salient events capturing the user's attention, often referred to as bottom-up attention [7].

When different sources of information and multiple tasks are competing for the user's attention, the correct management of attention is a critical component for performance in human-machine-systems. Accident and error analysis reveal that failures of attention are frequent in air traffic control or on flight deck [8–10]. Noticeably in these studies is, that the cause of attentional failures is not always caused by excessive task demands or high workload, but by errors regarding the management of attention. The following different failures of attention were described in the literature:

- *Vigilance performance decrement.* When a user has to perform a monotonous task requiring sustained vigilance, the risk of failure to notice task-relevant stimuli increases over time [11].
- *Attentional tunneling & change blindness.* Due to wrong expectations of probable situations (e.g. rare events) or wrong prioritization of goals, a user focuses of their attention solely on a single task, information or display and possibly misses other task-relevant information [12].
- *Complacency.* In the context of decision support systems, a user accepts automation recommendations without required verification of necessary task information, therefore not paying attention to them [13].

Definition of these phenomena regarding their underlying cognitive mechanism is still debated. Regardless the cause, fatal consequence is often that task-relevant information is missed. A reliable measurement of attention could be used to inform adaptive systems, that counteract these failures by means of system adaption. Therefore, the applied metric of attention must determine in near-real-time what information is currently attended by the pilot.

### 2.1  Measurement of Attention in the Workplace

Most experiments in visual attention research were conducted in controlled environments. Simple tasks such as filtering, monitoring, or detection tasks were used to test hypothesis and refine models of attention [14, 15]. It is difficult to transfer these experimental designs to an operational workplace. More specifically, there are two challenges in the operational task context: First, the measurement should be non-intrusive and applied within the natural task situation of the workplace. Second, modern HMIs do not contain a single stimulus but a variety of different competing information in different representations such as maps, virtual displays, or numerical displays. Therefore, the correct identification of an attended **A**rea **o**f **I**nterest (AoI) is crucial to attention measurement in the workplace.

For this eye-tracking is the most promising to measure attention and has been used extensively in studies in the context of aviation (for a review we refer to [16, 17]). For example, the authors of [18, 19] evaluated gaze patterns that correlate with flight performance and how patterns between expert and novice pilots differ. In other studies, eye-tracking was used to evaluate the impact of automation on monitoring behavior [20] or to identify automation surprises in the cockpit [21].

In most studies, visual attention is measured with an accumulated metric (e.g., total dwell time), a relative metric (e.g., distribution of dwell time on AoI) or a combination of different base metrics (e.g., transition matrix). These metrics provide insight into the macro-level of pilot behavior and can describe general relationship between a certain behavior and performance. But there are only a few studies that view attention measurement as a classification problem with the central question: which information does the participant attend at the very moment? The authors of [22, 23] conducted research in this area. Both studies used a classifier based on EEG measurements to identify if an auditory alarm has been missed by a pilot and achieved medium classification rates. In the following, we want to focus on the use of eye-tracking to measure attention, because the cockpit workplace is dominated by visual tasks.

## 2.2 Attention Measurement as a Classification Problem

As a first approach for this classification problem, one could use every fixation on an area of interest (AoI) as an indication of visual attention on the displayed information. In our recent studies [24–26], we used this *naïve* classification and encountered three problems: First, not every fixation on a AoI guarantees that the user processed the displayed information, sometimes referred to change or inattentional blindness [20, 27]. Second, not every display element must be directly fixated because near-peripheral vision allows for perception of information [28]. This seems to be the case especially with graphical representation (e.g., objects on a map) or movement (e.g., moving altitude ladder). Third, we often failed to recognize a fixation on an AoI but, nevertheless, measured that the pilot controlled the system parameter via buttons or directly interacted with the touch screen. In these situations, we assume rather, that the eye-tracking failed to accurately measure fixation position than a *blind* interaction with the system. Based on these different problems, we want to evaluate the following three questions in our task setting:

- What are the properties of fixations that precede cognitive processing of a fixated AoI?
- What types of display elements allow for near-peripheral perception of task-relevant information?
- To what extend is interaction and visual attention aligned?

The answer to this question could be used to improve our fixation-based method. Therefore, we conducted a simulator experiment to collect data that provides a baseline for attention on AoIs in a natural task setting.

## 3   Experiment

The experiment was conducted in a simulator of a generic fast-jet cockpit (see Fig. 1). The participants controlled the aircrafts attitude with throttle and stick. The aircraft systems can be controlled via three touchscreens. System information was displayed on these screens and a Head-Up-Display (HUD) projected into the visuals of the outside world.

**Fig. 1.** Cockpit simulator with integrated eye-tracking

The participant's gaze was measured with a commercially available four-camera system (SmartEye Pro 0.3 MP) which was connected to our simulation software. The gaze could be tracked in the three head-down displays as well as in the HUD. For fixation classification of a gaze sample, we used the functionality provided by the manufacturer with a gaze angular velocity threshold of $\dot{\alpha} \leq 2\frac{°}{s}$.

### 3.1   Task

The experimental task consisted of monitoring continuous and discrete states of the aircraft. At previously unknown times, participants had to react when these states deviated from desired parameters (e.g., environmental changes). The participants had three continuous tracking tasks without using an autopilot: First, they had to track a route displayed in their tactical map, where only the route leg to the next waypoint was visible. A new route leg became visible with a previously unknown heading after reaching a waypoint (continuous state, Fig. 2; Area 3).

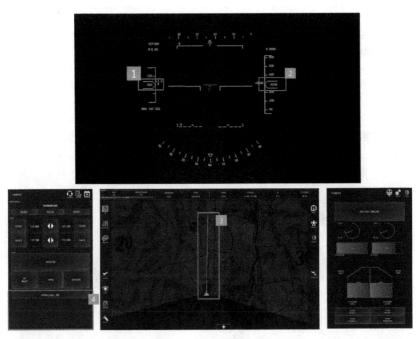

**Fig. 2.** Cockpit display for the participant. Areas of Interest in the experiment: (1) Altitude indicator, (2) Air speed indicator, (3) Position of aircraft and route to next waypoint, (4) message system (green on new message) (Color figure online)

Second, the participant had to track a specified altitude and velocity, both displayed in the HUD (continuous states, Fig. 2; Areas 1,2). The target altitude and velocity were specified and changed by a message received at previously unknown times. A new message was indicated by a green light in the left screen and had to be confirmed by a button click (discrete state, Fig. 2; Area 5). At unknown times, the aircraft altitude or velocity was disturbed by a simulated gust that changed the aircraft position or speed to a value beyond the target range. There were disturbances of altitude or velocity triggered with an average frequency of 3.5 times per minute. At no point in the trial, there was a disturbance of both variables at the same time. We simulated bad visibility to minimize the influence of spatial visual perception of the outside view. Therefore, change of velocity and altitude could only be recognized by perceiving HUD information. In the experiment, we distinguished between the following AoIs with different representations: Altitude indicator and ladder, speed indicator, route leg on map and message display. Each of the AoI was relevant to one specific task.

## 3.2  Procedure

At the beginning, the participants received a briefing about the simulator. Before the experimental trial, each participant was trained in the simulator for approximately one hour. During this training, they encountered the same tasks as in the experimental trial. Then, the eye-tracking was calibrated with mean accuracy of $1.04°$ ($SD_{acc} = 0.72°$). After that, the participants conducted the trial which lasted about 30 min.

## 3.3  Participants

We conducted the experiment with 10 participants, which had different levels of flight experience but no prior experience with the simulator. All participants had a sailplane pilot license (SPL). Half of the participants were pilots with a professional license. All participants were male with a mean age of 35.5 years ($\pm 13.2$ y). Their amount of flight hours varied between 500 and 29000 h. We had to exclude one participant from the analysis because of logging issues.

## 3.4  Data Processing

In conventional stimuli-response experiments, an attended stimulus can be objectively measured by the participant's response. We needed a similar method for the multi-task work environment such as the flight deck. For this, we used the following method inspired by [29] and displayed in Fig. 3.

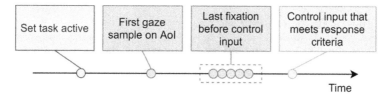

**Fig. 3.** Measurement timeline. Task (gray), gaze samples (blue) and pilot reaction (yellow). (Color figure online)

The participant's pursued their tracking tasks in parallel. As described, we changed the task-relevant state of the simulation in a way that required a timely response by the pilot (*set task active*). Subsequently, we measured the time when they performed the required action (*control input*). We used the conditions given Table 1 to classify the participants reaction in a task. The last fixation on the AoI before this reaction was labeled as attention directed towards the AoI. For the generation of the results, we only used these fixations to have error-free gaze data where attention lied on the task-related AoI.

During the experiment, we logged the aircraft state, gaze measurements and the participant's control input by throttle, stick or touchscreen.

**Table 1.** Condition to classify a reaction for altitude, velocity, route, and message task

| Task | Condition |
|---|---|
| Altitude task | Absolute change in elevator stick position >0.075° |
| | OR |
| | push pitch trim button |
| Velocity task | Relative Change in throttle position >10% |
| | OR |
| | push air brake button |
| Route task | Absolute change of aileron stick position >0.04° |
| Message task | Confirm message button |

## 4 Results

With the presented experimental design, we collected 990 samples of participants reacting to an active task from which 802 could be used for further processing. We ignored samples in two cases: When the reaction condition identified a reaction at the same time of setting a task active or when no reaction could be found until the task was completed. For all valid samples, we looked at three aspects: The fixation duration before control input, the analysis of the fixation's vicinity and the relationship between fixation position and interaction.

### 4.1 Analysis of Fixation Duration

Table 2 shows mean fixation durations for different sets of measured fixations. The data is plotted in Fig. 4.

**Table 2.** Fixation duration results

| Fixations | Mean [ms] | Std [ms] | N |
|---|---|---|---|
| All | 355 | 345 | 34151 |
| Before action | 409 | 394 | 802 |
| Task route | 268 | 191 | 68 |
| Task altitude | 313 | 321 | 266 |
| Task velocity | 466 | 411 | 415 |
| Task message | 599 | 560 | 53 |

When we compare the means of all fixations to the last fixations before a participant corrected a system state, we did not find a meaningful difference, which suggests that a fixation before action cannot be differentiated from a normal fixation. However, when we compare fixation durations by the different task related AoIs, there are differences in duration. Fixations on the message and velocity AoI are substantially longer than on the route or altitude AoI. These results show that, it can be perceived faster than numbers or text when information is represented graphically. Note, that altitude, opposed to velocity, is not solely represented as a number but change in altitude is visualized by a *moving* altitude ladder, which reduced fixation durations before reaction. Comparable to this, route information is displayed on a map where deviation between aircraft and route can be perceived without reading any numbers or text. Comparing velocity and message task, we explain the difference in fixation duration by a faster processing of a number with three figures (e.g., *400 [kts]*) than a text of 3–4 words (e.g., *IAS 400 kts ALT 5000 ft*). In summary, the fixation duration is dependent on the graphic representation of the task-related information which indicates that fixations should not be analyzed independently of the display properties.

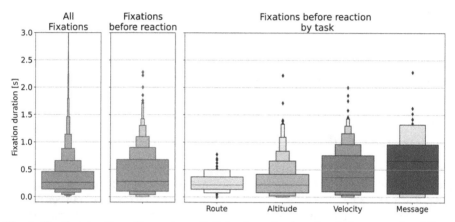

**Fig. 4.** Fixation durations. Comparison of all fixations, fixations just before a reaction (all vs. task-related) before participant action occurred compared to all measured fixation durations

### 4.2   Analysis of Fixation Vicinity

We varied the size of the radius analyzed in the vicinity of a measured fixation position (0.5°, 2°, 4.5°). An AoI was classified as attended if a fixation within this radius of the AoI was measured. Figure 5 shows the time between first fixation on a AoI and reaction in the associated task. We counted the occurrences of negative reaction times, where a reaction by the participant was registered before a fixation in the vicinity of the AoI was detected. With increasing vicinity radius, the number of these negative reaction times could be reduced, especially in the route task. This could interpretated that participant did not have to fixate the route in the map to collect sufficient information to execute a suitable reaction. A further increase of the radius resulted in increasing reaction times, especially in the velocity task. That means, that a fixation was classified as attention on task relevant AoI but no immediate reaction followed. We assume, that these long reaction times are rather false positive classifications than change blindness because of their high number of occurrences.

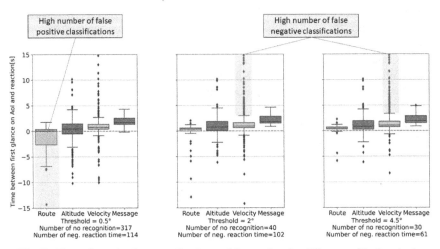

**Fig. 5.** Time of reaction between fixation and first action for different radii of analysis.

### 4.3  Interaction as Attention

We evaluated the interaction data to assess if interaction and visual attention on controlled parameter are aligned. The results confirmed that pilots tend to fixate the state of the aircraft while they are controlling it. Figure 6 shows the angular distance between fixation and AoI position at the time of an action, for example, the distance between airspeed indicator at the time of controlling the air brake or moving throttle. For all tasks, the majority of fixations lie within 1° angular radius on the AoI at the moment of control input. Notably, altitude showed two peaks at the distance of 10° and 20°. These points correspond to the center and the velocity indicator of the HUD. The reason for this is that participants noticed the moving altitude ladder without fixating the AoI and instantly reacted to this movement by moving the stick to adjust aircraft pitch.

Table 3 complements the histogram data and shows the mean angular distance for each task and the proportion of fixation-action samples within a radius of 2°.

### 4.4  Discussion

Our experimental design provided baseline data of fixations where attention is on a specific AoI. The results of the experiment can give insight into how to improve attention classification. First, the comparison of average duration between all and pre-action fixations showed no significant difference. However, our analysis showed that there are fixation properties dependent on the AoI design, where fixations are shorter when AoI is a graphic display as opposed to numeric or text display. These differences in fixation duration show that attention classification based of fixations should not be independent

Distance [°] to AoI at time of action

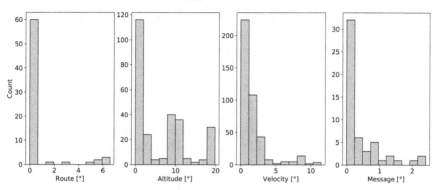

**Fig. 6.** Histogram of fixation distance to associated AoI at time of action

**Table 3.** For each task: angular distance at time of action and proportion of fixation-action samples within 2° radius.

| Task | Mean (SD) [°] | $N_{<2°}/N$ [−] |
|------|---------------|-----------------|
| Route | 0.56 (1.68) | 90% |
| Altitude | 6.30 (6.27) | 45% |
| Velocity | 1.61 (2.14) | 76% |
| Message | 0.39 (0.62) | 96% |

of the representation of an AoI. Second, we saw that graphical AoI must not be fixated directly to perceive the task-relevant information. Here, an increase of the AoI size can improve the measurement, but our data showed a trade-off between false negative and false positive classifications. Therefore, attention measurement could benefit from a better design of AoIs, for example, moving and graphic displays require greater AoIs as opposed to numeric or text displays. Third, our data showed that the control of an aircraft state is often accompanied by pilot attention towards the associated AoI. This could be used to improve attention classification. For example, when gaze cannot be measured robustly, control input can be used as a good proxy for visual attention on the associated state display.

**Limitations.** The participants of the experiment had different levels of expertise. This is a confounding factor, because it has been shown that experts require shorter dwell time on AoI to acquire information [18]. Further, the condition of stick and throttle input to identify the moment of reaction for altitude and velocity was not able to perfectly identify reaction times. The reason for this is, that these control inputs are continuous and not completely independent from each other. In some situations, participants controlled their speed by adjusting their pitch or, in other cases, there was no reaction because the aircraft coincidentally had the correct rate of descent or climb to acquire the desired altitude even after disturbance. Finally, the results of fixation vicinity analysis could be confounded by eye-tracking accuracy. The distance between fixation and AoI could be great at the time of action because the participant either did not have to fixate it or the measurement error was great. Finally, we only looked at gaze right before a participant's action, thus, the data is not representative for monitoring behavior.

## 5   Conclusion

In this contribution, we described attention measurement as a classification problem and presented an experimental design to collect baseline data in an aircraft cockpit. The results of our simulator experiment showed that classification by fixation on AoI is not an optimal approach but can be improved by adjusting AoIs and minimum fixation duration according to the representation of the information. In addition, interaction measurement can be used to validate or, to a certain extent, supplement eye-tracking for visual attention measurement. Our further research will focus on the application of the suggested improvements in attention-adaptive systems.

## References

1. Fortmann, F., Lüdtke, A.: An intelligent SA-adaptive interface to aid supervisory control of a UAV swarm. In: IEEE 11th International Conference on Industrial Informatics (INDIN), pp. 768–773 (2013)
2. Fortmann, F., Mengeringhausen, T.: Development and evaluation of an assistant system to aid monitoring behavior during multi-UAV supervisory control. In: Stary, C. (ed.) Proceedings of the 2014 European Conference on Cognitive Ergonomics-ECCE 2014, pp. 1–8. ACM Press, New York (2014)
3. Brand, Y., Schulte, A.: Design and Evaluation of a Workload-Adaptive Associate System for Cockpit Crews. In: Harris, D. (ed.) EPCE 2018. LNCS (LNAI), vol. 10906, pp. 3–18. Springer, Cham (2018). https://doi.org/10.1007/978-3-319-91122-9_1
4. Barrios, V.M.G., et al.: AdELE: a framework for adaptive e-learning through eye tracking. In: Proceedings of IKNOW 2004, pp. 609–616 (2004)
5. Wickens, C.D.: Attention: theory, principles, models and applications. Int. J. Hum. Comput. Interact. **37**, 403–417 (2021)
6. Remington, R.W., Loft, S.: Attention and multitasking. In: Boehm-Davis, D.A., Durso, F.T., Lee, J.D. (eds.) APA Handbook of Human Systems Integration, pp. 261–276. American Psychological Association, Washington (2015)
7. Wickens, C.D.: Noticing events in the visual workplace: the SEEV and NSEEV models. In: Hoffman, R.R., Hancock, P.A., Scerbo, M.W., Parasuraman, R., Szalma, J.L. (eds.) The Cambridge Handbook of Applied Perception Research, pp. 749–768. Cambridge University Press, New York (2015)
8. Jones, D.G., Endsley, M.R.: Sources of situation awareness errors in aviation. Aviat. Space Environ. Med. **67**, 507–512 (1996)
9. Shorrock, S.T.: Errors of perception in air traffic control. Saf. Sci. **45**, 890–904 (2007)
10. Kelly, D., Efthymiou, M.: An analysis of human factors in fifty controlled flight into terrain aviation accidents from 2007 to 2017. J. Safety Res. **69**, 155–165 (2019)
11. Thomson, D.R., Besner, D., Smilek, D.: A resource-control account of sustained attention: evidence from mind-wandering and vigilance paradigms. Perspect. Psychol. Sci. J. Assoc. Psychol. Sci. **10**, 82–96 (2015)

12. Wickens, C.D.: Attentional tunneling and task management. In: International Symposium on Aviation Psychology (2005)
13. Parasuraman, R., Manzey, D.H.: Complacency and bias in human use of automation: an attentional integration. Hum. Factors **52**, 381–410 (2010)
14. Styles, E.A.: The Psychology of Attention. Psychology Press, Hove (2005)
15. Pashler, H.E.: Attention. Psychology Press, Hove (1998)
16. Peißl, S., Wickens, C.D., Baruah, R.: Eye-tracking measures in aviation: a selective literature review. Int. J. Aerosp. Psychol. **28**, 98–112 (2018)
17. Ziv, G.: Gaze behavior and visual attention: a review of eye tracking studies in aviation. Int. J. Aviat. Psychol. **26**, 75–104 (2016)
18. Lounis, C., Peysakhovich, V., Causse, M.: Visual scanning strategies in the cockpit are modulated by pilots' expertise: a flight simulator study. PLoS ONE **16**, e0247061 (2021)
19. Brams, S., et al.: Does effective gaze behavior lead to enhanced performance in a complex error-detection cockpit task? PLoS ONE **13**, e0207439 (2018)
20. Sarter, N.B., Mumaw, R.J., Wickens, C.D.: Pilots' monitoring strategies and performance on automated flight decks: an empirical study combining behavioral and eye-tracking data. Hum. Factors **49**, 347–357 (2007)
21. Dehais, F., Peysakhovich, V., Scannella, S., Fongue, J., Gateau, T.: "Automation surprise" in aviation. In: Begole, B., Kim, J., Inkpen, K., Woo, W. (eds.) Proceedings of the 33rd Annual ACM Conference on Human Factors in Computing Systems, pp. 2525–2534. ACM, New York (2015)
22. Dehais, F., Roy, R.N., Scannella, S.: Inattentional deafness to auditory alarms: inter-individual differences, electrophysiological signature and single trial classification. Behav. Brain Res. **360**, 51–59 (2019)
23. Klaproth, O.W., Halbrügge, M., Krol, L.R., Vernaleken, C., Zander, T.O., Russwinkel, N.: A neuroadaptive cognitive model for dealing with uncertainty in tracing pilots' cognitive state. Top. Cogn. Sci. **12**, 1012–1029 (2020)
24. Schwerd, S., Schulte, A.: Experimental Validation of an Eye-Tracking-Based Computational Method for Continuous Situation Awareness Assessment in an Aircraft Cockpit. In: Harris, D., Li, W.-C. (eds.) HCII 2020. LNCS (LNAI), vol. 12187, pp. 412–425. Springer, Cham (2020). https://doi.org/10.1007/978-3-030-49183-3_32
25. Schwerd, S., Schulte, A.: Measuring the deviation between ground truth and operator awareness in a UAV management scenario: an eye-tracking approach. In: AIAA Scitech 2021 Forum. American Institute of Aeronautics and Astronautics, Reston (2021)
26. Schwerd, S., Schulte, A.: Operator state estimation to enable adaptive assistance in manned-unmanned-teaming. Cogn. Syst. Res. **67**, 73–83 (2021)
27. Mack, A.: Inattentional blindness. Curr. Dir. Psychol. Sci. **12**, 180–184 (2003)
28. Strasburger, H., Rentschler, I., Jüttner, M.: Peripheral vision and pattern recognition: a review. J. Vis. **11**, 13 (2011)
29. Dick, A.O.: Instrument scanning and controlling: using eye movement data to understand pilot behavior and strategies. National Aeronautics and Space Administration, Scientific and Technical Information Branch (1980)

# Is There a Relationship Between Pilot Stress and Short- and Long- Haul Flights?

Khai Sheng Sew[✉], Jongwoo Jung, Kin Wing Lo, Lucus Yap, and Silvia Pignata

University of South Australia, Mawson Lakes, SA 5095, Australia
sewky004@mymail.unisa.edu.au

**Abstract.** Past studies have been conducted to identify whether short-haul (SH) or long-haul (LH) pilots experience a higher level of stress during a single flight. An extensive literature review revealed high stress levels in both groups (i.e., LH pilots were more stressed than SH pilots, and vice versa). To investigate these mixed results, quantitative and qualitative survey data were collected from 49 international commercial airline pilots from various countries in the Asia-Pacific, Europe and in North America. The General Health Questionnaire–12 (GHQ-12) was used to measure the stress levels of pilots during the pandemic. The study found that there was no significant difference between the stress levels of SH pilots compared to the stress levels of medium-, long-, and ultra long-haul pilots. To further investigate stress levels, pilots' qualitative responses indicated that 75.5% of pilots were impacted by factors related to the COVID-19 pandemic, including increased stress associated with the uncertain future of the aviation industry, and income instability. In summary, this study aims to raise the attention of industry stakeholders such as aviation authorities and airlines of the need for targeted initiatives to support pilots who are most vulnerable to high-stress levelsas .

**Keywords:** Pilots · Stress · Short-haul or Long-haul · Covid-19

## 1 Introduction

As the world is continuously evolving, consumerism is on the rise. Associated with this are changes in the business models of airlines, where low-cost carriers (LCCs) have bloomed and prospered in recent years. Consequently, airlines now strive to keep their fleet in the air for as long as possible, achieving a high turnover rate and transporting more passengers for extra sales volume (Pels 2021). This growth may be negatively perceived by pilots, as higher turnover rates mean more flight legs which can lead to increased workloads and stress levels for pilots. The issue of work stress has been neglected by the aviation industry and pilots also tend to avoid the topic mainly due to concerns about medical certifications that require pilots to be both physically fit and mentally healthy, thus pilots may perceive that a slight compromise in these areas may cost them their licenses (Lollis et al. 2009). As a result, pilots may remain silent about any increases in psychological stress stemming from personal and/or work-related factors such as long flight hours or multiple flight legs in a typical working day.

© The Author(s), under exclusive license to Springer Nature Switzerland AG 2022
D. Harris and W.-C. Li (Eds.): HCII 2022, LNAI 13307, pp. 420–432, 2022.
https://doi.org/10.1007/978-3-031-06086-1_33

The result of a reactive approach towards the mental health of pilots was sadly demonstrated by the Germanwings Flight 9525 in 2015, where the co-pilot kept his mental illness from his employer and then committed suicide using a commercial airliner filled with passengers (Bureau d'enquêtes et d'analyses pour la sécurité de l'aviation civile 2015). The incident resulted in the tragic loss of 150 lives and cost the airline more than $300 m. Although attention focussed on the topic of pilots' mental health after the incident, there is a need for the aviation industry to take more initiatives to mitigate the issue as pilots are still reluctant to openly talk about their mental health.

### 1.1 Purpose and Importance

This study aims to investigate the vulnerability of certain categories of pilots (short-haul (SH) or long-haul (LH)) in experiencing higher psychological stress levels than their counterparts. The main objective of this research is to identify the potential relationship between the psychological stress levels of pilots and the number of hours they fly on a single flight. We hope to induce and spark positive actions from industry players, including civil aviation authorities and airlines, to act against this prevalent issue in order to maintain a healthy sky.

## 2   Literature Review

Extant research has sought to identify whether SH or LH pilots experience higher stress levels stemming from the nature of their work, with regard to flight hours. Due to mixed findings, this review seeks to paint a clearer picture on the topic. According to (Pasha and Stokes 2018), commercial airline pilots are constantly exposed to work-related stressors including, but not limited to, high workloads, disrupted circadian rhythms and the corporate instability of airlines (Little et al. 1990). As piloting a commercial aircraft is likely to be a stressful job, this review aims to identify whether SH or LH pilots experience a higher level of stress when performing their flight duties (Johnson 2019).

### 2.1   SH Pilots and Stress

According to research conducted by (Reis et al. 2013) the proportion of pilots experiencing mental fatigue directly related to their job was 94.1% for SH or medium-haul (MH) pilots compared to 89.3% of LH pilots. SH pilots experience a higher level of mental fatigue due to flying multiple flight legs in a typical duty day. For example, one study utilizing the NASA Task Load Index Scale demonstrated that mental and performance demands were essential components of workload during take-offs and landings (Lee and Liu 2003). This finding was supported by a study highlighting the increase in physiological activity in pilots during flights, especially during take-offs and landings where pilots' heart rates increased during landing, reaching a peak at or just before touchdown (Causse et al. 2012; Roscoe 1978). (Lee and Liu 2003) were also able to demonstrate that pilots' heart rates reached a high of 83.2 bpm during take-off and a staggering 88.6 bpm during landing. Further studies were able to demonstrate that heart rate responses in experienced pilots were influenced almost entirely by workload-related factors, not emotional factors (Roscoe 1978). In short, SH pilots experience a high level of stress due to increased demands with repeated cycles of take-offs and landings on a typical working day.

## 2.2  LH Pilots and Stress

A study that utilized the biopsychosocial model of the lived experience of commercial airline pilots revealed that pilot well-being is negatively affected by the nature of their work, especially for LH pilots (Cullen et al. 2021). This finding was related to biological issues such as long, irregular, and anti-social work hours with frequent time-zone changes, accompanied by circadian rhythm disruptions (Cullen et al. 2021). On top of these stressors, having to fly across multiple time zones has been shown to cause the human body to release stress hormones, leading pilots to experience high levels of stress on a LH flight (Bidaisee et al. 2019).

In addition, research conducted by (Guy 2006) recognized that workers who undertake shift work complained more about stress at work when their working schedule was less predictable. This result suggests that LH pilots are likely to be more prone to experience high-stress levels during work compared to SH pilots, as they often work irregular hours (Cullen et al. 2021; Lee et al. 2017). This finding was supported by several studies which looked at the relationship between long work hours and the psychosocial stress levels of workers. A positive correlation was identified between the two variables where the psychosocial stress levels of workers increase with longer work hours (Lee et al. 2017; Maruyama and Morimoto 1996; Sato et al. 2009). This finding also relates to LH pilots more than SH pilots as the former usually fly more than 16 h on a single trip while the latter fly less than three hours on a single trip.

Furthermore, research has also identified a positive correlation between hours on duty and the stress levels of individuals, suggesting that pilots who spend longer hours on duty tend to experience higher stress levels (Kasi et al. 2007). Our present study is based on the survey instrument used in the study by Kasi et al. with regard to employing the valid GHQ-12 instrument to measure the psychological well-being of pilots (Kapur et al. 1998; Kasi et al. 2007). It should be noted that this current review examined literature from 1978 to 2021, and that most studies reviewed were cross-sectional in nature.

## 2.3  Research Question

This research aims to highlight the issue of job stress in the aviation industry by demonstrating the putative relationship between the stress levels of pilots and the number of hours that they fly on a single trip. A detailed examination of this topic will help to tackle high stress levels amongst pilots in order to combat possible negative consequences such as mental illness. The literature presents evidence that supports both sides of the argument (i.e., LH pilots experience higher stress levels than SH pilots, and vice versa). As a result, the present study seeks to investigate the following research question:

RQ: Do pilots who fly short-haul routes (less than three hours on a single trip) have higher levels of psychological stress than pilots who fly on longer routes (medium-, long-, ultra-long-haul (ULH)) on a single trip?

## 2.4  Design

A cross-sectional survey design comprising a 26-item questionnaire, containing demographic, multiple-choice, and open-ended questions was used to gather data from commercial airline pilots. In addition, the General Health Questionnaire-12 (GHQ-12) measured the psychological well-being of participants. The GHQ-12 was selected as the stress level indicator as previous studies that measured the stress levels of the general population have demonstrated the validity and reliability of this instrument (Goldberg et al. 1997). Thematic analysis was used to analyse answers to open-ended questions in order to identify key themes and trends.

## 3  Methodology

An internet-based survey using Google Forms was conducted over a three-week period from mid September to November 2021. An online survey was chosen for reachability, anonymity, time and cost-efficient reasons.

### 3.1  Population and Sample

The participants comprised commercial pilots who currently fly SH, MH, LH or ULH flights. To recruit the sample, the researchers contacted several major airlines, including airline pilot associations but due to the study's tight time constraints the researchers elected to use a snowballing method of recruitment. The online questionnaire was distributed following approval from the Human Research Ethics Committee of the University of South Australia.

The sample comprised 49 commercial airline pilots. Twenty four pilots (49%) were SH pilots, 11 MH pilots (22%), 10 LH pilots (20%), and 4 ULH pilots (8%). Ninety eight percent (n = 48) of participants were male. Twenty one pilots (44%) were from the Asia-Pacific region, followed by 19 pilots (39%) from Europe, 8 pilots (16%) from North America, and one participant declined to declare which region he or she was from. Fifteen pilots (31%) were aged between 26 to 35 years, 12 pilots (25%) were aged between 36 to 45 years, 11 pilots (22%) were aged between 46 to 55 years, 9 pilots (18%) were aged over 55 years, and 2 pilots (4%) were below 25 years of age.

With regard to flight experience, 13 pilots (27%) had flown between 1,001 to 5,000 h, and 13 pilots (27%) had flown between 5,001 to 10,000 h. This was followed by 9 pilots (18%) who had flown more than 15,000 h, while 8 (16%) had flown between 10,001 to 15,000 h. Three pilots (6%) had flown below 300 h and three (6%) had between 301 to 1,000 flying hours.

The majority of 43 pilots (88%) were employed full-time, with 2 pilots (4%) employed part-time and 1 pilot (2%) based on contract. One other pilot (2%) was on leave without pay, and 2 pilots (4%) were made redundant due to COVID-19. With regard to relationship/family status, 33 pilots (67%) were married, followed by 7 pilots (14%) who were single, 6 pilots (12%) were dating, 2 pilots (4%) were divorced, and 1 pilot (2%) was separated. The majority of participants did not have a child.

## 3.2  Procedure

A link to the online survey was distributed via airlines, airline pilots' associations and pilots' groups on the social media platforms of Facebook and LinkedIn. Snowball sampling was used to achieve a larger sample as participants were asked to distribute the survey link to their networks and colleagues who were employed as commercial airline pilots.

## 3.3  Measures

The questionnaire contained demographic questions related to work role, region, gender, age, flying experience, employment type, and relationship/family status. The General Health Questionnaire-12 (GHQ-12) measure consisted of 12 statements to which respondents indicated their agreement on a four-point scale (0 = Not at all; 3 = Much more than usual; (Goldberg and Williams 1988).

## 3.4  Ethics Considerations

Ethical considerations included voluntary participation, informed consent, confidentiality, and participants' anonymity. Participants were notified that the questionnaire was voluntary and that the collected data would not be shared with employers or airlines. As suggested by (Murdoch et al. 2014), it was important to ensure that data was confidential and de-identified, as these factors may affect the response rate as well as participants' willingness to reveal sensitive information. Participants were also notified that there were no penalties or disadvantages for not participating in the survey. A Participant Information Sheet was provided to participants to ensure their informed consent.

## 3.5  Data Analysis Method

Responses to the survey were exported to Google Spreadsheet for analysis. Quantitative data as transferred to Microsoft Excel and analysed using ToolPak VBA functions. The responses to the GHQ-12 were given a score, based on the user's manual to obtain an average score for each individual. The relationship between the stress level and flight hours per trip was analysed using an independent samples t-test comparing the GHQ-12 scores of the SH pilots against the GHQ-12 scores from the sample of MH, LH and ULH pilots.

## 3.6  Thematic Analysis Method

Qualitative responses were exported to Microsoft Excel for thematic analysis which enabled responses to be categorised into themes and codes to allow a wide-scale understanding of the sample population (Boyatzis 1998). First, responses were grouped based on similar themes that the researchers had laid out prior to the study. Then, themes that emerged were added to the list of categories where keywords were used to identify themes. This process was completed independently by different researchers, then cross-checking was carried out to ensure the consistency of analysis. This process was undertaken to also ensure interrater reliability.

The researchers identified six main themes, namely "income", "job security", "quarantine", "time away from family", "lockdown" and "infected by COVID-19". Lastly, the frequencies of each keyword appearing in the responses were recorded to allow the presentation of findings in a bar chart.

## 4   Findings and Results

### 4.1   Mean GHQ-12 Score of Pilot Categories

The total mean GHQ-12 score for each of the four categories of pilots show that MH pilots reported the lowest level of stress (12), followed by SH pilots (12.96), ULH pilots (14.25) and LH pilots (15.3) reported the highest level of stress. Our study noted a positive relationship between the number of hours that pilots flew on a single trip with their stress levels (see Fig. 1), suggesting that pilots who fly longer hours on a single trip experience a higher stress level than pilots who fly shorter trips. This may be due to the nature of long-haul flight operations, where work-related stressors such as unpredictable working schedules, crossing multiple time zones which is associated with hormone disruptions, and anti-social work hours may be contributing to their stress levels (Bidaisee et al. 2019; Cullen et al. 2021). The impact of the COVID-19 pandemic and the ensuing disruptions to international long-haul flights are likely to have also impacted the stress levels of LH commercial pilots (Table 1).

**Table 1.** Median, Mean and Total GHQ scores for each pilot category

| Pilot category (N = 49) | Flight hours per trip | Median GHQ score | Total median GHQ score | Total mean GHQ score | Mean GHQ score |
|---|---|---|---|---|---|
| Short-haul pilots (n = 24) | 1−4 h | 0.96 | 11.50 | 12.96 | 1.08 |
| Medium-haul pilots (n = 11) | 5−9 h | 1.08 | 13.00 | 12 | 1 |
| Long-haul pilots (n = 10) | 10−14 h | 1.08 | 13.00 | 15.3 | 1.28 |
| Ultra-Long-haul pilots (n = 4) | 15 h and above | 1.21 | 14.50 | 14.25 | 1.19 |

**T-test Analysis:** An independent samples t-test was performed to investigate any differences between the sample of SH pilots and the other sample comprising MH, LH and ULH pilots. The 24 SH participants ($M = 13$, $SD = 5.92$) compared to the 25 MH, LH and ULH participants [$M = 13.68$, $SD = 6.32$] did not report significantly more stress, $t(47) = -0.39$, $p = .70$.

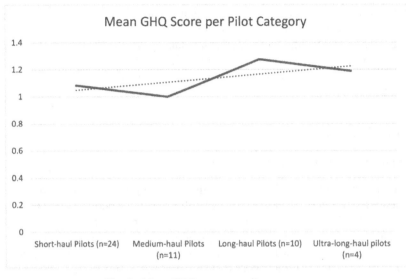

**Fig. 1.** Mean GHQ score per pilot category

### 4.2 Factors Affecting Stress Levels

To further investigate pilot stress levels, participants were asked to rank the top three factors that they believed impacted their stress levels. By applying a score-based app-roach, the researchers multiplied the first reported factors by 3, the second factors by 2 and the third by 1. It was discovered that the reported factor with the highest score was the 'changing nature of the industry', followed by 'anti-social hours' and then the 'divergence of values between pilots and management' (see Fig. 2). The divergence of values between pilots and management suggests that both entities hold differing views and perspectives towards matters. For example, this was evident when participants stated that "*management expiations need to change*", as well as the "*company used covid as leverage and succeeded in worsening contracts dramatically.*" These comments portray the reality of pilots' views in the context of the pandemic and are supported by (Cullen et al. 2021), who found that pilots experienced a disconnection between their values and those of their line managers.

### 4.3 Impact of COVID-19

As mentioned above, a majority of participants selected the "changing nature of the industry" as the factor that most impacted their stress levels. As this phenomenon is likely to be related to the impact of COVID-19, and in order to gather rich data about how participants were affected by COVID-19, all participants were asked to respond to an open-ended question. By applying thematic analysis, the researchers identified the categories of pilots who were most impacted by the pandemic, and also gained insights into their perceptions of the pandemics' impact (see Fig. 3).

Figure 3 shows that 82% of MH pilots were impacted by the COVID-19 pandemic, followed by 75% of ULH pilots, 70% of LH pilots and 46% of SH pilots.

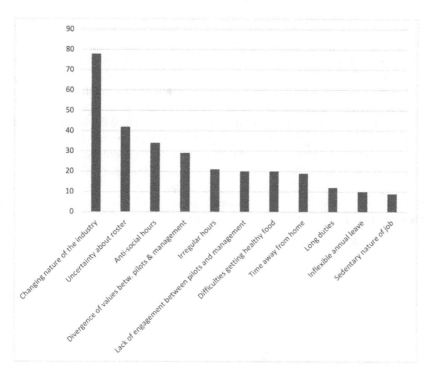

**Fig. 2.** Reported stress factors

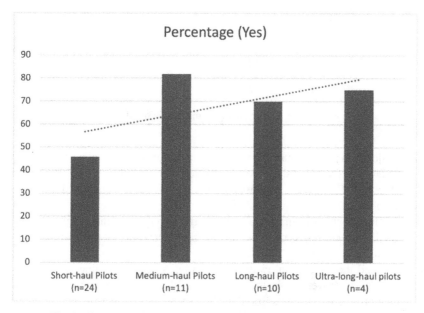

**Fig. 3.** Percentage of pilots impacted by COVID-19 per each category

Due to the small sample size of 49 participants, we were not able to undertake further quantitative analyses but did establish a trend line to demonstrate the positive relationship between the number of hours that pilots fly, with the percentage of pilots affected by COVID-19 (see Fig. 3). This result is likely due to the nature of flight operations during the pandemic where short-haul domestic flights were allowed to operate however, in most regions, the majority of long-haul international operations were halted. This finding is supported by statistics released by the International Civil Aviation Organization reporting that international passenger traffic plummeted by 50% as the number of passengers flown decreased by 2.7 billion in 2020 compared to 2019 (International Civil Aviation Organization [ICAO] 2021).

In analysing the qualitative responses to the question "Has COVID-19 impacted your wellbeing?", several themes were identified which included income, job security, quarantine, time away from family, lockdown and infected by COVID-19 (see Fig. 4).

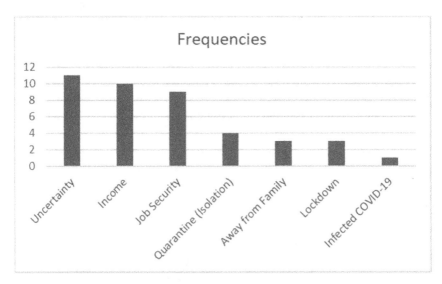

**Fig. 4.** Frequency of themes reported

The majority of participants reported that the aviation industry has an uncertain future and COVID-19 has affected their income and job significantly, with some participants losing their jobs. Participant responses were categorized and organized in themes as shown in Table 2.

It was found that pilots, in general, were currently experiencing a higher stress level than normal, with concerns revolving around the uncertainty of the industry, income, and job security. As expected, only LH and ULH pilots were stressed by the quarantine restrictions and the time spent away from family. At the same time, some SH pilots experienced an improvement in their well-being due to the pandemic as it provided them with more spare time and allowed them to spend more time with their families (see Table 3). A possible explanation for this result is that SH flights were not completely halted during the period, thus allowing SH pilots to continue flying throughout the

**Table 2.** Thematic analysis of responses showing negative impacts of COVID-19

| Theme | Example | Pilot category |
|---|---|---|
| Uncertainty | "It gets demoralising at times whenever there seems no sign of recovery in the industry yet" | Short-haul |
| | "More uncertainty in relation to career prospects" | Medium-haul |
| | "Uncertainty of the industry" | Long-haul |
| | "Stress of having young family and uncertain of future" | Ultra-long-haul |
| Income | "Only income has been affected" | Short-haul |
| | "In terms of income, yes. 50% pay cut" | Medium-haul |
| | "Loss of income" | Long-haul |
| Job security | "Stressed due to Layoffs" | Short-haul |
| | "Lost my career" | Medium-haul |
| | "Caused massive lay-offs" | Long haul |
| | "I am now unemployed" | Ultra-long-haul |
| Quarantine (Isolation) | "Isolation after the flights, unable to go out in layovers" | Long-haul |
| | "Stress of having to isolate or be sent into quarantine" | Ultra-long-haul |
| Away from family | "Can't be with family" | Long-haul |
| | "Yes, been away from family for too long" | Ultra-long-haul |
| Lockdown | "Lockdowns; no exercises and no social contracts" | Short-haul |
| | "The stress and mental strain of being lockdown" | Long-haul |
| Infected COVID-19 | "I had COVID early 2020" | Short-haul |

period. Conversely, LH operations were reduced to a minimum which resulted in LH pilots experiencing an adverse affect. However, overall, the results show that regardless of flight hours per trip, pilots have been impacted by the pandemic in various ways, which has also likely impacted their stress levels.

## 4.4 Strengths and Limitation

A clear strength of this study is that it aims to fill the knowledge gap within the aviation industry regarding the impact of flying hours in a single trip on a pilot's well-being and mental health. To date, this area has been overlooked and the adverse impact of the COVID-19 pandemic has only escalated the potential for harm for pilots and other workers in the industry. The present study has also identified pilots' views on both the negative and positive impacts of the pandemic and this rich information is vital to aviation managers and airlines who can initiate interventions and strategies to enhance

**Table 3.** Thematic analysis of responses showing positive impacts of COVID-19

| Theme | Example | Pilot category |
|---|---|---|
| Improved well-being | "It has improved my well-being significantly by giving much more time at home" | Short-haul |
| | "Improving my well-being. Reason is extra time with my family" | Short-haul |
| | "Had enjoyed time home" | Short-haul |
| | "Best time of my life because of extra free time" | Short-haul |

work environments and in particular, address the divergence of views between pilots and management.

There are, however, several limitations to this research, including: (1) the cross-sectional design (Sedgwick 2014); (2) the use of self-reported data which is dependent on the honesty of participants and could be affected by social desirability bias (Meleis & Dagenais 1980; Thea 2008); (3) the time constraints of the study which did not permit the researchers to achieve the targeted sample size; and (4) the ensuing small sample of 49 commercial pilots limits the generalizability of our findings. Finally, it was unfeasible to completely exclude factors external to the research such as the impact of COVID-19 which adversely affected the psychological stress levels of pilots.

## 5   Conclusion

As pilots are more susceptible to high-stress levels than the general population, this study has taken a step in identifying the category of pilots who are most vulnerable to stress and shows a trend related to the stress levels of pilots with the number of hours they fly in a single trip. The results suggest that LH and ULH pilots are more vulnerable than SH and MH pilots in experiencing higher levels of stress which could deteriorate the mental well-being of pilots when on duty and also impair their performance.

To date, minimal research has been undertaken on job stress in pilots, and this is also likely to be due to pilots being reluctant to openly talk about work-related stressors, which may, in the long run, threaten the safety benchmark of the aviation industry. Added to that is the negative impact of the recent pandemic, which only increases the need for aviation authorities to look deeper into pilot's mental health and well-being.

Lastly, this study induces a rethink on the requirements of medical certificates for pilots in that the sensitivity of mental health issues and stigmas may have prevented pilots from openly discussing mental well-being issues (Cullen et al. 2021; Lollis et al. 2009). Also, further research could look at external factors that can contribute to the high-stress levels of pilots (e.g., relationship and work-home conflict).

In summary, the qualitative responses obtained in the present study reveal a trend that commercial pilots who fly more than 10 h on a single trip experience a higher stress level compared to pilots who fly less than 10 h. It is also important to acknowledge that pilots are continuing to experience a higher than usual level of stress stemming from the impact of the COVID-19 pandemic. Therefore, this is an area where aviation authorities can play a part in mitigating this issue with targeted initiatives directed to the more vulnerable categories of pilots.

# References

Bidaisee, S.E.D.D., Bala, A.M.D., Uddin, S.M.P.H.: Depression in the skies: an occupational health issue among pilots. Int. Public Health J. **11**(4), 339-343 (2019). https://www.proquest.com/docview/2440011011?accountid=14649&forcedol=true

Boyatzis, R.E.: Transforming Qualitative Information: Thematic Analysis and Code Development. SAGE, New York (1998)

Bureau d'enquêtes et d'analyses pour la sécurité de l'aviation civile. Final Report. Alpes-de-Haute-Provence, France: Bureau d'enquêtes et d'analyses pour la sécurité de l'aviation civile Retrieved from (2015). https://www.bea.aero/uploads/tx_elydbrapports/BEA2015-0125.en-LR.pdf

Causse, M., Dehais, F., Faaland, P.-O., Cauchard, F.:. An analysis of mental workload and psychological stress in pilots during actual flight using heart rate and subjective measurements In: 5th International Conference on Research in Air Transportation (ICRAT 2012). Berkeley, United States (2012). https://oatao.univ-toulouse.fr/16202/

Cullen, P., Cahill, J., Gaynor, K.: A qualitative study exploring well-being and the potential impact of work-related stress among commercial airline pilots. Aviat. Psychol. Appl. Hum. Factors **11**, 1–12 (2021). https://doi.org/10.1027/2192-0923/a000199

Goldberg, D.P., et al.: The validity of two versions of the GHQ in the WHO study of mental illness in general health care. Psychol. Med. **27**(1), 191–197 (1997). https://doi.org/10.1017/s0033291796004242

Goldberg, D.P., Williams, P.: A Users' Guide to the General Health Questionnaire. GL Assessment, London (1988)

Guy, V. G.: Night work and shift work cause high stress levels. Eurofound (2006). https://www.eurofound.europa.eu/publications/article/2006/night-work-and-shift-work-cause-high-stress-levels

ICAO. Economic impacts of COVID-19 on civil aviation (2021). https://www.icao.int/sustainability/Pages/Economic-Impacts-of-COVID-19.aspx

Johnson, S.R.: The top 10 most and least stressful jobs. Business News Daily. (2019). https://www.businessnewsdaily.com/1875-stressful-careers.html

Kapur, N., Borrill, C., Stride, C.: Psychological morbidity and job satisfaction in hospital consultants and junior house officers: multicentre, cross sectional survey. BMJ (Clin. Res. Ed.) **317**(7157), 511–512 (1998). https://doi.org/10.1136/bmj.317.7157.511

Kasi, P., et al.: Studying the association between postgraduate trainees' work hours, stress and the use of maladaptive coping strategies. J. Ayub Med. Coll. Abbottabad JAMC **19**, 37–41 (2007)

Lee, K., Suh, C., Kim, J.-E., Park, J.O.: The impact of long working hours on psychosocial stress response among white-collar workers. Ind. Health **55**(1), 46–53 (2017). https://doi.org/10.2486/indhealth.2015-0173

Lee, Y.H., Liu, B.S.: Inflight workload assessment: comparison of subjective and physiological measurements. Aviat. Space Environ. Med. **74**(10), 1078–1084 (2003)

Little, L.F., Gaffney, I.C., Rosen, K.H., Bender, M.M.: Corporate instability is related to airline pilots' stress symptoms. Aviat. Space Environ. Med. **61**(11), 977–982 (1990)

Lollis, B.D., Marsh, R.W., Sowin, T.W., Thompson, W.T.: Major depressive disorder in military aviators: a retrospective study of prevalence. Aviat. Space Environ. Med. **80**(8), 734–737 (2009). https://doi.org/10.3357/asem.2484.2009

Maruyama, S., Morimoto, K.: Effects of long workhours on life-style, stress and quality of life among intermediate Japanese managers. Scand. J. Work Environ. Health **5**, 353–359 (1996). https://doi.org/10.5271/sjweh.153

Meleis, A.I., Dagenais, F.: Response bias and self-report of honesty. J. Gen. Psychol. **103**(2), 303–304 (1980). https://doi.org/10.1080/00221309.1980.9921010

Murdoch, M., et al.: Impact of different privacy conditions and incentives on survey response rate, participant representativeness, and disclosure of sensitive information: a randomized controlled trial. BMC Med. Res. Methodol. **14**(1), 90 (2014). https://doi.org/10.1186/1471-2288-14-90

Pasha, T., Stokes, P.R.A.: Reflecting on the germanwings disaster: a systematic review of depression and suicide in commercial airline pilots systematic review. Front. Psychiatry **9**, 86 (2018)

Pels, E.: Optimality of the hub-spoke system: a review of the literature, and directions for future research. Transp. Policy **104**, A1–A10 (2021). https://doi.org/10.1016/j.tranpol.2020.08.002

Reis, C., Mestre, C., Canhão, H.: Prevalence of fatigue in a group of airline pilots. Aviat. Space Environ. Med **84**(8), 828–833 (2013). https://doi.org/10.3357/asem.3548.2013

Roscoe, A.H.: Stress and workload in pilots. Aviat. Space Environ. Med. **49**(4), 630–633 (1978)

Sato, Y., Miyake, H., Thériault, G.: Overtime work and stress response in a group of Japanese workers. Occup. Med. (Lond) **59**(1), 14–19 (2009). https://doi.org/10.1093/occmed/kqn141

Sedgwick, P.: Cross sectional studies: advantages and disadvantages. BMJ Br. Med. J. **348**, g2276 (2014). https://doi.org/10.1136/bmj.g2276

Thea, F.V.D.M.: Faking it: social desirability response bias in self-report research. Aust. J. Adv. Nurs. **25**(4), 40–48 (2008). https://doi.org/10.3316/informit.210155003844269

# Evaluation of User Experience of Self-scheduling Software for Astronauts: Defining a Satisfaction Baseline

Shivang Shelat[1]([✉]), John A. Karasinski[2], Erin E. Flynn-Evans[2],
and Jessica J. Marquez[2]

[1] San Jose State University Research Foundation, San Jose, CA 95112, USA
sshelat@ucsb.edu
[2] NASA Ames Research Center, Mountain View, CA 94043, USA

**Abstract.** As NASA turns its sights to deep-space exploration, a greater focus on supporting crew autonomy has led to the development of Playbook, a self-scheduling software tool. Evaluating the user satisfaction of Playbook is essential in ensuring its usability for critical spaceflight operations. Satisfaction of an interface is often quantified with attitude surveys, such as the User Experience Questionnaire (UEQ). This paper demonstrates an application of the UEQ in comparing the user experience of Playbook interface designs for displaying graphical data. We lay the foundation for future user experience comparisons by defining a satisfaction baseline, which is crucial as more features are integrated into Playbook's interface. This work extends a validated user experience framework into a spaceflight domain, allowing optimization of human-computer interaction as future operational tools are developed.

**Keywords:** Spaceflight software · Self-scheduling · User experience · Usability

## 1 Introduction

Future NASA deep-space human exploration missions will require astronauts to behave and perform more autonomously from ground flight controllers. One manner to provide additional crew autonomy is to enable astronauts to manage their own sets of activities, or schedules, during spaceflight operations. Astronauts aboard the International Space Station (ISS) follow detailed schedules designed and supported by ground-station planners, but do not currently participate in the development of these schedules. Crew self-scheduling would allow planners and astronauts to collaborate, providing astronauts the ability to reschedule or manage their own timeline [17, 18]. Playbook, a mission planning and scheduling software tool, allows users to self-schedule by organizing mission activities on a user-friendly interface. The interface has a timeline that displays all of the scheduled activities for the crewmembers. If activities do not meet their constraints, the software highlights the scheduling violations in the user interface. This prompts crewmembers to reorganize their activities until they have a plan that is feasible and

D. Harris and W.-C. Li (Eds.): HCII 2022, LNAI 13307, pp. 433–445, 2022.
https://doi.org/10.1007/978-3-031-06086-1_34

violation-free. The design of the timeline allows astronauts, who are inexperienced planners, to build comprehensive schedules without any intervention from ground personnel [18].

A valuable practice in software development is to maximize the usability of system interfaces through user-focused research methods. Unusable systems pose risks to a variety of fields, and are often associated with high error rates, high workload, user discomfort, and poor productivity [1, 7, 9, 23, 27]. A human-centered design approach that evaluates the specifics of any human-computer interaction supports the creation of a usable system, which is vital to performing NASA operations [20]. The *Spaceflight Human-System Standard* specifies the need for a defined usability acceptance criteria for each NASA program [21], and asserts that a usable crew interface must allow users to achieve their tasks efficiently, effectively, and with satisfaction. Efficiency refers to the use of resources and time involved with completing a task, effectiveness refers to accuracy and the ability to complete the task, and satisfaction refers to the comfort and attitude carried towards the interface.

Maximizing satisfaction ensures that the user has a positive experience with the interface and is comfortable using it to perform operations. The International Organization for Standardization states that for the satisfaction of a system to be acceptable, the user experience from interacting with the system must meet the user's needs and expectations [14]. To verify that the interface of operational software meets user expectations, we must evaluate user experience when any changes are made to the software design. NASA's *Human Integration Design Handbook* [20] suggests that this evaluation procedure can be done by using quantitative measures of user experience, such as standardized questionnaires. If a researcher wanted to investigate whether a particular new design of a system met an acceptable level of satisfaction, they could compare user experience scores to a defined quantitative baseline derived from that same system [13, 15]. A baseline provides a simple approach to evaluating the user experience of new interfaces and enables frequent testing to confirm that users are satisfied with the system.

In this paper we demonstrate the use of the User Experience Questionnaire (UEQ) in comparing the user experience of different iterations of the Playbook interface. Additionally, we define a baseline satisfaction standard to assist evaluations of Playbook's user experience moving forward. The goal of the paper is to fulfill the need for a NASA program usability standard and to support a research approach that allows for the optimization of Playbook's interface as future designs are developed for operational use. By extending the UEQ's ability to evaluate user experience into the realm of operational spaceflight tools, we emphasize that a usability-oriented research approach in systems development is key to optimizing human-computer interaction.

## 2   The User Experience Questionnaire

The User Experience Questionnaire (UEQ) is a short, 3–5-min scale that was developed to quantify the user experience of interactive products such as business applications, web shops, and development tools [26]. Subjects respond to 26 items after interacting with a product, and computed scores can be used to evaluate how they felt and identify what facets of the user experience were positive or negative.

Each of the items provides a 7-point Likert scale between two adjectives with opposite meanings. Each item pertains to one of 6 subscales of the UEQ, and scores for each subscale can be computed on a calculator provided by the UEQ developers [24]. Scores can range from −3 to 3, with values between −0.8 and 0.8 representing a neutral evaluation, values greater than 0.8 representing a positive evaluation, and values less than − 0.8 representing a negative evaluation.

Each of the six subscales of the UEQ reflect an aspect of user experience [25]. The aspects are:

- *Attractiveness*: Do users like or dislike the product?
- *Perspicuity*: Is it easy to get familiar with the product?
- *Efficiency*: Can users solve their tasks with the product without unnecessary effort?
- *Dependability*: Does the user feel in control of the interaction?
- *Stimulation*: Is it exciting and motivating to use the product?
- *Novelty*: Is the product innovative and creative?

Attractiveness is considered to be an overall positive or negative impression of the product. Perspicuity, Efficiency, and Dependability are considered to be aspects of "hard user experience" and represent the pragmatic quality of the product. Users typically perceive products with greater pragmatic quality as easy-to-learn, efficient, and secure. Stimulation and Novelty are considered to be aspects of "soft user experience" and represent the hedonic quality of the product. Users typically perceive products with greater hedonic quality as interesting and leading-edge [25].

UEQ developers have proposed specific approaches that can be applied to evaluate a product's user experience. The first is to compare a product's scores to a provided benchmark that consists of a large number of responses from a variety of entities [26]. This comparison allows researchers to evaluate if the user experience of their product meets the expectations of the general user population. The calculator compares the average UEQ scores of entered data to this benchmark. It is important to note that the dataset of the benchmark does not distinguish between different product categories, and it includes data from products that are drastically different from Playbook, such as social networks and household appliances. The second proposed approach is to quantitatively determine whether a new version has an improved user experience by comparing average scores among each subscale to an older version. As developers redesign software to include new capabilities and features, we may expect to see a change in the user experience. Administering the UEQ to a sample of users allows for a quick and easy comparison between an old and new version of that software.

Researchers can also use the UEQ to determine how design changes affect the scores of different versions of their tools. While not as comprehensive as qualitative user feedback from usability testing, UEQ scores can inform educated guesses as to what design element affects which aspect when comparing multiple interfaces [25]. The delineation of the six dimensions by the UEQ allows for independent subscale comparisons that provide more insight into the strengths and flaws of a product than a single score alone. Additionally, we are able to prioritize different aspects of the UEQ based on the purpose of the entity we are evaluating. For Playbook, we care more about the goal-oriented aspects such as Perspicuity to maximize operational usability, and we care less about competing with other products in the market. We can apply comparative methods to reach conclusions about Playbook's user experience in order to guide design decisions and software development in the future.

## 3   User Interface Evaluations in HERA Campaign 4

### 3.1   Study Overview

In 2018, NASA conducted the fourth campaign in the Human Exploration Research Analog (HERA) to simulate deep-space missions. There were a multitude of research objectives during the campaign, including evaluating the effectiveness of different biomathematical sleep models in predicting crewmember fatigue [10]. In addition to having numerous physiological measures evaluated during the 45-day missions, a subset of HERA crewmembers was administered four Fatigue Interface Testing (FIT) sessions in which they used different designs of Playbook to solve scheduling problems. Each design involved using predictions from fatigue models to inform the user of how their performance would be expected to change based on their prior sleep and circadian rhythm phase. Model predictions were generated offline and integrated into Playbook's interface [11]. This integration is a prototyping technique called "Wizard of Oz" (WOZ), in which the user thinks that the software has certain capabilities, but a person has actually simulated these capabilities behind the scenes [3].

The four interfaces each displayed model predictions, but the presentation of information had different designs. Specifically, the design varied among the types of predictions of performance on a standard five-minute reaction time test (lapses [count of reaction times > 500 ms], mean response time in milliseconds, and mean speed [1000/reaction times] vs. only lapses), the number of models used (one model output vs. three model outputs), and the visual representations of the predictions. Crewmembers filled out the UEQ after each FIT session to give us a comprehensive impression of their user experience.

Participants were recruited through a variety of methods, from advertisements at NASA to appeals to the general public. Those who were selected were "astronaut-like." Individuals were divided to populate five separate missions of four members each [11]. In this investigation, we consider the eight HERA crewmembers of Missions 3 and 4, as they were the only crewmembers that completed the task with all four of the designs.

- *FIT Session 1*: Sleep model outputs (lapses, mean response time, and mean speed) for each scheduling scenario were presented in graph format in the context of their day's schedule (see Fig. 1).
- *FIT Session 2*: Sleep model output (lapses) for each scheduling scenario were presented in graph format alongside a red-green-yellow "heatmap", in the context of their day's schedule (see Fig. 2).
- *FIT Session 3*: Sleep model output (lapses) for each scheduling scenario were presented in graph format alongside a red-green-yellow "heatmap", in the context of their day's schedule. It also contained a legend for the graphs and data (see Fig. 3).

- *FIT Session 4*: Sleep model output (lapses) for three different models for each scheduling scenario were presented in graph format in the context of their day's schedule. Each graph was colored red-green-yellow accordingly (see Fig. 4).

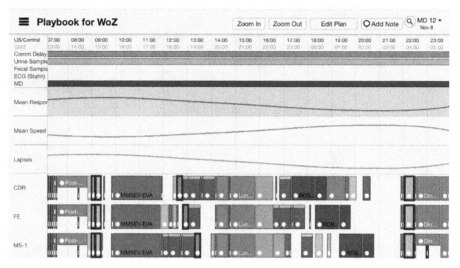

**Fig. 1.** FIT session 1 interface.

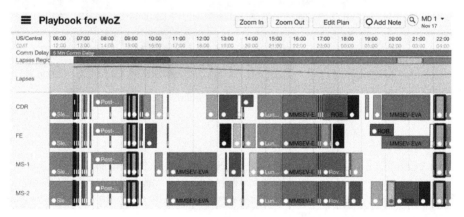

**Fig. 2.** FIT session 2 interface.

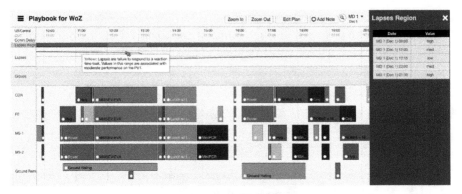

**Fig. 3.** FIT session 3 interface.

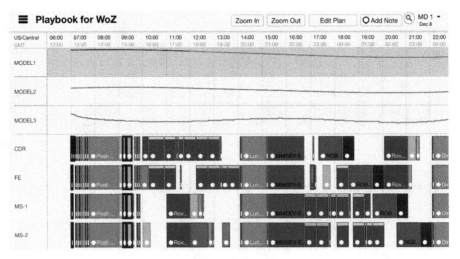

**Fig. 4.** FIT session 4 interface.

## 3.2 Results

HERA Campaign 4's exploration of user experience (see Fig. 5) showed steep differences in the Perspicuity aspect, particularly between FIT Sessions 1 and 3 and FIT Sessions 3 and 4. Because of these differences, we wanted to test an approach in comparing the user experience of different interfaces with the UEQ.

By attributing differences in the designs to the observed variation in the Perspicuity scores, we hypothesized that the crew preferred FIT 3 over FIT 1 because of the red-green-yellow lines, corresponding heatmap, and the legend for graphs/data. Additionally, we hypothesized that they did not prefer FIT 4 over FIT 3 because of the confusing (large) amount of model suggestions.

We chose to use a linear mixed-effect model to test the hypotheses because of the repeated measures experimental design. Each participant underwent each FIT Session,

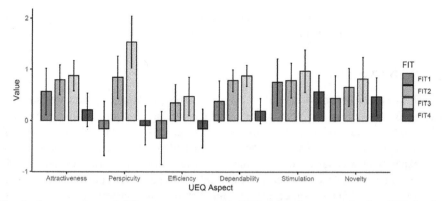

**Fig. 5.** A comparison of different scores on each UEQ subscale among the four FIT Session designs. Error bars represent the standard error.

resulting in dependency among the data. A linear mixed-effect model allows us to control for dependency by treating the repeated measurements of each subject as a random effect.

We ran the linear mixed-effect model analysis in R (version 4.0) [22] using the GAMLj package [12]. We included UEQ Value as the dependent variable and added fixed effects of UEQ Aspect and FIT Design, as well as the interaction between UEQ Aspect and FIT Design. We included Participant as a random effect. The model specification was as follows:

$$\text{Value} \sim \text{FIT\_Design} + \text{UEQ\_Aspect} + \text{FIT\_Design} : \text{UEQ\_Aspect} + (1 \mid \text{Participant})$$

The linear mixed-effect model detected statistically significant differences among UEQ aspects between different FIT designs, $F(3, 161) = 8.21$, $p < .001$. Post-hoc analysis with a Bonferroni adjustment showed that the Perspicuity of FIT 3 ($M = 1.53$, $SD = 1.44$) was significantly greater than the Perspicuity of FIT 1 ($M = -0.16$, $SD = 1.51$), $t(161) = -4.03$, $SE = 0.42$, $p < .05$. Additionally, the Perspicuity of FIT 4 ($M = -0.09$, $SD = 1.09$) was significantly lesser than the Perspicuity of FIT 3 ($M = 1.53$, $SD = 1.44$), $t(161) = 3.88$, $SE = 0.42$, $p < .05$. There were no other significant differences among matched UEQ aspects between the different conditions.

The HERA Campaign 4 analysis showed that the UEQ can be used to evaluate the user experience of different design iterations within Playbook. Similar research approaches like that of Campaign 4 can be used to detect significant differences in the user experience of an interface. To assist future user experience comparisons, we define a satisfaction baseline that consists of a more recent set of UEQ scores.

## 4 Developing a Playbook Satisfaction Standard

Our research study in HERA Campaign 4 only focused on the user experience of a specific Playbook feature for analog crewmembers and not about the Playbook tool in general. In order to consider future features that support and enable self-scheduling, we collected user experience data on Playbook as a whole. This allows us to create a standard that future design iterations of Playbook can be compared to so we can adequately compare integrated features and evaluate their effects on user experience.

### 4.1 Study Overview

In a study conducted remotely due to the COVID-19 pandemic, participants solved a number of scheduling and rescheduling problems using Playbook. Participants were split into two groups of subjects. 15 participants were instructed to schedule their task timeline and 16 participants were instructed to reschedule a predetermined task timeline. This experiment was designed to evaluate the differences in performance between the scheduling conditions (scheduling vs. rescheduling), type of task constraint (time range vs. requires vs. claim vs. ordering), and number of task constraints (33% vs. 66%) [8]. Each participant solved one baseline condition in which there were no scheduling constraints and 8 other conditions in which the type of constraint and the number of constraints varied. At the end of all the trials, they filled out the UEQ to evaluate their overall experience with Playbook. In this investigation, we only consider 30 participants because 1 subject in the rescheduling condition experienced a technology issue that interfered with their ability to respond to the UEQ.

### 4.2 Results

The results showed only minor differences between the conditions among each UEQ subscale (see Fig. 6), suggesting that there were no significant differences in user experience between using Playbook for scheduling and rescheduling.

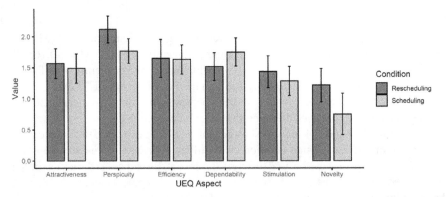

**Fig. 6.** Average UEQ scores for the scheduling and rescheduling conditions. Error bars represent the standard error.

To test for statistically significant differences between the scheduling and rescheduling conditions, we used a two-sample t-test assuming unequal variances. The results are shown in Table 1 and indicate that there were no significant differences between the two conditions. To create a larger, singular dataset that can serve as a satisfaction baseline for

**Table 1.** Results of a 2-sample t-test assuming unequal variances. There are no significant differences between the scheduling and rescheduling conditions. SD = standard deviation.

| Aspect | Scheduling | | Rescheduling | | $t$ | $df$ | $p$ |
| --- | --- | --- | --- | --- | --- | --- | --- |
| | Mean | SD | Mean | SD | | | |
| Attractiveness | 1.49 | 0.91 | 1.57 | 0.93 | 0.23 | 27.99 | 0.82 |
| Perspicuity | 1.77 | 0.76 | 2.12 | 0.83 | 1.20 | 27.82 | 0.24 |
| Efficiency | 1.63 | 0.91 | 1.65 | 1.19 | 0.04 | 26.23 | 0.97 |
| Dependability | 1.75 | 0.88 | 1.52 | 0.87 | -0.73 | 28.00 | 0.47 |
| Stimulation | 1.28 | 0.91 | 1.43 | 1.00 | 0.43 | 27.74 | 0.67 |
| Novelty | 0.75 | 1.29 | 1.22 | 1.04 | 1.09 | 26.79 | 0.28 |

**Table 2.** The descriptive statistics and UEQ benchmark comparison of the Playbook satisfaction baseline. An interpretation of the comparison is provided by developers of the UEQ [26]. For each aspect, N = 30. SD = standard deviation; CI = confidence interval; LL = lower limit; UL = upper limit.

| Aspect | Mean | SD | 95% CI | | Benchmark |
| --- | --- | --- | --- | --- | --- |
| | | | LL | UL | Comparison |
| Attractiveness | 1.53 | 0.90 | 1.20 | 1.85 | Above average |
| Perspicuity | 1.94 | 0.80 | 1.65 | 2.23 | Good |
| Efficiency | 1.64 | 1.04 | 1.27 | 2.01 | Good |
| Dependability | 1.63 | 0.87 | 1.32 | 1.94 | Good |
| Stimulation | 1.36 | 0.94 | 1.02 | 1.69 | Good |
| Novelty | 0.98 | 1.17 | 0.56 | 1.40 | Above average |

future design iterations of Playbook, we merged the UEQ responses from the scheduling and rescheduling participants.

Treating the UEQ data from this experiment as a singular dataset, we evaluated the user experience of this version of Playbook using methods outlined by the developers of the UEQ. Figure 7 is a visualization of each subscale and its performance relative to a provided benchmark which consists of a large bank of data from many entities. The results indicate that Playbook has been evaluated positively (>0.8) on each aspect of user experience. The calculator provided by the UEQ creators provides a benchmark comparison, which can be found in Table 2. "Above average" means that 25% of the benchmark products score higher and 50% score lower. "Good" means that 10% of the benchmark products score higher and 75% score lower [26]. The comparison shows that Playbook meets the user experience expectations of the general user population and scores highly among the products that make up the benchmark.

All aspects of the user experience of Playbook have been evaluated positively, with the highest score being Perspicuity and the lowest being Novelty. Relative to the provided UEQ benchmark, Playbook scores either above average or good in every aspect. As Playbook's goal is to maximize the user's operational ability, we are more focused on

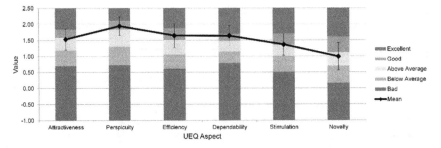

**Fig. 7.** Average scores for Playbook vs. the UEQ Benchmark. $> 0.8$ is a positive evaluation, between $-0.8$ and $0.8$ is neutral, and $< -0.8$ is negative. Error bars represent a 95% confidence interval.

the pragmatic subscales of Perspicuity, Efficiency, and Dependability, which all indicate a positive user experience. After applying the methods outlined by the developers of the UEQ, we can predict that users will have a positive attitude towards Playbook's interface and be comfortable using it to complete tasks. The dataset from this experiment can be used as a satisfaction baseline that future Playbook designs can be compared to in order to preserve the positive user experience.

## 5   Discussion

User satisfaction is an important aspect of the overall usability of a system. When completing tasks with an unsatisfying system, user needs and expectations are not met, causing negative attitudes towards the interface [14, 20]. To ensure an acceptable level of satisfaction, NASA's *Spaceflight Human-System Standard: Volume 2* states the need for each program to define a usability standard that includes a metric of satisfaction [21]. A satisfaction baseline allows for frequent testing to maintain a system's positive user experience as developers create new versions. It is therefore critical to develop and define a user experience standard that future Playbook versions and self-scheduling features can be compared to. This paper demonstrates the use of the User Experience Questionnaire (UEQ) in comparing the user experience of different Playbook interfaces and lays the foundation in evaluating Playbook satisfaction by defining a baseline. We have demonstrated the ability to measure and compare user satisfaction with the UEQ and detect differences in Playbook feature designs.

When comparing different biomathematical model design integrations of Playbook, we found that certain features significantly improved the Perspicuity of the interface. For example, the design iteration that only presented one modeled output (lapses) instead of three (lapses, mean response times, and mean speed) scored significantly higher on the Perspicuity aspect. This indicates that crewmembers preferred a single suggestion instead of multiple, which made interpreting the user interface confusing. Our investigation of the HERA Campaign 4 UEQ data showed that Playbook interfaces can be effectively evaluated by the UEQ and compared to one another.

The scheduling and rescheduling experiment gave us a novel UEQ dataset that measures the user experience of a general version of Playbook. After establishing that there were no significant differences in UEQ scores between the two experimental conditions, we merged the scores from all subjects into a baseline dataset that other Playbook versions can be compared to. Using methods outlined by UEQ developers, we established that Playbook has a positive user experience among each subscale. We now have the precedent and the means to make future user experience comparisons and ensure that Playbook provides a satisfying interface to its users.

Administering the UEQ to a pool of subjects after they interact with a new version of Playbook provides data that is easy to statistically compare against the satisfaction standard. We can then evaluate if an integrated feature significantly improves or worsens the user experience. If a feature increases human performance without significantly harming the user experience, we may be able to treat it as operationally usable.

## 5.1 Future Research

Future research should seek to further validate the ability of the UEQ to conclude that a system is sufficiently usable. To do this, UEQ scores can be compared to scores from a different questionnaire also designed to measure user experience, such as the System Usability Scale (SUS) [16]. The SUS is a brief, 10-item attitude questionnaire that evaluates the perceived usability of a system. Each item is a statement that describes how a user may have felt about the system that they interacted with, followed by a 5-point Likert scale (1 = strongly disagree, 5 = strongly agree). The final score can range from 1 to 100. NASA's *Human Integration Design Handbook* [20] explicitly states that usable systems receive a score of 85. Bangor, Kortum, & Miller have defined specific SUS score ranges that relate to acceptability ($< 50$ = unacceptable, 50–70 = marginal, $> 70$ = acceptable) [2, 4].

While the SUS has been used to evaluate the user experience of other NASA programs [5, 19] and is explicitly recommended by the *Human Integration Design Handbook* [20], the UEQ offers more insight into what distinct aspects of user experience have been affected by changes to an interface. While both measures have been used together in prior studies [6, 28], they have not been conjunctively applied in a spaceflight context. A comparison between Playbook's SUS and UEQ scores would shine light on the UEQ's ability to conclude that Playbook does indeed have an acceptable interface and positive user experience. If Playbook is evaluated positively by the SUS, it supports the conclusion that our UEQ analysis has yielded. It is also of interest to note whether the positive, negative, and neutral UEQ scores correlate with acceptability ranges of SUS scores as defined by Bangor, Kortum, & Miller [2].

To achieve this goal, future experiments should consider collecting both UEQ and SUS responses after administering experimental trials in Playbook. This would provide data to draw comparisons between the methods of evaluating Playbook's user experience and deriving meaningful conclusions in the future. By integrating two user experience frameworks in evaluating satisfaction, we contribute to research approaches in human-computer interaction supporting usable system development.

# References

1. Ahlstrom, U., Arend, L.: Color usability on air traffic control displays. Proc. Hum. Factors Ergon. Soc. Annu. Meet. **49**, 93–97 (2005). https://doi.org/10.1177/154193120504900121
2. Bangor, A., Kortum, P., Miller, J.: Determining what individual SUS scores mean: adding an adjective rating scale. J. Usability Stud. **4**, 114–123 (2009)
3. Bernsen, N.O., Dybkjær, H., Dybkjær, L.: Wizard of oz prototyping: how and when. In: CCI Working Papers in Cognitive Science and HCI., Roskilde, Denmark (1994)
4. Brooke, J.: SUS: a retrospective. J. Usability Stud. **8**, 29–40 (2013)
5. Burke, K.A., Wing, D.J., Haynes, M.: Flight test assessments of pilot workload, system usability, and situation awareness of tasar. Proc. Hum. Factors Ergon. Soc. Annu. Meet. **60**, 61–65 (2016). https://doi.org/10.1177/1541931213601014
6. Devy, N.P.I.R., Wibirama, S., Santosa, P.I.: Evaluating user experience of english learning interface using user experience questionnaire and system usability scale. In: 2017 1st International Conference on Informatics and Computational Sciences (ICICoS), pp. 101–106. IEEE, Semarang (2017)
7. Donahue, G.M.: Usability and the bottom line. IEEE Softw. **18**, 31–37 (2001). https://doi.org/10.1109/52.903161
8. Edwards, T., Brandt, S.L., Marquez, J.J.: Towards a measure of situation awareness for space mission schedulers. In: Ayaz, H., Asgher, U., Paletta, L. (eds.) Advances in Neuroergonomics and Cognitive Engineering, pp. 39–45. Springer International Publishing, Cham (2021). https://doi.org/10.1007/978-3-030-80285-1_5
9. Fairbanks, R.J., Caplan, S.: Poor interface design and lack of usability testing facilitate medical error. Joint Comm. J. Qual. Saf. **30**, 579–584 (2004). https://doi.org/10.1016/S1549-3741(04)30068-7
10. Flynn-Evans, E.E., et al.: Evaluation of the validity, acceptability and usability of biomathematical models to predict fatigue in an operational environment (2018)
11. Flynn-Evans, E.E., et al.: Changes in performance and bio-mathematical model performance predictions during 45 days of sleep restriction in a simulated space mission. Sci. Rep. **10**, 15594 (2020). https://doi.org/10.1038/s41598-020-71929-4
12. Gallucci, M.: GAMLj: general analyses for linear models. [jamovi module] (2019). https://gamlj.github.io/
13. Holm, J.E.W., du Plessis, E.: Usability - a full life cycle perspective. In: 2019 IEEE AFRICON, pp. 1–7. IEEE, Accra, Ghana (2019)
14. International Organization for Standardization: ISO Standard No. 9241–210:2019 (2019). https://www.iso.org/standard/77520.html
15. Jordan, P.W.: An Introduction to Usability. CRC Press, London (2020)
16. Jordan, P.W., Thomas, B., McClelland, I.L., Weerdmeester, B. (eds.): Usability Evaluation in Industry. CRC Press, London (1996)
17. Lee, C., Marquez, J., Edwards, T.: Crew autonomy through self-scheduling: scheduling performance pilot study. In: AIAA Scitech 2021 Forum. American Institute of Aeronautics and Astronautics, Virtual Event (2021)
18. Marquez, J.J., Hillenius, S., Kanefsky, B., Zheng, J., Deliz, I., Reagan, M.: Increasing crew autonomy for long duration exploration missions: self-scheduling. In: 2017 IEEE Aerospace Conference, pp. 1–10. IEEE, Big Sky (2017)
19. Meza, D., Berndt, S.: Usability/sentiment for the enterprise and enterprise. NASA (2014)
20. NASA: Human Integration Design Handbook (HIDH) (2010)
21. NASA: Space Flight Human-System Standard Volume 2: Human Factors, Habitability, and Environmental Health (Vol. 2). NASA-STD-3001 (2011)

22. R Core Team: R: A language and environment for statistical computing. [Computer Software] (2021). https://cran.r-project.org
23. Ratwani, R.M., Reider, J., Singh, H.: A decade of health information technology usability challenges and the path forward. JAMA **321**, 743 (2019). https://doi.org/10.1001/jama.2019.0161
24. Schrepp, M., Hinderks, A., Thomaschewski, J.: Applying the user experience questionnaire (UEQ) in different evaluation scenarios. In: Hutchison, D., et al. (eds.) Design, User Experience, and Usability. Theories, Methods, and Tools for Designing the User Experience, pp. 383–392. Springer International Publishing, Cham (2014)
25. Schrepp, M., Hinderks, A., Thomaschewski, J.: Construction of a benchmark for the user experience questionnaire (UEQ). Int. J. Interact. Multimedia Artif. Intell. **4**, 40 (2017). https://doi.org/10.9781/ijimai.2017.445
26. Schrepp, M., Hinderks, A., Thomaschewski, J.: User experience questionnaire (UEQ), https://www.ueq-online.org/
27. Viitanen, J., Hyppönen, H., Lääveri, T., Vänskä, J., Reponen, J., Winblad, I.: National questionnaire study on clinical ICT systems proofs: physicians suffer from poor usability. Int. J. Med. Inform. **80**, 708–725 (2011). https://doi.org/10.1016/j.ijmedinf.2011.06.010
28. Yulianto, D., Hartanto, R., Santosa, P.I.: Evaluation on augmented-reality-based interactive book using system usability scale and user experience questionnaire. J. RESTI (Rekayasa Sistem dan Teknologi Informasi) **4**, 482–488 (2020). https://doi.org/10.29207/resti.v4i3.1870

# Pilot Fatigue Evaluation Based on Eye-Movement Index and Performance Index

Hongjun Xue[1], Xiaotian Chen[1], Xiaoyan Zhang[2(✉)], Ziqi Ma[1], and Kai Qiu[3]

[1] School of Aeronautics, Northwestern Polytechnical University, Xi'an, China
[2] School of Marine Science and Technology, Northwestern Polytechnical University, Xi'an 710072, China
zxyliuyan@163.com
[3] Beijing Aeronautical Technology Research Center, Beijing, China

**Abstract.** Flight fatigue has always been an important factor affecting flight safety, but how to control and identify the state of fatigue is still an unsolved problem. The aim of this study is to explore the changing rules of eye-movement indicator and performance indicator of pilots under fatigue state by building a fatigue model of task load to excite fatigue, so as to provide reference for fatigue identification and evaluation. Thirty participants attended the experiment, which was required to complete three sets of flight parameters dynamic monitoring and control mission of varying difficulty in a controlled laboratory environment. The eye-movement indicators (blink duration time, average saccade amplitude, average pupil diameter) and performance indicators (accuracy, response time) of 30 subjects were measured in three groups of tasks. The experimental results showed that the blink duration time, average saccade amplitude, average pupil diameter and response time were all significantly affected by fatigue, but the accuracy rate was not significantly affected. According to the analysis of experimental data, it is concluded that the blink duration time increases first and then decreases with the increase of fatigue degree. Saccade amplitude average decreased with the increase of fatigue degree. Pupil diameter size decreases gradually with fatigue degree. These eye-movement indexes show good significance and can be used as good indicators to identify and evaluate fatigue state. Fatigue degree also has a significant effect on the response time. When the task load exceeds a certain degree, the response time will increase exponentially, which seriously affects the operation speed of pilot. The experimental results have important reference significance for the identification and evaluation of pilot fatigue.

**Keywords:** Pilots · Flight fatigue · Eye-movement indexes · Performance

## 1 Introduction

With the continuous improvement of technological level, the air transport industry has also developed by leaps and bounds. According to statistics from the Civil Aviation Administration of China, in 2019, the annual passenger traffic at China's airports reached 135,169,000 [1]; in 2020, the annual passenger traffic at China's airports decreased due to the epidemic, but still reached 85,715,000 [2]. With the rapid increase in air traffic, shift work, long-distance flights, and frequent take-offs and landings for short-haul flights have led to an increasing workload for pilots [3], which has led to an increasingly common phenomenon of pilot fatigue.

Fatigue has become a phenomenon that cannot be ignored during flight. Fatigue is a common cause of aviation accidents. According to the National Transportation Safety Board (NTSB), 105 of the 144 accidents, or 74% of the total, were caused by human factors, and most of them were related to pilot fatigue [4]. The results of the European Cockdeck Association survey also showed that 92% of German pilots experienced fatigue problems, and 93% said they had experienced operating errors due to fatigue, while only 23% reported fatigue incidents [5]. Flight fatigue is already one of the most important influences on flight safety [6], so research into the identification and evaluation of pilot fatigue is essential highly.

How to identify and evaluate the fatigue state of pilots is also a hotpot of research for scholars at home and abroad. At present, the method of pilot fatigue evaluation is mainly including subjective and objective assessment methods [7]. The NASA-TLX is the most widely used subjective evaluation method [8]. Zhong et al. [9] conducted a study on the validity and applicability of the NASA-TLX for evaluating fatigue, and the results of the study showed that the NASA-TLX as an evaluation tool showed good levels of reliability and validity. The subjective scale is widely used because of its simplicity and low cost, but it also has obvious disadvantages. The subjective evaluation method is highly susceptible to external stimuli and one's own subjective feelings, which can affect the level of fatigue and judgement of the pilot, and has poor real-time performance [10]. The objective evaluation method is mainly through physiological signal measurement and image analysis techniques [11]. The measurement of physiological signals mainly includes the detection of heart rate, blood oxygen saturation etc. Fatigue detection of physiological signals can determine whether a pilot is fatigued, but the detection of physiological signals is more complex and not easy to use in practical scenarios [12]. And physiological signal can be affected by individual differences. Fatigue assessment methods for image analysis are mainly based on the analysis of video of the pilot's facial region, more commonly as an eye movement indicator. In most cases, the information is fed into the brain through the eyes. The eye contains information about many important parameters that can be used as an important basis for fatigue detection. Parisay M et al. [13] proposed a new evaluation method based eye-movement measurements focusing on detecting fatigue during work. Li Shi [14] analysed the changes of eye-movement indicators in different degrees of fatigue and non-fatigue states through eye tracking techniques, and concluded that eye-movement indicators could effectively detect the fatigue and non-fatigue states of the subjects. At present, the available studies can show that there is a close relationship between the state of the eyes and the fatigue state of a person [15]. When a person is in fatigue, the pupil diameter and saccade etc. will change accordingly, but the variation degree and trend between eye-movement index and fatigue degree in flight activities need to be further studied.

In summary, the identification and evaluation of pilot fatigue is an important research direction. This paper focuses on pilot fatigue identification and evaluation methods. By simulating flight parameters dynamic monitoring and control mission, performance and eye-movement data in experiment are statistically analyzed to explore changes of eye-movement and performance levels under different fatigue states.

## 2  Method

### 2.1  Design and Variables

#### 2.1.1  Design

According to previous studies [16], the fatigue models commonly used nowadays are: task load, hypoxia, sleep deprivation, alcohol stimulation, etc. [17]. In this study, the task load fatigue model, which is most suitable for the working mode of civil aviation pilots, was selected for experimental design. Based on scholars' research on the workload of civil aviation pilots [18], this experiment chosen time pressure, flight time, and difficulty of flight task to excite the fatigue. The experiment task was to simulate the pilot flight parameters of the dynamic monitoring process, subjects need to be on display to monitor seven flight parameters of simulation, as shown in Table 1. Once the abnormal flight parameters, flight parameters need to be corrected immediately and within a limited time.

**Table 1.** Parameters and range of monitoring

| Status parameters | Normal value range |
|---|---|
| Airspeed | 90–130 |
| Barometric height | 1200–1800 |
| Angle of pitch | −20–+20 |
| Angle of roll | −30–+30 |
| Angle of yaw | Target heading ±5 |
| Engine speed | 1800–2700 |
| Cylinder temperature | 120–200 |

#### 2.1.2  Variable

The experimental independent variable was set as three groups of flight parameters dynamic monitoring and control mission with different task intensity, namely, the high-load task without any prompt information when the certain flight parameters was abnormal, medium-load task with only visual cues when certain flight parameters was abnormal, and low-load task with both visual and auditory cues when certain flight parameters was abnormal.

The dependent variable measured experimentally include eye-movement indicators (average pupil diameter, average saccade amplitude and blink duration time) and performance indicators (accuracy and response time). Based on the available research results, blink duration time, average saccade amplitude and average pupil diameter, which have good significance and stability, were selected as the eye-movement indicators for analysis [19]. Eye-movement indicators are mainly used to assess the fatigue state, and performance indicators are used to indicate the cognitive state and manipulation level in the fatigue state. Response time refers to the total time taken from the time the monitoring instrument malfunctioned to the time the subject identified the malfunction and responded accordingly. The response time is used to assess the subject's manipulation level in different states of fatigue. Accuracy is the percentage of the total number of malfunction identified correctly and corrected by the subject. The indicator is used to assess the subject's cognitive accuracy in different states of fatigue.

## 2.2  Participants

Thirty university students with a background in aviation knowledge participated in this study. The subjects had an average age of 22.39 years and an average visual acuity of 5.0 in the left and right eyes. They all had normal vision and hearing, no colour blindness or colour weakness, no cognitive impairment or hearing impairment, and could correctly identify the experimental clues. At the same time, 2 days before the start of the experiment, all the subjects were required to go to bed in strict accordance with the prescribed schedule and rest system, and should not take any drugs or drinks that may affect the central nervous system.

## 2.3  Equipment and Procedures

### 2.3.1  Equipment

The experiments were conducted on a civil aircraft cockpit simulation test platform, as shown in Fig. 1. The flight simulation system consists of a flight control computer, an aircraft display computer, a navigation display computer, a status monitoring computer, a view generation computer as well as the aircraft dynamics simulation software Flight Gear. It is capable of imitating mission scenarios, dynamically responding to pilot control inputs, generating aircraft dynamics parameters, etc. The experimental mission interface program is based on the flight simulation software Flight Gear 2018.3.5, using the C++ programming language for independent development of the flight monitoring and manoeuvring mission software.

The experimental equipment is mainly the IView X HED eye-tracking device made in Germany, as shown in Fig. 2. The eye-tracking device mainly consists of a helmet, an IView X companion computer, a transmission cable and a power cable. There are two cameras on the helmet, one of which is used to capture the fixation of the subject as they gazes at the target object with a semi-lens reflection, so that the position of the eye and pupil can be easily identified and calibrated. Thus obtaining the measurement indicators of the three basic forms of eye movements: blink, fixation and saccade, as well as the degree of eyelid closure and changes in pupil diameter. The other is used to record the image of the driver's gaze at the target object, which can be superimposed with the image of the previous camera to determine the position of the subject's gaze and also determine the area of interest of the subjects. One of the advantages of the equipment is that the test data can be transferred to the IView X software on the accompanying computer, stored and processed. And the supporting analysis software Begaze can be used to process the experimental test data, which is convenient to carry out research on the characteristics of the subjects.

**Fig. 1.** Civil aircraft simulation experiment platform

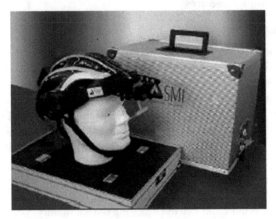

**Fig. 2.** IView X HED

### 2.3.2 Procedure

Before the start of the experiment, the subject were introduced to the purpose and process of the experiment. Later, they were informed of the safety requirements of the experiment, and were trained and tested on the task. The formal experiment starts with the research assistant to debug the experimental procedures and experimental equipment. Subjects wore the experimental equipment under the guidance of the assistant, signed the Informed experimental consent. They performed the three tasks in order of low, medium and high. After a single task was completed, the subject took a 10– 30 min break and filled in the KSS (karolinska sleepiness scale) to record the subject's state after the task and ensure that the subject remained awake for the next set of tasks. The experiment was over until the subjects completed all the tasks in three sets of different intensities.

### 2.4    Data Analysis

The data was statistically analysed by third party statistical analysis software SPSS 26.0. The K-S (Kolmogorov-Smirnov) test and the S-W (Shapiro-Wilk) test, usually used to test whether data distribution is normal distribution. With the K-S test selected when the sample size is more than 2000 and the S-W test selected when the sample size is less than 2000 [20]. Null hypothesis H0: the data meet the normal distribution ($P > 0.05$); Alternative hypothesis H1: the data does not satisfy the normal distribution ($P < 0.05$).

The homogeneity of variance test was carried out on the data satisfying the normal distribution. Null hypothesis H0: the variance between the data is equal ($P > 0.05$); Alternative hypothesis H1: variances between the data are not equal ($P < 0.05$). ANOVA and Bonferroni tests were performed for the data of three or more groups satisfying the homogeneity test of variance, and Tamhane postmortem test was performed for the data not satisfying the homogeneity test of variance. Non-parametric hypothesis tests were performed on data that did not satisfy the normal distribution [21]. The Kruska-Wallis H-test was selected for analysis of variance for samples of three and more. Null hypothesis H0: there was a significant difference in the data ($P < 0.05$); Alternative hypothesis H1: there was no significant difference in the data ($P > 0.05$).

## 3    Results

### 3.1    Eye-Movement Indicators

### 3.1.1    Blink Duration Time

Statistical analysis was conducted on the collected blink duration time. K-S test was used to test the normality of blink duration time under three groups of tasks. The results of the test showed that the low, medium and high load tasks did not conform to a normal distribution, as shown in Table 2, therefore, the non-parametric test was selected. The results of the non-parametric test showed that there was a significant difference in blink duration time ($H = 346.407$, $P = 0.000 < 0.05$) between the subjects in the three task groups, as shown in Table 3. Comparing three sets of tasks in pairs, as shown in Table 4, there were significant differences between the low-load task and medium-load task, the medium-load task and high-load task, and the low-load task and high-load task, with the variation tendency shown in Fig. 3. The subjects' blink duration time reached the longest during the medium-load task, followed by the low-load task, while it was the shortest during the high-load task.

**Table 2.** Tests for normality of blink duration time

| Workload | Kolmogorov-Smirnov test | | |
|---|---|---|---|
| | Statistics | Freedom | Significance |
| Low-load | 0.284 | 11500 | 0.000 |
| Medium-load | 0.237 | 12047 | 0.000 |
| High-load | 0.341 | 12605 | 0.000 |

**Table 3.** Non-parametric statistics of blink duration time

| Workload | Kruska-Wallis H | | | |
|---|---|---|---|---|
| | Rank average | Statistics | Freedom | Significance |
| Low-load | 17585 | 346.407 | 2 | 0.000 |
| Medium-load | 19496 | | | |
| High-load | 17168 | | | |

**Table 4.** Comparison of blink duration time in pairs

| Workload (I) | Work load (J) | Test statistics (I-J) | Standard error | Adjusting for prominence |
|---|---|---|---|---|
| Low-load | Medium-load | −1910.534 | 134.067 | 0.000 |
| Medium-load | High-load | −2327.627 | 132.466 | 0.000 |
| High-load | Low-load | 417.093 | 135.541 | 0.006 |

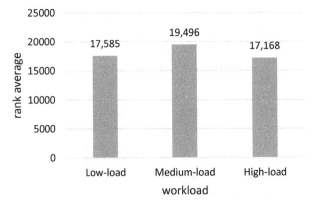

**Fig. 3.** Variation tendency of blink duration time

### 3.1.2   Average Saccade Amplitude

Statistical analysis was conducted on the collected average saccade amplitude. S-W test was used to test the normality of average saccade amplitude under three groups of tasks. The test results showed that the high-load task ($P = 0.001 < 0.05$) did not conform to a normal distribution, as shown in Table 5, therefore a non-parametric test was selected. The results of the non-parametric test showed that there was a significant difference in the average saccade amplitude ($H = 7.388$, $P = 0.025 < 0.05$) of the subjects under the three groups of tasks, as shown in Table 6. Comparing three sets of tasks in pairs, as shown in Table 7, there was a significant difference in average saccade amplitude between low-load and high-load, and no significant difference between low-load and medium-load, and medium-load and high-load, and the change tendency in the three groups of tasks is shown in Fig. 4. The average saccade amplitude showed a decreasing trend as the task load increased. It was greatest at low load, and decreased sequentially at medium-load and high-load.

**Table 5.** Test for normality of average saccade amplitude

| Workload | Shapiro-Wilk test | | |
|---|---|---|---|
| | Statistics | Freedom | Significance |
| Low-load | 0.936 | 30 | 0.070 |
| Medium-load | 0.934 | 30 | 0.062 |
| High-load | 0.856 | 30 | 0.001 |

**Table 6.** Non-parametric statistics of average saccade amplitude

| Workload | Kruska-Wallis H | | | |
|---|---|---|---|---|
| | Rank average | Statistics | Freedom | Significance |
| Low-load | 54.70 | 7.388 | 2 | 0.025 |
| Medium-load | 45.43 | | | |
| High-load | 36.37 | | | |

**Table 7.** Comparison of average saccade amplitude in pairs

| Workload (I) | Work load (J) | Test statistics (I-J) | Standard error | Adjusting for prominence |
|---|---|---|---|---|
| Low-load | Medium-load | 9.267 | 6.745 | 0.509 |
| Medium-load | High-load | 9.067 | 6.745 | 0.509 |
| High-load | Low-load | 18.333 | 6.745 | 0.020 |

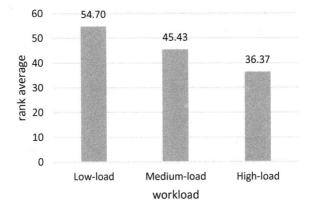

**Fig. 4.** Variation tendency of average saccade amplitude

### 3.1.3  Average Pupil Diameter

Statistical analysis was conducted on the collected average pupil diameter. k-S test was used to test the normality of average pupil diameter under three groups of tasks. The results of the test showed that the low, medium and high load tasks did not conform to a normal distribution, as shown in Table 8, so a non-parametric test was chosen. The results of the non-parametric test showed that there was a significant difference in average pupil diameter (H = 2729.132, P = 0.000 < 0.05) of the subjects under the three groups of tasks, as shown in Table 9. Comparing three sets of tasks in pairs, as shown in Table 10, there were significant differences in average pupil diameter between low and high load, low and medium load, and medium and high load, and the change tendency is shown in Fig. 5. There was a decreasing trend in pupil diameter size as task load increased. Average pupil diameter was greatest at low-load task, and began to show a significant decrease at medium-load task, and showed a significant decrease at high-load task, when average pupil diameter was the smallest under all three groups of tasks.

**Table 8.** Normality test for average pupil diameter

| Workload | Kolmogorov-Smirnov test | | |
|---|---|---|---|
| | Statistics | Freedom | Significance |
| Low-load | 0.069 | 48394 | 0.000 |
| Medium-load | 0.070 | 49557 | 0.000 |
| High-load | 0.087 | 60093 | 0.000 |

**Table 9.** Non-parametric statistics of average pupil diameter

| Workload | Kruska-Wallis H | | | |
|---|---|---|---|---|
| | Rank average | Statistics | Freedom | Significance |
| Low-load | 87551 | 2729.132 | 2 | 0.000 |
| Medium-load | 77849 | | | |
| High-load | 73122 | | | |

**Table 10.** Comparison of average pupil diameter in pairs

| Workload (I) | Work load (J) | Test statistics (I-J) | Standard error | Adjusting for prominence |
|---|---|---|---|---|
| Low-load | Medium-load | −9702.741 | 276.838 | 0.000 |
| Medium-load | High-load | −4726.488 | 275.351 | 0.000 |
| High-load | Low-load | 14429.229 | 278.655 | 0.000 |

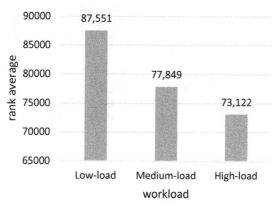

**Fig. 5.** Variation tendency of average pupil diameter

## 3.2  Performance Indicators

### 3.2.1  Accuracy

Statistical analysis was conducted on the performance data collected. Given that there was only one accuracy obtained under each set of tasks, it was not possible to conduct ANOVA on their data, so the coefficient of variation was used for the accuracy to determine the degree of dispersion between the accuracy of the groups. In general, a coefficient of variation of less than 15% can be considered as no significant difference between the data [22], and the results of the statistical analysis are shown in Table 11. The results showed that there was no significant difference in the accuracy under the three groups of tasks, as shown in Table 12.

**Table 11.** Descriptive statistics of task manipulation performance for the three groups

| Workload | Correct | Disposal errors | Undetected failure | Normal state misjudgment | Total | Accuracy |
|---|---|---|---|---|---|---|
| Low-load | 1056 | 70 | 10 | 13 | 1149 | 92% |
| Medium-load | 1001 | 87 | 5 | 12 | 1105 | 91% |
| High-load | 733 | 67 | 61 | 37 | 898 | 83% |

**Table 12.** Analysis of variance in accuracy

| Average value | Variance | Coefficient of variation | Contrast values |
|---|---|---|---|
| 0.89 | 0.052 | 0.058 | 0.15 |

### 3.2.2  Response Time

Statistical analysis was conducted on the collected response time. K-S test was used to test the normality of response time under three groups of tasks. The result showed that the low-load task ($p = 0.000 < 0.05$), medium-load task ($p = 0.000 < 0.05$) and high-load task ($p = 0.000 < 0.05$) did not conform to a normal distribution, as shown in Table 13, Therefore the non-parametric test was chosen. The results of the non-parametric test showed that there was a significant difference in the response time of the subjects under the three groups of tasks ($H = 1121.876$, $P = 0.000 < 0.05$), as shown in Table 14. Comparing three sets of tasks in pairs, as shown in Table 15, showed that there were significant differences between low and medium load, medium and high load, and low and high load. The change tendency in response time for the three groups of tasks is shown in Fig. 6. The response time showed an increasing trend as the task load increased. At low-load task, the response time was the shortest, at medium-load task the response time increased significantly and at high-load task the reaction time was again longer.

**Table 13.** Tests for normality of response time

| Workload | Shapiro-Wilk test | | |
|---|---|---|---|
| | Statistics | Freedom | Significance |
| Low-load | 0.605 | 1546 | 0.000 |
| Medium-load | 0.750 | 1490 | 0.000 |
| High-load | 0.901 | 1228 | 0.000 |

**Table 14.** Non-parametric statistics of response time

| Workload | Kruska-Wallis H | | | |
|---|---|---|---|---|
| | Rank average | Statistics | Freedom | Significance |
| Low-load | 1253 | 1121.876 | 2 | 0.000 |
| Medium-load | 1392 | | | |
| High-load | 2591 | | | |

**Table 15.** Comparison at response time in pairs

| Workload (I) | Work load (J) | Test statistics (I-J) | Standard error | Adjusting for prominence |
|---|---|---|---|---|
| Low-load | Medium-load | −611.202 | 44.692 | 0.000 |
| Medium-load | High-load | −961.698 | 47.447 | 0.000 |
| High-load | Low-load | 1572.899 | 47.057 | 0.000 |

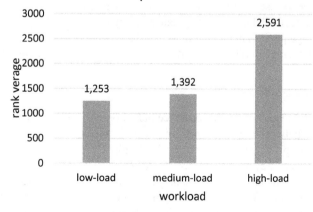

**Fig. 6.** Variation tendency of response time

## 4  Discussion

The negative impact of flight fatigue on flight effectiveness and safety is well known. It is very important to identify and evaluate pilot fatigue state to prevent flight fatigue. In this study, based on previous work, a task load fatigue model was constructed to explore the tendency of eye movement changes and performance changes in fatigue states.

### 4.1  Eye-Movement Indexes

The experimental results of the eye-movement index show that the level of fatigue gradually increased as the task load increased. The blink duration time of the subjects also increased, but began to decrease when fatigue reached a certain level. This is due to the body's resistance to fatigue, which has been confirmed in previous studies [19]. When the subjects reached a certain level of fatigue, because they had to complete the task, the subjects resisted the fatigue by blinking quickly. The average saccade amplitude tended to decrease with increasing task load. Average saccade amplitude is the span from the beginning of saccade to the end of saccade, that is, the range of eyes jumping between two consecutive fixation points [12]. The results of the experiment showed that the subjects' average saccade amplitude showed significant differences under the three group of tasks, which was consistent with Li's verification that average saccade amplitude could be used as an eye-movement indicator to detect fatigue state [13]. In our study, we also found the subjects' attention was relatively concentrated and their working state was good in the low-load task. At this time, the average saccade amplitude was also the largest, while in the medium-load task and the high-load task, the average saccade amplitude decreased in turn. It indicated that the degree of attention had begun to decrease at this moment, which seems to indicate that the average saccade amplitude of the subjects presents a downward trend when the fatigue degree deepens. Average Pupil diameter showed a decreasing trend with increasing task load. Average pupil diameter is a good indicator of the pilot's level of tension and fatigue [23]. The results of the experiment showed that subjects showed significant differences in pupil diameter size under the three groups of tasks, which again argued for the previous conclusion that pupil diameter size could be a good indicator to assess work status [24]. Further research into the trend of change found that average pupil diameter was greatest during the low-load task. As the task load increased, average pupil diameter decreased and the range of vision narrowed. It can be speculated that average pupil diameter decreases as fatigue levels increase.

### 4.2  Performance Indexes

The experimental results of the performance indicators showed that there was no significant difference between the correctness of the subjects under the three groups of tasks. This seemed to imply that the different levels of fatigue did not have a significant effect on the cognitive accuracy of the subjects. JC Sun et al. [16] also studied the performance levels of subjects in the fatigue state and they found that the performance changed significantly before and after the task, with a significant decrease in correctness. Comparing the results of the experiment we made, although there was no significant difference in correctness under the three groups of tasks, it could be seen that the overall change showed a decreasing trend. The trend of change was theoretically the same, only the degree of change differed. In terms of response time, there were significant differences between the three groups of tasks. Subjects had significantly shorter response times in the low-load task, significantly longer response times in the high-load task, and response times in this state even reached twice as long as in the low-load task. This indicates that fatigue has a significant effect on reaction speed and that increased fatigue significantly reduces the flexibility of the subjects' reactions, which can be quite fatal for pilots when dealing with malfunctions and emergencies.

### 4.3 Summary

In summary, the research results of experiment can provide some guidance for pilot fatigue identification and evaluation. Firstly, this experiment successfully constructed a fatigue model of task load, simulated three groups of workload states with different intensities, and derived the change tendency of fatigue state under different workload states. Secondly, the experiment verified the significance of blink duration time, saccade amplitude average and pupil diameter size as pilot fatigue state evaluation indexes, which could better reflect the fatigue state of pilots. Thirdly, at different levels of fatigue, the subjects' cognitive accuracy was not greatly affected, and they could still make judgments and responses, but the response time of operation was greatly affected. The task load increasing in a gradient, while the response time was exponentially longer. When scheduling flight tasks, the impact on pilot manoeuvre performance should be taken into account, and the duration and intensity of the task should be arranged as appropriate to prevent the pilot from working too hard and compromising flight safety.

### 4.4 Limitation and Future Studies

There are also some shortcomings in this study. For example, the task load modeling is more biased towards mental fatigue and ignores the physical load that may be involved in the flight process. Together with the physical load, the range and degree of variation in various eye-movement indicators and performance levels need to be further examined. In addition, the fault handling in the monitored manoeuvring task in this study was a one-off correction. The real fault handling situation is much more complex. Subsequent studies could make the fault handling process more difficult to make the simulation closer to the real flight process.

## 5    Results

This study explored the effects on pilots' fatigue state under three groups of task load, as well as the tendency of change in eye-movement indicators and performance under different fatigue states. The study showed that as task load increased, subjects' fatigue levels significantly deepened. Blink duration time, saccade amplitude average and pupil diameter size all showed significant changes with increasing fatigue, and performance also decreased significantly with increasing fatigue. The results of the experiment have important implications for the identification and assessment of fatigue in pilots and for improving flight safety.

# References

1. Civil Aviation Airport Production Statistics Bulletin for 2019 [EB/OL]. Civil Aviation Administration of China, p. 3 (2020)
2. Civil Aviation Airport Production Statistics Bulletin for 2020 [EB/OL]. Civil Aviation Administration of China, p. 4 (2021)
3. Powell, D., et al.: Pilot fatigue in short-haul operations: effects of number of sectors, duty length, and time of day. Aviat. Space environ. Med. **78**, 698–701 (2007)
4. Long, X.: Research on the influencing factors of pilot fatigue and methods to overcome it. Sci. Technol. Inf. **24**, 190–193 (2013)
5. Feng, W.: Theoretical analysis and application effect study of fatigue risk management provisions in CCAR-121 (R5). Civil Aviation University of China (2019)
6. Sun, R., Feng, W.: A comparative study on pilot fatigue risk management regulations at home and abroad. J. Civ. Aviat. (2019)
7. Wei, L., Long, H.J.: To review the progress of flight fatigue detection methods and mitigation measures (2018)
8. Hill, S.G.: Comparison of four subjective workload rating scales. Hum. Factors: J. Hum. Factors Ergon. Soc. **34**(4), 429–439 (1992)
9. Zhong, X., et al.: Research on the reliability and validity of NASA-TLX as a measurement of subjective fatigue after vienna psychological test. Chin. J. Ergon. (2018)
10. Guan, C.-C., Shen, C., Cheng, S., Zhang, T., Ma, J., Hu, W.: A study of a physiological electrical stimulation recovery task performance protocol for a sleep deprivation fatigue model. Occup. Health **36**(19), 90–95 (2020)
11. Saini, V.: Driver drowsiness detection system and techniques: a review. Int. J. Comput. Sci. Inf. Technol. **5**, 4245–4249 (2014)
12. Fu, C.: Study on the physiological and oculomotor characteristics of drivers under fatigue. Harbin Institute of Technology (2011)
13. Parisay, M., Poullis, C., Kersten-Oertel, M.: FELiX: fixation-based eye fatigue load index a multi-factor measure for gaze-based interactions. In: 2020 13th International Conference on Human System Interaction (HSI). IEEE (2020)
14. Li, S.: A comparative study of eye movement characteristics in fatigue and non-fatigue states. Henan University of Technology (2018)
15. Xiong, J., Yang, Z., Li, Y.: A study on mental fatigue assessment. Clin. Med. Res. Pract. **1**(012), 186–189 (2016)
16. Sun, J., et al.: Analysis of blood oxygen saturation in brain tissue under mental fatigue state by near infrared spectroscopy. Progr. Mod. Biomed. Sci. **015**(034), 6697–6700 (2015)
17. Hoedlmoser, K., et al.: Event-related activity and phase locking during a psychomotor vigilance task over the course of sleep deprivation. J. Sleep Res. **20**(3), 377–385 (2011)
18. Wang, L.J., et al.: The research of the influencing factors system of the civil aviation pilots' workload. Chin. J. Ergon. (2016)
19. Yu, C., Xu, J.: Analysis of eye movement parameters in fatigue detection. Sci. Technol. Wind **428**(24), 196–197 (2020)
20. Luo, W., et al.: Selection of normality test method based on SPSS. Chin. Hospit. Stat. (001), 48–51 (2015)
21. Chen, J.: Experimental design of nonparametric test and its application in SPSS software practice. J. Xingtai Polytech. **36**(01), 95–100 (2019)
22. Zhang, R.: Theory and Application of Spatial Variation. Science Press (2005)
23. Niu, S.F., et al.: Analysis on eye movement indices based on simulated flight task of fighter pilots. Progr. Mod. Biomed. (2013)
24. Jinfei, M.A., Chang, R., Gao, Y.: An analysis of empirical validity on pupil diameter size in driver fatigue measurement. J. Liaoning Norm. Univ. (Soc. Sci. Edn.) (2014)

# Study on the Mechanism of Pilot Fatigue on Performance

Hongjun Xue[1], Ziqi Ma[1], Xiaoyan Zhang[2]([⊠]), Xiaotian Chen[1], Kai Qiu[3], and Jie Li[3]

[1] School of Aeronautics, Northwestern Polytechnical University, Xi'an, China
[2] School of Marine Science and Technology, Northwestern Polytechnical University, Xi'an 710072, China
zxyliuyan@163.com
[3] Beijing Aeronautical Technology Research Center, Beijing, China

**Abstract.** The Unmanned Aerial Vehicle (UAV) cruise surveillance study is one type of encountered human-aircraft interaction tasks. The aim of this study was to examine the relationship between the pilot fatigue and performance. Thirty participants attended this experiment where they were recorded the performance under three task-loads which can cause different level of fatigue. Results indicated that the Low-Load and Medium-Load which this study set can guarantee better performance, and the High-Load can cause a significant drop in performance. The difficulty of the real mission should be avoided by setting a task that is equivalent to the High-Load in this experiment.

**Keywords:** UAV cruise surveillance · Simulation · Pilot fatigue · Task-load · Performance

## 1 Introduction

There are several factors that can affect flight safety, which include weather, mechanical failure, flight to the pilot fatigue [1], etc. The human which as the central-positioned factor of the system is required higher demands by the improvement of technologies and equipment. In the 21st century, the aviation into the era of 'people-centered' automation, human factor will be the key influence factor of aviation safety in a long period. However, fatigue is one of the most important human factors which can affect aviation safety. According to the statistic of the National Aeronautics and Space Administration (NASA), 52,000 of the 261,000 secret incident reports sent to the aviation safety reporting system have been classified as fatigue caused, accounting for 21% of the total [2]. The factors leading to pilot fatigue are various and complex, which can be divided into two categories: external factors and internal (personal) factors, the two categories both can be subdivided into several specific factors as the secondary indicators. Generally, flight fatigue is not affected by single factor, but the result of cumulative effects of multiple factors, among which the most important ones can be summarized as sleep problems, workload problems, flight environment factors and the pilot's physiological factors [3]. The influences of sleep factors on pilots mainly are divided into sleep deprivation and sleep disorders. Workload is an abstract concept that usually reflects the degree of pressure when a person doing his job. Different levels of workload can cause different effects on pilot fatigue. Environmental factor mainly refers to the cockpit environment and flight environment. The pilot working in the cockpit will be influenced negatively by the vibration, noise, radiation, poor light environment and the narrow space, etc., which will cause the body fatigue easily. Internal factors mainly refer to personal factors of a pilot, which include age, physical factors, psychological factors, flight skills and life factors [4]. The way that pilot fatigue affects flight safety needs to be explained from the perspective of the occurrence mechanism of fatigue. The theory of "protective inhibition" and the theory of "systemic adaptation syndrome" are widely recognized currently. The two theories consider fatigue as an external manifestation of body ability to protect or recover from overload by reducing some parts of its function.

Since pilot fatigue has a great impact on flight safety, researchers have carried out a series of studies on flight fatigue. In order to ensure flight safety, Chen et al. [5] established a real-time fatigue detection system of helicopter pilots based on eye state recognition by using 'Percent of eyelid closure over the pupil over time'(PERCLOS) method to ensure the flight safety. By comparing the advantages and disadvantages of fatigue risk management regulations of various countries, Feng [6] established a bio-mathematical model to make theoretical interpretation of the revised contents of CCAR-121 (R5) P, and conducted a survey on airline companies to optimize and confirm the effect of CCAR-121 (R5) P on alleviating pilot fatigue and improving flight safety. Based on the theoretical knowledge of software engineering, Li [7] analyzed the requirements of airlines for fatigue monitoring, then added various fatigue factors into the linear regression model to establish the pilot-flight fatigue value matrix model, and used 'Probabilistic Matrix Factorization' (PMF) model to establish flight recommendation model. Combined with the basic post-flight rest period stipulated by CAAC, the optimization model of post-flight rest period is established. Finally, he integrated the three models into the pilot fatigue monitoring and management system to form a unified management and ensure the flight safety. Cheng [8] verified the reliability through tests and adopted the posture chart measurement method to distinguish the mental and physical fatigue of pilots, she independently designed the posture chart for military pilots. By taking the heart rate as the fatigue analysis index and selecting the performance such as yawning and tear-flowing as the fatigue evaluation index, Sun [9] drew the fatigue characteristic curve of flight cadets and established the flight quality evaluation model, then verified the influence of fatigue on flight quality through the collected data of flight cadets. Luo et al. [10] constructed the fatigue state index by extracting the rhythmic waves of EEG signals, and proposed the fatigue state classification algorithm of Gamma deep belief network based on the periodic changes of each channel of EEG signals to identify and classify the brain fatigue state of pilots and ensure flight safety.

Pilot fatigue can be studied from multiple perspectives with different methods. Excluding extraneous variables, fatigue can be quantified by the accumulation of a constant work load over time, and the degree of fatigue can be expressed indirectly by measuring the work load. Researchers focused more on the subjective feelings of pilots and measured pilot fatigue through subjective scales in the initial stage of the study. This article conducted a study into the mechanism of pilot's fatigue degree to task per-formance based on independent designed tests of pilot fatigue monitoring. By making a pilot produce different degree of fatigue and recording the fatigue performance data under this degree of fatigue, the researchers can explore the existing pattern between the two variables and create important significance for early warning of pilot fatigue and precaution of accidents.

## 2  Method

### 2.1  Design

According to the main task performance measurement method, a single factor-variable display interface, three-level design task was employed in this study to test the performance variation of pilots under different fatigue states. The independent variables of this study are flight monitoring operation tasks with three different difficulty levels while the dependent variables include subjective questionnaire survey and performance data.

The task is to simulate the pilot's dynamic monitoring of the flight parameters in the cruising state of the UAV. During the task, subjects need to conduct real-time monitoring with seven parameters, including the flight attitude parameters (pitch angle, roll angle and heading angle), airspeed, pressure altitude and engine parameters (engine speed and engine temperature). If an abnormal state is found, the test subjects need to eliminate the abnormal quickly by pressing the corresponding button on the keyboard, the adjustment methods corresponding to each specific flight parameter are shown in Table 1. The difficulty levels differentiate promptly based on the degree of information. The basic layout of the three tasks' interfaces is the same. The first task provides a combination of visual and auditory cues for the subjects while the second task provides visual cues for them only, and the third task does not provide any cues.

**Table 1.** Status parameter operation method

| States parameters | Normal range | Exceed | Below |
|---|---|---|---|
| Airspeed | 90−130 | Delete | Insert |
| Pressure altitude | 1200−1800 | Page Down | Page Up |
| Pitch angle | −20 − +20 | ↓ | ↑ |
| Roll angle | −30 − +30 | ← | → |
| Heading angle | Target ±5 | Keypad 0 | Keypad Enter |
| Engine speed | 1800−2700 | Keypad 1 | Keypad 7 |
| Engine temperature | 120−200 | Keypad 2 | Keypad 8 |

The subjective fatigue questionnaire evaluates the workload mainly or the current fatigue state directly by testing object's own experience and feeling. This intuitive method has great flexibility and is able to reflect a certain fatigue degree. Hart et al. [11] established the NASA-TLX evaluation method whose core idea is that workload is considered as a multi-dimensional concept. After a large number of investigations and studies, they determined six factors affecting the workloads: Mental Demand (MD), Physical Demand (PD), Time Demand (TD), Performance (PE), Effort Level (EF) and Frustration Level (FR), the specific description of each factor is shown in Table 2. Since the scale is simple and easy to operate without any other redundant measures, this method is widely used in the subjective measurement of human workload. Karolinska Sleepiness Scale (KSS) method divides people's mental state into 9 levels for measurement, the specific descriptions of each level is shown in Table 3. This questionnaire is simple and easy to operate. It is able to evaluate the state of test subjects before and after the task or in the process of the task, so that real-time fatigue degree of test subjects can be obtained more quickly [12].

**Table 2.** NASA-TLX's six factors description

| Factors | Description |
| --- | --- |
| Mental Demand | The amount of activity in the brain or perception (i.e., thinking, decision making, calculating, remembering, searching) |
| Physical Demand | The amount of physical type of activity (pushing, pulling, turning, control activities, etc.) |
| Time Demand | Refers to the speed or rhythm of work operation, whether it is too fast or too slow |
| Performance | Operators' satisfaction with their performance |
| Effort Level | The effort required to complete the operation (mental and physical) |
| Frustration Level | The magnitude of operator frustration during task execution |

**Table 3.** Description of each level of the KSS

| Karolinska Sleepiness Scale (KSS) | Select a state |
| --- | --- |
| 1 = extremely alert | |
| 2 = very alert | |
| 3 = alert | |
| 4 = rather alert | |
| 5 = neither alert nor sleepy | |
| 6 = some signs of sleepiness | |
| 7 = sleepy, no effort to stay awake | |
| 8 = sleepy some effort to stay awake | |
| 9 = very sleepy, great effort to stay awake, fighting sleep | |

Performance data are divided into accuracy rate and response time. Accurate rate is the proportion of correct operation in the total number of tasks executed. Response time refers to the time required for the body to make a response to the stimulus. In this experiment, reaction time refers to the response time taken from the failure of flight instruments to the discovery of the fault by the pilot and the corresponding manipulation. Response time is an important index to evaluate flight fatigue. From the perspective of verifying the relationship between performance and fatigue state, the selection of response time as performance data analysis is more representative, which reflects more intuitively the performance of the test object.

## 2.2 Participants

In this experiment, participants were eligible if they were self-reported with normal or corrected- to-normal vision and normal color vision. Thirty university students (15 males and 15 females; mean age = 22.4 years) participated in our study. The subjects should have the ability to correctly recognize the prompt information of the experimental setting. Two days before the start of the experiment, all the subjects were required to follow a strict accordance with the prescribed schedule and rest system and should not take any drugs or drinks that may affect the central nervous system. In addition, they were provided written informed consent before their participation.

## 2.3 Materials

Apparatus. The test mission is controlled by the UAV cruise surveillance, which was developed by the institute of man-aircraft efficacy design and research evaluation at Northwestern Polytechnic University. The equipment used for the whole experiment is

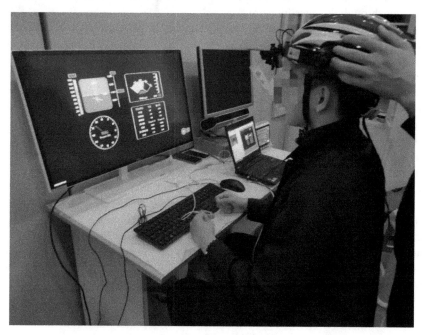

**Fig. 1.** Experiment apparatus

shown in Fig. 1. The simulation system was developed using C++ programming language and Qt interface design to simulate the maneuvering interface during the UAV cruise. The system is able to control the flight parameters with random failures and record the operation records of the test subjects in the background.

## 2.4 Procedures

Before the start of the experiment, there are two steps to prepare in order to make the whole test running properly. In the test debugging stage, the research assistant should debug the test software, test instruments, test equipment, test environment and test platform. The software debugging process mainly target the flight monitoring and control tasks to ensure that there are not any fluctuations and lag occurring on the software interface within 6 h and the background data records are normal and complete. The test environment is selected in a space with no sunlight, stable light source, quiet and no noise, and a temperature of about 25 °C.

In the pre-experimental phase, a trained research assistant first explains the study's background to the participants, helps subjects understand the experimental process. Later, the research assistant instructs the participants to sign the safety requirements and complete personal spatial ability questionnaire. After passing the pre-experimental training test, the subjects perform three tasks in turn, each of which lasts for 1 h. Assistant should use the KSS scale to ensure consistent subject status before each task. After each task, subjects fill in the NASA-TLX scale to quantify the difficulty of the task. The subjects have sufficient rest time to eliminate the fatigue state after performing one set of tasks, and started the next set of experimental tasks after the fatigue state is confirmed to be gone through the questionnaire.

During the experiment, the flight parameters on the interface change randomly in terms of the appearance of an abnormal parameter every 10−30 s. The test subject is supposed to monitor the changes of the parameters on the interface at all times and identify the abnormalities in time so that to make the corresponding operation as specified. After the test subject finishes the response operation, the abnormal information is eliminated and restored to normal immediately regardless of the correct result. The task operation interface is shown in Fig. 2.

Four kinds of results are probably generated during the task: correct, incorrect disposal, no fault found, and normal state misjudgment. If the subject finds the fault within the specified time and makes the corresponding disposal manipulation in time, it is correct, and then the system will record the reaction time; If the subject finds the fault within the specified time but makes the wrong disposal manipulation, it is disposal error; If the subject does not find the fault in the system within the specified time, it is no fault, and then the system will automatically correct and record once that no fault is found; If the system does not find the fault, which means the subject misjudged the working state of the system and made the disposal manipulation, that is, the normal state misjudgment. The program automatically records the correct rate and reaction time of the subject.

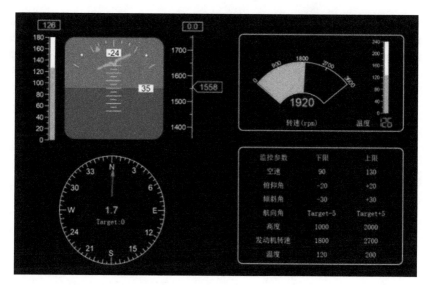

**Fig. 2.** Task operation interface

## 2.5 Date Analysis

Shapiro-Wilk test is performed first to examine whether variables were normally distributed, and the normality of the performance and perception measures are verified (p > 0.05). If the test passes, the data are subjected to Chi-square test, when the Chi-square test is satisfied, variance analysis (ANOVA) and Bonferroni post hoc comparison test are used for three work-load tasks, when the Chi-square test is not satisfied, using Tamhane post hoc test for data, as for analyzing the differences between two groups satisfying the normal distribution, using independent samples t-test. If the test does not pass, the data are tested for nonparametric hypotheses, the Kruska-Wallis test is chosen to analyze the variance for three work-load tasks and the Mann-Whitney U test is used to analyze the variance for two samples. Statistical analyses were performed with IBM SPSS 22 (Chicago, Illinois, USA).

The NASA-TLX scale is analyzed by assigning different weights to the six dimensions, where the weights are assigned by the two-by-two matching method, and the weighted average is obtained by combining the weights and the scores are obtained for each dimension, which are used as the quantitative score of task difficulty in this experiment is the workload score.

## 3   Result

### 3.1   Task-Load

The NASA-TLX scale data were weighted and summed for each task difficulty by the weighting coefficients in Table 4. Overall scores for the difficulty of the three tasks could be obtained (No. 1 Task = 34.31, No. 2 Task = 39.15, No. 3 Task = 51.20). The overall calculation of NASA-TLX data revealed that the evaluation scores gradually increased with gradually decreasing information cues of the three tasks which could be learned to a gradually increase in difficulty. Based on this result, the tasks are named as Low-Load task, Medium-Load task and High-Load task. In order to make fuller use of the data, the three task load data were calculated for each experimental subject. The distribution of the calculated individual data is shown in Fig. 3.

**Table 4.** Wight of each factor.

|  | MD | PD | TD | PE | EF | FR |
|---|---|---|---|---|---|---|
| No. 1 task | 1 | 3 | 3 | 2 | 5 | 1 |
| No. 2 task | 2 | 3 | 2 | 2 | 4 | 2 |
| No. 3 task | 5 | 2 | 1 | 2 | 2 | 3 |

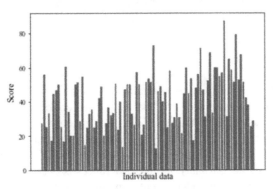

**Fig. 3.** The calculated individual data

### 3.2 Reaction Time

Reaction Time (RT) is an important indicator to evaluate flight fatigue. The awaken pilot will be in a high-level working state so that the RT will be shorter, while the sleepy pilot will become obviously sluggish so that the RT will be relatively longer. Choosing RT as performance data to analysis is more representative and can more visually reflect the performance of the test subjects.

The experimental data of RT were analyzed to obtain the variability the change pattern of RT within a fixed time interval (1 h). The SW method was chosen to test the normality of RT for the three different load-tasks, as shown in Table 5, Low-Load Task ($P = 0.000 < 0.05$), Medium-Load Task ($P = 0.000 < 0.05$) and High-Load Task ($P = 0.000 < 0.05$) did not have significant effect, so nonparametric hypotheses was chosen to test the data. As is shown in Fig. 4. The results of the average rank of RT showed that in the Low-Load Task condition (AR = 1.253) was shorter than that in the Medium-Load

Task condition (AR = 1.392) and significantly shorter than that in the High-Load Task condition (AR = 2.591); The test result of the chosen KW method showed that there was a significant difference in RT (H = 1121.876, P = 0.000 < 0.05) under the three different load-tasks. As shown in Table 6, the RT of the three load-tasks were compared pairwise where significant differences were found between any groups (P = 0.000).

**Table 5.** Reaction Time normality test

|  | Kolmogorov-Smirnov | | | Shapiro-Wilk | | |
|---|---|---|---|---|---|---|
| Task load | Statistics | DOF | Significance | Statistics | DOF | Significance |
| Low-load | 0.183 | 1546 | 0.000 | 0.605 | 1546 | 0.000 |
| Medium-load | 0.129 | 1490 | 0.000 | 0.750 | 1490 | 0.000 |
| High-load | 0.116 | 1228 | 0.000 | 0.901 | 1228 | 0.000 |

**Table 6.** Pairwise comparative variability of Reaction Time

| Task load (I) | Task load (J) | Statistics (I-J) | Standard error | Significance |
|---|---|---|---|---|
| Low-Load | Medium-Load | −611.202 | 44.692 | 0.000 |
| Medium-Load | High-Load | −961.698 | 47.447 | 0.000 |
| High-Load | Low-Load | 1572.899 | 47.057 | 0.000 |

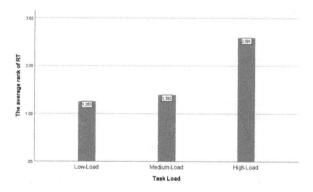

**Fig. 4.** The average rank of RT under the three loads

## 4   Discussion and Conclusion

The experiment was conducted by the controlled variable method, confirming that the pilots were in a consistent state before the start of each group of tasks by using KSS scale. The KSS data verified a progressively deeper fatigue produced on the experimental subjects in three tasks where found a high degree of similarity between the trend in NASA-TLX data and that in degree of fatigue. This study decided to quantify the level of fatigue using task difficulty scores.

With NASA-TLX results as fatigue level values and RT data as performance values, linear regression was used to fit fatigue and performance relationship curves. The curve was fitted by linear regression. As shown in Fig. 5, the change trend of the curve fitted by cubic relationship was consistent with the data, and as shown in Fig. 6, the value of the cost function reached the allowed range. Increased reaction time corresponds to decreased performance; The trend transformation of the curve gave the final result as shown in Fig. 7. The curve fitting process was implemented programmatically in python3.4.

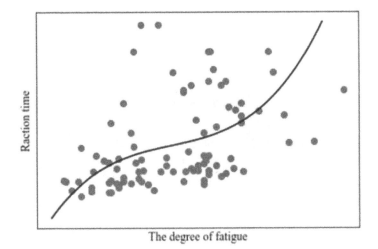

**Fig. 5.** Relationship between reaction time and fatigue levels

In the UAV cruise surveillance task, the relationship curve of fatigue and performance is divided into three main parts. In the low fatigue level, performance is at a high level, and increasing fatigue level causes a more significant drop of performance; In the media fatigue level, performance is more stable and do not fluctuate with changes in fatigue; Entering the high fatigue level range, performance decreases rapidly as fatigue level increases. According to the task difficulty load set in this experiment, the task-load range should be set between low and medium load, which will allow pilots to maintain good performance for a long time. When the task-load range is in high load, pilots' working hours should be strictly controlled to prevent excessive fatigue accumulation from affecting flight safety.

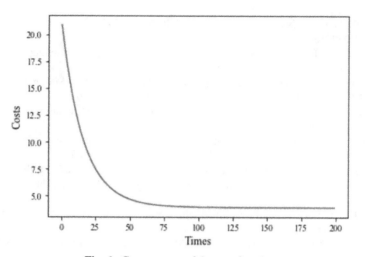

**Fig. 6.** Convergence of the cost function

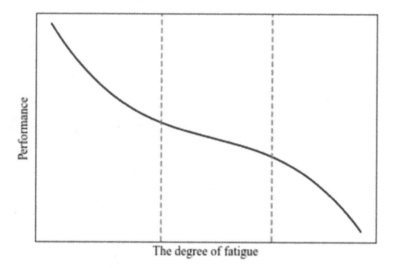

**Fig. 7.** The relationship between fatigue and performance

# References

1. Long, X.: And to overcome the method of pilot fatigue factors. Sci. Technol. Inform. **24**, 190–193 (2013)
2. McCallum, M., Sanquist, T., Mitler, M.: Commercial transportation operator fatigue management reference. In: Prepared for the US Department of Transportation Research and Special Programs Administration, pp. 200–205 (2003)
3. Loewenthal, K.M., Eysenck, M., Harris, D.: Stress, distress and air traffic incidents: job dysfunction and distress in airline pilots in relation to contextually-assessed stress. Stress Health **16**(3), 179–183 (2015)

4. Cao, B., Yang: Study and analysis of pilot flight fatigue. Chin J. Convalescent Med. **19**(10), 920–922 (2010)
5. Chen, X., Liu, L.: A design of military helicopter pilot fatigue real-time monitor system based on the eye state. Electron. Test. **12**, 60–61 (2019)
6. Feng, W.: Theoretical Analysis and Application Effect of Fatigue Risk Management in CCAR-121(R5), pp. 1–4. Civil Aviation University of China, Tianjin (2019)
7. Li, X.: Research of Pilot Fatigue Assessment Model and Application, pp. 15–23. Dalian University of Technology, Dalian (2016)
8. Cheng, S.: Study on discriminant method for mental and physical fatigue of pilots based on posturography, pp. 33–45. Air Force Medical University, Xi'an (2018)
9. Sun, J.: Study on Fatigue Characteristics and Flight Quality Evaluation of Flying Students Based on Physiological Index Measurement, pp. 36–51. Civil Aviation University of China, Tianjin (2018)
10. Luo, J., Qiu, D., Ren, W.: Pilots' brain fatigue state inference based on gamma deep belief network. Acta Electron. Sin. **48**(6), 1062–1070 (2020)
11. Hart, S.G., Legaip, S.: Development of NASA-TLX (Task Load Index). Results Empirical Theor. Res. **52**(6), 139–183 (1988)
12. Kaida, K., Takahashi, M., Akerstedt, T.: Validation of the Karolinska sleepiness scale against performance and EEG variables. Clin. Neurophysiol. **117**(7), 1574–1581 (2006)

# Preliminary Research on Evaluation Index of Professional Adaptability for Airline Transport Pilot

Mengxi Zhang[1], Lei Wang[1(✉)], Ying Zou[1], Jiahua Peng[1], Yiwei Cai[1], and Shu Li[2]

[1] College of Safety Science and Engineering, Civil Aviation University of China, Tianjin, China
mxzhangzhang@163.com, wanglei0564@hotmail.com
[2] Flight Academy, Civil Aviation University of China, Tianjin, China

**Abstract.** Combining with the professional characteristics of airline transport pilots and requirements of implementing pilots' Professionalism Lifecycle Management (PLM) system put forward by Civil Aviation Administration of China (CAAC), this study aims to examine the initial evaluation index of professional adaptability for airline transport pilot. Based on literatures review and analysis, the cognitive ability, operation and professional ability, social-interpersonal ability and personality traits were selected and included in the initial index system. Meanwhile, this study pointed out that the primary indices could be optimized through the implementation of expert method and data analysis in next step. The initial evaluation index system would also be a basis for developing final professional adaptability evaluation tools, which could be used for airline transport pilots' selection and evidence-based training in future.

**Keywords:** Professional adaptability · Evaluation index · Airline transport pilot · Flight safety

## 1 Introduction

Human factors are considered to cause over 70% of aviation accidents and have been widely recognized as a key element to ensure flight safety and efficiency [1, 2]. Among that, pilot's psychological traits and states are two of the most critical human factors. Currently, psychological evaluation has become a necessary step in the selecting and training for pilots all over the world [3].

In 2021, the Civil Aviation Administration of China (CAAC) proposed out a plan of implementing Professionalism Lifecycle Management (PLM) system for promoting airline transport pilots' post competence. The PLM system is regarded as an important tool for the selection and training of civil aviation transport pilots in China. As a trait affected by the interaction of congenital and environmental factors [4], professional adaptability is an essential psychological factor for pilots. Meanwhile, some inherent risks from the psychological defects of professional adaptability cannot be controlled or mitigated through flight training, or the training cost is hard to accept. The ability to deal with emergency events is closely related to pilot's professional adaptability. Therefore, evaluating professional adaptability of pilots is helpful to select the suitable candidates. Monitoring pilot's psychological risks in their professionalism lifecycles can effectively ensure flight safety, save training costs and improve training efficiency.

Based on previous studies, we have proposed out a floating iceberg model of pilots' psychological competence. As shown in Fig. 1, the bottom of the iceberg is professional adaptability which is defined as a kind of professional competences and social competences formed on the basis of personality traits and cognitive abilities [5].

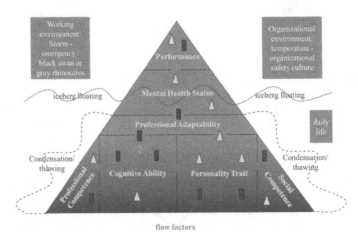

**Fig. 1.** Floating iceberg model of pilots' psychological competence [5]

The aim of this study is to propose out the initial professional adaptability evaluation index for airline transport pilot, as the basis for developing practical evaluation tools. This study intends to summarize the literatures referring to psychological competence and capability evaluation in civil aviation industry, and tries to reveal the coherence between pilots' post competence and professional adaptability.

## 2   State of Art of Evaluation Methods and Index

To improve flight safety, pilot's flight training community has begun to shift from the traditional task-based training to competency-based training and assessment globally.

In the 1980s, the Federal Aviation Administration (FAA) launched the Advanced Qualification Program (AQP), which was the first attempt by industry regulators to integrate non-technical competencies such as crew resource management (CRM) into the training system [6]. The FAA requires that American airline transport pilots must accept an annual psychological examination, including neurocognitive and personality assessments. Neurocognitive assessment includes intelligence test (especially the Wechsler Adult Intelligence Scale) and tests assessing executive functions such as decision-making speed and decision-making ability. Minnesota Multiphasic Personality Inventory-2 (MMPI-2) is generally used for personality assessment. In the early years of 20th century, the four-dimensional model of non-technical skills training evaluation (NOTECHS) proposed by the Joint Aviation Authorities (JAA) believed that the non-technical skills of airline transport pilots consisted of four categories, such as Cooperation, Leadership and Managerial Skills, Situation Awareness and Decision-making [7]. Helmreich et al. [8] proposed out five non-technical skill evaluation indices based on the investigation and analysis of human factors skills of airline transport pilots, including Team Management and Communication, Situational Awareness and Decision-making, Automatic Management, Special Situation Treatment and Technical Proficiency. Subsequently, in 2013, the International Civil Aviation Organization (ICAO) proposed out eight kinds of pilot's capabilities, including application of procedures and compliance with regulations, communication, flight path management-automation, flight path management-manual control, leadership and teamwork, problem solving and decision-making, situation awareness and management of information, workload management, and stipulated that pilots at any stage of the professional lifecycle must possess and develop these eight competencies[9]. The European Aviation Safety Agency (EASA) listed "knowledge" as the ninth competency. On this basis, according to the principles of crew resource management, EASA proposed that psychological assessment should include cognitive abilities, personality traits, operational and professional competencies, and social competences [10]. In the Guidance Material and Best Practices for Pilot Aptitude Testing (PAT) developed by the International Air Transport Association (IATA), six dimensions were proposed, namely English language proficiency, basic ability, composite abilities, operational abilities, social-interpersonal abilities and personality traits [11].

In the 1990s, CAAC began to pay attention to pliot's psychological selection and evaluation. After introducing pilot selection system developed by Deutsche Lufthansa (LH) and the Deutsches Zentrum für Luft-und Raumfahrt (DLR) [12], it was found that the best psychometric predictors for the different stages of Chinese airline transport pilot training were psychomotor ability, mental concentration, spatial ability, and English language proficiency in multi-tasking assignments. Space perception, also called flight space orientation, is considered as the most core element of the flight capability structure [13]. During flight in extreme environments, crew members must confront interpersonal problems such as interpersonal tension, decreased cohesion, deprivation of interpersonal relationships, and catharsis [14]. If pilots' cooperation ability is poor, the entire team and mission will be exposed to substantial risks. Therefore, the evaluation of individual cooperation ability in the selection stage is necessary, it can provide reference and guarantee for the smooth progress of subsequent team formation and training. You et al. [15] put forward that flight cognitive ability is the comprehensive reflection of pilot's psychological quality, the foundation of flight technical level, and the core element for pilots to ensure flight safety and successfully complete flight tasks. As a special profession, pilots require good attention, judgment, decision-making ability, spatial orientation ability, etc. The comprehensive performance of these abilities on the individual is the flight cognition ability. The pilot capability evaluation index proposed by Sun [16], Jiao [17], Li [18] et al., all cover spatial perception, judgment, decision-making ability, working memory, mathematical reasoning, etc. Among them, the pilot capability evaluation index built by Jiao, also includes communication ability. These indices are consistent with the eight-capability structure of ICAO.

The professional and operational ability of pilots are the basis for them to acquire flight operational skills. And the control of individual consciousness of the body's fine movement coordination is called psychomotor ability, which is the process from perception to motor response and the ability to coordinate with each other [19]. This ability includes three aspects, namely motor activity, sensory activity and coordination. Coordination, accuracy, flexibility, reaction speed and control ability are main characteristics of psychomotor ability. The study found that psychomotor ability covers a variety of basic elements and can be summarized into 11 categories, namely, orientation reactions, reaction time, aiming, accurate control, speed control, wrist-hand speed, wrist-finger speed, arm movement speed, arm-hand stability, finger agility and limb movement coordination [20]. The elements mentioned above play a key role in becoming a good pilot. Therefore, the psychomotor ability test is an important part of pilot ability selection [21].

Flight safety is closely related to the pilot's individual safety or risk awareness level. Everyone has the tendency or willingness to take risks, which is called risk propensity [22]. People who are prone to taking risks or taking risky actions have a high-risk operation tendency, which leads to a higher accident rate. Risk tolerance [23] is a personality trait that refers to the amount and degree to which an individual is willing to accept risks in order to achieve a specific goal. Hazardous attitude [24] is a common and relatively persistent perception, which plays a mediating role in the process of risk tolerance impacting pilots' aviating safety behaviors. Hazardous attitudes that can affect pilot aviating behaviors include macho, anti-authority, impulsiveness, obedience, and invulnerable [25]. Training for these hazardous attitudes can effectively improve and enhance the decision-making level of pilots in the short term [26]. O'Hare D et al. [27] used risk tolerance to predict pilot safety performance. Ji et al. [28] found that after controlling for the effects of pilot age and flight hours, risk tolerance had a significant negative predictive effect on pilots' driving safety behavior. Wang et al. [29] found that there is a correlation between the risk mental characteristics constituted by risk tolerance and hazardous attitudes and the flight operation level, and the lower the mental risk, the better the operational level. In addition, emotional stability is also an important aspect of evaluating mental risk. The emotional stability of pilots is closely related to their response to emergencies and their rapid and effective operations [30].

In a summary, there have been lots of researches focused on basic cognitive ability structure and evaluation of pilots. Although more attention was paid to pilots' teamwork and communication ability, there is a lack of tools with better measurable consistency and reliability. It was proposed that psychomotor ability and the professional adaptabilities such as risk tolerance are crucial to flight safety, and these professional adaptability indices are consistent with the core competency and skill requirements of airline transport pilots. These studies mentioned above provide a basis and direction for research on selection of the evaluation index of pilot's professional adaptability.

## 3    Review on Application of Evaluation Tools

European civil aviation industry has always led the development and application of professional adaptability assessment tools, and many tools have been applied in practice. In the early stage, the tools recognized and applied include: the US Aviation Cadet Qualifying Examination (ACQE), the US Air Force Pilot Candidate Selection Method (PCSM) test, and the Computer Assisted Test 4 (CAT4) designed by the Aerospace Psychology Department of the DLR, the Vienna Test System (VTS) created by SCHUHFRIED in Austria, the Global Pilot Selection System (GPSS) developed by the EASA, et al. After the Germanwings crash in 2015, EASA has strengthened the research and application of pilot psychological evaluation tools, which include the Pilot Aptitude Testing system (PAT), the Computerized Pilot Aptitude Screening System (COMPASS), etc.

The development and application of pilot psychological selection tools in civil aviation of China started relatively late. Since the 1990s, China has introduced a complete set of pilot psychological selection system from DLR [31]. The evaluation contents of this system mainly include professional basic knowledge, operation ability, personality quality and psychomotor ability, etc. At the same time, Chinese researchers independently developed a number of pilot psychological selection tools, such as DXC psychological instruments and the basic flight ability question library [32], etc. These tools, which can evaluate pilots' spatial perception, digital reasoning, attention, decision-making, judgment, working memory, responsiveness, etc., have been applied in some airlines.

Some mature psychological assessment tools of pilots' professional adaptability and their characteristics are summarized in Table 1 below:

**Table 1.** Typical evaluation tools for pilot's professional adaptability

| Evaluation tool | Characteristics of evaluation tools |
| --- | --- |
| The ADAPT psychological selection and evaluation tool platform | Based on test dimension and stage in the IATA-PAT evaluation matrix, Symbiotics, a company in Europe, has developed an online pilot psychological selection evaluation tool platform – ADAPT. The test items include knowledge assessment (Maths Test, Physics Test, Aviation Knowledge Test, etc.), Cognitive Reasoning Test, Control and Co-Ordination (Ball Game) Practice Test, Future Aptitude Selection Tool (FAST) and the ADAPT Personality Questionnaire (APQ), which is expected to measure the professional suitability of flight cadets and pilots at all stages of the pilots' professionalism lifecycle |

(*continued*)

**Table 1.** (*continued*)

| Evaluation tool | Characteristics of evaluation tools |
|---|---|
| DXC series multiple psychological evaluation instrument | Air Force Medical University in China has developed DXC series multiple psychological evaluation instrument, including psychological evaluation and cognitive ability test. The scale parts include the most widely used psychological, neurological and psychiatric scales, mainly include: Minnesota Multiphasic Personality Inventory (MMPI), Sixteen Personality Factor Questionnaire (16PF), Eysenck Personality Questionnaire (EPQ), Symptom Checklist 90 (SCL-90), Brief Psychiatric Rating Scale (BPRS), Scale for Assessment of Negative Symptoms (SANS), etc The instrument can be used not only for psychological counseling, psychological auxiliary diagnosis, but also for cognitive ability, engineering ergonomic evaluation |
| Psychomotor ability evaluation instrument | Based on computer and external stick equipment, the pilot's psychomotor ability evaluation tool adopts single person and single machine mode. The test items include three-dimensional motion control ability test, hand-eye coordination test, bimanual coordination test, man-machine function distribution test, etc. [33, 34] 。 |
| Pilot Risk Tolerance Scale (Hunter,2002) | Risk tolerance scale developed on the base of Hunter (2002) consists of 16 scenarios depicting aviation situations. These include: aircraft system failure risk tolerance (three items), crew operation risk tolerance (six items) and flight weather risk tolerance (seven items) Participants are asked to imagine whether they accept the decision-making or operation behaviors in the situation description when facing these flight situations and indicate his level of acceptance with five options presented: definitely no approval (1) to definitely approval (5) to rate the likelihood that they would personally be willing to undertake the flight, and then average together to gain an overall score of risk tolerance. Individuals with higher scores are more willing to take more risk [35] |

(*continued*)

**Table 1.** (*continued*)

| Evaluation tool | Characteristics of evaluation tools |
| --- | --- |
| New Hazardous Attitude Scale Among Pilots (Hunter,2006) | This scale contains six factors, namely, self-confidence (six items), impulsive (five items), worry/anxiety (four items), macho (three items), antiauthority (three items) and resignation (four items). The participants are provided with 24 contexts, and the Likert scale ranging from 5 (strongly agree) to 1 (strongly disagree) was used for responses. A mean score on each of the hazardous attitude is constructed on the basis of the items measuring the attitude. Individuals with higher scores are more likely having negative attitude towards aviation safety [36] |
| Sixteen Personality Factor Questionnaire (16PF) [53] | It contains 16 main personality traits. Primary Scales: Warmth (A), Reasoning (B), Emotional Stability (C), Dominance (E), Liveliness (F), Rule-Consciousness (G), Social Boldness (H), Sensitivity (I), Vigilance (L), Abstractedness (M), Privateness (N), Apprehension (O), Openness to Change (Q1), Self-Reliance (Q2), Perfectionism (Q3), Tension (Q4) Global Scales: Extraversion, Anxiety Neuroticism, Tough-Mindedness, Independence, Self-Control It is a comprehensive measure to distinguish the basic personality factors and secondary factors of normal people, and is applicable to a wide range of fields and people |
| Eysenck Personality Questionnaire (EPQ) [59] | Evaluation dimensions: Neuroticism(N), Extraversion(E) and Psychoticism(P), Lie(L). It is used to evaluate the personality type, and then indirectly measure the mental health status of people, which is widely used in medical, judicial, education and other fields, suitable for a variety of test population |

(*continued*)

**Table 1.** (*continued*)

| Evaluation tool | Characteristics of evaluation tools |
| --- | --- |
| Minnesota Multiphasic Personality Inventory (MMPI) [60] | There are two test versions of MMPI: an adult version, the MMPI-2, and an adolescent version, MMPI-A. The MMPI-2 is a 567-item inventory comprised of symptoms, beliefs, and attitudes in adults above age18<br>MMPI-2 includes 10 clinical scales, namely: Hypochondriasis (Hs), Depression (D), Hysteria (Hy), Psychopathic deviation (Pd), Paranoid thinking (Pa), Psychasthenia (Pt), Schizophrenia (Sc), Hypomania (Ma), Masculinity-femininity (Mf), Social introversion (SI). It is currently the main psychological selection tool for Chinese airline transport pilots, which can not only provide medical diagnosis, but also be used for normal people personality assessment |

As seeing from above table, the previous pilot selection evaluation systems and tools mainly focused more on assessment of basic ability and personal characteristics, and few researches on psychomotor ability test and risk personality measurement have been carried out. The evaluation items basically covers the dimensions and indices required by airline transport pilot's professional adaptability. Some indices (such as cognitive ability, personality characteristics, etc.) have been determined as necessary items for pilot selection by airlines and flight training schools. However, some indices (such as social ability, psychomotor ability, etc.) have not been widely incorporated into the pilot's psychological selection.

## 4   Preliminary Evaluation Index of Professional Adaptability of Airline Transport Pilots

Based on the literature review of non-technical skill model, crew resource management model, information processing model, the basis of pilot psychological selection and evaluation, and the requirement of pilots psychological competence, we initially choose cognitive abilities (including spatial perception ability, logical reasoning ability, information processing ability), operational and professional abilities, social-interpersonal abilities (including leadership, teamwork ability, and communication ability), and personality traits (including general personality characteristics and risk personality characteristics) as the evaluation indices of professional adaptability.

Combining with the psychological assessment tools, the indices were analyzed, summarized, divided, and deleted according to the flight task procedures and pilot's professional characteristics. We confirmed the initial professional adaptability indices of airline transport pilots (Table 2).

**Table 2.** Primary evaluation indices on professional adaptability of airline transport pilots

| Leve 1 | Level 2 | Description | Reference sources |
|---|---|---|---|
| Cognitive ability | Position perception<br>Speed perception | The pilot's ability to identify and judge the ground-to-air target, flight state, position, and the spatial relationship between himself and the flight environment. It is not only related to the identification and judgment of direction, but also the judgment and control of flight speed, altitude, and aircraft attitude [37] | Sun [16], Jiao [17], Li [18], Luo [32], Chen [38] You [39], Mou [40], Caponecchia [41] |
| | Numerical reasoning<br>Spatial reasoning | The pilot's understanding and reaction time about number relations, reflecting the development level of a person's abstract thought [42] | You [15], Li [18] |
| | Judgement | The ability to embody individual values into action through choices and selections | Jiao [17], Li [18], Mou [40] |
| | Decision-making ability | The ability to select or adjust the direction, content and pattern of relevant activities in a period of time in the future in order to achieve a certain goal | Jiao [17], Li [18], You [39], Mou [40], Caponecchia [41],Zhang [43], Flin, [44], Fowlkes, J [45], Song [46] |
| | Attention | The attention span, allocation, and stability | Jiao [17], Li [18], Luo [29], Chen [35],You [37], Caponecchia [39] |

(*continued*)

**Table 2.** (*continued*)

| Leve 1 | Level 2 | Description | Reference sources |
|---|---|---|---|
| | Short-term memory | The ability of an individual to store and maintain information in current thinking activities [15], including visual short-term memory and auditory short-term memory | Jiao [11], Li [12], Luo [32], You [39], Caponecchia [41] |
| | Reaction capacity | The process of rapid detection and response to stimulates | Wang [47], Mou [40] |
| Operational and professional ability | Hand-eye coordination ability | Hand-eye coordination refers to the ability of the physiological reflex of eye nerve conduction to quickly reflect on the movement [48] | EASA [10], IATA [11], Whittudor [34], Miao [49], Qi [50], Wei [33] |
| | Bimanual coordination ability | Bimanual coordination ability refers to the ability of the body to coordinate the activities of both hands and all parts of the body in time and space to complete the action reasonably and effectively in the process of completing a task. It is a comprehensive ability, mainly investigating the quality of speed control, balance, and coordination | |

(*continued*)

**Table 2.** (*continued*)

| Leve 1 | Level 2 | Description | Reference sources |
|---|---|---|---|
| Social-interpersonal ability | Teamwork ability | Two or more individuals working together to contribute the resources they owned, and achieve agreed solutions by sharing them [51] | Jiao [17], Chen [35], Zhang [43], You [39], Mou [40], Flin [44], Fowlkes [45], Yang [52] |
| | Communication ability | The ability to accurately understand and effectively express information | |
| Personality and attitude | 16 Personality Factors | Primary Scales: Warmth (A), Reasoning (B), Emotional Stability (C), Dominance (E), Liveliness (F), Rule-Consciousness (G), Social Boldness (H), Sensitivity (I), Vigilance (L), Abstractedness (M), Privateness (N), Apprehension (O), Openness to Change (Q1), Self-Reliance (Q2), Perfectionism (Q3), Tension (Q4) Global Scales: Extraversion, Anxiety Neuroticism, Tough-Mindedness, Independence, Self-Control | Cattell & Mead [53], Gao [54] |
| | Emotional stability | It refers to the situation that human's emotional state fluctuates with the variation of external (or internal) conditions | Du [55], Li [56], Ren [57], Cartera [58] |
| | Risk tolerance | The quantity and extent of an individual to accept risks for a certain purpose | Hunter [33, 36], Ji [28], Wang [29] |

(*continued*)

**Table 2.** (*continued*)

| Leve 1 | Level 2 | Description | Reference sources |
|---|---|---|---|
| | Hazardous attitude | A kind of learned and lasting perception, and the specific proneness of an individual to respond to others, situations, and events related to hazards | Hunter [35, 36], Ji [28], Wang [29] |

# 5  Conclusion

Based on literatures review and analysis in the field of aviation psychology, the present study preliminarily proposed out the evaluation dimensions and indices of the professional adaptability for airline transport pilots.

In the preliminary evaluation indices of the professional adaptability, some of them (such as cognitive ability, personality trait, etc.) have been recognized as necessary items for pilot selection by airlines and civil aviation administrators. However, some indices (such as social ability, psychomotor ability, etc.) have not been widely introduced into the current pilot's psychological selection procedure. At the same time, some indices lack practical evaluation tools.

Finally, these professional adaptability evaluation indices concluded in this study are primary indices with incompleteness. The follow-up study will be carried out to design and implement semi-structured questionnaires to obtain data from pilots and flight experts, and then establish the final professional adaptability evaluation index system based on analyzing these data.

In the next step, the evaluation method will be put forward, and the evaluation model based on flight training scenarios will be developed. Our final goal is to develop the professional adaptability evaluation tools for airline transport pilots, which can provide effective support for selection and training of safer pilots.

**Acknowledgments.** The authors would like to appreciate the support of the National Natural Science Foundation of China (grant no. 32071063) and Tianjin Graduate Science and Innovation Research Project (grant no. 2021YJSS110).

# References

1. Maurino, D.E., Reason, J., Johnston, N., et al.: Beyond aviation human factors: safety in high technology systems. Hum. Factors Eng. **3**, 55–57 (1998)
2. Civil aviation safety report of China. Aviation Safety Office of Civil Aviation Administration of China, 2021, Beijing (2020)
3. Bor, R., Eriksen, C., Hubbard, T., King, R.E. (eds.): Pilot Selection Psychological Principles and Practice. CRC Press, London (2019)

4. Civil Aviation Administration of China (CAAC): Roadmap for the Construction and Implementation of the Airline Transport Pilots Professionalism Lifecycle Management System in China (2020). In Chinese
5. Li, S., Wang, L., Zeng, M.: Floating iceberg model of psychological competence towards airline transport pilots' professionalism lifecycle management system. In: Harris, D., Li, W.-C. (eds.) Engineering Psychology and Cognitive Ergonomics: 18th International Conference, EPCE 2021, Held as Part of the 23rd HCI International Conference, HCII 2021, Virtual Event, July 24–29, 2021, Proceedings, pp. 28–37. Springer, Cham (2021). https://doi.org/10.1007/978-3-030-77932-0_3
6. Civil Aviation Administration of China AC-121-FS-2018–130: Flight Operation Style. Civil Aviation Administration of China (2018). in Chinese
7. Avermaete, J.A.G., Kruijsen, E.A.C.: NOTECHS. The evaluation of non-technical skills of multi-pilot aircrew in relation to the JAR-FCL requirements. EC NOTECHS project final report: NLR-CR-98443, Amsterdam (1998)
8. Helmreich, R., Butler, R., Taggart, W., et al.: The NASA/University of Texas/Federal Aviation Administration Line/LOS checklist: A behavioral-based checklist for CRM skills assessment (Version 4.4) [computer software]. NASA/University of Texas/Federal Aviation Administration Aerospace Group, Austin, TX (1997)
9. International Civil Aviation Organization (ICAO): Doc 9995, Manual of Evidence-base Training, First Edition (2013)
10. European Aviation Safety Agency (EASA): AMC1 CAT. GEN. MPA. 175 (b) Endangering Safety. Annex III to ED Decision 2018/012/R
11. International Air Transport Association (IATA): Pilot Aptitude Testing, Guidance Material and Best Practices, 3rd edn. (2019)
12. Hoermann, H.J., Luo, X.: Empirical evaluation of a selection system for Chinese student pilots. Space Med. Med. Eng. 15(1), 6–11 (2002)
13. Song, X., Ge, X., Zhang, K., Wang, D., Ge, L.: Research and application of spatial orientation ability in different environments. Space Med. Med. Eng. 34(04), 328–338 (2021)
14. Zhang, Q., Bai, B.: Some psychological problems in manned spaceflight. Space Med. Med. Eng. (02), 69–73 (1999)
15. You, X., Ji, M.: Compilation of airline flight aptitude selection test. Psychol. Res. 1(01), 43–50 (2008)
16. Sun, R., Peng, T.: Research on measurement scheme design and model of flight cognitive ability. Chin. J. Saf. Sci. 20(11), 47–51 (2010)
17. Jiao, S.: Research on competency model of civil aviation pilots. Civil Aviation University of China (2019)
18. Li, Q., Sun, J., Ma, J., Hu, W.: Pilot competency analysis and establishment of discriminant equation for excellent flight cadets. Occup. Health 35(03), 363–366 (2019)
19. James, A.H., Schaller, C.A.: Information Systems Auditing and Assurance. South-western College Publish, Cincinnati (2000)
20. Liu, W.: Design Pattern Training Course. Tsinghua University Press, Beijing (2012)
21. Freeman, E.: Head First Design Pattern. China Power Press, Beijing (2007)
22. Zhou, Y., Shu, L., John, D., et al.: The neural correlates of risk propensity in males and females using resting-state fMRI. Front. Behav. Neurosci. 8, 2 (2014)
23. Murray, S.R.: FACE: fear of loss of face and the five hazardous attitudes concept. Int. J. Aviat. Psychol. 9(4), 403–411 (1999)
24. Hunter, D.R.: Risk perception among general aviation pilots. Int. J. Aviat. Psychol. 16(2), 135–144 (2006)
25. Berlin, J.I., Gruber, E.V., Holmes, C.W., Jensen, P.K., Lau, J.R., Mills, J.W.: Pilot judgment training and evaluation—Vol. 1 (Rep. No. DOT/FAA/CT–81/56–I). Federal Aviation Administration, Washington, DC (1982)

26. Diehl, A.: The effectiveness of training programs for preventing aircrew 'error'. In: 6 th International Symposium on Aviation Psychology, Columbus, OH, pp. 640–655 (1991)
27. O'Hare, D.: Pilots' perception of risks and hazards in general aviation. Aviat. Space Environ. Med. **61**(7), 599–603 (1990)
28. Ji, M., Yang, S., Zhao, X., et al.: The influence of risk tolerance on pilots' driving safety behavior: the role of risk perception and risk attitude. Acta Psychol. Sinica **43**(11), 1308–1319 (2011)
29. Wang, L., Dong, C., Yang, X., et al.: Study on the correlation between risk psychology and operation level of civil aviation pilots. China Safety Sci. J. **29**(6), 37 (2019)
30. Judge, T.A., Bono, J.E.: Relationship of core self-evaluations traits—self-esteem, generalized self-efficacy, locus of control, and emotional stability—with job satisfaction and job performance: a meta-analysis. J. Appl. Psychol. **86**(1), 80–92 (2001)
31. Luo, X.: Revision of German aerospace center pilot paper pen test system. Chin. J. Aerosp. Med. **14**(4), 213–216 (2003)
32. Luo, M.: Establishment of flight basic ability test question bank and equivalent analysis and construction of college entrance examination score prediction model. Air Force Medical University (2007)
33. Wei, H.: Application of psychomotor ability in civil aviation pilot selection. Air Force Medical University (2013)
34. Hui, D., Hu, W., Li, X., et al.: Development and application of psychomotor ability test software. Comput. Technol. Dev. **24**(4), 155–157 (2014)
35. Hunter, D.R.: Risk perception and risk tolerance in aircraft pilots. DOT/FAA/AM-02/17. Federal Aviation Administration, Washington, DC (2002)
36. Hunter, D.R.: Measurement of hazardous attitudes among pilots. Int. J. Aviat. Psychol. **15**(1), 23–43 (2005)
37. Zong, Y., et al.: Research on spatial cognitive characteristics of flight orientation. Chin. J. Aerosp. Med. (02), 28–31 (2003)
38. Chen, K., Ban, D.: Construction of post competency model for land aviation pilots. J. Third Mil. Med. Univ. **39**(08), 705–710 (2017)
39. You, X., Ji, M.: Construction of multidimensional evaluation scale for route driving safety behavior. Psychol. Bull. **41**(12), 1237–1251 (2009)
40. Mou, H., Zhang, H.: Analysis on the structure of non-technical skills of civil aviation pilots. Stud. Psychol. Behav. **14**(02), 241–246 (2016)
41. Caponecchia, C., Zheng, W.Y., Regan, M.A.: Selecting trainee pilots: Predictive validity of the WOMBAT situational awareness pilot selection test. Appl. Ergon. **73**, 100–107 (2018)
42. Wang, Y., Liu, C.: Development of processing speed, working memory and digital reasoning ability. J. Psychol. Sci. (05) 1081-1085 (2006)
43. Zhang, Y., et al.: Construction of competency model of armed police sergeant. Chinese J. clin. psychol. **18**(03), 293–296 (2010)
44. Flin, R., Martin, L., Goeters, K.M., et al.: Development of the NOTECHS (non-technical skills) system for assessing pilots' CRM skills. Hum. Factors Aerosp. Saf. **3**(2), 95–117 (2003)
45. Fowlkes, J.E., Lane, N.E., Salas, E., et al.: Improving the measurement of team performance: the TARGETs methodology. Mil. Psychol. **6**(1), 47–61 (1994)
46. Song, C.: Research on the construction of safety capability dimension of transport pilots. Civil Aviation Flight University of China (2016)
47. Wang, L., Pei, Y.: The impact of continuous driving time and rest time on commercial drivers' driving performance and recovery. J. Safety Res. **50**, 11–15 (2014)
48. Yang, B.: Outline of Psychological Experiment. Peking University Press, Beijing (1986)
49. Liu, X., Lin, Y., Miao, D., et al.: Comparison of pilots' psychomotor ability and flight performance. J. Fourth Mil. Med. Univ. (8), 747–749 (2001)

50. Qi, J., Liu, X., Huangfu, E., et al.: Construct validity analysis of five spatial-ability tests. Negative **24**(021), 1993–1995 (2003)
51. Li, H.: Design and development of pilot team cooperation ability test system. Civil Aviation Flight University of China (2011)
52. Yang, S., Li, J.: Research on the structure model of civil aviation pilot's comprehensive safety capability based on DEMATEL-ISM method. Saf. Environ. Eng. **25**(04), 169–174 (2018)
53. Cattell, H.E.P., Mead, A.D.: The sixteen personality factor questionnaire (16PF). In: Boyle, G.J., Matthews, G., Saklofske, D.H. (eds.) The SAGE Handbook of Personality Theory and Assessment, Vol. 2. Personality Measurement and Testing, pp. 135–159 (2008)
54. Gao, Y., Li, H., Wang, Y.: Research on personality traits and mental health of civil aviation pilots based on 16PF. China Saf. Sci. J. **21**(4), 13–18 (2011)
55. Du, X.: Study on the impact of pilots' emotional stability on flight safety and countermeasures. Sci. Technol. Inform. (25), 231–233  (2011)
56. Hao, B., Li, J.: The influence of pilots' personality traits on job performance. Chin. J. Ergon. **22**(02), 62–66 (2016)
57. Ren, H., Liu, Q., Liu, J., et al.: Study on the correlation between work emergency and personality of military pilots. Chin. J. Convalescent Med. **21**(4), 291–294 (2012)
58. Michelle, N., Shioa, J.W., Kalat, S., et al.: Emotional psychology. Chinese Light Industry Press (2015)
59. Gong, Y.: Revision of eysenck personality questionnaire in China. Psychol. Commun. (04) 13–20 + 67 (1984). https://doi.org/10.16719/j.cnki.1671-6981.1984.04.004.html
60. Ji, S., Dai Z.: Minnesota Multiphasic Personality Questionnaire. Science Press (2004)

# The Assessment of Aviation Situation Awareness Based on Objective Behavior Methods

Hao Zhou, Yanyu Lu[✉], and Shan Fu

School of Electronic Information and Electrical Engineering, Shanghai Jiao Tong University, Shanghai 200240, People's Republic of China
luyanyu@sjtu.edu.cn

**Abstract.** Situation awareness assessment is one of the current focuses of aviation human factors research. In response to the current demand for real-time and interpretable situation awareness measurement, this study adopts a behaviour-based assessment approach and designs a simulated cockpit interface for the experiment. The response time is assessed as the performance indicator. The experimental periods can be divided into two categories: continuous and intermittent, depending on the way in which the tasks are performed. During the intermittent periods, the state differences in situation awareness are compared and analyzed from three main perspectives: First, the comparative analysis of situation awareness between different situation conditions. Second, the comparative analysis of situation awareness between Peripheral Visual Perception and Gaze Perception. Third, the hierarchical analysis of situation awareness of gaze perception data. It is found that there are significant differences in the states of situation awareness between some different conditions, which means that the criteria for assessing situation awareness should vary with situation conditions. This study paves the way for future analysis of real-time situation awareness.

**Keywords:** Aviation · Situation awareness assessment · Real-time · Intermittent period

## 1 Introduction

According to statistics, more than 70% of commercial aircraft flight accidents are caused by human errors. With the development of modern aircraft manufacturing technology, the number of accidents caused by human factors far exceeds those caused by mechanical failure, weather and other unforeseen circumstances. Aviation human factors have therefore long played an important part in the study of aviation safety.In the aviation industry, human factor researches cover a wide range of areas in the design,construction, operation, management and maintenance of products and systems in the aviation industry,with the goal of optimizing the relationship between operators, technology and the environment in order to eliminate or reduce errors in operations.

One important source of human errors is the decision error, and loss of situation awareness is an important cause of the decision error. Situation awareness (SA) has been studied for a long time, and many models describing it exist to date. Of all these models, Endsley's three-level model is the most developed and has been used and studied by many other researches. In this model SA consists of three levels: perception,comprehension, and projection. Perception refers to the pilot's ability to perceive key task-related elements of the surrounding environment within a certain time and space. Comprehension is based on perception and requires pilots to be able to integrate and understand perceived information based on mission requirements and operational objectives. Projection is the highest level of SA which is based on perception and comprehension. It requires the pilot to make predictions for the near future based on his or her own judgment of the environment.

Measuring SA is an important means of understanding the pilot's cognitive state with respect to the current situation. By measuring SA, it is possible not only to obtain the reasons for the pilot's human errors, but even to predict how the pilot will perform. SA measurements can be divided into two main categories: subjective methods and objective methods. The main form of the subjective approaches is the post-test self-evaluation, where each subject fills in an evaluation scale of his or her overall SA after the experiment is completed. Previous work of this type mainly includes Situation Awareness Rating Technique (SART) [1], Situation Awareness Rating Scales Technique (SARS) [2], Cranfield Situation Awareness Scale (CSAS) [3], Crew Awareness Rating Scale (CARS) [4, 5] and so on. The advantages of post-exp self-evaluation are mainly its simplicity and convenience. For the fact that it is performed after the test, it is not invasive to the experiment process. However, the disadvantages of these methods are also obvious: One reason is that sometimes the subject cannot know whether he or she is in a good or bad state of SA. Therefore, the self-evaluation method measures more of the subject's confidence in his or her SA state [6]. Moreover, the method requires the subject to recall the entire experiment, which also depends to some extent on the level of memory. Another type of subjective form is the observer's evaluation, where an expert on the sidelines evaluates the SA of the subject by observing his or her performance during the experiment. The representative method is Situation awareness behavioral rating scale (SABARS) [7]. This method is non-invasive like the self-assessment, but it has been questioned whether it measures SA [8].

Objective methods can be further divided into two main categories: direct methods and indirect methods. The representative techniques of the former are Freeze-Probe Techniques and Real-Time Probe Techniques. The most famous of the Freeze-Probe Techniques is Situation Awareness Global Assessment Technique (SAGAT) proposed by Endsley [9], which requires a subject matter expert to develop a series of relevant questions examining the three levels of SA states before the experiment. The screen is frozen at random moments during the experiment and the subject is asked to recall the immediate situation and answer the relevant questions. Then the correctness of the answers is used as an assessment of current SA.A representative method of the real-time probe technique is the Situation Present Assessment Method (SPAM) [10], which, like SAGAT, gives a question probe during the experiment, but does not freeze the screen. The response time and the content of the answer are used as an assessment of SA. SPAM is somewhat less intrusive,but the degree of reduction cannot be estimated, and it is difficult to apply to complex and dynamic environments because SA questions in

SPAM need to be formulated in real time. In addition, although the probe approach is able to measure SA in real time states, its temporal resolution is poor due to the limitation of the number of probes [11].

Indirect methods can also be divided into two categories, one of which uses the subject's physiological data to assess the state of SA. The other method uses the subject's behavior performance. There have been many studies using physiological data to assess SA, such as EEG, ECG, EYE and EDA [12]. The correlation of the results between these physiological data and other methods of measurement has been validated to varying degrees, suggesting that there is some feasibility in using physiological data to assess SA, but the use of physiological data alone lacks significant persuasive power, which is due to the complexity of interpretation of physiological data. In order to obtain high temporal resolution measures of SA in a highly dynamic aviation environment in a non-invasive manner and give interpretable accounts, behavior measure is a feasible approach. By capturing subjects' eye-movement behaviors and manipulation behaviors in real time from high sampling rate sensors, real-time situation cognitive states of subjects can be analyzed.

In this study, a simulated experimental setting is designed by integrating several basic flight elements. The behavior responses of different subjects to different events are compared to analyze the SA according to two categories of behavioral performance indicators: eye-movement and manipulation. Experimental periods are first divided into two categories according to the tasks: continuous and intermittent. In the continuous periods, subjects are required to perform tasks that requires continuous operation, while in the intermittent periods, subjects take actions only in unusual situations. Intermittent periods are the main research periods of this study, and the behavioral performance indicator of SA used in this study is response time, which has been used as a measure of SA in other studies [13]. In this paper, response time is replaced by action response time (ART), which can further be subdivided into eye movement reaction time (ERT) and comprehension response time (CRT) in order to discuss SA in a hierarchical manner. The main research content of this paper are: First, factors that affect the overall SA, including workload changed by adjusting tracing tasks and different abnormal event designs. Second, the differences between using peripheral vision (PV) and central vision (CV) to perceive events. Third, further exploration of the evaluation indicators of different levels of SA for events perceived using CV.

## 2    Materials and Methods

### 2.1    Subjects

Eight volunteers (six males and two females) from Shanghai Jiao Tong University, ranging in age from 22 to 30 (mean 25), participated in this experiment. All subjects have normal or corrected normal vision and are right-handed. Prior to the start of the formal experiment, each subject underwent a 10-min training procedure.

### 2.2    Materials

**Hardware.** The main experimental platform for this experiment is on an 18-in. monitor with a display resolution of 1920 × 1080 and a refresh rate of 60 Hz. Other equipment used during the experiment contains a keyboard and a joystick. The subjects' eye movement is recorded by a portable head-mounted eye-tracking device (TOBII Glasses3, see Fig. 1). Eye-movement data is recorded at 100 Hz on an SD memory card, which is then transferred to a computer for further processing and analysis, mainly for mapping of gaze points in the panorama, data pre-processing and calculation of other eye-movement metrics. The eye-movement equipment will be calibrated before the start of the experiment.

**Software.** The layout of common elements in the flight task, such as alarm lights, instruments, fuel management, communication and target tracking, are simulated and simplified in the study and finally are integrated into a comprehensive multitasking experimental interface by using the built-in software (see Fig. 2). The software can also be used to set and execute the relevant experimental procedures, including recording the environmental variables and the operator's keystrokes in the experiment and saving them as a readable file with a frequency of 50 Hz. The software uses Microsoft Visual Studio as the development platform, C++ as the development language, and OpenGL as the basic development library.

**Fig. 1.** Experiment scene.

## 2.3 Tasks

**Target Tracking.** The target tracking task module is located on the top-center side of the interface (see Fig. 3, 3). The tracking target is a free-moving circle with a blue dot in its center. Two modes exist for this task: manual and automatic. In the manual mode, the subject is asked to manipulate the joystick to control the tracking box, and the task is to keep the target circle in the center of the tracking frame as much as possible. In the automatic mode, the tracking box will track the target circle automatically and the subject can focus more on other tasks.

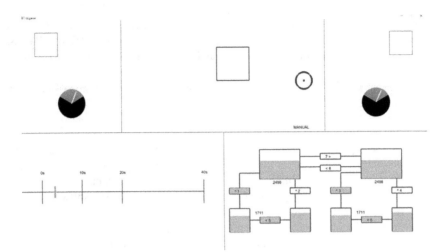

**Fig. 2.** Experiment software interface.

**Abnormal Events Response.** The abnormal event response task module is arranged on the left and right sides of the experimental interface (see Fig. 3, 1 and 2), which contains two parts, one is the alarm light event. The alarm light is usually colorless in the normal state,while in the alarm state, the light will turn red (see Fig. 4, left). The subject needs to press the corresponding button as a response, and then the abnormal event will be eliminated. Instruments are placed below the alarm lights, and each of them has a yellow pointer. The blue area indicates the normal area, while the black area is the abnormal area. The pointer oscillates in the normal zone during normal times and oscillates out of the normal zone when an abnormal event occurs (see Fig. 4, right). As with the alarm light event, the subject needs to notice the instrument abnormality event and press the corresponding button in time to eliminate the abnormal event.

**Communication Response.** The communication response task module is located at the bottom left of the interface (see Fig. 3, 4). In the event, response is similar to the abnormal event response. The subject has 5 s to press the corresponding button after the green bold line is slid to the '0s' position to indicate the response to the communication event. And then the event bar will be eliminated. The difference is that the event already appears in the schedule bar before reaching '0s'. By observing the position of the event on the schedule bar, the subjects can roughly determine how long it is before the communication event occurs. By observing the position of the event on the schedule bar, the subject can know the time before the event occurrence and make arrangements and plans in advance.

**Fuel Management.** The fuel management task module is located at the bottom right of the interface (see Fig. 3, 5).The module consists of 6 simulated fuel tanks with 8 simulated pumps. The upper two tanks are the main fuel tanks, which are consumed at a certain rate. The lower left tank is the supply tank, which feeds the main tank. The lower right-hand side is the reserve tank, which can supply both the main tank and the supply tank. The transfer of oil is controlled by eight pumps, the direction of which is marked by arrows. The flow rate of the pumps varies. At random moments some pumps will fail (turn red) and the subject cannot operate the pump. After a certain time, the pump failure eliminates itself. The central task of the module is to maintain the oil volume of the left and right main tank at 2000 to 3000. In addition, the difference between the oil volume of the left and right main tank should not exceed 50.

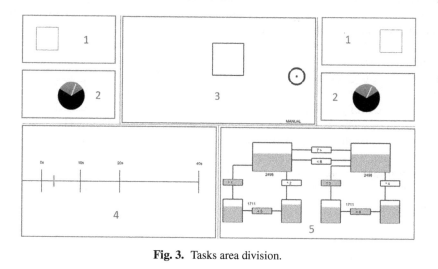

**Fig. 3.** Tasks area division.

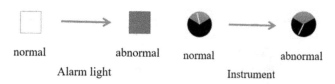

normal        abnormal     normal        abnormal

Alarm light            Instrument

**Fig. 4.** Alarm light and instrument events

## 2.4 Experiment Design

In this study, the experiment is divided into two types of time periods (see Fig. 5). The first type is the continuous period, in which subjects perform tasks that are continuous. In this experiment the communication task, the target tracking task and the fuel management task belong to this type. Although the communication task requires the subjects to respond after the bar reaches '0s', the subject has already looked ahead before. So the subject's normal responses are not caused by the '0s' events. The second type is the intermittent period, in which subjects complete tasks that do not require attention at all times, but only when an abnormal event occurs. In this experiment, the alarm light and instrument monitoring tasks belong to this type.

The experiments are arranged around the tracking module, with the tracking part alternating between automatic and manual modes, each lasting about 4 min. The number of alarm light events and instrument events are set at the same level, but the moment of occurrence and sequence are randomized. The appearance of communication events is a Poisson process with a time constant of 20 s. The appearance of pump failures is also a Poisson process with a time constant of 15 s. The repair time meets a uniform distribution of 10 to 20 s. While performing the continuous tasks, Subjects are subjected to a number of intermittent tasks and they need to response to them in time.In the automatic mode, the continuous tasks include oil management and communication. In the manual mode, in addition to the two tasks above, the continuous tasks also include target tracking. In both two modes, the abnormal events response tasks are included in intermittent tasks. The experiment specifies the highest priority for the disposal of such tasks. The overall prioritization is arranged as follows: alarm light > instrument > communication > fuel management = target tracking.

This study focuses on the research of the SA states during intermittent periods. There are several issues that can be studied in these periods: First, factors that affect the overall SA, including workload and different abnormal event designs. Second, the differences between using peripheral vision and central vision to perceive events. Third, further exploration of the evaluation indicators of different levels of SA for events perceived using central vision.

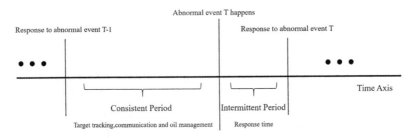

**Fig. 5.** Experimental periods division.

**Effect of Subjects' Workload and Interface Design on Overall SA.** There is a certain correlation between workload and SA. In addition, different interface designs also have effect on SA. As a result, the effects of subjects' workload is investigated through using the automatic or manual tracking mode, while the factor of interface design is studied through comparing alarm light and instrument abnormal event.

**Central Vision vs Peripheral Vision.** Through the eye-movement study, it is found that events during intermittent periods do not necessarily need to be perceived by subjects using central vision (CV) every time. Peripheral visual (PV) is common during such periods. Therefore, it is meaningful to make comparison between CV and PV. The percentage of total events perceived by PV and CV will be analyzed. Moreover, the action response time (ART) of subjects using PV and CV will also be compared.

**Hierarchical Analysis of SA.** According to the Endsley's SA model, SA is constructed by three levels:perception, comprehension and projection. To understand the SA state more deeply, it is of great import importance to make hierarchical analysis of SA. Although it is hard to find the distinction between comprehension and projection, finding the boundary between perception and the other two is relatively simple. In this study, only those events perceived by CV can make further analysis because the hierarchical analysis needs the eye reaction time (ERT) which is the evaluation indicator of perception and the comprehension response time (CRT) which the evaluation indicator of comprehension and projection.

## 2.5  Data Processing

**Response Time.** In this study, response time is used as the evaluation indicator. To make deeper research on SA, the response time is subdivided here. Firstly, the key response time of the subjects to events is named as action response time (ART), which is the indicator of the overall SA. Then, to distinguish the SA1 (perception) and SA2/3 (comprehension and projection), ART will be further subdivided into eye reaction time (ERT) and comprehension response time (CRT). ERT, which refers to the time required from the occurrence to the point of eye movement fixation to the target AOI, only happens in those events perceived by central vision (CV). Similar to ERT, CRT which refers to ART minus ERT is also can only be extracted in CV events (see Fig. 6).

In the past researches on SA using the eye tracker, eye movement indicators such as fixation duration, fixation counts and saccade frequency are widely used. Eye reaction time (ERT) is rarely used because few researches use response time for SA hierarchical analysis. ERT is also an important indicator for SA1 (perception). CRT is another indicator which is seldom used while it can reflects the SA2/3 state (comprehension and projection) of the subjects from the side.

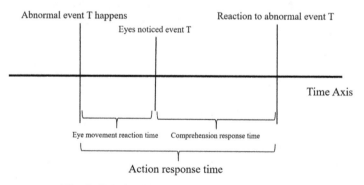

**Fig. 6.** Relationship between ART, ERT and CRT.

**Statistical Methods.** SPSS 25 is used as the main analysis tool in this study. Due to data volume limitations and the non-normality of some of the distributions, the statistical tests used in this study included the paired t-test, Wilcoxon signed-rank test, and Kruskal-Wallis H-test (K-W test). The normality test used is the Shapiro-Wilk method.

## 3   Results

The workload variation in this experiment comes from that whether the tracking mode is automatic or manual. The event type variables also contain two types: alarm light events and instrument events. Combining the workload and event types, four types of data are obtained, which are alarm light-manual tracking (Alt-Man), alarm light-automatic tracking (Alt-Aut), instrument-manual tracking (Ins-Man), and instrument-automatic tracking (Ins-Aut). The following content of the study results will be analyzed around the four types of data for comparison.

### 3.1   Effect of Subjects' Workload and Interface Design on ART

It is necessary to perform normality test on all subjects' data in the four types of data before comparing them.And then in each type, to test whether there is statistical variability in the distribution of all subjects' data, which determines whether subjects' data can be used as the analysis data. It is tested that all subjects did not satisfy the normality assumption in each type, and that the overall distribution test between subjects finds significant differences. This established that the statistical comparison method uses nonparametric methods. What's more, the data of all subjects cannot be directly compared as a whole to compare the differences between the two types of data.

To address the inter-subject differences, the subjects are divided into two categories overall as follows, one with longer overall ART (subject 3, 7, 8) and the other with shorter (subject 1, 2, 4, 5, 6):

1) The respective mean values of each subjects' data is calculated and sorted.
2) Data is divided into two groups with same amount of subjects according to the sorting order of mean values.
3) If subject differences still exist in one group, the group with differences will choose the data of the subject whose mean value is the closest to that of all data and transfer it to the other group.
4) Perform the above until there are no inter-subject differences within either group.
5) If the data of a subject cannot be put into any group to eliminate the differences, then this part of the data will be discarded.

It is found that in four conditions the subject can be divided into two groups with the same subjects and the final comparison can be seen below (see Table 1). After screening, the distribution differences are analyzed again within the respective groups, and it is found that there is no difference in the distribution of ART between the subjects in these two categories. Therefore, the ART under different conditions can be compared within the high ART group and the low ART group, respectively.

**The Effect of The Workload with The Same Abnormal Event Type.** The following figure compares the difference between the high and low ART group for different workloads respectively (see Fig. 7). It is shown that the change in workload in this experimental design does not cause significant differences in subjects' ART in the same type of event whether in the high or low ART group (Alt: LART: p = 0.290, HART: p = 0.485; Alt: LART: p = 0.693, HART: p = 0.187).

**Table 1.** ART comparison of the high and low ART group (unit: ms)

|  | High ART group ART mean (std) | Low ART group ART mean (std) |
|---|---|---|
| Alt-Man | 1075 (316) | 840 (160) |
| Alt-Aut | 1236 (990) | 875 (145) |
| Ins-Man | 3159 (3792) | 1165 (412) |
| Ins-Aut | 1880 (1079) | 1224 (880) |

**The Effect of Different Abnormal Event Types with The Same Workload.** The following figures compare the ART variability of response times for the high and low reaction time groups for different events,respectively (see Fig. 7). Unlike the fixed event type, under the same workload, subjects in the high and low reaction time groups had significant ART variability between alarm light and instrument events. (Man: LART: p = 0.001, HART: p = 0.000; Aut: LART: p = 0.006, HART: p = 0.000), with significantly higher ART for instrument than alarm light.

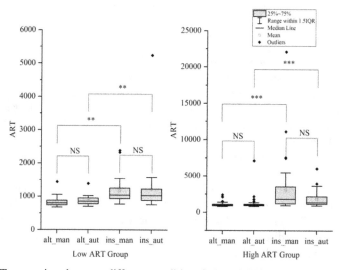

**Fig. 7.** ART comparison between different conditions in low and high ART group. (*: p < 0.05, **: p < 0.01, ***: p < 0.001, NS: p > 0.05)

### 3.2  Central Vision vs Peripheral Vision

It is found that not all event responses are perceived using central vision (CV). This part of the study will first analyze whether there is variability in the proportion of events perceived using peripheral vision (PV) versus those perceived using CV, and subsequently compare ART for events perceived using PV versus those perceived using CV.

**Proportion of CV vs Proportion of PV.** The number of PV response proportions and CV response proportions are the same for each subject, and the data under the same condition does not satisfy normality. So Wilcoxon's signed rank test for paired samples is performed directly. The results of the test are found that (see Table 2) when the occurrence is an alarm light event, the proportion of PVP used by the subjects is significantly higher than that of FP, regardless of the tracking pattern. While there is always no significant difference between the two proportions when an abnormal instrument event occurs.

**Table 2.** Matching test results of the proportion of PVP and FP under different conditions

|  | FP mean (Std) | PVP mean (Std) | p |
|---|---|---|---|
| Alt-Man | 0.34 (0.15) | 0.66 (0.15) | 0.019 |
| Alt-Aut | 0.28 (0.22) | 0.71 (0.22) | 0.026 |
| Ins-Man | 0.56 (0.09) | 0.44 (0.09) | 0.102 |
| Ins-Aut | 0.53 (0.36) | 0.46 (0.36) | 0.815 |

**Differences of ART between Events Perceived by CV and PV.** Before formally comparing ART, it is still necessary to test for normality and subsequently for distributional differences in the data for each subject in each of the four categories of CV and PV separately. It is found that most of the subjects' data in the four categories does not meet the normality assumption, and then a non-parametric K-W test will be used next. And after doing the between-subjects difference test for each of the four categories of cases, it is found that there is no significant difference in the data between subjects under automatic tracking, while there is a significant difference between subjects under manual tracking. Using a similar method as in Sect. 3.1, the group of subjects is divided into two parts in the analysis of manual tracking according to the method in Sect. 3.1, the low ART group (subject 2, 4, 5, 6) and the high ART group (subject 1, 3, 7, 8) (comparison can be seen in Table 3). The data distribution between individual subjects within the same group is tested to be insignificantly different after regrouping.

**Table 3.** ART comparison of the high and low ART group (Unit: ms)

|  | High ART group ART mean (Std) | Low ART group ART mean (Std) |
|---|---|---|
| CV-Alt-Man | 1300 (420) | 913 (194) |
| PV-Alt-Man | 1043 (270) | 825 (99) |
| CV-Ins-Man | 3450 (2695) | 1434 (1087) |
| PV-Ins-Man | 4347 (6808) | 1331 (790) |

After statistical analysis, it can be found that during automatic target tracking, all subjects have significantly lower ART using PV than that using CV, regardless of whether the occurring event is the alarm light or the instrument (see Fig. 8, Alt-Aut: p = 0.001; Ins-Aut: p = 0.002). In contrast, there are different statistical patterns between the low-ART and high-ART groups when manually tracking the target.There is no significant difference of ART between PV and CV in the low ART group regardless of the event that occurs (see Fig. 8, Alt-Man: p = 0.227; Ins-Man: p = 0.439), while there is a significant difference in the high ART group for both events that occurs (see Fig. 9, Alt-Man: p = 0.004; Ins-Man: p = 0.040).

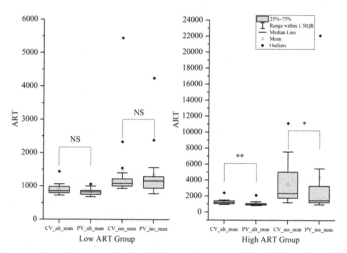

**Fig. 8.** ART comparison in low and high ART group between CV and PV under manual tracking.

### 3.3  Hierarchical Comparison of ART

For the experimental Intermittent periods in this study, not all data can be analyzed hierarchically, mainly because of the presence of PV. In this part of the results study, ART using CV will be compared across conditions and used as an indicator for different layers of SA.

Before hierarchical comparison, the ART of CV data is compared. The test for differences in distribution between subjects in the four categories is first done and found to be significantly different. So here too it is necessary to first divide the subjects into two groups with different ART (the classification method is the same as that in Sect. 3.1 and comparison can be seen in Table 4). The low ART group has subject 2, 4, 5, 6 and the high one has subject 1, 3, 7, 8. The test after regrouping finds that there are no significant differences between subjects within the groups. Using the non-parametric K-W test, the paired analysis of variance shows that in the high ART group, there is a significant difference in ART corresponding to different event types under fixed workload (see Fig. 10, Alt-Man/Alt-Aut, p = 1.000; Ins-Man/Ins-Aut, p = 0.380; Alt-Man/Ins-Man, p = 0.007; Alt-Aut/Ins-Aut, p = 0.000). While there is no significant difference in

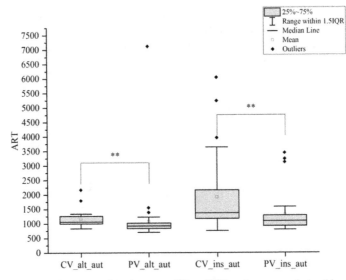

**Fig. 9.** ART comparison between CV and PV under automatic tracking.

ART corresponding to different workloads under fixed event types, which is the same as the results in Sect. 3.1. While slightly different from the previous results in the low ART group (see Fig. 10, Alt-Man/Alt-Aut, p = 0.882; Ins-Man/Ins-Aut, p = 1.000; Alt-Man/Ins-Man, p = 0.030; Alt-Aut/Ins-Aut, p = 0.345), only in the fixed workload type, there is a significant difference between the ART of alarm lights and instrument events when tracking manually, and pairwise comparative variability is not present for the remaining cases.

The statistical comparison between ERT and CRT likewise requires analyzing whether there are differences in the distribution of data for all subjects in different types of time periods, and after analysis it can be learned that there is no significant difference between ERT and CRT for all subjects under different conditions, so the data for all subjects are directly used as statistical data for comparison.

The following discussion is whether there is a significant difference between ERT and CRT at different periods. From the figure (see Fig. 11, Alt-Man/Alt-Aut, p = 0.381; Ins-Man/Ins-Aut, p = 0.575; Alt-Man/Ins-Man, p = 0.777; Alt-Aut/Ins-Aut, p = 1.000), it can be seen that in the comparison of pair types with fixed workload or fixed event type, there is no significant difference. And in terms of CRT's test (see Fig. 11, Alt-Man/Alt-Aut, p = 0.432; Ins-Man/Ins-Aut, p = 0.331; Alt-Man/Ins-Man, p = 0.762; Alt-Aut/Ins-Aut, p = 1.000), there is no significant difference in all types of periods overall.

**Table 4.** ART comparison of CV perceived events between the high and low ART group (Unit: ms)

|  | High ART group ART mean (Std) | Low ART group ART mean (Std) |
|---|---|---|
| Alt-Man | 1300 (420) | 913 (193) |
| Alt-Aut | 1162 (331) | 1160 (379) |
| Ins-Man | 3450 (2695) | 1434 (1087) |
| Ins-Aut | 1999 (1215) | 1749 (1294) |

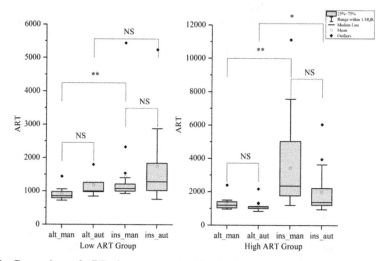

**Fig. 10.** Comparison of ART of events perceived by CV between different conditions in low and high ART group.

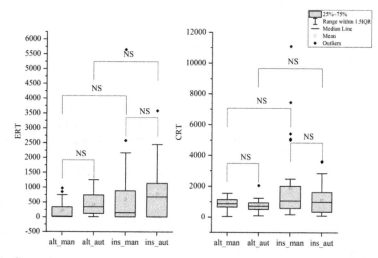

**Fig. 11.** Comparison of ERT and CRT of events perceived by CV between different conditions.

# 4  Discussion

## 4.1  Effect of Subjects' Workload and Interface Design on Overall SA

ART is used as an indicator to evaluate the overall SA. The longer the time, the lower the level of the overall SA state of the subjects. The analysis of the variability of the ART in the results corresponds to the division of the overall SA status into two groups: the high SA group and the low SA group.

The analysis of the results shows that under the condition of fixed event type, the workload changed in this experiment does not cause a significant difference in SA, regardless of the group of subjects with a high level of overall SA or a low level. According to the inverted U-shaped relationship curve between workload and performance [14], it indicates that the workload levels in this experiment are basically in the central part, so the changes in workload does not trigger significant differences in overall SA.

When the workload is fixed and the overall SA status is significantly different between the high SA and low SA groups under changing event types, the overall SA is better for the alarm light than the instrument. This variability mainly comes from the degree of significance of the appearance of the two events. The alarm light occurs from a white background color to a red alarm state that allows subjects to respond more quickly than the instrument's change in pointer position, and thus achieve a better SA state.

## 4.2  Central Vision vs Peripheral Vision

The results is shown that there is no significant difference in the proportion of subjects using CV versus PV when there is an instrument event. However, during the alarm light event, subjects use PV significantly more frequently than CV. The alarm light events require less perceptual and cognitive resources from subjects, so subjects tend to use less attention to response to the event. Whereas for the instrument event, the increased of perceptual and cognitive demands makes the subjects' choice between using CV and PV much less variable. As is in Sect. 4.1, ART is used here as an indicator of overall SA status to compare and analyze the overall SA state of CV and PV in different conditions.

According to the results it can be found that the inter-subject differences differ depending on whether the tracking is manual or automatic. In the automatic case, there are no differences in the inter-subject distribution, while in the manual case the differences are significant. This suggests that in the lower workload all subjects are likely to be in a more similar state of SA. While in the higher workload, subjects show significant differences in SA. It can be inferred that workload and SA show a non-linear negative relationship, and that the degree of non-linearity is determined by the subjects' individual difference.

In the automatic tracking condition, there are significant differences in the ART contrast between all subjects using CV and PV. In this case, the subjects are generally in a more relax state, and the events to which they response using PV indicates a better mastery of the surroundings (corresponding to a good SA), whereas the responses using CV are likely due to a sudden attention to the event after a long period of inattention, corresponding to a worse SA state.

In the manual situation, there is no significant difference in ART between CV and PV for the low ART group, whereas there is for the high ART group. This is mainly due to the fact that the low ART group (better SA state group) tends to be more of a personal random choice using the two types of perception types under higher load rather than a choice made due to being influenced by the current situation. So the SA states corresponding to the two types of perception modalities do not differ significantly in this category of subjects. In contrast, the SA state of the high ART group (worse SA state group) under high load resembles its SA state under low work load, so the use of PV is more likely to represent a better mastery of their environment, and the use of CV corresponded much to a sudden response after ignoring the event for a longer period of time.

### 4.3 Hierarchical Analysis of SA

It is possible to perform SA hierarchical analysis in the data where CV occurs. ERT is used as an indicator for SA1 analysis. CRT, which can be calculated by subtracting ERT from ART, is used as an indicator for understanding. The lower the reaction time, the better the corresponding SA state. Due to the hierarchical relationship of SA, a good SA2 presupposes a good SA1. Thus the CRT can not be directly used as an indicator of SA2. The final SA2 state is obtained by combining CRT on the basis of the evaluation of SA1.

In the analysis of the results, it can be found that overall SA differs significantly in the condition of fixed workload and changed event type, but does not differ significantly when assigned to either the perception or the comprehension layer. This suggests that the SA differences that occur between alarm light and instrument do not originate in the perceptual or comprehension layer alone. The source of variability is more complex.

## 5  Conclusion

This study use a behavior-based approach to assess SA in real time and interpretability in the current aviation environment. A simulated experimental interface for different flight elements is designed. The experimental periods are divided into continuous and intermittent periods according to the types of tasks performed. This study focuses on the SA state during intermittent periods and uses reaction time as the assessment indicator of SA.

The results revealed that the interface design has significant effect on the overall SA. The alert light with more obvious alarm signal is more possible for subjects to get good SA state than the instrument. The comparison between Peripheral vision and central vision show that people are more used to use PV to perform tasks with conspicuous appearance than CV and different workload causes different overall SA pattern. In general, those who use PV is more possible to have better SA under lighter workload. Finally, the hierarchical analysis of SA shows that the significant differences can be found in overall SA while not in individual level.

In conclusion, the results in the study demonstrated that eye-movement and behavioral performance indicators can be used to assess subjects' SA states in real time. The

SA criterion representing good or bad state in different types of conditions should also be different, and more data is still need to be obtained for further analysis to get a clear threshold for SA state segmentation.

# References

1. Taylor, R.M.: Situational awareness rating technique (SART): the development of a tool for aircrew systems design. In: Proceedings AGARD AMP Symposium Situational Awareness Aerospace Operations, pp. 1–17 (1990)
2. Waag, W.L., Houck, M.R.: Tools for assessing situational awareness in an operational fighter environment. Aviat. Space Environ. A13–A19 (1994)
3. Denney, K.: Cranfield situation awareness scale: user's manual. Applications Psychology Unit College Aeronautics, Cranfield University, Cranfield, UK (1997)
4. McGuinness, B., Foy, L.: A subjective measure of SA: the crew awareness rating scale (CARS). In: Proceedings 1st human performance, Situation Awareness, automation conference, Savannah, GA, USA, pp. 286–291 (2000)
5. McGuinness, B., Ebbage, L.: Assessing Human Factors in Command and Control: Workload and Situational Awareness Metrics. BAE Systems Advanced Technology Centrer, Bristol, UK (2002)
6. Endsley, M.R.: Toward a theory of situation awareness in dynamic systems. Hum. Factors **37**(1), 32–64 (1995)
7. Matthews, M.D., Beal, S.A.: Assessing Situation Awareness in Field Training Exercises. US Military Aca, West Point, NY, USA (2002)
8. Nguyen, T., Lim, C.P., Nguyen, N.D., Gordon-Brown, L., Nahavandi, S.: A review of situation awareness assessment approaches in aviation environments. IEEE Syst. J. **13**(3), 3590–3603 (2019)
9. Endsley, M.R.: Measurement of situation awareness in dynamic systems. Hum. Factors **37**(1), 65–84 (1995)
10. Durso, F.T., Hackworth, C.A., Truitt, T.R., Crutchfield, J., Nikolic, D., Manning, C.A.: Situation awareness as a predictor of performance for en route air traffic controllers. Air Traffic Control Quart. **6**(1), 1–20 (1998)
11. Bacon, L.P., Strybel, T.Z.: Assessment of the validity and intrusiveness of online-probe questions for situation awareness in a simulated air-trafficmanagement task with student air-traffic controllers. Saf. Sci. **56**, 89–95 (2013)
12. Zhang, T., Yang, J., Liang, N., et al.: Physiological measurements of situation awareness: a systematic review. Hum. Factors (2020)
13. Endsley, M.R.: The divergence of objective and subjective situation awareness: a meta-analysis. J. Cogn. Eng. Decis. Making (2020)
14. Schnell, T., Cornwall, R., Walwanis, M., Grubb, J.: The quality of training effectiveness assessment (QTEA) tool applied to the naval aviation training context. In: Schmorrow, D.D., Estabrooke, I.V., Grootjen, M. (eds.) Foundations of Augmented Cognition. Neuroergonomics and Operational Neuroscience. LNCS (LNAI), vol. 5638, pp. 640–649. Springer, Heidelberg (2009). https://doi.org/10.1007/978-3-642-02812-0_73

# Author Index

Bengler, Klaus 189
Benichou, Gregory 373
Bettiga, Debora 149
Burr, Wesley S. 97

Cai, Yiwei 473
Carim Junior, Guido 384
Chan, Wesley Tsz-Kin 245
Chen, Nongtian 253
Chen, Xiaotian 446, 461
Chen, Xinyi 3

Di Dalmazi, Michele 149
Du, Feng 33
Duan, Wenxuan 164

Feng, Guo 179
Flynn-Evans, Erin E. 433
Fottner, Johannes 189
Friedrich, Maik 265
Fu, Shan 290, 349, 488
Fu, Xinyun 279
Fu, Yao 179
Fujikake, Kazuhiro 108

Gong, Yang 279
Guo, Zizheng 179

Harazawa, Makoto 108
He, Miao 124
Hemingray, Caroline 279
Hua, Yue 290
Hudson, Peter 373

Iwai, Yoshio 18
Iwasaki, Fuyuko 18

Jakobi, Jörn 265
Jiang, Ao 279
Jiang, Jiali 33
Jung, Jongwoo 420

Kamiya, Naoki 108
Karasinski, John A. 433
Karatas, Nihan 108

Karvonen, Hannu 49
Kenny, Shane 300
Korek, Wojciech Tomasz 314, 326

Laarni, Jari 49
Lapointe, Jean-François 225
Lastusilta, Toni 49
Lemaire, Noémie 225
Li, Bingxin 33
Li, Harry X. 64
Li, Jie 461
Li, Junhui 253
Li, Ranran 179
Li, Shiyue 3
Li, Shu 473
Li, Wen-Chin 74, 245, 300, 314, 326
Li, WenKai 279
Li, Xianxue 339
Li, Yueqing 85
Liang, Yung-Hsiang 326
Liesenfeld, Andreas 3
Lin, John J. H. 326
Liu, Ang 349
Liu, Yanfang 33, 124
Lo, Kin Wing 420
Lohmann, Gui 384
Lone, Mudassir 314
Lu, Linghai 314
Lu, Yanyu 290, 488

Ma, Ziqi 446, 461
Man, Yongzheng 253
Mancuso, Vincent 64
Mandolfo, Marco 149
Manikath, Elizabeth 74
Mannawaduge Dona, Chanika 358
Marquez, Jessica J. 433
McCarthy, Pete 373
McGuire, Sarah 64
Mizzi, Andrew 384

Ning, Weifeng 253
Nishiyama, Masashi 18

Omeroglu, Fatih Baha 85

Peng, Jiahua   473
Pignata, Silvia   358, 420
Pollanen, Marco   97
Prasch, Lorenz   189

Qin, Kuo   212
Qiu, Kai   446, 461
Quinby, Francis   97

Ram, Angeline   397
Reynolds, Michael G.   97

Saffre, Fabrice   49
Schmidtler, Jonas   189
Schulte, Axel   408
Schwerd, Simon   408
Sew, Khai Sheng   420
Shang, Yan   164
Shelat, Shivang   433
Stringhini, Chiara   149

Takeuchi, Shuhei   108
Tanabe, Hiroko   108
Tanaka, Takahiro   108
Timmermann, Felix   265
Top, Felix   189

Väätänen, Antti   49
Vinson, Norman G.   225

Wang, Huiyun   164
Wang, Lei   473
Wang, Xiaoyu   124
Wang, Zhen   349
Wei, Zheng   33
Westland, Stephen   279
Wu, Yao-Sheng   137
Wu, ZiJian   279

Xue, Hongjun   446, 461

Yamamoto, Tsuneyuki   108
Yang, Tong   33
Yao, Xiang   279
Yao, Yao   3
Yap, Lucus   420
Yoshihara, Yuki   108

Zhang, Huihui   124
Zhang, Jingyu   164, 179, 212
Zhang, Liang   124
Zhang, Mengxi   473
Zhang, Xiaoyan   446, 461
Zhang, Yijing   212
Zhou, Hao   488
Zou, Xiangying   164
Zou, Ying   473